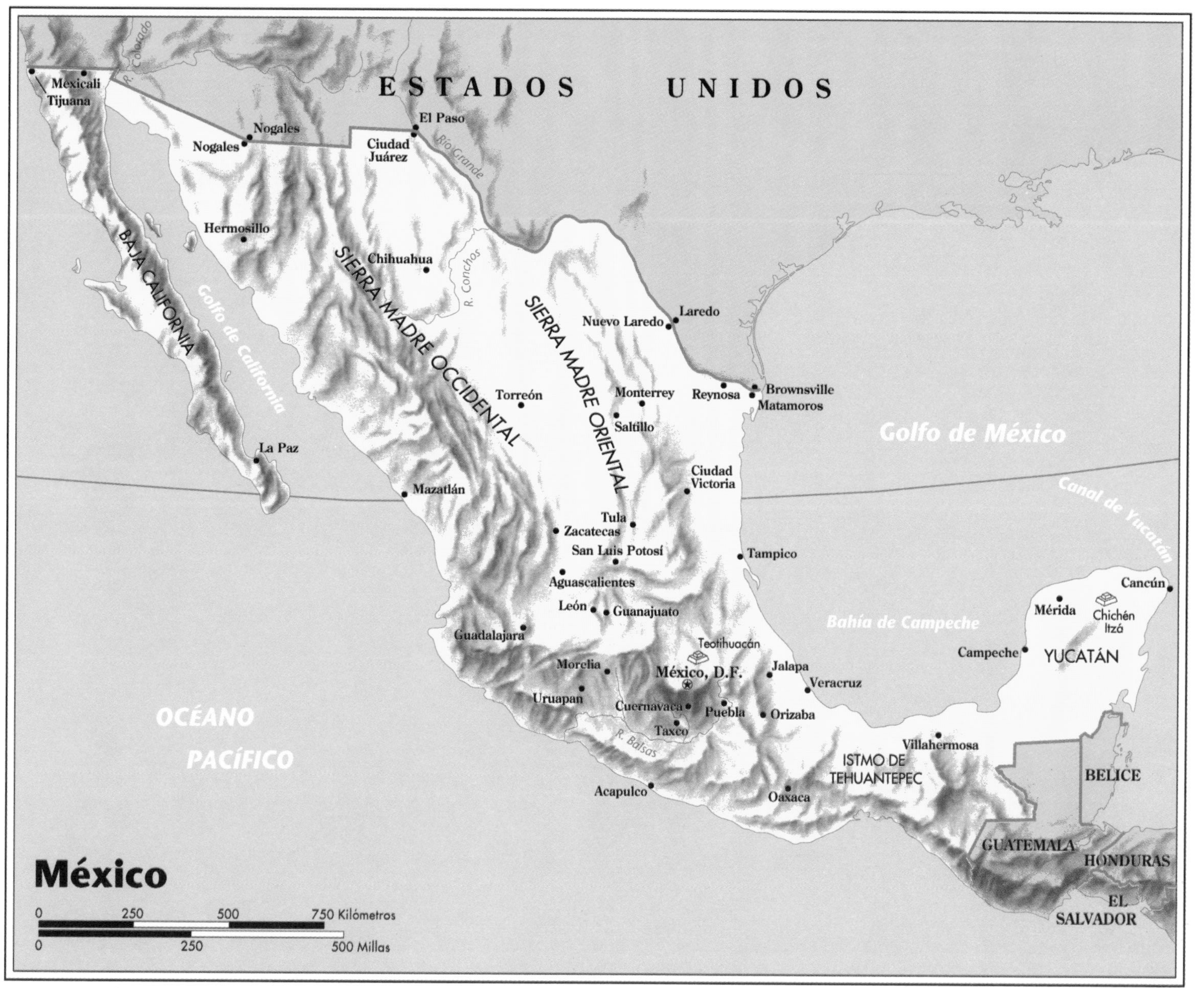
México
ESTADOS UNIDOS
Mexicali
Tijuana
R. Colorado
Nogales
Nogales
Ciudad Juárez
El Paso
Río Grande
Hermosillo
Chihuahua
R. Conchos
BAJA CALIFORNIA
Golfo de California
SIERRA MADRE OCCIDENTAL
SIERRA MADRE ORIENTAL
Nuevo Laredo
Laredo
Torreón
Monterrey
Saltillo
Reynosa
Brownsville
Matamoros
Golfo de México
La Paz
Mazatlán
Ciudad Victoria
Tula
Zacatecas
San Luis Potosí
Tampico
Canal de Yucatán
Aguascalientes
León
Guanajuato
Guadalajara
Bahía de Campeche
Cancún
Mérida
Chichén Itzá
Campeche
YUCATÁN
Teotihuacán
México, D.F.
Morelia
Uruapan
Cuernavaca
Taxco
Puebla
Jalapa
Veracruz
Orizaba
R. Balsas
OCÉANO PACÍFICO
Villahermosa
ISTMO DE TEHUANTEPEC
BELICE
Acapulco
Oaxaca
GUATEMALA
HONDURAS
EL SALVADOR
0 250 500 750 Kilómetros
0 250 500 Millas

Caminos

INSTRUCTOR'S ANNOTATED EDITION

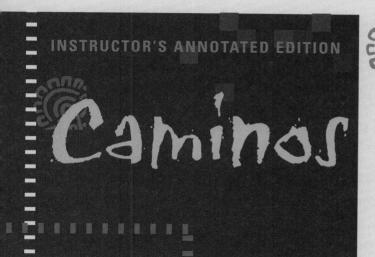

Caminos

Joy Renjilian-Burgy
Wellesley College

Ana Beatriz Chiquito
Massachusetts Institute of Technology
University of Bergen, Norway

Susan M. Mraz
Tufts University

HOUGHTON MIFFLIN COMPANY
Boston New York

Director, Modern Language Programs: **E. Kristina Baer**
Development Manager, Modern Language Programs: **Beth Kramer**
Development Editor: **Kristin Swanson**
Project Editor: **Harriet C. Dishman**
Senior Production/Design Coordinator: **Jennifer Waddell**
Manufacturing Coordinator: **Priscilla Abreu**
Marketing Manager: **Patricia Fossi**

Cover Design: **Minko T. Dimov, MinkoImages**

Printed in the U.S.A.

Library of Congress Catalog Card Number: 98-72078

Instructor's Annotated Edition ISBN: 0-395-81539-8

23456789-DW-03 02 01 00 99

Preface

Caminos is a video-integrated introductory Spanish program that develops students' language learning within an authentic and exciting cultural context. The ***Caminos*** program facilitates students' acquisition of speaking, listening, reading, and writing skills through a dramatic video set in a variety of locations throughout the Spanish-speaking world. Join your students in solving the mystery of the missing Jaguar Twins of Mexico as it is told through the ***Caminos del jaguar*** video program!

AUTHORS' PHILOSOPHY

The ***Caminos*** program combines text, video, CD-ROM, audio, and Internet technologies in a way that immerses students in the culture and language of Spanish-speaking countries and exposes them to the rich diversity of native speakers of Spanish. With this program, students learn not only the semantics and syntax of Spanish, but they also gain exposure to non-verbal communication. The video enlivens the registers of speech required in a variety of social situations to make the learning tasks compelling, especially through culturally enriching themes. The dynamic video narrative of ***Caminos del jaguar*** provides students with an opportunity to visit a variety of sites, to appreciate the vitality and complexity of the Spanish-speaking world, and to gain a heightened awareness of its great civilizations, past and present.

Video is an ideal medium to offer real-time aural and visual access to other cultures. The principal goal of ***Caminos*** is to use natural language in cultural settings that highlight and support language learning in order to stimulate student motivation and self-confidence. In the ***Caminos del jaguar*** video program, language combines with culture within a dramatic, entertaining narrative. Since myth and folklore play an essential part in Hispanic cultures, the video incorporates them into a plot that interweaves adventure, romance, and humor.

The video is filmed on location in Mexico, Spain, Puerto Rico, Costa Rica, Ecuador, and the United States, providing short, teachable segments that offer exciting, interesting, and contextualized situations for language practice. Although many other programs offer video materials to supplement their print materials, ***Caminos*** is a truly video-integrated program on several levels.

- The video demonstrates communicative functions in context and models grammatical structures in the context of natural speech. These functions and corresponding grammatical structures are then presented and practiced explicitly in the textbook.
- Instructors can use the video in the classroom or in the lab. With its short segments and the accompanying activities in the textbook, it can easily be integrated into regular classroom instruction.

The cultural content of the video is reinforced by cultural materials that run throughout the textbook, including popular and literary texts and images from other Spanish-speaking locations that reflect the legacy of the Spanish-speaking world. As we enter the new century, it is increasingly important for students to become more informed global citizens and to use their critical-thinking skills to make cross-cultural connections. The cultural content of ***Caminos*** and ***Caminos del jaguar*** is designed with these goals in mind.

Vocabulary and grammar play a critical role in the development of language acquisition because they permit the learner to use a structural and thematic framework in an ever-expanding approach to linguistic tasks. Grammar and vocabulary are consistently spiraled throughout the ***Caminos*** program, providing learners with a sense of growth and accomplishment as language instruction moves from basic concepts to more complex ones. This kind of reinforcement fosters meaningful language acquisition and prepares students to become culturally literate, motivated language learners.

The technology ancillaries reinforce the internal spiraling and recycling across textbook chapters. Repeated exposure to the same material in the video, the audio CD program, the CD-ROM and the ***Caminos*** web site gives students the opportunity to re-experience the same information through a variety of media. The ***Caminos*** program immerses students in a rich, authentic context that allows them to encounter and re-encounter the chapter's functions, vocabulary, grammar, and culture in various kinds of learning environments. This design lets students pursue their language acquisition through the channels that are most useful to them, whether they are video-, audio-, print-, or computer-based.

PROGRAM FEATURES

By combining pedagogically sound print materials and a culturally vibrant video story, the ***Caminos*** program includes the following features.

For Students

Features	Benefits
Fully integrated video and textbook, rather than video used as an add-on ancillary to supplement the textbook	• Encourages student success in self-expression in Spanish and interaction with others • Provides a culturally rich context for language learning and acquisition of non-verbal communication tasks • Promotes a high-interest, contextualized learning experience
Textbook and video that also integrate audio, CD-ROM, the Internet and a program-specific web site, as well as authentic reading selections	• Presents a complete multimedia learning environment • Provides a variety of authentic input • Allows for natural recycling of textbook and video content

Features	Benefits
Thematic presentation of vocabulary integrates relevant cultural materials	• Presents vocabulary in a context that students can use immediately and apply to the chapter's cultural material • Teaches students to examine the ways that language and culture interact by highlighting critical thinking and cross-cultural communication
Strategy-oriented practice: • The **Vistas y voces** section contains previewing activities that activate students' prior knowledge and ask them to make predictions about content of the video segment • Reading strategies are presented in the first **etapa** of each chapter and practiced in both of the chapter's reading selections • The **En resumen** section of each chapter presents a writing strategy and then teaches students to apply it to a specific writing task • The **Investiguemos por Internet** section of **En resumen** teaches students strategies for using the Internet to expand their language-learning context	• Supports diverse learning styles • Promotes higher-order thinking skills • Teaches beginning students ways to approach and work successfully with authentic materials
Functionally sequenced grammar presentations that recycle structures and vocabulary	• Encourages mastery of essential language elements through consistent re-entry of structures and vocabulary
En resumen section that synthesizes chapter content	• Summarizes chapter functions and contents for final practice before evaluation • Allows students to integrate the chapter functions, content, vocabulary, and structures in meaningful oral and written practice

Features	Benefits
Completely integrated four-skills approach to language-learning	• Ensures that students practice reading, writing, speaking, and listening with equal emphasis • Teaches students the way each skill supplements and reinforces the others (i.e., listening and writing, reading and writing, etc.)

For Instructors

Features	Benefits
Short, manageable video segments of approximately 7 to 12 minutes each, with corresponding activities in the textbook	• Makes it possible to incorporate video into regular classroom instruction • Reduces time instructors spend in preparing video lessons
Flexible format for diverse curricular needs	• Adapts to diverse teaching styles, such as using video in the classroom or in the language lab • Adapts to courses with a range of contact hours, for two or three semesters or for three or four quarters of instruction
Textbook and video that also integrate audio, CD-ROM, the Internet and a program-specific web site, as well as authentic reading selections	• Presents a complete multimedia learning environment that will reinforce students' understanding of Spanish • Increases student motivation

TEXTBOOK ORGANIZATION

The ***Caminos*** textbook is made up of a preliminary chapter and twelve chapters. The twelve chapters begin with a chapter opener. This serves as an advance organizer for the chapter content. It contains two visuals from the video with brief statements that preview the chapter's video content. It also lists the chapter functions, structures, culture topics, readings, reading/writing strategies, and Internet strategies.

Each of the twelve chapters is divided into two **etapas**, using the following organization:

- **Pistas y palabras** This vocabulary section opens with a visual or written clue (such as a map, an illustration, a postcard, a short article, an e-mail message, etc.). It introduces the **etapa** vocabulary, which is related to some aspect of the video content for the **etapa**. The vocabulary is presented and practiced here and later reinforced through cultural information, video activities, grammar presentations, and readings.
- **Enlace cultural** This section, which may appear once or twice per **etapa,** is typically integrated into the **etapa** vocabulary presentation. These notes introduce interesting cultural topics relating to the Spanish-speaking world and give students a context in which to do cross-cultural communication. They are always followed by a discussion-style activity.
- **Vistas y voces** This section is dedicated to video anticipation, viewing, and comprehension activities. Each video segment (approximately 7–12 minutes each) can be watched either in the classroom or assigned for viewing in the language lab ahead of time. Some of the activities, such as the comprehension questions, can be assigned for students to do as homework or in the lab, while other pair and group activities may be done in class, such as those that have students dramatize episodes from the video in groups. This section also highlights the use of the chapter functions and provides activities for personalization.
- **Lengua** This is a formal presentation of grammar. Most presentations begin with additional input in the form of light-hearted illustrations or conversations that highlight the structure that is presented. This feature encourages students to infer grammatical form, meaning, and use prior to the formal presentation of grammar. Following each grammar presentation are varied activities that range from controlled to more open-ended and allow for recycling of previous structures and vocabulary.
- **Lengua en acción** This feature appears either in the **Pistas y palabras** or **Lengua** sections of the text. Its linguistic presentations give students extra information about language usage on an as-needed basis. Topics include items such as false cognates, idiomatic expressions, language register, forms of address, grammatical forms used lexically, and more.
- **Lectura** The reading selections include both authentic, unadapted selections, as well as edited and author-written pieces. Cultural and literary readings are representative of the Spanish-speaking regions covered in the textbook and the video and include a variety of genres. **Etapa A** presents a reading strategy that focuses students on critical approaches to

reading. This strategy is then recycled and reapplied to the **Etapa B** reading selection.

The culminating sections of the chapter appear after the chapter's two **etapas:**

- **En resumen** This section gives students the opportunity to practice the four language skills while reviewing the structures, functions, and culture of the entire chapter. In addition, the section explicitly provides additional communicative practice, a different Internet activity for each of the twelve chapters, and a different writing strategy and task for each chapter.
- **Vocabulario** The vocabulary list includes all of the active vocabulary from the chapter's two **etapas** organized alphabetically with English translations for easy reference.

The ***Caminos*** textbook also contains the following materials:

- **Preliminary chapter** This short introductory section introduces students to the characters they will meet in ***Caminos del jaguar*** and serves as a reference as they progress through the video.
- **End vocabulary** There are complete Spanish/English and English/Spanish glossaries at the end of the textbook. These include both the active vocabulary from the chapter presentations and the recognition vocabulary from the video, culture, and reading sections.
- **Appendices** Complete verb charts, a list of common prefixes and suffixes, and a list of classroom expressions are included for ready reference by students.

PROGRAM COMPONENTS

The complete ***Caminos*** introductory college Spanish program includes the following components:

Student Text The textbook is intended for use in introductory college programs. Its four-skills approach combines oral, listening, reading and writing practice, and culture, with a fully-integrated three-and-a-half-hour video.

The twelve chapters of the textbook correlate to the six geographical locations in the video and include information, cultural notes, and readings about countries not featured in the video, to give a more complete representation of the Hispanic world.

Instructors' Annotated Edition Contains helpful point-of-use information, pedagogical support in the form of margin annotations, plus many answer keys.

***Caminos del jaguar* Video Program** The video program consists of three and a half hours of authentic video footage filmed on location and featuring an exciting, action-packed mystery that incorporates myth, folklore, and local regional culture. The video was filmed in Mexico, Spain, Costa Rica,

Puerto Rico, Ecuador, and the United States. The video program is divided into two 7- to 12-minute segments per chapter, for a total of twenty-four segments.

Activities Manual This separate student ancillary provides additional vocabulary and grammar practice for each chapter. It also contains writing practice that ties specifically into the writing strategy presented in the **En resumen** section of each chapter. Listening practice is provided through special listening comprehension activities that relate directly to video content and are tied to segments provided on the audio CDs, packaged with the Manual. An answer key with answers for selected activities is included at the end of the Manual.

Audio CDs These CDs contain audio clips taken from the video soundtrack. Students can listen to key scenes from the ***Caminos del jaguar*** video program on their own, at their own pace, in order to reinforce their understanding of the story. The audio CDs, packaged with the Activities Manual, provide the listening input that relates to the listening activities in the Manual.

Instructor's Resource Manual with Test Bank This component includes a complete testing program with tests, listening scripts, and answers. In addition to the testing program, it includes the complete video script for the ***Caminos del jaguar*** video program, the script for the audio CDs, and an introduction about the integration of the ***Caminos*** program components.

Caminos del jaguar* Video Activities Manual** This manual contains the video activities from the textbook and can be used with the ***Caminos del jaguar video program in any introductory-level Spanish course.

Caminos* Web Site** This multifaceted, text-specific web site is available to adopters only. It contains video-based activities related to the ***Caminos del jaguar video program; self-test activities in which students may practice chapter grammar; and a task-based activity section that requires students to explore the World Wide Web and submit their findings to their instructor.

Caminos* CD-ROM** This is a state-of-the-art multimedia program designed to improve students' Spanish. It features full-motion video clips from the ***Caminos del jaguar video program, record-and-playback options, and a variety of interactive activities. It also includes links to the ***Caminos*** web site.

Instructor's Resource Kit This component contains the Instructor's Resource Manual, the audio CDs, and the ***Caminos*** CD-ROM.

CREATING COURSE SYLLABI FOR *CAMINOS*

Depending on the number of class and laboratory meetings per week, instructors may create course syllabi for utilization of the ***Caminos*** program. The following outlines offer suggestions for organization of two-semester, three-semester, and three-quarter system courses.

Two-Semester Syllabus (3 or 5 class periods per week)

Semester One		Semester Two	
Week	**Chapter**	**Week**	**Chapter**
1	Preliminary Chapter	1	Review Chapters 1-6
2	1A	2	7A
3	1B	3	7B
4	2A	4	8A
5	2B	5	8B
6	3A	6	9A
7	3B	7	9B
8	Review/ Midterm	8	Review/ Midterm
9	4A	9	10A
10	4B	10	10B
11	5A	11	11A
12	5B	12	11B
13	6A	13	12A
14	6B	14	12B
15	Review/ Final	15	Review/ Final

Three-Semester Syllabus (3 class periods per week)

Semester One		Semester Two		Semester Three	
Week	**Chapter**	**Week**	**Chapter**	**Week**	**Chapter**
1	Preliminary Chapter	1	Review Chapters 1-4	1	Review Chapters 5-8
2	1A	2	5A	2	9A
3	1A/1B	3	5A/5B	3	9A/9B
4	1B	4	5B	4	9B
5	2A	5	6A	5	10A
6	2A/2B	6	6A/6B	6	10A/10B
7	2B	7	6B	7	10B
8	Review/ Midterm	8	Review/ Midterm	8	Review/ Midterm
9	3A	9	7A	9	11A
10	3A/3B	10	7A/7B	10	11A/11B
11	3B	11	7B	11	11B
12	4A	12	8A	12	12A
13	4A/4B	13	8A/8B	13	12A/12B
14	4B	14	8B	14	12B
15	Review/ Final	15	Review/ Final	15	Review/ Final

Three-Quarter Syllabus (5 class periods per week)

Quarter One		Quarter Two		Quarter Three	
Week	**Chapter**	**Week**	**Chapter**	**Week**	**Chapter**
1	Preliminary Chapter	1	Review Chapters 1-4	1	Review Chapters 5-8
2	1A	2	5A	2	9A
3	1B	3	5B	3	9B
4	2A	4	6A	4	10A
5	2B	5	6B	5	10B
6	3A	6	7A	6	11A
7	3B	7	7B	7	11B
8	4A	8	8A	8	12A
9	4B	9	8B	9	12B
10	Review/ Final	10	Review/ Final	10	Review/ Final

If your introductory Spanish course has fewer contact hours than the courses outlined above, you can use the ***Caminos*** program successfully by following some or all of the suggestions below.

- Have students view the video in the lab before coming to class. They should also do the previewing activities and some of the comprehension activities on their own.
- Have students read the **Enlace cultural** sections before coming to class. Limit the time you spend on them in class to the discussion activity at the end of each section.
- Have students read the grammar explanations in the **Lengua** sections before they come to class. Answer any questions about the explanations that students may have and then focus class time on having students do the activities.
- Have students read the **Lectura** selection in either **Etapa A** or **Etapa B** rather than reading both selections.
- Have students write summaries of their Internet searches rather than give classroom presentations about them.

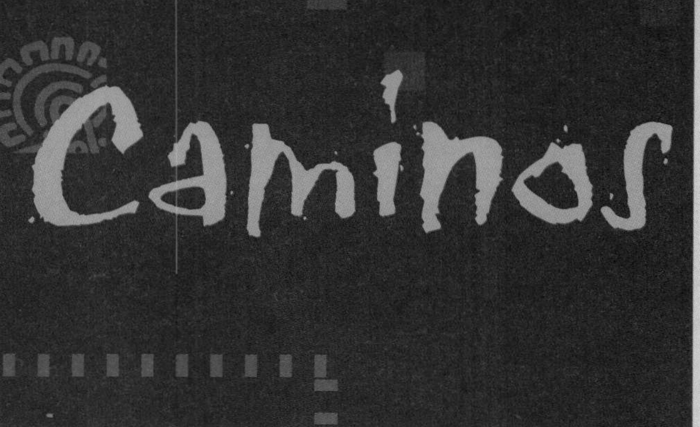
Caminos

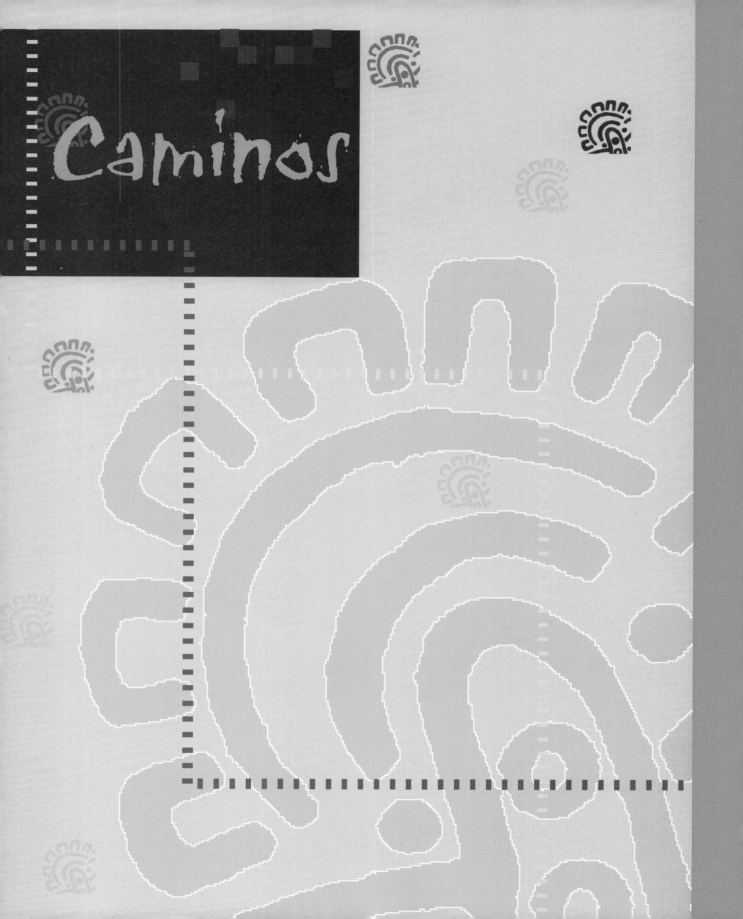

Joy Renjilian-Burgy
Wellesley College

Ana Beatriz Chiquito
Massachusetts Institute of Technology
University of Bergen, Norway

Susan M. Mraz
Tufts University

HOUGHTON MIFFLIN COMPANY
Boston New York

Director, Modern Language Programs: **E. Kristina Baer**
Development Manager, Modern Language Programs: **Beth Kramer**
Development Editor: **Kristin Swanson**
Project Editor: **Harriet C. Dishman**
Senior Production/Design Coordinator: **Jennifer Waddell**
Manufacturing Coordinator: **Priscilla Abreu**
Marketing Manager: **Patricia Fossi**

Cover Design: **Minko T. Dimov, MinkoImages**

Printed in the U.S.A.

Library of Congress Catalog Card Number: 98-72078

Student Text ISBN: 0-395-81538-X

23456789-DW-03 02 01 00 99

Abrazos y besos a mi marido, Donísimo, el don de dones; a mis gemelos-hijos-jaguares-bostonianos Lucien y Sarkis; a Ángela y Mukhul; y a mis queridos padres, hermanas y suegros. Los quiero mucho. (JRB)

Para mi querida familia con todo amor, en especial para mis padres, Lucio y Ofelia, mi marido, Ivar, y mi hijo, Edvard. (ABC)

To my loving family, especially my mother Margie Mraz, my father John Mraz (1920-1997), my sister Mary Beth, her family (Terry, Angela, Malissa, P.J.), and to my constant companion and friend, Jesse. (SMM)

And to all of our students and friends who have inspired and guided us throughout this project.

Acknowledgments

We would like to thank the Modern Language Department of Houghton Mifflin Company, College Division, for believing in ***Caminos*** and for supporting us throughout the different stages of development and production: Kristina Baer, Director of Modern Language Programs; Beth Kramer, Development Manager; and Lydia Mehegan, Editorial Assistant. Special thanks to Kris Swanson for her helpful insights, humor, and support. We also wish to thank Sylvia Madrigal for her creativity and dedication in converting our video ideas into a vibrant, exciting videoscript and to Video Publishing Group for creating the video. To Mary-Anne Vetterling we express our deepest thanks for all her contributions to this project. Heartfelt thanks also to Harriet Dishman of Elm Street Publications whose attention to detail and whose continual enthusiasm helped finalize our project, and to Cécile Delagouttière, Katherine Lincoln, Grisel Lozano-Garcini, and Luz Garcés-Galante for their very careful copyediting and proofreading.

At Wellesley College, I would like to express my gratitude to the Wellesley College Spanish Department for your enduring love and professional support on all my caminos; to the Knapp Media Center, for providing a spacious, state-of-the-art multimedia environment in which to develop interactive teaching and learning materials; to the Education Department, for your partnership in so many educational endeavors; to the Mellon Minority Fellows for your sisterhood and help; and to Nicole Barraza, Norma Huizar, and Patricia Sciaraffa, for your constant contributions and assistance.

—*Joy Renjilian-Burgy*

Special thanks to Professor Steven Lerman and to my colleagues at MIT for their inspiration and for providing such a wonderful and creative working environment, to Deputy Director Sverre Spildo of the University of Bergen for his crucial support, and to all my colleagues at the MIT and Bergen Spanish Departments for their encouragement and help.

—*Ana Beatriz Chiquito*

At Tufts University, I would like to thank the members of the Department of Romance Languages for their inspiration and for creating such a collegial atmosphere in which to teach and learn. To my mentors from West Virginia University who inspired me: Joseph F. Renahan, Dr. Michael E. Reider, and Dr. Joseph A. Murphy. I also want to thank my friends for their constant support and encouragement, especially Sandy Earnest, Lynne Barsky, Sandy Guadano, Barbara Clark, Amy Orrell, Judy McArthur, and Phil Charles. A special thanks to Alison Safford for her friendship and for enduring my strange and long working hours, piles of manuscript, and for being a special aunt to Jesse.

—*Susan M. Mraz*

We would like to gratefully acknowledge the contributions of our reviewers:

Karen Berg, *College of Charleston*
Judy Berry-Bravo, *Wichita State University*
Kathleen Boykin, *Slippery Rock University*
Christina A. Buckley, *Tulane University*
Maxine Cirac, *Western Nevada Community College*
Dr. Richard K. Curry, *Texas A & M University*
Robert L. Davis, *University of Oregon*
Ozzie F. Díaz-Duque, *The University of Iowa*
Dr. A. Raymond Elliott, *University of Texas at Arlington*
Sally Eyles-Goldfarb, *Vanderbilt University*
Rob Freeman, *Delaware Technical Community College*
Herschel Frey, *University of Pittsburgh*
María Dolores Goddard, *Xavier University*
Janis Halpern, *Indiana State University*
Ronald M. Harmon, *California State University at Fullerton*
Ellen Haynes, *University of Colorado*
Dr. Irene B. Hodgson, *Xavier University*
Phillip Johnson, *Baylor University*
Teresa H. Johnson, *Saint Louis University*
Jerry W. Larson, *Brigham Young University*
Isabel C. Livosky, *Knox College*
Donna McMahon, *California State University at San Bernardino*
Glenn Morocco, *LaSalle University*
Ellen C. Nugent McArdle, *Raritan Valley Community College*
Anne I. Pomerantz, *University of Pennsylvania*
Cristina A. Sanicky, *California State University–Chico*
Dennis L. Seager, *Oklahoma State University*
Vilma Silverman, *San Diego Mesa College*
Beverly Turner, *Truckee Meadows Community College*
Elizabeth Vargas Dowdy, *Manatee Community College*
Joseph Weyers, *College of Charleston*
Nancy Zechiedrich, *Westark College*
Francisco Zermeño, *Chabot College*

TABLE OF CONTENTS

CAPÍTULO Preliminar

1 ¿Arqueóloga o criminal?

CAPÍTULO 2 ¿Dónde está Nayeli?

CAPÍTULO 3 ¿Qué revela el sueño de la abuela?

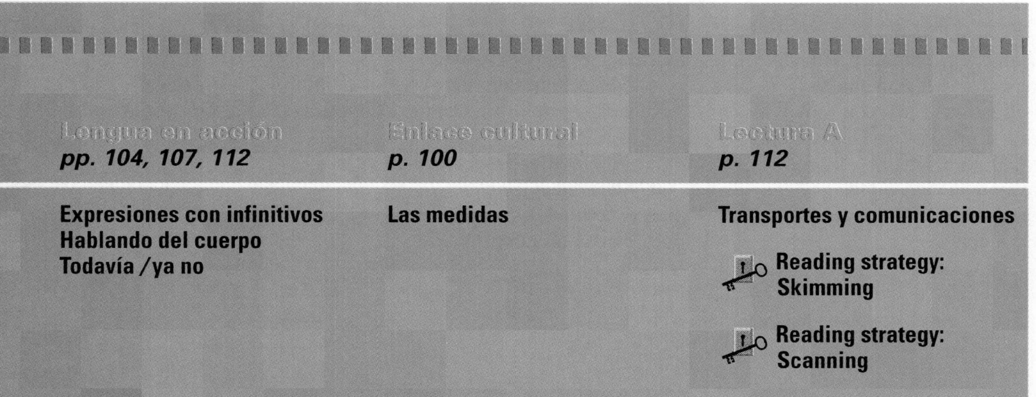

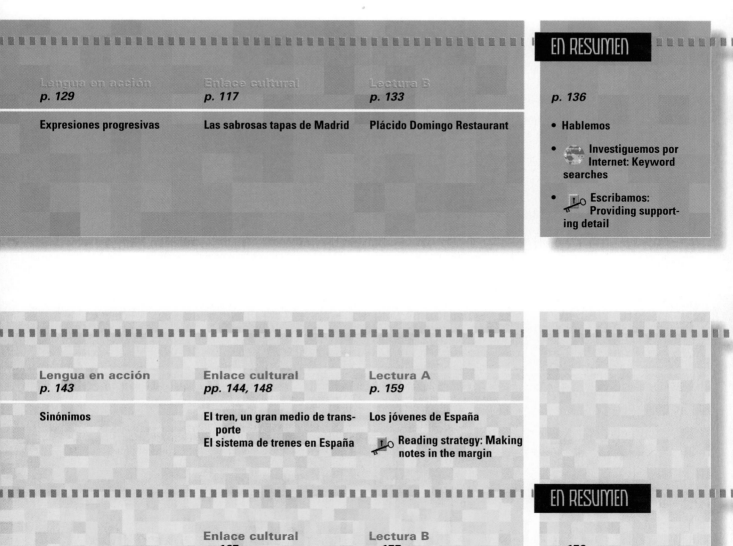

CAPÍTULO 8 ¿Qué plan secreto tiene Zulaya?

CAPÍTULO 9 ¿Tiene Armando la solución?

Reference Section

Lengua en acción *p. 497*	Enlace cultural *pp. 492, 494*	Lectura B *p. 499*	EN RESUMEN *p. 502*
Special use of lo	Lenguas en contacto Semblanzas latinas	¡BRAVO a los hispanos!	• Hablemos • Investiguemos por Internet: Using synonyms and word combinations • Escribamos: Editing your own work

Los héroes gemelos, Yax-Balam y Hun-Ahau

Capítulo preliminar

Video Guide to *Caminos del jaguar*

Saludos (*Greetings*)

Presentaciones (*Introductions*)

Nacionalidad (*Nationality*)

Join us as we follow the story of two students, Adriana and Felipe, who begin their journey down an unexpected path where the forces of good and evil (los Buenos y los Malos) battle over the fate of the Jaguar Twins Yax Balam and Hun-Ahau. Will these Mayan Hero Twins be reunited and returned to Mexico or will they fall into the wrong hands forever?

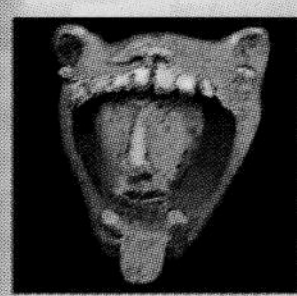

Video Guide to Caminos del jaguar

Familiarize yourself with some of the characters who provide drama and suspense in the ***Caminos del jaguar*** video that accompanies your textbook ***Caminos***. Use this to guide your international journey in pursuit of the missing Jaguar Twins.

The Jaguar Twins (Los héroes gemelos)

Yax-Balam (YASH-BA-LAM) and Hun-Ahau (U-NA-HOW) are classical mythical twin figures from Mayan lore who symbolize the triumph of good over evil. They have legendary powers affecting the fate of their nation. They are the focal point for this exciting mystery.

Nayeli Paz Ocotlán

Born of a Mexican mother and a Spanish father, Nayeli was raised in New York City and studied at the Universidad Autónoma de México (UNAM). She is now a well-known professor of archeology at the Universidad de Puebla, where she is dedicated to locating and preserving missing Mexican artifacts. She is an expert on the story of the Jaguar Twins and has recently published the book *Los héroes gemelos de Xibalbá*. Hernán, her husband, died in the Mexican earthquake of 1985. Nayeli feels responsible for his death.

Doña Gafasnegras

Doña Gafasoscuras is another one of her nicknames, but her real name is Mariluz Gorrostiaga Hinojosa. Born and raised in Mexico City, she was one of Nayeli's first students in Puebla and has always been jealous of her.

Adriana Reyes Tepole

Born in San Antonio, Adriana Reyes Tepole grew up in Guayaquil, Ecuador, where her father worked in a United Nations project. When she was twelve, the family then returned to Texas, the birthplace of her father. Her mother is from Puebla, Mexico. Adriana recently studied at the Universidad de Puebla and lived with her maternal grandparents. Currently a graduate student in archeology at the University of Texas at San Antonio, she won a summer fellowship to go on an excavation with Nayeli.

Felipe Luna Velilla

For many years, Felipe lived with his Venezuelan father in Caracas before returning to Miami to live with his Cuban mother and stepfather. He did his undergraduate studies in archeology at the University of Miami and is doing graduate work at the University of Texas at San Antonio. He also has been awarded a summer fellowship to go on a dig with Nayeli.

La abuelita (Grandmother)

Nayeli's grandmother lived in Puebla all her life and Nayeli was her favorite grandchild. She has passed away but visits Nayeli through her vivid dreams. Nayeli adored her grandmother and dreams of her often.

Mysterious Ring-fingered Man

Friend or foe? You decide.

Doña Carmen Quesada Araya

Doña Carmen, an art collector, lives on a ranch outside of San José, Costa Rica. Nayeli is her godchild, and has been very close to her for years. Nayeli's mother and doña Carmen were art history majors and best friends in college. After Nayeli's mother died, doña Carmen funded Nayeli's college studies.

Armando de Landa Chávez

Armando is a Mexican entrepreneur who helps to fund Adriana and Felipe's summer travels.

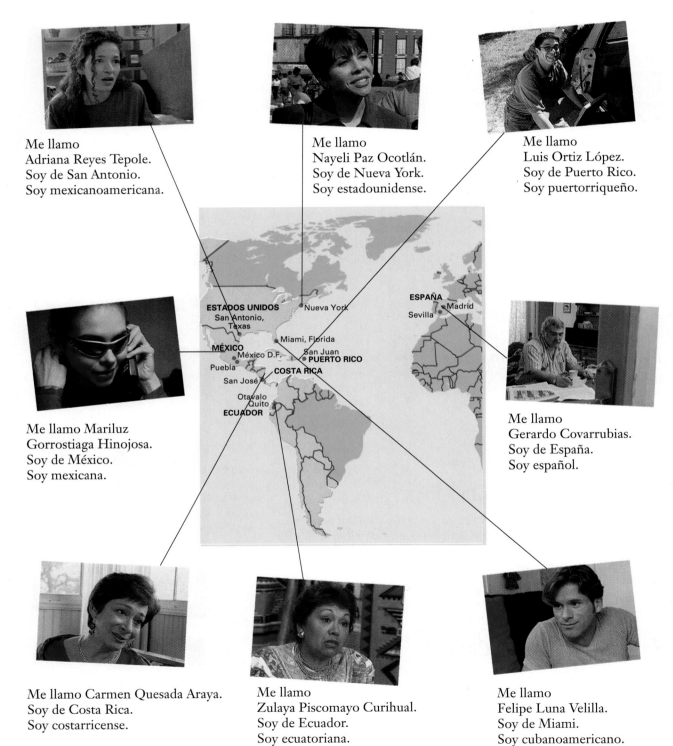

Me llamo
Adriana Reyes Tepole.
Soy de San Antonio.
Soy mexicanoamericana.

Me llamo
Nayeli Paz Ocotlán.
Soy de Nueva York.
Soy estadounidense.

Me llamo
Luis Ortiz López.
Soy de Puerto Rico.
Soy puertorriqueño.

Me llamo Mariluz
Gorrostiaga Hinojosa.
Soy de México.
Soy mexicana.

Me llamo
Gerardo Covarrubias.
Soy de España.
Soy español.

Me llamo Carmen Quesada Araya.
Soy de Costa Rica.
Soy costarricense.

Me llamo
Zulaya Piscomayo Curihual.
Soy de Ecuador.
Soy ecuatoriana.

Me llamo
Felipe Luna Velilla.
Soy de Miami.
Soy cubanoamericano.

Nacionalidades

Country / island	For females	For males	*English*
Alemania	alemana	alemán	*German*
Argentina	argentina	argentino	*Argentine*
Bolivia	boliviana	boliviano	*Bolivian*
Brasil	brasileña	brasileño	*Brazilian*
Canadá	canadiense	canadiense	*Canadian*
Chile	chilena	chileno	*Chilean*
China	china	chino	*Chinese*
Colombia	colombiana	colombiano	*Colombian*
Corea	coreana	coreano	*Korean*
Costa Rica	costarricense	costarricense	*Costa Rican*
Cuba	cubana	cubano	*Cuban*
Cuba + Estados Unidos	cubanoamericana	cubanoamericano	*Cuban American*
Ecuador	ecuatoriana	ecuatoriano	*Ecuadorian*
El Salvador	salvadoreña	salvadoreño	*Salvadoran*
España	española	español	*Spanish*
Estados Unidos	estadounidense	estadounidense	*from the U.S.A.*
Francia	francesa	francés	*French*
Guatemala	guatemalteca	guatemalteco	*Guatemalan*
Honduras	hondureña	hondureño	*Honduran*
Inglaterra	inglesa	inglés	*English*
Italia	italiana	italiano	*Italian*
Japón	japonesa	japonés	*Japanese*
México	mexicana	mexicano	*Mexican*
México + Estados Unidos	mexicano-americana	mexicano-americano	*Mexican American*
Nicaragua	nicaragüense	nicaragüense	*Nicaraguan*
Panamá	panameña	panameño	*Panamanian*
Paraguay	paraguaya	paraguayo	*Paraguayan*
Perú	peruana	peruano	*Peruvian*
Portugal	portuguesa	portugués	*Portuguese*
Puerto Rico	puertorriqueña	puertorriqueño	*Puerto Rican*
República Dominicana	dominicana	dominicano	*Dominican*
Rusia	rusa	ruso	*Russian*
Uruguay	uruguaya	uruguayo	*Uruguayan*
Venezuela	venezolana	venezolano	*Venezuelan*

Saludos (Greetings)

Buenos días

—Buenos días. ¿Qué tal?	*Good morning. How's it going?*
—Muy bien, ¿y tú?	*Very well, and you?*
—Bastante bien, gracias.	*Quite fine, thanks.*

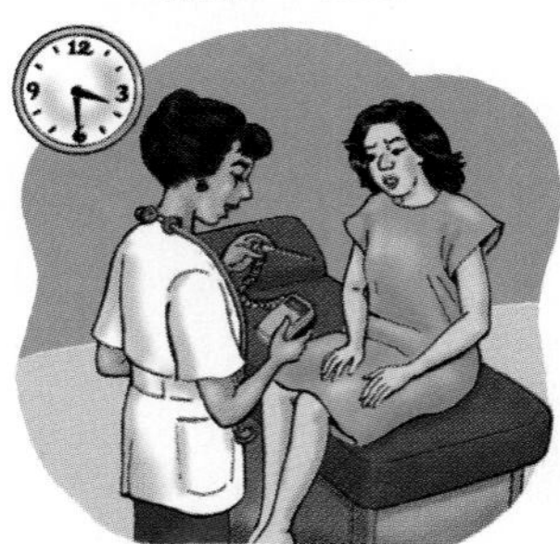

Buenas tardes

PACIENTE:	Buenas tardes, doctora. ¿Qué hay de nuevo?	*Good afternoon, doctor. What's new?*
DOCTORA:	Nada en particular. ¿Qué tal usted?	*Nothing special. How's everything with you?*
PACIENTE:	Muy mal, bastante mal.	*Very bad, quite bad.*
DOCTORA:	¿Verdad? Lo siento.	*Really? I'm sorry.*

Buenas noches

—Buenas noches.	*Good night.*
—Buenas noches. Hasta mañana.	*Good night. See you tomorrow.*
—Adiós. Hasta pronto.	*Good-bye. See you soon.*
—Chao.	*Bye-bye.*

Write **encantado** (for a male) and **encantada** (for a female) on the board. Explain that they mean "delighted" and are used as much as **mucho gusto**. Also practice **El gusto es mío.** Divide the class in halves to model the dialogue, with one group taking the role of Pablo and the other that of Sara.

- Note that **buenos días** is normally used from sunrise to noon; **buenas tardes** from noon through approximately suppertime; and **buenas noches** after the evening meal.

1 **Saludos.** Recombine expressions from the three conversations above to create a conversation around the theme of greetings. Work with a partner.

Presentaciones (Introductions)

En la cafetería

SARA:	Hola. ¿Cómo te llamas?	*Hello. What's your name?*
PABLO:	Me llamo Pablo. ¿Y tú?	*My name is Pablo. And you?*
SARA:	Me llamo Sara.	*My name is Sara.*
PABLO:	Mucho gusto.	*Pleased to meet you.*
SARA:	Igualmente.	*Likewise.*

En la oficina

RAFAEL:	Hola. ¿Cómo se llama usted?	*Hello. What's your name?*
MIRTA:	Me llamo Mirta Pérez. ¿Y usted?	*My name is Mirta Pérez. And you?*
RAFAEL:	Me llamo Rafael Ramírez.	*My name is Rafael Ramírez.*
MIRTA:	Mucho gusto.	*Pleased to meet you.*
RAFAEL:	Igualmente.	*Likewise.*

En la sala de clase

—Buenos días, profesora.	*Good morning, professor.*
—Buenos días. ¿Cómo te llamas?	*Good morning. What is your name?*
—Me llamo David Romero Solar. ¿Y usted?	*My name is David Romero Solar. And you?*
—Me llamo Susana Alegría Ramírez.	*My name is Susana Alegría Ramírez.*
—Mucho gusto, profesora Alegría.	*Pleased to meet you, Professor Alegría!*
—El gusto es mío. ¡Bienvenido, David!	*The pleasure is mine. Welcome, David!*

2 **El gusto es mío.** Look at the conversations above. With whom would you use the following phrases?

¿Cómo te llamas? / ¿Y tú? ______________________

¿Cómo se llama usted? / ¿Y usted? ______________________

Point out that **tú** *(informal you)* is used with people you would address by their first name, such as friends and classmates. **Usted** *(formal you)* is utilized respectfully for older family members and professionals.

3 **¿Cómo te llamas?** Practice introducing yourself to three classmates. Follow the model of the conversation between Pablo and Sara.

4 **¿Cómo se llama usted?** Using the conversation above as a model, role play with different classmates three formal introductions as though you were: (a) head of your school, (b) president of your country, and (c) a famous celebrity.

You may wish to tell your students that they must address you as **usted**.

Nacionalidad (Nationality)

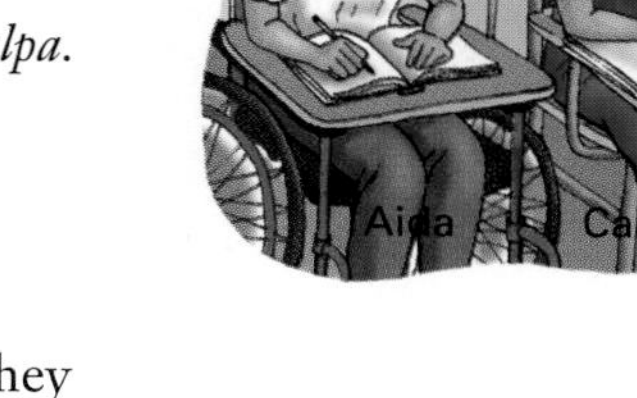

CAELA:	¿De dónde eres?	*Where are you from?*
AIDA:	Soy de La Paz. Soy boliviana. ¿Y tú?	*I am from La Paz. I am Bolivian. And you?*
CAELA:	Soy hondureña. Soy de Tegucigalpa.	*I'm Honduran. I am from Tegucigalpa.*
AIDA:	Mucho gusto.	*It's a pleasure.*
CAELA:	El gusto es mío.	*The pleasure is mine.*

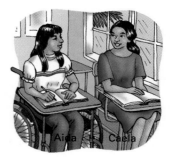

5 **¿De dónde eres?** Go around the room asking four classmates where they are from and what their nationality is. Follow the model of the conversation above.

Answers to Actividad 6:
1. puertorriqueña
2. alemana
3. español
4. cubanoamericana
5. italiano
6. argentina
7. francés
8. mexicana
9. inglés
10. canadiense

Refer students to Appendix C for a comprehensive list of classroom expressions.

6 Nacionalidades. How many of these people do you recognize? Identify their nationalities. Refer to the nationality chart and the map on pages 4–5. Be sure to use the nationality that corresponds to a female or a male.

1. Rosie Pérez
2. Claudia Schiffer
3. Antonio Banderas
4. Gloria Estefan
5. Luciano Pavarotti
6. Gabriela Sabatini
7. Jacques Chirac
8. Frida Kahlo
9. Monty Python
10. Jim Carrey

7 ¡Hola! In pairs, role play the video characters from the opening presentation on pages 2–4. Use the information about their names and nationalities to create a conversation in which you practice greetings, introductions, and expressions of courtesy.

Palabras y expresiones útiles

¿Cómo se dice...?	*How do you say . . .?*
con permiso	*excuse me*
de nada	*you're welcome*
don (D.)	*(Sr., Mr.) with first name*
doña (Dña.)	*(Mrs., Ms.) with first name*
El gusto es mío.	*The pleasure is mine.*
en grupos	*in groups*
en parejas	*in pairs*
gracias	*thanks*
hasta la vista	*until we meet again*
no sé	*I don't know*
perdón	*pardon*
por favor	*please*
¿Qué quiere decir...?	*What does . . . mean?*
regular	*OK*
señor (Sr.)	*Mr.*
señora (Sra.)	*Mrs.*
señorita (Srta.)	*Miss*
Sí, cómo no.	*Of course.*
también	*also*

CAPÍTULO 1

1A

LOCALIDAD: Estados Unidos/ México

¿Arqueóloga o criminal?

1B

The journey begins as Adriana and Felipe prepare to join their archaeology professor, Nayeli, on an excavation dig. However, something unexpected happens to change the course of events—and their lives—completely.

Vocabulary themes
- Describing things in a room
- Identifying colors
- Counting from 0 to 100
- Stating day and date
- Stating month and date
- Talking about academic subjects
- Expressing likes and dislikes
- Describing people

Language structures
- Talking about specific and nonspecific things and people
- Identifying gender of nouns
- Talking about several persons or things
- Coordinating gender and number
- Describing people and things
- Discussing actions in the present
- Asking and responding to questions
- Telling time

Culture topics
- El teléfono
- El sistema universitario en el mundo hispano

Readings
- Titulares
- Tres estudiantes de la universidad

Reading/writing strategies
- Recognizing cognates/prefixes
- Creating a cluster diagram

Internet strategy
- Using Internet addresses

ETAPA A

Pistas y palabras

I. Describing things in a room

¿Qué hay en el cuarto?

Make a transparency of the bedroom. Point to individual words and have students repeat them individually and in chorus. You might also make a copy of the picture without labels and have students practice the vocabulary orally or in a written fashion as a spot-quiz.

Point to various items in the classroom. Have students identify them in Spanish. Do the same with pictures of your office, a dormitory, and so on.

1. una silla
2. una pared
3. una mochila
4. un sillón
5. unos libros
6. una calculadora
7. unas llaves
8. una alfombra
9. un escritorio
10. un reloj
11. un florero
12. una ventana
13. un radio
14. un cuaderno
15. una lámpara
16. una computadora
17. un lápiz
18. una rosa
19. una planta
20. una impresora
21. una cartera
22. un teléfono
23. un cartel
24. un bolígrafo / una pluma
25. un calendario
26. un estante
27. unos papeles
28. una cama
29. una televisión
30. un basurero

(No) Hay means *there is (not)* or *there are (not)*.

Palabras y expresiones útiles

la bolsa	*purse*	la pizarra	*blackboard, chalkboard*
el borrador	*eraser*	el pupitre	*writing desk*
la carpeta	*folder*	la regla	*ruler*
la habitación	*room*	la residencia	*dormitory*
el mapa	*map*	la sala de clase	*classroom*
la mesa	*table*	la tiza	*chalk*
la oficina	*office*	la universidad	*university*

1 **El cuarto.** Work with a partner to list as many things in your bedroom as you can.

▶ **Modelo:** —*¿Qué hay en el cuarto?*
—*Hay una silla.*

Walk around the room and help students with **Actividades 1** and **2.** Have students report on their lists.

2 **Cosas que no hay en el cuarto.** Now list five to eight things that are *not* in your room. Take turns naming them with a partner.

▶ **Modelo:** *No hay una alfombra.*

II. Identifying colors

¿De qué color es?

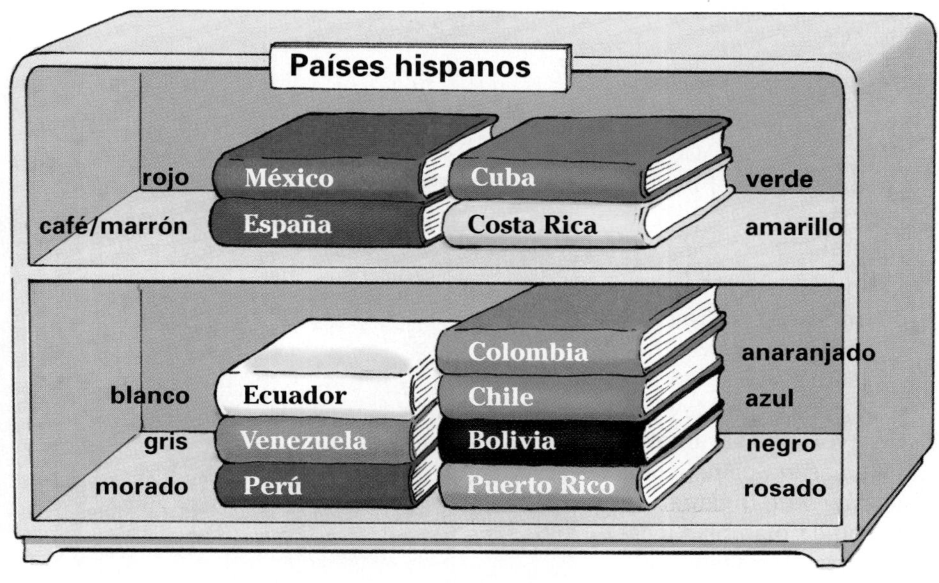

Other word for *brown* is **pardo.** *Pink* is also known as **rosa.**

3 **Los colores.** Name the colors of the books on the bookshelf. Work with a partner. Follow the model.

▶ **Modelo:** *¿De qué color es el libro de Bolivia?*
Es negro.

Practice: Point to different objects in the classroom, the cover of this book, your own and students' clothing and ask **¿De qué color es?**

4 **¡Colores, colores, colores!** What colors do you associate with the following?

1. Coca-Cola
2. Irish Spring soap
3. The Energizer Bunny
4. Howard Johnsons
5. Ivory Snow
6. Pepsi
7. Burger King
8. M&M's

Answers to Actividad 4:
1. marrón/rojo
2. verde
3. gris y rosado
4. anaranjado / azul
5. blanco
6. rojo, blanco, azul
7. anaranjado
8. todos los colores (amarillo, verde, marrón, anaranjado, azul)

III. Counting from 0 to 100

Contemos de cero a cien

Practice: Have students repeat the numbers in chorus. Then have them count off. Write numbers on the board and use sources such as pictures of sports figures, speed-limit signs, and address numbers.

Point out that numbers in the twenties can be written as one word or as three: **veintitrés** or **veinte y tres.** Numbers higher than thirty must be written as three words: **cuarenta y seis.**

Números de 0–100

0	cero	10	diez	20	veinte	30	treinta
1	uno	11	once	21	veintiuno	40	cuarenta
2	dos	12	doce	22	veintidós	50	cincuenta
3	tres	13	trece	23	veintitrés	60	sesenta
4	cuatro	14	catorce	24	veinticuatro	70	setenta
5	cinco	15	quince	25	veinticinco	80	ochenta
6	seis	16	dieciséis	26	veintiséis	90	noventa
7	siete	17	diecisiete	27	veintisiete	100	cien / ciento*
8	ocho	18	dieciocho	28	veintiocho		
9	nueve	19	diecinueve	29	veintinueve		

Use **cien for 100 and **ciento** for anything above 100 (**ciento uno, ciento dos...**)*

Practice: Bring a phone to class or simulate one. Have students simulate brief conversations like the following to practice **residencia** (**Actividad 5**) and number vocabulary:
—Aló. ¿Residencia Rioja?
—No. Es la Residencia Flores.
—¿No es 2–75–21–93?
—No. Es 19–83–22–45.
—Adiós.
—Adiós.

ENLACE CULTURAL

El teléfono

In Spanish-speaking countries, there are several ways to answer the telephone. **Aló** is used in many places. In Mexico, it is typical to say **Bueno,** whereas in Spain, people answer with **Dígame.** In some Colombian locations, people answer with **A la orden.**

Un teléfono público en Alcalá de Henares, España.

Telephone numbers can have five, six or seven digits, depending on the size of the city. Today, most large and medium-sized cities have seven digits; smaller ones may have five or six digits. In Santiago, the capital of Chile, the number for the American Embassy there is 232–2600, and would be read aloud as **dos, treinta y dos, veintiséis, cero, cero.** In San Luis Potosí, Mexico, the number of the American Consulate is 2–1528 and would be read aloud: **dos, quince, veintiocho.**

5 En grupos. Work in groups and determine how many undergraduates (*estudiantes de pregrado*) and master's degree students (*estudiantes de maestría*) live in different dormitories and boarding houses at a university in Spain.

▸ **Modelo:** —*¿Cuántos estudiantes de pregrado hay en la Residencia Omega?*
—*Hay cuarenta y cinco.*

Follow-up: Practice this question-and-answer activity with students. Make an overhead of the chart and point to the different **residencias** while asking questions of individual students.

	Residencia Rosales	Residencia Rioja	Residencia Flores	Residencia Omega	Residencia Moderna	Residencia Internacional
Estudiantes de pregrado	89	23	75	45	14	55
Estudiantes de maestría	43	11	42	12	8	24

6 ¿Cuál es el número? Work in groups saying the telephone numbers aloud.

1. Corporación Agroamazonas, Riberalta, Bolivia. Teléfono: 852–8426
2. Transflora Cargo, Bogotá, Colombia. Teléfono: 415–0188
3. Biblioteca Nacional de Venezuela, Caracas. Teléfono: 564–1717
4. Embajada de los Estados Unidos en La Paz, Bolivia. Teléfono: 43–0251
5. Consulado de los Estados Unidos en Nuevo Laredo, México. Teléfono: 4–0512

In addition, have students give the school's number, the number at your office, the number for the police.

7 Números importantes. You need to make up a class list of phone numbers and addresses for five of your classmates. Complete the following chart with this information. Follow the model.

▸ **Modelo:** —*¿Cuál es tu* (your) *número de teléfono?*
—*Es cinco, veinticuatro, cuarenta y nueve, setenta y seis.*
—*¿Cuál es tu dirección?*
—*Es dos, tres, nueve Miller Hall.*

Divide the class into groups or let students mingle informally. Then, have them report on the information they have gathered. When they give out a phone number, write it on the board so that the student can be sure it is correct.

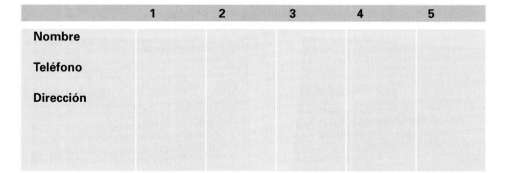

	1	2	3	4	5
Nombre					
Teléfono					
Dirección					

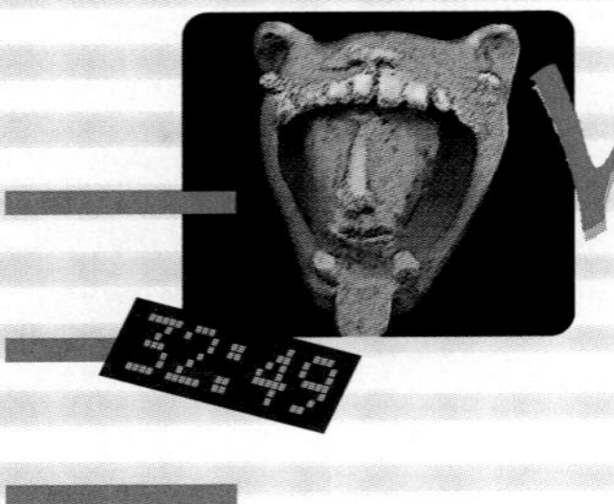

Vistas y voces

I. Preparémonos

1 Anticipación. Answer these questions in pairs.

A. **1.** Describe your university campus or the place where you are studying.
2. Which faculty members do you visit during office hours? What furniture, objects, posters do they have in their offices? What kind of computer?
3. What kinds of newspaper articles does your city/university publish? Are they available on the Internet?

B. Review chapter opening photo 1A. What do you think Nayeli is writing in the note? Who is the person behind her? What is going to happen next?

32:50

Para comprender mejor

el cuchillo	*knife*	el pelo castaño	*brown hair*
Di que sí.	*Say yes.*	el sueño	*dream*

2 Secuencia. In pairs, number the video action shots in the order in which you think the action will occur in the video you will watch.

Identify the characters in these photos (Adriana, Felipe, Nayeli, doña Gafasoscuras) and write their names on the board. Make an overhead of these pictures, cut them up, project them on the screen, and move them around according to the order in which the class would like them to be.

Correct order of video action shots: 3, 1, 2, 4

1.

2.

3.

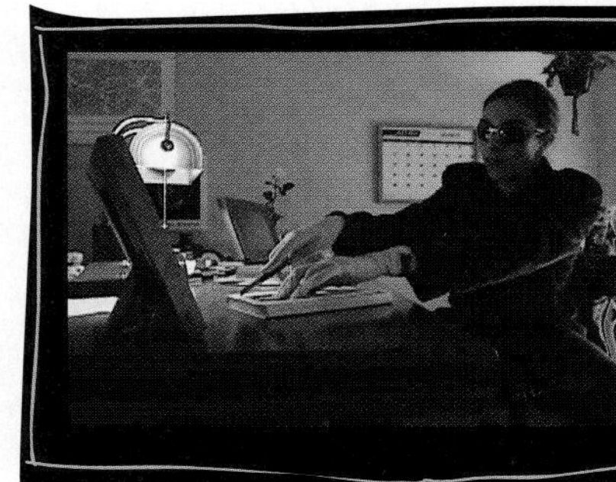
4.

II. Miremos y escuchemos

3 **Colores.** What color clothing are the characters wearing in the video? While watching the video, place a checkmark next to the colors they are wearing.

Explain that **Doña Gafasoscuras** is a nickname (*Lady Sunglasses*). Before showing the video, review colors by pointing to classroom objects. Have students say the color in Spanish.

	Nayeli	Adriana	Felipe	Doña Gafasoscuras
amarillo				
anaranjado				
azul				
blanco				
gris				
café, marrón				
morado				
negro				
rojo				
rosado				
verde				

III. Comentemos

4 **Asociación.** Working in groups, match each character with an associated item or items: 1) Nayeli; 2) Felipe; 3) Adriana; 4) Doña Gafasoscuras.

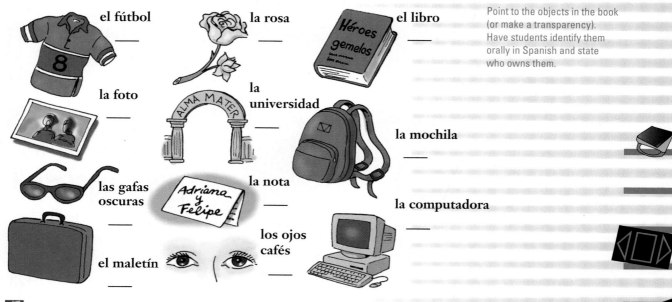

Point to the objects in the book (or make a transparency). Have students identify them orally in Spanish and state who owns them.

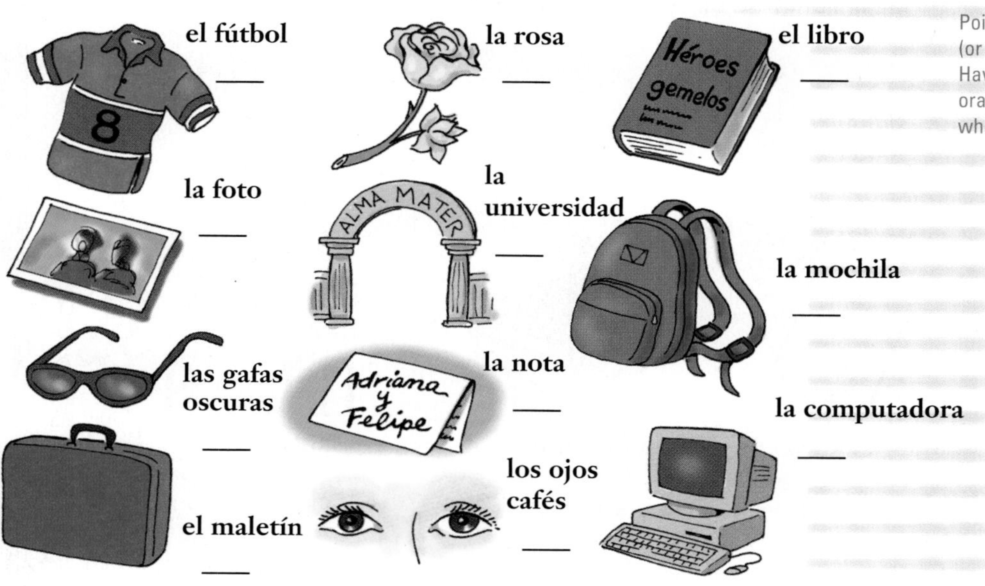

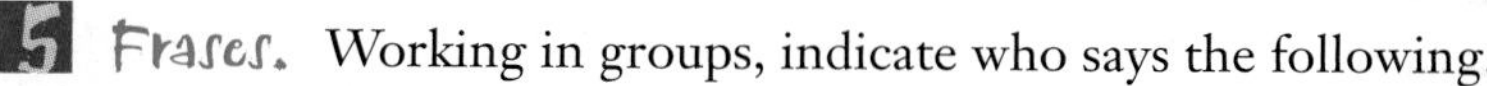

5 **Frases.** Working in groups, indicate who says the following.

1. "Tengo que hablar con Felipe Luna."
2. "Mi sueño es ser arqueóloga."
3. "Qué organizada eres, Adriana, qué organizada eres."
4. "Arqueóloga... ¡Ja!"

Answers to Actividad 5:
1. Adriana
2. Adriana
3. Felipe
4. Doña Gafasoscuras

Lengua

I. Talking about specific and nonspecific things and people

A. Indefinite articles (a, an, some)

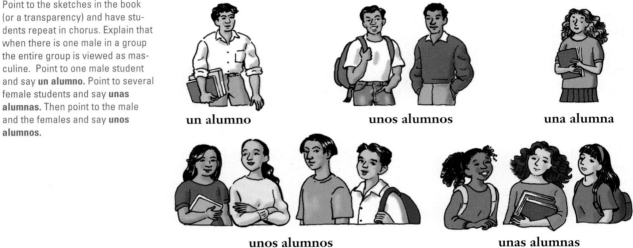

Point to the sketches in the book (or a transparency) and have students repeat in chorus. Explain that when there is one male in a group the entire group is viewed as masculine. Point to one male student and say **un alumno.** Point to several female students and say **unas alumnas.** Then point to the male and the females and say **unos alumnos.**

The indefinite article has four forms.

	Masculine	Feminine
Singular	un	una
Plural	unos	unas

B. Definite articles (the)

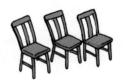

Have students repeat words with articles. Then point to chair(s) and book(s) and have students respond appropriately (**el libro, las sillas**).

The definite article has four forms.

	Masculine	Feminine
Singular	el	la
Plural	los	las

Lengua en acción

Nacionalidades, títulos y profesiones

Mention that adjectives of nationality are not capitalized in Spanish.

- When describing somebody's nationality or profession, Spanish doesn't use an indefinite article unless an additional adjective follows the description.

Felipe es futbolista.	*Felipe is a soccer player.*
Felipe es un futbolista cubanoamericano.	*Felipe is a Cuban American soccer player.*
Nayeli es arqueóloga.	*Nayeli is an archaeologist.*
Nayeli es una arqueóloga excelente.	*Nayeli is an excellent archaeologist.*

- When talking *about* people with titles, such as **señor, señora, señorita,** and **doctor/a,** the definite article is used.

El doctor Medina es mexicano.	*Dr. Medina is Mexican.*
La señorita Reyes es chicana.	*Ms. Reyes is Chicana.*

- However, when talking directly *to* a person with a title, the definite article is not used.

Doctor Medina, ¿cómo está usted?	*Doctor Medina: How are you?*
Señorita Reyes, ¿cuál es su número de teléfono?	*Ms. Reyes: What is your phone number?*

II. Identifying gender of nouns

Masculine and feminine forms

Nouns in Spanish are either masculine or feminine.

- Usually, nouns that refer to males are masculine and nouns that refer to females are feminine.

Masculine	Feminine	
el doctor	**la** doctora	*doctor*
el profesor	**la** profesora	*teacher*
el señor	**la** señora	*Mr., Mrs.*

- Nouns that refer to people and end in **-e** or **-ista** are either masculine or feminine. Gender is specified by the context or by modifiers such as articles.

Masculine	Feminine	
el artista	**la** artista	*artist*
el estudiante	**la** estudiante	*student*
el paciente	**la** paciente	*patient*

- Most nouns that refer to things and end in **-o** are masculine while most feminine nouns end in **-a.**

Masculine		Feminine	
el calendari**o**	*the calendar*	la bols**a**	*the bag*
el florer**o**	*the vase*	la calculador**a**	*the calculator*
el libr**o**	*the book*	la impresor**a**	*the printer*

The gender of nouns with other endings is not obvious. Some endings may give a clue about the gender of the noun.

- Nouns ending in **-ión, -dad, -tad** are usually feminine.

la lección	*lesson*	la actividad	*activity*	la tempestad	*storm*
la televisión	*television*	la cantidad	*quantity*	la libertad	*liberty*

- Nouns ending in **-ma** are usually masculine.

el clima	*climate*	el idioma	*language*
el sistema	*system*	el problema	*problem*
el tema	*theme*	el programa	*program*

- Nouns ending in **-e** may be masculine or feminine.

la clase	*class*	**el** arte	*art*
la gente	*people*	**el** cine	*movie theater*

You will need to learn these on a case-by-case basis.

- Common exceptions are:

el día	*day*	la mano	*hand*	el mapa	*map*

After students have finished **Actividad 1,** call on them individually or in chorus. Instructor says **un señor** and students answer **el señor.**

1 Práctica. Working with a classmate, replace the indefinite article **un** or **una** with the definite article **el** or **la**.

► **Modelo:** *un libro*
el libro

1. un señor
2. una estudiante
3. una calculadora
4. un florero
5. una composición
6. un tema
7. un doctor
8. una paciente
9. una mano
10. una arqueóloga

2 *¿Qué es?* Indicate whether each noun is masculine, feminine or both, by writing the definite article **el, la,** or both of them in front of each noun. Then, say the words aloud. Work with a partner.

Have students close their books. State words at random from the list and have students supply the definite article: **arte / el arte.**

______	arte	______	idioma
______	artista	______	impresora
______	bolsa	______	estudiante
______	calendario	______	mapa
______	dentista	______	oportunidad
______	cine	______	papel
______	clase	______	profesor
______	día	______	señora

LENGUA EN ACCIÓN

Gente (People)

- When discussing people, it is useful to know these terms. Notice the masculine and feminine forms.

el/la	abuelo/a	*grandfather, grandmother*	la	madrastra	*stepmother*
			la	madre	*mother*
el/la	alumno/a	*pupil, student*	la	mujer	*woman*
el/la	amigo/a	*friend*	el/la	niño/a	*child*
el/la	chico/a	*boy/girl*	el/la	novio/a	*boyfriend/ girlfriend*
el/la	compañero/a de clase	*classmate*	el	padrastro	*stepfather*
el/la	compañero/a de cuarto	*roommate*	el	padre	*father*
			el/la	profesor/a	*teacher*
el/la	estudiante	*student*	el	señor	*gentleman, Mr.*
el/la	hermanastro/a	*stepbrother/sister*			
el/la	hermano/a	*brother/sister*	la	señora	*lady, Mrs.*
el/la	hijastro/a	*stepson/daughter*	la	señorita	*young lady, Miss, Ms.*
el	hombre	*man*			

Show pictures from magazines and have students use the vocabulary words and practice masculine and feminine forms.

III. Talking about several persons or things

Plural of nouns

- Nouns ending in a vowel generally add **-s** to form the plural.

Singular	Plural	
la cas**a**	las casa**s**	*houses*
el niñ**o**	los niño**s**	*children*
la noch**e**	las noche**s**	*nights*

Add that words ending in **-ión** lose their accent in the plural: **nación / naciones.**

- Nouns ending in a consonant add **-es.**

Singular	Plural	
la activida**d**	las activida**des**	*activities*
el pape**l**	los pape**les**	*papers*

- When adding **-es** to nouns ending in **z,** the **z** changes to **c.**

Singular	Plural	
el lápiz	los lápi**ces**	*pencils*
la luz	las lu**ces**	*lights*

IV. Coordinating gender and number

Nouns and adjective agreement

Adjectives must agree in gender and number with the nouns they modify. Adjectives with a final **-o** in the singular have four endings: **-o, -os, -a, -as.** They usually follow the nouns they modify.

Singular		Plural	
el radio blanc**o**	*the white radio*	los radios blanc**os**	*the white radios*
la silla blanc**a**	*the white chair*	las sillas blanc**as**	*the white chairs*

Adjectives ending in **-es, -án,** and **-dor** do have four forms and are the exception to this rule: **inglés, inglesa; catalán, catalana; trabajador, trabajadora.**

Adjectives that end in any other letter have two forms, singular and plural.

Singular		Plural	
el libro interesant**e**	*the interesting book*	los libros interesant**es**	*the interesting books*
la clase interesant**e**	*the interesting class*	las clases interesant**es**	*the interesting classes*

Answers to Actividad 3:
1. unas
2. unos
3. unos
4. unos
5. unas
6. unos/unas
7. unas
8. unas

3 **¿Masculino o femenino?** Identify the correct indefinite article of these words.

1. ______ actividades
2. ______ bailes
3. ______ carteles
4. ______ cuartos
5. ______ doctoras
6. ______ estudiantes
7. ______ impresoras
8. ______ televisiones

4 Los artículos definidos. For each noun, give the correct definite article. Then make each example plural.

1. ______ cuaderno ________
2. ______ día ________
3. ______ lápiz ________
4. ______ mano ________
5. ______ papel ________
6. ______ reloj ________
7. ______ silla ________
8. ______ teléfono ________

Answers to Actividad 4:

1. el cuaderno/los cuadernos
2. el día/los días
3. el lápiz/los lápices
4. la mano/las manos
5. el papel/los papeles
6. el reloj/los relojes
7. la silla/las sillas
8. el teléfono/los teléfonos

5 Una historia interesante. Read the following short text and complete it with the missing definite or indefinite article. If no article is needed, leave the space blank.

Adriana es ________ chica de San Antonio. Es ________ estudiante de arqueología en ________ Universidad de Tejas en San Antonio. ________ papá de Adriana se llama Alberto y es ________ profesor de historia. ________ mamá de Adriana es ________ dentista.

Answers to Actividad 5:
una, —-, la, El, —-, La, —-

6 Cosas y colores. Work in pairs to describe the objects and their colors in this drawing.

► **Modelo:** *—¿Qué hay en la oficina?*
—Hay cuatro lápices amarillos.

Assign **Actividad 6** as written homework before having students describe these objects orally. After a few minutes of pair work, point to the objects to elicit oral responses. Collect the assignment to check for spelling.

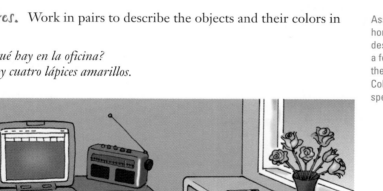

V. Describing people and things

A. Descriptive adjectives: People

Have students read the sentences in the talkbubbles out loud. Ask them who is (**quién**) **es alto, bajo,** and so on.

LENGUA EN ACCIÓN

Cortesía

In some countries it is more polite to say **mayor** (*older*) or **grande** instead of **viejo/a** (*old*) to describe someone's age.

Also, the term **gordo/a, gordito/a** (*fat*) is often used as a term of affection.

Assign **Actividad 7** as homework and/or do orally in class with books closed. Be sure to check that students add **-es** to **señor** and **profesor.**

7 **¿Cuál es el plural?** Change the following phrases from the singular to the plural. Follow the model.

▸ **Modelo:** *la mujer rubia*
las mujeres rubias

1. la chica grande
2. el señor alto
3. el hombre interesante
4. la niña morena
5. la alumna inteligente
6. el profesor rubio
7. la doctora alta
8. la profesora interesante
9. el chico moreno
10. el chico gordito

B. Descriptive adjectives: Things

Have students read aloud the sentences accompanying the drawings. Have them guess the meaning of the adjectives, or say the English and have them give the Spanish. Practice with questions such as **¿Qué es nuevo?** Make a transparency with the Spanish sentences (or just the adjectives) eliminated.

La computadora es nueva.

La computadora es vieja.

La mesa es grande.

La mesa es pequeña.

El coche es rápido.

El coche es lento.

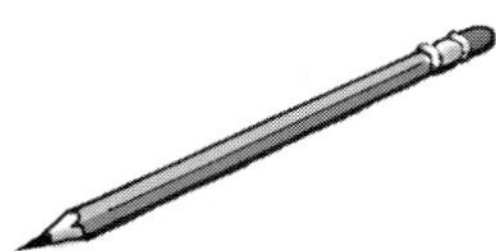
El lápiz es largo.

El lápiz es corto.

8 **¿Cuál es el singular?** Write the following phrases in the singular. Make all changes necessary. Then practice both the plural and the singular forms with a partner.

▸ **Modelo:** *las mochilas rojas*
la mochila roja

1. los coches amarillos
2. las computadoras rápidas
3. los mapas viejos
4. los teléfonos azules
5. los escritorios pequeños
6. las bolsas verdes
7. las impresoras grises
8. los libros interesantes
9. los radios negros
10. los números grandes

C. Subject pronouns

In Spanish, pronouns are used to clarify or emphasize the subject. In most cases they are optional because you can tell what the subject is by looking at the verb ending.

Singular		Plural	
yo	*I*	**nosotros/nosotras**	*we*
tú	*you*	**vosotros/vosotras**	*you*
usted (Ud.)	*you*	**ustedes (Uds.)**	*you*
él	*he*	**ellos**	*they*
ella	*she*	**ellas**	*they*

Vos is used instead of **tú** in Argentina, Costa Rica, Paraguay, Uruguay, and elsewhere in Latin America. Explain carefully the formal, informal singular and plural forms of *you.* Students should always address a figure of authority as **usted** and a student as **tú**.

- **Tú** is a pronoun for people you address by first name.
- **Usted (Ud.)** is a pronoun used for people you respect or don't know well.
- **Vosotros/vosotras** is an informal pronoun used only in Spain for people you address by first name.
- **Ustedes (Uds.)** is a formal plural pronoun in Spain. In Latin America, it is formal or informal and designates only the plural.
- **Nosotras, vosotras,** and **ellas** are used when referring to all-female groups.

D. *Ser* (*to be*)

The forms of **ser** are irregular.

Practice the forms of **ser** orally with students. Point out that **son** and **es** each have three possible subjects, referred to as the "second or third person singular and plural," which can take the form of pronouns or proper names. Explain that any subject that includes **y yo** takes the **nosotros** form.

Singular			Plural		
yo	**soy**	*I am*	nosotros/nosotras	**somos**	*we are*
tú	**eres**	*you are*	vosotros/vosotras	**sois**	*you are*
usted	**es**	*you are*	ustedes	**son**	*you are*
él	**es**	*he is*	ellos	**son**	*they are*
ella	**es**	*she is*	ellas	**son**	*they are*

Ser has many uses. In Spanish, **ser** is used to describe the following:

People	Felipe **es** alto. Nosotros **somos** bajos.	*Felipe is tall.* *We are short.*
Occupation	Adriana y Felipe **son** estudiantes. Armando, **¿es** usted profesor?	*Adriana and Felipe are students.* *Armando, are you a professor?*
Things	La computadora **es** nueva. Los gemelos **son** importantes.	*The computer is new.* *The twins are important.*
Identity	¿**Eres** Roberto? No, **soy** Felipe.	*Are you Roberto?* *No, I'm Felipe.*
Origen	Los gemelos **son** de México. **Somos** del* sur de México.	*The twins are from Mexico.* *We are from Southern Mexico.*
Nationality	Ellos **son** mexicanos. Doña Carmen **es** costarricense, ¿verdad?	*They are Mexican.* *Doña Carmen is Costa Rican, right?*
Substance: what things are made of	La computadora **es** de plástico. Los floreros **son** de barro.	*The computer is made of plastic.* *The vases are made of clay.*

****De** (of) plus **el** (the) form the contraction **del** (of the).*

- Notice that the first letter of each usage spells the word *POTIONS*. Mnemonic devices such as this can help you remember the rules.

- When describing someone or something with more than one adjective, the adjectives are connected with **y** (*and*).

  Felipe es alto **y** guapo. — *Felipe is tall and handsome.*

- If the word **y** appears before a word that starts with **i-** or **hi-**, it changes to **e**.

  Adriana es simpática **e** inteligente. — *Adriana is friendly and intelligent.*
  Ella estudia arqueología **e** historia. — *She studies archaeology and history.*

LENGUA EN ACCIÓN

Expresiones enfáticas

Spanish makes descriptions emphatic in many ways. Some common ways are:

- **muy** + adjective

El libro es **muy** interesante.	*The book is very interesting.*
La computadora es **muy** vieja.	*The computer is very old.*
La clase es **muy** buena.	*The class is very good.*

- adjective + **-ísimo/s, -ísima/s**

El libro es **interesantísimo.**	*The book is very interesting.*
La computadora es **viejísima.**	*The computer is very old.*
La clase es **buenísima.**	*The class is very good.*

Notice that if the adjective ends in a vowel, you drop the vowel and add the ending. If the adjective ends in a consonant, you usually add just the ending. As with all other adjectives, these agree in gender and number.

La lección es dificil**ísima.** — *The lesson is very difficult.*

Add that with **rico** (*rich*) there is a spelling change in **riquísimo.**

E. Negation

- Simple negation is formed by adding **no** before the verb.

  Marcela **no** es de México. — *Marcela is not from Mexico.*
  El libro **no** es amarillo. — *The book is not yellow.*

- To answer a question negatively, start the sentence with **no.**

  ¿La ventana es grande? — *Is the window large?*
  No, la ventana **no** es grande. — *No, the window is not large.*

9 ¿Cómo son? Complete the following sentences to describe various people and things.

1. Las clases...
2. Los profesores...
3. La universidad...
4. El libro de español...
5. Mi compañero/a de cuarto...
6. Mi mamá...
7. Tom Cruise y Nicole Kidman...
8. La pluma...
9. Los estudiantes...
10. Yo...

Answers to Actividad 10:
1. es / Él es dominicano.
2. son / Ellos son (estadounidenses) norteamericanos.
3. es / Ella es española.
4. es / Ella es guatemalteca.
5. es / Ella es mexicana.
6. es / Ella es chilena.
7. soy / (Answers will vary.)
8. es / (Answers will vary.)

10 ¿De dónde son? Working with a partner, state where these people are from and their nationalities.

▶ **Modelo:** *Gabriela Sabatini es de Buenos Aires. Ella es argentina.*

1. Juan Luis Guerra ______ de Santo Domingo. __________.
2. Henry Cisneros y su familia ______ de Texas. __________.
3. Arantxa Sánchez ______ de Barcelona. __________.
4. Rigoberta Menchú ______ de Chimel, Guatemala. __________.
5. Laura Esquivel ______ de México D.F. __________.
6. Isabel Allende ______ de Santiago. __________.
7. Yo ______ de __________. __________.
8. Mi compañero/a de cuarto ______ de __________. __________.

11 Así es. Write a brief description of one of your classmates on a piece of paper. Your instructor will collect these and hand them out at random to read. Try to guess who the person is.

Lectura A

Introducción

In the newspaper headlines (**titulares**) that you will be reading in this section, you will encounter words in Spanish that look very much like words that you know in English. These Spanish words that have a similar spelling and meaning as English words are called *cognates*. The strategies that follow will help you identify them in a text.

You may need to do some contrastive drills to help students hear the difference between the English and Spanish pronunciation of word pairs such as *optimist* / **optimista.**

Reading strategy: Recognizing cognates

Knowing cognates can help you increase your vocabulary tremendously! The following is a list of adjectives that can be used to describe things, people, or places. Listen to your instructor and pronounce these words to hear how they compare to similar words in English.

arrogante	importante	pesimista
egoísta	insuficiente	popular
elegante	interesante	profesional
emocional	internacional	realista
evidente	nacional	sentimental
excelente	natural	terrible
final	oportunista	tradicional
futbolista	optimista	transparente
horrible	original	tropical
idealista	persistente	universal

1 **¿Qué quiere decir?** What do the words in the preceding list mean?

2 **Categorías.** The cognates listed fall into four categories according to their endings. List them in the following chart. The first one is done for you.

Ending = *-nte*	Ending = *-ista*	Ending = *-al*	Ending = *-ible*
arrogante			

Answers to Actividad 2:
-nte: elegante, evidente, excelente, importante, insuficiente, interesante, persistente, transparente
-ista: egoísta, futbolista, idealista, oportunista, optimista, pesimista, realista
-al: emocional, final, internacional, nacional, natural, original, profesional, sentimental, tradicional, tropical, universal
-ible: horrible, terrible

What are the comparable endings for these groups of words in English?

Reading strategy: Identifying prefixes

By adding prefixes to some cognates you can greatly expand your vocabulary. Here are some examples of the prefix **in-,** a very common prefix in Spanish and English. Note that in Spanish **in-** is spelled **im-** before **b** and **p.**

3 **Opuestos.** Complete the chart with the opposites of the given words.

► **Modelo:** *conveniente/inconveniente*
perfecto/imperfecto

in-		im-	
dependiente estable flexible formal tolerante		probable personal posible paciente popular	

Answers to Actividad 3:
independiente
inestable
inflexible
informal
intolerante
improbable
impersonal
imposible
impaciente
impopular

4 **¿Positivo o negativo?** Considering both groups of cognates, which of the adjectives are positive in meaning? Negative? Both? Work in pairs and write down the adjectives below the corresponding heading.

Write the lists of positive and negative adjectives on the board.

positivo	**negativo**	**positivo y negativo**
________	________	________
________	________	________

Titulares

a. ¡Bacterias resistentes en hospitales! ________

b. Estudiantes de universidad: ¿optimistas o pesimistas? ________

c. LA FAMILIA MODERNA: UNA INSTITUCIÓN EN CRISIS ________

d. *Los héroes mayas: ¿leyenda o realidad?* ________

e. Cinema espectacular: Misión imposible ________

f. ASESINADO IMPORTANTE ARTISTA DE TELEVISIÓN ________

g. Clima inestable en el trópico ________

h. Mafias internacionales son un problema enorme ________

i. *Importante arqueóloga visita el Museo Nacional* ________

Have students read these headlines out loud.

Answers to Actividad 5:
1. h
2. g
3. e
4. d
5. b
6. c
7. f
8. i
9. a

5 *Crónicas.* What kind of text is behind the headlines? Match the Spanish headlines above to the following English sentences by writing down the corresponding letter in front.

1. ________ "American agents will be cooperating with Interpol . . ."
2. ________ "Heavy winds are expected in the whole region . . ."
3. ________ "His performance in this movie is very convincing . . ."
4. ________ "Interpretation of history is a matter of our social and cultural context . . ."
5. ________ "Not all teachers agree on the causes of this problem among young people . . ."
6. ________ "The number of divorces and one-person households has increased dramatically . . ."
7. ________ "The author of this terrible crime is still at large . . ."
8. ________ "This important institution is honored by the scientist's presence . . ."
9. ________ "Modern antibiotics are useless against these new strains . . ."

6 *Titulares.* Write your own headlines using the vocabulary from this chapter and as many cognates as possible.

ETAPA B

Pistas y palabras

I. Stating day and date: Days of the week

Una agenda típica

Read the schedule out loud with students. Have each student say one day of the week. Ask students what their (least) favorite day is.

Days of the week are not capitalized in Spanish.
Days of the week are masculine: **el lunes** = *(on) Monday* / **los lunes** = *(on) Mondays.*
To state the day, use the following model.

¿Qué día es hoy?	*What day is today?*
Hoy es martes.	*Today is Tuesday.*

Assign **Actividad 1** as homework or have students do this in pairs before you ask them the questions individually. Note that **estudia** is used as vocabulary here. Verbs will be formally introduced later.

1 **¿Qué estudia?** *(What does she study?)* Answer the following questions according to the schedule above.

1. ¿Qué estudia los lunes?
2. ¿Estudia historia? ¿Cuándo?
3. ¿Qué estudia los jueves?
4. ¿Cuándo estudia música?
5. ¿Qué estudia los viernes?
6. ¿Qué estudia los martes?
7. ¿Estudia mucho los sábados?

Answers to Actividad 1:

1. Estudia historia y arqueología.
2. Sí. Estudia historia los lunes, miércoles y viernes.
3. Estudia música y química.
4. Estudia música los jueves.
5. Estudia historia y arqueología.
6. Estudia arte y química.
7. No, no estudia mucho los sábados.

II. Stating month and date: Months of the year

***¿En qué mes estamos?** (What month is it?)*

Have students repeat the months after you and then go around the class with each student naming a month. Watch for the **z** in **marzo,** the **a** in **mayo,** the **o** in **agosto** and the **o** in **octubre.** Ask students what month their birthdays (**cumpleaños**) are in.

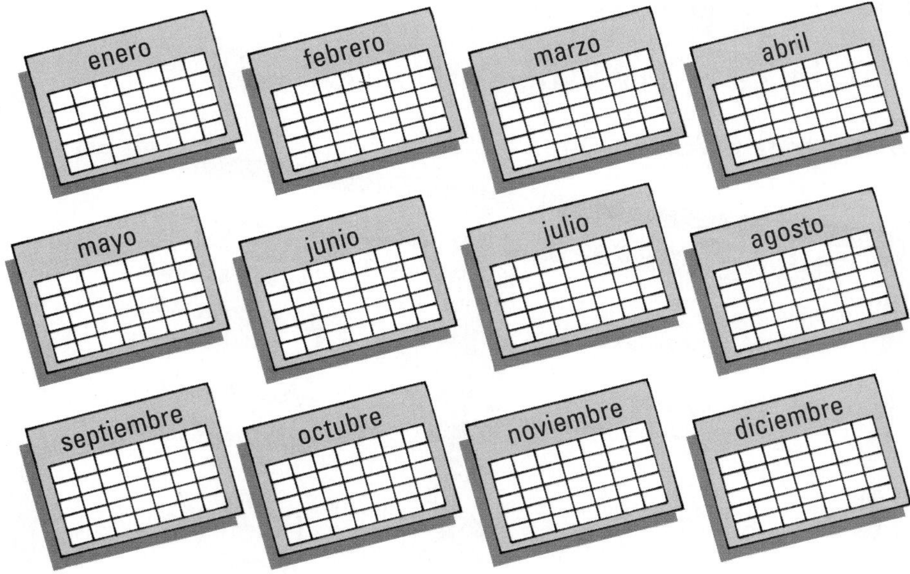

Months are not capitalized in Spanish. To state the day and date, use the following model.

¿Qué fecha es hoy?	*What is today's date?*
Hoy es el veintitrés de septiembre.	*Today is September 23.*

If you are stating the first day of the month, use the ordinal number **primero.**

Hoy es **el primero** de septiembre.	*Today is September 1.*

2 ¿Qué fecha es? State the following dates in Spanish.

1. December 9
2. October 15
3. July 4
4. August 10
5. January 1
6. March 13
7. May 31

Answers to Actividad 2:
1. Es el nueve de diciembre.
2. Es el quince de octubre.
3. Es el cuatro de julio.
4. Es el diez de agosto.
5. Es el primero de enero.
6. Es el trece de marzo.
7. Es el treinta y uno de mayo.

3 Fechas importantes. Write the dates for the following occasions. Then practice them with a classmate.

► **Modelo:** *Independence Day, USA*
el cuatro de julio

1. Valentine's Day
2. Thanksgiving Day this year
3. Columbus Day
4. Christmas
5. New Year's Day
6. The first day of spring vacation
7. Your birthday
8. Your sister or brother's birthday
9. The first day of fall classes
10. The last day of exams this term

Answers to Actividad 3:
1. el catorce de febrero
2. el ____ de noviembre
3. el doce de octubre
4. el veinticinco de diciembre
5. el primero de enero

6–10. Answers will vary.

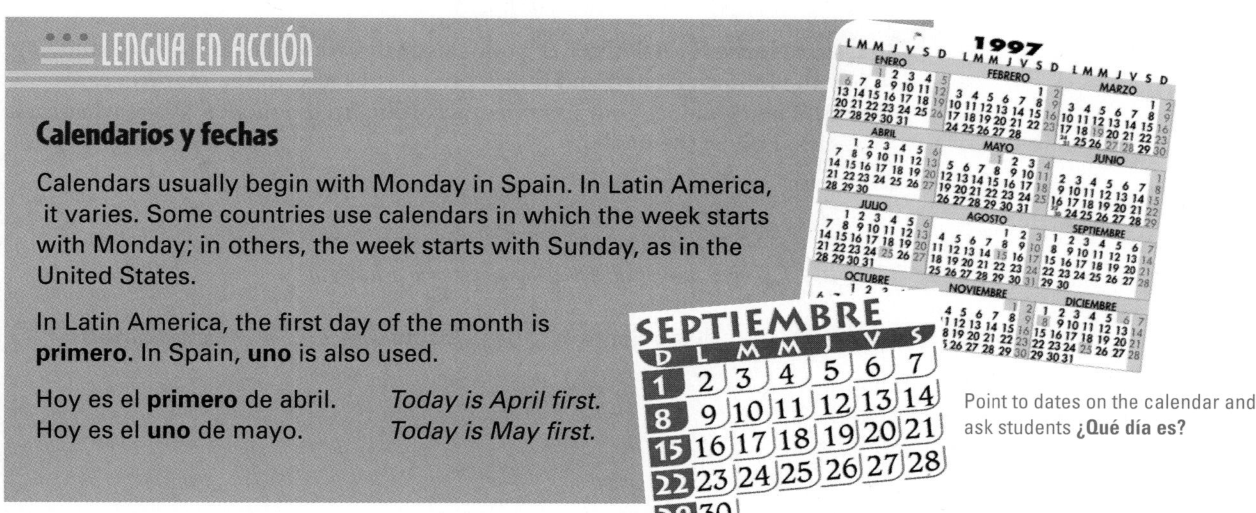

LENGUA EN ACCIÓN

Calendarios y fechas

Calendars usually begin with Monday in Spain. In Latin America, it varies. Some countries use calendars in which the week starts with Monday; in others, the week starts with Sunday, as in the United States.

In Latin America, the first day of the month is **primero.** In Spain, **uno** is also used.

Hoy es el **primero** de abril.	*Today is April first.*
Hoy es el **uno** de mayo.	*Today is May first.*

Point to dates on the calendar and ask students **¿Qué día es?**

III. Talking about academic subjects

En la universidad

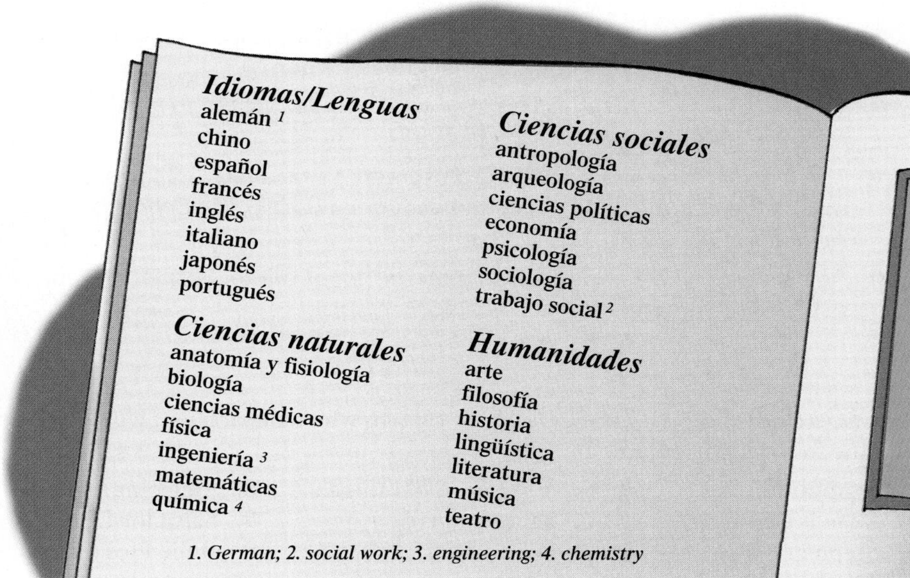

Idiomas/Lenguas
alemán [1]
chino
español
francés
inglés
italiano
japonés
portugués

Ciencias naturales
anatomía y fisiología
biología
ciencias médicas
física
ingeniería [3]
matemáticas
química [4]

Ciencias sociales
antropología
arqueología
ciencias políticas
economía
psicología
sociología
trabajo social [2]

Humanidades
arte
filosofía
historia
lingüística
literatura
música
teatro

1. German; 2. social work; 3. engineering; 4. chemistry

4 *Asociaciones.* What subject areas do you associate with these words? Use your knowledge of cognates.

1. el átomo
2. el cadáver
3. el laboratorio
4. el oxígeno
5. la composición
6. las elecciones
7. la fórmula
8. la infección
9. los números
10. la psicosis
11. la sociedad
12. la trompeta

Answers to Actividad 4:
1. física/química
2. anatomía y fisiología
3. química/biología
4. biología/química
5. inglés
6. ciencias políticas
7. matemáticas/química
8. ciencias médicas
9. matemáticas
10. psicología
11. sociología
12. música

5 **¿Qué estudias?** Ask three of your classmates what classes they are studying. Copy the following chart and fill in three classes next to the **materia** categories. Then conduct your interview according to the model. Write what each one says. Follow the model.

▸ **Modelo:** —*¿Qué estudias?*
—*Estudio matemáticas.*
—*¿Estudias sociología?*
—*No, no estudio sociología, estudio psicología.*

	Estudiante 1	Estudiante 2	Estudiante 3
Materia 1 Materia 2 Materia 3			

LENGUA EN ACCIÓN

Cognados falsos

A false cognate, sometimes called **falso amigo,** is a word in Spanish that looks like a word in English but has a different meaning. Some examples are found when talking about academic subjects.

- To ask what someone's major is, you say **¿Cuál es tu (su) (*your*) especialización?** The word **mayor** in Spanish means *older.*
- To attend class is **asistir a clase.** The verb **atender** means *to take care of, to pay attention to.*
- The *faculty* of a university is **el profesorado. La facultad** in Spanish means the *School* as in **La facultad de humanidades,** *The School of Humanities.*
- An academic subject matter is **la materia,** not **el sujeto. El sujeto** often refers to the grammatical subject of a sentence.

Answers to Actividad 6:
1. psicología
2. física
3. literatura
4. ciencias políticas
5. ciencias médicas
6. antropología
7. filosofía
8. ciencias políticas
9. arte
10. música

To supplement this exercise bring books to class from different disciplines or point to students' books using adjectives such as **interesante, práctico, fascinante, moderno, popular** to describe the subject matter.

6 **¿Qué enseña?** *(What does he/she teach?)* In which department would you find the following people?

1. Sigmund Freud
2. Isaac Newton
3. Stephen King
4. Abraham Lincoln
5. Florence Nightingale
6. Jane Goodall
7. Aristotle
8. Malcolm X
9. Salvador Dalí
10. Billie Holiday

7 **Preferencias.** Based on your preferences, give a name of an academic subject that matches the descriptions.

1. una materia de ciencias naturales
2. una materia práctica
3. una materia fascinante de humanidades
4. un idioma moderno
5. una materia de ciencias sociales muy popular

IV. Expressing likes and dislikes

Palabras y expresiones útiles

alquilar videos	*to rent videos*	mirar la televisión	*to watch television*
dar un paseo	*to take a walk*	navegar por Internet	*to surf the Web*
estar con amigos	*to be with friends*	practicar deportes	*to play sports*
estudiar	*to study*	trabajar	*to work*
hacer ejercicio	*to exercise*	viajar	*to travel*

Practice: Bring in pictures from magazines that illustrate pastimes and have students identify them.

- To say that someone likes to do something, you use the following structures.

  Me gusta + *infinitive*

  Me gusta mirar la televisión. *I like to watch TV.*

  Te gusta + *infinitive*

  Te gusta estudiar. *You like to study.*

- To say that someone likes one thing or many things, you use the following structures.

  Me gusta + *singular noun*

  Me gusta la clase de español. *I like Spanish class.*

  Me gustan + *plural noun*

  Me gustan las clases. *I like my classes.*

  Te gusta + *singular noun*

  Te gusta el fútbol. *You like soccer.*

  Te gustan + *plural noun*

  Te gustan el fútbol y el volibol. *You like soccer and volleyball.*

At this point introduce only the **me/te gusta/gustan** forms. The **gustar** construction will be covered in greater depth in a later chapter.

8 ¿Qué te gusta? With a partner, ask each other what you like to do.

▶ **Modelo:** —*¿Te gusta leer libros?*
—*Sí, me gusta leer libros.* or: —*No, no me gusta leer libros.*

1. ¿Te gusta el arte?
2. ¿Te gusta dar paseos?
3. ¿Te gustan las clases de arte?
4. ¿Te gustan los videos?
5. ¿Te gusta navegar por Internet?
6. ¿Te gusta el fútbol?
7. ¿Te gustan los deportes?
8. ¿Te gusta caminar?
9. ¿Te gusta la música jazz?
10. ¿Te gusta hablar con amigos?

After the pair activity ask students individually what they do and don't like to do on different days of the week.

9 ¿Qué te gusta hacer? In pairs, find out five activities your partner likes and doesn't like to do during the week. Follow the model.

▶ **Modelo:** —*¿Qué te gusta hacer los lunes?*
—*Me gusta estudiar y escuchar música.*
—*¿Qué no te gusta hacer?*
—*No me gusta hacer ejercicio.*

	lunes	martes	miércoles	jueves	viernes	sábado	domingo
Me gusta	*estudiar, escuchar música*	*hacer ejercicio*					
No me gusta							

V. Describing people: Adjectives of personality

Have students describe the people in the drawings with adjectives from the list.

¿Cómo son?

Adjetivos		**Opuestos**	
agradable	*pleasant*	desagradable	*unpleasant*
bueno/a	*good*	malo/a	*bad*
cómico/a	*funny*	serio/a	*serious*
divertido/a	*enjoyable*	aburrido/a	*boring*
extrovertido/a	*outgoing*	introvertido/a	*timid*
generoso/a	*generous*	envidioso/a	*envious*
honesto/a	*honest*	mentiroso/a	*liar*
inteligente, listo/a	*intelligent*	estúpido/a, tonto/a	*stupid*
moderno/a	*modern*	tradicional	*conventional*
optimista	*optimistic*	pesimista	*pessimistic*
organizado/a	*organized*	desorganizado/a	*disorganized*
simpático/a, amable	*nice, friendly*	antipático/a	*unfriendly*
trabajador/a	*hard-working*	perezoso/a, flojo/a	*lazy*

10 ¿Cómo son? Describe the following people. Include both physical and personality traits (see pages 22, 23, and 34).

1. Jimmy Smits
2. el/la presidente de la universidad
3. un/a compañero/a de clase
4. Oprah Winfrey
5. Jim Carrey
6. Frankenstein
7. Howard Stern
8. Whoopi Goldberg
9. Cindy Crawford
10. el/la profesor/a de español

Tape an index card containing the name of a famous person to a student's back, or write the name on the board, with the student facing the class. Have the student say adjectives until he or she guesses the name. Continue with the other students.

11 Adriana y Felipe. Read the description and then answer the questions.

Adriana y Felipe son estudiantes de arqueología en los Estados Unidos. Adriana es morena. Ella es inteligente, amable y atractiva. Felipe es moreno. Es futbolista, muy simpático y trabajador.

1. ¿Quiénes son estudiantes de arqueología?
2. ¿Es mexicana la universidad?
3. ¿Cómo es Adriana?
4. ¿Quién es futbolista?
5. ¿Cómo es Felipe?
6. ¿Quién es simpático?

12 Encuesta. Choose five of the characteristics listed at the beginning of section V that describe you. Then circulate among classmates to find three other people with the same characteristics.

▸ **Modelo:** —*Soy organizada, ¿y tú?*
—*No soy organizada. Soy desorganizada.*
—*Soy optimista, ¿y tú?*
—*Sí, soy optimista también.*

13 Video cita. You have decided to join the new video dating service that is offered for free on campus. Prepare a self-portrait of yourself for your video. Remember to include the information in these lists.

nombre	de dónde eres	tres materias que estudias
nacionalidad	tres pasatiempos	tres características físicas y personales

ENLACE CULTURAL

El sistema universitario en el mundo hispano

Tres estudiantes en México.

When students enter the university in Hispanic countries, they are usually accepted for specialized undergraduate programs (**pregrado**), such as humanities, law, medicine, engineering or agronomy, in which they receive a professional degree. Generally student work is assessed on a scale of 1 to 10, with 7 as a passing grade or on a scale of 1 to 5, with 3 as a passing grade.

Usually, students in Spanish-speaking countries live at home while they pursue their university education. If they attend a university far away from their hometown, they often live with relatives, in a dormitory called a **residencia estudiantil**, in a **pensión** (boarding house), or in shared apartments. In Spain, they may also live in large dormitories called **colegios mayores**.

Have students give names to the students in the picture, describe them, and state what they study.

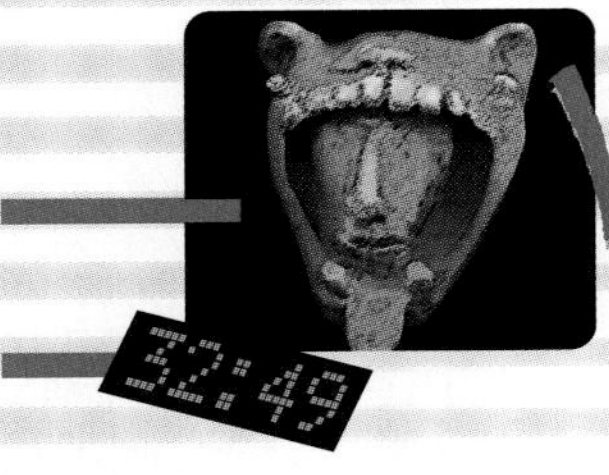

VISTAS Y VOCES

I. Preparémonos

1 Anticipación. Answer these questions in pairs.

A. **1.** ¿Qué materia es tu pasión?
2. ¿Eres optimista o pesimista?
3. ¿Qué pasatiempos te gustan? (dar un paseo, jugar al fútbol, estar con amigos y amigas, alquilar videos, etc.)
4. ¿Te gusta la aventura?

B. Review chapter opening photo 1B. What do you think that Adriana and Felipe observe in the Hero Twins book?

Para comprender mejor

el gemelo	*twin*	nadie	*nobody*
la leyenda	*legend*	se trata de	*it is about*

2 Secuencia. In pairs, number the video action shots in the order in which you think the action will occur in the video you will watch.

Correct order of video action shots: 3, 1, 2, 4

1.

2.

3.

4.

II. Miremos y escuchemos

3 ¿Cómo son? While watching the video, check off the words that are used to describe these characters.

	Adriana	Felipe	ambos (*both*)
agradable			
exagerado/a			
fascinante			
inteligente			
optimista			
profesional			
romántico/a			
simpático/a			
trabajador/a			

III. Comentemos

4 ¿Quién? Check off where each character is from originally.

Answers to Actividad 4:
Nayeli es de Nueva York.
Adriana es de San Antonio.
Felipe es de Miami.

	Nayeli	Adriana	Felipe
Miami			
San Antonio			
Nueva York			

5 Frases. Working in groups, indicate who says the following.

1. "Pero te vas a México, tres meses con Felipe 'Futbolista' Luna, y yo aquí con mis libros."
2. "Adriana es muy agradable, ...muy simpática."
3. "Sí, la arqueología es fascinante."
4. "Eres optimista, Arturo. Esta chica sólo vive para trabajar..."
5. "Y tú, mi amigo, eres un romántico incurable..."
6. "Voy a México a aprender, a investigar, a trabajar. No voy para empezar un romance sin importancia."
7. "¿Pasatiempos? Yo paso el tiempo estudiando."
8. "El libro de Nayeli. Acaba de salir: 'Los héroes gemelos de Xibalbá.'"
9. "Estoy listo para la aventura de mi vida."
10. "Tú y yo, como los héroes gemelos, vamos a triunfar sobre los malos."

Answers to Actividad 5:
1. amiga de Adriana
2. Felipe
3. Felipe
4. Felipe
5. Arturo
6. Adriana
7. Adriana
8. Adriana
9. Felipe
10. Felipe

6 Miremos otra vez. After watching the scene again, check to see if you have ordered the video action shots in the appropriate sequence.

Lengua

I. Discussing actions in the present

Present indicative of regular -ar, -er, and -ir verbs

Use different colors of chalk to demonstrate the concept of stem and endings. Use verbs other than those in the chart in the text. Or, prepare transparencies with lists of stems in one color before class and write in the endings in another color during class.

Él canta.

Ellos corren.

Ella sube la escalera.

Verbs have two parts. The meaning is carried by the *stem.* The *ending* indicates the subject and the tense. For example, you already know the verb **estudiar.** Its stem is **estudi-** and its endings show the person and tense: **estudi*o*, estudi*as*,** and so on.

- Verbs in Spanish belong to one of three conjugations: Infinitives ending in **-ar** (**cantar,** *to sing*), infinitives ending in **-er** (**correr,** *to run*), and infinitives ending in **-ir** (**subir,** *to climb*).
- Regular verbs are conjugated by dropping the **-ar, -er,** or **-ir** ending of the infinitive and adding endings to the stem that reflect tense and person. The present indicative tense of regular verbs is formed as follows.

Remind students that when you have proper names, the **él, ella, ellos,** and **ellas** forms of the verbs are used: **Celina habla = Ella habla; Celina y Jorge hablan = Ellos hablan.**

Subject	Regular *-ar* verbs	Regular *-er* verbs	Regular *-ir* verbs
yo	cant**o**	corr**o**	sub**o**
tú	cant**as**	corr**es**	sub**es**
él	cant**a**	corr**e**	sub**e**
ella	cant**a**	corr**e**	sub**e**
usted	cant**a**	corr**e**	sub**e**
nosotros/nosotras	cant**amos**	corr**emos**	sub**imos**
vosotros/vosotras	cant**áis**	corr**éis**	sub**ís**
ellos	cant**an**	corr**en**	sub**en**
ellas	cant**an**	corr**en**	sub**en**
ustedes	cant**an**	corr**en**	sub**en**

- The present indicative tense describes actions that happen in the present.

Yo estudio arqueología.	*I study/I am studying/I do study archaeology.*
Celina habla inglés.	*Celina speaks/does speak English.*
Nosotros bebemos leche.	*We drink/We are drinking/We do drink milk.*

Here are some common verbs that are regular in the present.

-*ar* verbs

acabar	*to finish*	escuchar	*to listen*	necesitar	*to need*
andar	*to walk, to ride*	estudiar	*to study*	pagar	*to pay*
ayudar	*to help*	investigar	*to research*	terminar	*to complete, to finish*
bailar	*to dance*	lavar	*to wash*	trabajar	*to work*
buscar	*to look for*	llamar	*to call*	usar	*to use*
cantar	*to sing*	llegar	*to arrive*	viajar	*to travel*
comprar	*to buy*	llevar	*to carry, to wear*	visitar	*to visit*
desear	*to wish for*	mandar	*to send*		
empacar	*to pack*	mirar	*to look at*		

-*er* verbs

aprender	*to learn*
beber	*to drink*
comer	*to eat*
comprender	*to understand*
correr	*to run*
creer	*to believe*
deber	*to ought to, to owe*
leer	*to read*
vender	*to sell*

-*ir* verbs

abrir	*to open*
decidir	*to decide*
describir	*to describe*
descubrir	*to discover*
escribir	*to write*
imprimir	*to print*
recibir	*to receive*
subir	*to go up, to climb*
vivir	*to live*

1 **Actividades estudiantiles.** The following sentences describe different students' activities. Complete them with the correct present tense form of the verb in parentheses.

1. Yo __________ (comprar) una mochila.
2. Elena ______ (hablar) tres idiomas.
3. Juan y Pepe ______ (trabajar) en la biblioteca.
4. Camila ________ (tocar) la trompeta en la banda universitaria.
5. Carmen y yo ___________ (desear) estudiar en el Perú.
6. Nosotros ________ (comer) en la cafetería todos los días.
7. Alicia ________ (escribir) cartas a su familia en la computadora.
8. Muchos estudiantes _______ (vivir) en residencias.
9. Los alumnos _________ (decidir) un plan importante.

Answers to Actividad 1:
1. compro
2. habla
3. trabajan
4. toca
5. deseamos
6. comemos
7. escribe
8. viven
9. deciden

2 **La vida en la universidad.** Paloma is on the phone telling her sister about a few of her academic activities for this week. What does she say? Use the phrases below in the **yo** form.

1. estudiar para un examen
2. escribir una composición en inglés
3. visitar el museo de arte
4. investigar en el laboratorio de física
5. mirar un video de antropología

Practice: Ask students what their own academic activities are.

Answers to Actividad 2:
1. estudio
2. escribo
3. visito
4. investigo
5. miro

Practice: Give a model sentence and a series of subject cues: **Yo debo trabajar mucho. Ellos / Ellos deben trabajar mucho.**

Lengua en acción

Expresiones con infinitivos

The verbs **desear, necesitar, deber,** and **decidir** are most often used with an infinitive.

Deseo vender el coche.	*I want to sell the car.*
Necesitamos comer.	*We need to eat.*
Debes trabajar mucho.	*You should work a lot.*
Deciden estudiar en la biblioteca.	*They decide to study in the library.*

The construction **acabar** + **de** + infinitive means *to have just done* or *to have just completed* an action.

Acabo de comer.	*I have just eaten.*
Acabamos de vender el coche.	*We have just sold the car.*

After completing this exercise, ask students **¿Qué deseas hacer? / ¿Qué necesitas hacer? / ¿Qué debes hacer?** State that **hacer** means *to do* and that they usually use another verb in their answer.

3 La lista de Javier. Write in complete sentences the social activities that Javier and his friends plan to do this weekend. Use **desear, necesitar,** or **deber** + infinitive. Follow the model.

► **Modelo:** *alquilar un video*
Ellos necesitan alquilar un video.

1. correr en el parque
2. bailar salsa
3. visitar el museo
4. trabajar mucho
5. escuchar música
6. salir hoy
7. escribir la composición
8. comer tacos
9. recibir las cartas
10. aprender español

Write verb expressions on the board. Act out a few situations and ask students **¿Qué acabo de hacer?** They answer: **Usted acaba de escribir una composición, hacer ejercicios,** and so on.

4 Actividades recientes. You have just visited with all of your friends. When you return to your room, your roommate asks you what your friends have just done. Report what they have done using **acabar de** + infinitive. Follow the model.

► **Modelo:** *Enrique (comer)*
Enrique acaba de comer.

1. Patricio (escuchar) música clásica
2. Paco y Graciela (comprar) pizza
3. Elvira (escribir) una composición en italiano
4. Alicia y su compañera de cuarto (dar) un paseo
5. Rodrigo y yo (terminar) un experimento en el laboratorio de física
6. Mario (hacer) ejercicios con amigos
7. Yo (visitar) a amigos

5 Querido amigo/Querida amiga. Write a postcard to a friend to tell him/her about university life. Include at least two sentences about each of the following: the university, the professors, classes, and new friends. Use as many different verbs as possible.

II. Asking and responding to questions

A. Question formation: Yes/No questions

There are three ways of asking questions in Spanish when only a **sí** or a **no** is required as an answer. Notice also how each question is answered.

- Raising the voice at the end of a statement.

—¿Manuel estudia ruso?	*Does Manuel study Russian?*
—Sí, él estudia ruso.	*Yes, he studies Russian.*
—¿Ellos viven en Acapulco?	*Do they live in Acapulco?*
—No, ellos viven en Veracruz.	*No, they live in Veracruz*

- Adding a tag word at the end of a statement.

  Note the English words that correspond to these expressions. Tag questions have the same sentence structure as statements, except for the addition of the tag words. Some common tag words are: **¿sí?**, **¿no?**, **¿(no es) verdad?**, and **¿(no es) cierto?**

—El portero abre la puerta, **¿no?**	*The doorman opens the door, doesn´t he?*
—Sí, él abre la puerta.	*Yes, he does open the door.*
—Olga habla inglés, **¿verdad?**	*Olga speaks English, doesn´t she?*
—No, ella no habla inglés.	*No, she doesn´t speak English.*

- Inverting the word order of subject and verb.

  Note how the response to the question reestablishes the original order of the sentence.

—¿Es interesante el libro?	*Is the book interesting?*
—No, el libro no es interesante.	*No, the book isn´t interesting.*
—¿Son deliciosos los chocolates?	*Are the chocolates delicious?*
—Sí, los chocolates son deliciosos.	*Yes, the chocolates are delicious.*

B. Question formation: Information questions

Interrogative words are used for questions that require an informative response, rather than a simple *yes* or *no*.

Point out that these words, when interrogative, have accents. Note that *who* = **quién** in the singular and **quiénes** in the plural.

—¿**Qué** pasa hoy? ¡Hay mucha gente aquí!	*What is going on today? There are a lot of people here.*
—Hoy hay una celebración importante.	*There is an important celebration today.*
—¿Y **por qué** hay una celebración?	*And why is there a celebration?*
—Porque la excavación es un éxito.	*Because the excavation is a success.*
—¿Y **cuál** excavación es?	*And which excavation is it?*
—La excavación arqueológica maya.	*The Mayan archaeological excavation.*
—¿Y **quién** es el director de la excavación?	*And who is the director heading the excavation?*
—No es un director. Es una directora.	*It is not a male director. It is a female director.*

—Bueno, ¿**cómo** se llama la directora? — *Well, what is the director's name?*
—Se llama Nayeli Paz Ocotlán. — *Her name is Nayeli Paz Ocotlán.*
—¡Ah! Y ¿**de dónde** es la profesora Paz? — *Ah, and where is Professor Paz from?*
—Es mexicanoamericana, de Nueva York. — *She is Mexican-American, from New York.*
—¿**Quiénes** son los asistentes de la profesora? — *Who are the professor's assistants?*
—Son dos estudiantes, Adriana Reyes y Felipe Luna. — *They are two students: Adriana Reyes and Felipe Luna.*
—¿**Cuándo** termina la celebración? — *When does the celebration end?*
—Termina hoy por la noche, muy tarde. — *It ends tonight, very late.*

The interrogatives *how much* (**cuánto/a**) and *how many* (**cuántos/as**) agree with the noun they modify in gender and number. They also carry a written accent.

¿Cuánt**a** cervez**a** bebes? — *How much beer do you drink?*
¿Cuánt**as** lámpar**as** hay en la habitación? — *How many lamps are in the room?*
¿Cuánt**o** caf**é** tomas? — *How much coffee do you drink?*
¿Cuánt**os** estudiant**es** son de Madrid? — *How many students are from Madrid?*

Possible answers to Actividad 6:

1. ¿Qué bebe Celina?
2. ¿De qué es la computadora?
3. ¿Qué hablan ustedes?
4. ¿Qué miran Paula y Lucía?
5. ¿Qué hay en la universidad? / ¿Dónde hay muchos coches?
6. ¿Cuántos estudiantes de español hay en la clase?
7. ¿Qué video es interesante?
8. ¿De dónde son ustedes?
9. ¿Cuándo caminas?
10. ¿De qué es el libro?

6 Preguntas. Create a question for each of the following answers using interrogative question words such as **¿qué, ¿cómo?, ¿cuándo?, ¿dónde?, ¿cuánto(a/os/as)?, ¿de dónde?**

► **Modelo:** *En la ciudad hay tres museos.*
¿Cuántos museos hay en la ciudad? ¿Dónde hay tres museos?

1. Celina bebe leche.
2. La computadora es de plástico.
3. Nosotros hablamos francés.
4. Paula y Lucía miran dos videos españoles.
5. En la universidad hay muchos coches.
6. Hay veinte estudiantes de español en la clase.
7. El video "Misión imposible" es interesante.
8. Nosotros somos de Santiago de Chile.
9. Yo camino los sábados.
10. El libro es de papel.

7 La vida universitaria. Choosing from the three infinitives provided, ask a classmate one question about the academic and social life of his or her roommate.

► **Modelo:** *viajar / estudiar / comer*
¿Dónde estudia tu compañero/a de cuarto?

1. vivir / correr / trabajar
2. escuchar / mirar / describir
3. escribir / hablar / leer
4. comer / beber / llevar
5. deber / recibir / abrir
6. cantar / practicar / bailar
7. pagar / vender / comprar
8. vivir / visitar / viajar
9. imprimir / escribir / investigar
10. llegar / viajar / mandar

8 ¿Cómo es? Work with two classmates to discuss life at your university.

▸ **Modelo:** —*¿Son interesantes las clases? fácil / malo / difícil*
—*Sí, las clases son interesantes y fáciles.* or:
—*No, las clases son malas y difíciles.*

1. ¿Son buenos los médicos universitarios? inteligente / tonto / malo
2. ¿Es grande la universidad? hermoso / feo / viejo
3. ¿Son jóvenes los profesores de español? alto / bajo / gordo
4. ¿Es bonita la residencia? nuevo / feo / malo
5. ¿Es fácil el español? interesante / difícil / aburrido
6. ¿Es bueno el clima de la ciudad? hermoso / malo / frío
7. ¿Son simpáticos los estudiantes? / inteligente / antipático / optimista

9 Mi vida universitaria. Using the information from **Actividad 8** write six sentences describing university life on your campus.

10 Actividades diarias. Write down five questions to ask a classmate about his or her daily activities at home or at the university. Then work in pairs to ask and answer each other's questions.

III. Telling time

A. The clock: ¿Qué hora es? *(What time is it?)*

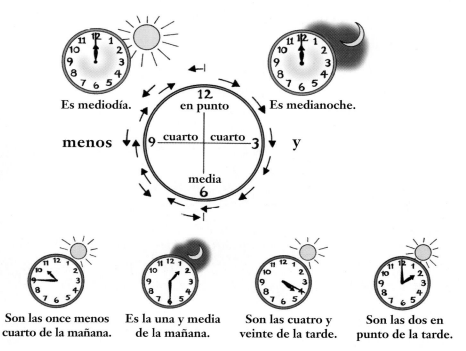

Bring a large clock (real or cardboard) to class or create a variety of clocks on transparencies. Remember that there are some students who have had more practice with digital clocks.

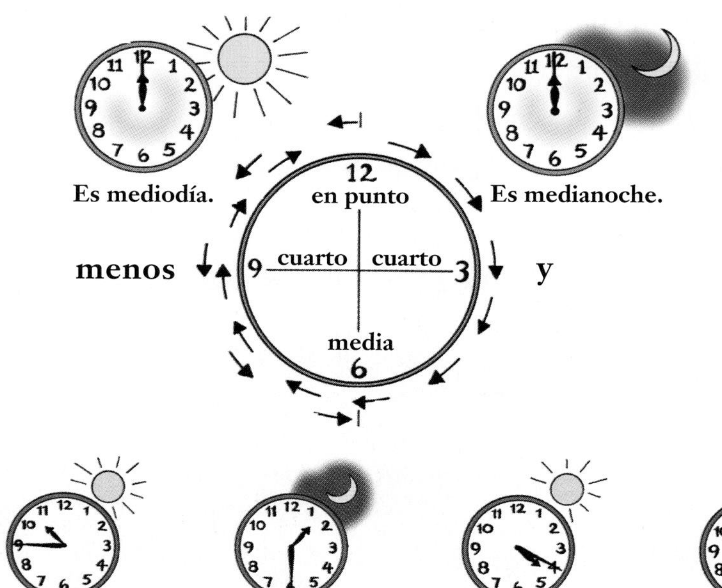

Son las once menos cuarto de la mañana.	Es la una y media de la mañana.	Son las cuatro y veinte de la tarde.	Son las dos en punto de la tarde.

- In many Spanish-speaking countries, the question is also formed as **¿Qué horas son?**
- Time is expressed using the verb **ser.** As you can see, time that has already passed is added to the hours using **y.** Time before the hour is expressed with the hour + **menos** + minutes.

B. Time expressions

State that **tarde** can also mean *evening* and is abbreviated **p.m.** **Noche** is also used for **p.m.** and means *night*. It is normally used to refer to p.m. after sunset.

Por la noche

CAROLINA: ¡Hay una fiesta fantástica en la universidad!
LUISA: ¿A qué hora es la fiesta?
CAROLINA: Es a las nueve y media **de la noche.**
MARIO: ¡Qué lástima! *(Too bad!)* Yo estudio **por la noche.**
LUISA: Y yo trabajo **por la noche.**
CAROLINA: ¡Qué mala suerte!

Useful time expressions:

por la mañana *morning* (general time period)

Mireya toma café **por la mañana.** *Mireya drinks coffee in the morning.*

por la tarde *afternoon* (general time period)

Ellos miran la televisión **por la tarde.** *They watch TV in the afternoon.*

por la noche *evening/night* (general time period)

Esteban y Lucía trabajan **por la noche.** *Esteban y Lucía work at night.*

specific time + **de la mañana**

El autobús llega **a las seis de la mañana.** *The bus arrives at six in the morning.*

specific time + **de la tarde**

La clase es **a las tres de la tarde.** *The class is at three in the afternoon.*

specific time + **de la noche**

La visita es **a las siete de la noche.** *The visit is at seven p.m.*

- Time can also be expressed in Spanish using a.m. and p.m. Lower case letters are preferred.

  Voy al cine a las 7.30 **p.m.** *I'm going to the movie theater at 7:30 p.m.*

LENGUA EN ACCIÓN

El horario de veinticuatro horas

In daily life, a 12-hour time format is usual in the Hispanic countries. However, a 24-hour time table is preferred in Spain for transportation itineraries, official events, and so on. In this time format, 12 midnight is 00:00 hours.

El autobús sale a las **23.35** horas. *The bus leaves at 11:35 p.m.*

After students do this exercise in pairs, ask the entire class what the times are, first in 24-hour time, then in a.m./p.m. format. To convert from 24-hour time to 12-hour time, subtract 12 from the time given: 18.00 = 6.00 p.m.

11 ¿Qué hora es? Take turns with a partner to tell the time on each clock below. Use the 24-hour clock.

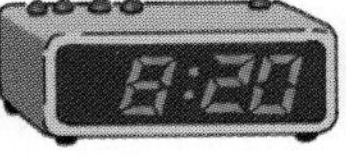

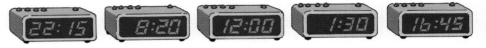

12 Hora mundial. You are in San Francisco and have to communicate with friends in eight cities, located in eight different time zones. Following the model, ask your partner what time it is in each location.

▸ **Modelo:** —*¿Qué hora es en San Antonio?*
—*En San Antonio son las dos de la mañana.*

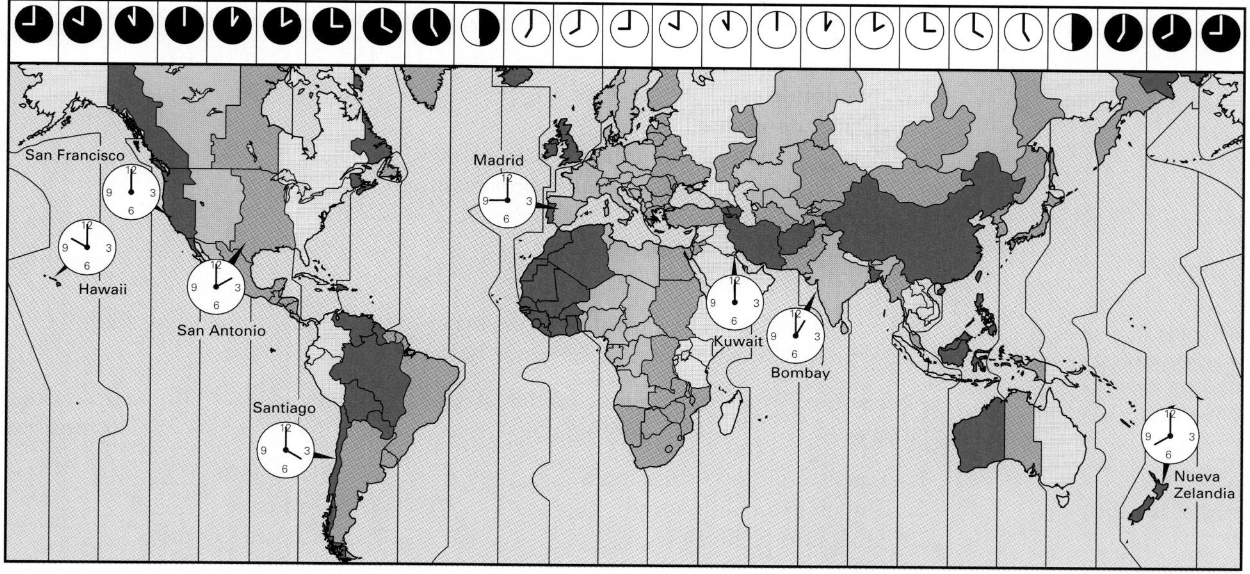

13 ¿Cuál es la rutina? In pairs, ask each other these questions.

1. ¿Cuándo estudias tú, por la noche o por la mañana?
2. ¿A qué hora comes?
3. ¿Te gusta ir a clase a las seis de la mañana?
4. ¿Cuándo lees el correo en la computadora?
5. ¿A qué hora miras videos?

Lectura B

Introducción

In this reading selection you will meet three university students from different parts of the Spanish-speaking world.

Prelectura

1 El mapa. With a classmate, review the names and locations of Spanish-speaking countries and islands that you studied in the introductory chapter on pages 4 and 5. Then, complete each of these ideas orally.

1. Las tres islas de habla española en el Mar Caribe son Puerto Rico, La República Dominicana y ______.
2. Venezuela es un país al ______ del continente suramericano.

Practice: Have students imagine they are in other cities, such as Boston, Miami, Chicago, Denver, and San Diego and figure out what those local times are relative to other places in the world. If your students are from different cities, use their hometowns.

Answers to Actividad 12:
1. En Nueva Zelandia son las ocho de la noche.
2. En Hawaii son las diez de la noche.
3. En San Francisco es medianoche.
4. En San Antonio son las dos de la mañana.
5. En Santiago son las cuatro de la mañana.
6. En Madrid son las nueve de la mañana.
7. En Kuwait es (el) mediodía.
8. En Bombay son las dos de la tarde.

Answers to Actividad 1:
1. Cuba
2. norte
3. Nicaragua, Panamá
4. Argentina, Bolivia, Colombia. (If students choose **Brasil,** remind them that Portuguese, not Spanish, is spoken in **Brasil.**)
5. Europa

Bring a map to class to have students name the different countries as you point to them.

3. En Centroamérica hay seis naciones de habla española: Guatemala, Honduras, El Salvador, Costa Rica, ______ y ______.
4. A, B y C son las primeras letras de tres países de Suramérica. ¿Qué países son? A______, B______ y C______.
5. España y Portugal forman parte del continente de ______.

2 Persona a persona. Working with a classmate, ask each other these questions.

1. ¿De dónde eres?
2. ¿Qué lenguas hablas?
3. ¿Cuántas materias estudias? ¿Cuáles son?
4. En tu opinión, ¿qué especialización es difícil?
5. ¿Qué días trabajas?
6. ¿Qué deseas ser en el futuro?

Answers to Actividad 3:
1. la universidad
2. inteligente
3. ecuatoriana
4. optimistas
5. familia
6. literatura
7. especialización
8. emocionales

3 Palabras internacionales. Construct meaningful sentences by adding one of the provided words to each sentence below.

especialización	emocionales	la universidad	literatura
familia	inteligente	ecuatoriana	optimistas

1. Los estudiantes estudian en ______.
2. Soy un estudiante muy ______.
3. Me llamo Celina y soy ______.
4. Mis amigos y yo somos muy ______.
5. Vivo con mi ______.
6. ¿Estudias ______?
7. El español es mi ______.
8. Ella tiene problemas ______.

Tres estudiantes universitarios

Read the following passages using your knowledge about cognates. First, study the photos. Then, while you read, underline the words that you recognize as cognates and read them aloud to learn about the students.

Have students describe the people in the photos and write down on the board the adjectives students use.

Me llamo Luis González. Soy mexicano, de la ciudad de Chihuahua. Soy estudiante de doctorado° y estudio psicología clínica. Tengo° clases los lunes, miércoles y viernes. Los martes y jueves, trabajo en un laboratorio de biología. Deseo ser psicólogo en el futuro, tener° una práctica en la capital y ayudar a las personas con problemas emocionales. Me gusta practicar el fútbol.° Soy una persona flexible y optimista. Mi vida es fantástica.

Ph.D.
I have
to have
soccer

Mi nombre es Janet Quesada y soy dominicana. Hablo inglés y español. Vivo con mi familia en un apartamento, en la ciudad de Nueva York, en los Estados Unidos. Estudio italiano como especialización en la universidad. Soy poeta bilingüe y actriz. Me gusta ir al teatro y ver telenovelas° en la televisión. También,° bailo danzas afrocaribeñas. Es difícil tener auto en la ciudad y yo uso transporte público. En el futuro deseo ser profesora de lengua, literatura y cultura.

soap operas / Also

¡Hola! Soy española y me llamo Beatriz Iraeta. Soy alta y rubia. Soy de Granada pero vivo en Madrid, una ciudad enorme con millones de personas. Ando en motocicleta. Me gusta escribir música original contemporánea y los sábados toco la guitarra y canto en discotecas con un grupo de amigos universitarios. Estudio antropología en la Universidad Complutense de Madrid. En el futuro deseo ser antropóloga y viajar a Asia, a África y a las Américas para trabajar.

Postlectura

4 Preguntas. Answer the following questions with a classmate. Then write your answers.

1. ¿De dónde es Luis? ¿Cómo es?
2. ¿Dónde vive Janet? ¿Cómo es? ¿Qué desea ser en el futuro?
3. ¿Cómo es Beatriz? ¿De dónde es? ¿En qué universidad estudia?
4. ¿Qué especialización tiene Luis?
5. ¿Quién desea trabajar en África?
6. ¿Qué materia estudia Janet?
7. ¿Dónde canta Beatriz los sábados?
8. ¿Qué deporte practica Luis?
9. ¿Quién escribe música contemporánea?
10. ¿Quién es poeta?

5 Retratos. Write a description in Spanish of three famous people. Then, working in groups of three, read your descriptions and have your classmates guess who they are.

Answers to Actividad 4:

1. Luis es de la ciudad de Chihuahua. Es flexible y optimista.
2. Janet vive en la ciudad de Nueva York. Es artística. En el futuro desea ser profesora de lengua, literatura y cultura.
3. Beatriz es alta y rubia. Es de Granada. Estudia en la Universidad Complutense de Madrid.
4. Luis estudia psicología clínica.
5. Beatriz desea trabajar en Africa.
6. Janet estudia italiano.
7. Los sábados Beatriz canta en discotecas.
8. Luis practica el fútbol.
9. Beatriz escribe música contemporánea.
10. Janet es poeta.

As a group activity have students concentrate on the description of one famous person. Then have one spokesperson from each group read his or her group's description. Have the class guess who the person is.

En resumen

I. Hablemos

1 ¡Personas con...! Arrange the class with all seats in a circle. There is one chair for each student except for one volunteer. The volunteer starts this activity by standing in the middle of the class and calling out a descriptive phrase like: **Personas con mochilas verdes.** All students with green bookbags must stand up and search for a seat that is *different* from the one they are sitting in. At this time, the volunteer must also find a seat leaving one student without a seat. This student calls out the next description. The game continues for at least five rounds.

2 Una entrevista con Letterman. Some of the main characters from the video have been invited to appear on the David Letterman show. In groups of three or four, prepare an interview for the class. One member plays the role of Letterman and the others choose one of the main characters from the video. Choose from Adriana, Felipe, Gafasnegras, and Nayeli.

II. Investiguemos por Internet

Using Internet addresses

The Internet and the World Wide Web are important means of communication and reference resources. In this section, you will learn vocabulary and strategies to find and use available information in Spanish, and to increase your learning enjoyment of the Spanish language.

Show students what this homepage looks like through a photocopy of the printout if you do not have access to the Internet in your school or classroom.

3 El sitio Web. Your first activity will be to find the Web site of the Houghton Mifflin Company. When you are on this site, search for the title of this book to access its home page.

Here are some useful words to start with. You will encounter these words many times on Spanish Web sites.

Vocabulario informático

buscar	*to search*	la página principal (la página inicial)	*home page*
la búsqueda	*search*	la red	*the Net, Internet*
el navegador	*browser*	el sitio Web	*Web site*
navegar por Internet	*to surf the Internet*		

4 Palabras. Select three words presented in the *Vocabulario informático* and create one sentence with each one. You may want to review the adjectives and verbs that you have learned in this chapter.

► **Modelo:** *El navegador Netscape es bueno.*
La página principal de Houghton Mifflin es **http://www.hmco.com**

III. Escribamos

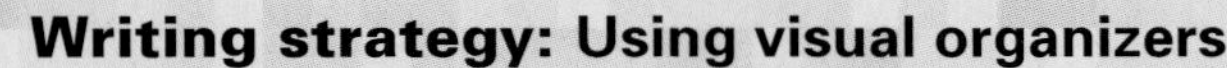

Writing strategy: Using visual organizers

When beginning to write in a new language, it is a good idea to use strategies that help you organize your thoughts. Although you might be tempted to write in English and then translate your writing into Spanish, you will be a better writer if you apply some of the suggestions provided in this textbook. At the end of each workbook segment, you will practice these strategies in a section called *Escribamos*.

Writing strategy: Creating a cluster diagram

One common visual organizer is called a cluster diagram. It allows you to see the connection between main topics and details and will help you find the words that you will need to write in Spanish.

1. Choose your topic and write it in the center of a piece of paper. Circle it.
2. Focus on the main ideas for your topic. Write them down, circle them, and connect them to your topic.
3. Think about these main ideas and write any related words around them until you have a diagram that looks like this one.

Strategy in action

Turn to *Escribamos* in the Workbook to practice the strategy of creating a cluster diagram.

5 La vida universitaria. You have been chosen by the university to write an article (in Spanish) on university life for incoming freshmen from Mexico. Use a cluster diagram to organize your thoughts before writing your article.

Vocabulario

En el cuarto

la alfombra	*rug*	**el libro**	*book*
el basurero	*waste basket*	**la llave**	*key*
el bolígrafo (la pluma)	*pen*	**el mapa**	*map*
la bolsa	*purse*	**la mesa**	*table*
el borrador	*eraser*	**la mochila**	*bookbag, backpack*
la calculadora	*calculator*	**la oficina**	*office*
el calendario	*calendar*	**el papel**	*paper*
la cama	*bed*	**la pared**	*wall*
la carpeta	*folder*	**la pizarra**	*blackboard, chalkboard*
el cartel	*poster*	**la planta**	*plant*
la carta	*letter*	**el pupitre**	*writing desk*
la cartera	*wallet*	**el radio**	*radio*
la computadora	*computer*	**la regla**	*ruler*
el cuaderno	*notebook*	**el reloj**	*watch, clock*
el escritorio	*desk*	**la rosa**	*rose*
el estante	*bookshelf*	**la silla**	*chair*
el florero	*flower vase*	**el sillón**	*arm chair*
la habitación	*room*	**el teléfono**	*telephone*
la impresora	*printer*	**la televisión**	*television*
la lámpara	*lamp*	**la tiza**	*chalk*
el lápiz	*pencil*	**la ventana**	*window*

Colores

amarillo/a	*yellow*	**morado/a**	*purple*
anaranjado/a	*orange*	**negro/a**	*black*
azul	*blue*	**rojo/a**	*red*
blanco/a	*white*	**rosa, rosado/a**	*pink*
café (marrón)	*brown*	**verde**	*green*
gris	*gray*		

Números de 0 a 100

(See p. 12)

Gente/Personas

(See p. 19)

Descripción de personas y cosas

alto/a	*tall*	**delgado/a**	*thin*
bajo/a	*short (height)*	**difícil**	*difficult*
bueno/a	*good*	**feo/a**	*ugly*
corto/a	*short (length)*	**gordo/a**	*fat*

grande	*big, large*	**moreno/a**	*dark-complexioned*
guapo/a	*handsome, good-looking*	**nuevo/a**	*new*
importante	*important*	**pelirrojo/a**	*red-headed*
inteligente (listo/a)	*intelligent*	**pequeño/a**	*small*
joven	*young*	**rápido/a**	*fast*
largo/a	*long*	**rubio/a**	*light-complexioned, blonde*
lento/a	*slow*		
malo/a	*bad*	**viejo/a**	*old (for a person or thing)*
mayor	*older*		

Días de la semana

lunes	*Monday*	**viernes**	*Friday*
martes	*Tuesday*	**sábado**	*Saturday*
miércoles	*Wednesday*	**domingo**	*Sunday*
jueves	*Thursday*		

Meses del año

enero	*January*	**julio**	*July*
febrero	*February*	**agosto**	*August*
marzo	*March*	**septiembre**	*September*
abril	*April*	**octubre**	*October*
mayo	*May*	**noviembre**	*November*
junio	*June*	**diciembre**	*December*

En la universidad

la especialización	*major*	**la residencia**	*dormitory*
la facultad	*School*	**la sala de clase**	*classroom*
la materia	*academic subject*	**la universidad**	*university*
el profesorado	*faculty*		

Idiomas / Lenguas

alemán	*German*	**inglés**	*English*
chino	*Chinese*	**italiano**	*Italian*
español	*Spanish*	**japonés**	*Japanese*
francés	*French*	**portugués**	*Portuguese*

Pasatiempos

alquilar videos	*to rent videos*	**jugar al volibol**	*to play volleyball*
caminar	*to walk*	**leer libros**	*to read books*
dar un paseo	*to take a walk*	**mirar la televisión**	*to watch television*
escribir cartas	*to write letters*	**navegar por Internet**	*to surf the Web*
escuchar música	*to listen to music*	**pintar**	*to paint*
estar con amigos	*to be with friends*	**practicar deportes**	*to play sports*
estudiar	*to study*	**tocar la guitarra**	*to play the guitar*
hablar con amigos	*to talk with friends*	**trabajar**	*to work*
hacer ejercicio	*to exercise*	**viajar**	*to travel*

Adjetivos de personalidad

aburrido/a *boring*
agradable *pleasant*
antipático/a *unfriendly*
bueno/a *good*
cómico/a *funny*
desagradable *unpleasant*
desorganizado/a *disorganized*
divertido/a *enjoyable, amusing*
envidioso/a *greedy, envious*
estúpido/a (tonto/a) *stupid*
extrovertido/a *outgoing*
generoso/a *generous*
honesto/a *honest*
inteligente, listo/a *intelligent*
introvertido/a *timid*
malo/a *bad*
mentiroso/a *(lying) / liar*
moderno/a *modern*
optimista *optimistic*
organizado/a *organized*
perezoso/a (flojo/a) *lazy*
pesimista *pessimistic*
serio/a *serious*
simpático/a (amable) *nice, friendly*
trabajador/a *hardworking*
tradicional *conventional*

Verbos -ar, -er, -ir

(See p. 39)

Tiempo, hora y fecha

(See p. 43)

Palabras y expresiones útiles

acabar de *to have just done or completed an action*
con *with*
hay *there is, there are*
me gusta/n *I like*
muy *very*
no *no*
sí *yes*
te gusta/n *you like*
norte *north*
este *east*
oeste *west*
sur *south*

CAPÍTULO 2

LOCALIDAD: México

2A

¿Dónde está Nayeli?

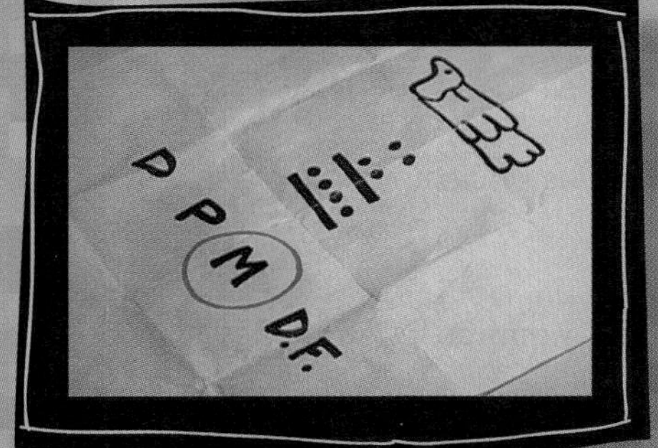

2B

A stranger plays a pivotal role in the search for Nayeli and the missing Jaguar Twin. Will the mysterious note hold the clue to their whereabouts?

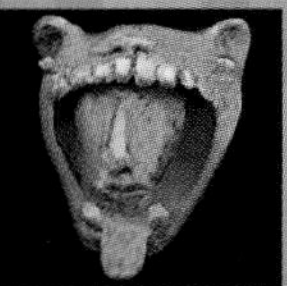

Vocabulary themes

- Describing an apartment
- Describing places in a city
- Talking about weather
- Talking about seasons, weather, and appropriate clothes
- Describing how you feel

Language structures

- Expressing possession
- Describing actions
- Expressing location with *estar*
- Describing people and places
- Describing direction
- Expressing obligation and mental or physical conditions
- Using common expressions with *tener*

Culture topics

- La cerámica, adorno urbano y doméstico
- La temperatura

Readings

- Puebla, una ciudad importante
- Oaxaca maravillosa

Reading/writing strategies

- Asking questions
- Brainstorming ideas

Internet strategy

- Searching for Spanish sites

ETAPA A

Pistas y palabras

I. Describing an apartment

Se vende apartamento en la Colonia Villareal.

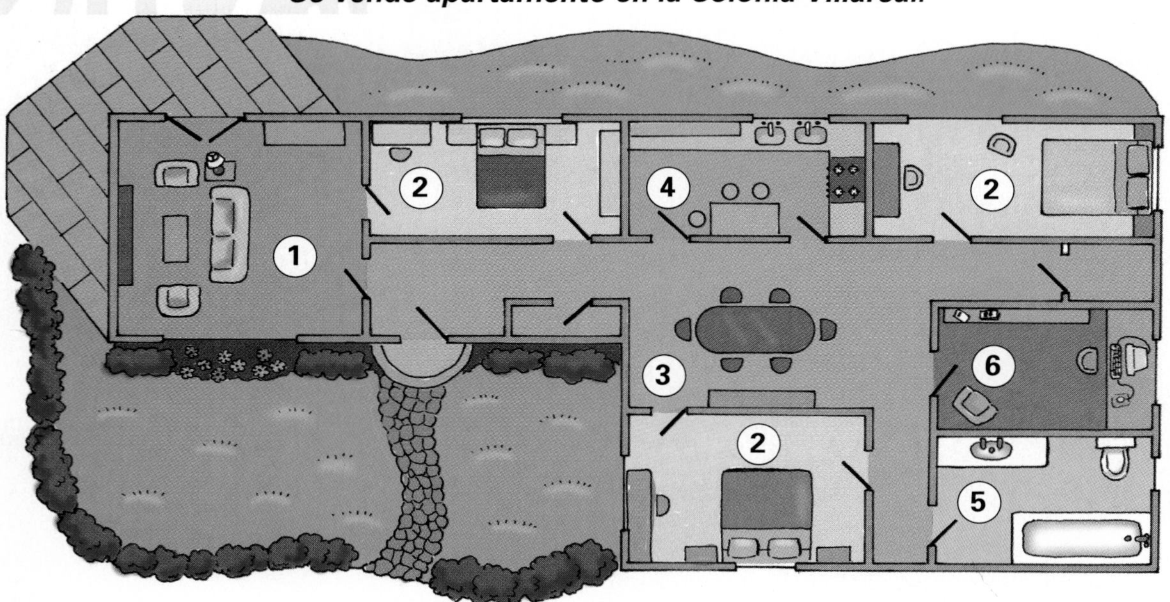

Use a transparency of the floor plan or hold your book open in front of the class. Have students repeat the names of the rooms.

1. una sala con terraza al jardín
2. tres dormitorios/alcobas grandes
3. un comedor amplio (*big*)
4. una cocina moderna
5. un cuarto de baño completo
6. una oficina privada

Note that **recámara** and **pieza** also mean bedroom.

Note that **alberca** is also used for *swimming pool.*

Palabras y expresiones útiles

el alquiler	*rent*	el/la inquilino/a	*tenant*
el balcón	*balcony*	el pasillo	*hallway*
la bañera	*bathtub*	la piscina	*swimming pool*
la calefacción	*heat*	el piso	*floor*
la cancha de tenis	*tennis court*	el ropero/armario	*closet*
el cuarto	*room*	barato/a	*inexpensive*
la ducha	*shower*	caro/a	*expensive*
el/la dueño/a	*owner*		

Have each student take a sheet of paper and divide it into two columns, one headed **necesito** and the other **deseo.**

1 ¿Qué necesito en un apartamento? You need to look for a new apartment. Before you go to the rental agency, make a list of five things that you need in an apartment and five things that you want but are not essential.

After doing **Actividad 2,** ask the pairs or groups to repeat their final lists orally.

2 Necesito compañero/a. You decide that it would be more economical to live with a roommate. Compare your list with that of a classmate's and come up with a final list of things you need/want in your apartment.

3 **Buscamos apartamento.** You and your roommate go to the rental agency to look for an apartment. Fill out the following rental application.

Before students do **Actividad 3,** go over it in class using your or a well-known person's name. Point out that in addresses **calle** is first, followed by the number. (Ask students to write out all the numbers.) The next day, distribute the completed applications randomly so that no student has his or her own. Have groups of four decide which application they accept.

SOLICITUD DE ALQUILER

CIUDAD Y FECHA: ______________________

DATOS PERSONALES:
Apellido(s): ____________ Nombre(s): ____________
Dirección: ______________________
Ciudad: ________ Estado: ________ Zona postal: ______
Teléfono: ________ Fax: ________ Correo electrónico: ________
Sexo: Masculino ___ Femenino ___ Edad: _____ años
Documento de identificación: ______________________
Profesión: ______________________

TIPO DE RESIDENCIA:
Casa: ___ Apartamento: ___ Número de dormitorios: ___
Ascensor: Sí ___ No ___
Bañera: Sí ___ No ___ Ducha: Sí ___ No ___
Balcón: Sí ___ No ___ Jardín: Sí ___ No ___
Terraza: Sí ___ No ___ Garaje: Sí ___ No ___
Cancha de tenis: Sí ___ No ___ Campo de golf: Sí ___ No ___
Piscina: Sí ___ No ___

SERVICIOS NECESARIOS:
Electricidad: ___ Gas: ___ Aire acondicionado: Sí ___ No ___
Calefacción central *(central heating)*: Sí ___ No ___

ALQUILER:
Máximo alquiler al mes: $ ________

4 **El apartamento ideal.** You have found the perfect apartment. Work with a partner to discuss the following floor plan. Discuss the number of rooms, the things that you like and don't like. Follow the model.

After students have finished doing **Actividad 4**, go around the room and ask them randomly **¿Qué (no) te gusta? / ¿Cuántos/as...hay?**

▸ **Modelo:** —*¿Cuántas alcobas hay?*
—*Hay tres alcobas.*
—*¿Hay un jardín?*
—*No, no hay un jardín, hay un balcón.*

II. Describing places in a city

¿Qué hay en la ciudad?

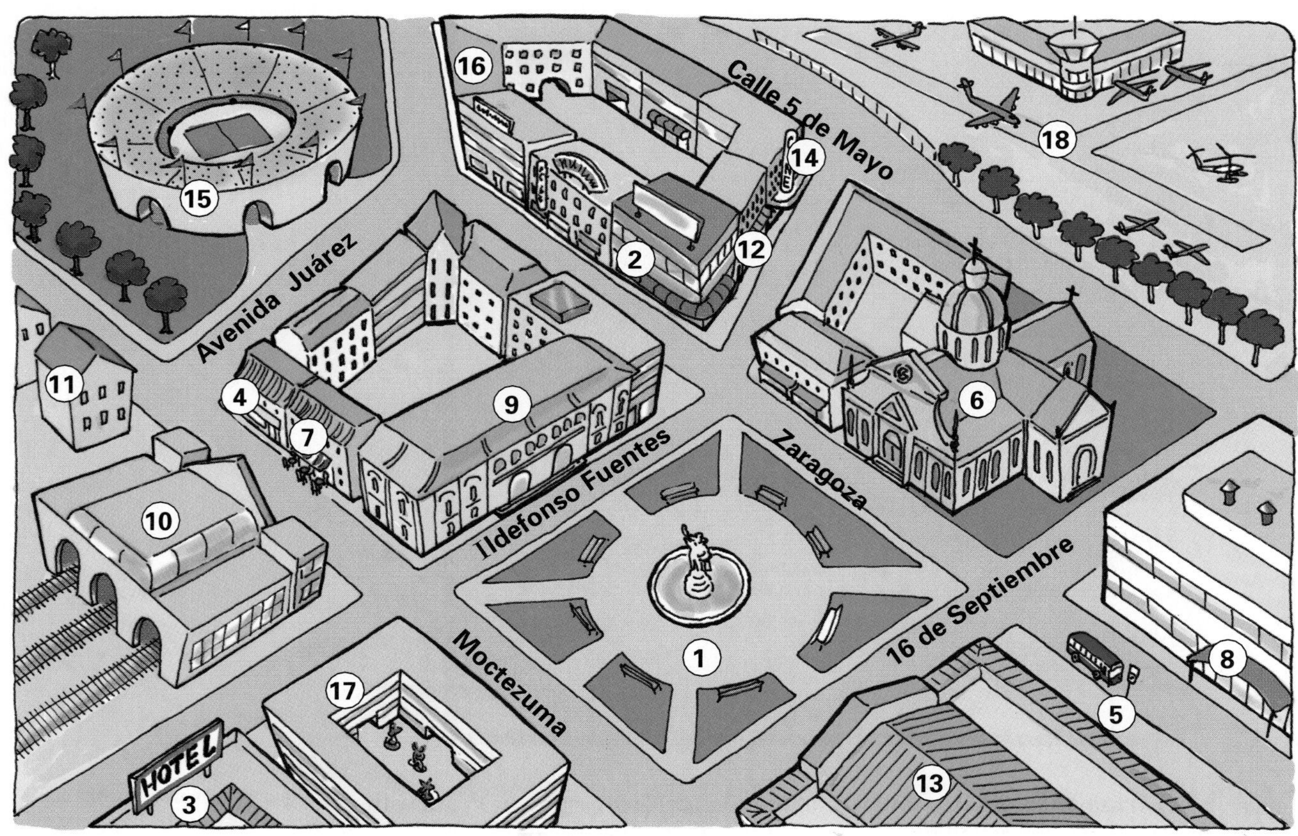

Have students repeat the city vocabulary. **Practice:** Name a famous local place and have students tell you what it is in Spanish. (For example, McDonald's, the Ritz, La Guardia, and so on.)

1. la plaza/el zócalo
2. la tienda
3. el hotel
4. la librería
5. la parada de autobús
6. la iglesia
7. el café
8. el hospital
9. el correo
10. la estación de tren
11. la casa
12. el restaurante
13. la biblioteca
14. el cine
15. el estadio
16. el centro comercial
17. el museo
18. el aeropuerto

After students have completed **Actividad 5**, ask them **¿Dónde está?** questions.

5 ¿Dónde está? Work with a partner to identify and locate the buildings in the illustration. Follow the model.

▶ **Modelo:** —*¿Dónde está la tienda?*
—*Está en la calle Zaragoza.*

6 Una ciudad ideal. Create your own city by drawing and labeling an original city plan. Include at least seven buildings and places from the city map on page 56.

Assign **Actividad 6** as homework. Students can do this on paper, on their own transparencies or on a large piece of cardboard. Remind students to give their streets Spanish names.

7 Los planes. Now work with a partner to compare the maps of your city plans. Follow the model.

► **Modelo:** —*¿Hay un restaurante en la ciudad?*
—*Sí, hay un restaurante, (No, no hay un restaurante.)*
—*¿Dónde está el restaurante?*
—*Está en la Calle 5 de Mayo.*

As an additional activity, have students present their plan to the class, describing in Spanish at least two buildings: **El museo es pequeño y amarillo y está en la Calle Diego Rivera.**

8 ¿Qué haces? *(What do you do?)* Now work in groups of three. Choose one of your maps and state what things you do in the buildings shown. Use the following list of activities and follow the model.

► **Modelo:** —*¿Qué haces en la biblioteca?*
—*Leo libros en la biblioteca.*

beber café	mandar postales (*post cards*)
caminar	mirar arte
comer	mirar a la gente
comprar	mirar una película
esperar el autobús	pagar mucho dinero
estudiar	tomar el tren
hablar con amigos	ver televisión

Have students also ask **¿Qué no haces?** questions. **Practice** (**yo** and **usted** forms): Have each student report on one thing their friend does in a particular building. Also, ask students **¿dónde?** questions with these expressions: **¿Dónde compro libros?**

Mirar televisión is also used.

ENLACE CULTURAL

La cerámica: adorno urbano y doméstico

La Cocina de Santa Rosa.

The town of Puebla in Mexico is well known for its Talavera ceramic objects and tiles (**azulejos**). Beautiful Talavera tiles adorn today's homes, fountains, and buildings in Puebla, and artists continue to create ceramic objects in many colors and forms, such as plates, cups, and vases. In addition, Talavera tiles with numbers and patterns may be used to identify a particular residence. Talavera ceramics were influenced by Spanish-Arabic and Chinese artisans. Even though silver, as well as Chinese porcelain, were valued more than the local Talavera tiles by the wealthy Mexicans during Colonial times, today these tiles are considered works of art and are very valuable.

If you have any ceramic tiles from your travels be sure to show them to your class. For further information, do a word search on the World Wide Web for **Talavera**.

VISTAS Y VOCES

Show the difference between **cartas** and **notas** by bringing in a Post-it note and a letter. Point out the difference between **noticias** and **telenovelas.** Have students describe a favorite TV program.

I. Preparémonos

1 Anticipación. Answer these questions in pairs.

A. **1.** ¿A quiénes escribes notas? ¿Escribes en la computadora o escribes a mano?
2. ¿Qué bebes tú por la mañana, café o té?
3. ¿Cómo se llama tu profesor/a favorito/a? ¿Cómo es? ¿Qué enseña?
4. ¿Te gusta la televisión? ¿Miras las noticias? ¿Son buenas o malas?

B. Review chapter opening photo 2A.
1. Who do you think the man wearing a jacket and a tie is?
2. What does he want?

Para comprender mejor

el periódico	*newspaper*	buscar	*to look for*
la prensa	*press (news)*	preocupado/a	*worried*
encontrar	*to find*	raro/a, extraño/a	*strange*
escribir a mano	*to write by hand*	(no) (lo) sé	*I do (not) know*
el detective	*detective*	siento	*I regret*
la noticia	*news*	¡Qué mala suerte!	*What bad luck!*

Write 1, 2, 3, 4 on the board and then take a poll as to what position each group has put each video scene. Practice numbers and briefly introduce the ordinals **primero, segundo, tercero, cuarto.**

2 Secuencia. In pairs, number the video action shots in the order in which you think the action will occur in the video you will watch.

1.

2.

3.

4.

II. Miremos y escuchemos

3 Palabras importantes. Circle the items you hear and see in this segment.

periódico	nota	taxi
computadora	café	plantas
flores	flores	universidad
fútbol	camión	televisión
jaguar	autobús	bolsa

III. Comentemos

4 Frases. Working in groups, indicate who says the following.

1. "Yo también busco a Nayeli. Soy un colega de ella."
2. "¿Qué quieren ustedes? ¿Son de la prensa?"
3. "Nayeli es mi profesora. Le ruego, por favor, quiero ayudarla."
4. "Veo la televisión. Sé lo que está pasando."
5. "Nayeli Paz Ocotlán es nuestra criminal. ¡Tenemos que encontrarla!"

5 Opinión. Answer these questions in groups.

1. ¿Cómo se llama la universidad?
2. ¿Quiénes llegan a la universidad?
3. ¿Cómo se llama el señor?
4. ¿De quién es la foto en el periódico?
5. ¿Cómo se llama la señora que está en la casa de Nayeli?
6. ¿Cómo es el jaguar? ¿grande? ¿pequeño?

6 Miremos otra vez. After watching the scene again, check to see if you have ordered the video action shots in the appropriate sequence.

Comentemos.
Write on the board: **Adriana, Felipe, Armando, Esperanza, el detective, el señor del anillo, el chofer de Sevilla.** Be sure students read the questions before viewing. A hint for question 1: **un colega** is masculine. (Ask students how you know that.)

Answers to Actividad 4:
1. Armando
2. Esperanza
3. Adriana
4. Esperanza
5. el detective

Answers to Actividad 5:
1. Universidad de las Américas
2. Adriana, Felipe y Armando
3. Se llama Armando de Landa Chávez.
4. la foto de Nayeli
5. La señora se llama Esperanza.
6. *Answers will vary.*

Actividad 5
Put students in groups of three to five and assign one question to each group. Have a spokesperson from each group answer that group's question for the class.

Correct order of video action shots: 1, 2, 3, 4

Lengua

I. Expressing possession

A. Possessive adjectives

For review, have students describe the houses and the cars using the adjectives in the talk bubbles as well as colors.

Stress that there is no *'s* in Spanish. The literal English translation is *the car of Alvaro* and *the house of Benito.*

¡Me gusta el auto de Álvaro! Es grande, moderno y bonito.
Sí, pero su casa es pequeña y vieja.
La casa de María y Benito es grande, moderna y bonita, pero yo tengo un auto fantástico.
Es cierto, nuestra casa es elegante.
¡Y tu perro es maravilloso también!

There are many ways to express possession. Look at the conversation above and find these expressions in Spanish.

Alvaro's car	María and Benito's house
his house	I have a fantastic car
our house	your dog

In English, words such as *my, your, his, her, their,* and *our* are called possessive adjectives. In Spanish, they must agree in number (singular/plural) with the nouns they modify. This is how they are expressed in Spanish.

mi auto	*my car*	su perro	*(his, her, their, your) dog*
tu**s** auto**s**	*your cars*	su**s** perro**s**	*(his, her, their, your) dogs*

Possessive adjectives		
Before singular nouns	**Before plural nouns**	**English**
mi	mis	*my*
tu	tus	*your (informal singular)*
su	sus	*her, his, your (formal singular and plural, informal plural), its, their*
nuestro/a	nuestros/as	*our*
vuestro/a	vuestros/as	*your (informal plural)*

Notice that **nuestro/nuestra** and **vuestro/vuestra** also change to agree with the noun they modify in gender (masculine/feminine) as well as in number.

To stress agreement, take some pictures of cars from magazines and give them to a student, stating **tus autos.**

nuestr**o** apartament**o**	*our apartment*	nuestr**a** cas**a**	*our house*
nuestr**os** apartament**os**	*our apartments*	nuestr**as** cas**as**	*our houses*

1 Práctica. Replace the English word in parentheses with the appropriate Spanish possessive adjective. Then practice the completed phrases with a partner.

► **Modelo:** ______ *mochila* (my)
mi mochila

1. ______ computadoras (*his*)
2. ______ auto (*our*)
3. ______ ducha (*their*)
4. ______ compañera de cuarto (*my*)
5. ______ pisos (*our*)
6. ______ correo electrónico (*her*)
7. ______ balcón (*your, familiar*)
8. ______ aeropuertos (*our*)
9. ______ estadio (*their*)
10. ______ hospital (*your, formal*)

2 Posesión. Create sentences using the correct possessive adjective.

► **Modelo:** *el libro / Paco*
Es su libro.

1. la clase / nosotros
2. las mochilas / Uds.
3. la pluma / yo
4. el apartamento / los Gómez
5. el estéreo / Pepín
6. el portafolio / tú
7. el auto / papá
8. la computadora / ella

Answers to Actividad 2:
1. Es nuestra clase.
2. Son sus mochilas. (Note: the verb is **son** because **mochilas** is plural.)
3. Es mi pluma.
4. Es su apartamento.
5. Es su estéreo.
6. Es tu portafolio. (Note: the possessive adjective has no accent while the subject pronoun **tú** does.)
7. Es su auto.
8. Es su computadora.

B. Phrases with de

- In Spanish, possession can also be expressed using **de.**

El auto **de** Álvaro es grande, moderno y bonito.	*Álvaro's car (lit., the car of Álvaro) is big, modern, and beautiful.*
La casa **de** María y Benito es grande, moderna y bonita.	*María and Benito's house (lit., the house of María and Benito) is big, modern, and beautiful.*

- Since **su/s** can refer to several owners, the phrases **de él, de ella, de ellos/ ellas, de Ud.,** and **de Uds.,** are often used to indicate the specific person or persons.

—¿Es su casa?	*Is it their house?*
—Sí, es la casa de ellos.	*Yes, it's theirs.*

Expand the example **es su casa** and have students clarify it as *it is his house; it is your* (singular) *house.* Stress that **él** is a subject pronoun meaning *he,* whereas **el** (no accent) is an article meaning *the.* Review the fact that when speaking *about* someone, one uses the definite article in Spanish

- As you learned in Chapter 1, when the preposition **de** precedes the article **el,** they contract to form **del.** Note that it doesn't form a contraction with the pronoun **él,** as in the sample sentences below.

—¿Quiénes son Adriana y Felipe?	*Who are Adriana and Felipe?*
—Adriana y Felipe son estudiantes de la profesora Paz Ocotlán.	*Adriana and Felipe are students of Professor Paz Ocotlán.*
—¿También son estudiantes **del** señor de Landa?	*Are they also Mr. de Landa's students?*
—No, son solamente estudiantes **de ella,** no **de él.**	*No, they are only her students, not his.*

- You can also use **ser** + **de** + a noun or pronoun to express possession.

—¿**De quién** es la casa grande?	*Whose large house is it?*
—Es **de María y Benito.**	*It's María and Benito's.*
—¿Es el perro **de Álvaro?**	*Is it Álvaro's dog?*
—Sí, es **de él.**	*Yes, it's his.*

Es de can also be translated *it belongs to.* Note the accent on **quién** and the fact that *whose* is translated **de quién,** whereas in the previous section *who* is translated as **quiénes** (no **de**). (See a later note in this lesson for an explanation of when **quiénes** is used.)

Answers to Actividad 3:
1. El auto es de Paquita.
2. El estéreo es de mi compañero/a de cuarto.
3. Las plumas son del profesor Salinas.
4. El teléfono celular es de los señores Vera.
5. Los papeles son de la estudiante de español.

3 Preguntas. Answer the questions.

▶ **Modelo:** —*¿De quién es la televisión? (la señora Pérez)*
—*La televisión es de la señora Pérez.*

1. ¿De quién es el auto? (Paquita)
2. ¿De quién es el estéreo? (mi compañero/a de cuarto)
3. ¿De quién son las plumas? (el profesor Salinas)
4. ¿De quién es el teléfono celular? (los señores Vera)
5. ¿De quién son los papeles? (la estudiante de español)

After students have finished **Actividad 4**, ask **¿de quién?** questions: **¿De quién es el libro?**

4 ¿De quién es? Column A has a list of articles, and column B has a list of possible owners. Take turns asking each other questions about who owns what. Work with a partner and follow the model.

▶ **Modelo:** A: *¿De quién es el portafolio?*
B: *El portafolio es del Sr. Luna.*

A: *¿De quién son los papeles?*
B: *Los papeles son de las alumnas.*

A	B
1. portafolio	1. el señor Luna
2. libros	2. la señora francesa
3. teléfonos	3. él
4. estéreos	4. los papás de Adriana
5. calculadora	5. unos turistas ingleses
6. apartamento	6. el señor Chávez
7. radio	7. ellos
8. llave	8. Mario
9. silla	9. un profesor
10. dormitorio	10. el estudiante

After students have completed **Actividad 5,** ask the class to report by first asking **¿Qué hay?** (Write the items on the board.) Then ask **¿De quién son?** Write the answers on the board.

5 ¿Qué hay aquí? Working in pairs, make a list of six things seen in the classroom or at home. Then ask your partner who owns them. Take turns.

▶ **Modelo:** —*En la clase hay muchos cuadernos.*
—*¿De quién son?*
—*Son de los estudiantes.*

C. The verb tener

The verb **tener** is used to express possession in the same way the verb *to have* is used in English.

—¿**Tienen** Uds. clase de sociología al mediodía?	*Do you have sociology class at noon?*
—No, al mediodía **tenemos** clase de álgebra.	*No, at noon, we have algebra class.*
—¿**Tienes** buenas amigas?	*Do you have good friends?*
—Sí **tengo** muchas buenas amigas.	*Yes, I have many good friends.*

The verb **tener** is irregular, meaning that the stem of its present-tense forms does not follow the same model presented for the regular verbs in Chapter 1. Notice, however, that the endings are the same as for the other **-er** verbs.

Singular		Plural	
yo	**tengo**	nosotros/nosotras	**tenemos**
tú	**tienes**	vosotros/vosotras	**tenéis**
él/ella, Ud.	**tiene**	ellos/ellas, Uds.	**tienen**

LENGUA EN ACCIÓN

Quién/Quiénes

Questions that use **de quién** are usually answered by sentences with possessives. When asking questions of this kind, you may use the plural **de quiénes** if you think that several people are the owners.

¿**De quiénes** son los autos?	*Whose cars are these?*
El auto azul es de Isabel y el auto rojo es de Juliana.	*The blue car is Isabel's and the red car is Juliana's.*

6 *¿Qué tiene?* Using the correct form of the verb **tener,** answer the questions.

1. ¿Qué tiene el profesor?
2. ¿Qué tienen las dos chicas?
3. ¿Qué tiene la señora?
4. ¿Qué tiene el hombre?
5. ¿Qué tienen las muchachas?
6. ¿Qué tienen los novios en la mano?

Answers to Actividad 6:
1. Tiene un libro azul.
2. Tienen dos perros marrones (color café/castaños/pardos).
3. Tiene unas llaves.
4. Tiene una guitarra.
5. Tienen unas mochilas rojas.
6. Tienen un calendario.

7 **Posesiones.** Some students are in the cafeteria eating and talking. Answer the questions they ask each other. Use the correct form of **tener.** Work in pairs.

1. ¿Tiene tu familia un auto viejo o nuevo?
2. ¿La universidad de tu amigo tiene televisión de cable?
3. ¿Cuántos cursos tiene tu compañero/a de cuarto? ¿Cuáles son?
4. ¿Tienes un apartamento o una casa?
5. ¿Quién tiene un calendario con las fechas de las vacaciones?

II. Describing actions

A. Irregular yo verbs in the present tense

La cocina de Daniel

I know how to prepare
I make / dishes (food) /
I set the table /
I go out / cooking

Yo **sé** preparar° comidas deliciosas. Los domingos, invito a mis amigos y **hago**° platos° exquisitos. **Pongo** la mesa° y comemos en el jardín o en la terraza. Después, **salgo**° con ellos al cine o a una discoteca. Son buenos amigos y todos tienen la misma opinión: "¡la cocina° de Daniel es excelente!"

As you have learned, some verbs in Spanish are irregular in the present tense. The following groups of verbs are easy to remember because they are irregular only in the first person (**yo**) form. The other forms follow the same pattern as other verbs you have learned. It will be easier to remember if you group them according to their similarities.

- **-go** verbs add a **g** before the **-o** in the **yo** form.
- **-zco** verbs add a **z** before the **-co** in the **yo** form.

Here is how you conjugate these verbs.

	-go verbs salir *to leave*	-zco verbs conducir *to drive*	Irregular verbs ver *to see*	 saber *to know*
yo	**salgo**	**conduzco**	**veo**	**sé**
tú	**sales**	**conduces**	**ves**	**sabes**
él/ella, Ud.	**sale**	**conduce**	**ve**	**sabe**
nosotros/nosotras	**salimos**	**conducimos**	**vemos**	**sabemos**
vosotros/vosotras	**salís**	**conducís**	**veis**	**sabéis**
ellos/ellas, Uds.	**salen**	**conducen**	**ven**	**saben**

Common verbs with irregular *yo* forms

-go verbs		-zco verbs	
hacer (hago)	*to do; to make*	conocer (conozco)	*to know, be familiar with*
poner (pongo)	*to put, place*	traducir (traduzco)	*to translate*
traer (traigo)	*to bring*	conducir (conduzco)	*to drive*
		producir (produzco)	*to produce*

8 **Una invitación.** Linda meets Pablo and they talk about going to the movies. Complete the following sentences with the correct forms of the present tense.

LINDA: ¡Hola, Pablo! ¿ _________ (saber) tú si hay películas buenas hoy?
PABLO: Sí, hay muchas. Yo _________ (conocer) un teatro muy bueno. Allí presentan películas francesas.
LINDA: ¿Películas francesas? ¡Yo no _________ (saber) francés! ¿Tienen subtítulos?
PABLO: No, no tienen, pero yo _________ (traducir) muy bien el francés.
LINDA: ¡Pablo, qué tonto eres! Es una broma (*joke*), ¿verdad?
PABLO: ¡Claro que es una broma! Las películas tienen subtítulos. ¡Vamos al cine; yo _________ (conducir)!
LINDA: ¡Y yo pago, vamos!

Answers to Actividad 8:
1. Sabes
2. conozco
3. sé
4. traduzco
5. conduzco

9 **Rutinas.** Alicia writes to her cousin about her weekly routine. Complete the following story with verbs from the list. You may use each verb more than once.

beber	hacer	traducir
conducir	comer	poner
ir		

Hola Patricia, mi rutina siempre es igual. Los domingos, (yo) _________ mi coche a la universidad. Por la mañana, (yo) _________ a la biblioteca y (yo) _________ las tareas para el lunes. Por la noche, mis amigas y yo _________ a un café muy bueno, _________ pizza o _________ un café. El lunes por la mañana, (yo) _________ al gimnasio y _________ ejercicio. Los lunes, miércoles y viernes hay clases de humanidades; en la clase de latín, (yo) _________ de latín a inglés y vice versa. Los sábados (yo) _________ los libros en el escritorio y no estudio.

Answers to Actividad 9:
1. conduzco
2. voy
3. hago
4. vamos
5. comemos
6. bebemos
7. voy
8. hago
9. traduzco
10. pongo

10 ¡Yo también! See what the following people do and then say whether or not you do these things.

► **Modelo:** —*Nosotros salimos de la casa a las siete, ¿y tú?*
—*Yo también* (also) *salgo a las siete.* [or]
—*No, no salgo a las siete. Salgo a las siete y media.*

1. Ricardo sale para México, ¿y tú?
2. Nosotros conducimos autobuses grandes, ¿y tú?
3. Los estudiantes hacen fiestas fantásticas, ¿y tú?
4. El profesor sale temprano, ¿y tú?
5. María y Pepe ponen la mesa muy bien, ¿y tú?
6. Mis amigos y yo viajamos los sábados, ¿y tú?
7. Ella pone la mesa antes de comer, ¿y tú?
8. El señor Rulfo conoce bien a mucha gente, ¿y tú?
9. Tu compañera traduce la tarea al inglés, ¿y tú?
10. Ellos viven en Madrid, ¿y tú?

B. Common expressions with poner and salir

These are some common expressions with **poner** and **salir.**

After having students repeat these expressions, ask questions: **¿Quién sale con Marta?**

poner la mesa	*to set the table*
poner una carta en el correo	*to mail a letter*
salir de	*to leave from a place*
salir para	*to leave for a place*
salir con	*to leave with*
salir a	*to go out to*

Practice: Expand question 1 in **Actividad 11** by asking **¿Y en tu familia...?** For question 2, exchange **los viernes** for other days of the week. For question 3, exchange **por la mañana** with **por la tarde,** and so on.

11 ¿Quién hace qué? Answer the questions, using **poner** and **salir.**

1. ¿Quién pone la mesa en tu familia?
2. ¿A dónde sales los viernes?
3. ¿A qué hora tienes que poner las cartas en el correo por la mañana?
4. ¿Con quiénes salen tú y tus amigos los fines de semana?

For a quick drill on this point show a series of pictures of people and things and ask students individually **¿Qué ves?**

C. The personal a

A direct object is a word that receives the action of the verb.

I see the *house.*	(*House* is the direct object.)
I see *Marcos.*	(*Marcos* is the direct object.)

In Spanish when the direct object is a person, you need to place an **a** in front of that person's name or reference. This is called the "personal **a.**"

Veo la casa.
but: Veo **a** Marcos. Veo **a** mi amigo. *(I see my friend.)*

Answers to Actividad 12:

1. —	4. —
2. a	5. —
3. —	6. a

12 Práctica. Write the personal **a** where needed and make any other necessary changes.

1. Escucho _________ música contemporánea.
2. Veo _________ Leonardo.

3. ¿Usted desea vender __________ su teléfono celular?
4. Compramos __________ la mochila verde.
5. ¿Vas a leer __________ nuestro libro para la clase de historia?
6. ¿Conoce Ud. __________ Roberto Méndez?

LENGUA EN ACCIÓN

Saber, conocer

The verbs **saber** and **conocer** both mean *to know* in English. In Spanish **saber** is used to express knowledge about facts or things that people know how to do. **Conocer** means to meet someone or to be acquainted with persons, places, or things.

¿Sabes la dirección de Hernando?	*Do you know Hernando's address?*
Lola **sabe** español.	*Lola knows Spanish.*
No **conoces** Madrid, ¿verdad?	*You don't know Madrid, do you?*
Conozco a tu amigo Ignacio.	*I know your friend Ignacio.*

Like **de** + **el** forming **del,** the preposition **a** combined with **el** forms the contraction **al** (**a** + **el** = **al**).

Conozco al presidente de México.	*I know the president of Mexico.*
Conocemos a la enfermera Ríos.	*We know Nurse Ríos.*

13 *¿Quién sabe qué?* Say what these people know or know how to do. Use **saber** or **conocer.** Follow the model.

▸ **Modelo:** *Elena / inglés*
Elena sabe inglés.

1. Berta / muchos secretos
2. nosotros / Madrid
3. Verónica / bailar
4. ellos / a la Profesora Paz
5. usted / la hora
6. el chico / un buen restaurante mexicano
7. yo / español
8. el profesor / nuestros nombres
9. yo / a Adriana
10. Gil y yo / traducir al inglés

Answers to Actividad 13:
1. sabe
2. conocemos
3. sabe
4. conocen
5. sabe
6. conoce
7. sé
8. sabe
9. conozco
10. sabemos

14 *Necesito un hotel.* Teodoro is going to Colombia and is looking for a hotel. His friend, Aida, gives him information. Complete their conversation with the correct form of **saber** or **conocer.**

TEODORO: El lunes viajo a Colombia. ¿Tú __________ un hotel bueno allí?
AIDA: Sí, __________ un buen hotel. Se llama El Tequendama y está en Bogotá.
TEODORO: ¿ __________ tú la dirección exacta?
AIDA: No, no __________ la dirección exacta, pero tengo el número de teléfono del hotel.
TEODORO: ¡Qué bien! Mil gracias. Deseo __________ Bogotá.

Answers to Actividad 14:
1. conoces
2. conozco
3. Sabes
4. sé
5. conocer

III. Expressing location with estar

Las frutas están en el plato.

Los niños están en la escuela.

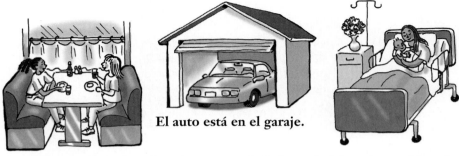

Las chicas están en la cafetería.

El auto está en el garaje.

Isabel y su bebé están en el hospital.

Write the six forms of **estar** on the board or on a transparency with the endings color coded. Note the accents on all forms but **yo** and **nosotros,** and that the stem of the verb is **est-**.

The verb **estar** indicates the location of persons or objects. Note that the first person singular is irregular and the second and third persons singular and plural carry written accents.

Singular		Plural	
yo	**estoy**	nosotros/nosotras	**estamos**
tú	**estás**	vosotros/vosotras	**estáis**
él/ella, Ud.	**está**	ellos/ellas, Uds.	**están**

After students have finished **Actividad 15** in pairs ask **¿Dónde están?** questions of individual students, using these sentences as models.

15 **¿Dónde están mis cosas?** You are constantly misplacing things, but luckily you have a roommate who remembers where you put them. You call him/her to ask for help. Work with a partner and follow the model.

▸ **Modelo:** *llaves / mochila*
—¿Dónde están mis llaves?
—Están en tu mochila.

1. cuadernos / cama
2. radio / cuarto de baño
3. mi libro de español / portafolio
4. reloj / escritorio
5. papeles / estante
6. teléfono / mesa
7. cuaderno / laboratorio de ciencias

16 ¿Dónde están? Work in pairs. Ask your partner where the articles and the people in the house or apartment can be found. Make a list of all the things or people in the room. Follow the model.

▸ **Modelo:** *televisión*
—¿Dónde está la televisión?
—La televisión está en la cocina.

Answers to Actividad 16:

1. dormitorio: cama, niño, computadora, escritorio, silla
2. comedor: mesa, cuatro sillas, estéreo
3. jardín: plantas, señor, silla, periódico
4. baño: bañera, ducha, señora
5. cocina: mesa, televisión
6. sala: lámpara, teléfono, sillón, alfombra

Lectura A

Introducción

In this reading, you will learn about the location of Puebla and its most important buildings downtown.

Reading strategy: Asking questions
Preparing yourself to read in another language is an important step to achieve strong reading skills. One way to help you understand and remember ideas is to ask yourself questions before you read, while you are reading, and after you read.

1 Antes de leer. Ask yourself these questions before you read.

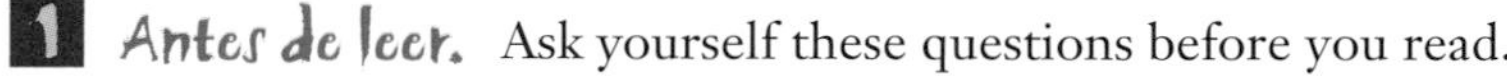

1. What does the title tell me about the topic of the reading?
2. Do I already know anything about the topic?
3. What information do the pictures and captions tell me about the article?
4. ¿...?

2 *Al leer.* Ask yourself these questions while you are reading.

1. What is the topic of the article? Have I guessed correctly after reading the title of the article?
2. Which vocabulary words related to the topic do I already know? (Review in Spanish the buildings and places you find in a city.)
3. Can I get the gist of the reading without looking things up in a dictionary?
4. Which words are essential for me to know to understand the passage?
5. Which words can I gloss over and still understand the reading?
6. Do I understand what this paragraph is telling me?
7. ¿...?

Puebla, una ciudad importante

high plain

average

La ciudad de Puebla de los Ángeles es la capital del estado de Puebla y está en el altiplano° central de México. Está a noventa minutos de la ciudad de México en automóvil, a tres horas de la ciudad de Oaxaca, a tres horas y media del Puerto de Veracruz y a seis horas de Acapulco. La temperatura media° varía entre 20°C y 30°C.

Baroque / brick / stone

stucco

onyx / marble / gold / designed

Puebla es famosa por sus estructuras barrocas° de ladrillo° rojo, piedra° gris, estuco° blanco y por los espectaculares azulejos de Talavera. La Catedral de Puebla tiene altas torres y un hermoso altar con adornos de ónice°, mármol° y oro°, diseñado° por un arquitecto de origen español, Manuel Tolsá.

valuable / Some

La Biblioteca Palafoxiana es un hermoso edificio de la época colonial. Tiene más de 40.000 libros, todos muy valiosos°. Algunos° especialistas

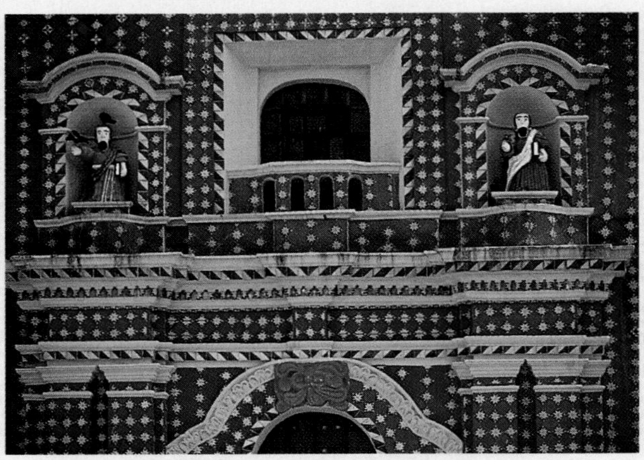

La casa de las muñecas, Puebla, México.

consideran la Capilla° de la Virgen del Rosario como la octava° maravilla° del mundo por los impresionantes adornos interiores. El Convento Colonial de Santa Rosa es hoy un museo de cerámica. El Museo Amparo, con muchos adelantos tecnológicos, es uno de los más modernos de América Latina.

Chapel
eighth
wonder

La Capilla de la Virgen del Rosario, Puebla, México.

3 Después de leer. After you read, ask yourself these questions.

1. What is the main idea of the reading?
2. What themes or topics does the reading contain?
3. Which words do I need to look up to help me better understand the reading?
4. ¿...?

4 Edificios. Work with a partner to complete these ideas based on the reading.

1. ¿Dónde está Puebla?
2. ¿A cuántas horas en automóvil está Puebla de Oaxaca? ¿de la capital? ¿del Puerto de Veracruz? ¿de Acapulco?
3. ¿Cuál es la temperatura media de la ciudad?
4. Menciona cinco edificios importantes de Puebla.
5. ¿De dónde es el arquitecto de la Catedral de Puebla? ¿Cómo se llama?
6. Según los especialistas, ¿qué tipo de maravilla es la Capilla del Rosario?
7. ¿Qué colores tienen los edificios del centro de la ciudad?
8. ¿Hay un museo de cerámica en Puebla?
9. En Puebla hay un museo tecnológico muy moderno. ¿Cómo se llama?
10. ¿Qué biblioteca menciona la lectura? ¿Cuántos libros hay allí?

5 Mi ciudad. Describe your city and the important sites and buildings in it.

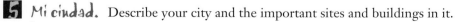

Answers to Actividad 4:

1. Puebla está en el altiplano central de México.
2. Puebla está a tres horas de Oaxaca, a noventa minutos de la ciudad de México, a tres horas y media del Puerto de Veracruz, y a seis horas de Acapulco.
3. La temperatura media es 25°C.
4. Los edificios importantes son: la Catedral, la biblioteca Palafoxiana, la Capilla de la Virgen del Rosario, un museo de cerámica (antes el Convento Colonial de Santa Rosa), El Museo Amparo.
5. El arquitecto es de España. Se llama Manuel Tolsá.
6. Es la octava maravilla del mundo.
7. Los edificios del centro tienen los colores rojo, gris y blanco.
8. Sí, hay un museo de cerámica en Puebla.
9. El museo tecnológico se llama El Museo Amparo.
10. Menciona la biblioteca Palafoxiana que tiene más de 40.000 volúmenes.

ETAPA B

Pistas y palabras

I. Talking about weather

¿Qué tiempo hace? (What's the weather like?)

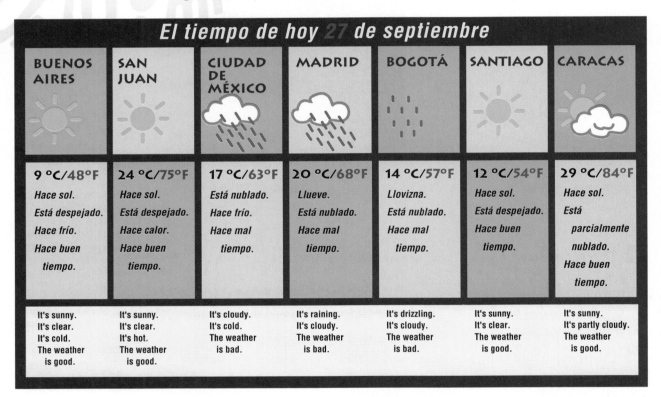

El tiempo de hoy 27 de septiembre

BUENOS AIRES	SAN JUAN	CIUDAD DE MÉXICO	MADRID	BOGOTÁ	SANTIAGO	CARACAS
9 °C/48°F	24 °C/75°F	17 °C/63°F	20 °C/68°F	14 °C/57°F	12 °C/54°F	29 °C/84°F
Hace sol. Está despejado. Hace frío. Hace buen tiempo.	*Hace sol. Está despejado. Hace calor. Hace buen tiempo.*	*Está nublado. Hace frío. Hace mal tiempo.*	*Llueve. Está nublado. Hace mal tiempo.*	*Llovizna. Está nublado. Hace mal tiempo.*	*Hace sol. Está despejado. Hace buen tiempo.*	*Hace sol. Está parcialmente nublado. Hace buen tiempo.*
It's sunny. It's clear. It's cold. The weather is good.	It's sunny. It's clear. It's hot. The weather is good.	It's cloudy. It's cold. The weather is bad.	It's raining. It's cloudy. The weather is bad.	It's drizzling. It's cloudy. The weather is bad.	It's sunny. It's clear. The weather is good.	It's sunny. It's partly cloudy. The weather is good.

Bring in pictures from magazines to have students practice *Palabras y expresiones útiles.*

Palabras y expresiones útiles

las condiciones del tiempo	*weather conditions*
los grados centígrados/Celsius	*degrees centigrade/Celsius*
el pronóstico del tiempo	*weather forecast*
la temperatura máxima/mínima/media	*highest/lowest/average temperature*
El tiempo está despejado/nublado.	*The weather is clear/cloudy.*
Hace mucho calor/frío/viento.	*It's very hot/cold/windy.*
Hace un poco de frío/calor/viento.	*It's a little cold (chilly)/warm/windy.*
Llovizna un poco/mucho.	*It's drizzling a little/a lot.*
Llueve un poco/mucho.	*It's raining a little/a lot.*
Nieva un poco/mucho.	*It's snowing a little/a lot.*
Tiene buen/mal clima.	*It has good/bad climate.*

1 El tiempo. Work with a partner to describe the weather report in each city. Follow the model.

▶ **Modelo:** —*¿Qué tiempo hace en Buenos Aires?*
—*Hace buen tiempo. Hace sol y está despejado.*
—*¿A cuánto está la temperatura?*
—*La temperatura está a 9°C.*
—*¿Hace frío?*
—*Sí, hace frío.*

2 ¿Qué tiempo hace? Work with a partner asking questions about the weather and temperatures in the cities listed below. Follow the model.

▶ **Modelo:** —*¿Hace buen tiempo en Asunción?*
—*No, no hace buen tiempo.*
—*¿Llueve?*
—*Sí, llovizna un poco.*
—*¿A cuánto está la temperatura máxima?*
—*La temperatura máxima está a 30 grados centígrados.*
—*Entonces hace calor.*

After **Actividades 1** and **2**, ask the entire class to tell you where certain conditions take place: **¿Dónde hace frío?**

INFORME METEOROLÓGICO

Septiembre 27 Ciudad	**Temp. máxima en °C**	**Temp. mínima en °C**	**Temp. media en °C**	**Condiciones del tiempo**
Asunción, Paraguay	30	19	27	Llovizna.
La Paz, Bolivia	14	0	7	Parcialmente nublado. Tiempo seco.
Málaga, España	25	17	21	Vientos fuertes. Muy nublado.
Quito, Ecuador	17	10	14	Llueve. Muy nublado.
San José de Costa Rica	24	29	18	Parcialmente nublado. Tiempo seco.

scale

Mention a few temperatures in Fahrenheit and Celsius and ask students, **¿hace calor/hace frío...?**, and so on.

ENLACE CULTURAL

Escala° Celsius y escala Fahrenheit

In the United States, temperatures are expressed on the Fahrenheit scale (°F), and in Hispanic countries, on the Celsius or centigrade scale (°C). A temperature of 32°F corresponds to 0°C. Use the following formula to convert from Fahrenheit to Celsius and vice-versa: °C = (°F – 32) / 1.8. For the conversion from Celsius to Fahrenheit: °F = (°C x 1.8) + 32. Decimals of 5 and higher round off to the number above, while decimals below 5 drop down a number.

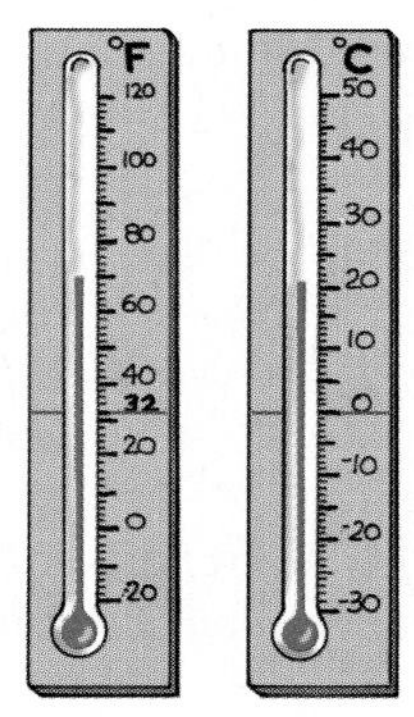

La temperatura

In Latin America, temperatures vary with the altitude of the site and its distance from the Equator. When it is winter in January in the United States, the countries south of the Equator have summer, and vice versa. High mountain locations close to the Equator vary in climate according to their altitude above sea level. The lowlands are warm and higher altitudes are progressively cooler.

El Pico de Orizaba, en los estados de Puebla y Veracruz, México.

II. Talking about seasons, weather, and appropriate clothes

Bring in some of these articles of clothing or magazine pictures. Have students identify them in Spanish.

A. *¿Qué llevo?* (What do I wear?)

B. ¿En qué estación estamos? (What season is it?)

Go over the seasons and point to articles of clothing (or pictures) you brought in, having students associate a season with each article.

la primavera

el verano

el otoño

el invierno

3 ¿Qué llevo? Work in small groups to discuss the things you will need in the different weather conditions and seasons. Follow the model.

▸ **Modelo:** —*¿En qué estación hace sol?*
—*Hace sol en el verano.*
—*¿Qué llevas cuando hace sol?*
—*Cuando hace sol, llevo unos pantalones cortos.*

4 ¿Cuál es la estación? Work with a partner to identify the season for each month where you live. Then describe what the weather is like in each month. Follow the model.

After students have finished **Actividad 4,** ask them in what months certain weather conditions typically exist in the town or city where their university or college is located: **¿Cuándo hace calor aquí?** Ask students which is their favorite season: **¿Qué estación te gusta más?**

▸ **Modelo:** *julio*
—*¿En qué estación estamos en julio?*
—*Estamos en verano.*
—*¿Qué tiempo hace?*
—*Hace buen tiempo.*

1. julio
2. enero
3. agosto
4. junio
5. abril
6. noviembre
7. mayo
8. septiembre
9. febrero
10. diciembre
11. octubre
12. marzo

III. Describing how you feel

¿Cómo están?

Palabras y expresiones útiles

alegre	*happy*	enamorado/a	*in love*
aliviado/a	*relieved*	entusiasmado/a	*enthusiastic*
alterado/a	*upset*	listo/a	*ready*
borracho/a	*drunk*	nervioso/a	*nervous*
calmado/a	*calm*	preocupado/a	*worried*
deprimido/a	*depressed*	seguro/a	*sure*
desilusionado/a	*disappointed*		

Have each student report on one or two of the students interviewed. Ask questions such as **¿Quiénes están contentos?** of the class as a whole, having students raise their hands. Ask **¿Cómo estás?/¿No estás contento/a?** of those students who do not raise their hands.

5 Entrevista. Interview six of your classmates to ask them how they are today. Report your findings to the class.

▸ **Modelo:** —*¿Cómo estás?*
—*Estoy preocupado/a.*
—*¿Y tú?*
—*Estoy contento/a.*

After students complete **Actividad 6,** ask them what adjectives would be appropriate for each situation. Write them on the board to help students become visually acquainted with this vocabulary.

6 Reacciones. How would you feel in the following situations? Write your reactions and then share them with a classmate.

▸ **Modelo:** Your paycheck is late.
Estoy preocupado/a.

1. You have an exam tomorrow.
2. You just found your true love.
3. You have the flu.
4. Your favorite aunt died.
5. You passed your most difficult class.
6. Your roommate stole some money.

7 Emociones. Complete these ideas.

1. Estoy contento/a cuando...
2. Estoy triste cuando...
3. Estoy enojado/a porque...
4. Estoy cansado/a porque...
5. Estoy desilusionado/a porque...

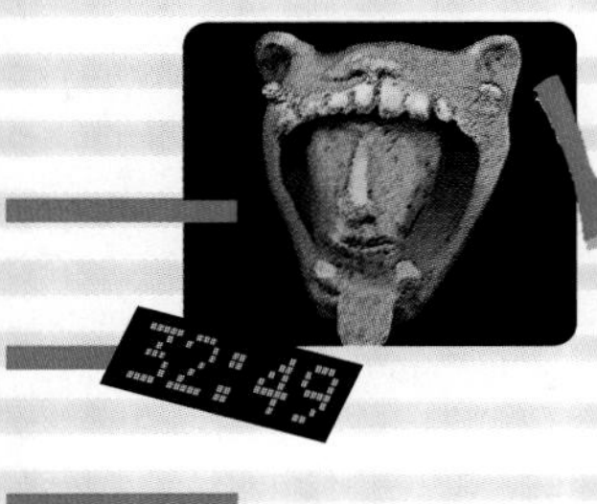

VISTAS Y VOCES

I. Preparémonos

1 Anticipación. Answer these questions in pairs.

A. **1.** ¿Qué tipo de códices hay en tu país? ¿Tienen números? ¿letras? ¿arte?
2. Cuando tú viajas, ¿te gusta viajar en autobús, en tren o en avión?
3. ¿Tienes computadora en tu cuarto? ¿Es grande o pequeña? ¿De qué color es?
4. ¿Tienes un/a buen/a amigo/a en la universidad? ¿Quién es?

B. Review chapter opening photo 2B.
What do you think that this glyph is going to reveal?

Before students view the video, review in which countries are **Dresden (Alemania), París (Francia), Madrid (España),** and **Distrito Federal (México).**

Para comprender mejor

a solas	*alone*	la tarjeta de crédito	*credit card*
el avión	*plane*	el vuelo	*flight*
la ciudad	*city*	ayudar	*to help*
el códice	*codex, ancient manuscript*	el dinero	*money*
confiar	*to confide in*	el jeroglífico	*glyph*
estar en peligro	*to be in danger*	el presentimiento	*premonition*
el lugar	*place*	el/la reportero/a	*reporter*
el pájaro	*bird*	en efectivo	*cash*

2 Secuencia. In pairs, number the video action shots in the order in which you think the action will occur in the video you will watch.

Ask students to name the characters in the pictures.

1.

2.

3.

4.

II. Miremos y escuchemos

3 **¿Verdadero o falso?** While you are watching the video, put a checkmark next to the phrases that are true.

1. ______ Adriana estudia el jeroglífico.
2. ______ Armando escucha la conversación de Adriana y Felipe.
3. ______ Felipe y Adriana tienen mucho dinero.
4. ______ Armando es amigo de Esperanza.
5. ______ La nota es para Adriana.
6. ______ Nayeli llama a Armando por teléfono.
7. ______ Una reportera habla de Nayeli en la televisión.

True statements: Numbers 1, 2, 7.

III. Comentemos

4 **Frases.** Working in groups, indicate who says the following.

1. "Cuatro códices, en cuatro ciudades: Dresden, París, Madrid, Distrito Federal."
2. "¡Madrid! ¡Nayeli está en Madrid!"
3. "Los boletos aéreos, una tarjeta de crédito, un poco de efectivo, una computadora para facilitar la comunicación."
4. "Aquí está la nota para el señor Raúl Guzmán."
5. "Oye, ¿qué tiempo hace en junio en Madrid?"
6. "Todo está bajo control."
7. "Si los gemelos no están juntos, no tendremos paz ni armonía económica en México."

Answers to Actividad 4:
1. Adriana
2. Adriana
3. Armando
4. Adriana
5. Felipe
6. Armando
7. Reportera

5 **Opinión.** Answer these questions in groups.

1. ¿Cómo están Adriana y Felipe? ¿Contentos o preocupados? ¿Por qué?
2. ¿Qué revela el códice a Adriana sobre dónde está Nayeli?
3. ¿Qué ofrece Armando a Adriana y Felipe? En tu opinión ¿es bueno o malo Armando?
4. Armando habla con una señora por teléfono. ¿Cómo es ella? ¿Es buena o mala?
5. ¿Qué mira Armando?

Answers to Actividad 5:
1. Están preocupados. Nayeli no está en su oficina.
2. Revela que Nayeli está en Madrid.
3. Les ofrece boletos, dinero y una computadora.
4. *Answers will vary.*
5. *Answers will vary.*

6 **Miremos otra vez.** After watching the scene again, check to see if you have ordered the video action shots in the appropriate sequence.

Correct order of video action shots: 2, 1, 3, 4

Lengua

I. Describing people and places

A. Adjective placement

As you have learned, adjectives usually follow the nouns they describe. In Spanish when two adjectives modify the noun, they are joined by **y.**

unas tiendas elegantes	*some elegant shops*
un mercado mexicano	*a Mexican market*
las iglesias viejas y coloniales	*the old, colonial churches*
la plaza grande y hermosa	*the large and beautiful plaza*

However, numbers, possessive adjectives, and definite and indefinite articles precede the noun.

cuarenta alumnos	*forty students*	una hora	*an hour*
mis papeles	*my papers*	cuatro ciudades	*four cities*
las clases	*the classes*		

B. Bueno, malo, grande

The adjectives **bueno** *(good)*, **malo** *(bad)* and **grande** *(big)* can appear either before or after the noun they describe. When **bueno** and **malo** appear before a singular masculine noun they change to **buen** and **mal. Grande** changes to **gran** before any singular noun. Notice that **grande** has a different meaning depending on its placement.

¿Es Armando un **buen** hombre?	
¿Es Armando un hombre **bueno?**	*Is Armando a good man?*
¿Es Armando un **mal** hombre?	
¿Es Armando un hombre **malo?**	*Is Armando a bad man?*

But:

Puebla es una **gran** ciudad.	*Puebla is a great city.*
México D.F. es una ciudad **grande.**	*Mexico City is a large city.*

1 Repaso. Make the necessary changes in gender and number in the text that follows. Work in pairs.

Nayeli es una arqueóloga __________ (importante) y __________ (famoso). Ella es también una __________ (grande) profesora. Felipe y Adriana son estudiantes muy __________(trabajador). Son __________ (joven) y muy __________ (bueno) investigadores de arqueología. Ellos viajan a __________ (diferente) partes del mundo __________ (hispano) para buscar a Nayeli.

Answers to Actividad 1:

1. importante
2. famosa
3. gran
4. trabajadores
5. jóvenes
6. buenos
7. diferentes (You may wish to point out that here **diferentes** goes before the noun for emphasis.)
8. hispano

2 Tu opinión. Use **buen/o, malo/o,** and **gran/de** to express your opinion about the following. Then, compare your answers orally with a partner.

Nueva York / ciudad	CNN / canal
Toyota / coche	Tiger Woods / golfista
Gloria Estefan / cantante	*USA Today* / periódico
IBM 123 / computadora	

Assign this as homework. After students have compared each other's answers, ask them for 1-2 sentences per phrase. Collect the papers to check for placement and agreement of adjectives.

II. Describing direction: Coming and going

A. Ir and venir

Ask for 2 student volunteers, one to read the part of Leticia and the other to read the part of Juan.

This implies she is at the party.

LETICIA:	Oye, Juan, ¿por qué no **vienes** a la fiesta ahora?	*Hey, Juan, why don't you come to the party now?*
JUAN:	Me gustaría, pero no tengo auto y no hay autobuses hoy.	*I would like to, but I don't have a car and there are no buses today.*
LETICIA:	¡**Voy** a tu casa inmediatamente en mi auto y tú **vienes** a la fiesta conmigo, ¿verdad?	*I'll go to your house immediately by car and you will come to the party with me. O.K.?*
JUAN:	¡Perfecto! Hasta luego, entonces.	*Perfect! I'll see you later, then.*
LETICIA:	Hasta luego.	*See you later.*

In the conversation above, what verb is used to talk about going from point A to point B? From point B to point A?

In Spanish, the verb **ir** (*to go*) is used to describe motion from point A (where the speaker is) to point B, and **venir** (*to come*) to talk about motion from point B to point A (where the speaker is). These verbs are irregular and are conjugated below.

Write these verbs on the board and have students repeat the verb forms in chorus after you. Then give a quick check drill using subject and infinitive to help students internalize verb endings.

	ir	venir
yo	**voy**	**vengo**
tú	**vas**	**vienes**
él/ella, Ud.	**va**	**viene**
nosotros/nosotras	**vamos**	**venimos**
vosotros/vosotras	**vais**	**venís**
ellos/ellas, Uds.	**van**	**vienen**

B. Ir + a + location

Ir + **a** + location indicates destination. Its use is similar to English.

Have students repeat the sentences in chorus after you.

Ustedes **van a** la universidad.	*You go to the university.*
Vamos mucho **al** cine.	*We go to the movies a lot.*
Mañana **voy a** la estación de tren.	*Tomorrow I am going to the train station.*

3 Los viajes. Work with a partner and create questions and answers with these elements.

nosotros		la piscina	mañana
los estudiantes		el mercado	el lunes
nuestros amigos	**ir a**	la clase	en mayo
yo	**venir de**	la universidad	el martes
tú	**venir a**	la plaza	en junio
ustedes		la cancha de tenis	el miércoles
ellas		mi casa	el domingo

▶ **Modelo:** —*¿A dónde vamos nosotros mañana?*
—*Vamos a mi casa.*

After students have completed questions and answers for **Actividad 3,** have each group contribute one sentence orally with you writing it on the board.

Adónde can be either one or two words.

4 ¿Adónde van? The following people are going to different places. Create sentences indicating their destinations.

▶ **Modelo:** *las mamás y sus hijos / parque*
Las mamás y sus hijos van al parque.

1. Gonzalo / el centro comercial
2. nosotros / las clases de español
3. ellas / el estadio
4. Liliana / la tienda
5. ustedes / el mercado
6. tú / la discoteca
7. el doctor / el hospital
8. los chicos / el museo
9. yo / la universidad
10. Adriana y Felipe / Madrid

This illustrates the use of **ir a** + noun where **a** is translated and it means *to* (*towards*). Remind students that the preposition **a** should be used in every answer.

Answers to Actividad 4:
1. Gonzalo va al centro comercial.
2. Nosotros vamos a las clases de español.
3. Ellas van al estadio.
4. Liliana va a la tienda.
5. Ustedes van al mercado.
6. Tú vas a la discoteca.
7. El doctor va al hospital.
8. Los chicos van al museo.
9. Yo voy a la unversidad.
10. Adriana y Felipe van a Madrid.

5 Itinerario de buses. You and your partner are in Puebla. Take turns asking each other where the buses are headed and where they come from using the information in the **salidas** (*departures*) and **llegadas** (*arrivals*) tables. Follow the model.

▶ **Modelo:** —*¿A dónde va el bus de las 6.45 a.m.?*
—*El bus de las 6.45 a.m. va a México D.F.*
—*¿De dónde viene el bus de las 11.40 a.m.?*
—*El bus de las 11.40 a.m. viene de Veracruz.*

After students have completed **Actividad 5**, go around the class asking **¿Adónde va?** and **¿De dónde viene?** questions.

Llegadas a Puebla	
6.30 a.m.	México D.F.
8.30 a.m.	Toluca
9.50 a.m.	Cuernavaca
11.05 a.m.	Taxco
11.40 a.m.	Veracruz
11.45 a.m.	México D.F.
1.10 p.m.	Acapulco
2.10 p.m.	Cuernavaca
4.05 p.m.	Taxco
6.30 p.m.	Veracruz
9.45 p.m.	Oaxaca

Salidas de Puebla	
6.45 a.m.	México D.F.
9.50 a.m.	Toluca
11.05 a.m.	Cuernavaca
11.30 a.m.	Taxco
12.15 p.m.	Veracruz
12.45 p.m.	México D.F.
2.15 p.m.	Acapulco
3.05 p.m.	Cuernavaca
5.55 p.m.	Taxco
8.45 p.m.	Veracruz
10.30 p.m.	Tlapa

As the two verbs **ir** and **venir** can be a source of confusion to English speakers, remind students before doing **Actividad 6,** that the use of one or the other depends on where the speaker is. Tell them that when answering the door, you say **ya voy** in Spanish whereas in English you say *I'm coming.* In Spanish you also say **ir y venir** whereas in English you say *coming and going.* To do **Actividad 6,** have students in groups of 3-4 report on the trips they have organized.

6 ¿Quién va y quién viene? You coordinate the schedule of several groups of tourists traveling to and from Puebla. You are an agent in Puebla and there are other agents in the other cities listed in the bus timetables. Use the tables to ask each agent which bus the tourists are traveling with.

▸ **Modelo:**

You, in Puebla: *¿En qué bus va el grupo de turistas argentinos a Veracruz?*
Your agent in Veracruz: *El grupo de turistas argentinos viene a Veracruz en el bus de las 8.45 p.m.*
You, in Puebla: *¿En qué bus viene el grupo de turistas chinos a Puebla?*
Your agent in Veracruz: *El grupo de turistas chinos va a Puebla en el bus de las 11.40 a.m.*

Draw a triangle on the board. Put the names of the buildings in the corners and the names of the characters on the sides with arrows indicating the directions they took in going from one building to another. Then it becomes clear that Isabel is lying because in **3** she states that **el señor elegante viene del correo al banco,** revealing with the use of **viene** that she was at the bank, not at the restaurant, as she states, falsely, in **4.**

7 Testimonio falso. You are the prosecutor in a theft trial listening to the deposition of Isabel Iriarte. Each one of Isabel's descriptions indicates where each person involved is heading, from where, and Isabel's whereabouts: **¿Banco?, ¿Correo?, ¿Restaurante?** For each sentence, draw an arrow to indicate the direction of the person and Isabel's position. Explain why her explanation is false.

La señorita Isabel Iriarte explica *(explains)*:

1. A las 8 a.m., los dos chicos van del correo al restaurante.
2. A las 8 a.m., la chica joven sale del banco y va al restaurante.
3. A las 8 a.m., el señor elegante viene del correo al banco.
4. A las 8 a.m., cuando la señora anciana va al banco, yo estoy aquí, en el restaurante.

C. Making future plans with ir

Have two students act out the dialogue in front of the class.

PATRICIA:	¡Hola Mauro! ¿Adónde vas?	*Hi, Mauro! Where are you going?*
MAURO:	¡Hola Patricia! **Voy al** aeropuerto.	*Hi, Patricia! I'm going to the airport.*
PATRICIA:	Y ¿cómo **vas a** llegar allá?	*And how are you going to arrive there?*
MAURO:	En autobús, pero ¡es muy tarde ya!	*I'm taking a bus, but it's already very late!*

PATRICIA:	Si no llegas al aeropuerto, no **vas a** tener vacaciones. Yo te llevo! **¡Vamos!**	*If you don't arrive at the airport, you won't have a vacation. I'll take you. Let's go.*
MAURO:	¡Acepto! ¡Eres una buena amiga!	*I accept. You are a good friend.*

1. Ir + a + *infinitive*

The verb **ir** may also be used to discuss the immediate future as part of the construction **ir** + **a** + infinitive. It is comparable to the English expression *going to.*

No sé cómo **voy a** pagar el viaje.	*I don't know how I am going to pay for the trip.*
¿Y dónde **vamos a** conseguir el dinero?	*And where are we going to get the money?*

Review briefly the conjugation of **ir.** Then practice with personal questions of individual students: **¿Vas a estudiar mucho esta noche? ¿Vas a comer? ¿Qué vas a hacer?**

2. Vamos

Vamos and **vamos a** + infinitive are usually used to mean *Let's go* somewhere or do something.

¡Vamos a tomar helados!	*Let's go and have some ice cream!*
Bueno, **¡vamos!**	*Fine, let's go.*

After going over the examples, have a few students create some suggestions for the class with **vamos a** expressions.

8 **¿Es posible o no?** Work in pairs. Look at the list of things your partner would like to do depending on the circumstances. Compare each numbered item on your list with your partner's list to see what he or she will do given the conditions on your list.

After students have done **Actividad 8,** go around the class and ask **¿Qué vas a hacer si hay...?**

► **Modelo:** *A. Hay programas interesantes.* *B. mirar la televisión*
—¿Qué vas a hacer si hay programas interesantes?
—Voy a mirar la televisión.

A	B
1. Hace buen tiempo.	**1.** salir al parque
2. Tienes dinero.	**2.** comprar una computadora
3. Llega el autobús pronto.	**3.** llegar temprano a la escuela
4. La paella es buena.	**4.** comer mucho
5. El examen es mañana.	**5.** estudiar hoy
6. El auto es elegante.	**6.** conducir por la ciudad
7. Tus amigos vienen hoy.	**7.** ir al aeropuerto
8. Hay oportunidad.	**8.** comprar un carro Honda
9. Es sábado.	**9.** bailar en la discoteca
10. El profesor es bueno.	**10.** estudiar español

9 **¡Vamos!** Plan some fun events with your family and friends, using the expression **Vamos a** + infinitive. Follow the model.

Have students do **Actividad 9** together, in chorus. Then ask students what they really plan to do with their family and friends.

► **Modelo:** *comer en un buen restaurante*
Vamos a comer en un buen restaurante.

1. escuchar al cantante Marc Anthony
2. ir a un concierto de los Rolling Stones
3. comprar un coche importado
4. bailar en nuestra discoteca favorita
5. hacer y comer pizza
6. organizar una fiesta
7. escribir cartas de amor
8. tocar la guitarra y cantar

III. Expressing obligation and mental or physical conditions

Tener que

Tener que + infinitive is used to express obligation or the commitment to do something or behave in a certain way.

Tengo que confiar en él.	*I have to trust him.*
Tenemos que ir a Madrid.	*We have to go to Madrid.*
Tienen que buscar a Nayeli.	*They have to look for Nayeli.*

LENGUA EN ACCIÓN

Deber

The verb **deber** *(should)* is used to talk about duties or things that you are expected to do.

Debo trabajar el lunes.	*I should work on Monday.*
Debemos asistir a todas las clases.	*We should attend all classes.*

Using common expressions with tener

Tener is used in many high-frequency expressions.

Make transparencies or draw stick figures on the board and ask **¿Qué tiene?** Then act out these expressions yourself and have students answer with **Usted tiene...** Follow up by going around the class and asking **¿Qué tienes tú?**

Tiene frío.

Tiene calor.

Tiene hambre.

Tiene sed.

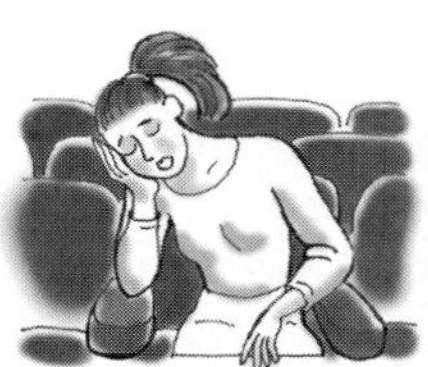

Tiene sueño.

Tiene miedo.

Tiene prisa.

Tiene cinco años.

Some other expressions with **tener** are:

- **tener ganas de** + *infinitive* — *to really want to do something*

  Adriana **tiene ganas** de ir a Madrid. — *Adriana wants to go to Madrid.*

- **tener razón** — *to be right*

  —Nayeli está en peligro. De eso estamos seguros. — *Nayeli is in danger. Of that we are sure.*

  —**Tienes razón.** — *You're right.*

10 Responsabilidades. You and your friends have a lot to do before you can relax during the weekend. Create sentences describing everybody's obligations.

▶ **Modelo:** *yo / escribir / las cartas*
Yo tengo que escribir las cartas.

1. nosotros / terminar la composición
2. Cristián / leer la novela
3. yo / hacer los ejercicios de gramática
4. Miguel / vender su estéreo
5. Isabel / ayudar a su mamá en casa
6. Eduardo / lavar el auto de papá
7. Bernardo / comprar comida para la familia
8. Guillermo y Daniel / ir al centro comercial
9. Juana y Pedro / alquilar los videos
10. Rosa / pagar los libros

11 ¿Qué tengo? Create complete sentences by matching a situation (column A) with an expression with **tener** (column B). Follow the model.

▶ **Modelo:** *Hay poco tiempo. / tener prisa*
Si hay poco tiempo, tengo prisa.

A	B
1. Veo un tigre (*tiger*).	1. tener hambre
2. Compro un buen libro.	2. tener miedo
3. No hay agua.	3. tener sed
4. Hace mucho sol.	4. tener ganas de leer
5. Es invierno.	5. tener sueño
6. Tengo muy poco tiempo.	6. tener frío
7. Es medianoche.	7. tener calor
8. No hay comida.	8. tener prisa
9. Estoy seguro/a.	9. tener razón

Lectura B

Introducción

This reading takes you on a tour of different cities and sites in the state (**el estado**) of Oaxaca on the Mexican Pacific Coast.

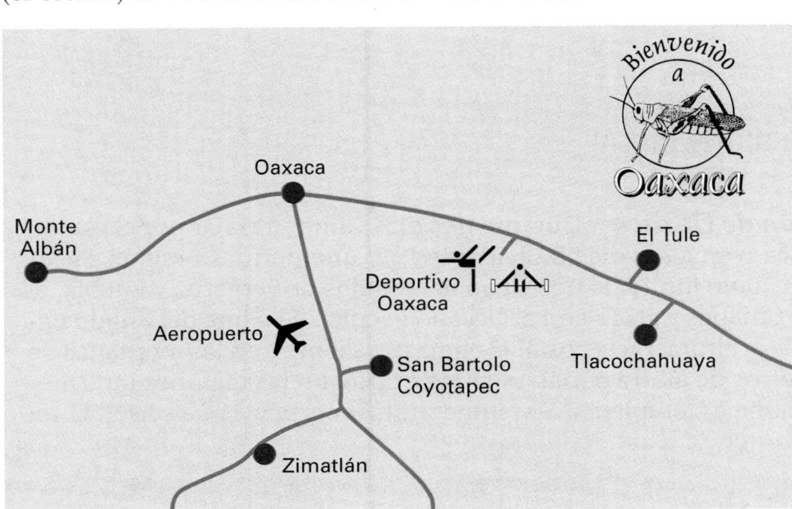

Prelectura

1 ***Atracciones turísticas.*** Which of the sites in column A would you like to visit? First, number the sites in order of priority. Then, match the reasons in column B to your selections. Compare your choices with a partner's.

	A	B
	el correo	Allí venden artículos típicos.
	el estadio	El arte me gusta mucho.
	las discotecas	La historia local es importante.
	los cines	Me gusta bailar y hablar con mucha gente.
	los edificios famosos	Me gusta mucho la arquitectura.
	los mercados populares	Me gustan los deportes.
	los monumentos históricos	Tienen platos deliciosos.
	los museos de arte	Voy mucho al cine en mis vacaciones.
	los restaurantes de comidas típicas	Yo escribo y mando cartas en mis vacaciones.

2 ***¿Qué ciudades te gustan?*** The table below describes weather conditions and main attractions in five imaginary cities. Which of them would you like to visit? Number them in your order of priority. Compare your choices with a partner's.

#	Ciudades	Temperatura media	Mes	Atracciones
	Ciudad A	30°C	junio	Tiene buen clima y hace mucho sol. Tiene parques y plazas muy hermosos, y museos interesantes.
	Ciudad B	4°C	diciembre	Su comida es deliciosa y su gente es muy simpática. Su clima es frío.
	Ciudad C	12°C	agosto	Hay enormes tiendas y mercados típicos.
	Ciudad D	28°C	septiembre	Hay monumentos históricos y ruinas arqueológicas muy famosas.
	Ciudad E	21°C	abril	No hace frío, pero llueve mucho. Sus restaurantes y discotecas son fenomenales.

¡Oaxaca maravillosa!

La región de Oaxaca Durante tres días vamos a viajar por el estado de Oaxaca. Van a ser días inolvidables° en una hermosa región mexicana. El estado limita° al norte con los estados de Veracruz y Puebla, al este con Chiapas y al sur con el Océano Pacífico. El clima del estado depende° de la altura. En la costa° el clima es caliente y en las montañas de 2.000 metros de altura o más, el clima es frío. En las regiones intermedias, el clima es templado.° Su temperatura en primavera es de 25°C, en

unforgettable
borders
depends / coast
temperate

Remind students to read for meaning and not to look up every word. In class have each student read one sentence out loud. Help them with pronunciation when they need it but do not interfere too much. At the end you may wish to focus in on keywords such as **Oaxaca, Veracruz** (for the **x**, the **v** and **z**), **Patio** (for the **a**), **hotel** (for the silent **h**); **bellas** (for the **ll**), **museo** (for the **u**) and **viaje** (for the **v** and **j**).

Una playa en Puerto Escondido, México.

La zona arqueológica de Monte Albán, Oaxaca, México.

El centro histórico, Oaxaca, México.

verano y en otoño es de 22°C, y en invierno es de 16°C.

Martes Hoy vamos a visitar la ciudad de Oaxaca. Por la mañana, vamos al centro histórico de la ciudad; allí está el acueducto español de San Felipe, en uso hasta° 1940. También vamos a visitar el Museo de Arte. Por la tarde, vamos al Museo Regional de Antropología e Historia. Finalmente,° vamos al Zócalo, Plaza de la Constitución (existe desde el año 1529), y la cena es a las 8.30 de la noche. Vamos a cenar en el restaurante El Patio, en nuestro camino° a Mitla, a 46 kilómetros de la ciudad. Regresamos a Oaxaca, al hotel Casa Colonial.

in use until

Finally

way

Miércoles Hoy salimos temprano para ver las bellas pirámides zapotecas° de Monte Albán y el museo de la ciudad. El camino es corto y regresamos a Oaxaca para almorzar en el restaurante La Abuelita. Por la tarde hay tiempo para comprar artículos típicos de Oaxaca.

Zapotec

Jueves, viernes y sábado El jueves, salimos en auto para Puerto Escondido, un pintoresco° puerto° en la Costa Esmeralda del Océano Pacífico mexicano. Es un viaje largo porque está a 318 kilómetros al sur de Oaxaca. El puerto es un paraíso y el centro turístico más antiguo de la región. Tiene playas° muy buenas y exquisitos restaurantes. Regresamos a Oaxaca el sábado por la tarde.

picturesque / port

beaches

Postlectura

3 Viaje turístico. Answer in writing the following questions about the tour in Oaxaca.

1. ¿Dónde está el estado de Oaxaca?
2. ¿Cómo son las temperaturas en las diferentes estaciones? ¿Dónde hace frío? ¿Y dónde hace calor?
3. ¿Qué van a visitar los turistas en el centro de Oaxaca?
4. ¿Cuántos años tiene el Zócalo de Oaxaca? ¿Cómo se llama?
5. ¿A dónde van a cenar los turistas el martes?
6. ¿A qué hora van a ir a cenar?
7. ¿Qué hay en Monte Albán?
8. ¿Dónde van a almorzar los turistas el miércoles?
9. ¿Cómo es el clima de Puerto Escondido? ¿Cómo es la ciudad?
10. ¿Cómo es la Costa Esmeralda: el clima, la temperatura, el agua?

1. El estado de Oaxaca limita al norte con los estados de Veracruz y Puebla, al este con Chiapas, y al sur con el Océano Pacífico.
2. Las temperaturas varían. En general hace calor en el verano y hace frío en el invierno. Hace calor en la costa y hace frío en las montañas de más de 2.000 metros de altura.
3. Los turistas van a visitar el acueducto, el Museo de Arte y el Museo Regional de Antropología e Historia.
4. El Zócalo tiene muchos años (369 en 1998). Se llama La Plaza de la Constitución.
5. El martes los turistas van a comer en el restaurante El Patio.
6. Van a ir a cenar a las 8.30 de la noche.
7. Hay bellas pirámides zapotecas en Monte Albán.
8. El miércoles los turistas van a almorzar en el restaurante La Abuelita.
9. El clima de Puerto Escondido es caliente (porque está en la costa). La ciudad es el centro turístico más antiguo de la región.
10. El clima de la Costa Esmeralda es un paraíso. Es caliente y tiene playas muy buenas.

4 Me gusta, no me gusta. List five sites mentioned in the reading and say whether you like them or not and why. Compare your selections with a partner's.

► **Modelo:** *Me gusta... porque tiene buenos restaurantes.*
No me gusta... porque hace mucho calor.

5 Me gusta la comida. Look at the two restaurant ads and write two sentences describing the food they serve. You will find the Spanish word for **Oaxacan** in one of the ads. Use it! Work with a partner and ask each other if you like the food you have described.

After doing **Actividad 5**, have student volunteers report on what they like.

6 Un sitio. Describe a site that you like, using some of the adjectives and expressions that you have learned.

Minimum 35 words in Spanish. Have a few student volunteers read their papers to the class and collect all papers.

En resumen

I. Hablemos

1 La casa de mis sueños *(My dream house).* Draw and label an original floor plan for your dream house. Then present your plan to the class.

These should be very brief talks (less than one minute each).

2 El canal del tiempo. You have just landed a new job with the weather channel. You are expected to give an updated weather report for your home town; Mexico City, México; Madrid, Spain; and Buenos Aires, Argentina. Prepare a weather report for all four cities. Work in groups and compare your reports to those of your classmates. Use the information provided in this chapter.

Divide the class into groups of 4. Have groups report on the weather in the different cities. Make sure they are realistic about what they say.

II. Investiguemos por Internet

Searching for Spanish sites

When searching for Spanish sites, the first thing you must do is to write in Spanish the word or words for which you are searching. The most popular search engines have a Spanish version and offer links to search engines in Spanish. The Houghton Mifflin Web site will give you updated links to useful sites and to Web browsers in Spanish.

Usually, when you write several words in a phrase, you should use quotation marks; in this way, the search engine will read them as a phrase and not word-for-word. You may also want to read the instructions of the browser you are using on how to refine your search. Following these instructions, you will access more relevant and useful sites for your purposes.

3 Pronóstico del tiempo de hoy. You may want to search for actual weather reports in Spanish for the four cities that you have selected. Review the Spanish words that you have learned related to weather and type them in as keywords in your search. Start with the following keywords one-by-one: **tiempo, clima, pronóstico del tiempo.**

If your students do not have access to the Internet, you can still print out information and photocopy it for them from either your own home account or from a cyber café or your local library, or a friend who can send you a printout.

Vocabulario informático

la guía Internet/el directorio Internet	*Internet guide*	la palabra clave	*keyword*
el motor de búsqueda/ el buscador Internet	*search engine*		

III. Escribamos

Writing strategy: Brainstorming ideas

Before writing an essay or a report, it is often useful to brainstorm your ideas, especially with a partner or in a group. In order to do this effectively, write only in Spanish.

1. Write down your ideas on paper as they occur to you. They can be single words, phrases, or questions.
2. Write quickly and in no particular order. Do not stop to evaluate which ideas are good.
3. Once the ideas are written, read the list and circle the ideas that you will use in your writing.

The following is a possible brainstorm for an essay that describes your apartment.

Have students repeat the words on this brainstorm list and then add words of their own, which you or a student volunteer can write on the board.

grande	me gusta
cocina fea	azul
comer	novio arrogante
no hay sofá	jardín bonito
2 pisos	hace frío
buena compañera	dormitorio pequeño

Strategy in action

Turn to *Escribamos* in the Workbook to practice the strategy above.

Show students how to write a letter with an opening such as **Muy estimado/a:** and a closing such as **Atentamente.**

4 Nuestra universidad. You have been chosen to be the host for an international student coming to visit your campus and the city where you live. Before he or she arrives you write a letter that describes four interesting places in town to visit and two to three activities to do on campus. Before writing your letter, use the diagram to brainstorm your ideas.

Vocabulario

El apartamento

el alquiler	*rent*
el balcón	*balcony*
la bañera	*bathtub*
barato/a	*inexpensive*
la calefacción	*heat*
la cancha de tenis	*tennis court*
caro/a	*expensive*
la cocina	*kitchen*
el comedor	*dining room*
el cuarto	*room*
el cuarto de baño	*bathroom*
el dormitorio (la alcoba)	*bedroom*
la ducha	*shower*
el/la dueño/a	*owner*
el/la inquilino/a	*tenant*
el jardín	*garden*
la oficina	*office*
el pasillo	*hallway*
la piscina	*swimming pool*
el piso	*floor*
el ropero (armario)	*closet*
la sala	*living room*
la terraza	*terrace*

La ciudad

el aeropuerto	*airport*
la biblioteca	*library*
el café	*café*
la casa	*house*
el centro comercial	*shopping district*
el cine	*movie theater*
el correo	*post office*
la estación de tren	*train station*
el estadio	*stadium*
el hospital	*hospital*
el hotel	*hotel*
la iglesia	*church*
la librería	*bookstore*
el museo	*museum*
la parada de autobús	*bus stop*
la plaza (el zócalo)	*city square, plaza*
el restaurante	*restaurant*
la tienda	*store*

Expresiones con poner y salir

(See p. 66)

Tiempo y clima

las condiciones del tiempo	*weather conditions*
Está despejado.	*It's clear.*
Está nublado.	*It's cloudy.*
el grado (centígrado/Celsio)	*degree (centigrade/Celsius)*
Hace buen tiempo.	*The weather is good.*
Hace (mucho) calor.	*It's (very) hot.*
Hace fresco.	*It's cool.*
Hace (mucho) frío.	*It's (very) cold.*
Hace mal tiempo.	*The weather is bad.*
Hace sol.	*It's sunny.*
Hace (mucho) viento.	*It's (very) windy.*
Llovizna (mucho/un poco).	*It's drizzling (a lot/a little).*
Llueve (mucho/un poco).	*It's raining (a lot/a little).*
Nieva (mucho/un poco).	*It's snowing (a lot/a little).*
el pronóstico del tiempo	*weather forecast*
la temperatura	*temperature*
Tiene buen/mal clima.	*It has a good/bad climate.*

Ropa

el abrigo	*coat*	**el impermeable**	*raincoat*
las botas	*boots*	**los pantalones**	*pants*
la bufanda	*scarf*	**los pantalones cortos**	*shorts*
la chaqueta	*jacket*	**el paraguas**	*umbrella*
las gafas de sol	*sunglasses*	**el sombrero**	*hat*
la gorra	*cap*	**el suéter**	*sweater*
los guantes	*gloves*	**el traje de baño**	*bathing suit*

Estaciones del año

el invierno	*winter*
el otoño	*autumn*
la primavera	*spring*
el verano	*summer*

Descripción de personas con estar

aliviado/a	*relieved*	**enfermo/a**	*sick*
alterado/a	*upset*	**enojado/a**	*angry*
borracho/a	*drunk*	**entusiasmado/a**	*enthusiastic*
calmado/a	*calm*	**listo/a**	*ready*
cansado/a	*tired*	**nervioso/a**	*nervous*
contento/a	*content, happy*	**preocupado/a**	*worried*
deprimido/a	*depressed*	**seguro/a**	*sure*
desilusionado/a	*disappointed*	**triste**	*sad*
enamorado/a	*in love*		

Expresiones con tener

(See p. 84)

Verbos

conducir	*to drive*	**producir**	*to produce*
conocer	*to know, be familiar with*	**saber**	*to know*
		salir	*to leave*
esperar	*to wait*	**tener**	*to have*
estar	*to be*	**traducir**	*to translate*
hacer	*to do; to make*	**traer**	*to bring*
ir	*to go*	**venir**	*to come*
ir a (+ infinitive)	*going to (+ infinitive)*	**ver**	*to see*
poner	*to put, place*		

Adjetivos posesivos

(See p. 60)

CAPÍTULO 3

LOCALIDAD:
España

3A

3B

The trucker, el señor Covarrubias, plots to keep the jaguar twin for himself, but the jaguar has other plans. While Adriana continues to search for Nayeli, doña Gafasoscuras finds an ingenious way to keep track of Nayeli's every move.

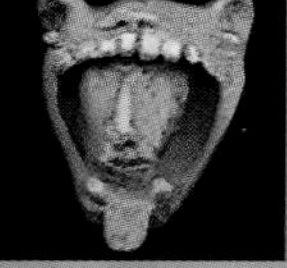

¿Qué revela el sueño de la abuela?

Vocabulary themes

- Describing means of transportation
- Checking into a hotel
- Talking about large quantities
- Ordering food
- Setting the table
- Shopping for food

Language structures

- Describing actions in the present
- Describing daily routines
- Describing how actions are done
- Expressing negation
- Pointing out people, things, and places
- Describing actions in progress
- Using *ser* and *estar*

Culture topics

- Las medidas
- Las sabrosas tapas de Madrid

Readings

- Transportes y comunicación
- Plácido Domingo Restaurant

Reading/writing strategies

- Skimming
- Scanning
- Providing supporting detail

Internet strategy

- Keyword searches

ETAPA A

Pistas y palabras

I. Describing means of transportation

A. El viaje de una tarjeta postal

In Puerto Rico, buses are commonly called **guaguas.** Other names for *car* are **carro, auto, automóvil, máquina.**

To review **llegar** from Chapter 1, ask students how they arrive on campus: **¿Quiénes llegan en metro? ¿Cómo llegas tú a la universidad?**

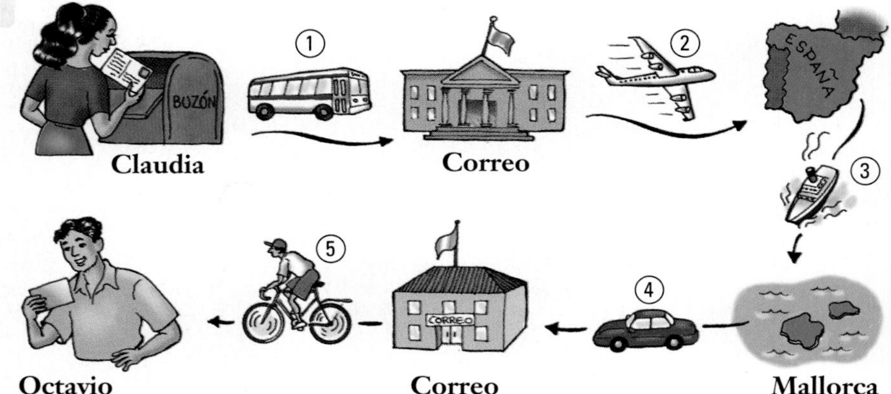

In Mexico **camión** means *bus,* while in other Hispanic countries it means *truck.*

1. el autobús/el camión
2. el avión
3. el barco
4. el coche
5. la bicicleta

B. Otros medios de transporte

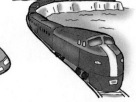

el metro **la moto/motocicleta** **a pie** **el taxi** **el tren/ferrocarril**

Point out that the definite article is not used after **en** when speaking about modes of transportation in general. Bring to class pictures of different modes of transportation to have students practice the construction **en tren, en barco,** and so on.

To say *by,* **en** is frequently used with means of transportation:

Voy en tren/coche/barco. To say *on foot,* use **a pie.**

1 **La ruta de la tarjeta.** Trace the route of the postcard. Follow the model.

▸ **Modelo:** *La tarjeta va al correo en autobús.*

1. La tarjeta va a España...
2. La tarjeta va a Mallorca...
3. La tarjeta va al correo...
4. La tarjeta va a la casa de Octavio...

Answers to Actividad 1:
1. en avión
2. en barco
3. en coche
4. en bicicleta

2 ¿Cómo se va? How do the following people and things reach their destination? Use your imagination! Follow the model.

▸ **Modelo:** *los estudiantes / a la universidad*
Los estudiantes van a la universidad en metro.

Additional words for **Actividad 2: limosina, helicóptero, nave espacial, monopatín, tabla de patinar sobre ruedas.**

1. la Secretaria de Defensa / a la Casa Blanca
2. mis amigos / a la universidad
3. la señora Fernández / al Caribe
4. los empleados / al trabajo
5. una carta / a los amigos en México
6. Jay Leno / al canal de NBC
7. yo / al cine
8. la doctora / al hospital
9. los amigos / al museo

3 ¿Cómo se va? Working in pairs, ask each other these questions about the transportation used by family and friends.

1. ¿Van tus padres al trabajo en transporte público?
2. Si vives en la universidad, ¿cómo viajas a casa en tus vacaciones?
3. Si vives en casa o en un apartamento, ¿cómo vas a la escuela?
4. ¿Te gusta viajar en motocicleta? ¿Por qué?
5. ¿Es fácil ir al centro de tu ciudad a pie?
6. Si vas a Europa, ¿vas en barco o en avión?
7. ¿Adónde vas en taxi? ¿Cuándo?
8. ¿Cómo va tu compañero/a de cuarto al banco?
9. Cuando vas a comprar ropa, ¿cómo llegas a las tiendas?

II. Checking into a hotel

Necesitamos una habitación

1. el huésped
2. la huésped
3. el ascensor
4. el botones
5. el buzón
6. la conserje
7. la llave
8. la maleta
9. la recepción
10. el recepcionista

Palabras y expresiones útiles

el almuerzo	*lunch*
el viaje	*trip*
Aquí tengo mi confirmación.	*Here is my confirmation.*
¿Cómo quiere Ud. pagar?	*How do you want to pay?*
con cheques de viajero	*with traveler's checks*
con desayuno	*with breakfast*
con media pensión	*with breakfast and lunch*
con tarjeta de crédito	*with a credit card*
¿Cuánto cuesta... ?	*How much does . . . cost?*
¿Dónde puedo cambiar el dinero?	*Where can I exchange money?*
¿En qué le(s) puedo servir?	*How can I help you?*
en seguida	*right away*
hacer una llamada de larga distancia	*to make a long distance phone call*
hacer una llamada por cobrar	*to make a collect call*
Lo siento.	*I'm sorry.*
no fumar	*no smoking*
Quiero pagar con dinero en efectivo.	*I want to pay cash.*
Quisiera una habitación doble/sencilla.	*I would like a double/single room.*
¿Tiene(n) Ud(s). reservación?	*Do you have a reservation?*

Answers to Actividad 4:
1. la maleta
2. la tarjeta de crédito
3. la llave
4. la habitación / la cama
5. la recepción
6. la recepción
7. el ascensor

4 **¿Qué es?** Write the correct word that matches each definition.

1. Cuando viajas, pones mucha ropa (*clothing*) allí.
2. Es dinero plástico para pagar la habitación del hotel.
3. Es una cosa para abrir la puerta.
4. Allí descansas en el hotel.
5. Allí reciben los turistas la llave de la habitación.
6. Allí pagas para mandar una tarjeta postal.
7. Es un aparato para ir al piso doce (*twelfth floor*).

5 **Símbolos internacionales.** Match the international hotel symbols with their meanings.

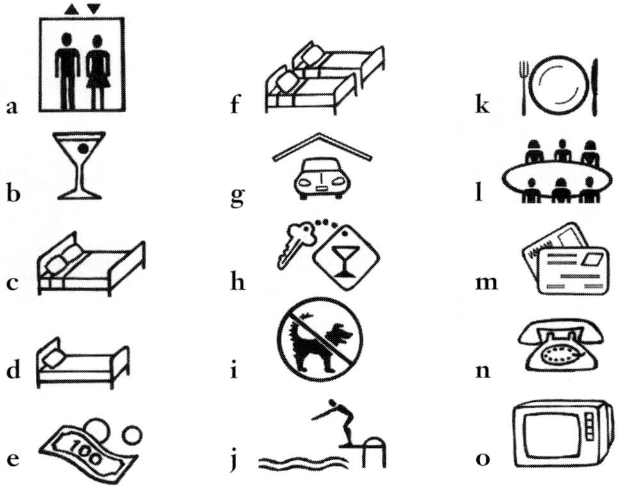

Note that **estacionamiento** is also used for *parking*.

___piscina
___dos camas sencillas
___tarjetas de crédito
___cama sencilla
___cambio de moneda (*money exchange*)
___restaurante
___salón de conferencias
___teléfono
___ascensor
___bar
___aparcamiento
___cama doble
___televisión
___perros no (*no dogs*)
___minibar

a b c d e f g h i j k l m n o

6 **¿Qué necesitas?** What hotel amenities will you need in the following situations?

▶ **Modelo:** *Tienes hambre.*
Necesito ir al restaurante.

1. No tienes dinero.
2. Debes llamar a tu madre.
3. Tus maletas son muy grandes.
4. Tu habitación está en el piso (*floor*) veinticuatro.
5. Tienes sed.
6. Quieres hacer ejercicio.
7. Tienes hambre a la medianoche y el restaurante está cerrado (*closed*).
8. Llegas al hotel en coche.

Answers to Actividad 6:
1. Necesito ir al banco.
2. Necesito un teléfono.
Necesito hacer una llamada de larga distancia.
Necesito hacer una llamada por cobrar.
3. Necesito un (una) botones.
4. Necesito un ascensor.
5. Necesito ir al bar/restaurante.
6. Necesito ir a la piscina.
7. Necesito el minibar.
8. Necesito el aparcamiento.

7 **Entre nosotros.** Role-play the following situation with a partner.

Turista:	**Recepcionista:**
You are traveling through Spain by bicycle. After a difficult day, you arrive at your hotel very tired. When you arrive the receptionist tells you that he or she doesn't have your reservation. You have a copy of your confirmation. Do whatever you can to get a room for the night.	A young bicyclist arrives at your hotel, but you can't find his or her reservation in the computer. There's a medical conference (**congreso**) in the hotel and the only (**única**) room is in the basement (**sótano**). Do your best to solve this dilemma.

To follow-up, have students give you first the complaints, using **necesito,** and then the solutions. Write the sentences on the board.

8 **Querido amigo/Querida amiga.** You are on vacation. Write a postcard to your best friend. Tell him or her where you are staying. Describe the hotel and tell him or her what you like and don't like to do there. Include any special information about your vacation.

Have students draw their vacation site on one side of a 5 x 7 card and on the other do the written assignment for **Actividad 8.** Have them exchange postcards and present orally their classmates' creations.

III. Talking about large quantities

A. Los números de 100 a 2.000.000

Los números de 100 a 2.000.000			
100	cien	700	setecientos
101	ciento uno	800	ochocientos
200	doscientos	900	novecientos
201	doscientos uno	1.000	mil
300	trescientos	1.999	mil novecientos noventa y nueve
400	cuatrocientos	2.000	dos mil
500	quinientos	1.000.000	un millón
600	seiscientos	2.000.000	dos millones

Point out the irregular forms for **500, 700, 900.** Note that **quinientos** is related to *quincentennial;* **setecientos** to **setenta; novecientos** to **noventa.** Have students state the current date and year while you write it in words on the board. Contrast *nineteen hundred and ninety nine,* in English with the use of **mil** for *thousands* in Spanish.

Note that in Spanish, numbers are separated by a period and not by a comma.

With large, complex numbers Spanish uses the **y** only in numbers from sixteen to 99: **mil novecientos noventa *y* nueve.**

B. ¿Cómo contamos los números en español?

any number + **uno**	• **Uno** changes to **una** in front of a feminine noun: *401 rooms* = cuatrocientas **una** habitaciones • Just as with the indefinite articles, **uno** changes to **un** in front of a masculine noun: *301 hotels* = trescientos **un** hoteles • Numbers ending in *one* (**uno/una**) do not have a plural form: *301 students* = trescientos **un** estudiantes *301 pounds* = trescientas **una** libras
cien	• **Cien** is used when the number begins with *exactly* 100: *100,000* = **cien mil (100.000)** *100,000,000* = **cien millones (100.000.000)**
ciento	• **Ciento** is used from **101** to **199**; it doesn't change its form. *103 tourists* = En el hotel hay **ciento tres** turistas. *101 tourists* = En el hotel hay **ciento un** turistas. *101 rooms* = En el hotel hay **ciento una** habitaciones.
doscientos a novecientos	• The numbers from **200** to **900** agree in gender with the nouns they modify. These words are always plural. *200 rooms* = **doscientas** habitaciones *300 dollars* = **trescientos** dólares
mil	• **Mil** remains unchanged and does not agree in gender or number with the nouns it modifies: *1,000 pesetas* = **mil pesetas** *2,000 students* = **dos mil alumnos**
millón	• **Millón** agrees in number (**millones**) with the noun it modifies. *1,005,093 pesos* = **un millón, cinco mil, noventa y tres** pesos *2,400,671 dollars* = **dos millones, cuatrocientos mil, seiscientos setenta y un** dólares
cientos de	• **Cientos de** is not used to count. It only expresses *hundreds of.* *I have hundreds of friends.* = Tengo **cientos de** amigos.
miles de	• **Miles de** is not used to count. It only expresses *thousands of.* *I have thousands of dollars.* = Tengo **miles de** dólares.
un millón de/ millones de	• **Un millón de/millones de** is used to count only when the number is exact. Otherwise **millones** follows the other rules above. *1,000,000 dollars* = **un millón de** dólares *5,000,000 dollars* = **cinco millones de** dólares *but* *5,100,401 pesetas* = **cinco millones, cien mil, cuatrocientas una** pesetas

9 **Eventos históricos.** Write out the following dates in Spanish. Then work with a partner to see if you can match the dates in column **B** with the events in column **A.**

A	B
1. la llegada de Cristóbal Colón a las Américas	a. 1/1997
2. la llegada de los moros (*Moors*) a España	b. 2/9/1964
3. la segunda guerra mundial (WWII)	c. 9/17/1970
4. la muerte de Jimi Hendrix	d. 711
5. los Packers de Green Bay ganan el Superbowl contra (*against*) los Patriots	e. 1492
	f. 1776
6. la Independencia de los Estados Unidos	g. 1941
7. la disolución de la Unión Soviética	h. 1992
8. los Beatles cantan en el "Ed Sullivan Show"	

10 **¿Cuánto cuesta una habitación?** Look at the prices of the different hotel rooms, and then work with a partner to compare the prices. Follow the model. (Note that the prices for double rooms depend on the kind of view they have.)

▶ **Modelo:** —*¿Cuánto cuesta una habitación individual con media pensión en agosto?*
—*Cuesta quince mil doscientas cincuenta pesetas.*

Answers to Actividad 9:

1. e. (mil cuatrocientos noventa y dos)
2. d. (setecientos once)
3. g. (mil novecientos cuarenta y uno)
4. c. (el diecisiete de septiembre de mil novecientos setenta)
5. a. (enero de mil novecientos noventa y siete)
6. f. (mil setecientos setenta y seis)
7. h. (mil novecientos noventa y dos)
8. b. (el dos de septiembre de mil novecientos sesenta y cuatro)

Ask students what monetary unit they would expect to use in Marbella (peseta or Euro). Find out the current exchange rate from your local bank and have students convert the rates into dollars. Review the names of the seasons and ask students when the rates are the highest and why. Ask students when they would go to Marbella, what kind of room they would like and why.

TARIFAS

Único hotel de 3 estrellas en el centro de Marbella y al borde (border) *del mar, lugar* (place) *tranquilo*

	1° de enero al 15 de julio *1° de octubre al 31 de diciembre*			*16 de julio al 30 de septiembre*		
PRECIOS POR DÍA (PESETAS)	**Habitación**	**Habitación con desayuno**	**Media pensión**	**Habitación**	**Habitación con desayuno**	**Media pensión**
Doble montaña	12.300	15.000	22.200	14.400	17.100	24.300
Doble lateral mar	14.500	17.200	24.400	16.600	19.300	26.500
Doble frontal mar	16.500	19.200	26.400	18.700	21.400	28.600
Doble con salón	20.000	22.700	29.900	25.000	27.700	34.900
Individual	9.100	10.450	14.050	10.300	11.650	15.250
Semisuite	25.000	27.700	34.900	31.300	34.000	41.200
Suite	30.200	32.900	40.100	36.500	39.200	46.400

TEMPORADA DE INVIERNO
Larga estancia 10% Dto.*
Oferta especial de fines de semana
Servicios incluídos, excepto I.V.A. 7%**

SERVICIOS SUELTOS
Desayuno - Bufet... 1.350
Media pensión... 4.950
Almuerzo o cena... 3.600
Pensión completa... 6.880

*descuento *(discount)*
**I.V.A. is a sales tax: *Value-added tax (VAT)*

ENLACE CULTURAL

Las medidas

Casi todos los países del mundo usan el sistema métrico, basado en múltiplos de diez. Tres medidas importantes en este sistema son: el **metro,** medida de longitud;° el **litro,** medida de volumen; y el **gramo,** medida de peso.° Un metro equivale° a 3,3 pies° y a 1,1 yardas aproximadamente. Un centímetro equivale a 0,4 pulgadas.° Un kilómetro equivale aproximadamente 0.6 millas. Un litro equivale a 1,057 *quarts.* Una onza° tiene 28,35 gramos y un kilo equivale a 2,2 libras° americanas. Los prefijos **mega** y **giga** son también parte del sistema decimal. En electricidad, por ejemplo, un millón de vatios es un **megavatio**° y mil millones de vatios son un **gigavatio.**

length
weight / equals / feet
inches
ounce
pounds
megawatt

Ask students what **L, m, cm,** and **kg** mean in Spanish.

Note that the comma is used where the period is used in the U.S. for numbers and vice versa. Be aware that 10^9 watts = 1 gigawatt. Avoid using the term **billion.** In the U.S. *1 billion* = 10^9 whereas in other countries **1 billion** = 10^{12}.

Longitud		Volumen		Peso	
Nombre	**Metros**	**Nombre**	**Litros**	**Nombre**	**Gramos**
kilómetro	1.000	kilolitro	1.000	kilogramo	1.000
hectómetro	100	hectolitro	100	hectogramo	100
decámetro	10	decalitro	10	decagramo	10
metro	**1**	**litro**	**1**	**gramo**	**1**
decímetro	0,10	decilitro	0,10	decigramo	0,10
centímetro	0,01	centilitro	0,01	centigramo	0,01
milímetro	0,001	mililitro	0,001	miligramo	0,001

Discusión en grupos

En grupos de tres, adivinen (*guess*) las siguientes medidas: (a) la estatura (*height*) de cada persona en metros y centímetros; (b) el peso de su mochila; (c) el volumen de las bebidas favoritas de cada compañero/a; (d) la distancia en kilómetros de su casa a la universidad; (e) el tamaño (*size*) del disco de la computadora de un/a compañero/a, en megabyts o gigabyts. Cada grupo le presenta los resultados a la clase.

Vistas y voces

I. Preparémonos

1 Anticipación. Answer these questions in pairs.

A. **1.** ¿Cuál es el medio de transporte más popular en tu ciudad: el metro, el autobús o los autos?
2. ¿Vas a la escuela a pie o en transporte público?
3. ¿Te gustan los hoteles grandes o pequeños? ¿Por qué?
4. ¿Tienes agenda? ¿De qué color es? ¿Qué escribes en tu agenda?
5. ¿Usas el teléfono mucho? ¿A quién llamas? ¿Por cuántos minutos hablas y de qué?

B. Review chapter opening photo 3A.
Who do you think these two people are? Why are they behind the couch? What is going to happen next?

Para comprender mejor

cálmate	*relax, calm down*	la naturaleza	*nature*
desde aquí	*from here*	No es culpa tuya.	*It's not your fault.*
la dirección	*address*	No seas así, cariño.	*Don't be like that, love.*
está bien, está bien	*O.K., O.K.*	Parece que...	*It seems that...*
el lío	*trouble*	por supuesto	*of course*
luego	*then*	querido/a	*dear*
el/la huésped	*guest*	el chofer	*driver*
la buena suerte	*good luck*	el sueño	*dream*
mejor	*better*	el terremoto	*earthquake*
la muerte	*death*		

2 Secuencia. In pairs, number the video action shots in the order in which you think the action will occur in the video you will watch.

1.

2.

3.

4.

II. Miremos y escuchemos

Point out that the **Portero** pronounces the **Paz** in Nayeli's surname with the Castilian **theta,** whereas the other characters use the Latin American pronunciation(s).

3 Acción. While watching the video, number the following sentences in the order in which the action occurs.

______ Adriana y Felipe hablan con el portero.
______ Doña Gafasoscuras pone un microfonito en la agenda de Nayeli.
______ El empleado de la compañía de transporte no quiere ayudar a Nayeli.
______ Adriana y Felipe van al hotel Prisma.
______ Hay problemas en la casa de los señores Covarrubias.
______ Doña Gafasoscuras espía por la ventana.
______ Nayeli escribe el nombre y la dirección del chofer en un papelito.
______ La abuela le habla a Nayeli en un sueño.
______ El portero habla de la rutina de Nayeli.
______ Nayeli busca el nombre del chofer.
______ Nayeli va a la compañía de transporte.

Answers to Actividad 3:
The sentences should read in the following order:
5, 3, 9, 4, 2, 7, 11, 1, 6, 10, 8

III. Comentemos

4 Comprensión. Answer the following questions in groups.

1. ¿Cómo es la abuelita de Nayeli? ¿quién es Hernán?
2. En este episodio, ¿de qué desastre natural habla la abuelita en el sueño?
3. ¿Quién tiene el jaguar?
4. ¿Cómo es el portero del Hotel Prisma?
5. ¿Dónde está la agenda de Nayeli? ¿Qué hace doña Gafasoscuras?
6. ¿Cómo está el empleado de la compañía de transportes?

Possible Answers to Actividad 4:
1. La abuela es vieja/viejita/anciana y simpática. Hernán es el esposo muerto de Nayeli.
2. Habla del terremoto de México en 1985.
3. El chofer de la compañía de transporte tiene el jaguar en su casa.
4. El portero es simpático.
5. La agenda está en su habitación. Doña Gafasoscuras investiga la habitación de Nayeli y deja un microfonito.
6. Está frustrado.

5 Acciones y opiniones. Describe, in Spanish, an action or opinion of the following characters in this episode.

1. el chofer
2. la esposa del chofer
3. Felipe y Adriana
4. doña Gafasoscuras
5. el portero
6. Nayeli

6 ¿Qué pasa en nuestra ciudad? Working in pairs, create a conversation in the present tense between Nayeli and the employee of the transport company about the missing jaguar. Then act out the role-play.

7 Miremos otra vez. After watching the scene again, check to see if you have ordered the video action shots in the appropriate sequence.

Order of video action shots: 4, 2, 3, 1

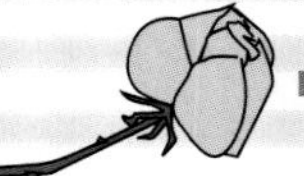

Lengua

I. Describing actions in the present

Present indicative of stem-changing verbs

Esta tarde

MAURO: Aquí está el hotel Prisma. ¡Por fin **encontramos** nuestro hotel!
ROSALÍA: Sí, ¡por fin! Yo **pienso** dormir toda la tarde.
MAURO: Pues yo no voy a dormir. Esta tarde **prefiero** ir a un buen restaurante.
ROSALÍA: ¡Ah! Buena idea. Me **muero** de hambre. Vamos al restaurante Plácido Domingo.
MAURO: ¿Entonces no **duermes** esta tarde?
ROSALÍA: No, yo **pido** la habitación y tú **consigues** la dirección del restaurante. ¿De acuerdo?
MAURO: ¡Sí, de acuerdo!

Stem-changing verbs

Stem-changing verbs have the same present tense endings as the regular **-ar, -er,** and **-ir** verbs, but they have a vowel change in the stem.

	e > ie: empezar *to start, begin*	**o > ue: volver** *to return*	**e > i: servir** *to serve*	**u > ue: jugar** *to play (games, sports)*
yo	emp**ie**zo	v**ue**lvo	s**i**rvo	j**ue**go
tú	emp**ie**zas	v**ue**lves	s**i**rves	j**ue**gas
él/ella, Ud.	emp**ie**za	v**ue**lve	s**i**rve	j**ue**ga
nosotros/nosotras	empezamos	volvemos	servimos	jugamos
vosotros/vosotras	empezáis	volvéis	servís	jugáis
ellos/ellas, Uds.	emp**ie**zan	v**ue**lven	s**i**rven	j**ue**gan

Notice that the **nosotros** and **vosotros** forms do not have a stem change.

Some common stem-changing verbs

e > ie		**o > ue**		**e > i**	
c**e**rrar	*to close*	alm**o**rzar	*to have lunch*	cons**e**guir	*to obtain, get*
com**e**nzar	*to begin*	c**o**ntar	*to count*	cons**e**guir	*to get, obtain*
emp**e**zar	*to begin*	c**o**star	*to cost*	d**e**cir	*to say, tell*
ent**e**nder	*to understand*	d**o**rmir	*to sleep*	p**e**dir	*to ask for*
n**e**var	*to snow*	enc**o**ntrar	*to find*	pers**e**guir	*to follow, pursue*
p**e**nsar	*to think*	ll**o**ver	*to rain*	s**e**guir	*to follow*
p**e**rder	*to lose*	m**o**strar	*to show*	s**e**rvir	*to serve*
pref**e**rir	*to prefer*	m**o**rir	*to die*		
qu**e**rer	*to want*	p**o**der	*to be able to*		
recom**e**ndar	*to recommend*	pr**o**bar	*to try, taste*		
		rec**o**rdar	*to remember*		
		s**o**ñar (con)	*to dream (about)*		
		v**o**lver	*to come back, return*		

Write the **yo** and **nosotros** forms of each of these verbs on the board. Point out that **conseguir, perseguir,** and **seguir** have irregular **yo** forms: **consigo, persigo, sigo.**

- **Decir** also has an irregular form in the first-person singular: **yo digo.**

¡Yo siempre **digo** sí y tú siempre d**i**ces no! *I always say yes and you always say no!*

- The verbs **llover** *(to rain)*, **nevar** *(to snow)*, and **costar** *(to cost)* are used, as in English, usually in the third person singular.

Una llamada por cobrar **cue**sta mucho dinero. *A collect call costs a lot of money.*
En invierno n**ie**va y hace frío. *It snows and it's cold in the winter.*
En el desierto no ll**ue**ve mucho. *It doesn't rain much in the desert.*

LENGUA EN ACCIÓN

Expresiones con infinitivos

■ The verbs **empezar** and **pensar** are frequently used with infinitives.

empezar a + infinitive — *to begin, start to do something*

El chofer y su esposa **empiezan a** correr. — *The driver and his wife begin to run.*

Nayeli **empieza a** buscar al chofer. — *Nayeli begins to look for the driver.*

pensar + infinitive — *to plan, intend*

Adriana y Felipe **piensan viajar** a Sevilla. — *Adriana and Felipe plan to travel to Sevilla.*

Pensamos ir a la compañía de transporte para buscar a Nayeli. — *We plan to go to the transport company to look for Nayeli.*

1 **Los planes de Vicente.** Fill in the correct forms of the verbs in the following passage. Then answer the questions that follow.

Yo __________ (pensar) viajar por Andalucía y __________ (ir) a empezar mi viaje en Madrid y después yo __________ (querer) visitar Granada, Málaga y Jerez. Yo __________ (preferir) ir en verano porque no __________ (llover) mucho. Luis Fernando, mi amigo andaluz, __________ (decir) que yo __________ (poder) dormir y comer en su casa. Es fantástico porque yo sé que su madre __________ (servir) comidas deliciosas todos los días.

Now answer the following questions about Vicente's plans.

▸ **Modelo:** —*Vicente piensa empezar su viaje en Granada, ¿verdad?*
—*No, Vicente piensa empezar su viaje en Madrid.*

1. Vicente quiere dormir en un hotel, ¿verdad?
2. Vicente no puede comer en casa de Luis Fernando, ¿verdad?
3. En Andalucía llueve mucho en verano, ¿verdad?
4. Vicente prefiere ir a Andalucía en invierno, ¿no?
5. Vicente no piensa visitar Sevilla, ¿verdad?

Answers to Actividad 1:
pienso
voy
quiero
prefiero
llueve
dice
puedo
sirve

Answers to Actividad 1 (Vicente):
1. No, Vicente quiere dormir en la casa de Luis Fernando, su amigo andaluz.
2. Sí, Vicente puede comer en la casa de Luis Fernando.
3. No, en Andalucía no llueve mucho en verano.
4. No, Vicente prefiere ir a Andalucía en verano.
5. No, Vicente no piensa visitar Sevilla.

2 **¿Qué quieres hacer?** You are planning a tour around town and discuss with a friend the best places to go. Follow the model.

▸ **Modelo:** *el cine / la discoteca*
—*¿Quieres ir al cine?*
—*No, prefiero ir a la discoteca.*

1. el teatro / el museo
2. el restaurante español / el restaurante alemán
3. el parque / el correo
4. el banco / la universidad
5. la piscina del hotel / la playa
6. la catedral / la plaza central

II. Describing daily routines

Reflexive verbs and reflexive pronouns

To discuss many daily routines in Spanish, you use a class of verbs called reflexives. Identify who performs and who receives the action of the verbs in these illustrations.

Susana lava al perro. **Miranda se baña.** **Roberto se lava los dientes.**

When the subject both performs and receives the action of the verb, as in **B** and **C** above, the action is called reflexive.

To make a verb reflexive, Spanish uses the pronouns in boldface.

Subject pronoun	Reflexive pronouns	Conjugated verb: *lavar*	*(to wash)*
yo	**me**	lavo	*I wash myself.*
tú	**te**	lavas	*You wash yourself.*
él/ella, usted	**se**	lava	*He washes himself. She washes herself. You wash yourself.*
nosotros/nosotras	**nos**	lavamos	*We wash ourselves.*
vosotros/vosotras	**os**	laváis	*You (plural) wash yourselves.*
ellos/ellas, ustedes	**se**	lavan	*They wash themselves. You (plural) wash yourselves.*

- Reflexive verbs do not mean only *myself*, *yourself*, and so on in English. They can sometimes be expressed as *to get*. **Yo me visto.** = *I get dressed.* **Ella se levanta.** = *She gets up.*
- To identify that a verb is reflexive, the infinitive is usually listed with **-se** attached to the end.
- Reflexive pronouns are placed before a conjugated verb. When reflexive verbs are used together with an infinitive, the reflexive pronouns may be attached to the end of the infinitive or may go before, as they do with a conjugated verb.

Los chicos van a vestir**se.** *The boys are going to get dressed.*
Los chicos **se** van a vestir.

Note that many of these verbs are stem changers. Other irregular verbs in the list are **ponerse, irse**.

Common reflexive verbs			
acostarse (ue)	*to lie down*	levantarse	*to get up*
afeitarse	*to shave*	maquillarse	*to put on makeup*
alojarse (hospedarse)	*to stay (in a hotel)*	peinarse	*to comb one's hair*
		ponerse la ropa	*to put on clothes*
bañarse	*to take a bath*	preocuparse	*to worry*
cepillarse	*to brush*	probarse (ue)	*to try on*
desayunarse	*to have breakfast*	quedarse	*to stay*
despertarse (ie)	*to wake up*	quitarse la ropa	*to take off one's clothes*
divertirse (ie)	*to enjoy oneself*		
dormirse (ue)	*to fall asleep*	secarse	*to dry off*
ducharse	*to take a shower*	sentarse (ie)	*to sit down*
irse	*to go away, leave*	sentirse (ie)	*to feel*
lavarse	*to get washed*	vestirse (i)	*to get dressed*

Some common words to use with these verbs are:

la cara *face*
los dientes *teeth*
las manos *hands*
el pelo *hair*

To express the sequence of the things you do, use words such as:

primero	*first*	entonces	*then, at that time*
luego	*later, then, next*	por fin	*finally*
después	*after*		

Primero me despierto a las seis de la mañana, **luego** me baño, y **por fin** me visto.

First, I wake up at six in the morning, then I take a bath, and finally, I get dressed.

LENGUA EN ACCIÓN

Hablando del cuerpo

When talking about parts of the body, use the article in Spanish and not the possessive adjective, as we do in English.

Nos lavamos **las** manos. — *We wash our hands.*
Tienes que cepillarte **los** dientes. — *You have to brush your teeth.*

3 **Nuestras rutinas.** You are describing the routines of several people. Follow the model to complete your descriptions. Remember to change the reflexive pronouns to agree with the subjects.

▸ **Modelo:** *tú / despertarse temprano todos los días*
Tú te despiertas temprano todos los días.

1. yo / ducharse con agua caliente
2. usted / levantarse tarde
3. las chicas / ponerse el sombrero sevillano
4. el señor / afeitarse por la mañana
5. Marina / secarse el pelo
6. tú / vestirse con ropa moderna
7. ustedes / divertirse mucho en la discoteca

Answers to Actividad 3:
1. me ducho
2. se levanta
3. se ponen
4. se afeita
5. se seca
6. te vistes
7. se divierten

In #3 explain that **sombrero** is singular because each person puts on only one hat versus the English, *They put on their hats,* in which the focus is on the total number of hats, rather than on each individual.

4 **¿Cuándo haces tus actividades?** Ask the following people when they are going to do the activities indicated. Follow the model.

▸ **Modelo:** *Luis / afeitarse mañana*
—Luis, ¿cuándo te vas a afeitar? or: *Luis, ¿cuándo vas a afeitarte?*
—Me voy a afeitar mañana. or: *Voy a afeitarme mañana.*

1. Cecilia / bañarse temprano
2. Cristina y María Teresa / secarse el pelo por la mañana
3. Raúl / acostarse tarde
4. Nubia / ponerse las botas hoy
5. Daniel / levantarse a las seis
6. tú y yo / divertirse en la discoteca esta noche
7. Gil /cepillarse los dientes por la mañana

Answers to Actividad 4:
1. se va a bañar / va a bañarse
2. se van a secar / van a secarse
3. se va a acostar / va a acostarse
4. se va a poner / va a ponerse
5. se va a levantar / va a levantarse
6. nos vamos a divertir / vamos a divertirnos
7. se va a cepillar / va a cepillarse

5 Día típico. What does Felipe do on a typical day? Look at the pictures and decide in which order Felipe would do the following activities. Number the activities in a logical order, then write a sentence to describe each action shown in the picture. Use reflexive verbs.

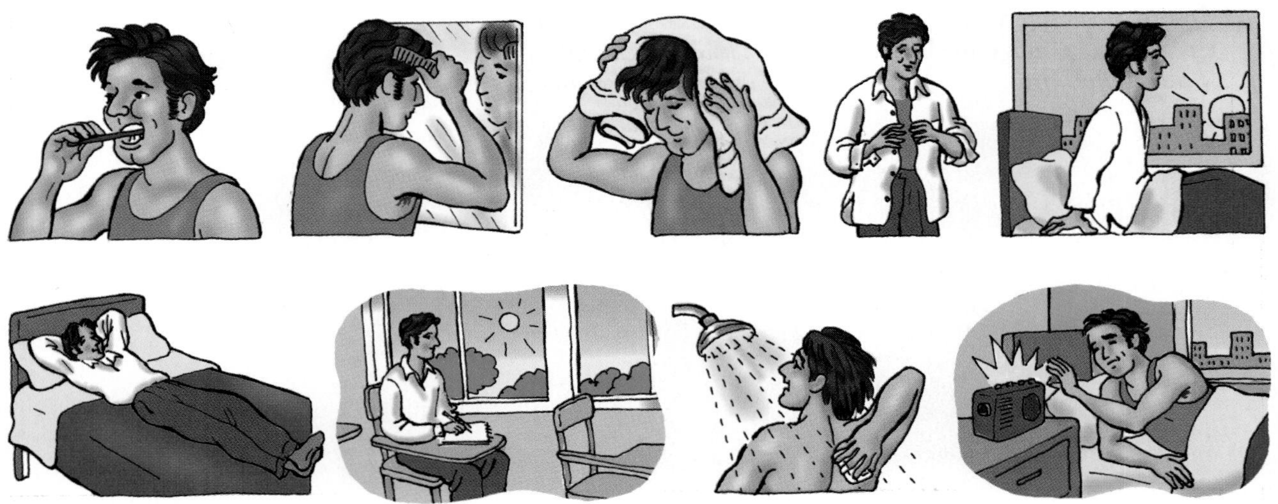

6 Mi rutina diaria. Write a short paragraph describing your daily activities. Include the order in which you do them and at what time you do them.

▸ **Modelo:** *Primero, me despierto a las seis y media de la mañana.*

III. Describing how actions are done

Adverbs ending in -mente

Adverbs of manner describe how an action is done. These adverbs are usually formed in Spanish by adding **-mente** to the singular form of the adjective. If the adjective has -**a** and **-o** endings, **-mente** is added to the feminine form. No changes are necessary when the adjective ends in another vowel or in a consonant. The **-mente** ending in Spanish corresponds to the *-ly* ending of many English adverbs (*easy* > *easily*).

rápido	rápid**amente**	*rapidly*
impaciente	impaciente**mente**	*impatiently*
fácil	fácil**mente**	*easily*

You may wish to mention that when two or more adverbs appear in a sentence, only the last one has the suffix **-mente.** The others (if they are regular) appear in their feminine form.

Adriana y Felipe hablan con el portero **impacientemente.**	*Adriana and Felipe speak with the porter impatiently.*
Nayeli puede ir a la compañía de transporte **fácilmente.**	*Nayeli can go to the transport company easily.*
El chofer maneja **rápidamente.**	*The chauffeur drives rapidly.*

- Written accents on the adjectives are retained when the **-mente** ending is added.

fácil fácilmente   rápido rápidamente

7 **¿Cómo se dice?** Give the correct adverb for the following adjectives.

1. difícil
2. elegante
3. frecuente
4. fuerte
5. lento
6. moderno
7. normal
8. perezoso
9. profesional
10. claro
11. regular
12. serio
13. tímido
14. tradicional

8 **¿Cómo hacen las cosas?** Use adverbs to tell how the following people do the activities indicated.

▸ **Modelo:** *El examen es fácil. Yo hago el examen fácilmente.*

1. La explicación de Julia es muy clara. Julia explica las cosas muy __________.
2. Mis conversaciones con Luis son agradables. Luis y yo conversamos __________.
3. Mi trabajo es muy duro. Yo trabajo __________.
4. Ese tren es muy lento. Ese tren anda muy __________.
5. La ropa de Verónica es elegante. Verónica se viste __________.
6. Carlos es un escritor profesional. Carlos escribe __________.
7. Los aviones modernos son rápidos. Los aviones modernos viajan __________.
8. Tú eres muy tímido. Tú hablas muy __________.

Answers to Actividad 8:
1. claramente
2. agradablemente
3. duramente
4. lentamente
5. elegantemente
6. profesionalmente
7. rápidamente
8. tímidamente

9 **¿Cómo hacemos las cosas?** Ask each other the following questions about habits and actions, using adverbs. Work in pairs.

1. ¿Manejas el coche de la familia rápidamente? ¿lentamente?
2. ¿Llegan a clase puntualmente los estudiantes de tu universidad?
3. ¿Hablas con tus amigos/as por teléfono frecuentemente? ¿infrecuentemente?
4. ¿Trabaja tu compañero/a pacientemente? ¿impacientemente?
5. ¿Los estudiantes de tu escuela se visten elegantemente los sábados por la noche?
6. ¿Te duchas inmediatamente después de levantarte todos los días?
7. ¿Puede hablar abiertamente la gente de tu país?
8. ¿Generalmente sales a comer con tu familia o con amigos?
9. ¿Usualmente practicas deportes solo/a o con otra persona?

IV. Expressing negation

Affirmative and negative expressions

Affirmative expressions		Negative expressions	
algo **todo**	*something, anything* *everything*	**nada**	*nothing*
todos, todas **alguien** **algún, alguno** **algunos, algunas**	*everybody, all* *someone, somebody* *a, an, some* *some*	**nadie, ningún, ninguno**	*no one, nobody, none*
(o) ... o	*either . . . or*	**ni ... ni**	*neither . . . nor*
siempre **todos los días** **a veces**	*always* *every day* *sometimes, at times*	**nunca, jamás**	*never*
también	*also, too*	**tampoco**	*neither, either*

To use negative and affirmative expressions:

- You can make a sentence affirmative or negative by placing the appropriate expression either before or after the verb. If you use it after the verb in negative expressions, you must put **no** in front of the verb.

Nayeli **siempre** se aloja en el mismo hotel. — *Nayeli always stays in the same hotel.*
Nayeli se aloja **siempre** en el mismo hotel.

Doña Gafasoscuras **nunca** va a perder de vista a Nayeli. — *Sunglasses will never lose sight of Nayeli.*
Doña Gafasoscuras **no** va a perder de vista a Nayeli **nunca.**

- **Nadie** and **alguien** refer to people and require the personal **a** when used as direct objects.

—¿Nayeli ve **a alguien** sospechoso? — *Does Nayeli see someone suspicious?*
—No, **no** ve **a nadie** sospechoso. — *No, she doesn't see anyone suspicious.*

- All forms of **alguno** and **ninguno** agree in gender with the noun they modify. Notice that they drop the **-o** before the noun in the masculine singular form. **Ninguno** does not usually have a plural form and is mostly used in the singular form.

Nayeli necesita **alguna** información sobre el chofer. — *Nayeli asks for some information about a driver.*
El empleado **no** le da **ninguna** información sobre el chofer. — *The employee doesn't give her any information about the driver.*

—¿Tienen Felipe y Adriana **algún** problema con el portero? — *Do Felipe and Adriana have any problems with the porter?*
—No, no tienen **ningún** problema con el portero. — *No, they don't have any problems with the porter.*

10 **Los contrarios.** Change the following affirmative statements to make them negative. Some statements require two changes.

▸ **Modelo:** *Necesito comer algo antes de la reunión.*
No necesito comer nada antes de la reunión.

1. Nosotros viajamos en tren o en avión.
2. Quiero hablar con algún director.
3. Ellos siempre hablan por teléfono con alguien.
4. Todos los días tomamos el metro.
5. Alguien siempre llama a Rosario por la mañana.
6. Teresa va a divertirse y Rafael también.
7. Todas las postales tienen la dirección correcta.
8. Tengo todo listo para las vacaciones.
9. Elena siempre llega tarde a todas partes.

Answers to Actividad 10:
1. Nosotros no viajamos ni en tren ni en avión.
2. No quiero hablar con ningún director.
3. Ellos nunca hablan por teléfono con nadie.
4. Nunca tomamos el metro.
5. Nadie llama nunca a Rosario por la mañana.
6. Teresa no va a divertirse ni Rafael tampoco. / Ni Teresa ni Rafael van a divertirse.
7. Ninguna postal tiene la dirección correcta.
8. No tengo nada listo para las vacaciones.
9. Ella nunca llega tarde a ninguna parte.

11 **Sucede todos los días.** You have just returned from a vacation and are answering your friend's questions about your experiences. Unfortunately, it was not a very good trip and you are quite negative about it.

▸ **Modelo:** *¿Hay muchos hoteles de cinco estrellas?*
No, no hay ningún hotel de cinco estrellas.

1. ¿Sirven siempre buena comida en el hotel Prisma?
2. ¿Tienen alguna oferta especial para el verano?
3. ¿Hay televisión en todas las habitaciones?
4. ¿Hacen algunas fiestas para los visitantes?
5. ¿Conoces alguna compañía de transportes allí?

Answers to Actividad 11:
1. Nunca sirven buena comida en el hotel Prisma.
2. No tienen ninguna oferta especial para el verano.
3. No hay televisión en ninguna habitación.
4. No hacen ninguna fiesta para los visitantes.
5. No conozco ninguna compañía de transporte allí.

12 **Nunca el domingo.** This is your weekly schedule for this semester. Follow the model to create a list of five activities that you usually do and five activities that you usually do not do. Use affirmative and negative expressions.

▸ **Modelo:** *Los martes me levanto a las ocho de la mañana y los miércoles también.*
Nunca me levanto temprano los domingos.
Los lunes no veo televisión ni los sábados tampoco. or
No veo televisión ni el sábado ni el domingo.

Mi agenda semanal

lunes	martes	miércoles	jueves	viernes	sábado	domingo
levantarme a las 6 a.m.	levantarme a las 8 a.m.	levantarme a las 6 a.m.	levantarme a las 9 a.m.	levantarme a las 5 a.m.	levantarme a las 7 a.m.	dormir y dormir
tomar el bus: 7 a.m.	tomar el bus: 9 a.m.	tomar el bus: 7 a.m.	tomar el bus: 10 a.m.	tomar el bus: 7 a.m.	tomar el bus: 8 a.m.	tomar el bus: 11 a.m.
clase de ciencias	clase de ciencias	clase de ciencias	clase de ciencias	clase de ciencias	clase de fotografía	clase de fotografía
almorzar con Isabel	almorzar con Isabel	almorzar con Isabel	almorzar con Isabel	almorzar con Isabel	almorzar con Isabel	almorzar con René
clase de arte	clase de geografía	clase de literatura	hacer tareas	clase de arte	clase de cine	tomar la siesta
hacer tareas o ver televisión	cenar con Marta y Cecilia	hacer tareas	hacer tareas o ver televisión	hacer tareas	ir a la discoteca	jugar cartas

Lengua en acción

Todavía (still) / ya no (not any more)

- **Todavía** can be placed before or after the verb.

¿**Todavía** está Nayeli en Sevilla? *Is Nayeli still in Sevilla?*
¿Está Adriana **todavía** en Madrid? *Is Adriana still in Madrid?*

- The negative expression **ya no** is placed before the verb.

Felipe **ya no** está preocupado. *Felipe is not worried anymore.*
Esas tapas de pescado **ya no** me gustan. *I don't like those fish tapas anymore.*

Answers to Actividad 13:
1. ¿Todavía tienen los estudiantes clases a las ocho de la mañana? —No, ya no tienen...
2. ¿Todavía comen mis compañeros pizza en el almuerzo? —No, ya no comen...
3. ¿Todavía estudian los estudiantes de español en grupos? —No, ya no estudian...
4. ¿Todavía pide la policía del colegio informes de los estudiantes? —No, ya no pide...
5. ¿Todavía tienen las chicas y los chicos tiempo libre por las tardes? —No, ya no tienen...
6. ¿Todavía sirve el restaurante del colegio helados para el postre? —No, ya no sirve...

13 Todavía. You are trying to find out what is going on in school. There are many things that people have recently stopped doing. Create questions and answers for your investigation. Follow the model.

▸ **Modelo:** *usar el sistema americano de medidas / los profesores*
¿Todavía usan los profesores el sistema americano de medidas?
No, ya no usan el sistema.

1. tener clases a las ocho de la mañana / los estudiantes
2. comen pizza en el almuerzo / mis compañeros
3. estudiar en grupos / los estudiantes de español
4. pedir informes de los estudiantes / la policía de la universidad
5. tener tiempo libre por las tardes / las chicas y los chicos
6. servir helados para el postre / el restaurante de la universidad

Lectura A

Introducción

In this selection you will learn about various means of transportation and communication in Spain.

Reading strategy: Skimming

When you want to learn information quickly from written materials, skimming and scanning are two reading strategies that you can apply. Skimming is the technique of quickly eliciting the general idea or main focus of the text or article.

Quickly look at any headings, titles, and obvious cognates (which were presented in chapter one), as well as visuals which your instructor may give you. Skimming is very useful in reading in Spanish. Skim this selection and then do the activities that follow.

Transportes y comunicaciones

Es bien sabido° que el sector de transportes y comunicaciones es fundamental para el buen desarrollo° económico, cultural y social de un país. España ha realizado° una gran inversión° en infraestructuras en los últimos años hasta situarse a la altura° de cualquier país de su entorno.°

known
development
has made / investment
level / area

Viajar en avión En el año 2000 se habrán invertido° en España más de 500.000 millones de pesetas en reformas y ampliación° de aeropuertos. Muchas ciudades españolas están comunicadas por rutas aéreas a la vez° que desarrollan un gran tráfico internacional. Sólo el aeropuerto de Madrid-Barajas recibe más de 16.000.000 de pasajeros al año. Su tráfico es, fundamentalmente, de líneas regulares, nacionales y extranjeras.° En cambio,° Palma de Mallorca, por ejemplo, tiene un 77% de vuelos charter.

will have invested
expansion
at the same time
foreign
On the other hand

Avión en el aeropuerto de Palma de Mallorca.

En barco En cuanto al° tráfico de pasajeros por mar, varias° ciudades españolas (Valencia, Barcelona, Málaga) comunican habitualmente la Península con las islas Baleares y Canarias y con el norte de África. La compañía naviera° más importante es la Transmediterránea, que transporta pasajeros y automóviles. Los puertos más importantes para el tráfico de mercancías° son: Barcelona, Bilbao, Valencia y Vigo, entre° otros.

Regarding / several
boating
merchandise / among

En tren Más de 13.000 kilómetros de vía° enlazan° los pueblos y las ciudades de España. Debido a° la orografía° accidentada° del terreno, en España todavía° existen recorridos° auténticamente pintorescos.° Pero en los últimos 30 años las líneas ferroviarias° y los trenes han experimentado una modernización espectacular que se ha traducido° no solamente en una mayor rapidez sino en la mejora° de la calidad de los servicios de atención al cliente. Por ejemplo: el tren de alta velocidad, AVE, es capaz° de recorrer la distancia Madrid-Sevilla (538 km)

track / connect
Because of / contour / rough
still / routes / picturesque
railway network
has been translated
improvement
capable

Confort, rápidez y seguridad en los recorridos del AVE, tren de alta velocidad.

en 2 horas y 45 minutos. Existe el proyecto de una vía para el AVE que enlazará° España con Francia a comienzos del siglo° XXI.

will connect
century

En automóvil Más de 162.000 km de carreteras° surcan° el territorio; de ellas, 2.022 km son autopistas° (de peaje°), y cerca de 6.000 km de autovías y carreteras de doble calzada° (gratuitas°). El número de vehículos matriculados° en toda España es de 18.218.000 (datos de 1994); de ellos, más de 13 millones son automóviles.

roads / go through
expressways / toll
divided highways / free
registered

Modernas carreteras de España.

1 Información general. In the selection above, skim the headings of the text for the types of transportation in Spain. In pairs, ask each other, **¿Cuáles son las cuatro categorías de transportes en España?** Then, examine the photos, taking turns reading the captions under each one to gather further information rapidly about the content of the selection. Ask each other, **¿Cuáles son los cognados y qué significan?**

2 Impresiones generales. What overall impressions about **transportes españoles** do you get immediately from skimming the reading?

Reading strategy: Scanning

Scanning is a reading strategy that is often used in conjunction with skimming, especially if there is an abundance of new vocabulary. In scanning, you look for specific details that support the general information learned.

3 Características. After scanning this selection, jot down one basic characteristic of each **medio de transporte.**

1. avión __________
2. barco __________
3. tren __________
4. automóvil __________

4 Detalles. Complete the following information, which elicits details regarding transportation in Spain.

1. Los transportes son importantes para el desarrollo __________, cultural y __________ de España.
2. Más de __________ millones de pasajeros pasan por el aeropuerto de Madrid que se llama __________.
3. Algunos barcos españoles van a las Canarias y al norte de __________.
4. Los puertos más importantes para el tráfico de mercancías son Barcelona, __________ , __________ y __________.
5. Los trenes españoles tienen más de 13.000 __________ de vías. Esto equivale a __________ millas.
6. El número de autos matriculados en 1994 es __________.
7. En España hay __________ kilómetros de carreteras.

Answers to Actividad 4:
1. económico, social
2. dieciséis, Barajas
3. África
4. Bilbao, Valencia, Vigo
5. kilómetros, 7800
6. 18.218.000
7. 162.000

ETAPA B

Pistas y palabras

I. Ordering food

¿Qué van a tomar?

1. la camarera
2. la cerveza
3. las gambas (L. Am.: los camarones)
4. la jarra
5. el vino tinto
6. la carta/el menú
7. la cuenta
8. la tortilla española

You can find pictures of these dishes either on the Internet, in Spanish cookbooks, or in the recipe section of *Vanidades* or other magazines in Spanish. Point out the difference between a Mexican tortilla (made with corn) and the Spanish potato, onion, and egg tortilla. The **queso manchego** is from the region in Spain called La Mancha (also famous for Don Quijote). **Vino tinto** is *red wine;* the expression **vino rojo** is not used in Spain, although it may be used in Latin America. Bring any menus from Hispanic restaurants you may have collected in your travels. You can also find them on the Internet and share printout with class.

Palabras y expresiones útiles

el almuerzo	*lunch*
la cena	*dinner*
la comida	*food, dinner in some places, lunch in others*
el desayuno	*breakfast*
la hambre	*hunger*
el jugo (el zumo)	*juice (L. Am., Sp.)*
la papa (la patata)	*potato (L. Am., Sp.)*
el pedido	*order*
el plato principal	*main dish*
la propina	*tip*
las tapas	*appetizers (Sp.)*
cenar	*to have dinner*
dejar	*to leave (behind)*
disfrutar	*to enjoy*
ligero/a	*light*
rico/a	*rich, delicious*
sabroso/a	*delicious, tasty*

¡A sus órdenes!	*At your service!*
La carne está dura.	*The meat is tough.*
La comida está muy salada/dulce.	*The food is too salty/sweet.*
La cuenta, por favor.	*The check, please.*

estar listo/a	*to be ready*
Estoy muerto/a de hambre.	*I'm starving, famished.*
Me falta (el tenedor).	*My (fork) is missing.*
Me gustaría...	*I would like . . .*
¿Podría traer la cuenta, por favor?	*Could you bring the check, please?*
Los precios están por las nubes.	*The prices are high (in the clouds).*
¿Qué desean comer/beber?	*What do you want to eat/drink?*
¡Qué hambre!/¡Tengo mucha hambre!	*I am very hungry!*
¿Qué nos recomienda?	*What do you recommend to us?*
¿Qué recomendaría Ud.?	*What would you recommend?*
Quisiera pedir...	*I would like to order . . .*
El servicio es deficiente.	*The service is not acceptable.*
La sopa está fría.	*The soup is cold.*
El zumo/jugo de naranja está amargo/ácido.	*The orange juice is bitter/sour.*

Point out that **quisiera pedir** is very polite and **me gustaría** moderately so.

Precio en pesetas

Entremeses	Tortilla española	350	***Appetizers***	*Spanish omelette with potatoes and onions*
	Chorizo y pan	450		*Sausage and bread*
	Pulpo o calamar frito	850		*Fried octopus or squid*
	Queso manchego	500		*Manchego (goat) cheese*
Sopas	Gazpacho	400	***Soups***	*Gazpacho (cold vegetable) soup*
	Sopa de pollo	500		*Chicken soup*
	Sopa de pescado	600		*Fish soup*
	Sopa del día	450		*Soup of the day*
Ensaladas	Ensalada mixta	600	***Salads***	*Mixed salad*
	Ensalada sencilla	300		*Green salad*
	Ensalada rusa	400		*Potato salad*
Entradas	Especialidad de la casa:		***Entrées***	*Specialty of the house:*
	Paella valenciana	1.400		*Paella valenciana*
	Pescado del día al horno	1.100		*Baked fish of the day*
	Gambas al ajillo	900		*Shrimp in garlic sauce*
	Chuletas de cerdo con legumbres	800		*Pork chops with vegetables*
	Bistec asado con patatas fritas	1.100		*Steak with French fries*
Postres	Helado de chocolate, vainilla o fresa	300	***Desserts***	*Chocolate, vanilla, or strawberry ice cream*
	Fruta del día	200		*Fruit of the day*
	Flan	300		*Baked egg custard*
Bebidas	Sangría – 1 litro	900	***Drinks***	*Beverage of wine, soda or juice, and fruit pieces*
	Agua mineral con/sin gas	250		*Mineral water (carbonated/uncarbonated)*
	Té o café	200		*Tea or coffee*
	Refrescos variados	250		*Assorted soft drinks*
	Zumo de naranja	500		*Orange juice*
	Cerveza	250		*Beer*
	Vino tinto/blanco	150		*Red/white wine*
	Batido de frutas	250		*Blended fruit beverage*

*151 **pesetas** = 1 USA *dollar* (1999)

1 **En el café.** Work with a partner to decide what you are going to eat.

Before doing **Actividad 1,** point out that **tengo ganas de** means *to feel like.* Using the menu, have students figure out how much each of these meals will cost in pesetas and then estimate the cost in dollars using the current rate of exchange.

▸ **Modelo:** *ensalada mixta y vino blanco / paella valenciana y vino tinto*
—¿Qué vas a pedir?
—Quisiera una ensalada mixta y un vino blanco. ¿Y tú?
—Tengo ganas de pedir una paella valenciana y un vino tinto.

1. chuletas de cerdo / ensalada rusa y la sopa del día
2. pescado del día al horno y agua mineral con gas / bistec con patatas fritas
3. tortilla española / chorizo
4. helado de chocolate / flan y café con leche
5. pescado del día / sopa de pescado y ensalada mixta
6. gazpacho y chorizo / batido de banana y piña

2 **Una cena importante.** You are dining with a friend in a nice restaurant. Work with a partner and talk about the things you like and don't like.

▸ **Modelo:** *las chuletas de cerdo / calientes*
—¿Te gustan las chuletas de cerdo?
—No, no me gustan porque están calientes. or:
—Sí, me gustan porque están calientes.

1. el helado de chocolate / amargo
2. el postre de piña / dulce y delicioso
3. la ensalada con pulpo frito / buenísima
4. las patatas con carne / duras
5. sopa de pollo / muy caliente
6. los quesos manchegos / salados
7. los batidos de frutas / sabrosos
8. las tapas / picantes
9. la sopa de tomate / fría
10. el café / muy fuerte

ENLACE CULTURAL

Las sabrosas tapas de Madrid

Un bar de tapas en la Plaza Mayor, Madrid, España.

¡Comer tapas es una costumbre° muy española! Las tapas son pequeñas porciones de comida que las tabernas y los bares de la ciudad sirven con vino o cerveza. En platos grandes y pequeños, ponen jamón, queso, pescado, aceitunas, mariscos y carne. Los madrileños toman las tapas especialmente como entremeses antes del almuerzo, a las tres de la tarde o antes de la cena, a las diez de la noche. Muchas veces, las familias o los amigos van de bar en bar en Madrid para comer tapas y hablar de la política, de la economía, del trabajo, de los estudios y de la vida en general.

custom

Bring a menu from a tapas bar you have visited or create one of your own, using cookbooks and the Internet as sources of information.

Discusión en grupos

1. ¿Qué son las tapas madrileñas? ¿Qué tipos de tapas sirven los bares?
2. ¿De qué hablan frecuentemente los madrileños mientras (*while*) comen tapas? Y ustedes, ¿de qué hablan mientras comen en un restaurante?
3. Ustedes van a preparar tapas esta noche. ¿Qué van a servir?

Bring these kitchen items to class. Have students tell you where to place them, using the words from **Actividad 4.**

II. Setting the table

Pepito pone la mesa.

3 **¡Ay, Pepito!** Pepito is helping out in his parents' restaurant by setting the tables. Help him out by giving him a list of where to put things on the table.

a la izquierda ***(on the left)***	**en el centro** ***(in the center)***	**a la derecha** ***(on the right)***	**delante** ***(in front)***

4 **Te toca a ti.** *(It's your turn.)* Use the list above to draw and label a typical place setting. Work with a partner.

5 **¡Hay una mosca (fly) en mi sopa!** You are at a restaurant with some friends and everything is going wrong. The food is cold and the table is missing some important items. Use your imagination to create an interesting conversation. With a partner practice and present the conversation to the class.

6 **Entre nosotros.** Role-play the following situation with a partner.

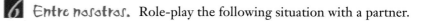

Turista:	**Camarero/a:**
After a whole day of sightseeing in Sevilla, you want to eat at a restaurant called "Los Arcos." You're very hungry and could eat everything on the menu, but really want to try **sangría, tapas, paella,** and dessert.	Today has been a difficult day. The cook is sick and the only person who knows anything about cooking is the dishwasher. In addition, there are no desserts, shrimp, or wine. Try to resolve the situation.

III. Shopping for food

¿Qué hay en las tiendas?

In Spain, **carne de vaca/buey** is also used. In Latin America, **carne de res** is preferred.

Point out that **-ería** is a common suffix added to words to denote the store where they are sold or made. Ask students what they think is sold at a **lechería**, and a **zapatería.** Bring in pictures or real food items to practice the vocabulary with a "**¿Qué es esto?**" drill.

7 ¿Cuánto cuesta? Work with a partner to identify the prices of the items in the stores. Follow the model.

► **Modelo:** —*¿Qué hay en la frutería?*
—*En la frutería hay tomates.*
—*¿Cuánto cuestan los tomates?*
—*Los tomates cuestan ochenta pesetas por kilo.*

8 ¿Qué necesitas comprar? With a friend, you are preparing dinner for some important guests. First, read the descriptions of your guests. Decide what you need to buy for the dinner. Then create a shopping list.

El Sr. Martín: Es un hombre muy tradicional. Todos los días come carne, papas y pan. Nunca come legumbres, siempre come ensalada y jamás come postre. No toma vino y bebe agua con todas las comidas.

La Sra. López: Es vegetariana y no come nada de carne roja. A veces come pescado o mariscos, pero no le gustan ni el pulpo ni el calamar. Le encantan las frutas y los postres. A veces bebe agua mineral y otras veces bebe jugo de naranja o limonada.

La señorita Morales: Sus platos favoritos son las sopas y las ensaladas, todo con mucho chile, pero sin sal. Solamente come pollo y no le gustan las carnes rojas ni el pescado ni los mariscos. Bebe agua o vino blanco con sus comidas. No le gustan las cosas dulces.

Give students either real or "home-made" pesetas. Try to make sure that students don't have quite enough money, so that they can bargain (**regatear**) with the clerk.

9 De compras. You need to go shopping for the ingredients for the meal you planned in **Actividad 8.** With a partner create a conversation between the store clerk (**el/la dependiente**) and the shopper (**el/la cliente**).

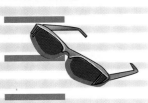

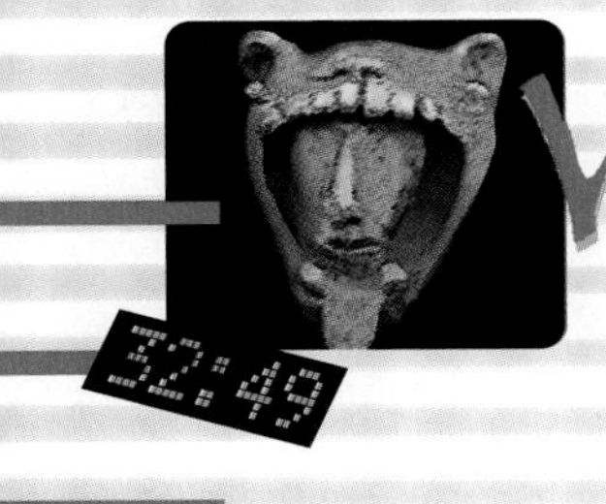

VISTAS Y VOCES

I. Preparémonos

1 Antcipación. Answer these questions in pairs.

A. **1.** ¿En qué café comes tú? ¿Cómo es? ¿Cuál es su especialidad? ¿Son simpáticos/as los/las camareros/as?
2. ¿Cuál es tu bebida favorita? ¿Qué ingredientes tiene?
3. ¿Cuál es tu plato favorito? ¿Qué ingredientes tiene?
4. ¿Te gustan las flores? ¿De qué colores?

B. Review chapter opening photo 3B.
Why do you think that Adriana is glaring at the clerk? What is he telling her? Where is Nayeli?

Para comprender mejor

alterado/a	*upset*	la especialidad	*specialty*
calmado/a	*calm*	insoportable	*unbearable*
¡Dios mío!	*My goodness!*	el peligro	*danger*
Eso sí que está claro.	*That's clear.*	la regla	*rule*

Answers to Actividad 2:
3, 2, 1, 4

2 Secuencia. In pairs, number the video action shots in the order in which you think the action will occur in the video you will watch.

1.

2.

Before viewing make students aware that the waiter will be addressing Adriana and Felipe with the **vosotros** form because they are in Spain.

3.

4.

II. Miremos y escuchemos

3 ¿Quién/es? While watching and hearing this episode, check off the emotions or conditions associated with these characters.

	Portero	Nayeli	Adriana	Felipe	Empleado
1. Tiene miedo.					
2. Está preocupado/a.					
3. Está alterado/a.					
4. Está calmado/a.					
5. Tiene hambre.					
6. Está en peligro.					
7. Tiene mala suerte.					
8. Está frustrado/a.					

III. Comentemos

4 Frases. In groups, tell to whom these characters speak and where.

El personaje	La frase	¿A quién habla y dónde?
Adriana	"¿Por qué no nos traes dos entremeses, los más populares de la casa? Y también un gazpacho para mí."	*al camarero; en el café*
Empleado de la compañía de transportes	"Mire, señorita, yo estoy perfectamente calmado. Es usted y su amiga, la profesora, quienes están alteradas."	
Adriana	"Esta situación es muy seria. No hay tiempo para las reglas."	
Empleado de la compañía de transportes	"¡Dos clientes impertinentes en un solo día!"	
Felipe	"Tengo la información que necesitamos."	
el portero	"¡Qué horror! Voy a llamar a la policía."	
Felipe	"Nayeli está en mucho peligro, eso sí que está claro."	

5 Comprensión. Answer these questions in groups.

1. ¿Qué comen Adriana y Felipe en el café? ¿Qué bebe Adriana?
2. ¿ Adónde van los dos después de comer allí?
3. ¿Cómo es el empleado de la compañía de transportes?
4. ¿Qué le muestra Adriana al empleado de la compañía de transportes?
5. ¿Por qué está alterada Adriana con el empleado?
6. ¿Cómo reacciona Felipe? ¿Cómo consigue la información que él y Adriana necesitan?
7. ¿Cómo encuentra Nayeli su habitación en el hotel, ordenada o desordenada?
8. ¿De qué color es la rosa que recibe Nayeli?

Answers to Actividad 3:
1. Tiene miedo: Nayeli
2. Está preocupada: Adriana, Nayeli
3. Está alterada: Nayeli, Adr-iana
4. Está calmado: el portero, Felipe
5. Tiene hambre: Felipe
6. Está en peligro: Nayeli
7. Tiene mala suerte: Nayeli
8. Está frustrado: Felipe, empleado de la compañía de transportes Está frustrada: Adriana, Nayeli

Answers to Actividad 4:
1. empleado: a Adriana en la compañía de transportes
2. Adriana: al empleado en la compañía de transportes
3. Empleado: a nadie/a sí mismo (*to himself*)
4. Felipe: a Adriana y al portero en la habitación de Nayeli
5. el portero: a Adriana y Felipe en la habitación de Nayeli
6. Felipe: a Adriana y al portero en el hotel

Answers to Actividad 5:
1. Comen dos entremeses y un gazpacho. Adriana bebe agua mineral con gas.
2. Van a la compañía de transportes.
3. Es alto, tiene el pelo largo, es amable, pero está impaciente.
4. Le muestra una foto de Nayeli.
5. Porque él no le quiere dar información.
6. Felipe reacciona con calma y lee el documento de transporte secretamente.
7. Encuentra la habitación muy desordenada.
8. Es una rosa roja.

Lengua

I. Pointing out people, things, and places

A. Demonstrative adjectives and pronouns

Look at the following drawing and try to identify which objects the persons are talking about.

¿De qué hablan?

Cecilia, esas flores rojas me gustan mucho.

Sí, son muy bonitas, pero prefiero aquellas flores amarillas.

No, aquellas flores no me gustan. Prefiero éstas.

- Demonstrative adjectives are used to point out persons or objects. Demonstrative adjectives modify a noun and have three main forms: *here, close to me* (**este**); *there, close to you* (**ese**); or *over there, away from both of us* (**aquél**). These adjectives agree in gender and number with the noun they modify.

Esta compañía de transportes es buena.	*This transportation company is good.*
Ese señor está alterado.	*That man is upset.*

- Demonstrative pronouns are used to replace the noun. These pronouns have the same forms as the adjectives, but carry a written accent over the stressed vowel to mark their function as pronouns. Demonstrative pronouns agree with the gender and number of the nouns they replace.

Me gusta mucho este café, **aquél** no.	*I like this café very much, not that one.*
Prefiero esta tortilla. **Ésa** está muy salada.	*I prefer this tortilla. That one is very salty.*

- The neuter demonstrative pronouns are used to refer to something indefinite or abstract: an object, an event, or an idea. Note that the neuter pronouns don't have written accents.

Esto representa un problema enorme.	*This represents an enormous problem.*
Eso no me parece bien.	*That doesn't seem fine to me.*

Demonstrative adjectives	Demonstrative pronouns		Neuter demonstrative pronouns	
este, esta	**éste, ésta**	*this (one)*	**esto**	*this*
estos, estas	**éstos, éstas**	*these*		
ese, esa	**ése, ésa**	*that (one)*	**eso**	*that*
esos, esas	**ésos, ésas**	*those*		
aquel, aquella	**aquél, aquélla**	*that (one)*	**aquello**	*that*
aquellos, aquellas	**aquéllos, aquéllas**	*those*		

B. Adverbs of location

When practicing these sentences act out the situation. You first point to a student's books while stating the first sentence; the student states the second one, and you the third. Add **necesito aquellos libros en la biblioteca** to illustrate the concept of *far away.*

When using demonstrative adjectives and pronouns, the following adverbs of place are useful to describe the relative location of things: **aquí,** *here;* **allí (ahí),** *there;* **allá,** *over there.*

—Por favor, necesito **esos** libros.	*Please, I need those books.*
—¿Cuáles libros? **¿Éstos** que están **aquí?**	*Which books? These here?*
—Sí, **ésos** que están **allí.**	*Yes, those there.*

Answers to Actividad 1:
1. ésa
2. ése
3. aquéllos
4. ésa
5. ése
6. ésas
7. aquélla
8. ésos
9. ése

1 **¿Preferencias?** Use demonstrative pronouns to make comparisons about the following foods. Follow the model.

▸ **Modelo:** *Este café está fuerte hoy,* (that one) *no.*
Este café está fuerte hoy, ése no.

1. Me gusta más esta ensalada que (*that one*).
2. Mi tío favorito come este tipo de pescado, no (*that one*).
3. Estos atletas corren más que (*those, in the distance away from both speakers*).
4. Esta pizza de vegetales es deliciosa, pero (*that one*) no.
5. ¿Quieres este pan o (*that one*)?
6. Prefiero estas galletas, no (*those*).
7. Esta tortilla española es pequeña; (*that one, away from both speakers*) es grande.
8. Estos postres tienen chocolate; (*those*) tienen piña.
9. Este café es de Colombia; (*that one*) es de Costa Rica.

2 **¿Cuáles galletitas?** Two friends are planning to buy a dessert for dinner. Complete their conversation using demonstrative adjectives or demonstrative pronouns. Look closely at the drawing to establish the most appropriate demonstrative adjectives or pronouns to use, based on where the people are standing.

ROMEO: ¡Mira, Julieta, _________ galletas María parecen muy ricas!
JULIETA: No, Romeo, no me gustan, quiero _________ galletitas con piña.
ROMEO: De acuerdo, pero ¿ves alguna galletita de chocolate?
JULIETA: Claro, mira, _________ son de chocolate.
ROMEO: ¡Qué bien! Voy a comprar _________ galletas de chocolate y _________ mazapanes.
JULIETA: Y yo quiero comprar también _________ pastelitos de coco y _________ galletas de almendra. ¿Quieres probar _________ pastelitos de coco?
ROMEO: Por supuesto, quiero probar de todo. ¡Nuestra cena va a ser estupenda!

Answers to Actividad 2:
1. estas
2. aquellas
3. éstas
4. esas / estos
5. esos / estas
6. esos

3 **¿Preferencias?** You and a friend are talking about foods. Work with a partner to form the demonstrative pronouns in your comparisons. Follow the model.

► **Modelo:** *¿Cuál helado prefieres, éste o* (that one)?
—*¿Cuál helado prefieres, éste o ése?*
—*Prefiero éste.*

1. ¿Cuál sopa de pollo te gusta, ésta o (*that one*)?
2. ¿Cuál plato prefieres, (*this one*) o ése?
3. ¿Cuáles quesos deseas, éstos o (*those*)?
4. ¿Cuál chorizo está más picante, (*this one*) o aquél?
5. ¿Cuáles tapas quieres, (*these*) o ésas?
6. ¿Cuál carne está más rica, ésta, ésa o (*that one, away from both speakers*)?
7. ¿Cuál sopa está más caliente, ésta o (*that one*)?

Answers to Actividad 3:
1. ésa
2. éste
3. ésos
4. éste
5. éstas
6. aquélla
7. ésa

4 **Restaurante Delicias.** Using the vocabulary you have learned in this chapter, do a role-play in a restaurant. Ask questions of each other and the waiter about the different foods and dishes for each course for dinner.

II. Describing actions in progress

A. Present progressive tense

¿Qué están haciendo?

1. Ernesto está hablando por teléfono.

2. Los amigos están comiendo pizza.

3. La gente está saliendo del cine.

The present progressive tense describes actions in progress. It is formed with the verb **estar** and the *present participle*. The present participle is formed by dropping the **-ar**, **-er**, or **-ir** ending of the verb and adding **-ando** for **-ar** verbs and **-iendo** for **-er** and **-ir** verbs.

To emphasize that the present progressive is a verb tense, conjugate a sample verb on the board with **estar** and the present participle. Stress that in the present progressive *nothing* can come between **estar** and the present participle.

Present participle of regular verbs

-ar	-er	-ir
hablar: habl**ando**	comer: com**iendo**	salir: sal**iendo**

Present participle of stem-changing verbs

- Stem-changing verbs ending in **-ar** and **-er** have regular present participle forms. Stem-changing verbs ending in **-ir** have irregular forms.

e > i	e > i	o > u
s**e**ntir: s**i**ntiendo	s**e**rvir: s**i**rviendo	d**o**rmir: d**u**rmiendo

- The stem-changing reflexive verbs that end in **-ir** also follow the same rule, except that they add the reflexive pronoun on the end. Note that the accent is marked in this case.

e > i	e > i	o > u
div**e**rtirse: div**i**rtiéndose	v**e**stirse: v**i**stiéndose	m**o**rirse: m**u**riéndose

- Reflexive pronouns can precede the verb or can be attached to the end of the participle. Notice the written accent when adding the pronoun to the end.

Nayeli está alojándo**se** en el hotel Prisma. *Nayeli is staying at the Prisma hotel.*
Nayeli **se** está alojando en el hotel Prisma.

Irregular present participles

Some verbs like **leer** and **construir** have irregular present participles. Other verbs that follow this model are: **traer, oír, creer, caer,** and most verbs ending in **-uir** (**incluir, destruir,** etc.).

Felipe **está leyendo** la dirección.	*Felipe is reading the address.*
Mis amigos **están construyendo** una casa nueva.	*My friends are building a new house.*

Adverbial phrases used with participles

Adverbs of manner or time are frequently used with the present progressive tense.

en este momento	*at this moment*
ahora	*now*
ahora mismo	*at this very moment, right now*

En este momento todos están buscando a Nayeli.	*At this moment, everyone is looking for Nayeli.*
Y **ahora,** ¿qué están haciendo Adriana y Felipe?	*And now, what are Adriana and Felipe doing?*
Ellos están hablando con el empleado **ahora mismo.**	*They are speaking with the employee right now.*
Todos están trabajando **tranquilamente.**	*Everyone is working calmly.*

5 **¿Qué están haciendo?** Use the present progressive tense to describe what the following people are doing.

6 En este momento... What do you think the following people are doing right now? Work with a partner.

▸ **Modelo:** —*¿Qué están haciendo tus padres en este momento?*
—*Creo que están trabajando.*

1. tus padres
2. tus compañeros/as de cuarto
3. tus amigos/as
4. tu profesor/a de matemáticas
5. tu profesor/a de español
6. el presidente de los Estados Unidos
7. los camareros de una cafetería
8. las personas en un restaurante
9. la policía de tu ciudad
10. los turistas en tu región
11. los choferes de los autobuses
12. Y ¿qué estás haciendo tú?

B. Ongoing actions

The present progressive tense indicates only that an action is in progress at the moment we describe it. To indicate how long it has been going on, you may use these two expressions. Note that both expressions use verbs in the present tense.

- **llevar** + expression of time + present participle

¿Cuánto tiempo **llevas estudiando** español?	*How long have you been studying Spanish?*
Llevo tres años **estudiando** español.	*I have been studying Spanish for three years.*

Stress that here **hace** and **que** are invariable both in form and position. So, too, is the expression **¿Cuánto tiempo hace que?** + present tense. The **no** goes before the variable verb.

- **hace** + expression of time + **que** + present tense

—¿Cuánto tiempo **hace que trabajas** en esa compañía?	*How long have you been working at that company?*
—**Hace** tres años **que** trabajo allí.	*I have been working there for three years.*
—¿Cuánto tiempo **hace que no** ves a tu novio?	*How long has it been since you have seen your boyfriend?*
—**Hace** dos semanas **que no** veo a mi novio.	*I haven't seen my boyfriend for two weeks.*

Answers to Actividad 7:
1. Llevo poco (tiempo) trabajando...
2. Llevo dos años administrando...
3. Llevo mucho tiempo escribiendo...
4. Llevo tres meses conduciendo...
5. Llevo algunos años recibiendo...
6. Llevo toda la vida haciendo...
7. Llevo algún tiempo preparando...
8. Llevo seis semanas sirviendo...

7 Experiencia profesional. You are hiring people for a company and need to assess their level of expertise in each field. Work with a partner and use **usted,** which is the socially preferred form of address for this situation. Ask the necessary questions following the model.

▸ **Modelo:** *vender tiquetes de avión / tres años*
—*¿Cuánto tiempo lleva usted vendiendo tiquetes de avión?*
—*Llevo tres años vendiendo tiquetes de avión.*

1. trabajar en una agencia de viajes / poco
2. administrar un hotel / dos años
3. escribir reportes / mucho tiempo
4. conducir taxis / tres meses
5. recibir turistas en los hoteles / algunos años
6. hacer comidas / toda la vida
7. preparar guías turísticas / algún tiempo
8. servir comidas rápidas / seis semanas

8 Falta de tiempo. You have been working very hard, even on weekends. Answer the following questions about all the things that you haven't had time to do because of your work load.

▶ **Modelo:** *ir a la discoteca / dos semanas*
—¿Cuánto tiempo hace que no vas a la discoteca?
—Hace dos semanas que no voy a la discoteca.

1. ver televisión / un mes
2. visitar a los amigos / una semana
3. tener tiempo libre / seis meses
4. ir al cine / mucho tiempo
5. comer en un restaurante / quince días
6. tener vacaciones / un año
7. conversar con mis amigas / tres días
8. preparar comida en casa / varios meses

Answers to Actividad 8:
1. Hace un mes que no veo...
2. Hace una semana que no visito...
3. Hace seis meses que no tengo...
4. Hace mucho tiempo que no voy...
5. Hace quince días que no como...
6. Hace un año que no tengo...
7. Hace tres días que no converso...
8. Hace varios meses que no preparo...

LENGUA EN ACCIÓN

Expresiones progresivas

■ **seguir/continuar** + present participle means *to continue/to be still doing something.*

El empleado **sigue/continúa** trabajando.	*The employee continues/is still working.*
¡No puedo **seguir/continuar** pidiendo información a ese señor!	*I can't continue asking that man for information.*
Gafasnegras **sigue/continúa** persiguiendo a Nayeli, y Adriana **sigue/continúa** preocupándose.	*Sunglasses is still/continues pursuing Nayeli and Adriana continues worrying.*

Write out the complete conjugation of **seguir** and **continuar,** paying special attention to stem changes and accents. **(sigo, sigues, sigue, seguimos, seguís, siguen / continúo, continúas, continúa, continuamos, continuáis, continúan).**

9 Práctica. Follow the model to indicate a progressive action in the present tense.

▶ **Modelo:** *¿Estás trabajando en el mismo restaurante? (seguir)*
¿Sigues trabajando en el mismo restaurante?
Sí, sigo trabajando en el mismo restaurante.

1. ¿Comes los mismos platos de pulpos y camarones cuando vas a o estás en Madrid? (seguir)
2. ¿Tus compañeros/as de apartamento estudian matemáticas? (continuar)
3. ¿Tus padres y tú visitan a los abuelos en Venezuela todos los veranos? (seguir)
4. ¿Venden allí la deliciosa paella española? (continuar)
5. ¿Preparas ensalada de camarones todas las noches para la cena? (seguir)
6. ¿Compras frutas para el postre en el mismo supermercado? (continuar)

Point to the appropriate drawings when students recite the sentences in chorus, as a way to make them conscious of the story line.

III. Using ser and estar

You have already learned the general uses of **ser** and **estar** (*to be*). The following short story summarizes the different ways these two verbs are used.

Mini historia de amor—El noviazgo (*The courtship*)

A. Ser:

1. states identity.

La novia **es** Juliana Castro; el novio **es** Luis Orozco. — *The fiancée is Juliana Castro; the fiancé is Luis Orozco.*

2. describes origin of things and people.

Luis **es** de Buenos Aires y Juliana **es** de Quito. — *Luis is from Buenos Aires and Juliana is from Quito.*

3. states occupation or profession of persons.

Juliana **es** médica y Luis **es** arquitecto. — *Juliana is a doctor and Luis is an architect.*

4. describes nationality.

Él **es** argentino y ella **es** ecuatoriana. — *He is Argentinean and she is Ecuadorian.*

5. describes things and people.

Juliana **es** una chica muy bonita y Luis **es** un chico encantador. — *Juliana is a very beautiful girl and Luis is a charming boy.*

6. describes what things are made of.

El anillo de Juliana **es** de oro y tiene un diamante enorme. — *Juliana's ring is made of gold and has an enormous diamond.*

7. states where events take place.

La boda **es** en la iglesia de San Felipe. — *The wedding is in the church of San Felipe.*

La boda (*The wedding*)

B. Estar:

8. describes location of places, buildings, and so on.

La iglesia de San Felipe **está** en el centro de la ciudad, cerca del parque. — *The church of San Felipe is downtown, close to the park.*

9. describes where people and things are at a certain moment.

Cuando la novia llega, algunos invitados **están** en el parque, pero Luis ya **está** en la iglesia. — *When the bride arrives, some guests are in the park, but Luis is already at the church.*

10. states how things look or are at a certain moment.

La novia **está** muy hermosa hoy, con su vestido blanco y largo. Luis también **está** guapísimo, con su traje negro. — *The bride is very beautiful today, in her long, white dress. Luis is also very handsome, in his black suit.*

Son novios y están enamorados
1
2
3
4
5
6
7
8
9
10
11
12

11. describes emotional or physical states.

Todos **están** muy contentos: la novia, el novio y los invitados; pero una amiga de Juliana, Berta, **está** muy emocionada y...	*Everyone is very happy: the bride, the groom, and the guests; but a friend of Juliana's, Berta, is very moved and . . .*

12. describes ongoing actions with the present progressive tense.

...**está** llorando muchísimo. Pero, muy cerca, hay un chico muy guapo mirando a Berta intensamente...	*. . . she is crying a lot. But, very close by there is a very handsome guy looking intensely at Berta . . .*
¡Cupido **está** preparando un nuevo romance!	*Cupid is preparing a new romance!*
FIN	*THE END*

Answers to Actividad 10:
1. Es Juliana Castro.
2. Es de Quito.
3. Es de Buenos Aires.
4. Es médica. Es arquitecto.
5. Algunos invitados están en el parque.
6. Está muy hermosa.
7. Están contentos.
8. Es en la iglesia de San Felipe.
9. Está en el centro de la ciudad.
10. Está guapísimo.

10 ¿Cuánto sabes? Answer the following questions about the mini-story.

1. ¿Quién es la novia?
2. ¿De dónde es la novia?
3. ¿De dónde es el novio?
4. ¿Cuál es la profesión de Juliana? ¿y la profesión de Luis?
5. ¿Dónde están los invitados cuando llega la novia?
6. ¿Cómo está la novia ese día?
7. ¿Cómo están todos los invitados?
8. ¿Dónde es la boda?
9. ¿Dónde está la iglesia?
10. ¿Cómo está Luis ese día?

Answers to Actividad 11:
1. Es el presidente de los Estados Unidos.
2. Son los coches.
3. Son las flores.
4. Es el agua.

11 ¡Adivina! Guess what the riddle is describing.

1. Es presidente de un país grande e importante. Su casa es blanca y está en la capital del país. ¿Quién es?
2. Son prácticos. Pueden ser grandes, pequeños, viejos, nuevos, bonitos y feos, buenos y malos, caros y baratos. Están generalmente en las calles contaminando el aire. Otras veces están en el garaje de la casa. ¿Qué son?
3. Son hermosas. Son de muchos colores y formas. Tienen perfume. Generalmente están en los jardines, pero a veces están adornando las casas. ¿Qué son?
4. Es clara y transparente. Está en el mar (*ocean*) y en los ríos (*rivers*), en el aire y en las nubes. En invierno es nieve y en verano puede ser vapor (*mist*). ¿Qué es?

12 ¡Ahora, adivina tú! Now, make a riddle and ask one partner to guess what it is.

Answers to Actividad 13:
1. es
2. es
3. está
4. está
5. está
6. está
7. están

13 Un crimen. Fill in the blanks with the necessary forms of **ser** or **estar** in this story about Nieves.

Nieves __________ una chica hermosa y simpática; __________ hija de un hombre muy rico de la ciudad. Hoy Nieves __________ inmensamente triste porque nadie quiere hablar con ella. Solamente su padre __________ allí, pero también él __________ triste y preocupado. Toda la gente __________ en el salón de la casa de Nieves y todos __________ hablando con interés y curiosidad. La casa

_________ grande y las habitaciones _________ elegantes, pero _________ terriblemente desordenadas: las sillas no _________ en su sitio y los libros _________ en el piso. En el salón de la casa hay un detective. _________ un hombre alto y _________ interrogando a todas las personas. Cuando acaba de interrogar, dice: "Este crimen _________ imperdonable" *(unforgivable)* y después, sale de la casa con Nieves. En la calle, el coche de la policía _________ esperando a Nieves y al detective.

8. es
9. son
10. están
11. están
12. están
13. Es
14. está
15. es
16. está

14 *Mi historia.* Now create your own mini-story, demonstrating at least three uses of **ser** and three uses of **estar.**

Lectura B

Introducción

In this selection you will learn about a restaurant owned by a famous Spanish-speaking opera star.

Prelectura

1 *Asociaciones.* ¿Qué cosa de la columna **B** asocias con las palabras de la columna **A**?

A	B
1. paella	_________ a. postre
2. tortilla española	_________ b. bebida
3. sangría	_________ c. sopa
4. flan	_________ d. entremés
5. sopa de pescado	_________ e. entrada

2 *¿Te gusta o no te gusta?* Working in pairs, inquire about each other's preferences, asking the following question: **¿Te gusta o no te gusta?**

1. la ensalada
2. la ópera
3. comer en restaurantes
4. Mel Gibson
5. cocinar

3 *Información necesaria.* Read the following background information before you go on to the reading itself.

Plácido Domingo es un tenor de Madrid. Tiene mucho éxito en la ópera. En el mundo hispano, Plácido Domingo es muy importante porque también interpreta las canciones populares de México, Chile, Argentina y otros países latinos. Es el padre de tres hijos; José, el mayor, Plácido y Álvaro. Su hijo Plácido escribe canciones para su padre. "Tres tenores" es el nombre de un concierto de Plácido con

otro gran cantante español, José Carreras, y con el distinguido tenor italiano Luciano Pavarotti. *Mis primeros cuarenta años* es el título del libro de memorias de Plácido Domingo. El siguiente artículo de la revista *Cristina* dice que Plácido, además de° ser un cantante extraordinario, tiene en Nueva York un restaurante español que sirve tapas, paella y mucho más.

besides

cocina°

cuisine

Plácido Domingo Restaurant

Plácido Domingo.

¿Por qué un restaurante de comida española... y por qué en Nueva York? Para el superastro° de la ópera Plácido Domingo, la respuesta° es muy sencilla:° "Porque amo esta ciudad, pero siempre pensé° que la comida de mi país no estaba° bien representada", dice. "Y, francamente, para tener un lugar donde cenar a las 12 de la noche, después de terminar mi actuación en la Ópera Metropolitana".

superstar
answer
simple
thought / was not

Donde, por cierto, ha cantado° como los mismísimos° ángeles durante 28 temporadas° consecutivas.

he has sung
same / seasons

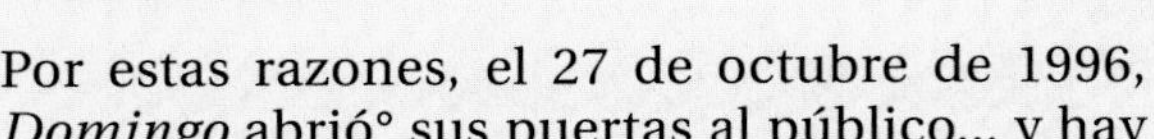

Por estas razones, el 27 de octubre de 1996, *Domingo* abrió° sus puertas al público... y hay una larga lista de luminarias que almuerzan en el elegante salón y cenan *filet mignon* y sopa de azafrán° con albóndigas° en la terraza, a la luz de las velas° y rodeadas° por la frondosa° vegetación. Algunas de las celebridades que han visitado° *Domingo*: la diva Beverly Sills, El Rey Juan Carlos de España y su esposa, la Reina Sofía — quienes, según° Nick Marco, el administrador, "son muy amables y se tomaron fotos con los meseros"° — y el actor australiano Mel Gibson, quien se sentó° en la mesa de Plácido y su esposa Marta, a jugar a las cartas° con los hijos del tenor.

opened
saffron / meatballs
candles / surrounded / lush
have visited
according to
waiters
sat
cards

Paella "Plácido Domingo".

Siempre que Domingo está en Nueva York, se le puede ver° cenando en su propio restaurante, acompañado por su querida Marta... y otros noctámbulos como él.

one can see him

Postlectura

3 Resumen. Write a short summary of three sentences about Plácido Domingo. Then read your work aloud to a classmate. Then, studying his photo, answer the question, **¿Cómo es Plácido?**

4 Quiero saber. Scan the reading selection to elicit the following details about Plácido Domingo, his family and his restaurant.

1. Plácido Domingo es un superastro de __________
   a. rock and roll.
   b. ópera.
   c. música jazz.

2. Domingo abrió un restaurante español en __________
   a. Nuevo México.
   b. Madrid.
   c Nueva York.

3. ¿Dónde canta Plácido cuando está en Nueva York?
   a. en la Ópera de Milán
   b. en la Ópera Metropolitana
   c. en la Ópera de México

4. ¿A qué hora cena Plácido generalmente?
   a. al mediodía
   b. a medianoche
   c. a las dos de la tarde

5. ¿Qué celebridades cenan con él y su familia?
   a. los reyes de España
   b. los reyes de Inglaterra
   c. los reyes de Dinamarca

6. ¿Quién se sentó a jugar a las cartas con los hijos de Plácido?
   a. la diva Beverly Sills
   b. el actor Mel Gibson
   c. el administrador Nick Marcos

7. ¿Cómo se llama la esposa de Plácido?
   a. María
   b. Mercedes
   c. Marta

Answers to Actividad 4:
1. b.
2. c.
3. b.
4. b.
5. a.
6. b.
7. c.

5 Tengo hambre. Working with a partner, study the photo of the meal. Take turns describing the different ingredients in the paella, plus the other foods and drink. Then, tell each other what your Spanish food preferences are for each of these items.

1. entremeses
2. comidas
3. ensaladas
4. bebidas
5. postres

6 Los cognados. Using five cognates from the selection, write original sentences in Spanish. Then, read them aloud to each other in groups.

En resumen

I. Hablemos

1 De viaje. You and a friend are planning to spend the summer in Spain. You each have limited resources ($750). Negotiate an itinerary of cities and sites to visit, where to stay and what to eat. Choose to travel to a minimum of four places and use at least three different means of transportation. Use the map in the front of the book for reference. Work with a partner.

2 El cuarto de Nayeli. After Adriana and Felipe leave for Sevilla, the doorman calls the police to report the break-in of Nayeli's room. Create a telephone conversation between the police and the doorman to describe Nayeli and the condition of the room. Be sure to use **ser** and **estar** for your descriptions and the present tense.

II. Investiguemos por Internet

Keyword searches

Searching the Internet successfully requires some practice selecting keywords, using the available search engines and following their guidelines for keyword search. For faster searches in Spanish, set the language of your browser to Spanish, if this option is available. If you need help with your search, look for it on the Houghton Mifflin Web site (http://www.hmco.com). In the activities below, you will be looking for food recipes and for measurement units in the metric system. You may want to review the vocabulary for the chapter to come up with useful keywords.

Vocabulario informático	
el/la cibernauta	*cyberspace surfer*
el enlace	*link*
el/la internauta	*Internet surfer*

This can be done either in a computer lab or as a homework assignment with students bringing in printouts of the most interesting page they find. Make transparencies or come to class with some of your own "favorite sites." If you have a homepage on the Web you might wish to place links to the best sites students have found as a way to share information.

3 Actividad para internautas. Work in groups and find one of the following categories of foods: (1) Two dishes—from any Hispanic country—that contain rice as the main ingredient, and in addition, seafood, chicken, or red meat. (2) Two dishes from Spain. (3) Two desserts. Report to the class the names of the dishes that you have selected, where they are from, and the ingredients. Keep a record of the keywords that you have used and report them to the class. Try **recetas de cocina** as your first keyword; other keywords could be **platos típicos** or **platos regionales.** If you have a specific country in mind, you may start looking for the country information first. Sometimes, recipes for regional dishes are listed as part of the country information, for example under the *tourism* (**turismo**) or *restaurants* (**restaurantes**) sections.

4 Cibernautas en acción. Work in groups and find the standard symbols for the metric measures listed in the "Las medidas" *Enlace cultural.* Be aware that on the Internet, you may also find the metric system listed under the International System of Units (**SI** or **SI** system), which is an extension of the metric system and is now the standard throughout the world. You may search in English or in Spanish. Start with one the following keywords: *metric system,* **sistema internacional de unidades, sistema métrico.**

III. Escribamos

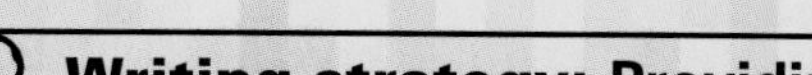

Writing strategy: Providing supporting detail

One way of making your writing interesting for the reader is to provide details about your topic that support or explain your main idea. The result is more vivid and convincing prose.

Main idea:

Doña Gafasoscuras es mala.

Supporting detail:

Ella siempre lleva gafas de sol.
Ella persigue a Nayeli.
Piensa robar el jaguar.
Pone un microfonito en la agenda de Nayeli.

Sample passage:

Doña Gafasoscuras es una persona muy mala. No sabemos quién es, pero la conocemos por sus famosas gafas de sol. Desde el primer capítulo de la historia, ella sigue a Nayeli porque piensa robar el jaguar. Desordena la habitación de Nayeli y pone un microfonito en su agenda para saber donde está Nayeli.

Strategy in action

Turn to *Escribamos* in the Workbook to practice the writing strategy of providing supporting detail.

5 Mi viaje. Choose one of the places you selected in **Actividad 1** and write a postcard to a close friend describing either the city or a specific place in the city. Write a main idea and some supporting detail.

6 Querido compañero/Querida compañera. Put yourself in the place of Felipe or Adriana. Select one of the themes below and write an e-mail of ten sentences. Use **ser, estar,** and other present-tense verbs.

Temas

1. Felipe escribe a su compañero de cuarto, Arturo, y describe cómo es Adriana y comó es España.
2. Adriana escribe a su compañera de cuarto, Patricia, y describe cómo es Felipe y cómo es España.

Assign this as homework. The e-mail can be either ficticious or real and can be sent to you to edit and possibly post a compilation of the students' responses on the Internet for all to share.

Vocabulario

Medios de transporte

a pie	*on foot*	**el coche**	*car*
el autobús	*bus*	**el metro**	*subway*
el avión	*plane*	**la moto/motocicleta**	*motorcycle*
el barco	*boat*	**el taxi**	*taxi*
la bicicleta	*bike*	**el tren (ferrocarril)**	*train*

En el hotel

el almuerzo	*lunch*
el ascensor	*elevator*
Aquí tengo mi confirmación.	*Here is my confirmation.*
el/la botones	*bellhop*
el buzón	*mailbox*
la cama	*bed*
el cambio de moneda	*money exchange*
¿Cómo quiere Ud. pagar?	*How do you want to pay?*
con cheques de viajero	*with traveler's checks*
con desayuno	*with breakfast*
con media pensión	*with breakfast and lunch*
con tarjeta de crédito	*with a credit card*
el/la conserje	*concierge*
¿Cuánto cuesta...?	*How much does . . . cost?*
¿Dónde puedo cambiar el dinero?	*Where can I exchange money?*
¿En qué le(s) puedo servir?	*How can I help you?*
en seguida	*right away*
la habitación	*room*
hacer una llamada de larga distancia	*to make a long distance phone call*
hacer una llamada por cobrar	*to make a collect call*
el/la huésped	*guest*
la llave	*key*
Lo siento.	*I'm sorry.*
la maleta	*suitcase*
no fumar	*no smoking*
la piscina	*swimming pool*
Quiero pagar con dinero en efectivo.	*I want to pay cash.*
Quisiera una habitación doble/sencilla.	*I would like a double/ single room.*
la recepción	*reception*
el/la recepcionista	*receptionist*
el salón de conferencias	*conference room*
la tarjeta de crédito	*credit card*
¿Tiene(n) Ud(s). reservación?	*Do you have a reservation?*
el viaje	*trip*

Números grandes

(See page 97.)

Palabras afirmativas y negativas

(See page 110.)

En el restaurante

A sus órdenes.	*At your service.*
el almuerzo	*lunch*
el azúcar	*sugar*
la bebida	*drink*
el café	*coffee*
el/la camarero/a	*waitperson*
La carne está dura.	*The meat is tough.*
la carta (el menú)	*menu*
la cena	*dinner*
cenar	*to have dinner*
la cerveza	*beer*
la comida	*food, meal*
La comida está muy salada/dulce.	*The food is too salty/sweet.*
la copa	*wine glass*
la cuchara	*spoon*
la cucharita	*teaspoon*
el cuchillo	*knife*
la cuenta	*check, bill*
La cuenta, por favor.	*The check, please.*
dejar	*to leave*
el desayuno	*breakfast*
disfrutar	*to enjoy*
la ensalada	*salad*
la entrada	*entrée*
el entremés	*appetizer*
Estoy muerto/a de hambre.	*I'm starving, famished.*
la jarra	*pitcher*
ligero/a	*light*
listo: estar listo/a	*to be ready*
el mantel	*table cloth*
Me falta (el tenedor).	*My (fork) is missing.*
Me gustaría...	*I would like . . .*
el pedido	*order*
la pimienta	*(black) pepper*
el platillo	*saucer*
el plato	*dish, plate*
el plato fuerte	*main dish*
¿Podría traer la cuenta, por favor?	*Could you bring the check, please?*
el postre	*dessert*
Los precios están por las nubes.	*The prices are high (in the clouds).*
la propina	*tip*
¿Qué desean comer/beber?	*What do you want to have (to eat/drink)?*
¡Qué hambre! / ¡Tengo mucha hambre!	*I am very hungry!*
¿Qué nos recomienda?	*What can you recommend to us?*
¿Qué recomendaría Ud.?	*What would you recommend?*
Quisiera pedir...	*I would like to order . . .*
rico/a	*rich, delicious*
la sal	*salt*
el servicio	*service*
El servicio es deficiente.	*The service is not acceptable.*
la servilleta	*napkin*
la sopa	*soup*
las tapas	*appetizers (Spain)*
la taza	*cup*
el té	*tea*
el tenedor	*fork*
el vaso	*glass*
el vino (tinto/blanco)	*(red/white) wine*
Un vino tinto/blanco, por favor.	*A glass of red/white wine, please.*
el zumo (jugo)	*juice*

Comidas

el aceite de oliva	*olive oil*
el apio	*celery*
el bizcocho (el pastel)	*cake*
el bollo	*hard roll*
el cabrito	*goat*
el calamar	*squid*
el cangrejo	*crab*
la carne	*meat*
la carne de vaca (res)	*beef, Sp. (L. Am.)*
la carnicería	*meat market*
la cebolla	*onion*
la chuleta de puerco	*pork chop*
la fruta	*fruit*
la frutería	*fruit stand*
la galleta	*cookie*
la gamba (el camarón)	*shrimp*
el huevo	*egg*
la langosta	*lobster*
la leche	*milk*
la lechuga	*lettuce*
las legumbres	*vegetables*
la mandarina	*tangerine*
la manzana	*apple*
la naranja	*orange*
la ostra	*oyster*
el pan	*bread*
la panadería	*bread bakery*
la patata (la papa)	*potato*
el pepino	*cucumber*
la pera	*pear*
la pescadería	*fish market*
el pescado	*fish*
el pimiento verde/rojo	*green/red pepper*
la piña	*pineapple*
el plátano	*banana*
el pollo	*chicken*
el pulpo	*octopus*
el queso	*cheese*
la ternera	*veal*
el tomate	*tomato*
la uva	*grape*
la zanahoria	*carrot*

Adjetivos demostrativos

(See page 124.)

Verbos

almorzar (ue)	*to have lunch*
cerrar (ie)	*to close*
comenzar (ie)	*to begin*
conseguir (i)	*to get, obtain*
contar (ue)	*to count*
costar (ue)	*to cost*
decir (i)	*to say, tell*
dormir (ue)	*to sleep*
empezar (ie)	*to begin*
encontrar (ue)	*to find*
entender (ie)	*to understand*
llover (ue)	*to rain*
morir (ue)	*to die*
mostrar (ue)	*to show*
nevar (ie)	*to snow*
pedir (i)	*to ask for*
pensar (ie)	*to think*
perder (ie)	*to lose*
perseguir (i)	*to follow, pursue*
poder (ue)	*to be able to*
preferir (ie)	*to prefer*
probar (ue)	*to try; to taste*
querer (ie)	*to want*
recomendar (ie)	*to recommend*
recordar (ue)	*to remember*
seguir (i)	*to follow, to continue*
servir (i)	*to serve*
volver (ue)	*to come back, return*

Verbos reflexivos

(See page 106.)

Adverbios

ahora	*now*
ahora mismo	*at this very moment, right now*
después	*after*
en este momento	*at this moment*
entonces	*then*
luego	*later, then*
por fin	*finally*
primero	*first*

CAPÍTULO 4

LOCALIDAD: España

4A

¿Está en peligro el jaguar?

4B

Nayeli desperately tries to get information from the trucker regarding the jaguar's whereabouts. Meanwhile, an ominous figure shadows Adriana through the streets of Sevilla.

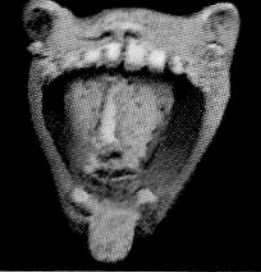

Vocabulary themes

- Talking about train travel
- Expressing location
- Making travel plans
- Using ordinal numbers
- Talking about location

Language structures

- Describing to whom and for whom actions are done
- Establishing relationships through prepositions
- Retelling simple past events
- Indicating when actions were completed
- Avoiding redundancy

Culture topics

- El tren, un gran medio de transporte
- El sistema de trenes en España
- España

Readings

- Los jóvenes de España
- La encantadora ciudad de Sevilla

Reading/writing strategies

- Making notes in the margins
- Creating a time line

Internet strategy

- Identifying country domains

ETAPA A

Pistas y palabras

I. Talking about train travel

A. ¡Todos a bordo!

▲ *Salidas y llegadas.*

◄ *Estación de Atocha, Madrid, España.*

1. los pasajeros
2. el billete/el boleto
3. la llegada
4. la salida

Palabras y expresiones útiles

el andén	*track*	el maletero	*porter*
el asiento	*seat*	la plaza	*place/seat*
la demora	*delay*	la taquilla	*ticket window*
el horario	*schedule*	el tiquete (pasaje de ida y vuelta)	*round trip*
el itinerario	*itinerary*		

bajar (del tren)	*to get off (the train)*
estar/llegar a tiempo	*to be/arrive on time*
estar/llegar atrasado/a	*to be late/arrive late*
ir/salir con destino a	*leave/depart with destination to*
no fumar	*no smoking*
subir (al tren)	*to board (the train)*
tardar en llegar/salir	*to take (too much) time to arrive/leave*

¿Cuánto cuesta? ¿Cuánto es?	*How much is it?*
¿En qué les puedo servir?	*How may I help you?*
¡Que tenga/n un buen viaje!	*Have a good trip!*

LENGUA EN ACCIÓN

Sinónimos

There are several ways to say *ticket* in Spanish. In some countries like Spain, **el billete** is used for transportation, sporting events and the lottery, while in others like Mexico, **el boleto** is also used. Other synonyms are:

el tiquet(e) = ticket or receipt
el pasaje = fare or ticket
la plaza = place, seat
la entrada = ticket to the movies, sports event, theater, and so on

1 **Hablando de viaje.** Working with a partner, create complete sentences in the present tense with the words provided in the columns. Use each subject and verb at least once. Then read your sentences aloud to another classmate to compare answers.

A	B	C
la empleada	escribir	de Toledo
nosotros	llegar	el equipaje
tú	llevar	a Madrid
el maletero	no tener	un mensaje
yo	salir	atrasado/a
el tren	subir	a tiempo
los pasajeros	viajar	la reservación
	volver	al ascensor
	estar	a las 9.00
		al tren

2 **¿A qué hora llega?** Discuss the AVE train schedule with a classmate. Follow the model.

► **Modelo:** —*¿A qué hora llega el tren a Tarragona?*
—*Llega a las once menos cinco de la noche.*

—*¿A qué hora sale el tren de Tarragona?*
—*Sale a las once menos cuatro de la noche.*

Point out that the train originates in Barcelona and terminates in Seville. With the map of Spain in this chapter, trace the route of the train.

INTERNET ADDRESS: http://www.renfe.es

TREN HOTEL: Madrid=>Sevilla Santa Justa

ESTACIÓN	Llegada	Salida	ESTACIÓN	Llegada	Salida
BARCELONA-SANTS	—	22:00	MADRID-PUERTA DE ATOCHA	05:28	05:33
TARRAGONA	22:55	22:56	CIUDAD REAL	06:38	06:39
REUS	23:11	23:12	CÓRDOBA CENTRAL	07:48	07:50
LLEIDA	00:10	00:11	SEVILLA SANTA JUSTA	08:50	—
ZARAGOZA-EL PORTILLO	01:49	01:50	Antonio Machado No circula 24 y 31-12-96.		

ENLACE CULTURAL

El tren, un gran medio de transporte

El AVE es un tren muy moderno de alta velocidad° que funciona en España desde° 1992, el año de la Exposición Mundial de Sevilla. Este tren va de Madrid a Sevilla en dos horas y cuarenta y cinco minutos. Allí presentan películas, hay música y venden comidas y bebidas.

high speed
since

En Madrid y en otras ciudades hispanas, la gente viaja también en trenes interurbanos° o en metro, por ejemplo en la Ciudad de México; en Santiago de Chile; en Caracas, Venezuela; en Buenos Aires, Argentina y en Medellín, Colombia.

commuter trains

El AVE.

En contraste con el AVE, el tren que va a Machu Picchu, en los Andes peruanos, sube poco a poco° hasta la cima° de la gran montaña. Es el tren que sube a más altura° en el mundo.

little by little
top
height

Discusión en grupos

1. ¿Hay trenes en la ciudad donde ustedes viven?
2. ¿Hay en los Estados Unidos trenes de alta velocidad, trenes interurbanos, metro?
3. ¿En qué región de los Estados Unidos hay más trenes? ¿Qué transportan estos trenes?
4. Menciona tres características de trenes que conoces en los Estados Unidos.

El tren que va de Cuzco a Machu Picchu, Perú.

B. ¿En qué les puedo servir?

—¿En qué les puedo servir?
—Queremos comprar dos billetes de Madrid a Sevilla.
—¿En qué tren prefieren viajar?
—¿Cuál es el tren más económico?
—El interurbano es el más económico, pero tarda en llegar.
—No, nosotros tenemos prisa. ¿Cuál es el más rápido?
—El AVE. Solamente tarda dos horas y cuarenta y cinco minutos.
—¡Eso está muy bien! ¿Cuánto cuesta un billete en el próximo AVE?
—¿De ida y vuelta?
—No, solamente el billete de ida.
—¿En qué clase?
—En segunda clase,° por favor.
—Cada billete cuesta 8.900 pesetas. Son 17.800 pesetas por los dos.
—Está bien, entonces dos billetes por favor.
—Aquí tienen ustedes sus billetes. Los asientos son el A1 y el A2 en el vagón número 4.
—¿Dónde está el andén?
—Está allí, a la izquierda.°
—Muchas gracias, señor.
—¡Qué tengan un buen viaje!

second class

to the left

3 Comprensión. Answer the questions based on the conversation.

1. ¿Cuántas personas viajan?
2. ¿Adónde van?
3. ¿Cuándo quieren viajar?
4. ¿Compran billetes de ida y vuelta?
5. ¿En qué tren deciden viajar? ¿Por qué?
6. ¿Cuánto cuestan los dos billetes?
7. ¿Piensan viajar en primera clase?

Answers to Actividad 3:
1. dos
2. a Sevilla
3. pronto
4. no, sólo de ida
5. en el AVE. Es más rápido.
6. 17.800 ptas.
7. No, en segunda.

Answers to Actividad 4:
1. e
2. d
3. f
4. g
5. a
6. b
7. c

4 ¡Todos a bordo! Working with a partner, complete the following situations in the train station with an appropriate answer. Then put the completed sentences in a logical order.

1. La empleada de la taquilla les dice:	a. Nayeli.
2. El tren sale del	b. de ida.
3. Hay	c. vagón número 4, asientos A1 y A2.
4. En la taquilla,	d. andén número 2.
5. Felipe y Adriana se preocupan por	e. ¡Qué tengan un buen viaje!
6. Los boletos son	f. muchos pasajeros en el tren.
7. Adriana y Felipe suben al	g. Felipe compra dos billetes para Sevilla en el AVE.

5 ¿Y tú? In pairs, ask each other these questions.

1. ¿Cuál es tu medio de transporte favorito—el avión, el tren, el auto, el autobús?
2. ¿Cuál es el medio de transporte favorito en tu ciudad y por qué?
3. ¿Qué medios de transporte usa tu familia?
4. ¿Camina mucho la gente en tu ciudad? ¿Camina al trabajo?
5. ¿Cómo van tú y tus compañeros/as de sus casas a la universidad? ¿Y cómo regresan?

6 Viaje urgente. Read the descriptions of the roles of passenger and employee. Then, with a partner, create a conversation between the two.

Pasajero/a:	Empleado/a:
You are in Madrid and have just received bad news: a member of your family is ill and is in the hospital in Cádiz. You have to travel on the next train, but there's a problem: there are no tickets left. Convince the ticket agent to send you to Cádiz as fast as possible. Review the conversation on page 145 for help. Here are some useful expressions: **pagar con tarjeta de crédito** **viaje urgente** **primera clase** **Tengo que llegar/ir.** **por favor**	Today is your first day on the job and you are a little nervous. Your boss (**el/la jefe/a**) is observing you. You want to impress him/her (**impresionar al jefe/a la jefa**). How will you handle this passenger? Look at the map of trains in Spain in the next *Enlace cultural* on page 148 for ideas on how to get to Cádiz. Here are some useful expressions: **No es posible ..., Es imposible ..., No puedo ...** **el tren de mañana / de la tarde / de las 3 p.m.** **más caro** **No hay billetes en ese tren.** **Lo siento (*I am sorry*).**

II. Expressing location

¿Quién está delante de la profesora Jaramillo?

Carlitos está **entre** el Sr. y la Sra. Coronado.
La profesora Jaramillo está **delante de** la Sra. Coronado.
Ricardo está **detrás de** Federica.
Paula está **al lado de** Ricardo.
Las bolsas están **debajo de** los asientos.
Las maletas están **encima del** portaequipajes.
El Sr. Coronado está **lejos de** *(far from)* Federica.
La profesora Jaramillo está **cerca de** *(close to)* la Sra. Coronado.

7 **¿Dónde están?** Tell where the following people are located. Follow the model.

▸ **Modelo:** *Carlitos Coronado / El Sr. Coronado*
Carlitos Coronado está al lado del Sr. Coronado.

1. la Sra. Coronado / Carlitos Coronado
2. Manuel Mendoza / Federica
3. la profesora Jaramillo / Paula y la Sra. Coronado
4. Ricardo / Federica
5. Manuel / Ricardo
6. Carlitos Coronado / Ricardo
7. el portaequipajes / las maletas

Answers to Actividad 7:
1. al lado de
2. al lado de
3. detrás de Paula y delante de la Sra. Coronado
4. delante de
5. cerca de/delante` de
6. detrás de
7. debajo de

Have students try to deduce the meaning of **portaequipajes.** Give them a hint that **equipaje** = *luggage.*

8 ¿Dónde estás? Write a list of four classmates. Then, ask a partner where each one is located. Work in pairs to compare the locations of the eight people on your two lists.

► **Modelo:** **Persona A** 1. *Alison* **Persona B** 1. *Sean*

—*¿Dónde está Alison?*
—*Alison está lejos de Sean.*

ENLACE CULTURAL

El sistema de trenes en España

En España, las líneas de trenes van, básicamente, en dos direcciones: (a) las líneas que salen y llegan a Madrid: Líneas Radiales° y (b) las líneas que salen y llegan a otras ciudades: Líneas Transversales.°

radial
cross

Discusión en grupos

¿Cómo es el sistema de trenes de su país? ¿Existen trenes en su región?

For **Actividad 9**, bring in pictures or postcards of some of the cities on the map.

9 Descripción. Look at the map of the *Enlace cultural* and select two of the train lines. Then write a short description of how the cities on these lines are located in relation to one another. Use prepositions.

► **Modelo:** *Madrid está lejos de Sevilla, pero cerca de Aranjuez.*
En la línea de Madrid a Linares, Manzanares está entre Alcázar y Linares.

10 A escribir. Write a brief paragraph describing the photograph of Atocha at the beginning of the chapter on page 142. Use at least five prepositions.

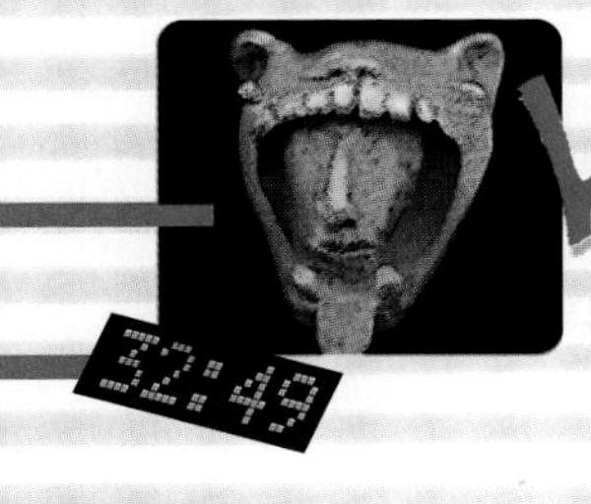

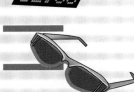

VISTAS Y VOCES

I. Preparémonos

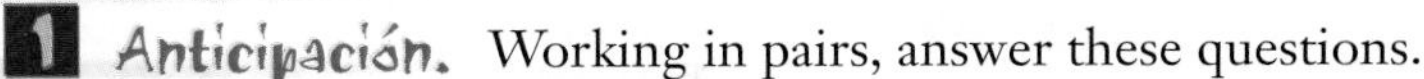

1 Anticipación. Working in pairs, answer these questions.

A. **1.** ¿Cómo es la estación de tren o de autobuses que está más cerca de tu escuela?
2. ¿Cuántas personas usan esa estación en una semana? ¿La usas tú? ¿Por qué sí? ¿Por qué no?
3. ¿Qué objeto de arte valioso admiras mucho? ¿Cómo es? ¿Dónde está?
4. ¿Hay muchos robos en tu ciudad? ¿Qué roban los ladrones (*thieves*): obras de arte, dinero, radios, televisiones?

B. Review chapter opening photo 4A. What do you think that Felipe is doing at the Atocha train station in Madrid? Where are he and Adriana going? Why? What is going to happen next?

Para comprender mejor

el asunto	*matter*	No me cae nada mal.	*He's OK.*
cuidar	*to take care of*		
de todos modos	*anyway*	No se preocupe.	*Don't worry.*
de veras	*really*	No vale la pena.	*It's not worth it.*
desgraciadamente	*unfortunately*	Olvídelo.	*Forget it.*
enseguida	*right away*	por si acaso	*just in case*
esconder	*to hide*	reaccionar	*to react*
Estoy de acuerdo.	*I agree.*	recorrer	*to travel all around*
ilegal	*illegal*	el robo	*robbery*
Lo siento.	*I'm sorry.*	rogar	*to beg*
lucrativo/a	*profitable*	sacar	*to take (away)*
mientras	*while*	sacudir	*to shake*
mover	*to move*	sucio/a	*dirty/shady*
el negocio	*business*	Vámonos.	*Let's go.*

Enseguida can also be written as **en seguida.**

2 Secuencia. In pairs, describe what you see happening in each video action shot. Then, order them in a logical sequence.

Correct order of video action shots: 2, 1, 4, 3

1.

2.

3.

4.

II. Miremos y escuchemos

3 ¿Verdadero o falso? While watching this episode, mark **V** (**verdadero**) for each true statement and **F** (**falso**) for each false one. Then, correct the false ones.

1. ______ El chofer y su esposa hablan de vender el jaguar.
2. ______ Adriana empieza a tener interés romántico en Felipe.
3. ______ Felipe y Adriana van a Sevilla en avión.
4. ______ El chofer le da un papelito a Nayeli.
5. ______ Nayeli le indica al chofer que es ilegal tener el jaguar.
6. ______ Doña Gafasoscuras escucha la conversación de Nayeli en la casa del chofer.
7. ______ El chofer espera tres semanas y después manda el jaguar el Ecuador.

Answers to Actividad 3:
1. F—El chofer y su esposa hablan de enviarlo al Ecuador.
2. V
3 F—Felipe y Adriana van a Sevilla en tren. (el AVE)
4. V
5. V
6. V
7. F—El chofer manda el jaguar a Quito, Ecuador enseguida.

III. Comentemos

4 Comprensión. In groups, answer the following questions.

1. ¿Cómo se llama el señor Covarrubias?
2. ¿Qué tiene el chofer del camión en las manos?
3. ¿Por qué hace el chofer un negocio "sucio" con el jaguar?
4. ¿Cómo reacciona (*reacts*) la esposa del chofer? ¿Qué coincidencias ocurren?
5. ¿Cómo se llama la estación de tren en Madrid?
6. ¿Adónde van Adriana y Felipe? ¿Cómo y en qué clase?
7. ¿Detrás de (*behind*) qué se esconden los señores Covarrubias?
8. ¿Cómo describe Nayeli el robo del jaguar? Según el chofer, ¿dónde está el jaguar?
9. ¿Cómo están los Covarrubias al final de esta escena?

Answers to Actividad 4:
1. Se llama Gerardo.
2. el jaguar
3. es mucho dinero y poco trabajo
4. La esposa tiene miedo. Las cosas se mueven.
5. Puerta de Atocha
6. a Sevilla; en tren, en segunda clase
7. detrás del sofá
8. Nayeli indica que es un asunto ilegal. El señor Covarrubias mandó el jaguar al Ecuador.
9. Los dos están nerviosos y tienen miedo.

5 ¿Estás de acuerdo? Working in groups, compare the different ideas you have with regard to the following statements based on this episode. Tell if you agree (**estoy de acuerdo**) or disagree (**no estoy de acuerdo**) and the reason (**razón**).

1. El crimen no paga.
2. El dinero es la seguridad más importante de la vida.
3. Unas personas tienen mala suerte.
4. Está bien decir mentiras si la familia está en peligro.

6 Miremos otra vez. After watching this episode again, check to see if you have arranged the video action shots in the correct sequence.

Lengua

I. Describing to whom and for whom actions are done

A. Indirect-object pronouns

To illustrate the concept of indirect objects, take your textbook and give it to a student. Point out that you didn't touch the student, only the book. The student is indirect (a recipient of your action), while the contact you have with the book is direct.

Mis padres **me** compran un estéreo.
Las Girl Scouts **nos** venden galletitas.

My parents buy ***me*** *a stereo.* *The Girl Scouts sell* ***us*** *cookies.*

Indirect objects indicate *to* or *for* whom an action is done. Read the examples and identify who receives the action of the verb. The highlighted pronouns in Spanish and English indicate the indirect objects: the stereo is bought *for me* and the cookies are sold *to us.*

Indirect-object pronouns			
me	*to (for) me*	**nos**	*to (for) us*
te	*to (for) you*	**os**	*to (for) you*
le	*to (for) him, her, you*	**les**	*to (for) them, you*

- Indirect-object pronouns can precede the conjugated verb or can be attached to the end of the infinitive or the present participle.

  Te voy a decir una cosa. — *I am going to tell you something.*
  Voy a decir**te** una cosa.

  Nayeli **le** está haciendo preguntas. — *Nayeli is asking him questions.*
  Nayeli está haciéndo**le** preguntas.

Stress that normally these objects go *right* before the conjugated verb. When the sentence is negative, the **no** precedes the pronoun: **No te voy a decir... / No voy a decirte. / No te digo.**

- In Spanish, the indirect-object pronoun is mandatory in almost all cases, but the prepositional forms are optional.

  El chofer **le** da un papelito. *or* — The driver *gives her* a piece of paper.
  El chofer **le** da un papelito **a ella.** — The driver gives a piece of paper *to her.*

Some common verbs that take indirect-object pronouns are:

Note that the **zc** for **agradecer** and **ofrecer** are for the **yo** forms only.

agradecer (zc)	*to thank*	ofrecer (zc)	*to offer*
contar (ue)	*to tell*	pagar	*to pay (for)*
contestar	*to answer*	pedir (i)	*to ask for*
dar	*to give*	pegar	*to hit; to stick*
decir (i)	*to tell, say*	preguntar	*to ask a question*
escribir	*to write*	preparar	*to prepare*
explicar	*to explain*	regalar	*to give a gift*
hablar	*to speak*	servir (i)	*to serve*
mandar / enviar	*to send*	vender	*to sell*

B. Prepositional pronouns

Clarify this construction by writing on the board the following and highlighting with different colors the subjects, indirect objects, and objects of prepositions:
Pepe me da el libro a mí.
Pepe te da el libro a ti.
Pepe le da el libro a usted/a él/a ella/a Felipe.
Pepe nos da el libro a nosotros/a nosotras.
Pepe os da el libro a vosotros/a vosotras.
Pepe les da el libro a ustedes/ a ellos/a ellas/a Felipe y Adriana.

Note that **mí** has an accent while **ti** does not. This is to distinguish it from the possessive pronoun **mi**.

Prepositional pronouns follow a preposition and have the same form as the subject pronouns except for the first person (**mí**) and second person (**ti**) singular forms.

Prepositional pronouns	
mí	*me*
ti	*you*
él/ella, usted	*him/her, you (singular)*
nosotros/nosotras	*us*
vosotros/vosotras	*you*
ellos/ellas, ustedes	*them, you (plural)*

- Indirect-object pronouns can be clarified or emphasized by using one of these expressions:

  a + person's name or word referring to a person
  a + prepositional pronoun

Nayeli **le** está haciendo preguntas **al señor** Covarrubias.	*Nayeli is asking Mr. Covarrubias questions.*
Nayeli **le** está haciendo preguntas **al empleado.**	*Nayeli is asking the employee questions.*
Te voy a decir una cosa **a ti.**	*I am going to tell you something.*

Answers to Actividad 1:
1. le
2. le
3. les
4. me
5. Te
6. nos
7. les
8. me
9. les
10. les

1 *¿A quién?* Say the correct form of the indirect-object pronoun which corresponds to the underlined noun(s) or pronoun(s) in each sentence.

1. Adriana ________ dice a Felipe que está preocupada por Nayeli.
2. Felipe ________ contesta a Adriana que van a seguir buscando a Nayeli.
3. Algunas personas ________ pagan dinero al chofer y a su esposa.
4. Mi compañero de apartamento ________ está vendiendo su estéreo a mí.
5. ¿________ digo la verdad a ti sobre Nayeli y los héroes gemelos?
6. Tino ________ va a regalar a nosotros boletos para el cine, ¿verdad?
7. Nayeli ________ escribe una carta a Felipe y a Adriana.
8. Mis amigos ________ van a contar un secreto a mí.
9. La profesora ________ habla a los estudiantes sobre Puerto Rico.
10. ¡Yo ________ agradezco mucho a ustedes los hermosos regalos de boda!

2 **Preguntas personales.** Ask a classmate the following questions.

▸ **Modelo:** —*¿Quién te da regalos? (mi amigo Juan)*
—*Mi amigo Juan me da regalos.*

1. ¿Quiénes te hablan por teléfono? (mis amigos)
2. ¿Quién te escribe cartas? (la gente)
3. ¿Quién les prepara la comida en casa? (yo)
4. ¿Quién les enseña español en la clase? (la profesora)
5. ¿Quién te agradece? (todo el mundo)
6. ¿Quién les pide su opinión? (nadie)
7. ¿Quiénes te dicen la verdad? (algunas personas)
8. ¿Quién te paga el alquiler de tu casa? (mis padres)

3 **¿De quién hablas?** Combine the cued words to form complete sentences.

▸ **Modelo:** *la profesora / preguntar (a los estudiantes)*
La profesora les pregunta a los estudiantes.

1. ellos / contestar las preguntas (a la profesora)
2. el chofer del camión / enviar el jaguar (a alguien)
3. los médicos / ofrecer ayuda (a nosotros)
4. ustedes / servir la cena (a mamá)
5. Armando / escribir correo electrónico (a Adriana y Felipe)
6. alguien / regalar una rosa (a Nayeli)
7. Tomasito nunca / pegar (a su perro)
8. mi mamá / pedir un favor (a mí)
9. el chico / hablar (a la chica)
10. usted / explicar la lección (a nosotros)

Answers to Actividad 3:

1. Ellos le contestan las preguntas a la profesora.
2. El chofer del camión le envía el jaguar a alguien.
3. Los médicos nos ofrecen ayuda a nosotros.
4. Ustedes le sirven la cena a mamá.
5. Armando les escribe correo electrónico a Adriana y Felipe.
6. Alguien le regala una rosa a Nayeli.
7. Tomasito nunca le pega a su perro.
8. Mi mamá me pide un favor a mí.
9. El chico le habla a la chica.
10. Usted nos explica la lección a nosotros.

C. The verb *gustar* and similar verbs

- As you have learned, the verb **gustar** is used with the indirect-object pronouns **me** and **te.**

Me gustan los trenes rápidos.	*I like fast trains.*
Te gusta viajar en tren.	*You like to travel by train.*

- The following table shows how **gustar** is used with the other indirect-object pronouns.

Me gusta(n).	*I like it/them.*	**Nos** gusta(n).	*We like it/them.*
Te gusta(n).	*You like it/them.*	**Os** gusta(n).	*You (plural) like it/them.*
Le gusta(n).	*He/She likes it/them. You (formal) like it/them.*	**Les** gusta(n).	*They/You (plural) like it/them.*

At this point students need to know only two forms of this verb: **gusta** and **gustan.** Write a sentence on the board and translate it literally, pointing out that the Spanish and English word orders are opposites.
Les gusta el libro. = *To them is pleasing the book.*
Me gustan los libros. = *To me are pleasing the books.*
The expressions *is pleasing* and *are pleasing* help students see whether the verb should be singular or plural.

- Remember that **gustar** agrees in number with the thing/s liked. Use **gusta** when followed by a singular noun or an infinitive. Use **gustan** when followed by a plural noun.

¿Te **gusta** el AVE?	*Do you like el AVE?*
No, no me **gustan** los trenes.	*No, I don't like trains.*
Me **gusta** viajar en avión.	*I like to travel by plane.*

- Many Spanish verbs are used in a similar way to **gustar.** Some common verbs that follow this pattern are:

caer bien/mal	*to like/dislike (a person)*
encantar	*to delight, enchant, like very much*
faltar	*to lack, need; to be left (to do)*
fascinar	*to fascinate*
importar	*to matter, be of concern*
interesar	*to interest, be of interest*
molestar	*to bother, annoy*
parecer	*to seem, appear to be*
preocupar	*to worry*

Nos encanta comer tapas.	*We love to eat tapas.*
¿**Te** molesta viajar en avión?	*Does it bother you to travel by plane?*

- As with other verbs that take indirect objects, the preposition **a** + noun or **a** + prepositional pronoun can be used to emphasize or clarify the recipient of the action.

A mí me fascina viajar.	*Traveling fascinates me.*
¡**A nosotros** nos encantan los hoteles de cinco estrellas!	*Five star hotels delight us!*
A Felipe y Adriana les preocupa el problema de Nayeli.	*Nayeli's problem worries Felipe and Adriana.*
Al dependiente le molestan los clientes impertinentes.	*Impertinent clients annoy the clerk.*

- When verbs like **gustar** are used with a reflexive verb, the corresponding reflexive pronoun is attached to the infinitive.

Nos gusta **divertirnos** mucho.	*We really like to have fun.*
A Nayeli le gusta **alojarse** en el hotel Prisma.	*Nayeli likes to stay at the Prisma Hotel.*

4 ¿Te gusta? You and a friend are talking about what you like to do on a trip. Following the model, ask each other questions about the following information. Remember to modify the pronoun of reflexive verbs.

► **Modelo:** *levantarse temprano y viajar por la mañana*
—¿Te gusta levantarte temprano y viajar por la mañana?
—No, no me gusta levantarme temprano y viajar por la mañana. or:
—Sí, me gusta levantarme temprano y viajar por la mañana.

1. desayunar tarde y sentarse a leer
2. dar paseos por la ciudad y divertirse mucho
3. dormir mucho y despertarse tarde
4. irse en tren para Sevilla
5. viajar con un guía turístico
6. ducharse en la mañana
7. cenar comida española

5 *Gustos.* Working with a partner, ask each other the following information. Then write down the answers for the next activity.

▸ **Modelo:** *gustar / las ensaladas de tomate*
—¿Te gustan las ensaladas de tomate?
—Sí, me gustan las ensaladas de tomate. or:
—No, no me gustan las ensaladas de tomate.

1. fascinar / los restaurantes españoles
2. encantar / las canciones románticas
3. interesar / las novelas de misterio
4. gustar / los libros para jóvenes
5. molestar / el problema del tráfico
6. importar / la ecología
7. fascinar / las nuevas tecnologías
8. gustar / el cine mexicano
9. encantar / el centro de Sevilla

Answers to Actividad 5:
1. te fascinan
2. te encantan
3. te interesan
4. te gustan
5. te molesta
6. te importa
7. te fascinan
8. te gusta
9. te encanta

6 *Cosas especiales.* Work with a classmate to ask about the tastes of different people. Remember to use the personal **a.** Follow the model.

▸ **Modelo:** *gustar leer por las tardes (ellas)*
—¿Les gusta a ellas leer por las tardes?
—Sí, les gusta leer por las tardes. or:
—No, no les gusta leer por las tardes.

1. gustar tomar el café negro (a ustedes)
2. fascinar comer platos mexicanos (a ellos)
3. importar hacer las tareas (a ella)
4. interesar aprender chino (a ti)
5. molestar acostarse temprano (a usted)
6. interesar mirar la televisión (a ti)
7. encantar comprar frutas frescas (a él)

Answers to Actividad 6:
1. a ustedes les gusta
2. a ellos les fascina
3. a ella le importa
4. a ti te interesa
5. a usted le molesta
6. a ti te interesa
7. a él le encanta

7 *¿Te importa?* You have to prepare a report for your sociology class. Following the model, ask four to six students questions and write the answers on the survey below. Write **M** for **mucho, P** for **poco,** and **N** for **nada.** What is the total for each column?

For **Actividad 7,** make sure that students have a list of each other's phone numbers and e-mail addresses to facilitate communication.

▸ **Modelo:** *la ecología*
—Marcela, ¿te importa la ecología?
—Sí, me importa mucho.

Nombre del/de la estudiante	La ecología	El dinero	Los amigos	Las clases
Marcela	M			
Total				

Have students read their summaries for **Actividad 8** to the class. As a follow-up ask, **¿Qué más les importa a los estudiantes de esta universidad?**

8 **Mi informe.** Write a summary, using the information from **Actividad 7.** Follow the model.

▸ **Modelo:** *La ecología les importa mucho. No les importa nada a X estudiantes.*

9 **¿Te caen bien o mal?** Work in pairs. Make a list of persons you know or of fictional characters from TV, film, or literature. Then ask each other which persons in the list you like or dislike. Follow the model.

▸ **Modelo:** *Nayeli*
—¿Te cae bien Oprah? or:
—¿Te parece simpática Oprah?
—Sí, me parece simpática. Ella me cae bien. or:
—No, me parece antipática. Ella me cae mal.

II. Establishing relationships through prepositions

Perspectivas

Prepositions establish relationships between different parts of a sentence and can show where people or things are located in space. Prepositions can also state direction, position in space, sequence in time, or abstract relationships between objects, events, and persons. This chart summarizes the most common prepositions.

After going over the prepositions with students, ask them the following questions based on the drawing:

1. **¿Dónde están los libros de ella? (Están sobre la silla.)**
2. **¿Dónde están las revistas de ella? (Están en el suelo y al lado de la cama.)**
3. **¿Dónde está su ropa? (Está fuera del armario.)**
4. **¿Dónde están las galletas y la Coca-Cola? (Están en el escritorio entre los papeles y los libros.)**
5. **¿Dónde está la ropa de él? (Está dentro del armario.)**
6. **¿Dónde están los papeles, libros y lápices de él? (Están sobre el escritorio.)**

Simple prepositions		**Compound prepositions**	
a	*to, for*	**al lado de**	*beside, to/on the side of*
bajo	*under*	**antes de**	*before*
con	*with*	**arriba de**	*up, on top of, above*
de	*from, of*	**cerca de**	*close to, near*
desde	*from, since*	**debajo de**	*underneath, below*
durante	*during*	**delante de**	*in front of*
en	*in, on, at*	**dentro de**	*inside of*
entre	*between, among*	**después de**	*after*
hacia	*toward*	**detrás de**	*behind, in back of*
hasta	*until*	**encima de**	*above, on top of, over, on*
para	*for, to, in order to*	**enfrente de**	*right in front of, across from*
por	*for, by means of*	**frente a**	*across from*
sin	*without*	**fuera de**	*outside of*
según	*according to*	**junto a**	*side-to-side with, close to*
sobre	*about, over, on top of*	**lejos de**	*far from*

- As you already know, when pronouns follow a preposition, the forms of the first and second person singular change to **mí** and **ti.** All the others retain the form of the subject pronoun.

- The preposition **con** has its own forms for the first and second persons singular.

The preposition *con*	
conmigo	*with me*
contigo	*with you*
con él/ella/usted	*with him/her/you*
con nosotros/nosotras	*with us*
con vosotros/vosotras	*with you*
con ellos/ellas/ustedes	*with them (masc./fem.)/you*

- **Entre** (*between, among*) is used differently than the other prepositions because subject pronouns are always used with it.

¡**Entre tú y yo** no hay secretos!	*There are no secrets between you and me!*
Esta información es un secreto **entre nosotros.**	*This information is a secret among us.*
No entiendo qué sucede **entre ellos.**	*I don't understand what is going on between them.*

Answers to Actividad 10:
1. para / para
2. con / con
3. conmigo / contigo
4. de / de
5. sin / sin
6. en

10 Conversaciones. You are in a discoteque and overhear the following comments and questions. Complete each one with a preposition from the list below. You can use some prepositions more than once.

con	contigo	detrás de	para
conmigo	de	en	sin

1. —¡Estas flores son _________ ti, mi amor!
   —¿Son _________ mí las flores? ¡Qué cariñoso eres!
2. —¿Quién está _________ Marianela?
   — Francisco, su primo, está _________ ella.
3. —¿Quieres ir al cine _________ mañana?
   — No gracias, no puedo ir _________.
4. —¿Eres la hermana _________ Jorge Vázquez?
   — Sí, soy la hermana mayor _________ él.
5. — Tú sabes que no puedes vivir _________ mí, ¿verdad?
   — Sí, yo sé muy bien que no puedo vivir _________ ti.
6. —¿Dónde está mi billete de tren?
   — Está _________ tu mochila.

For **Actividad 11,** help students check themselves by having each group give you one sentence at a time for a volunteer student to write on the board.

11 En la estación de autobuses. After studying the drawing, work with a classmate to talk about where things are in the bus station. Use as many of the prepositions you have learned as possible. Follow the model. Then compare with other classmates to see who has located correctly the most things and people.

► **Modelo:** —*¿Dónde están los periódicos y las revistas?*
— *Los periódicos y las revistas están fuera del kiosko.*
—*¿Y el perrito, dónde está?*
— *El perrito está...*

12 **¡Colas para todo!** Working with a partner, describe where the people are in the line to buy bus tickets.

For **Actividad 12,** have students give names to the different characters in the drawing.

▸ **Modelo:** —*El señor anciano está detrás de la señora alta, ¿verdad?*
—*No, el señor anciano está enfrente de ella.*

13 **¿Dónde están?** While you tell a partner where things are in your bedroom, he or she will make a rough sketch placing the objects according to your instructions. Switch roles. Then check each other's work. Use the questions below and create your own activity.

As a follow-up to **Actividad 13** bring in doll house furniture or make drawings and have students tell you where to place the different items.

1. ¿Dónde está tu cama, tu lámpara, tu silla... ?
2. ¿En qué lugar está tu computadora?
3. ¿Qué cosas hay al lado de tu computadora?
4. ¿Tienes un teléfono en tu cuarto? ¿Dónde está?
5. ¿Qué tienes en la pared?
6. ¿Dónde están la puerta y la ventana? ¿Hay balcón?
7. ¿...?

Lectura A

Introducción

As Felipe and Adriana travel to Spain, you will learn about that country's young people and the problems and pressures they face.

Reading strategy: Making notes in the margin

A useful reading strategy is to make notes in the margin of the text you are reading. This strategy allows you to react actively to the ideas in the reading selection. Here are some suggestions to apply this technique:

a. While you are reading, jot down in the margin one or two themes in Spanish which highlight the content of the reading;
b. Next, put down short questions in Spanish about particular ideas of importance related to the themes, as though you were in a dialog with the author;
c. Mark down your ideas in the margin in response to the reading's content;
d. Finally, make short-hand references to other written materials you have read which relate to this reading.

Los jóvenes° de España

young people

El 77% de los jóvenes españoles (entre 15-29 años de edad°) vive en la casa de sus padres, según datos° del Ministerio de Trabajo° y Asuntos° Sociales. Aproximadamente tres de cada cuatro jóvenes dependen de su familia hasta los 30 años, un fenómeno social forzado por el desempleo° y el elevado precio° de las residencias.

age
data / Labor
Affairs
unemployment / price

Un reciente estudio del Instituto de la Juventud° indica que desde 1984 a 1995 se duplicó el número de jóvenes que no son independientes. De éstos, el 62% de los muchachos salen de su domicilio° familiar° cuando se casan,° lo que° hacen más tarde que en otros tiempos.

Youth
dwelling / family
get married / which

El prototipo del joven español de hoy es el de un soltero° que valora° mucho la generación de sus padres; es conservador, estudioso y descontento porque no encuentra° trabajo. Los jóvenes contemporáneos necesitan 130.000 pesetas al mes para ser independientes, pero los más pobres ganan solamente° unas 90.000 pesetas.

single person / values
find
only

Una familia española.

1 ¿Verdadero o falso? Working with another person, read each sentence and write **V** if the idea about the reading is true (**verdadero**) or **F** if it is false (**falso**).

1. ________ Los jóvenes españoles salen de la casa de su familia cuando tienen quince años.
2. ________ Entre los jóvenes españoles no hay desempleo.
3. ________ Muchos jóvenes viven en sus casas hasta los 30 años.
4. ________ El prototipo del joven español es el de un chico liberal, casado y contento.
5. ________ Más del 50% de los jóvenes españoles vive con su familia hasta su matrimonio.
6. ________ Generalmente, un joven no puede vivir independientemente con menos de 100.000 pesetas al mes.

Answers to Actividad 1:
1. **F**
2. **F**
3. **V**
4. **F**
5. **V**
6. **F**

2 Números y más números. With a classmate, orally practice the numbers and dates from the reading.

3 Nuestras reacciones. Working in groups of four, make a chart of your group's reactions to the reading by comparing the notes you made in the margin. Follow these steps: (1) Jot down the themes that you have identified, (2) fill in your questions, (3) write down your ideas about each theme, (3) then add the references to other materials that you may already know.

	Preguntas	Mi idea	Otra referencia
Tema 1 Muchos jóvenes dependen de sus padres.			
Tema 2			
Tema 3			

4 Análisis. Discuss the following questions. You may also be asked to write a short paragraph in Spanish on one of the topics, using the vocabulary from the reading.

1. Compara las condiciones económicas de España y tu país con referencia al porcentaje de desempleo.
2. ¿Cuáles son tus probabilidades de conseguir trabajo después de tu graduación?
3. ¿Cuáles son las carreras profesionales que los jóvenes prefieren actualmente?
4. ¿Les gusta a los jóvenes de tu edad vivir con sus padres mientras estudian en la universidad?
5. ¿Por qué es importante ser independiente? ¿Qué significa para ti?

ETAPA B

Pistas y palabras

I. Making travel plans

En la agencia de viajes

BORINQUEN

CRUCERO CARIBEÑO

Disfrute° de una fantástica aventura en Puerto Rico, a bordo de los espectaculares barcos° de la compañía Cruceros S.A. — Enjoy / ships

Duración: 9 días y 8 noches
Precio: 925 dólares americanos
Incluye desayuno continental. Otras comidas son adicionales.

ATRACCIONES

Comida Buffet • Bar a bordo° — on board
Discoteca nocturna° • Tiendas — nightly
Clases de baile con excelentes instructores

GIMNASIO COMPLETO CON:

Ejercicios aeróbicos en grupo
Médico especialista en medicina deportiva
Equipos de ejercicios con pesas° — weights
Masaje terapéutico° — therapeutic massage

¡VIAJE A COSTA RICA!

Excursión de ecoturismo

Aproveche esta oportunidad de viajar a una selva tropical, de disfrutar los espectaculares volcanes y las hermosas playas de Costa Rica.

Duración: 7 días y 6 noches
Precio: 750 dólares americanos

INCLUYE

Pasaje aéreo desde Miami hasta San José
Transporte local
Guías especializados
Comidas típicas
Alojamiento en campamento o en casas particulares

Palabras y expresiones útiles

la excursión	*tour*
el folleto	*brochure*
el/la guía	*tour guide*
la guía	*guidebook*
el paquete	*package tour*
el pasaporte	*passport*
las vacaciones	*vacation*
el vuelo	*flight*

¡Buen viaje!/¡Feliz viaje!	*Have a nice trip!*
estar/irse de vacaciones	*to be/to go on vacation*
viajar	*to travel*

1 **¿Cuál viaje prefieres?** With a partner, compare the two posters on page 162 and tell which of the trips you would associate with the things in the list below. Then tell your partner which tour you prefer and why.

animales	nadar
caminar mucho	volcanes
bailes	comidas típicas
plantas y flores	sol y calor
agua	ecoturismo
insectos	aventura
comer mucho	comprar cosas
hacer ejercicio	

2 **En la agencia de viajes.** In groups of three, create a conversation in a travel agency in Spanish.

For **Actividad 2**, get a number of brochures from your local travel agency and distribute them among the "travel agents" in your groups.

Situation: Two friends (students A and B) are planning a trip together. They go to a travel agent to discuss where to go. Negotiate a vacation package that will suit all of their needs.

Student A	Student B	Travel Agent
You are a biology major and are interested in learning about tropical vegetation and animals. You only have a two-week vacation coming up and money is not a problem.	You want to get away to a relaxing and fun vacation spot in the Caribbean or in Central America. You love sports and swimming. You have a one-week vacation and are able to spend around $800 to go with your friend.	You are close to meeting your quota of sales for the month. You need to sell at least $1500 in package tours. You are able to offer customers a discount if they travel together.

II. Using ordinal numbers

Borinquen, crucero caribeño

Primer día	Por la mañana	Llegada de los pasajeros a Miami desde diferentes ciudades.
		Una limosina espera a cada uno de los pasajeros en el aeropuerto. Por favor, avísenos° su hora de llegada a Miami. (El precio de la excursión no incluye propinas.°)
	13.30	Almuerzo en el hotel con los guías del crucero y todos los participantes de la excursión. El precio del hotel incluye impuestos.°
Segundo día	7.30	Transporte desde el hotel al puerto en autobús. Los pasajeros deben estar listos en la recepción del hotel a las 7.25 de la mañana.
	8.30	Salida del crucero para San Juan.
	14.00	Llegada a San Juan.
Tercer día	8.00–15.00	Excursión y tour de la isla. (Opcional)
Cuarto día		Día libre° para recreo° o compras.
Quinto día	8.30	Paseo a la Isla Vieques.
	19.30	Cena y baile a bordo. Todas las noches hay un espectáculo diferente con las mejores orquestas y los mejores artistas del país.
Sexto día	8.45	Excursión en barco para pescar° en nuestras aguas cristalinas. (Opcional)
Séptimo día		Día libre para descansar.
Octavo día	8.30	Paseo a la Isla de Culebra.
	22.30	Excursión a las mejores discotecas para gozar° de las actividades nocturnas de la ciudad.
Noveno día	8.30	Salida del crucero para Miami.
	14.00	Llegada a Miami. Salida de Miami a sus países de residencia.

let us know
tips
taxes
free / recreation
to fish
to enjoy

- Ordinal numbers in Spanish (**primero, segundo, tercero...**) generally appear in front of the noun they modify and agree in gender and number.*

  segundo viaje *second trip* **cuarta** excursión *fourth excursion*

- Notice in the itinerary above that **primero** and **tercero** drop the **-o** in front of a masculine noun.
- Normally, after **décimo** (*tenth*), the cardinal numbers are used.

  el día **once** *the eleventh day*

** Notable exceptions are names of monarchs: Carlos V (quinto), (Charles the 5th).*

3 Comprensión. Answer these questions from the information found in the poster and in the itinerary.

1. ¿A qué país va el crucero?
2. ¿Cómo se llama la excursión?
3. ¿De qué ciudad sale y a qué hora?
4. ¿Qué atracciones ofrecen los buques de la compañía Cruceros S.A.?
5. ¿Cuánto cuesta el viaje? ¿Qué cosas no incluye el precio de la excursión?
6. ¿En qué van los pasajeros del aeropuerto al hotel en Miami?
7. ¿Qué excursiones opcionales hay para los pasajeros?
8. ¿Qué ofrece el gimnasio del barco?
9. ¿Qué días libres tienen los turistas?

Answers to Actividad 3:
1. Va a San Juan, Puerto Rico.
2. Borinquen
3. Sale de Miami a las 8.30.
4. Comida buffet, bar a bordo, discoteca nocturna, tiendas, clases de baile con excelentes instructores
5. Cuesta 925 dólares americanos. No incluye los almuerzos ni las cenas todos los días. No incluye el vuelo de ida y vuelta a Miami. No incluye las cosas opcionales.
6. Van en limosina.
7. Excursión y tour de la isla, excursión en barco para pescar.
8. Ejercicios aeróbicos en grupo, médico, pesas, masaje
9. El cuarto día y el séptimo día.

4 Un día libre. Create your own itinerary for your free day. Follow the model.

▸ **Modelo:** *Primero, voy a despertarme muy tarde. Segundo...*

Before doing **Actividad 4,** review reflexive verbs from Chapter 3.

5 Unas vacaciones increíbles. Create your own brochure for a vacation that you want to take. Be sure to include the destination, price, what the package includes, and special offers. Share your brochure with your classmates.

III. Talking about location

La geografía

Bring in any photos or postcards you may have of these cities.

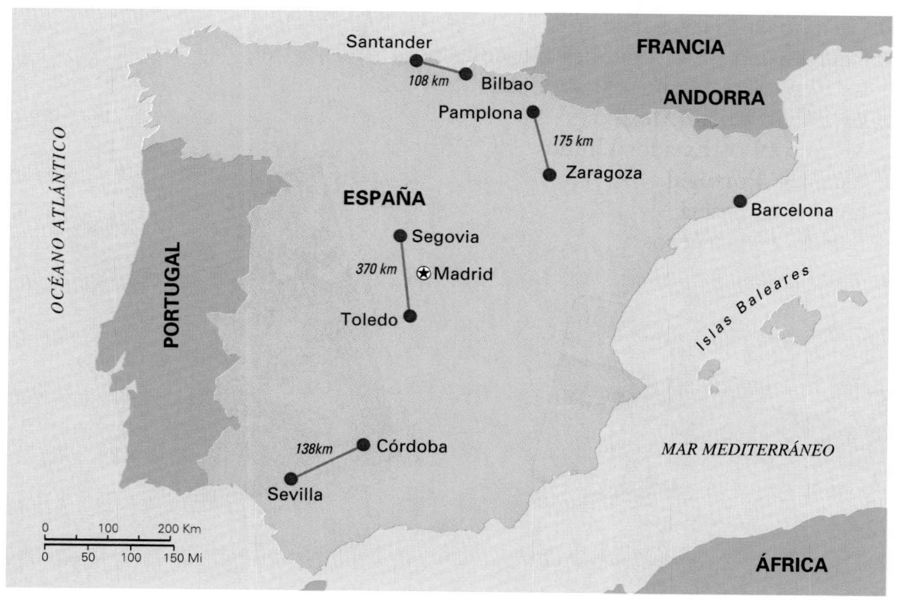

Segovia está a 370 km (*kilometers*) al norte de Toledo.
Sevilla está a 138 km al oeste de Córdoba.
Zaragoza está a 175 km al sur de Pamplona.
Bilbao está a 108 km al este de Santander.

6 Viajando en bicicleta. You and your friend want to tour five Spanish cities by bicycle. Use the chart to fill in your itinerary and routes. You can travel at a speed of 10 miles/hour. (1 mile = 1.6 kilometers)

De	A	¿Cuántos kilómetros?	¿Cuántas millas?
Barcelona	Lérida	150 km al oeste	240 millas al oeste
1.			
2.			
3.			
4.			
5.			

7 La clase de geografía. Refer to the maps on the inside front and back covers of this book in order to answer the following questions about the geography of the Spanish-speaking world.

► **Modelo:** *Costa Rica / Panamá*
Costa Rica está al noroeste de Panamá.*
Panamá está al sureste de Costa Rica.*

1. México / Guatemala
2. Honduras / Nicaragua
3. Guatemala / Honduras
4. Puerto Rico / La República Dominicana
5. La República Dominicana / Cuba
6. Baja California / México
7. México / Los Estados Unidos
8. España / Portugal
9. España / Francia
10. España / Marruecos

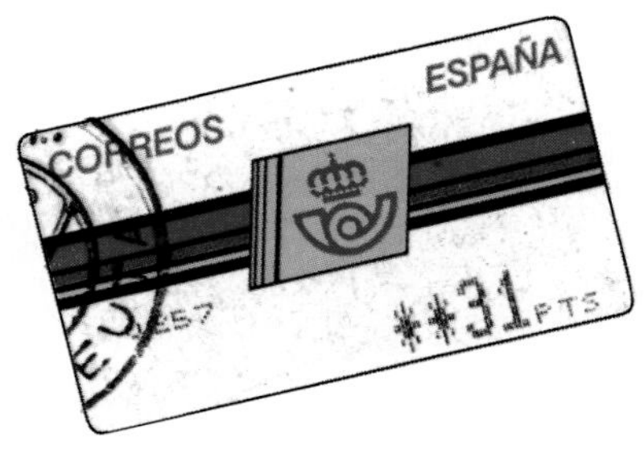

* ***noreste*** = *northeast,* ***noroeste*** = *northwest,* ***sureste*** = *southeast,* ***suroeste*** = *southwest,* ***central*** = *central*

Bring in some of your own photos or postcards of Granada and Córdoba and/or have students look up these cities on the Internet.

ENLACE CULTURAL

España

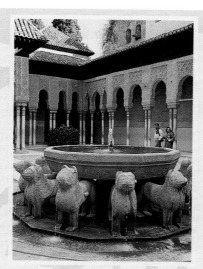

España está en la Península Ibérica, tiene casi 40 millones de habitantes y un área de 504.750 km² (kilómetros cuadrados°). Es un país montañoso y tiene un clima muy variado. Al norte está el Mar Cantábrico; al oeste, el Océano Atlántico; al este el Mar Mediterráneo y al sur, África del Norte, a casi 13 kilómetros de la costa española. Los montes Pirineos están al noreste y separan el país del resto del continente Europeo.

España es un país multicultural y sus habitantes hablan varios idiomas: español, vasco,° catalán,° gallego° y mallorquín.° La historia española también tiene influencia de muchas culturas importantes: la cultura cristiana, la judía° y la cultura islámica o musulmana°. Por ejemplo, en Granada está la Alhambra, un hermoso palacio de arquitectura musulmana. En sus jardines° está el famoso Patio de los leones.°

Patio de los leones en la Alhambra.

La famosa Mezquita° de Córdoba está en esa ciudad. Su construcción empezó en el año 785 y terminó en el año 985; tiene 850 columnas de casi 4 metros de altura° y dentro de ella hay una iglesia cristiana del siglo XVI. En Córdoba hay también una sinagoga del siglo IV, en honor del gran filósofo y médico judío, Maimónides.

square

Basque / Catalan / Galician / Mallorcan

Jewish / Muslim

gardens / lions

Mosque

height

Discusión en grupos

La Mezquita de Córdoba.

1. ¿Cuáles son tres culturas importantes en la historia de España? ¿Dónde podemos ver la influencia de estas culturas?
2. ¿Qué idiomas hablan en España?
3. Describan un monumento o un lugar representativo de una cultura de su país o de su región.
4. Además del inglés, ¿qué idiomas hablan los habitantes de los Estados Unidos? ¿Qué idiomas hablan sus compañeros/as de clase?

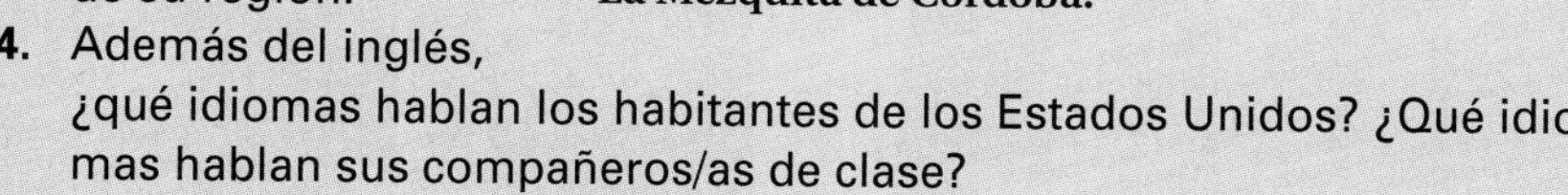

Answers:
1. cristiana, judía, islámica o musulmana. La Alhambra, la Mezquita de Córdoba y la iglesia cristiana dentro de la mezquita, la sinagoga de Córdoba.
2. español, vasco, catalán, gallego, mallorquín
3. and 4. *Answers will vary.*

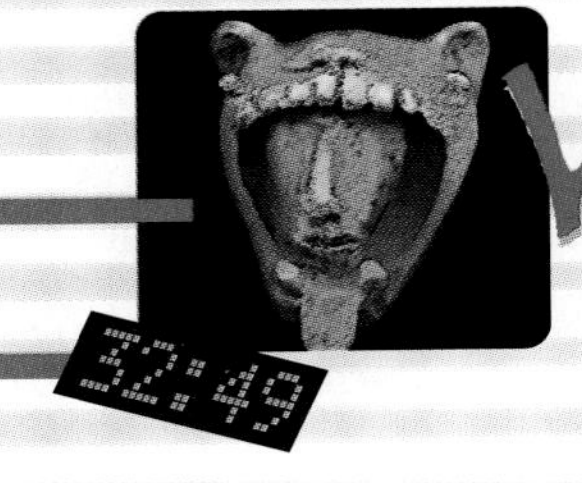

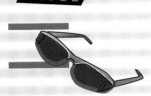

Vistas y voces

I. Preparémonos

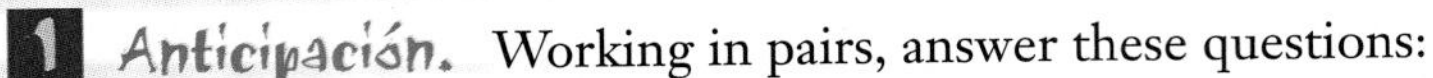

1 Anticipación. Working in pairs, answer these questions:

A. **1.** Menciona una biblioteca importante o un archivo nacional o regional. ¿Qué tipo de documentos tiene? ¿En qué ciudad está?

2. ¿Te gusta visitar la biblioteca de tu ciudad o de tu universidad? ¿Qué tiene?

3. ¿Recibes mensajes de correo electrónico? ¿Quién te escribe?

4. ¿Te dan miedo las cosas, ciudades o personas desconocidas (*unknown*)?

B. Review chapter opening photo 4B. What do you think the **Archivo de las Indias** is? Do you believe that Adriana is going to find Nayeli there? What do you think that Adriana learns there?

Para comprender mejor

el archivo	*archive, document*	ni idea	*haven't got a clue*
asustado/a	*frightened*	¡Oye!	*Listen! Hey!*
averiguar	*to find out*	parar de	*to stop (doing)*
besar	*to kiss*	¡Qué alivio!	*What a relief!*
deshacerse de	*to get rid of*	¡Qué gusto!	*What a pleasure!*
espantoso/a	*frightening*	¡Qué susto!	*What a scare!*
estar a punto de	*to be about to*	recoger	*to pick up*
la isla	*island*	vigilar	*to watch*

2 Secuencia. In pairs, describe the action occurring in each video action shot.

1.

2.

3.

4.

II. Miremos y escuchemos

3 Observaciones. While watching this episode, circle the letter of the correct answer.

1. En el hotel, Felipe y Adriana reciben un mensaje de correo electrónico de esta persona. ¿Cómo se llama?
   a. Nayeli Paz Ocotlán b. Armando de Landa c. Gerardo Covarrubias
2. Alguien está contentísimo de saber que los boletos para Puerto Rico están en el aeropuerto de Barajas en Madrid. ¿Quién es?
   a. el chofer del camión b. el agente de viajes c. Felipe
3. En el hotel, Adriana mira el libro de Nayeli. ¿Cuál es el título del libro?
   a. *El camino del jaguar* c. *La tumba de Pacal*
   b. *Los héroes gemelos de Xibalbá*
4. Nayeli sale de la agencia de viajes después de comprar un boleto de avión. ¿Adónde va?
   a. a Puerto Rico b. al Ecuador c. a Costa Rica
5. Los eventos de este episodio ocurren en la ciudad de
   a. Sevilla. b. San Juan. c. Quito.

Answers to Actividad 3:
1. b
2. c
3. b
4. b
5. a

III. Comentemos

4 Comprensión. In groups, answer the following questions.

1. ¿Cuál es el número de la casa de los Covarrubias?
2. ¿Sabe la señora Covarrubias dónde está su esposo? ¿Cómo está ella?
3. Adriana va al Archivo General de Indias. ¿La acompaña Felipe?
4. ¿De quién recibe Felipe un correo electrónico? ¿Qué dice su mensaje?
5. ¿Quién persigue a Adriana? ¿Cómo está ella al regresar al hotel?
6. ¿De quién es la foto que hay en el libro que Adriana lee en la habitación del hotel?
7. ¿Qué le cuenta Adriana a Felipe?
8. ¿Qué le cuenta Felipe a Adriana?
9. ¿Para dónde es el boleto de avión que compra Nayeli?
10. ¿Parece Nayeli triste, alegre o preocupada cuando recibe la rosa?

Answers to Actividad 4:
1. 7 (siete)
2. La señora Covarrubias no sabe dónde está su esposo. Ella está nerviosa (preocupada).
3. No la acompaña Felipe.
4. Felipe lee un correo electrónico de Armando de Landa. Dice que Nayeli está bien y que está esperándolos en San Juan, Puerto Rico.
5. El señor del anillo raro persigue a Adriana. Adriana tiene miedo.
6. de Nayeli
7. Adriana le cuenta que un hombre de anillo raro la persigue.
8. que tienen un mensaje de correo electrónico de Armando y dice que Nayeli está bien y que él y Adriana tienen que ir a Puerto Rico
9. para Quito, Ecuador
10. parece alegre

5 Yo creo que... In pairs, discuss the following question: ¿Qué crees que van a hacer estas personas?

1. Nayeli: ¿Va a encontrarse con Felipe y Adriana? ¿Va a hablar con la policía?
2. Adriana y Felipe: ¿Van a hablar con el señor del anillo raro? ¿Van a tener una relación romántica?
3. El chofer del camión: ¿Va a volver a su casa? ¿Va a hablar con Nayeli otra vez? ¿Le va a pasar algo malo?
4. El hombre del anillo raro: ¿Va a perseguir a Adriana en Puerto Rico? ¿Va a capturar a Adriana?

6 Miremos otra vez. After viewing the episode, put the video action shots in the correct order.

Correct order of video action shots: 2, 1, 3, 4

7 ¡Qué gusto! In trios, describe Sevilla by answering the following question: ¿Qué cosas, sitios, personas y actividades observas en Sevilla en este episodio?

Lengua

I. Retelling simple past events

A. Preterite indicative of regular verbs

Un día fantástico

Querido Diario:

El viernes, por primera vez, Oscar **me llamó**° por teléfono y **me invitó**° a salir. El sábado **pasé**° un día fantástico. Oscar **llegó**° a las ocho de la noche. **Fuimos**° a un restaurante, **comimos**° y él **me contó**° muchas cosas sobre su vida. A mí **me pareció**° todo muy interesante. Cuando **salimos**° del restaurante, yo le **pregunté**°: "¿Te voy a ver otra vez?°" Y él me **contestó**:° "¡Sí! Me vas a ver muchas, muchas veces más."

he called me / he invited me
I had / he arrived
We went / we ate / he told me
it seemed to me
got out / I asked him / again
he answered

To talk about actions that were completed in the past, use the preterite. To conjugate regular verbs in the preterite, the endings shown on page 171 are added to the stem of the verb:

	-ar (llamar)	-er (comer)	-ir (salir)
yo	llam**é**	com**í**	sal**í**
tú	llam**aste**	com**iste**	sal**iste**
él/ella, usted	llam**ó**	com**ió**	sal**ió**
nosotros/nosotras	llam**amos**	com**imos**	sal**imos**
vosotros/vosotras	llam**asteis**	com**isteis**	sal**isteis**
ellos/ellas, ustedes	llam**aron**	com**ieron**	sal**ieron**

- Note that the first and the third persons singular have a written accent.
- Verbs that end in **-er** and **-ir** have identical forms in the preterite.

B. Preterite indicative of verbs with orthographic changes

- Verbs ending in **-car, -gar,** and **-zar** change spelling in the first person singular.

Felipe, te **busqué** en el hotel.	*Felipe, I looked for you at the hotel.*
Te **expliqué** lo que pasó con el hombre del anillo misterioso.	*I explained to you what happened with the man with the mysterious ring.*
Llegué al hotel muy asustada.	*I arrived at the hotel very frightened.*
Empecé a sentirme mejor al hablar contigo.	*I started to feel better talking to you.*

	c > qu (buscar)	g > gu (jugar)	z > c (abrazar)
yo	**busqué**	**jugué**	**abracé**
tú	buscaste	jugaste	abrazaste
él/ella, usted	buscó	jugó	abrazó
nosotros/nosotras	buscamos	jugamos	abrazamos
vosotros/vosotras	buscasteis	jugasteis	abrazasteis
ellos/ellas, ustedes	buscaron	jugaron	abrazaron

Other verbs with orthographical changes include:

c > qu		g > gu		z > c	
explicar	**expliqué**	llegar	**llegué**	comenzar	**comencé**
practicar	**practiqué**	pagar	**pagué**	empezar	**empecé**
tocar	**toqué**				

1 **Mi primer día de práctica.** Mario's internship at the city library started yesterday, and he describes to his friend Lupe what he did. Change all the verbs to the preterite to tell Mario's story in the past. Follow the model.

► **Modelo:** *Me levanté a las siete...*

Me levanto a las siete. Me ducho, desayuno, y tomo el autobús número setenta y tres para el trabajo. Llego a la biblioteca a las ocho y media. Bebo un café con leche con mi jefa y converso con ella sobre mis responsabilidades en el trabajo. Después llegan muchos clientes y me preguntan por libros de diferentes temas. A

Answers to Actividad 1:
1. me levanté
2. Me duché
3. desayuné
4. tomé
5. Llegué
6. Bebí
7. conversé
8. llegaron
9. preguntaron

10. almorcé
11. empezó
12. Llegaron
13. salí
14. cené

mediodía, almuerzo con mi jefa y con otro de los empleados en un pequeño café cerca de la biblioteca. Por la tarde, la gente empieza a llegar después de las cuatro. Llegan muchos chicos y chicas buscando material para sus proyectos. A las seis de la tarde, salgo para casa, pero antes ceno en el restaurante La buena mesa con Ricardo, otro de los chicos de la biblioteca. ¡Qué día tan interesante y productivo!

Answers to Actividad 2:
1. toqué
2. empecé
3. llegué
4. practiqué
5. abracé
6. pagué
7. jugué
8. busqué

2 Práctica. Answer the following questions, using the correct form of the preterite. Follow the model.

► **Modelo:** —*¿Explicaste el problema? (Sí)*
—*Sí, expliqué el problema.*

1. ¿Tocaste la guitarra en el concierto? (Sí)
2. ¿Empezaste tus lecciones de tenis? (No)
3. ¿Llegaste tarde esta mañana? (No)
4. ¿Practicaste fútbol el año pasado? (Sí)
5. ¿Abrazaste a tu novia durante la ceremonia de bodas? (Sí)
6. ¿Pagaste la cuenta de la tienda de ropa? (Sí)
7. ¿Jugaste al volibol anoche? (No)
8. ¿Buscaste el horario del tren? (Sí)

C. Preterite indicative of *ir* and *ser*

The verbs **ir** and **ser** are irregular in the preterite. Both have the same forms.

	ir / ser
yo	**fui**
tú	**fuiste**
él/ella, Ud.	**fue**
nosotros/nosotras	**fuimos**
vosotros/vosotras	**fuisteis**
ellos/ellas, Uds.	**fueron**

Answers to Actividad 3:
1. fue
2. fuimos
3. compramos
4. salimos
5. llegamos
6. visitaron
7. entramos
8. nos probamos
9. fuimos
10. comieron
11. bebí
12. visitamos
13. fuimos
14. conocimos
15. escuchamos
16. bailamos
17. salimos

3 Un fin de semana maravilloso. Nela describes her weekend in Boston. Use the preterite tense of each of the verbs in parentheses to complete her paragraph.

El fin de semana pasado _________ (ser) muy divertido. Mis amigas Rosa, Marta y yo _________ (ir) de vacaciones a Boston. Nosotras _________ (comprar) un viaje muy barato en la agencia de viajes "Viajes Boston". Nosotras _________ (salir) de Nueva York muy tarde el viernes por la noche y _________ (llegar) a la medianoche a la ciudad. El sábado, Rosa y Marta _________ (visitar) primero a su abuela que vive allí. Después, nosotras _________ (entrar) a la tienda Filene's y _________ (probarse) unos zapatos y unas chaquetas. El domingo, _________ (ir) a comer a un restaurante elegante en la calle Newbury. Marta y Rosa _________ (comer) pollo con arroz pero yo solamente _________ (beber) un jugo de frutas. Por la tarde, nosotras _________ (visitar) el Museo de Ciencias.

Por la noche nosotras __________ (ir) a una discoteca. Allí __________ (conocer) a unos chicos muy simpáticos, __________ (escuchar) música y __________ (bailar) toda la noche. Nosotras __________ (salir) de Boston el lunes a las 6.00 de la mañana. ¡Quiero regresar muy pronto!

4 **De viaje.** The Ramírez family went to Europe on vacation. Rogelio called his grandmother to tell her about the trip. Complete their conversation using the preterite.

ABUELA: Cuéntame (*tell me*), Rogelio, ¿cómo __________ (ser) las vacaciones en Europa?
ROGELIO: Abuela, __________ (ser) maravillosas.
ABUELA: ¡Qué bien! ¿Cuántos países __________ (visitar) ustedes?
ROGELIO: __________ (ir) a Francia, Italia y España. Nos encantaron todos.
ABUELA: ¿Qué medios de transporte __________ (usar) ustedes?
ROGELIO: Primero, nosotros __________ (volar) en avión a Italia donde __________ (visitar) los museos y el Vaticano; segundo, __________ (pasear) en coche por Francia, y luego, __________ (tomar) el tren a Barcelona.
ABUELA: ¿Qué les __________ (gustar) a ustedes en Barcelona?
ROGELIO: Papá y mi hermana Patricia __________ (nadar) en la playa y __________ (caminar) en la zona antigua de la ciudad. Ellos __________ (llegar) al hotel muy tarde. Abuela, toda la familia __________ (pasar) unas vacaciones deliciosas.
ABUELA: Pues, la próxima vez, ¡quiero ir yo también!

Answers to Actividad 4:
1. fueron
2. fueron
3. visitaron
4. Fuimos
5. usaron
6. volamos
7. visitamos
8. paseamos
9. tomamos
10. gustó
11. nadaron
12. caminaron
13. llegaron
14. pasó

5 **¿Qué hiciste ayer?** In pairs, ask each other two typical questions in the preterite for the following settings. Choose two verbs from each of the lists in parentheses.

▶ **Modelo:** En casa (leer / despertarse / limpiar / descansar)
—*¿Qué hiciste en casa ayer?*
—*Me desperté tarde y después limpié la cocina.*

1. En casa (comer / despertarse / limpiar / tocar música)
2. En la escuela (estudiar / escribir / escuchar / discutir)
3. En el gimnasio (correr / practicar deportes / usar las máquinas / caminar rápido)
4. En el cine (mirar / beber / hablar / reunirse con amigos)
5. En la tienda (comprar / buscar / pagar / probarse)
6. En el parque (caminar / practicar / jugar / correr)

6 **Querido Diario.** Write ten sentences in the preterite. Choose from the following verbs.

bailar	practicar	caminar
despertarse	levantarse	ducharse
llegar	empezar	ir
comprar	estudiar	trabajar
acostarse	jugar	tocar la guitarra
salir	buscar	comer

Compile a pop-quiz from sentences students hand in for the next class. To facilitate this, have students hand in diskettes or e-mail their answers to you in addition to the hard copy for class.

II. Indicating when actions were completed

Adverbs of time

You have already learned many adverbs of manner and time. Adverbs of time modify verbs and indicate when actions are completed.

¿Cuándo ocurrió?

—¿Me dices que Héctor chocó su coche **ayer?**
Are you telling me that Héctor crashed his car yesterday?

—Sí, pero no pasó nada grave.
Yes, but nothing serious happened.

—Y ¿a qué hora ocurrió el accidente?
At what time did the accident occur?

—**Anoche,** después de la cena.
Last night, after dinner.

—¡Vaya! Menos mal que Héctor está bien.
Well, it's a relief that Héctor is fine.

Adverbial expressions of time		
ayer	*yesterday*	El accidente ocurrió ayer. *The accident happened yesteday.*
anteayer	*the day before yesterday*	Compramos toda la comida anteayer. *We bought all the food the day before yesterday.*
anoche	*last night*	La visita de México llegó anoche. *The visitor from Mexico arrived last night.*
anteanoche	*the night before last*	Anteanoche no dormí nada. *I didn't sleep at all the night before last.*
la semana pasada	*last week*	Abrieron la nueva tienda la semana pasada. *They opened the new store last week.*
el fin de semana pasado	*last weekend*	Fuimos a bailar el fin de semana pasado. *We went dancing last weekend.*
el año pasado	*last year*	Terminé mis estudios el año pasado. *I finished my studies last year.*
el mes pasado	*last month*	Pagamos nuestras cuentas el mes pasado. *We paid our bills last month.*

Point out that in **fin de semana pasado, pasado** is masculine because it agrees with **fin.**

7 **Quiero saber...** With a partner, answer the following questions using the cues provided. Follow the model.

▸ **Modelo:** —*¿Cuándo visitaste la catedral de Sevilla? (la semana pasada)*
—*Visité la catedral de Sevilla la semana pasada.*

1. ¿Cuándo cenaste comida española? (ayer)
2. ¿Cuándo le explicaste la lección a Marta? (la semana pasada)
3. ¿Cuándo le compraste el regalo a Martín? (anteayer)
4. ¿Cuándo reservaste los billetes? (el jueves pasado)
5. ¿Cuándo pensaste en mí durante tu viaje? (anoche)
6. ¿Cuándo fuiste a la discoteca? (el sábado pasado)
7. ¿Cuándo saliste con tus amigos en Málaga? (anteanoche)
8. ¿Cuándo fuiste de vacaciones a Bolivia? (el mes pasado)
9. ¿Cuándo compraste el coche? (el año pasado)

8 **Preguntas personales.** With a partner, answer the following questions. Then report your findings to the class.

1. ¿Adónde fuiste ayer?
2. ¿Bailaste anteayer?
3. ¿Fuiste de vacaciones el año pasado? ¿Adónde?
4. ¿Escribiste composiciones el mes pasado? ¿Sobre qué temas?
5. ¿Estudiaste anoche?

III. Avoiding redundancy

Direct-object pronouns

Preparando el viaje

ADELAIDA: No encuentro mi maleta azul. **La** necesito para empacar mis cosas.
ARTURO: **La** tengo lista; aquí está la maleta. También tengo los tiquetes de avión.
ADELAIDA: **Los** tienes también, ¡qué bien! Mil gracias. ¿Y el dinero?
ARTURO: También **lo** tengo aquí. Supongo que fuiste a la embajada americana y sacaste las visas, ¿verdad?
ADELAIDA: ¿Las visas? Claro, fui ayer a la embajada para pedir**las.**
ARTURO: Es importante tener**las.**
ADELAIDA: Sí, **lo** sé. Sin visas no podemos viajar.

A direct object is the person or thing that directly receives the action of the verb. In the sentences above, **mi maleta azul** is the first direct object. Once the object is stated, it is replaced by a direct-object pronoun to avoid redundancy: ***La* necesito para empacar mis cosas.**

In the selection above, identify the remaining direct-object nouns that correspond to the pronouns in boldface.

The direct-object pronouns are:

me	*me*	**nos**	*us*
te	*you*	**os**	*you*
lo, la	*him, her, you*	**los, las**	*them, you*

Stress that, as with indirect-object pronouns, direct-object pronouns usually go right before the conjugated verb even when the sentence is negative. **Yo no lo escribo.** Also, as with indirect-object pronouns, in the progressive tense direct-object pronouns can go either right before the conjugated verb or attached to the end of the participle. To practice direct-object pronouns, give your student a book and ask **¿Lo recibiste? (Sí, lo recibí.**). Then give two books; a piece of chalk, then two pieces of chalk, asking the same question, but appropriately modifying the pronoun. Also ask **¿Me llamaste anoche? (No, no la/lo llamé.**). Draw a stick figure on the board and ask **¿Nos llamaste...? (No, no los llamé....)**

- Direct-object pronouns are placed immediately before the conjugated verb.

¿Y **los boletos?**	*And the tickets?*
Los recogemos en Barajas.	*We'll pick them up in Barajas.*

- Direct-object pronouns are attached to the end of the infinitive when the infinitive is in expressions such as **es importante** and **es necesario** or in prepositional expressions such as **para recibir*las*, para visitar*la*.**

Me gusta tener un buen mapa.	*I like to have a good map.*
Sí, es bueno tener**lo.**	*Yes, it's good to have it (one).*
¿Vas a visitar a tu prima en Barajas?	*Are you going to visit your cousin in Barajas?*
Sí, en este momento salgo para visitar**la.**	*Yes, I am leaving right now to visit her.*

- When the direct object is used together with a conjugated verb and an infinitive, for example, in expressions that you already know: **tengo que comprar, voy a hacer, acabo de escribir,** the pronoun can go either before the conjugated verb or attached to the end of the infinitive:

Tenemos que encontrar al chofer que llevó al jaguar.	*We have to find the driver who brought the jaguar.*
Lo tenemos que encontrar. *or* Tenemos que encontrar**lo.**	*We have to find him.*
Quiero pedir una habitación más grande.	*I want to ask for a larger room.*
La quiero pedir./Quiero pedir**la.**	*I want to ask for it.*

Before doing this exercise, remind students that the personal **a** indicates a direct object that is a person or an animal.

Answers to Actividad 9:

1. La quiero mucho.
2. Las compré.
3. Los miro.
4. Los turistas la escuchan.
5. Lo acuesto en su cama.
6. Lo desperté temprano.
7. ¿Lo llamó usted?
8. Lo podemos tomar/Podemos tomarlo.
9. La llamamos.

9 Sin repeticiones. Write sentences replacing the direct-object nouns with direct-object pronouns. Follow the model.

▸ **Modelo:** *Miranda compra los pasajes.*
Miranda los compra.

1. Quiero mucho a Manuela.
2. Compré unas gafas.
3. Miro los balcones de Sevilla.
4. Los turistas escuchan música.
5. Acuesto al niño en su cama.
6. Desperté a mi hermano temprano.
7. ¿Llamó usted al médico?
8. Podemos tomar el autobús.
9. Llamamos a nuestra profesora.

Answers to Actividad 10:

1. Sí, lo encontré.
2. Sí, las escribí.
3. Sí, lo compré.
4. Sí, lo recibí.
5. Sí, la estudié.
6. Sí, lo llamé.
7. Sí, las pagué.

10 Preguntas personales. You are getting ready for a trip to Uruguay and your brother asks you if you have everything ready. Answer his questions using direct-object pronouns.

▸ **Modelo:** *—¿Reservaste el hotel?*
—Sí, lo reservé.

1. ¿Encontraste tu pasaporte?
2. ¿Escribiste las cartas?
3. ¿Compraste el pasaje?
4. ¿Recibiste el dinero?
5. ¿Estudiaste la tarea de español?
6. ¿Llamaste al médico para las vacunas?
7. ¿Pagaste las cuentas?

11 **¿Qué me falta?** Your roommate wants to know all about your vacation plans. Answer his/her questions using direct-object pronouns. Follow the model.

▸ **Modelo:** *tener que comprar los billetes*
—¿Tienes que comprar los billetes?
—Sí, los tengo que comprar. or: *—Sí, tengo que comprarlos.*

1. tener que vender el auto
2. tener que reservar las habitaciones del hotel Ramos
3. acabar de preparar la cena
4. acabar de hacer las invitaciones
5. ir a invitar a los amigos
6. ir a celebrar la fiesta de cumpleaños
7. poder hablar español
8. querer conocer a gente
9. querer hacer muchos viajes

Lectura B

Introducción

Adriana y Felipe take the AVE train from Madrid to Sevilla and find out that they have to return to Madrid to catch a plane to Puerto Rico. While in Sevilla, they see that they have some time left before the AVE leaves and they decide to take a short tour of Sevilla. Let's see what they learn about the city.

Prelectura

1 **Una ciudad que conozco.** With a classmate, take turns describing a city to which each of you has traveled with family or friends. Answer the following questions and then compare your answers with those of other students.

1. ¿Cómo se llama la ciudad? ¿Dónde está? ¿Cuántos habitantes hay?
2. ¿Es una ciudad muy vieja o es muy nueva?
3. ¿Hay iglesias y edificios importantes? ¿Cómo son?
4. ¿Qué tipos de restaurantes tiene? ¿Hay muchas tiendas allí?
5. ¿Cuáles son los principales sitios turísticos de interés?
6. ¿Quién es alguna persona famosa de esa ciudad?
7. ¿Es famosa la ciudad por algún evento importante?

La encantadora° ciudad de Sevilla

charming

Sevilla es la cuarta ciudad de España. Tiene 704.857 habitantes y es la capital de la provincia de Andalucía. Hay parques hermosos y sus edificios tienen muy variados estilos arquitectónicos. La Catedral de Sevilla, de estilo gótico, es una de las más famosas del mundo; es la tercera en tamaño° después de la Catedral de San Pedro en Roma y la de San Pablo en Londres.° Los reyes° de España eligieron° la Catedral de Sevilla para la gran boda° de su hija, Elena, en 1996.

size

London / king and queen / chose / wedding

tower

bell tower
weather vane / view

Renaissance Baroque

outside

shore

Junto a la Catedral de Sevilla está La Giralda, que es una alta torre° rectangular de casi 117.5 metros de altura. En 1184 se empezó su construcción de arquitectura musulmana y en 1555 el arquitecto Hernán Ruiz adicionó el campanario,° como el de una iglesia cristiana, con una gran figura de bronce como veleta.° Desde la torre hay una magnífica vista° panorámica de la ciudad de Sevilla.

El Archivo de Indias, de estilo barroco-renacentista,° tiene muchos documentos sobre el comercio con las Américas durante la época de la colonización y colonia.

Como en Madrid, en Sevilla hay bares al aire libre° para comer tapas. En Sevilla, la hora más animada para disfrutar de las tapas es de la una a cuatro de la tarde, cerca de la orilla° del río Guadalquivir.

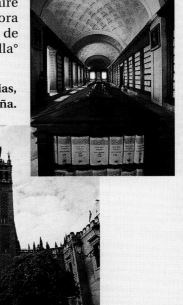

El Archivo General de Indias, Sevilla, España.

▲ La Catedral de Sevilla, España.
► La Giralda, Sevilla, España.

Answers to Actividad 2:
1. grande
2. La catedral de Sevilla
3. Elena, la hija de los Reyes de España / Los Reyes
4. alta, musulmana y cristiana, casi 117,5 metros
5. documentos sobre el comercio con las Américas
6. de la una hasta las cuatro de la tarde, en bares al aire libre cerca de la orilla del río Guadalquivir
7. *Answers will vary.*

Assign **Actividad 3** as homework and give students about a week to do this. You can either let them choose their cities or assign them. Students can find information in the library or on the Internet. Their talk should be delivered orally to the class and should be about two minutes long.

Optional: Una ciudad fascinante. Students write a half-page description of an attractive, touristic city in their country for the magazine *Viajes.* Include information answering the questions in **Actividad 1.**

Postlectura

2 Comprensión. In pairs, answer the following questions based on the reading.

1. ¿Es Sevilla una ciudad española grande o pequeña?
2. ¿Cuál es la tercera catedral más grande del mundo?
3. ¿Quién se casó en la Catedral de Sevilla? ¿Quién eligió la catedral para la boda?
4. ¿Cómo es la Giralda? ¿De qué estilo es? ¿Qué altura tiene?
5. ¿Qué hay en el Archivo de Indias?
6. ¿Cuáles son las horas más animadas para comer tapas en Sevilla? ¿Y dónde?
7. Describan qué más hay en las fotos de Sevilla.

3 Dos ciudades interesantes. You are a television reporter for the program "Vamos a viajar." You have to do research and give a short presentation with visuals about two cities in Spain. The title of your two-paragraph talk is "Vamos a viajar a dos fascinantes ciudades españolas."

En resumen

I. Hablemos

1 **¿Cómo es el campus?** How good are you at describing? Work with a partner to describe the location of five items or places on campus. Partner A describes where the items or places are in relationship to one another while Partner B draws them. Use only Spanish and do not use any visual cues. Check the accuracy of the drawing and switch roles.

2 **¿Adónde van los señores Covarrubias?** After sending the jaguar twin off to Ecuador, Sr. Covarrubias decides to take a little trip with his wife with the money he was paid to transport the jaguar. With a partner create a conversation between them to plan the trip. Choose at least three different locations and three different means of transportation to get there. Also discuss what activities they will do while hiding out on "vacation."

II. Investiguemos por Internet

Identifying country domains

Travel and tourist information on the Internet is extensive and you will find up-to-date facts about cities, tourist attractions, modes of transportation, hotels, and prices. In the Internet activities for this chapter, you will be looking for train information in Spain and for cruises in the Caribbean. For help, go to the Houghton Mifflin's Web site at any time.

When you are looking for information originating in a specific country, it is useful to look at the country domain of the Internet address. The domain will tell you where the server is registered. For example, the address **http://www.renfe.es** is in Spain because the last part of the address, **es**, corresponds to **España**.

3 **Viaje en tren.** As you have seen in this chapter, the Spanish railways company, RENFE (Red Nacional de Ferrocarriles Españoles) has a well-developed railway network. Work in groups to create a travel itinerary by train for your class. First, select one of these tours: (a) Madrid–Barcelona; (b) Sevilla–Madrid; (c) Huelva–Madrid. Then, look for the RENFE Web site. If you enter **RENFE** as a keyword, you may get many sites with related information. The selection will vary depending on the search engine you use. However, your best bet is to look for the main RENFE Web site. Try the address mentioned in *Investiguemos.*

You can make photocopies and/or transparencies from these Web sites in **Actividad 3** for use in the classroom.

4 **Un crucero maravilloso.** Imagine that you need to look for cruise information for some friends traveling to the Spanish-speaking Caribbean or to the "Mexican Riviera" (Puerto Vallarta, Mazatlán, Los Cabos, Acapulco). Work in groups and select one of the many tours offered on the Internet. Focus only on the most important facts, for example, departure and destination locations, dates, price, and special services. Try the word **crucero** as the first keyword or go directly to the information provided by the national tourism offices in Mexico or any of the Caribbean countries.

Vocabulario informático

dominio Internet	*Internet domain*

III. Escribamos

Writing strategy: Creating a time line

Another way to organize information visually is by use of a time line. This visual is good when planning to write about a sequence of events. This could be a sequence of events over a brief period of time or over a long period of time. By using a time line, it also helps you see the effects that earlier events have had on subsequent events.

▶ **Modelo:**

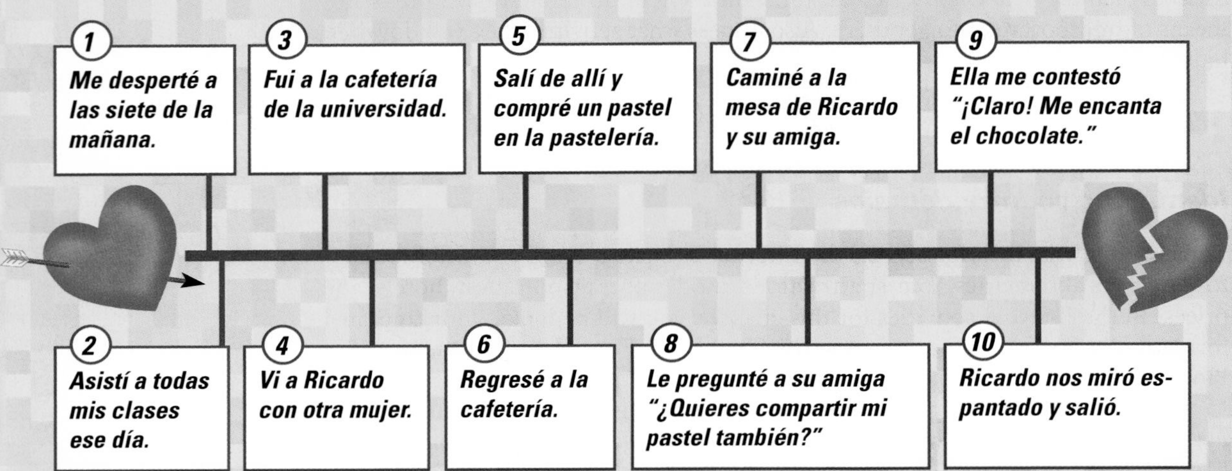

1 Me desperté a las siete de la mañana.
2 Asistí a todas mis clases ese día.
3 Fui a la cafetería de la universidad.
4 Vi a Ricardo con otra mujer.
5 Salí de allí y compré un pastel en la pastelería.
6 Regresé a la cafetería.
7 Caminé a la mesa de Ricardo y su amiga.
8 Le pregunté a su amiga "¿Quieres compartir mi pastel también?"
9 Ella me contestó "¡Claro! Me encanta el chocolate."
10 Ricardo nos miró espantado y salió.

Have a student volunteer read this paragraph out loud. Then, reread the paragraph as a group, changing all verbs to the third person singular (**ella**) and making all other necessary changes.

Primero me desperté a las 7.00 de la mañana. Asistí a todas mis clases ese día y luego fui a la cafetería para almorzar con mi novio, Ricardo. Llegué media hora antes de nuestra cita y vi a Ricardo ¡besando a otra chica! Ellos no me vieron. Fui a comprar un pastel de chocolate a la pastelería. Regresé a la cafetería y caminé a la mesa de Ricardo y su amiga. Le pregunté a su amiga "¿Quieres compartir mi pastel también?" Ella me contestó "¡Claro! Me encanta el chocolate." Ricardo nos miró espantado y salió. Ahora, su amiga Laura es mi mejor amiga y Ricardo está solo.

Strategy in action

Turn to *Escribamos* in the Workbook to practice the strategy of writing a time line.

Do **Actividad 5** collectively, with the class, with a student volunteer writing the sentences on the board.

5 Mi primer día de clase. Use a time line to record at least five things that happened on your first day of class. Then, write a brief paragraph to record the events of that day.

6 El diario de Adriana. The evening after being followed by the mysterious ring-fingered man, Adriana sits down to write the sequence of events in her journal. Use a time line to order the events and record what happened to her.

Vocabulario

Viajes en tren

el andén	*track, train platform*
el asiento	*seat*
bajar (de)	*to get down (from)*
el billete	*ticket*
el boleto	*ticket*
¿Cuánto cuesta?/ ¿Cuánto es?	*How much is it?*
de ida	*one way*
de ida y vuelta	*round trip*
la demora	*delay*
económico/a	*economical*
¿En qué le(s) puedo servir?	*How may I help you?*
estar/llegar a tiempo	*to be/arrive on time*
estar/llegar atrasado/a	*to be late/arrive late*
el horario	*schedule*
ir/salir con destino a	*leave/depart with destination to*
el itinerario	*itinerary*
la llegada	*arrival*
el/la maletero/a	*porter*
no fumar	*no smoking*
el pasaje	*ticket*
el/la pasajero/a	*passenger*
la plaza	*place, seat*
próximo/a	*next*
¡Que tenga(n) un buen viaje!	*Have a good trip.*
la salida	*departure*
segunda clase	*second class*
subir (al tren)	*to board (the train)*
la taquilla	*ticket window*
tardar en llegar/salir	*to take (too much) time to arrive/leave*
el tiquete	*ticket*
el vagón	*train car*

Planes de viaje

¡Buen viaje!/ ¡Feliz viaje!	*Have a nice trip!*
cada	*each*
estar/irse de vacaciones	*to be/go on vacation*
la excursión	*tour*
el folleto	*brochure*
gozar	*to enjoy*
el/la guía	*tour guide*
la guía	*guidebook*
los impuestos	*taxes*
libre	*free*
el paquete	*package tour*
el pasaporte	*passport*
pescar	*to fish*
la propina	*tip*
el recreo	*recreation*
las vacaciones	*vacation*
viajar	*to travel*
el vuelo	*flight*

Números ordinales

primero/a	*first*
segundo/a	*second*
tercero/a	*third*
cuarto/a	*fourth*
quinto/a	*fifth*
sexto/a	*sixth*
séptimo/a	*seventh*
octavo/a	*eighth*
noveno/a	*ninth*
décimo/a	*tenth*

Geografía

el norte	*north*
el sur	*south*
el este	*east*
el oeste	*west*
el noreste	*northeast*
el suroeste	*southwest*
el sureste	*southeast*
el noroeste	*northwest*

Preposiciones

(See page 157.)

Expresiones de tiempo

el año pasado	*last year*	**ayer**	*yesterday*
anoche	*last night*	**el fin de semana pasado**	*last weekend*
anteanoche	*the night before last*	**el mes pasado**	*last month*
anteayer	*the day before yesterday*	**la semana pasada**	*last week*

Verbos con complemento indirecto

(See page 152.)

Verbos como gustar

caer bien/mal	*to like/dislike (a person)*	**importar**	*to matter, be of concern*
encantar	*to delight; to enchant; to like very much*	**interesar**	*to interest, be of interest*
faltar	*to lack, need, be left (to do)*	**molestar**	*to bother, annoy*
fascinar	*to fascinate*	**parecer**	*to seem, appear to be*
		preocupar	*to worry*

CAPÍTULO 5

LOCALIDAD: Puerto Rico

5A

5B

¿Hay amor en la playa?

Believing that Nayeli is out of danger, Adriana and Felipe enjoy the beaches and explore the Puerto Rican rainforest. Little do they realize what perils lie ahead.

Have students give you as many adjectives as possible for the items in these pictures. Have one student write the words on the board. Be sure to review colors and agreement.

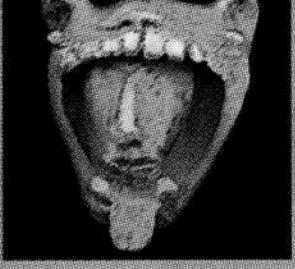

Vocabulary themes

- Talking about pastimes
- Traveling by airplane
- Identifying parts of the body
- Talking about family members
- Describing professions

Language structures

- Talking about the past
- Narrating a sequence of events with the preterite
- Describing ongoing actions and events in the past
- Telling time, weather, and age in the past
- Narrating a sequence of events with the imperfect
- Avoiding redundancy

Culture topics

- Un pasatiempo popular del Caribe
- Islas de sol y palmeras
- Celebraciones y comidas
- Festivales caribeños tradicionales

Readings

- Tres perlas del Caribe
- La creación del hombre y la mujer

Reading/writing strategy

- Using the dictionary

Internet strategy

- Looking for personal homepages

ETAPA A

Pistas y palabras

I. Talking about pastimes

After presenting these words and expressions, review the **tener** and **hacer frío/calor** expressions from Chapter 2.

Vamos a la playa.

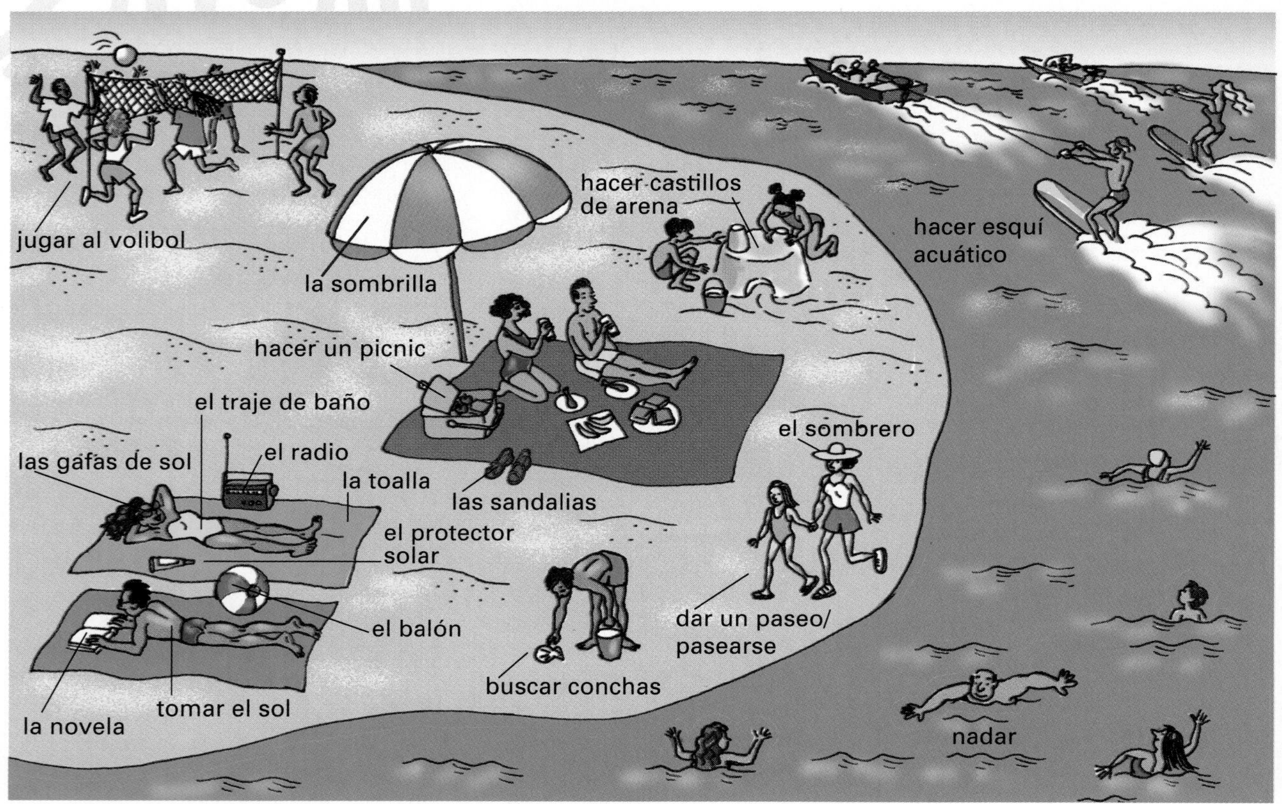

Introduce these verbs and review **gustar** expressions from Chapters 1 and 4 by asking **¿A quiénes les gusta...?** for each sport.

Palabras y expresiones útiles

bailar en una discoteca	*to dance in a club, disco*
broncearse	*to get a tan*
montar en bicicleta	*to go bicycling*
bucear	*to go skindiving, snorkeling*
correr	*to run, jog*
hacer surfing	*to surf*
ir de compras	*to go shopping*
ir de pesca (pescar)	*to go fishing*
montar a caballo	*to go horseback riding*
navegar en velero	*to go sailing*
protegerse	*to protect oneself*
quemar(se)	*to burn; to get a sunburn*

1 ¿Qué es? Choose the best vocabulary word to match each definition.

1. lugar (*place*) donde puedes bailar
2. algo (*something*) que usas para protegerte del sol
3. algo que puedes leer
4. algo que usas para hacer castillos en la playa
5. algo que buscas en la playa para una colección
6. algo que te pones en los pies (*feet*)
7. un animal grande y bonito
8. algo que usas cuando quieres escuchar música

Answers to Actividad 1:
1. discoteca
2. protector solar
3. novela, libro
4. arena
5. conchas
6. sandalias
7. caballo
8. radio

2 Me toca a mí. Now write three of your own definitions. Read them to a classmate and have him or her guess the answers.

3 Vamos a la playa. Create a list of four activities that you like to do on the beach and four that you do not like to do. Then find classmates with the same likes and dislikes as you. There are only two rules to follow: (1) You may ask only Yes/No questions; and (2) You may ask only one question of each classmate. Follow the model.

▸ **Modelo:** ANA: *Rodney, ¿te gusta montar en bicicleta?*
RODNEY: *No, no me gusta montar en bicicleta. ¿Te gusta jugar al volibol?*
ANA: *Sí, me gusta jugar al volibol.*

Actividades que me gustan	Estas actividades también les gustan a:
1. **jugar al volibol**	1. **Rodney**
2.	2.
3.	3.
4.	4.

Actividades que no me gustan	Estas actividades tampoco les gustan a:
1. **jugar al volibol**	1.
2.	2.
3.	3.
4.	4.

4 ¿A quién invito? With your completed list, decide whom you are going to invite to the beach to do which activities. Follow the model.

▸ **Modelo:** RODNEY: *Voy a jugar al volibol y voy a invitar a Ana.*
ANA: *Voy a montar en bicicleta y voy a invitar a Marcos.*

5 Necesito llevar... Work with a partner to make a list of the things you need to pack on your trip in order to do your favorite activities.

Bring dominoes to class. To review numbers, hold dominoes up in front of the class and ask students how many **puntos blancos/puntos negros** they see, or use drawings of dominoes or transparencies. For more information on dominoes, consult the World Wide Web.

ENLACE CULTURAL

Un pasatiempo popular del Caribe

En las islas caribeñas de habla española hay un pasatiempo que despierta mucho interés entre sus habitantes: el dominó. Lo juegan usualmente los hombres en los bares de las islas o al aire libre.° Este juego tiene veintiocho fichas° rectangulares, generalmente blancas y con puntos° negros, que representan los números del uno al seis. Los jugadores ponen las fichas con mucha gracia,° dando un golpe fuerte° en la mesa y pasan horas jugando y a veces también haciendo apuestas.° Mucha gente juega al dominó y uno de los grandes aficionados° a este juego es el presidente de Cuba, Fidel Castro.

outdoors
pieces
dots
flourish
hard hit
bets
fans

Un juego de dominó, La Habana, Cuba.

Discusión en grupos

Trabaja en grupos de tres. Cada persona describe un pasatiempo favorito que practica con la familia y uno que practica con los amigos.

Have student volunteers read out loud one sentence each. Explain that proverbs, such as **no hay mal que por bien no venga** (*Behind every cloud is a silver lining*) cannot be translated literally. In conjunction with a review of the parts of the body, other proverbs of interest are:
Ojos que no ven, corazón que no siente. *(Out of sight out of mind).*
En boca cerrada no entran moscas. *(Silence is golden.)*

II. Traveling by airplane

¡Qué viaje más interesante!

Una playa en San Juan, Puerto Rico.

Querida Alison,

Te mando un gran saludo desde San Juan. ¡Por fin estoy en la playa tomando sol! Te cuento° que mi viaje fue muy interesante. Primero, me desperté muy tarde y llegué al aeropuerto sólo veinte minutos antes del vuelo. El maletero me llevó al mostrador° rapidísimo y facturé el equipaje.° Llegué a la emigración° y no pude° encontrar mi pasaporte°! De repente° apareció° mi mamá con él. ¡Qué suerte° y qué buena mamá!

Let me tell you
counter
I checked in my luggage
emigration / I couldn't / passport / Suddenly / appeared / What luck!

Al llegar° a la puerta de salida° anunciaron que el avión estaba atrasado°. ¡Esperé en la sala de espera° por cuatro horas! Al subir° al avión, me quejé° de esto al aeromozo° y él me dio° un asiento en primera clase. ¡Sí, viajé en primera clase! Como dice mi mamá, "no hay mal que por bien no venga".° Cuando llegué a San Juan, pasé por la aduana° y después tomé un taxi para la residencia estudiantil.

Te mando una foto de las increíbles playas aquí. Son muy bonitas. Tienes que venir a visitarme.

Abrazos° de

Jesse

Upon arriving / departure gate / was late / waiting room Upon boarding / I complained / flight attendant / he gave me / "Behind every cloud is a silver lining" / customs

Hugs

Palabras y expresiones útiles

el/la aduanero/a	*customs agent*	aterrizar	*to land*
la clase turística	*coach class*	despegar	*to take off*
la escala	*layover*	estar a tiempo	*to be on time*
el/la piloto	*pilot*	hacer cola	*to wait in line*

6 Comprensión. Answer the following questions about the letter.

1. ¿Quién está de vacaciones?
2. ¿A quién le escribe Jesse?
3. ¿Dónde está él?
4. ¿Cuándo llegó al aeropuerto?
5. ¿Qué no tenía cuando llegó a la emigración?
6. ¿Quién lo ayudó? ¿Cómo?
7. ¿Con quién habló cuando subió al avión?
8. ¿En qué clase viajó Jesse a San Juan?
9. ¿Cómo llegó a la residencia estudantil?

Answers to Actividad 6:
1. Jesse
2. a Alison
3. en la playa en San Juan
4. veinte minutos antes del vuelo
5. su pasaporte
6. su mamá. Apareció con el pasaporte.
7. Habló con el aeromozo.
8. Viajó en primera clase.
9. Tomó un taxi.

7 Combinaciones. Create complete sentences in the preterite by combining the words from each column. You may use a verb or subject more than once.

A	B	C
Yo	miró	el equipaje
El maletero	aterrizó	a las tres
Mis amigos y yo	vendió	el pasaporte
El avión	llegué	tarde
El aduanero	llevó	atrasado
El empleado	nos despertamos	los boletos
Mis hermanos	compré	en la clase turística
	nos sentamos	por mucho tiempo
	facturó	la reservación
	llegaron	a tiempo

8 Querido amigo/Querida amiga. Write a postcard to a friend or family member describing an unforgettable (**inolvidable**) flight that you have taken.

III. Identifying parts of the body

¡Mamá, me quemé la espalda!

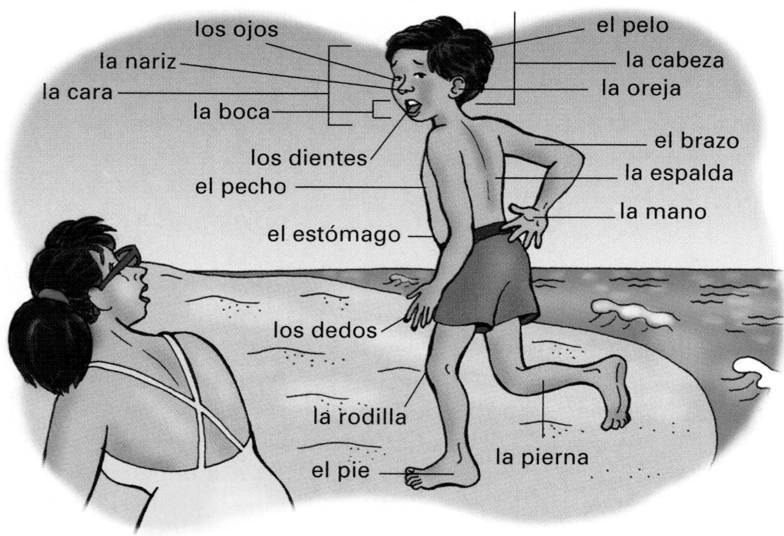

9 Asociaciones. What parts of the body do you associate with these activities?

1. jugar al volibol
2. bucear
3. escuchar música
4. comer
5. tocar la guitarra
6. montar en bicicleta
7. nadar en la playa
8. leer una novela
9. maquillarse

For **Actividad 10**, bring in pictures of **Caperucita Roja** and the **lobo** or have two artistic volunteers draw sketches of them on the board before students do this activity.

10 Para verte mejor. Little Red Riding Hood (**Caperucita Roja**) is on her way to grandmother's house. What body part is the wolf (**el lobo**) referring to when he says the following to Little Red Riding Hood? Follow the model.

► **Modelo:** *Para verte mejor.*
—¡Qué ojos tan grandes tienes!
—¡Para verte mejor!

1. Para escucharte mejor.
2. Para abrazarte mejor.
3. Para comerte mejor.
4. Para besarte mejor. (*to kiss you*)
5. Para saludarte mejor.
6. Para oírte mejor.

Review reflexive verbs from Chapter 3 regarding daily routines and assign as written homework. Have students read their sentences out loud in groups before handing them in.

11 Acciones reflexivas. Write complete sentences in the present tense by combining the words from each column. Be sure to use each verb and each subject at least once. Exchange papers and compare your creations.

A	B	C
yo	lavarse	las manos
tú	ponerse	el pelo
los niños	cepillarse	las sandalias
nosotros/as	peinarse	los dientes
tu mejor amiga	maquillarse	el cuerpo
mi hermano/a y yo	afeitarse	el traje de baño
ustedes	quitarse	la cara

ENLACE CULTURAL

Islas de sol y palmeras°

Cada año, millones de turistas visitan las islas del Caribe. Muchos van en avión o en barco a Puerto Rico, a Cuba y a la República Dominicana. En estas islas, el turismo es importante para su economía. La gente disfruta de° las hermosas y extensas playas, en un clima soleado de agradables temperaturas entre 27° y 29° C. El mar de estas regiones es de aguas cristalinas de color azul turquesa.° En las costas hay altas palmeras y hermosas flores de muchas variedades. El Caribe es conocido también por los arrecifes° de coral, las cascadas,° las aguas termales° y las cavernas. Dice la gente que en muchas de estas cavernas hay tesoros° muy valiosos que pertenecieron° a los piratas del Caribe hace varios siglos.

En esta idílica región hay también violentos huracanes que a veces° traen lluvias torrenciales y destrucción. La época de los huracanes es generalmente en los meses de junio, julio y agosto.

palm trees

enjoys

turquoise

reefs / waterfalls

hot springs

treasures

belonged

sometimes

La Playa de Varadero, la Habana, Cuba.

Read this selection out loud and have a student point out the locations of these places on a map. To review temperatures, ask students what 27 to 29 degrees centigrade is in Fahrenheit. Ask **¿Hace frío o hace calor en el Caribe?**

Discusión en grupos

Trabaja en grupos de tres o cuatro estudiantes. Pregunta sobre las playas importantes de tu región. ¿Dónde están? ¿Cómo son? ¿Qué hace la gente allí: nada, juega o practica algún deporte? ¿Cuáles son los meses más populares para ir a esas playas?

Un arrecife de coral en el Mar Caribe.

El huracán Hugo en Puerto Rico.

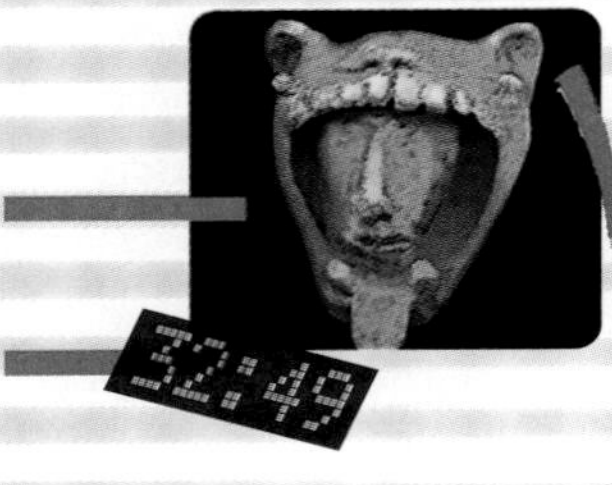

Vistas y voces

I. Preparémonos

1 Anticipación. Answer these questions in pairs.

A. **1.** ¿Cuál de los siguientes pasatiempos te parece más divertido hacer en la playa: navegar en velero, hacer castillos de arena, buscar conchas, hacer surfing? ¿Por qué?

2. ¿Pasas tus vacaciones con tu familia o con amigos? ¿Dónde se alojan: en un hotel, en una pensión o con amigos? ¿Cuál es tu lugar favorito para pasar las vacaciones?

3. ¿Cuáles son algunos pasatiempos divertidos en las diferentes estaciones del año?

B. Review chapter opening photo 5A on page 183. ¿Dónde están Adriana y Felipe y qué hacen? ¿Qué pasa entre estos dos jóvenes? ¿Van a ser novios? ¿Por qué crees que sí o que no?

Para comprender mejor

arreglado/a	*arranged*	la estadía	*stay*
bellísimo/a	*very beautiful*	guardado/a	*hidden*
crecer	*to grow*	la paloma	*dove*
cruzado/a	*crossed*	el pensamiento	*thought*
de una vez	*once and for all*	perder de vista	*to drop from sight*
desconocido/a	*unknown*	el recuerdo	*memory*
la desesperación	*desperation*	el ruidazo	*loud noise*
despedirse	*to say goodbye*	sin duda	*without a doubt*
el dolor	*pain*	valer la pena	*to be worth*

Correct order of video action shots: 3, 2, 1, 4

Answers to Actividades 3 and 4:
X's belong before numbers 2, 4, 5, 7, 9, 10
People who do the activities are:
2. una pareja
4. Nayeli, Gafasoscuras
5. muchos muchachos, Adriana y Felipe
7. Adriana y Felipe
9. Nayeli
10. unos muchachos

2 Secuencia. Study each scene of the video, and then describe what you think is going to happen in this episode. Work with a partner.

1.

2.

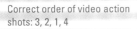

3.

4.

II. Miremos y escuchemos

3 Observaciones. While you view the video, put an **X** next to the activities that people do in this episode.

______ 1.	nadar	______ 6.	comer pan y queso
______ 2.	caminar por la playa	______ 7.	registrarse en el hotel
______ 3.	leer el periódico	______ 8.	mirar una película
______ 4.	hablar por teléfono	______ 9.	tener un sueño
______ 5.	jugar al volibol	______ 10.	hacer esquí acuático

4 Identificación. Now, write who does each of the different activities that you marked with an **X**.

III. Comentemos

5 Comprensión. Answer the following questions in groups.

1. ¿En qué ciudad están Adriana y Felipe?
2. ¿Qué piensa el empleado del hotel sobre la relación entre Adriana y Felipe?
3. ¿Cuáles son los números de las habitaciones de Adriana y Felipe? ¿Qué tipo de vista tienen?
4. ¿Qué tiempo hace en Sevilla? ¿Qué usan las señoras para protegerse?
5. ¿Con qué saludo contesta Nayeli el teléfono? ¿Qué malas noticias le da el señor y cómo reacciona ella?
6. ¿Qué hacen los muchachos que están en la playa? ¿Cómo describe Felipe la isla de Puerto Rico? ¿y ese momento en la playa con Adriana?
7. ¿De qué isla misteriosa habla Felipe con Adriana cuando está en la playa? ¿Qué dice él? ¿Cómo se siente él? ¿Qué hacen los dos después de hablar?
8. ¿Qué pájaro aparece? ¿De qué color? ¿Con quién sueña Nayeli? ¿Cómo es?
9. ¿A quién llama Nayeli? ¿Qué le dice? ¿Quién escucha la conversación telefónica? ¿Por qué no va a perder de vista a Nayeli?

6 Consejos de la abuela. Nayeli has a dream in which her grandmother speaks to her about her husband Hernán's death during the earthquake in Mexico. What are two things that **Abuelita** says to Nayeli?

7 Miremos otra vez. Watch the video again and order the scenes.

Answers to Actividad 5:

1. San Juan
2. El empleado piensa que Adriana y Felipe son esposos.
3. Adriana=103; Felipe=102; vista hermosa al mar
4. Está lloviendo (llueve) en Sevilla. Usan paraguas.
5. "Bueno"; El señor dice que Adriana y Felipe están en Puerto Rico. Nayeli está preocupada. Cree que puede ser peligroso.
6. Juegan al volibol, caminan, hacen esquí acuático. Felipe cree que Puerto Rico es bellísima. Felipe cree que ese momento en la playa es "perfecto".
7. Cuba; Felipe no conoce Cuba. Él está triste y curioso. Felipe y Adriana juegan al volibol.
8. una paloma blanca; Nayeli sueña con su abuelita. Ella es mayor y de pelo corto y blanco.
9. a Beatriz; Dice que no va a Quito. Gafasnegras; Dice que sabe lo que hace y que es experta.

Some possible answers to Actividad 6:

1. Lo que hiciste lo tuviste que hacer.
2. Los terremotos son parte de la naturaleza.
3. Hernán sabe que lo amas.
4. Los seres humanos importan más que las cosas.

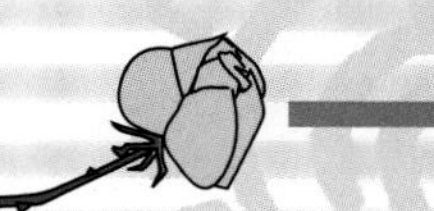

Lengua

Aterrizaje de emergencia: Have two students read and act out this dialogue out loud in front of the class.

I. Talking about the past

Preterite indicative of irregular verbs

Aterrizaje de emergencia

BÁRBARA: Pareces nerviosa, Jimena, ¿**pudiste**° hablar con el agente? — *could*

JIMENA: No, **no pude**,° pero alguien me **dijo**° que el avión no va a llegar hoy. — *was not able / said*

BÁRBARA: ¿Pero, **no supiste**° nada más? ¿Por qué **no vino**° el avión? — *didn't find out / didn't come*

JIMENA: Pues... parece que **tuvo**° problemas mecánicos... — *had*

BÁRBARA: ¡Dios mío! ¿No quieres decir que el avión se **cayó**°? — *fell*

JIMENA: ¡No, no, no es eso! El piloto **hizo**° un aterrizaje de emergencia y todos los pasajeros están bien. — *made*

BÁRBARA: ¡El piloto y sus pasajeros **tuvieron**° mucha suerte! — *had*

Irregular verbs can be grouped by the common changes they share in the stem. Grouping them by these similarities will help you remember them. Notice the following characteristics of the irregular verbs in the charts that follow and the ones highlighted in the conversation above.

- Verbs may belong to any one of the **-ar, -er,** or **-ir** conjugations.
- Verbs in groups **1** and **2** don't need accent marks.
- Verbs in group **3** (**huir**, **destruir**, **construir**, and so on) have written accents in the first and third persons singular as do regular verbs in the preterite.

Group 1: Irregular preterites with *i* or *u* in the stem

	tener > u	**Verbs like tener with u in the stem**	
yo	tuve	**andar** *(to walk; to go)*	and**uv-**
tú	tuv**iste**	**estar**	est**uv-**
él/ella, Ud.	tuv**o**	**haber**	**hub-**
nosotros/nosotras	tuv**imos**	**poder**	**pud-**
vosotros/vosotras	tuv**isteis**	**poner**	**pus-**
ellos/ellas, Uds.	tuv**ieron**	**saber**	**sup-**

	venir > i	**Verbs like venir with i in the stem**	
yo	vine	**querer**	qu**is**-
tú	vin**iste**	**hacer**	h**ic**-
él/ella, Ud.	vin**o**		
nosotros/nosotras	vin**imos**		
vosotros/vosotras	vin**isteis**		
ellos/ellas, Uds.	vin**ieron**		

- **Hubo** (*there was, there were*) is the preterite of **hay** (*there is, there are*). Like **hay**, there is only one form of this verb in the preterite.

No **hubo** problemas con las reservaciones.	*There were no problems with the reservations.*
En la lotería de hoy **hubo** sólo un ganador.	*In today's lottery there was only one winner.*
Hubo un problema en Sevilla: alguien persiguió a Adriana.	*There was a problem in Sevilla: someone chased Adriana.*

- **Hacer** has an orthographic change in the third person singular, in which **c** becomes **z** before the vowel **o**: yo **hi**<u>**c**</u>**e,** but él/ella/usted **hi**<u>**z**</u>**o**. This change keeps the pronunciation of all forms consistent.
- **Saber** in the preterite means *to find out; to learn.*

Group 2: Irregular preterites with a *j* in the stem

	decir
yo	dij**e**
tú	dij**iste**
él/ella, Ud.	dij**o**
nosotros/nosotras	dij**imos**
vosotros/vosotras	dij**isteis**
ellos/ellas, Uds.	dij**eron**

Verbs with endings like decir with j in the stem	
traer	traj-
conducir	conduj-
traducir	traduj-
producir	produj-

- This group of irregular verbs has a stem that ends in **j**. In addition to this change, **decir** has also a stem change from **e** to **i**.
- The endings of these verbs are the same as the endings of the **tener** and **venir** group except in the third-person plural where the ending is **-eron:** producir > produj**eron.**

Group 3: Irregular preterites with a *y* in the third-person

creer	
yo	cre**í**
tú	cre**íste**
él/ella, Ud.	cre**yó**
nosotros/nosotras	cre**ímos**
vosotros/vosotras	cre**ísteis**
ellos/ellas, Uds.	cre**yeron**

Verbs like creer with y in the ending of the third person	
caer	ca**y**-
leer	le**y**-
construir	constru**y**-
huir	hu**y**-
oír	o**y**-

- The unaccented **i** in the third person singular and plural becomes **y** between two vowels: **cayó, cayeron; leyó, leyeron; construyó, contruyeron; huyó, huyeron; oyó, oyeron.**
- These verbs have written accent marks in the first- and the third-person singular: **huí, huyó**.

1 ¿Qué hicieron? With a partner, create sentences about what people did.

▸ **Modelo:** *yo/ella/nosotros (poner los libros aquí)*
Yo puse los libros aquí.
Ella puso los libros aquí.
Nosotros pusimos los libros aquí.

1. ustedes/tú/Adriana (le [decir] la verdad a Felipe)
2. Felipe y su amigo/nosotros/él (venir a San Juan)
3. los estudiantes de Nayeli/ tú/yo (leer las instrucciones)
4. nadie/ella/ustedes (tener problemas con el itinerario)
5. nosotros/yo/la especialista (producir un nuevo motor)
6. todo el mundo/Felipe y Adriana/yo (oír el anuncio en la estación de Atocha)
7. el piloto/tú/Nayeli (ver la película en el avión)
8. Felipe y yo/los arqueólogos/la policía (venir a buscar al jaguar)

Answers to Actividad 2:
1. pusieron
2. hicieron
3. tuvimos
4. estuvieron
5. conduje
6. hubo
7. puso
8. huyó
9. pudimos

Bring in various magazine pictures and/or create some of your own of airport scenes. Ask the question **¿Qué pasó?**

2 Rutina en el aeropuerto. You have a summer job at the airport. Tell your friends what happened today at work. Use the preterite and follow the model.

▸ **Modelo:** *algunos pasajeros / traer artículos prohibidos al país*
¿Qué hicieron algunos pasajeros?
Algunos pasajeros trajeron artículos prohibidos al país.

1. los empleados / poner las revistas en el avión
2. las azafatas / hacer llamadas por el altavoz (*speaker*)
3. nosotros / tener que buscar a los niños perdidos
4. todos / estar en tres reuniones
5. yo / conducir a dos personas ancianas en silla de ruedas
6. haber / problemas con aviones atrasados
7. un terrorista / poner una bomba falsa
8. el terrorista / huir de la policía
9. por la noche, nosotros / poder descansar

3 Cosas. Work in groups of three or four students to create affirmative or negative sentences or questions with the elements in the columns below. Then, compare the sentences that you have created. Follow the model.

▸ **Modelo:** *Mis amigos dijeron tonterías.*

A	B	C
mis amigos	decir	la carta en el correo
mis padres	hacer	paella para la cena
los estudiantes	leer	aquí
yo	oír	el periódico de hoy
nosotros	poner	mentiras todo el tiempo
los chicos	tener	música rock
tú	venir	regalos a los niños
una compañía	dar	tonterías

II. Narrating a sequence of events with the preterite

Preterite and adverbial expressions of time

Viaje a Acapulco

1 ***Primero que todo*** **(*First of all*), el 15 de abril, un mes antes de viajar, Julia miró los folletos turísticos y preparó un plan de vacaciones.**

2 ***Cuando*** **(*When*) terminó, a las 3 de la tarde, llamó a la agencia de viajes para reservar el pasaje de avión.**

3 **El sábado 15 de mayo, el día antes de viajar, Julia compró *primero* (*first*) el pasaje de avión.**

4 ***Después*** **(*Afterward*) fue a comprar un nuevo traje de baño.**

5 ***Luego*** **(*Then*) por la tarde, compró sandalias y protector solar.**

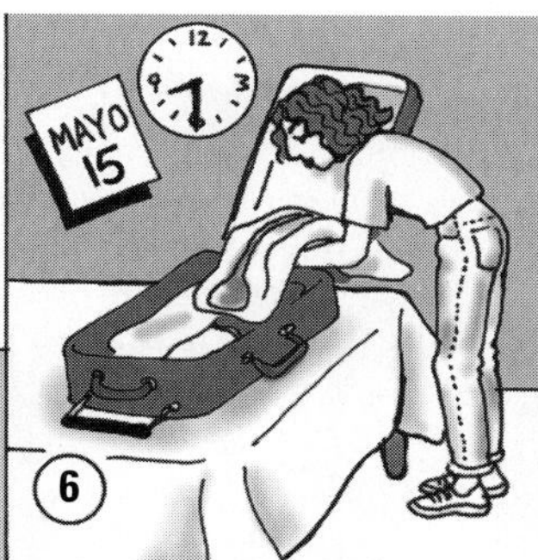

6 ***Por último*** **(*Finally*), empacó la maleta y preparó sus documentos de viaje.**

7 **¡*Ya* (*Now*) está todo listo!, dijo Julia mirándolo todo.**

8 ***Finalmente*** **(*Finally*), el domingo 16 de mayo, por la mañana, tomó el avión para Acapulco.**

- In a sequence of actions expressed with the preterite, adverbial expressions of time like the ones presented above can emphasize that each action is completed before the next one is started.
- If you need to emphasize that many things happened and were completed at the same time, you can use adverbial expressions like **cuando**, **simultáneamente**, and **al mismo tiempo (que)**.

Adriana sonrió **cuando** Felipe la miró.	*Adriana smiled when Felipe looked at her.*
Roberto llegó **al mismo tiempo** que Marta salió en su coche y Lucho llamó por teléfono.	*Roberto arrived at the same time that Marta drove away and that Lucho called.*

Before doing **Actividad 4**, this activity review time expressions and dates from Chapter 1.

4 Los planes de Julia. The drawing on page 195 shows Julia preparing her vacation to Acapulco. The words in boldface italics link the sequence of events in time. Using these words, work in pairs asking and answering questions about what Julia did. Look at the model below to get started.

▸ **Modelo:** *¿Qué hizo Julia primero que todo, un mes antes de viajar? ¿A qué hora? ¿Por la mañana o por la tarde?*

5 Mi propia historia. Using the adverbial expressions of time that you learned on page 174, write, in a mixed order, all you had to do to make plans for a vacation and what happened the day of your trip. Then, exchange descriptions with a partner and ask her or him to order all your activities in a logical sequence using adverbial expressions of time.

III. Talking about the past

Preterite indicative of stem-changing -ir verbs

Julia prefirió descansar.

LORENZO: ¿Ya llegó Julia de Acapulco?
PATRICIA: Sí, regresó anoche. Se **divirtió**° muchísimo. — *had a great time*
LORENZO: ¿Y dónde está? ¿Por qué no vino a clase?
PATRICIA: Es que **prefirió**° descansar hoy en casa. — *preferred, opted*
LORENZO: ¡Acaba de llegar de vacaciones! ¿Por qué está descansando?
PATRICIA: No **durmió**° mucho durante el viaje, ¿sabes? — *slept*
LORENZO: Mmm... supongo que sólo tuvo tiempo para divertirse.

Verbs that resemble **preferir** and **dormir** in the preterite have the same endings. However, their stems differ in the vowel they contain: it can be **i** or **u** correspondingly.

	preferir → i	**dormir → u**
yo	preferí	dormí
tú	prefer**iste**	dorm**iste**
él/ella, usted	pref**i**r**ió**	d**u**rm**ió**
nosotros/nosotras	prefer**imos**	dorm**imos**
vosotros/vosotras	prefer**isteis**	dorm**isteis**
ellos/ellas, ustedes	pref**i**r**ieron**	d**u**rm**ieron**

Verbs like preferir with i in the stem of third person	**Verbs like dormir with u in the stem of third person**
divertir(se) (ie, i)*	**morir (ue, u)**
pedir (i, i)	
repetir (i, i)	
seguir, perseguir (i, i)	
sentir(se) (ie, i)	
servir (i, i)	
sonreír (i, i)	

- In Chapter 4, review **-ar** and **-er** verbs with orthographic changes in the preterite.
- Stem-changing **-ir** verbs in the present are also stem-changing in the preterite. This change occurs only in the third person singular and plural in all stem-changing **-ir** verbs.
- The first- and third-person singular preterite forms carry the stress on the last syllable and have written accents.
- Notice that stem-changing **-ir** verbs have the same vowel change in the preterite and in the present progressive.

Julia está **sintiéndose** mejor hoy.	*Julia is feeling better today.*
Ella no se **sintió** bien ayer.	*She didn't feel well yesterday.*
Los niños **están durmiendo**.	*The children are sleeping.*
Ellos no **durmieron** bien anoche.	*They did not sleep well last night.*

6 ¿Qué hicieron? Create sentences in the preterite describing what the following people did.

► **Modelo:** *Adriana y Felipe (divertirse) en la playa*
Adriana y Felipe se divirtieron en la playa.

1. Los estudiantes (repetir) el examen hace un mes
2. Adriana y Felipe (no pedir) una habitación doble
3. Todos (dormir) mucho el fin de semana
4. Hernán, el esposo de Nayeli, (morirse) hace poco
5. Nayeli (sentirse) muy mal después del terremoto
6. Armando (preferir) un hotel de cinco estrellas
7. El chef del restaurante español (servir) comida exquisita

Answers to Actividad 6:
1. repitieron
2. no pidieron
3. durmieron
4. se murió
5. se sintió
6. prefirió
7. sirvió

The vowels in parentheses indicate the stem change in the present (ie**) and in the preterite (**i**).*

7 **Turistas alegres.** Imagine that you work for a travel company and are preparing an overview of a very successful one-day tour around Mexico City. Order the drawings in your preferred sequence and number them. Then, write a caption for each one using the linking words that you have learned. Finally, compare your work with a friend's.

Lectura A

Introducción

In this selection you will learn about the three Spanish-speaking islands of the Caribbean: Puerto Rico, la República Dominicana, and Cuba.

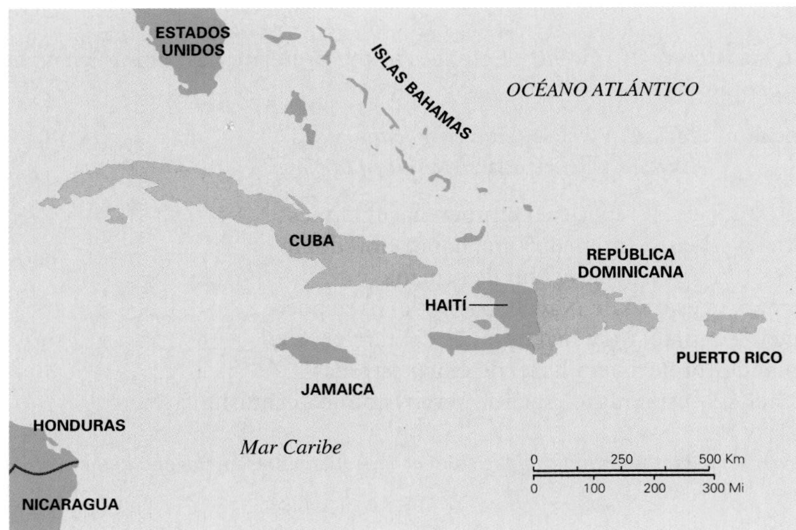

Reading strategy: Using the dictionary

When reading a text in Spanish, go through it several times, checking for words you already know, as well as cognates, which you have studied in earlier chapters. You should also try to guess the meaning of words you do not know through the context of the sentence and the text. Once you have followed these steps, then you can add the strategy of using the dictionary to confirm your guess. The dictionary will give you several meanings of a word. It is important to determine the grammatical form of the word because that may affect its meaning. Note the following facts about Spanish dictionaries.

- Verbs (**verbos**) appear in the infinitive form. If you are looking at a conjugated form, you will have to find the infinitive form before you start your search.
- The masculine and the feminine forms of nouns (**sustantivos**) are listed and marked *m.* and *f.*
- The masculine singular form of the adjective (**adjetivo**) is listed and marked *adj.*
- Idiomatic expressions (**expresiones idiomáticas**) are listed by their most important word. Sometimes you need several attempts to determine the main word.
- The letter **ñ** is listed as a separate letter after **n**. In older dictionaries, the letter **ll** (as in **llover**) and the letter combination **ch** were listed as separate letters, after **l** and **c** respectively.

Tres perlas del Caribe

Las tres islas caribeñas de habla española, Cuba, la República Dominicana y Puerto Rico, tienen una herencia° tricultural común: la indígena° de cada región, la española y la africana. Esta mezcla° étnica les da gran riqueza a sus tradiciones, a su música, a su literatura y a su vida diaria, pero cada isla tiene también su identidad propia. Estas perlas del Caribe comparten aspectos de su cultura, herencia y tradiciones con otras regiones hispanas como las costas caribeñas de Costa Rica, Panamá, Colombia y Venezuela.

heritage
indigenous / mix

Cuba Cuba es la más grande de las tres islas caribeñas. Fue el segundo lugar° al que llegó Cristóbal Colón.° Los españoles importaron a esclavos africanos para trabajar en las prósperas plantaciones de azúcar.° El azúcar lo llamaban "el oro blanco" por su valor económico en esa época. Con el tiempo, se mezclaron los africanos con los españoles para producir la rica mezcla racial que hoy existe en la isla. En 1959 hubo una revolución en Cuba y por más de treinta años, hasta 1990, Cuba estuvo bajo el socialismo de la Unión Soviética. Actualmente° la isla está en transición económica.

place / Christopher Columbus
sugar

Today

La República Dominicana La República Dominicana comparte° la misma isla que la República de Haití. Este país fue el primer centro administrativo español en América y sus habitantes indígenas, los taínos, la llamaban "Quisqueya". Según° Cristóbal Colón, esa isla era "la tierra más hermosa bajo los cielos".° La población de la isla tiene también herencia europea y africana debido a° los esclavos que llevaron a trabajar allí. Actualmente es un gran centro turístico en la región caribeña. Tiene bellas playas y hermosa arquitectura colonial. Tiene siete millones de habitantes.

shares
According to
in the world
because of

Puerto Rico Puerto Rico es la más pequeña de las tres islas hispanas y es un estado libre asociado° a los Estados Unidos. Los puertorriqueños pueden viajar libremente entre la isla y los EE. UU.° La población indígena de la isla de Puerto Rico, los taínos o arauacos, tenían° una sociedad bastante avanzada en esta bellísima isla de 175 kilómetros de largo° y 56 kilómetros de ancho.° Es la única región de los Estados Unidos que tiene el español y el inglés como lenguas oficiales. La gran cuestión es si los puertorriqueños quieren convertir la isla en el estado número 51 de los EE.UU. La población hoy en día° es de 3.646.000 millones de habitantes.

free associated state
U.S.
had
in length
in width
today

1 ¿Verdadero o falso? Write **V** if the following ideas are true (**verdadero**) or **F** if they are false (**falso**). Correct the false sentences.

______ 1. El azúcar fue importante para la economía de Cuba.
______ 2. Cuba es la más pequeña de las islas de habla española.
______ 3. Los taínos llamaban (*called*) "Quisqueya" a Puerto Rico.
______ 4. En las islas caribeñas de habla española hay una mezcla étnica de influencia indígena, española y africana.
______ 5. Puerto Rico es un estado libre asociado a los Estados Unidos.
______ 6. Cuba está bajo el socialismo de la Unión Soviética.
______ 7. Haití comparte la misma isla que Cuba.
______ 8. El español y el inglés son las lenguas oficiales de Puerto Rico.
______ 9. Puerto Rico tiene siete millones de habitantes.
______ 10. A Cristóbal Colón no le gustaba (*didn't like*) la isla de Quisqueya.

Answers to Actividad 1:
1. **V**
2. **F**—Puerto Rico es la más pequeña.
3. **F**—Llamaban "Quisqueya" a la República Dominicana.
4. **V**
5. **V**
6. **F**—Estuvo bajo el socialismo de la Unión Soviética entre 1959 y 1990.
7. **F**—Comparte la misma isla que la República Dominicana.
8. **V**
9. **F**—Tiene 3.646.000 millones de habitantes.
10. **F**—Según Colón, Quisqueya era "la tierra más hermosa bajo los cielos".

2 Buscando en el diccionario. Keep a list of the words that you needed to look up in the dictionary for this reading and compare them with a friend. Are there any that you could have guessed without looking them up? Which ones?

3 Compara y contrasta. Compare and contrast three different characteristics of Cuba, Puerto Rico, and the Dominican Republic. Which island do you find the most interesting? Why? Work with a partner.

4 Contéstalas. Work with a partner to answer the following questions.

1. ¿Hay islas en tu región? ¿Son importantes?
2. ¿Conoces alguna isla en el mundo? ¿Cuál? ¿Cómo es?
3. ¿Qué influencia étnica hay en tu región o estado?

ETAPA B

Pistas y palabras

I. Talking about family members

La familia de Velia

Me llamo Velia Rosas Suárez y tengo una **familia** muy grande. Mi **padre** se llama Pablo y mi **madre** se llama Marinela. Mis **padres** son muy simpáticos. Somos* cuatro **hermanos**. Mi **hermano** Roberto tiene treinta y cinco años y es alto y guapo. Su **esposa** se llama Aniela. Aniela es mi **cuñada**. Ellos tienen dos **hijos**: el **hijo** se llama Pedro y la **hija** se llama Leticia. Leticia tiene tres mascotas, un **conejo** que se llama Orejón, un **canario** que se llama Beto y una **tortuga**, Conchita. ¡Ella quiere ser veterinaria! Quiero mucho a mis **sobrinos.** ¡Soy su **tía** favorita!

Mi **hermana** mayor, Rosaura, tiene un **novio** que se llama Julio. Ellos están muy enamorados y van a casarse este verano. Mi hermana Maricarmen es soltera y se dedica mucho a sus estudios. Va a hacerse abogada. Ella tiene una **gata** que se llama Micifús.

¿Y yo? Yo estoy divorciada, no tengo hijos y vivo con mi **perrito** Sultán.

When talking about the number of people in a family, Spanish speakers often use* ***somos* *and not* ***son*** *to indicate how many people are in the family. This form includes themselves in the family portrait.*

Palabras y expresiones útiles

el/la abuelo/a	*grandfather/grandmother*
la adolescencia	*adolescence*
el/la bebé	*baby*
el/la bisabuelo/a	*great grandfather/great grandmother*
la edad adulta	*adulthood*
el/la nieto/a	*grandson/granddaughter*
la niñez	*childhood*
la nuera	*daughter-in-law*
el pariente	*family member, relative*
el/la primo/a	*cousin*
el/la suegro/a	*father/mother-in-law*
el yerno	*son-in-law*

Point out that **casarse** uses **con** and **enamorarse** uses **de** before nouns, versus the English *to get married* ***to*** and to *fall in love* ***with***.

casarse (con)	*to get married (to)*	estar separado/a	*to be separated*
dedicarse	*to dedicate oneself*	hacerse	*to become*
enamorarse (de)	*to fall in love (with)*	nacer (yo nazco)	*to be born*
estar casado/a	*to be married*	ser mayor	*to be older*
estar divorciado/a	*to be divorced*	ser menor	*to be younger*
estar enamorado/a	*to be in love*	ser soltero/a	*to be single*

Review names of other family members, on page 19, *Lengua en acción*.

1 La familia de Velia. Read the story on page 201 about Velia's family and label the family tree to indicate the relationship that each person has to Velia.

Answers to Actividad 2:
1. esposo
2. hijos
3. hijo
4. esposa
5. nietos
6. hija
7. novio

2 La familia de Marinela. If Marinela were telling the story about her family, the family relationships would change. Look at the family tree and describe the relationships between the following people from Marinela's point of view.

1. Me llamo Marinela y mi __________ se llama Pablo.
2. Tengo cuatro __________.
3. Mi __________ se llama Roberto.
4. Su __________ se llama Aniela.
5. Mis __________ son Pedro y Leticia.
6. Mi __________ mayor se llama Rosaura.
7. Rosaura tiene un __________ muy guapo.

Before doing **Actividad 3**, review dates from Chapters 1 and 3. Assign as homework. Students must write out all months and days in Spanish.

Answers to Actividad 3 (given as if the current year were 2000):
1. el veintitrés de febrero de 1942
2. el quince de mayo de 1970
3. el dos de febrero de 1985
4. el treinta de junio de 1964
5. el ocho de agosto de 1958
6. el primero de abril de 1965
7. el veintitrés de julio de 1993
8. el veintidós de diciembre de 1979

3 Feliz cumpleaños. Look at the family tree on page 201 and decide in what year each person was born. Note that the dates are written day/month/year in most Hispanic countries. Follow the model.

▶ **Modelo:** Pablo 10/3...
Pablo nació el diez de marzo del año (fill in year here).

1. Marinela 23/2
2. Rosaura 15/5
3. Leticia 2/2
4. Aniela 30/6
5. Julio 8/8
6. Roberto 1/4
7. Pedro 23/7
8. Maricarmen 22/12

4 Entre nosotros. Interview a partner about his or her family. Then draw a family tree that represents his or her family. Use questions as shown in the model.

▶ **Modelo:** *¿Cuántos hermanos tienes?*
¿Cómo se llaman?
¿Cuántos años tienen?

5 Mi familia. Write a paragraph about your family. Include a description of each family member, his or her relationship to you, name, age, and other interesting facts.

For **Actividad 5** stress that students may invent family trees. Set up appointments with each student to go over the paragraph and then have them present the material orally to the class.

You may wish to personalize the topic of **celebraciones y comidas** by asking students what their favorite celebration is and what foods they eat.

ENLACE CULTURAL

Celebraciones y comidas

En el mundo latino, las familias son muy unidas° y celebran juntas las fechas importantes y los días especiales. Una de las celebraciones más populares es la fiesta que se celebra cuando una chica cumple los quince años. Por la mañana el día de la celebración, la quinceañera° asiste a misa° en la iglesia con su familia. Después de misa hay una gran fiesta en su honor y la familia y los amigos bailan y sirven deliciosos platos.°

united

15-year-old birthday girl / mass

dishes

Unos platos típicos de Puerto Rico.

Otra de las celebraciones en muchas regiones hispanas es el "día del santo". Según la tradición cristiana, cada día del año está dedicado a un santo especial. Por ejemplo, el día 24 de junio es el día de San Juan y es el día del santo para las personas que se llaman Juan o Juana.

La manera de celebrar cada evento cambia dependiendo del tipo de evento y del país. Sin embargo,° uno de los elementos importantes de las celebraciones son las comidas. En el Caribe hay muchas comidas muy variadas y deliciosas. Entre los platos populares están el arroz con pollo, los frijoles y los tostones.° Las frutas tropicales como mangos, plátanos, guayabas° y piñas forman una parte importante de las comidas. La yuca° se prepara de muchas maneras y es también muy popular. Cada isla tiene un plato típico preferido: en Puerto Rico es el lechón asado;° en Cuba, comen mucho arroz con frijoles; y a la gente de la República Dominicana le gusta comer mondongo° y un guiso° de carnes y verduras° que se llama "sancocho".

Nevertheless

fried plantains

guavas / yucca

roast pig

tripe / stew / vegetables

Discusión en grupos

Describan los platos en la foto. ¿Cuáles son los cumpleaños especiales y cómo los celebran sus familias? ¿Qué otros eventos celebran? ¿Cómo pasan el día y qué platos típicos comen en esas ocasiones?

II. Describing professions

Somos vecinos *(neighbors).*

Laura Guzmán piensa ser *abogada* y su compañera Lourdes Vardi es *música*.

Los *artistas* trabajan intensamente. La *escultora* trabaja con madera (*wood*), mientras que el *fotógrafo* saca fotos (*takes pictures*).

Los hijos de los señores Terranova piensan ser *médicos*.

El *plomero* arregla el baño de la *farmacéutica* Aida Sosa.

El *cocinero* le sirve la comida a la familia Lara.

Una *pintora* pinta la sala de Eduardo Calasa.

Los *jardineros* trabajan en el jardín del Dr. Martín.

Pablo es *peluquero* y trabaja en la Peluquería Pablo.

Profesiones y oficios

For many professions, the masculine nouns end in **-o** and the feminine nouns end in **-a**:

el/la arquitecto/a	*architect*
el/la criado/a	*servant, maid*
el/la dueño/a	*owner*
el/la empleado/a	*employee*
el/la fotógrafo/a	*photographer*
el/la mecánico/a	*mechanic*
el/la médico/a	*doctor*
el/la psicólogo/a	*psychologist*
el/la químico/a	*chemist*
el/la secretario/a	*secretary*
el/la veterinario/a	*veterinarian*

Introduce also **el ama de casa** (*housewife*), which is feminine and that the plural is **las amas de casa.** The **el** is used to facilitate pronunciation. You may wish to state that at this point a number of words that begin with a stressed **a** or **ha** are feminine but are preceded by **el** when singular.

For other professions, the masculine nouns end in **-ero** and the feminine nouns end in **-era**:

el/la bombero/a	*fire fighter*	el/la enfermero/a	*nurse*
el/la carpintero/a	*carpenter*	el/la ingeniero/a	*engineer*
el/la cartero/a	*mail carrier*	el/la plomero/a	*plumber*
el/la consejero/a	*counselor*		

Masculine nouns ending in **-or** are made feminine by adding an **-a:**

el/la administrador/a de hogar	*household manager*
el/la contador/a	*accountant*
el/la doctor/a	*doctor*
el/la editor/a	*editor*
el/la profesor/a	*professor*
el/la programador/a de computadoras	*computer programmer*
el/la supervisor/a	*supervisor*
el/la trabajador/a	*worker*
el/la vendedor/a	*salesperson*

Nouns for professions ending in **-ista** or in **-e** have the same form for both masculine and feminine professions:

el/la agente de viajes	*travel agent*
el/la dentista	*dentist*
el/la electricista	*electrician*
el/la gerente	*manager*
el/la periodista	*journalist*
el/la recepcionista	*receptionist*

- Other occupations that have only one form are: **el/la atleta** (*athlete*), and **el/la policía** (*police officer*).
- Modern exceptions are **el jefe** (*male boss*) and **la jefa** (*female boss*), **el presidente**, and **la presidenta**.

Answers to Actividad 6:
1. el peluquero M
   la peluquera F
2. el cocinero M
   la cocinera F
3. el pintor M la pintora F
4. los médicos M
   las médicas F
5. el plomero M la plomera F
6. la farmacéutica F
   el farmacéutico M
7. la abogada F
   el abogado M
8. la música F el músico M
9. los artistas M
   las artistas F
10. la escultora F el escultor M
11. el fotógrafo M
    la fotógrafa F

Before students do **Actividad 7**, remind them that words not in the vocabulary list are likely to be cognates.

6 ¡Cámbialo! Identify the gender of the professions of the people in the apartment building on page 204 (written in boldface italics) by labeling them **F** for feminine and **M** for masculine. Then give the opposite form. Follow the model.

▸ **Modelo:** *los jardineros* (**M**)
las jardineras (**F**)

1. ______ **5.** ______ **9.** ______
2. ______ **6.** ______ **10.** ______
3. ______ **7.** ______ **11.** ______
4. ______ **8.** ______

7 Asociaciones. What profession/s do you associate with the following words?

1. las aspirinas
2. la pintura
3. las rosas
4. la bañera
5. el cepillo
6. el piano
7. el bistec
8. la justicia
9. el teléfono
10. el dinero
11. los animales

8 Querido amiguito. Complete the following letter with vocabulary from the list provided.

artistas	pintora	música	hijos
farmacéutica	cocinero	plomero	peluquero
jardineros	guitarra	criada	médico

Querido Mauro:

Saludos desde Puerto Rico. Aquí me estoy divirtiendo muchísimo, aunque° estudio demasiado. Mi compañera de cuarto se llama Lourdes y es _________. Toca la _________ y le gustan mucho el jazz y la música clásica. Nos llevamos° muy bien. Mis vecinos, los señores Lara, son muy simpáticos. Son muy ricos y tienen un _________ que prepara la comida y una _________ que limpia la casa.

Ayer, todos mis vecinos estuvieron muy ocupados. El Dr. Martín empleó a dos _________ para trabajar toda la tarde en el jardín. Pablo, el _________ tuvo quince clientes ayer. ¡Eso es mucho trabajo en un día! Una _________ vino a pintar el apartamento del vecino del 2B. Los dos _________ de los vecinos de abajo jugaron al "_________ y paciente"

°*although*

°*We get along*

Answers to Actividad 8:
1. música
2. guitarra
3. cocinero
4. criada
5. jardineros
6. peluquero
7. pintora
8. hijos
9. médico
10. farmacéutica
11. plomero
12. artistas

durante toda la mañana. La vecina del 3B es _________ y ayer, antes de salir para el trabajo, la llave° del agua se descompuso° y ella tuvo que llamar al _________ para arreglarla.° En el apartamento de al lado,° los _________ trabajaron toda la tarde. ¡Qué ruido!° Fue muy difícil para mí concentrarme° en los estudios.

faucet / broke
to fix it / next door
noise
to concentrate

Bueno, tengo mucho sueño y necesito descansar un rato.° ¡Me voy a acostar! Escríbeme pronto.

a little while

Abrazos de

Laura

9 En mi barrio *(neighborhood).* Write a description of five people in your neighborhood. Describe who they are, what they do, and what they are like.

ENLACE CULTURAL

Festivales caribeños tradicionales

En el Caribe hispano hay muchas tradiciones que celebran la herencia cultural. El festival puertorriqueño de **LeLoLai** festeja° la tradición indígena, española y africana de Puerto Rico con celebraciones folclóricas y musicales. En el mes de julio de cada año, se celebra en La República Dominicana el **Festival del merengue.** En este festival hay un concurso° anual de merengue,° en el que se elige a la pareja que mejor baila este ritmo, original de la isla. La historia afrocubana se festeja en Cuba con **comparsas,** grupos de danzas tradicionales, que desfilan° a través° de las calles de pueblos y ciudades.

celebrates
contest / Dominican rhythm
parade / through

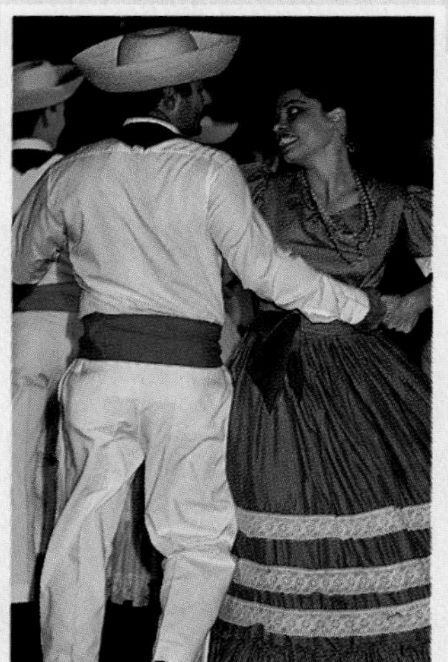

El festival LeLoLai en Puerto Rico.

Discusión en grupos

¿Cuáles son las celebraciones culturales más importantes del país o de una región del país? ¿En qué meses se realizan y qué actividades hay durante las celebraciones?

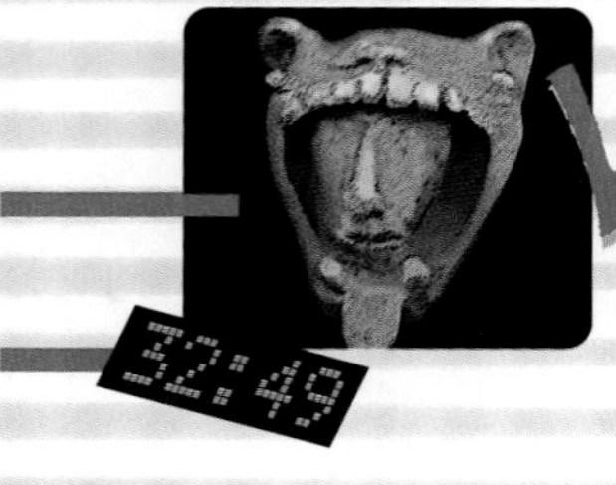

Vistas y voces

I. Preparémonos

1 Anticipación. Answer these questions in pairs.

A. **1.** ¿Tienes primos o primas? ¿Cuántos años tienen? ¿Qué tipo de actividades haces con ellos? ¿y con tus hermanos/as? ¿con tus amigos/as? ¿En dónde?
2. ¿Te sientes triste a veces? ¿Cómo combates tu tristeza? ¿Qué cosas te dan mucha alegría?
3. El sol y la luna son hermosos. ¿Cuál prefieres tú? ¿Por qué?

B. Review chapter opening photo 5B on page 183. ¿Quiénes son esos hombres vestidos de impermeables amarillos en el Yunque? ¿Para quién trabajan? ¿Qué crees tú que piensan hacer? ¿Crees que Adriana y Felipe están en peligro? Explica.

Para comprender mejor

adivinar	*to guess*	la lluvia	*rain*
ajá	*uh-huh*	el placer	*pleasure*
alegrarse	*to be happy*	por fin	*at last*
la alegría	*happiness*	por supuesto	*of course*
el/la bandido/a	*thug*	morder (ue)	*to bite*
la belleza	*beauty*	suceder	*to happen*
ladrar	*to bark*	tapado/a	*covered*
la lente	*lens*	la tristeza	*sadness*

Before viewing, present the English equivalent of the proverb in Actividad 8, *A dog's bark is worse than his bite.*

2 Secuencia. Describe what is happening in each video action shot. Then put them in a logical order and predict what is going to happen.

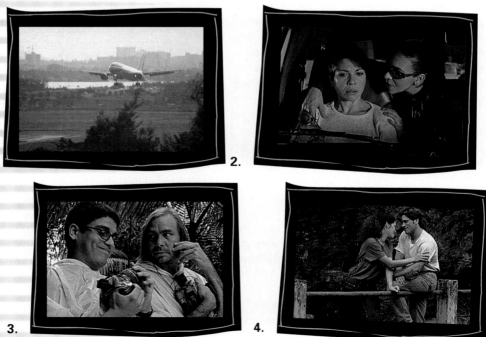

1.

2.

3.

4.

II. Miremos y escuchemos

3 Observaciones. In the chart below, write the items with which you associate the characters you see or hear in this episode, answering the question: **¿Con quién/es se asocian estas cosas o elementos?**

videocámara	impermeable	naturaleza
maleta	pantalones	árboles
puente	reloj	plantas
avión	gafas	lluvia
coche	paraguas	sol
cámara	ave	arena

Personaje	Las cosas
Adriana	
Felipe	
El bandido de pelo largo	
El bandido de pelo corto	
Gafasnegras	
Nayeli	

Actividad 3:
Answers will vary.

III. Comentemos

4 Comprensión. Answer the following questions in groups.

1. ¿Qué relación familiar hay entre los dos bandidos? ¿En dónde están?
2. ¿Cuál es la otra profesión de uno de ellos? ¿Cómo describe Luis a su primo?
3. ¿De qué hablan Felipe y Adriana mientras están en el puente? ¿Con qué elementos comparan al hombre y a la mujer?
4. ¿Cómo llega Nayeli a Puerto Rico? ¿Qué flor recibe? ¿Qué simboliza la flor?
5. ¿Quién está en el coche con Nayeli? ¿Cómo reacciona Nayeli?
6. ¿Qué le dice esa persona a Nayeli?

Answers to Actividad 4:

1. Son primos. Están en el Yunque.
2. Es programador. Luis dice que su primo está nervioso.
3. Hablan de la belleza de Puerto Rico y de una leyenda cubana; el sol y la luna
4. en avión; una rosa roja; Simboliza peligro.
5. Gafasnegras está en el coche. Nayeli tiene miedo.
6. Gafasnegras quiere saber dónde está el jaguar Yax-Balam.

5 Yo creo que... In pairs, discuss the following questions. Then, share your answers with the class.

1. ¿Qué crees que va a pasar con el jaguar en el próximo episodio?
2. ¿Dónde va a estar?
3. ¿Quién lo va a tener?

6 Miremos otra vez. After viewing the episode, put the video action shots in the correct order.

Correct order of video action shots: 4, 3, 1, 2

7 Somos primos. Describe the bandit cousins by answering the following questions: ¿Cómo son físicamente? ¿Qué hacen en el Yunque? ¿Cuántos años tienen? ¿Qué les interesa? ¿Qué efecto producen los primos en este episodio? ¿miedo? ¿susto? ¿humor? ¿tristeza?

8 Interpretación. Luis, el bandido, says **"Perro que ladra no muerde."** Is this true? Work in groups and give your opinion with a concrete example.

Lengua

I. Describing ongoing actions and events in the past

Imperfect indicative

You have learned the preterite to talk about completed actions in the past. In addition to this form, Spanish uses a second past form called the imperfect. Read the following passage and note the highlighted imperfect: How many times did each action happen? How long did it last? When did it start? When did it end?

Mi vecindario favorito

I was / we used to live / was
was / had

Cuando yo **era**° pequeña, **vivíamos**° en Palmas del Mar. Nuestra casa **estaba**° cerca de la playa, **era**° muy grande y **tenía**° palmeras en el jardín.

there were / I would go

En el vecindario **había**° muchos niños y frecuentemente yo **iba**° con ellos y con mis hermanos a nadar y a bucear en el mar.

we swam / she stayed

Mientras **nadábamos**,° mi mamá **se quedaba**° siempre con nosotros.

I felt

¡Yo me **sentía**° muy contenta!

- The imperfect corresponds to several forms in English: *I was doing, I used to do, I would often do, I did.*
- In general, the imperfect is used to describe how persons and places looked, how things used to be and what they used to do in the past. It is also used to describe past states of mind and feelings. The starting and completion points of these actions, events, and states are not important. The focus is placed only on the fact that they were *ongoing* at some time in the past.

A. Regular verbs in the imperfect

	-ar estar	-er tener	-ir sentir
yo	est**aba**	ten**ía**	sent**ía**
tú	est**abas**	ten**ías**	sent**ías**
él/ella, usted	est**aba**	ten**ía**	sent**ía**
nosotros/nosotras	est**ábamos**	ten**íamos**	sent**íamos**
vosotros/vosotras	est**abais**	ten**íais**	sent**íais**
ellos/ellas, ustedes	est**aban**	ten**ían**	sent**ían**

- Note that **-er** and **-ir** verbs have the same endings. Note also that **-er** and **-ir** verbs have written accents in all forms, while **-ar** verbs only have an accent on the **nosotros** form.
- All verbs that have stem changes in the present or the preterite are regular in the imperfect.
- **Había** is a form of the verb **haber** that is used for singular and plural, *there was, there were.* It is the imperfect equivalent of the present **hay** and the preterite **hubo**.

B. The only three irregular verbs in the imperfect

	ser	ir	ver
yo	**era**	**iba**	**veía**
tú	**eras**	**ibas**	**veías**
él/ella, usted	**era**	**iba**	**veía**
nosotros/nosotras	**éramos**	**íbamos**	**veíamos**
vosotros/vosotras	**erais**	**ibais**	**veíais**
ellos/ellas, ustedes	**eran**	**iban**	**veían**

LENGUA EN ACCIÓN

Iba a + infinitivo

You have used the expression **ir a** + infinitive to talk about future actions and events. When **ir** is in the imperfect tense, this expression has the following meaning:

Yo **iba a salir** cuando llegaron mis amigos.	*I was going to leave when my friends arrived.*
Las cosas no **iban a ser** como yo quería.	*Things were not going to be as I wanted.*

Some other questions for **Actividad 1**: ¿Cómo eran tus vecinos, tus parientes, tus amigos? ¿Qué hacía la gente? ¿Había un cine?

1 El vecindario de mis primos. A friend of yours visited relatives in another city. Ask your friend questions about their neighborhood (**el vecindario, la colonia, el barrio**). Then, present the description of the neighborhood to your class.

1. ¿Estaba cerca del centro de la ciudad?
2. ¿Cómo era? ¿grande? ¿pequeño?
3. ¿Había discoteca?
4. ¿Tenía muchas tiendas?
5. ¿Cómo eran las tiendas?
6. ¿Estaba cerca de la playa?
7. ¿Tenía buenos supermercados?
8. ¿Era deliciosa la comida en los restaurantes?
9. ¿La gente podía jugar al tenis? ¿al golf? ¿al básquetbol?
10. ¿Eran bonitos los edificios?
11. ¿Cómo era la plaza?
12. ¿...?

2 La vida cambia. With a friend, discuss how persons and things were before and how they are now. Then, present your findings to the class. Follow the model.

► **Modelo:** *Mi familia (ser)* *pequeña / mediana / regular / grande*
—¿Cómo era antes tu familia?
—Antes, mi familia era grande, pero ahora es pequeña.

1. Mi familia (ser)	pequeña / mediana / regular / grande
2. Nuestros abuelos (ser)	jóvenes / viejos / débiles / fuertes
3. Los árboles (estar)	amarillos / verdes / pequeños / grandes
4. Nosotros (tener)	mucho / poco / bastante dinero
5. Yo (estar)	casado/a / soltero/a / divorciado/a
6. (Haber)	mucho / poco interés por el turismo
7. Todo (ser)	caro / barato / excelente / de mala calidad
8. Esta ciudad (ser)	una cuidad pequeña / grande / importante / no importante
9. Yo (ser)	simpático/a / antipático/a / listo/a / inteligente
10. El teatro (ser)	popular / excelente / malísimo

3 Las costumbres diarias. Work in groups of three. Ask your partners what their daily routines were ten years ago. Use the imperfect tense of the verbs below plus expressions like **¿a qué hora? ¿cuándo? temprano, tarde, todos los días, frecuentemente**. Write down the answers. Then, present your findings to the class.

► **Modelo:** *levantarse*
—¿A qué hora te levantabas?
—Generalmente me levantaba a las seis.

1. levantarse
2. almorzar en casa
3. cenar con amigos
4. despertarse
5. hacer las tareas
6. jugar con la computadora
7. acostarse los fines de semana
8. regresar a casa
9. salir para el colegio
10. ver televisión

II. Telling time, weather, and age in the past

More uses of the imperfect

Eran las ocho de la mañana.

Eran las ocho de la mañana cuando yo salí de casa.

The imperfect is generally used to tell time as the background of a past event or action. The event or action that happens within this time scenario is expressed with the preterite: **Eran las ocho de la mañana** (time background) **...cuando yo salí** (action).

Álbum familiar

Éste es Eduardo cuando tenía tres años. Ese día hacía sol.
En esta foto, la abuelita tenía 25 años. Llovía cuando tomamos la foto.
Invierno de 1995. Pablito cuando tenía cinco años. Hacía muchísimo frío.

- Like time, age and weather are common boundaries that we use to place an event or action in the past, and are also expressed with the imperfect. The events and actions that happen within these age and weather scenarios are generally expressed with the preterite.

Hacía frío cuando tomamos la foto.	*It was cold when we took the photo.*
Yo **tenía** dieciséis años cuando aprendí a conducir un auto.	*I was sixteen years old when I learned how to drive a car.*
Mi hermana **tenía** veinte años cuando se casó con Roberto.	*My sister was twenty years old when she married Roberto.*

For **Actividad 4,** bring in a few of your own photos, especially old family pictures, and have the class describe them.

4 ¿Qué tiempo hacía cuando tomaron las fotos? Describe the photos on page 213 with as many details as you can. Use the prepositions and adjectives that you have learned to describe people and things. Look at the model for ideas.

► **Modelo:** La abuelita Elena era muy bonita. Tenía el pelo muy largo. Ahora lo tiene corto. El día que tomaron la foto, ella estaba junto a la ventana. Llevaba un vestido bonito. Hacía muy mal tiempo...

5 ¿Qué hora era? Work in pairs. Ask your partner what the weather was like and the time that he or she did the following activities.

► **Modelo:** *salir esta mañana (6 a.m.)*
—¿Qué hora era cuando saliste esta mañana?
—Eran las seis de la mañana cuando salí.
—¿Qué tiempo hacía?
—Llovía cuando salí.

1. tomar el desayuno (8 a.m.)
2. preparar las tareas ayer (9 p.m.)
3. ayudar a tu amigo/a anoche (7 p.m.)
4. servir la cena anoche (8 p.m.)
5. reservar las habitaciones (2 p.m.)
6. enviar las cartas ayer (10 a.m.)

6 ¿Cuántos años tenías? Contesta las preguntas sobre tu vida.

1. ¿Cuántos años tenías cuando empezaste los estudios en la universidad?
2. ¿Cuántos años tenías hace cinco años?
3. ¿Cuántos años tenían tus padres cuando se casaron?
4. ¿Cuántos años tenías cuando recibiste tu licencia de conducir?
5. ¿Cuántos años tenías cuando te enamoraste por primera vez?
6. ¿Cuántos años tenías cuando leíste tu primer libro?
7. ¿Cuántos años tenías cuando viste la "Guerra de las Galaxias"?

III. Narrating a sequence of events with the imperfect

Imperfect and adverbial expressions of time

Las mascotas de Fernando y sus hermanos

Yo *siempre* (*always*) coleccionaba insectos y los buscaba en el parque *con frecuencia* (*frequently*).

***Generalmente* (*Generally*), Tomás prefería los canarios, pero *a veces* (*sometimes*) también tenía gatos.**

***A menudo* (*Often*), el perro de Felicia saltaba en los muebles de la sala. ¡Y Felicia tenía perros *todo el tiempo* (*all the time*)!**

Unas veces **(*Sometimes*), las mascotas vivían en paz. *Otras veces* (*Other times*), había caos total.**

Todos los veranos **(*Every summer*) pasábamos unas semanas en el campo y jugábamos juntos.**

Todos los días **(*Every day*) nos acostábamos cansados y satisfechos.**

- The highlighted adverbial expressions in the art on pages 214–215 are not used exclusively with the imperfect, but they are useful to emphasize that these are things you used to do in the past.
- The imperfect may be used to express the sequence in which habitual actions used to happen. Adverbial expressions are helpful to highlight this relationship.

Primero, Nayeli **se levantaba**, después, **desayunaba** y **por último, salía a trabajar.**	*First, Nayeli used to get up, and then, she had breakfast, and lastly, she went to work.*

- If you want to emphasize that the past events were all happening at the same time, you can use adverbial expressions like **mientras**, **cuando**, **simultáneamente**, and **al mismo tiempo (que)**.

Mientras Nayeli **viajaba** a España, sus estudiantes la **buscaban** en Puebla.	*While Nayeli was traveling to Spain, her students were looking for her in Puebla.*
Felipe **leía** un mensaje de Armando **al mismo tiempo que** alguien **persiguía** a Adriana por las calles de Sevilla.	*Felipe was reading a message from Armando at the same time that someone was chasing Adriana through the streets of Sevilla.*

7 **¿Qué hacían?** Reread the story above and answer the following questions about Fernando, his brothers and sisters, and their pets.

1. ¿Qué coleccionaba Fernando? ¿Cuándo?
2. Y los hermanos de Fernando, Tomás y Felicia, ¿qué coleccionaban? ¿Todo el tiempo? ¿Siempre?
3. ¿Cómo era la mascota de Felicia? ¿Qué hacía la mascota a menudo?
4. ¿Vivían las mascotas siempre en paz?
5. ¿Adónde iban en el verano Fernando y su familia?
6. ¿Qué pasaba por la noche? ¿Siempre o solamente a menudo?
7. ¿Había cosas que pasaban simultáneamente en casa de Fernando, Tomás y Felicia?

Answers to Actividad 7:

1. Fernando coleccionaba insectos con frecuencia.
2. Tomás coleccionaba canarios y a veces gatos; Felicia coleccionaba perros todo el tiempo.
3. La mascota de Felicia era muy activa. A menudo saltaba en los muebles de la sala.
4. Unas veces vivían en paz. Otras veces había caos total.
5. Pasaban unas semanas en el campo.
6. Por la noche siempre se acostaban cansados y satisfechos.
7. Sí. Fernando, Tomás y Felicia jugaban con sus animales.

For **Actividad 8,** first have all pairs work together on questions; then have the groups exchange questions and have all groups working on answering the questions in pairs.

8 **¿Tienes mascota en casa?** Work in pairs. First, design a questionnaire of five to ten questions like the ones in **Actividad 7** about Fernando's family, friends, and pets. Then, answer the questions and present the answers to the class.

IV. Avoiding redundancy

Double-object pronouns

¿Está todo listo ya?

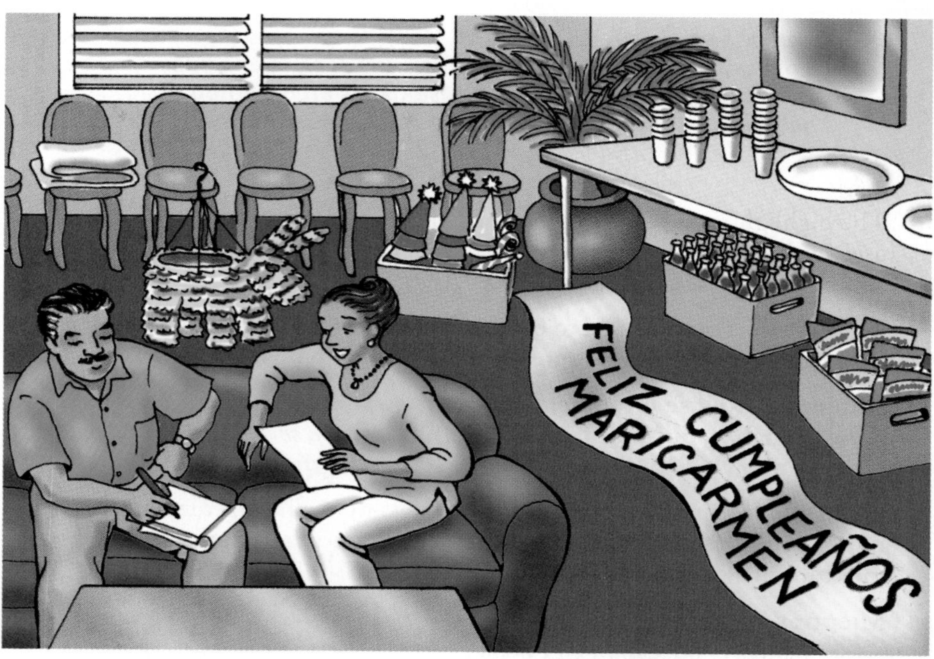

PEDRO: ¡La fiesta sorpresa de Maricarmen va a ser fenomenal!
MARISA: ¿Ya les mandaste las invitaciones a todos?
PEDRO: **Se las** mandé a casi todos. Me falta todavía enviár**sela** a Rosaura.
MARISA: **Se la** vas a enviar pronto, ¿verdad? ¿Ya pediste las flores?
PEDRO: Las flores **me las** envían a mi casa y yo las traigo el día de la fiesta.
MARISA: La torta de cumpleaños **nos la** trae Sofía dos horas antes de la fiesta.
PEDRO: ¿Estás segura? ¿Sofía **te lo** confirmó? Creo que no puede venir.
MARISA: Sofía no puede venir a la fiesta, pero sí puede traér**nosla**.
PEDRO: Bueno, pues no nos falta nada.
MARISA: Creo que ya está todo listo. Buen trabajo, ¡Maricarmen va a tener una magnífica sorpresa!

- You have already learned the direct- and the indirect-object pronouns. When you use both object pronouns in the same sentence, the indirect-object pronoun always precedes the direct-object pronoun.

La tienda **me** manda **las flores** a mi casa.	*The store sends me the flowers at my house.*
La tienda **me las** manda a mi casa.	*The store sends them to me at my house.*

- When the indirect-object pronouns **le** and **les** are used in the same sentence together with third-person direct-object pronouns, they change to **se**. The direct-object pronoun doesn't change form or position.

—¿Mandaste **las invitaciones** a **los chicos**?	*Did you send the invitations to the kids?*
—Sí, hoy **se las** mandé.	*Yes, I sent them today to them.*
—¿Mandaste **la invitación** a **Susana**?	*Did you send the invitation to Susana?*
—Sí, **se la** mandé.	*Yes, I sent it to her.*

- In verbal expressions with an infinitive, the two pronouns can be attached to the end of the infinitive. Generally, a written accent needs to be added to the infinitive.

—¿Vas a mandarle **los documentos a Adriana**?	*Are you going to send the documents to Adriana?*
—Sí, voy a **mandárselos.**	*Yes, I'm going to send them to her.*

- Since **se** can refer to any one of the third persons, it is usual to clarify its meaning with a prepositional pronoun, a noun, or a proper name.

¿Cuándo les mandaste las invitaciones a todos?	*When did you send the invitations to everyone?*
Se la mandé **a Rosana** ayer, pero **se las** mandé **a Jorge y Teresa** anteayer.	*I sent it to Rosana yesterday, but I sent them to Jorge and Teresa the day before yesterday.*

You may wish to mention that with double-object pronouns the second one almost always begins with **l** (**lo, la, los, la**) and that the order is the opposite of English: **Él me lo da** = (*lit.*) *He to me it gives.*

9 ***Una fiesta para los padres.*** Nora is planning a surprise anniversary party for her parents and her aunt Teresa offers to help her. Fill in the correct form of the direct and indirect pronouns in the passage.

TÍA: Nora, ¿es cierto que tú estás preparando la fiesta de aniversario de tus papás?
NORA: Sí tía, yo ______ ______ estoy preparando. Va a ser el seis de mayo.
TÍA: ¿Con quién la estás preparando? ¿Con Emilita?
NORA: Sí, Emilita ______ ______ está ayudando a preparar de principio a fin.
TÍA: ¿Quién te está comprando los refrescos?
NORA: Mi hermano Jorge ______ ______ está comprando. Vamos a servir vino, también.
TÍA: Necesitan música, ¿no? Nosotros podemos ayudarte también.
NORA: Sí, tía, ¿puedes comprarme el último CD de Celia Cruz? Quiero tocar______ durante la fiesta.
TÍA: Voy a llamar a la tienda ahora mismo y si tengo tiempo, ______ ______ compro yo misma.
NORA: Gracias. ¡Eres la tía más maravillosa del mundo!

Answers to Actividad 9:
1. se la
2. me la
3. me los
4. lo
5. te lo

Answers to Actividad 10:
(All questions will begin with **¿A quién le compraste...**)
1. Se lo compré a mi sobrina Mercedes.
2. Se las compré a mi tío Roberto.
3. Se la compré a mi hermana mayor.
4. Se lo compré a mi mamá.
5. Se los compré a mi novio/a.
6. Se las compré a todos.

Do this exercise with the entire class using props or pictures for the items mentioned.

10 **¿Para quién es?** You are going through your shopping list of gifts with a friend who is going to help you wrap up and mark all the gifts. Work with a partner following the model.

▶ **Modelo:** *estas medias / mi abuelita*
—¿A quién le compraste estas medias?
—Se las compré a mi abuelita Adela.

1. este traje de baño / mi sobrina Mercedes
2. estas entradas para el partido de fútbol / mi tío Roberto
3. esta novela de misterio / mi hermana mayor
4. este vaso de cristal / mi mamá
5. estos pantalones deportivos / mi novio/a
6. estas fotos del verano / todos

Answers to Actividad 11:
1. Sí, te lo presto.
2. Sí, te lo pido.
3. Sí, se las compro.
4. Sí, se lo traigo (os lo traigo).
5. Sí, se las escribo.
6. Sí, se lo traigo (os lo traigo).
7. Sí, se la digo.

After students have done **Actividad 11** in pairs, ask them the same questions individually but with the following pattern: **¿Me lo prestas a mí o se lo prestas a ella?** to vary the indirect-object pronouns. Be sure students answer you with **usted,** reminding them that the teacher is the "authority figure."

11 **¿Qué haces si...?** You would like to find out what your friends would do for you or other persons that need help. Work with a partner and ask each other questions, answering with direct- and indirect-object pronouns.

▶ **Modelo:** *—Si tus amigos se casan, ¿les regalas muchas flores?*
—Sí, se las regalo.

1. Si tengo frío y necesito un suéter, ¿me lo prestas?
2. Si vamos a un restaurante, ¿me pides un plato delicioso?
3. Si un/a amigo/a está enfermo/a, ¿le compras las medicinas?
4. Si necesitamos un libro, ¿nos lo traes?
5. Si tus amigos/as están de vacaciones, ¿les escribes muchas cartas?
6. Si necesitamos un protector solar, ¿nos lo traes?
7. Si la policía te pide decir la verdad, ¿se la dices?

12 **¿Y tú qué haces?** Work in pairs. Select from the questions below and ask each other which things you do and for whom. Follow the model.

▶ **Modelo:** *escribir tarjetas de cumpleaños*
—¿A quiénes les escribes tarjetas de cumpleaños?
—Se las escribo a mis amigos y a mi familia.

1. ayudar a poner la mesa
2. reservar las habitaciones en el hotel Prisma
3. servir buena comida
4. dar dinero para ir de compras
5. escribir muchas cartas
6. comprar regalos
7. hablar español
8. mandar una postal

Lectura B

Introducción

Legends are an important part of the Spanish-speaking world. Here is the legend that Felipe tells Adriana in the video episode about the creation of the first man and the first woman.

Prelectura

1 Términos. Working in pairs, match the terms in column **A** associated with the terms in column **B**.

A	B
1. sol	a. alegría
2. madre	b. hombre
3. mujer	c. tristeza
4. lágrimas (*tears*)	d. hijo
5. risa	e. luna

2 Yo prefiero leer... Check off the following list in order of preference of what you like to read. Then, compare your preferences to a classmate's and explain who your favorite authors/books/magazines, and so on, are and why you like to read them.

▶ **Modelo:** *Me gusta leer la poesía de Maya Angelou porque su lenguaje es hermoso y porque su poesía siempre tiene un mensaje importante.*

1. ______ novelas
2. ______ revistas (*magazines*)
3. ______ poesía
4. ______ leyendas
5. ______ cuentos (*stories*)
6. ______ cartas
7. ______ ensayos (*essays*)
8. ______ periódicos

3 ¿Y tu familia? Talking in groups, describe your family by responding to the following questions you ask of each other.

1. ¿Cómo se llaman tus abuelos? ¿Y tus padres?
2. ¿De dónde son tus abuelos? ¿De dónde son tus padres?
3. ¿Son grandes las familias de tus abuelos?
4. ¿Qué lenguas hablan en tu casa? ¿Y en la casa de tus abuelos?
5. ¿Cuántos hermanos tienes?
6. ¿Tienes celos (*Are you jealous*) de tus hermanos o primos? ¿Por qué?

Introducción a una leyenda cubana

The reading that follows is a Ciboney legend from Cuba. The Ciboneys were a group of indigenous people who lived in Cuba before the 15th century, along with other extinct cultures, like the Tainos. This legend is about the creation of man and woman. It was collected through oral tradition and later in written form around the 15th–16th centuries. Do not worry if you do not understand the meaning of every line. With a classmate, read the legend aloud and work through it together. Then, do the activities that follow.

La creación del hombre y la mujer

FELIPE: La leyenda dice que, Huión, el dios sol, creó a Hamao, el primer hombre. Hamao era muy feliz, pero de pronto,° empezó a sentirse muy solo…

suddenly

ADRIANA: …y entonces Huión creó a la primera mujer…

FELIPE: Casi, casi, adivinas°…, pero no, no la creó Huión. A la primera mujer la creó la luna.

you guess

ADRIANA: La luna. ¿Y cómo se llamaba esa primera mujer?

FELIPE: Se llamaba Guanaroca. Era muy bella, de piel color de oro° y de pelo negro. Un poco después, Guanaroca y Hamao tuvieron a Imao, su primer hijo.

gold

ADRIANA: ¿Y cómo era Imao?

FELIPE: Era un niño muy hermoso y su mamá lo quería muchísimo. Por todo esto, Hamao comenzó a tener un poco de celos° por él.

to be jealous

ADRIANA: ¿Celos? Un padre, ¡tener celos de su propio hijo!

FELIPE: Y por los celos, Hamao lo mató…

ADRIANA: ¿Qué dices? ¡Hamao mató a su propio hijo! ¿Y qué pasó° después?

happened

FELIPE: Pues, como era natural, Hamao se arrepintió° cuando vio° de la tristeza tan profunda de Guanaroca. Y entonces, Guanaroca lo perdonó, y tuvieron otro hijo. Se llamaba Caonao.

was sorry
realized

ADRIANA: ¿Y su padre lo mató también a él?

FELIPE: No, no, no lo mató, por el contrario, Hamao quería mucho a Caonao. Pero después éste creció y empezó a sentirse solo también.

ADRIANA: ¡Ya sé! Entonces, el dios Huión, le creó una mujer a él también.

FELIPE: Tampoco adivinaste° esta vez, porque a Jagua, la mujer de Caonao, también la creó la luna, la diosa de la noche, con uno de sus rayos lunares. ¡Zas!

did you guess

ADRIANA: ¡Ah! Ya entiendo. Primero, Huión creó a Hamao, el primer hombre. Luego, la luna, la diosa de la noche, creó a la primera mujer. ¡Qué interesante! Finalmente, ¿qué sucedió con Caonao y Jagua?

FELIPE: Pues, fueron muy felices. Pero, bueno, a ver, ¿cuál es el verdadero final de la historia? Que Guanaroca fue la madre de los primeros hombres y Jagua fue la madre de las primeras mujeres.

ADRIANA: ¡Qué bella historia! El principio° de la humanidad.
FELIPE: El sol y la luna.
ADRIANA: El hombre y la mujer.
FELIPE: ¡La tristeza y la alegría!

beginning

Postlectura

4 *Comprensión.* Complete the following ideas about the legend.

1. La leyenda es originalmente de la isla de ________.
a. La República Dominicana b. Cuba c. Puerto Rico

2. Huión era el dios ________ y creó a Hamao, el primer hombre.
a. sombra b. sol c. tierra

3. La luna creó a la primera mujer que se llamaba ________.
a. Guadalupe b. Guanaroca c. Georgina

4. Guanaroca era muy ________.
a. fea b. alta c. bella

5. El primer hijo de Guanaroca y Hamao se llamaba ________.
a. Ignacio b. Imao c. Isaac

6. Hamao, el padre de Imao, un día tuvo ________ de él y lo mató.
a. cuidado b. miedo c. celos

7. Guanaroca y Hamao tuvieron otro hijo que se llamaba ________.
a. Caonao b. Carlos c. Camilo

8. La luna, creó a ________, la mujer de Caonao.
a. Jorge b. Jagua c. Julián

9. La leyenda se trata ________.
a. del principio de la humanidad b. de la soledad de la luna y el sol c. de la muerte de los hijos y los padres

10. En tu opinión, ¿qué tono tiene la leyenda? Es ________.
a. feliz b. increíble c. triste

11. En tu opinión, esta leyenda es ________.
a. bonita b. difícil c. aburrida

Answers to Actividad 4:
1. b
2. b
3. b
4. c
5. b
6. c
7. a
8. b
9. a
10. *Answers will vary.* Have students explain their opinions.
11. *Answers will vary.* Have students explain their opinions.

5 *Un árbol genealógico.* Working with a classmate, draw and label a family tree based on the legend you have just read.

6 *Leyendas del mundo.* Working with a classmate, make up a story to describe a family tree you create. Present your story to the class.

7 *Mi leyenda.* Write a short legend of ten lines, in Spanish, about one of the following topics: **la familia, la escuela, el país, la luna, el sol, el agua, la tierra.** Then, read your legend to a classmate, comparing your creations.

En resumen

I. Hablemos

1 **Recuerdos.** You are attending your twenty-fifth high school reunion and run into an old friend. Reminisce about the things you used to do when you were in school. Review the uses of the preterite and imperfect.

2 **Entre enemigas.** When Sunglasses kidnaps Nayeli, they drive off to a secluded place. On the ride there, Nayeli tries to find out more about her kidnapper—who she is and why she is following her. With a partner, role-play the part of Nayeli and Sunglasses to complete the following conversation. Add four speeches.

NAYELI: ¿Cómo supo usted dónde estaba yo?
DOÑA GAFASOSCURAS: Es muy sencillo, señora arqueóloga. Puse un microfonito en la agenda y…

II. Investiguemos por Internet

Looking for personal homepages

Many people now have their own Web pages on the Internet with personal information and family pictures for anyone to see. Some of these pages also include a résumé and professional information for potential employers or clients.

3 **Mi página Web.** In this activity, you will present to the class information about three persons gathering data from their own Web pages. Work in groups and make a list of three people that you know or famous persons that you would like to know more about. If you have your own Web site, include yourself as one of the three persons. Access the Web sites and describe the information in them to your class. Give as many details as possible, especially if the sites have information about the person's family. Include a description of any photos or illustrations and whether there are links to other interesting Web sites. The White and Yellow Pages on the Internet may be useful in your search. Internet Guides may also be helpful.

Vocabulario informático	
Guía Internet	*Internet Guide*
Páginas amarillas	*Yellow Pages*
Páginas blancas	*White Pages*

III. Escribamos

Writing strategy: Using a dictionary

A dictionary is useful not only when reading a passage in Spanish. When used properly, it is also useful when writing a composition. To use a dictionary effectively, be sure to keep the following in mind.

1. There are many translations for some words. Do not use the first entry, but look for the translation that best suits your needs.
2. Once you have selected a word in the English–Spanish section, cross check its meaning in the Spanish–English section of the dictionary to assure accuracy.
3. When checking in the Spanish–English section, be sure to read any grammar notes that will tell you about irregular forms, different translations, and so on.
4. Always review the guide to using the dictionary to understand important symbols and abbreviations. Some common abbreviations are:

f femenino
m masculino
adv adverbio
adj adjetivo
s sustantivo (*noun*)

▶ **Modelo:** **fan**[1] (fan) **I.** s. (*paper*) abanico; (*electric*) ventilador *m*; AGR. aventadora **II.** tr. **fanned, fan-ning** (*to cool*) abanicar; FIG. (*to stir up*) avivar, excitar; AGR. aventar —intr. • **to f. out** abrirse en abanico

fan[2] (fan) s. FAM. (*enthusiast*) aficionado, hincha *m.*

suit (soot) **I.** s. (*garments*) traje *m*; (*set*) conjunto, juego; (*cards*) palo; (*court proceedings*) pleito; (*courtship*) galanteo, cortejo • **to follow s.** (*in cards*) jugar el mismo palo; (*as an example*) seguir el ejemplo **II.** tr. (*to accommodate*) ajustarse a, adaptarse a; (*to satisfy*) satisfacer; (*to dress*) vestir • **to s. oneself** hacer lo que uno quiere • **to s. to** adaptar a —intr. convenir

support (se-port') **I.** tr. (*weight*) aguantar, sostener, corroborar; (*a spouse, child*) mantener; (*a cause, theory*) sostener, respaldar; (*with money*) ayudar • **to s. onself** (*to earn one's living*) ganarse la vida; (*to learn*) apoyarse **II.** s. (*act*) apoyo; (*maintenance*) mantenimiento; ARQ., TEC. soporte *m.*

Strategy in action

Turn to *Escribamos* in the Workbook to practice the writing strategy of using a dictionary.

Answers to Actividad 4:
1. apoyo
2. ganarme la vida
3. traje/vestido
4. aficionado
5. me satisface/me conviene
6. abanicar
7. respalda
8. soporte
9. pleito
10. ventilador

4 Usando el diccionario. Use the dictionary entries to decide which word to use in place of the italicized words.

1. Can I count on your *support*?
2. I can't *support* myself on this salary.
3. I need a new *suit* for the wedding.
4. I'm a sports *fan*.
5. It *suits* me just fine.
6. It's hot outside and you need to *fan* yourself to keep cool.
7. My psychology instructor *supports* the Freudian school of thought.
8. The house has good *support* beams.
9. The plaintiff has filed a *suit* in the court.
10. Turn on the *fan*! It's hot in here.

5 Mi pariente favorito. Write a description of your favorite relative. Describe where this person was born, where he or she lives and what profession he or she has. Then tell an interesting story about something that has happened to him or her or to the both of you.

6 Querida Adriana. Nayeli has a dream in which she talks with Adriana. Write a conversation between the two of them where they discuss what happened to them in the two episodes in Chapter 5.

Vocabulario

Pasatiempos y recreos

bailar en una discoteca	*to dance in a club*
el balón	*beachball*
broncearse	*to get a tan*
bucear	*to go skindiving, snorkeling*
buscar conchas	*to look for shells*
hacer castillos de arena	*to build sand castles*
hacer esquí acuático	*to go water skiing*
hacer surfing	*to surf*
hacer un picnic	*to have a picnic*
ir de compras	*to go shopping*
ir de pesca (pescar)	*to fish*
montar a caballo	*to go horseback riding*
montar en bicicleta	*to go bicycling*
nadar	*to swim*
navegar en velero	*to go sailing*
la novela	*novel*
el protector solar	*sunscreen lotion*
protegerse	*to protect onself*
quemarse	*to get a sunburn*
la sandalia	*sandal*
la sombrilla	*umbrella*
la toalla	*towel*
tomar el sol	*to sunbathe*

Partes del cuerpo

la boca	*mouth*
el brazo	*arm*
la cabeza	*head*
la cara	*face*
el dedo	*finger/toe*
el diente	*tooth*
la espalda	*back*
el estómago	*stomach*
la mano	*hand*
la nariz	*nose*
el ojo	*eye*
la oreja	*ear*
el pecho	*chest*
el pelo	*hair*
el pie	*foot*
la pierna	*leg*
la rodilla	*knee*

De viaje

la aduana	*customs*
el/la aduanero/a	*customs agent*
al llegar	*upon arriving*
al subir	*upon boarding*
aparecer	*to appear*
aterrizar	*to land*
la clase turística	*coach class*
contar	*to tell*
de repente	*suddenly*
despegar	*to take off*
la emigración	*emigration*
la escala	*layover*
estar a tiempo	*to be on time*
estar atrasado/a	*to be late*
facturar el equipaje	*to check in luggage*
hacer cola	*to wait in line*
el mostrador	*counter*
el pasaporte	*passport*
el/la piloto	*pilot*
la puerta de salida	*departure gate*
quejarse	*to complain*
la sala de espera	*waiting room*

Familia, animales y vecinos

el/la abuelo/a	*grandfather/ grandmother*
la adolescencia	*adolescence*
el/la amigo/a	*friend*
el/la bebé	*baby boy/girl*
el/la bisabuelo/a	*great grandfather/ great grandmother*
el canario	*canary*
casarse	*to get married*
el/la chico/a	*child, young person*
el conejo	*rabbit*
el/la cuñado/a	*brother/sister-in-law*
dedicarse	*to dedicate/devote oneself*
la edad adulta	*adulthood*
enamorarse	*to fall in love*
la esposa	*wife*
el esposo/ marido	*husband*
estar casado/a	*to be married*
estar divorciado/a	*to be divorced*
estar enamorado/a	*to be in love*
estar separado/a	*to be separated*
la familia	*family*
el/la gato/a	*cat*
hacerse + *profession*	*to become + profession*
el/la hermano/a	*brother/sister*
el/la hijo/a	*son/daughter*
la madre	*mother*
el/la muchacho/a	*boy/girl*
nacer	*to be born*
el/la nieto/a	*grandson/ granddaughter*
la niñez	*childhood*
el/la niño/a	*baby, toddler, child*
la nuera	*daughter-in-law*
el padre	*father*
los padres	*parents*
el/la pariente	*family member, relative*
el/la perro/a	*dog*
el/la primo/a	*cousin*

ser adulto/a *to be an adult*
ser mayor *to be older*
ser menor *to be younger*
ser soltero/a *to be single*
el/la sobrino/a *nephew/niece*
el /la suegro/a *father/mother-in-law*
el/la tío/a *uncle/aunt*
la tortuga *turtle*
el vecindario *neighborhood*
el/la vecino/a *neighbor*
el yerno *son-in-law*

Profesiones y oficios

(See p. 205.)

Adverbios de tiempo

a menudo *often*
finalmente *finally*
generalmente *generally*
luego *then*
otras veces *other times*
por último *finally*
primero que todo *first of all*
unas veces *sometimes*
ya *now, already, yet*

CAPÍTULO 6

LOCALIDAD: Puerto Rico, Ecuador

6A

¿Cuál es el plan de Gafasnegras?

6B

While evil forces are about to descend on Nayeli, Adriana, and Felipe in Puerto Rico, a mysterious person picks up the Jaguar Twin in Ecuador.

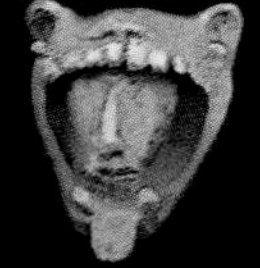

Vocabulary themes

- Talking about music and dance
- Talking about sports
- Discussing technology
- Talking about and looking for work

Language structures

- Indicating reason, duration, purpose, destination
- Using verbs that change meaning in the preterite
- Indicating how long ago a past action occurred
- Narrating in the past
- Expressing reflexive actions
- Stressing the action and not the subject
- Giving instructions and making requests

Culture topics

- Los fabulosos ritmos del Caribe
- El Yunque, esplendor ecológico
- El observatorio de Arecibo

Readings

- Algunos deportes caribeños
- Internet: La red mundial

Reading/writing strategies

- Skimming for main ideas
- Freewriting

Internet strategy

- Using Internet guides

ETAPA A

Pistas y palabras

I. Talking about music and dance

Baile y canto

YA ESTÁ SONANDO°

PROYECTO UNO *New Era*

En este tercer **disco** del **cuarteto** neoyorquino,° **producido** por el legendario Jellybean Benítez (quien **se hizo**° **famoso** trabajando con Madonna, Sting y Whitney Houston) para su nuevo **sello**° **bilingüe**, podemos escuchar R&B, *merengue*,° hip-hop y música house. Este **grupo** de jóvenes (de descendencia puertorriqueña y dominicana, pero **criados**° en la Gran Manzana°) mezcla **hábilmente**° el **sonido**° de las calles con el ritmo caribeño que llevan en la sangre.° (H.O.L.A. Recordings)

It's already playing
New York quartet
became
(record) label
rhythmic music of the Dominican Republic / raised / Big Apple / skillfully mixes / sound / blood

Patty Cabrera

bella y de las nuestras°

Tiene 28 años, nació en California, de madre puertorriqueña y padre cubano, y está considerada como una de las **cantantes**° de música religiosa más famosas del mundo. ¡Por eso la prestigiosa revista norteamericana *People* calificó° a Patty Cabrera como una de las personas más bonitas y **exitosas**° del mundo!

beautiful and one of ours
singers
named
successful

Have student volunteers read these passages aloud. Explain the role of the dieresis as a marker to ensure the pronunciation of the **u** in **bilingüe,** as opposed to **merengue,** which has no dieresis and in which the **u** is not pronounced.

For further information on Patty Cabrera, check the World Wide Web.

Palabras y expresiones útiles

los audífonos	*headphones*	la guitarra	*guitar*
el/la bailarín/ina	*dancer*	la música	*music*
la balada	*ballad*	el piano	*piano*
la batería	*drum set*	el ritmo	*rhythm*
el/la cantante	*singer*	la salsa	*salsa music*
el clarinete	*clarinet*	el saxofón	*saxophone*
el conjunto	*band*	el trombón	*trombone*
el disco compacto	*compact disc*	la trompeta	*trumpet*
la flauta	*flute*	el violín	*violin*
la grabadora (videograbadora)	*tape/video player/recorder*		
cantar	*to sing*	grabar	*to tape*
bailar	*to dance*		

1 **¿Verdadero o falso?** Read the following statements about the ads. Mark **V** for each true statement and **F** for each false one. Then, correct the false ones.

1. Patty Cabrera es una famosa cantante de jazz.
2. *New Era* trabaja con Whitney Houston y Sting.
3. Patty Cabrera tiene mucho éxito.

Answers to Actividad 1:
1. **F**—Ella canta música religiosa.
2. **F**—Jellybean Benítez trabaja con ellos.
3. **V**

4. *New Era* canta música salsa.
5. *New Era* canta en inglés y en español.
6. Patty Cabrera nació en Cuba.
7. *New Era* es de California.

4. **F**—*New Era* canta música R&B, merengue, hip-hop y house.
5. **V**
6. **F**—Nació en California.
7. **F**—*New Era* es de Nueva York.

Further information on these musicians is available on the World Wide Web.

2 Asociaciones. What instruments do the following people play? Compare your answers with a partner.

1. Elton John
2. Tito Puente
3. Miles Davis
4. Carlos Santana
5. Ringo Starr
6. Joan Baez
7. Itzak Perlman
8. Andrés Segovia
9. Kenny G.

Answers to Actividad 2:
1. piano
2. batería
3. trompeta
4. guitarra
5. batería
6. guitarra
7. violín
8. guitarra
9. saxofón

3 Preguntas personales. With a partner, answer these questions.

1. ¿Qué tipo de música te gusta?
2. ¿Te gusta bailar? ¿Dónde? ¿Cuándo?
3. ¿Cuál es tu conjunto musical favorito? ¿Por qué?
4. ¿Quién es tu cantante favorito/a? ¿Por qué?
5. ¿Quién era tu cantante favorito/a cuando tenías diez años? ¿Y cuando tenías 16 años? ¿Por qué?
6. ¿Tocas algún instrumento? ¿Cuál?
7. ¿Tocabas algún instrumento cuando eras niño/a? ¿Qué instrumento?
8. ¿Te gustaba practicar? ¿Por qué sí o por qué no?

ENLACE CULTURAL

Los fabulosos ritmos del Caribe

Dos parejas bailando en La Habana, Cuba.

El Caribe es famoso por su música y por sus bailes de origen africano. La música es un elemento omnipresente en la vida diaria de la gente, en los clubes, los bares, las casas, los carnavales y los festivales. Los ritmos tienen gran vitalidad, son muy expresivos e invitan al baile. Muchos de estos ritmos son populares internacionalmente, especialmente entre los países de habla española. La rumba y el cha-cha-cha son de Cuba, el merengue es de la República Dominicana y la cumbia tiene su origen en el caribe colombiano. La salsa tiene su origen en los ritmos de varios países caribeños y también recibió influencia de músicos latinos en los Estados Unidos.

Cuando las parejas bailan ritmos caribeños, el hombre y la mujer bailan juntos° con movimientos de caderas° rítmicos y sensuales y muchas veces con pasos° complejos como los pasos de la salsa. Estos ritmos pegajosos° los producen los músicos con varios instrumentos de percusión como el tambor,° la conga y las maracas.

close together / hips
steps / catchy
drum

Discusión en grupos

¿Qué instrumentos y bailes típicos conoces? ¿Cómo son? ¿Qué origen tienen? ¿Sabes bailar esos bailes típicos?

II. Talking about sports

¿Qué deportes practicas?

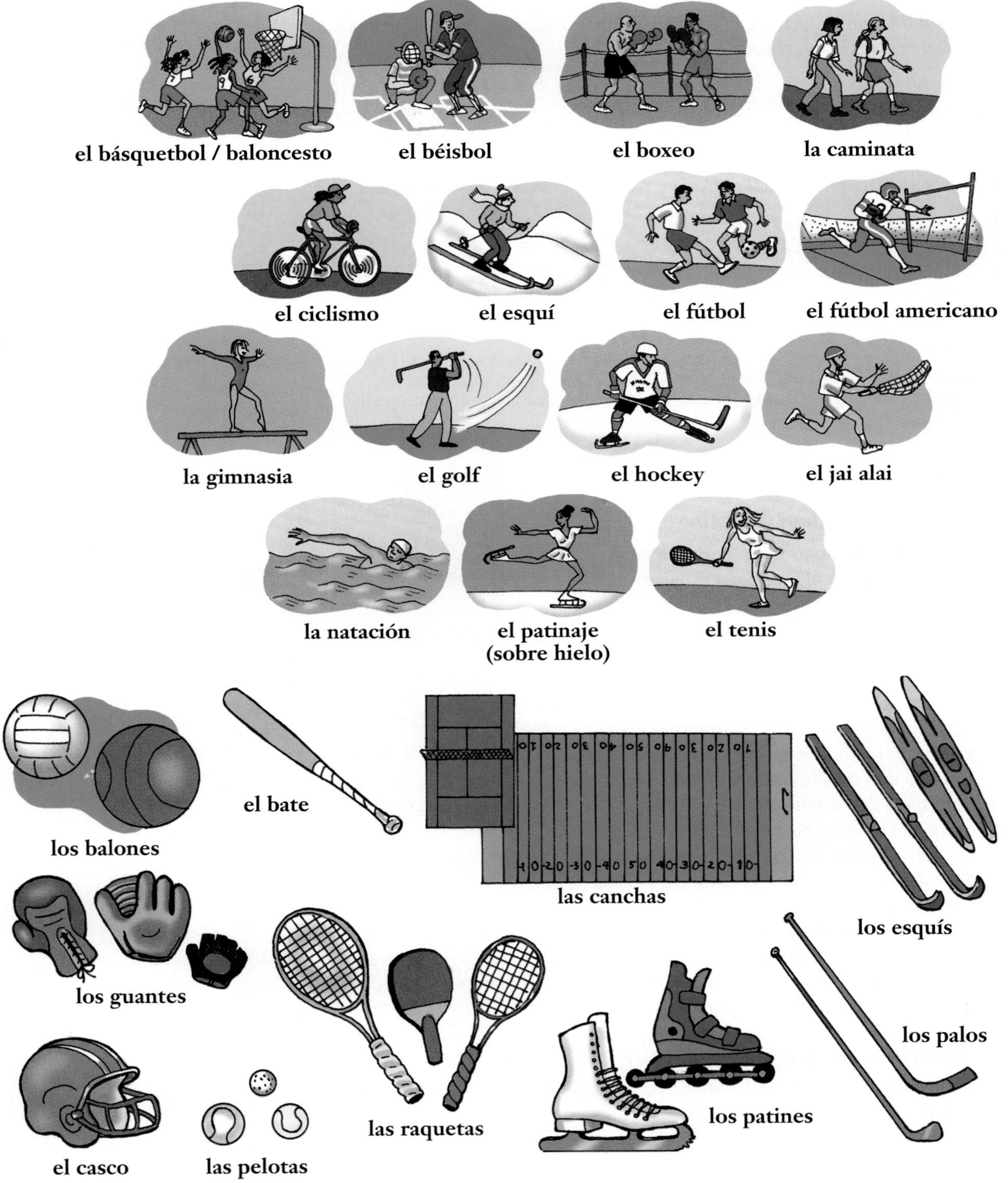

Palabras y expresiones útiles

el/la aficionado/a	*fan*	el uniforme	*uniform*
el/la deportista	*athlete, sports enthusiast*	ganar	*to win*
el equipo	*team*	gozar (de)	*to enjoy*
el/la espectador/a	*spectator*	patear	*to kick*
el/la jugador/a	*player*	patinar	*to skate*
el partido	*game*	perder	*to lose*
la pista	*ice rink, running track*		

4 **Busca la pareja.** Match the sports in the first illustration to the sporting equipment in the second. Follow the model.

▸ **Modelo:** *Para jugar al béisbol, necesitamos pelota, uniforme y bate.*

5 **¿Con qué se juegan estos deportes?** What parts of the body or sports equipment in column A do you use to do the activities in column B?

A		B	
la cabeza	las manos	jugar al tenis	tocar la guitarra
el balón	los pies	nadar	jugar al fútbol
la pelota	todo el cuerpo	jugar juegos de computadora	jugar al volibol
la raqueta			ciclismo

6 **Encuesta.** Ask four classmates the following questions about sports. Write down their answers and present them to the class.

¿Cuál es tu deporte favorito? ¿Por qué?
¿Quién es tu jugador/a favorito/a? ¿Por qué? ¿Qué deporte juega?
¿Cuál es tu equipo favorito? ¿Por qué?

ENLACE CULTURAL

El Yunque, esplendor ecológico

El coquí.

El Yunque, con 11.200 hectáreas, es uno de los más extraordinarios bosques pluviales° del Caribe. Está bajo la administración de los Estados Unidos; tiene más de 240 especies de árboles° y recibe un promedio° de 305 cm de lluvia al año. Hay dos impresionantes cascadas° y cientos de diferentes especies de animales, las que incluyen la boa puertorriqueña, el papagayo° y el coquí°. Esta gran riqueza° ecológica permite a los ecólogos estudiar plantas y animales, algunos de ellos en peligro° de extinción.

rainforests / *trees* / *average* / *impressive waterfalls* / *parrot / coqui frog* / *richness* / *danger*

Discusión en grupos

¿Qué bosques importantes hay en tu país o en tu estado? ¿Son necesarios? ¿Qué características tienen? ¿Cómo es el clima? ¿Qué tipo de plantas existen allí? ¿y qué tipo de animales? ¿Cuál es el animal más típico del área? ¿Cómo es?

Answers to Actividad 5:
1. la cabeza: jugar al fútbol
2. el balón: jugar al volibol
3. la pelota: jugar al fútbol, al tenis
4. la raqueta: jugar al tenis
5. las manos: jugar juegos de computadora; tocar la guitarra
6. los pies: ciclismo, jugar al fútbol
7. todo el cuerpo: nadar, jugar al volibol, jugar al fútbol, jugar al tenis

Expansion: Have students write about childhood sports preferences.

Cuando era niño/a... Escribe un párrafo describiendo qué deportes jugabas cuando eras niño/a. ¿Dónde? ¿Con quién? ¿Cuándo?

Adriana y Felipe are looking for Nayeli in Puerto Rico. This selection describes one of the ecological splendors of the island.

For the **Enlace cultural,** bring in pictures of El Yunque and/or have students find out about it on the World Wide Web.

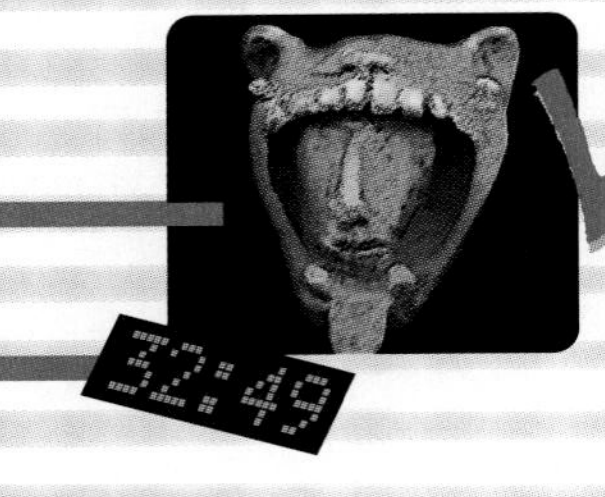

VISTAS Y VOCES

I. Preparémonos

1 Anticipación. In pairs, answer these questions.

A. 1. Si una persona extraña te persigue, ¿qué haces?
a) Corres rápidamente. b) La atacas. c) Gritas mucho.
2. ¿Qué situaciones te dan miedo?
3. ¿Cuál es el objeto más importante en tu cuarto? ¿Por qué?

B. Review chapter opening photo 6A on page 227.
¿Dónde está Nayeli? ¿Qué hace doña Gafasnegras con ella? ¿Qué piensas tú que va a pasar?

Para comprender mejor

afuera de	*outside of*	jurar	*to swear*
caerse	*to fall*	mágico/a	*magic*
el diseño	*design*	pálido/a	*pale*
extraño/a	*strange*	el secuestrador	*kidnapper*
hacer daño a alguien	*to harm someone*	el secuestro	*kidnapping*
involucrar	*to involve*	significar	*to mean*
		sonar	*to sound*

2 Secuencia. Put the video action shots in a logical order. Then, working in pairs, answer the following question: **¿Qué personaje va a hacerles daño a Nayeli, Adriana y Felipe? ¿Cómo?**

1.

2.

3.

4.

II. Miremos y escuchemos

3 **¿Verdadero o falso?** While watching this episode, mark **V** for each true statement and **F** for each false one. Then, correct the false sentences.

1. _______ Adriana y Felipe regresan a las habitaciones de su hotel.
2. _______ Adriana le dice a Felipe que ella vio al hombre del anillo en el hotel.
3. _______ El hombre del anillo entra a la habitación de Felipe.
4. _______ Adriana habla por teléfono con Nayeli.
5. _______ Adriana dice que tienen que alquilar un carro para buscar a Nayeli.
6. _______ Adriana no está preocupada.
7. _______ Nayeli comenta que los dos jóvenes van a necesitar un mapa de la isla.
8. _______ En Ecuador, Zulaya recoge el paquete con el jaguar gemelo.
9. _______ Felipe maneja al centro ceremonial indígena de Tibes afuera de Ponce.
10. _______ Adriana y Felipe se encuentran con los primos bandidos en el puente.

Answers to Actividad 3:

1. **V**
2. **V**
3. **F**—El hombre del anillo no entra en la habitación.
4. **V**
5. **V**
6. **F**—Adriana está preocupada.
7. **V**
8. **V**
9. **F**—Adriana maneja al centro ceremonial indígena de Tibes afuera de Ponce.
10. **V**

III. Comentemos

4 **Comprensión.** Answer the following questions in groups.

1. ¿Qué tiempo hace cuando Adriana y Felipe caminan al hotel?
2. ¿A quién ve Felipe al entrar a su habitación? ¿y Adriana?
3. ¿Quién llama a Adriana? ¿Qué tono tiene esa persona?
4. ¿Dónde y con quién está Nayeli?
5. ¿Es prisionera o invitada Nayeli? ¿Va todo bien?
6. ¿Por qué necesitan un coche y un mapa Adriana y Felipe?
7. ¿Cómo encuentra Adriana a Nayeli? ¿A qué ciudad tienen que ir Adriana y Felipe?
8. ¿Dónde tiene Felipe los mapas?
9. ¿Qué cosa rara ocurre con algunos paquetes en la oficina en el Ecuador?
10. ¿Cuándo llegó el paquete? ¿Qué encuentra Zulaya en el paquete?
11. ¿Qué coche sospechoso está en el parque ceremonial de Tibes en Ponce?
12. ¿Cómo está Gafasnegras—arrogante o humilde?

Answers to Actividad 4:

1. Hace sol y hace viento.
2. Felipe no ve a nadie. Adriana ve al hombre del anillo raro.
3. Nayeli; Tiene un tono raro.
4. Nayeli está con Gafasnegras y un hombre.
5. Es prisionera. Todo no va bien.
6. Tienen que buscar a Nayeli.
7. muy extraña; Tienen que ir a Ponce.
8. en la computadora
9. Se caen.
10. Hace dos días. Encuentra al jaguar.
11. el coche blanco que estaba en el aeropuerto para recoger a Nayeli
12. arrogante

5 **El mágico jaguar gemelo.** You are a reporter for your school newspaper and have to interview two Spanish students about this episode and the magical jaguar. Work in groups of three to sketch out key questions, and then role-play the scene for the class.

6 **Miremos otra vez.** After viewing the episode again, put the video action shots in the correct order.

Correct order of video action shots: 2, 3, 4, 1

7 **Mi personaje.** Invent another possible character for the next episode. Work in groups of four, with each student answering two of the questions below to create the total profile of the new character. Then, compare the description of your group's character with that of other groups.

ESTUDIANTE # 1: ¿Cómo se llama? ¿De dónde es?
ESTUDIANTE # 2: ¿Cuál es su profesión? ¿Está casado/a?
ESTUDIANTE # 3: ¿Cuántos años tiene? ¿Cómo es físicamente?
ESTUDIANTE # 4: ¿Es bueno o malo? ¿Qué va a hacer y a quién?

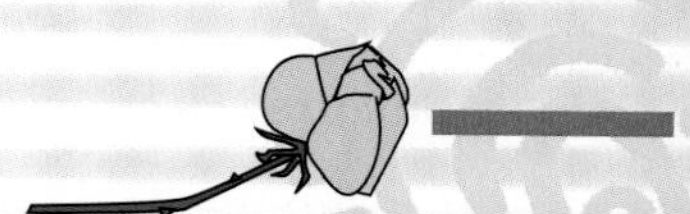

Lengua

I. Indicating reason, duration, purpose, destination

Por, para

¡Trabajo **por** mi equipo... y mi equipo es famoso **por** mí!
I work for my team's sake . . . and my team is famous because of me!

¡Mi equipo y yo trabajamos **para** ganar y **para** ser el mejor equipo del mundo!
My team and I work to win and to become the best team in the world!

Ayer jugué **por** Luis.
I played yesterday in Luis's place.

La copa es un regalo **para** mi novia.
The cup is for my girlfriend.

Jugué fútbol **por** todos los Estados Unidos.
I played soccer all around the United States.

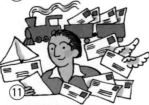

Salí temprano **para** el estadio.
I left early for the stadium.

Entrené sin pausa **por** tres horas.
I trained without stopping for three hours.

Tengo que entrenar **para** el cinco de mayo.
I have to train for May fifth.

Tenemos tres partidos **por** jugar. ¡Qué bien, solamente nos faltan tres!
This is good! We have three more games (left) to play.

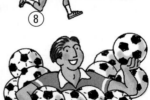

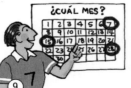

Tomás tiene muchos balones de fútbol **para** practicar.
Tomás has many soccer balls with which to practice.

Las cartas de sus aficionados le llegan a Tomás **por** aire, **por** tierra y **por** mar.
Letters from Tomás's fans arrive by air, by land, and by sea.

Tomás es muy famoso y da entrevistas **por** televisión. Él contesta las cartas **por** Internet y se comunica con su agente **por** correo electrónico.

Tomás is very famous and gives interviews on television. He answers his letters through the Internet and writes to his agent via e-mail.

Por and **para** correspond in general to the English preposition *for*. However, **por** and **para** are not interchangeable in Spanish and each one has its specific use. Sometimes they may also correspond to other English prepositions or expressions. Here is a summary of their uses and their corresponding structures in English. You have already learned some of them in earlier chapters.

por	para
1. Por expresses factors or reasons that influence someone to do something. **Por** also identifies the cause of something.	**2. Para** expresses the final intention or aim of an action—what you want to achieve with what you do. **Para** is usually followed by a verb in these cases.
3. Por expresses that an action is done in someone else's place or on behalf of someone.	**4. Para** indicates the recipient of an intended action—the indirect object.
5. Por expresses an ambigous location (English: *around*).	**6. Para** expresses concrete destination.
7. Por indicates duration of time.	**8. Para** indicates a deadline to meet.
9. Por is used to express *remaining to be/left* + verb.	**10. Para** indicates availability, when used with a verb.
11. Por is used to express how someone or something is transported or moved from one place to another.	
12. Por is also used when talking about means of communication or broadcast media.	

1 *¿Por o para?* Work in groups and discuss which preposition (**por / para**) is the best to use in each one of these situations. Don't translate the sentences, just think about the situation. You may want to review the examples about Tomás, the soccer player, before you start. Then, exchange your selections with another group and evaluate their answers.

Situación

1. Nayeli is still alive *because of* you, Adriana and Felipe!
2. I am always doing things *on your behalf*, but you never do anything *for* me!
3. Mr. de Landa, here is a letter *for* you.
4. We are young and have many years left *to* live.
5. I have so many things left *to* do!
6. You have to be done with the project *by* tomorrow morning.
7. Will you miss me, honey? I am going to be away *for* a whole month!
8. Adriana and Felipe are working hard *in order to* find Nayeli.
9. Would you please teach this class *for* me? I can't make it tomorrow.
10. Where are you *headed for* at this hour, Adriana?
11. Poor Juliana, she has lost her diamond ring. I am so sad *for* her!
12. Our teacher likes to shop at Pepe's *because of* their low prices.
13. *For* whom are all those gifts that you bought, Felipe?

Answers to Actividad 1:

1. por
2. por; para
3. para
4. por
5. por
6. para
7. por
8. para
9. por
10. para
11. por
12. por
13. para

Answers to Actividad 2:
1. por
2. para
3. para
4. por
5. por
6. por
7. por
8. para
9. por
10. para
11. para
12. por

2 ¿Por o para? Work with a partner and fill in the correct preposition in the following sentences.

1. Compramos el auto __________ su bajo precio.
2. Tenemos comida __________ tres días solamente.
3. Mis papás compraron una computadora __________ mí.
4. Vamos a estar en Cuba __________ una semana.
5. Quedan cinco lecciones __________ estudiar.
6. Mi amor, yo hago cualquier cosa __________ ti.
7. La casa me gustó mucho __________ sus grandes ventanas.
8. Voy a imprimir el documento __________ ellos.
9. Si te sientes mal, yo puedo ir __________ ti.
10. El jefe necesita el trabajo __________ mañana a las ocho a.m.
11. Ud. tiene que terminar __________ las cuatro. A esa hora cerramos la tienda.
12. Estuvimos en Santo Domingo y ¡viajamos __________ todas partes!

Disctronics
POR UBICACIÓN,°
POR ESPACIO,
POR COMODIDAD,°
POR AMBIENTE,°
POR ATENCIÓN,
POR VARIEDAD,
POR TODO . . .

°location
°comfort
°atmosphere

3 ¿Por qué compras allí? Imagine that you are a good client of Disctronics, a store that sells CD's. Study the Disctronic's ad and work with a partner asking and answering questions about why you like this store. Use the phrases below to ask your questions.

buena ubicación	gran comodidad
excelente atención al cliente	amplio espacio
gran variedad de productos	moderno ambiente

► **Modelo:** —*¿Es buena la ubicación de Disctronics?*
—*Es muy buena.*
—*¿Compras allí por eso?*
—*Sí, compro allí por su buena ubicación.*

Encourage students to think of reasons for buying CD's and using **Mundial Leasing** other than those found in the ads. Be sure they are using **por** and **para** correctly.

Have students start **Actividad 5** in class. As homework have them continue working in pairs on a brief (one-minute) oral presentation with props for the next class.

4 La respuesta es ¡Mundial Leasing! Imagine that you need to lease a new car or equipment for your company. You also need some advice on investments. Looking at the advertisement of the company *Mundial Leasing*, discuss with a partner where you can seek help. Look at the model for examples.

► **Modelo:** —*Necesito un auto nuevo para mi compañía.*
—*Pues, debes ir a Mundial Leasing para adquirir un auto nuevo.*

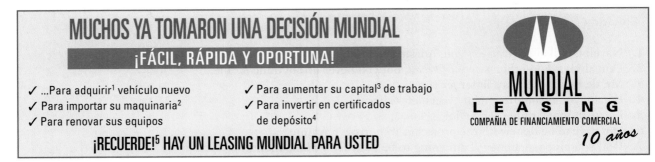

MUCHOS YA TOMARON UNA DECISIÓN MUNDIAL
¡FÁCIL, RÁPIDA Y OPORTUNA!

✓ ...Para adquirir[1] vehículo nuevo
✓ Para importar su maquinaria[2]
✓ Para renovar sus equipos
✓ Para aumentar su capital[3] de trabajo
✓ Para invertir en certificados de depósito[4]

¡RECUERDE![5] HAY UN LEASING MUNDIAL PARA USTED

MUNDIAL
LEASING
COMPAÑIA DE FINANCIAMIENTO COMERCIAL
10 años

[1]acquire; [2]machinery; [3]capital; [4]certificates of deposit; [5]remember

5 Mi negocio. Imagine that you have your own business. Choose a product or a service and work with a partner to create the perfect advertisement. The ads for *Disctronics* and *Mundial Leasing* are possible models.

II. Using verbs that change meaning in the preterite

Querer, poder, conocer, saber

Yolanda no pudo parar.

IRIS: Esta mañana **supe** que Yolanda está en el hospital.
LILIA: ¿Está enferma? ¡No lo sabía!
IRIS: No, no está enferma. La pobre tuvo un accidente ayer cuando patinaba. Iba muy rápido y no **pudo** parar.
LILIA: ¿Llevaba casco en la cabeza?
IRIS: Siempre lo lleva, pero ayer hacía calor y no **quiso** ponerse el casco, desgraciadamente.
LILIA: ¡Qué lástima!

The preterite expresses a completed action or its start and end points. Because of this characteristic, many verbs change meaning in the preterite. Here are some common verbs that change meaning.

Verbs	Present	Preterite
conocer	*to know*	*met/got acquainted with someone; visited a place the first time*
no conocer	*to not know*	*never met/got acquainted; never knew*
querer	*to want*	*intended to; wanted to do*
no querer	*to not want*	*refused; had no intention of doing*
poder	*to be able/can*	*was able to/managed to do something; found a way of doing it successfully*
no poder	*to be unable, cannot*	*tried and failed to do something*
saber	*to know*	*found out; realized*
no saber	*to not know*	*didn't find out*

Point out that the meaning of these verbs in the imperfect is basically the same as that for the infinitive. The new meaning is that associated with the preterite.

Nayeli **no quiso** involucrar a Felipe y Adriana.	*Nayeli refused to get Felipe and Adriana involved.*
Adriana y Felipe **supieron** por fin dónde estaba Nayeli.	*Adriana and Felipe found out at last where Nayeli was.*
Adriana **no supo** quién era el hombre que la persiguió en Sevilla.	*Adriana didn't find out who the man was that chased her in Sevilla.*
Zulaya **pudo** recoger el paquete en Quito.	*Zulaya managed to pick up the package in Quito.*

Answers to Actividad 6:
1. querían
2. conocieron
3. pudieron
4. quiso
5. supo
6. quería
7. sabía
8. supieron
9. quiso/quería

6 Un viaje por América. Olga and Rubén made a trip around the Caribbean. In the short story about their travels, write the correct form of **conocer, querer, poder,** and **saber** in the past (preterite or imperfect).

Olga y Rubén hicieron hace poco un viaje por el Caribe. Fueron a la República Dominicana porque ellos ______ (querer) conocerla. Olga y Rubén ______ (conocer) Santo Domingo y otras ciudades dominicanas. Ellos no ______ (poder) ir a Puerto Rico porque Rubén no ______ (querer = *refused*); él prefirió ir a Cuba, el país de sus antepasados. Cuando llegaron a Cuba, Olga ______ (saber) que los bisabuelos de Rubén eran de Aragón, España. Esto le pareció interesantísimo y ella ______ (querer) saber más sobre la familia de Rubén. Una señora cubana que ______ (saber) mucho sobre genealogía del país la ayudó. De esta manera, ellos ______ (saber) que un bisabuelo de Rubén ¡era puertorriqueño! Por esta razón, Rubén ______ (querer) buscar sus raíces (*roots*) en la isla de Puerto Rico y fueron allí después de salir de Cuba.

Before doing **Actividad 7,** review double negatives (Chapter 3).

7 Nunca. There were many things that people in earlier centuries never knew or could do. Work with a partner to create sentences about them, using the elements in columns A, B, and C. Remember to use double negatives if necessary.

▶ **Modelo:** *Mis bisabuelos no conocieron la televisión jamás.*

A	B	C
1. mis bisabuelos	conocer los clones de animales	nunca
2. Cristóbal Colón	poder viajar en avión	durante toda su vida
3. el presidente Lincoln	conocer la televisión	en su juventud
4. tus antepasados	poder enviar correo electrónico	jamás
5. Cleopatra	conocer los autos	en su época
6. la gente del siglo XIX	conocer la electricidad	el siglo pasado
7. ¿...?	¿...?	¿...?

8 ¿Cuál fue la razón? Work with a partner to find out why several of your friends didn't do what they were supposed to do. Follow the model.

▶ **Modelo:** *Miranda / hacer el trabajo (difícil)*
—¿Por qué no hizo Miranda el trabajo?
—Porque el trabajo era difícil y no pudo hacerlo.

1. Orlando / escribir la introducción (complicada)
2. Nubia y Roberto / seguir las instrucciones (poco claras)
3. Todos los miembros / hacer el trabajo (demasiado largo)
4. Mónica / revisar la ortografía (difícil)
5. Isabel / enviar el correo (mucho)

Answers to Actividad 8:
1. ¿Por qué no escribió Orlando la introducción? Porque la introducción era complicada y no pudo escribirla.
2. ¿Por qué no siguieron las instrucciones Nubia y Roberto? Porque las instrucciones eran poco claras y no pudieron entenderlas.
3. ¿Por qué no hicieron el trabajo todos los miembros? Porque el trabajo era demasiado largo y no pudieron hacerlo.
4. ¿Por qué no revisó Mónica la ortografía? Porque la ortografía era difícil y no pudo revisarla.
5. ¿Por qué no envió Isabel el correo? Porque el correo era mucho y no pudo enviarlo.

9 Mis experiencias. You are talking with a friend about a party that you attended yesterday. Work with a partner and ask each other questions about whom you met, interesting things that you found out, and so on.

► **Modelo:** *conocer / a personas interesantes*
—¿Conociste a muchas personas interesantes?
—Sí, conocí a una chica... or
—No, no conocí a nadie interesante.

1. saber / nuevas noticias sobre tu hermano/a
2. conocer / a la novia del profesor de español
3. poder / bailar salsa y tango
4. conocer / a algún hispanohablante
5. saber / cómo se llama el/la novio/a de tu mejor amigo/a
6. poder / tomar fotos de los invitados

III. Indicating how long ago a past action occurred

Hace + preterite

You have learned that the expression **hace** + time + **que** + verb in the present is used with the present indicative to state *for how long* an action *has been going on.*

Tell students to review **hace** expressions (Chapter 3) before reading this section. At this point, review preterite verb forms briefly (Chapters 4 and 5).

Hace + time + *que* + verb in the present

Hace tres días que estoy mal. — *I have been sick **for** three days.*

When the same expression is used with the verb in the preterite, it means the event happened a certain period of time *ago.*

Hace + time + *que* + preterite

—**¿Cuánto tiempo hace que** Adriana **habló** con Nayeli? — *How long ago did Adriana talk to Nayeli?*
—**Hace tres días que habló** con ella. — *She talked to her three days ago.*

—**¿Cuánto tiempo hace que** el hombre misterioso **persiguió** a Adriana? — *How long ago did the mystery man chase Adriana?*
—**Hace dos días que** la **persiguió.** — *He chased her two days ago.*

- The type of sentence above can also start with subject + verb in the preterite + **hace** + time expression.

Ella vio a ese hombre en Sevilla **hace tres días.** — *She saw this man in Sevilla three days ago.*
Nayeli salió del hotel **hace** solamente **una hora.** — *Nayeli left the hotel just an hour ago.*

Answers to Actividad 10:
(**Note:** All questions will begin with **¿Cuánto tiempo hace que...**, followed by the preterite.)
1. Hace muchísimo tiempo que me casé.
2. Hace pocos años que estuve en Puerto Rico.
3. Hace treinta años que hice esquí acuático.
4. Hace ochenta años que estudié piano.
5. Hace poco tiempo que produje películas de misterio.
6. Hace dos días que fui al médico.
7. Hace algunos años que jugué al tenis.
8. Hace demasiado tiempo que participé en el equipo de fútbol.

Students should write out all numbers in Spanish.

For **Actividad 11,** tell students to report their times in the average number of days for each question in each group. Tally the numbers on the board. On the left-hand side write the numbers of the questions; on top write numbers or names representing each group. Have a volunteer add up the numbers in each column and tell you their sums in Spanish. The group with the lowest number wins.

10 **Memoria de elefante.** You are interviewing a person that has just turned 100 years old. Work with a partner asking the questions below and use **usted** as the form of address. Follow the model.

▸ **Modelo:** *terminar escuela secundaria (82 años)*
—¿Cuánto tiempo hace que terminó usted la escuela secundaria?
—Hace ochenta y dos años que terminé la escuela secundaria.

1. casarse (muchísimo tiempo)
2. estar en Puerto Rico (pocos años)
3. hacer esquí acuático (30 años)
4. estudiar piano (80 años)
5. producir películas de misterio (poco tiempo)
6. ir al médico (dos días)
7. jugar al tenis (algunos años)
8. participar en el equipo de fútbol (demasiado tiempo)

11 **¿Eres deportista?** You are participating in your school program for adding more physical activities to students' daily life. Work in groups of three and record the answers. Then, present the answers to the class. Which is the most active group in class?

1. ¿Cuánto tiempo hace que bailaste con tus amigos?
2. ¿Cuánto tiempo hace que jugaste un deporte?
3. ¿Cuánto tiempo hace que caminaste por el parque?
4. ¿Cuánto tiempo hace que montaste en bicicleta?
5. ¿Cuánto tiempo hace que nadaste?
6. ¿Cuánto tiempo hace que corriste?
7. ¿Cuánto tiempo hace que subiste las escaleras (*stairs*) en vez de tomar el ascensor?
8. ¿Cuánto tiempo hace que caminaste a la universidad en vez de ir en coche o autobús?

IV. Narrating in the past

As you have learned, the preterite and the imperfect tenses are used to describe different types of past actions. The preterite focuses on whether the action in the past was *started or completed.* The imperfect focuses on whether the action was *ongoing* in the past. This characteristic of completed or ongoing action in the past is called the *aspect* of the verb. The main aspect of the preterite is *completion* and the main aspect of the imperfect is that the action, state, or event was *in progress* at the time in the past we are talking about. Sometimes, the selection of either the preterite or the imperfect is subjective and either form can be used.

A. The imperfect

The story below is about what happened to Lorenzo and his beloved Adelaida. It is written in two separate parts. In the first part, the *imperfect* describes the *background* or *scenario* of a happy day on the beach and all the expectations Lorenzo had for his relationship with Adelaida. We realize, at the end, that things didn't turn out as he expected. This first part also illustrates most of the uses of the imperfect. The second part, in the next section, will illustrate the uses of the preterite.

Read the story and then answer the questions about it.

MI PRIMER AMOR

Parte 1: Adelaida y yo éramos felices

The imperfect is used:	Me llamo Lorenzo Villarreal y ésta es la historia de un día feliz en la playa y de mi amor por Adelaida.
to set up a continous background or a scenario in which events or actions evolve or occur in the past.	**Era** un día de sol, como todos los días de verano. El cielo **estaba** azul y brillante. No **había** nadie en la playa. Con nosotros **estaban** solamente los pájaros y las olas (*waves*) del mar.
to describe ongoing mental, emotional, or physical states in the past.	**Me sentía** completamente feliz por primera vez. **Estábamos** juntos por fin. **¡Éramos** tan felices!
to describe how old a person was (*age*) in the past.	Adelaida **tenía** solamente veintitrés años y yo **tenía** veinticuatro.
to describe actions and events that were in progress in the past without emphasis on when they started or ended.	Adelaida me **quería** mucho. Y ¡yo la **adoraba** a ella!
to describe how people and things were in the past.	Para mí, ella **era** la mujer más hermosa del mundo, la más dulce, la más buena.
to describe repetitive or habitual past actions—what one used to do.	Desde ese primer día juntos, **íbamos** a esa playa con frecuencia y **tomábamos** el sol mientras **soñábamos** con el futuro, nuestro futuro.
to describe opinions, attitudes, and beliefs in the past using verbs like **creer, pensar**, and so on.	Yo **creía** que mi Adelaida **era** perfecta y al mismo tiempo pensaba que ella no **podía** engañarme (*betray*) jamás.
with **ir a** + *infinitive* to anticipate what was going to happen.	¡Pero las cosas no **iban a ser** como yo **quería**!

12 *¿Cómo era todo antes?* Work with a partner and answer the following questions about the story.

1. ¿Qué tiempo hacía ese primer día juntos?
2. ¿De qué color estaba el cielo ese día?
3. ¿Con quiénes estaban Lorenzo y Adelaida en la playa?
4. ¿Cómo se sentía Lorenzo? ¿Por qué?

Answers to Actividad 12:

1. Era un día de sol. / Hacía sol.
2. El cielo estaba azul.
3. Estaban con los pájaros y las olas del mar.
4. Se sentía completamente feliz porque por fin Adelaida y él estaban juntos.

5. Adelaida tenía 23 años; Lorenzo tenía 24 años.
6. Era la mujer más hermosa, dulce y buena del mundo.
7. Iban a la playa.
8. Hablaban del futuro.
9. No. Pensaba que no podía engañarlo jamás.
10. No, no creo porque Lorenzo dice: **Las cosas no iban a ser como yo quería.**

5. ¿Qué edad tenía Adelaida? ¿Qué edad tenía Lorenzo?
6. ¿Cómo era Adelaida, según Lorenzo?
7. ¿A dónde iban Lorenzo y Adelaida con frecuencia?
8. ¿De qué hablaban mientras tomaban el sol?
9. ¿Pensaba Lorenzo que Adelaida podía engañarlo?
10. ¿Crees que la Parte 2 de la historia va a tener un final feliz?

13 **Mi propia historia. Parte I.** You are going to write a story in two parts. Start by selecting the topic of a story. Then, write just the first part using the imperfect. Keep in mind a possible resolution that you will write later, in the next section. Invent your own theme or select one of the following.

Mi primer día en la universidad	Un viaje desastroso
Mi primer amor	Una lección de baile
Una fiesta de cumpleaños terrible	Mi carrera como atleta
La ilusión de mi vida	Tragedia en el concierto de rock

B. The preterite

In the second part, what happened, *the action*, is told by Lorenzo using the *preterite*. He tells us about all the events that lead to the end of his relationship with Adelaida and the sequence in which they occurred. This can also be viewed as the *plot* of the story. This part of the story illustrates most of the uses of the preterite. Note that the preterite may be used to talk about the weather when you want to state it as a fact and not just to open up the scenario of a story.

Read the story and then answer the questions about it.

MI PRIMER AMOR

Parte 2: Todo terminó

The preterite is used:	Me llamo Lorenzo Villarreal y ésta es la historia de lo que me sucedió con Adelaida, mi primer amor, un año después de ese día feliz en la playa.
to state facts in the past or to sum up a condition or state.	**Llovió** mucho el día de la mala noticia. **Fue** el día más terrible de mi vida.
to indicate the start or the end of an action, an event or a mental or physical state.	A las ocho de la mañana, el teléfono **empezó** a sonar (*ring*). Yo **quise** contestarlo, pero no **pude**. No **supe** por qué, pero me **dio** miedo.
to narrate completed actions that were repeated a number of times.	El teléfono **sonó** muchas veces más.
to narrate a sequence of completed past actions.	Finalmente, lo **contesté**. Adelaida me **dio** la noticia calmadamente: "Estoy enamorada de otro, lo siento mucho, Lorenzo." Cuando **escuché** estas palabras, **colgué** (*hung up*) el teléfono furiosamente y **pensé**:

to narrate actions that happened within a delimited period of time.	"Esto es injusto (*unfair*) ... durante un año **fuimos** novios..."
to state or sum up opinions, attitudes and beliefs as past completed actions, events, or facts.	Ahora solamente me queda su recuerdo. Ella **fue** el gran amor de mi vida; yo la **quise** y ella también me **quiso** ... alguna vez. ¡**Fui** tan feliz con ella!

14 ¿Qué sucedió? Answer the following comprehension questions about Lorenzo's story.

1. ¿Cómo fue ese día para Lorenzo?
2. ¿Qué tiempo hizo el día de la mala noticia?
3. ¿Qué pasó cuando sonó el teléfono?
4. ¿Cuántas veces sonó el teléfono?
5. ¿Qué hizo Lorenzo cuando escuchó las palabras de Adelaida?
6. ¿Durante cuánto tiempo fueron novios?
7. ¿Quiso Lorenzo mucho a Adelaida? ¿Y ella a él?
8. ¿Fue feliz Lorenzo con Adelaida? ¿Y ella con él?
9. ¿Qué fue Adelaida para Lorenzo?

Answers to Actividad 14:
1. Fue el día más terrible de su vida.
2. Llovió mucho. Hizo mal tiempo.
3. Él quiso contestarlo pero no pudo.
4. Sonó muchas veces.
5. Colgó el teléfono furiosamente.
6. Fueron novios por un año.
7. Lorenzo quiso mucho a Adelaida y ella también lo quiso.
8. Sí, fueron felices.
9. Ella fue el gran amor de su vida.

15 Mi propia historia. Review *Parte 1* and *Parte 2* of Lorenzo's story and use them as models to structure the second part of your own story.

C. Contrasting the preterite and the imperfect

In the story about Adelaida and Lorenzo, the scenario or background is a text composed of several sentences, all in the imperfect, and what happens within this space is told using the preterite. However, normally, when you are talking about the past, the two forms often appear in the same text. In this way, interest and suspense can be added to the composition or the conversation. When two or more actions, events, or states are in contrast, the imperfect is normally used to describe the background, the scenario, or the atmosphere, while the preterite is used to indicate discrete, completed actions in the past.

1. The scenario: Ongoing actions

It is useful to think about the type of scenario or background of your narration. It can play the role of a stage and just be there as the ongoing background of your story as in the following sentences:

Cuando **éramos** novios, Adelaida y yo **fuimos** al cine solamente una vez.	*When we were together, Adelaida and I went only once to the movies.*
Estaba lloviendo cuando **salí** de casa.	*It was raining when I left home.*
Adelaida tenía ventitrés años cuando la **conocí.**	*Adelaida was twenty-three when I met her.*
Eran las tres de la tarde cuando **salieron** Adriana y Felipe para Sevilla.	*It was three p.m. when Adriana and Felipe left for Sevilla.*

2. The scenario: Interrupted actions

The ongoing scenario or background may cease to exist when the ongoing action or actions are interrupted by something else. Adverbial expressions and other linking words are very useful to highlight this abrupt stop.

Camilo **patinaba** alegremente y **de pronto, se cayó.** — *Camilo was skating happily when suddenly, he fell.*

Mauro siempre miraba los partidos de fútbol, **pero** ese día no lo **hizo.** — *Mauro always used to watch the soccer games, but that day he didn't.*

Adelaida me **quería** mucho **hasta que** un día, **me olvidó.** — *Adelaida loved me very much until she just forgot me one day.*

3. Retelling: Indirect speech

Generally, the imperfect is used when retelling what someone said, thought, believed, wanted to do, or found out. Note the combination of the preterite and the imperfect and the use of **iba a** + infinitive to express *was going to.*

Adriana le contó a Felipe que alguien la **perseguía.** — *Adriana told Felipe that someone was chasing her.*

Doña Gafasnegras supo que Nayeli **iba a ir** al Ecuador. — *Sunglasses found out that Nayeli was going to Ecuador.*

Yo pensé que tú **eras** mi mejor amiga. — *I thought that you were my best friend.*

Alejandro me dijo que **iba a venir** hoy. — *Alejandro told me that he was coming today.*

Answers to Actividad 16:

1. regalaron
2. se descompuso
3. llevé
4. dijo
5. iba a costar
6. intenté
7. era/fue
8. pude
9. fue

Explain why #7 can be either imperfect or preterite

16 La nueva tecnología. Fill in the imperfect and the preterite in this reading about the computer your parents gave you.

Mis padres me __________ (regalar) una computadora nueva hace un año. Ya no la tengo porque __________ (descomponerse) hace un mes. Yo la __________ (llevar) a un especialista en computadoras, pero él me __________ (decir) que el trabajo __________ (ir a costar) mucho dinero. Yo __________ (intentar) componerla, pero __________ (ser) muy díficil y tampoco yo __________ (poder) hacer nada. Todo __________ (ser) inútil.

Answers to Actividad 17:

1. hacía
2. era
3. gustaba
4. tenía
5. me caí
6. llevaron
7. estaba
8. llegó
9. dijo
10. llevabas
11. te caíste
12. pregunté
13. llevaba
14. contestó
15. dijo

17 Practicando deportes. Complete the paragraph with the correct form of the preterite or imperfect.

Siempre __________ (hacer) deportes cuando __________ (ser) pequeña. A veces me __________ (gustar) mucho patinar. Una vez, cuando yo __________ (tener) diez años, patinaba con unos amigos, y de pronto, yo __________ (caerse). Ellos me __________ (llevar) al hospital. Mientras yo __________ (estar) en mi cama con mucho dolor, __________ (llegar) el médico y me __________ (decir): "Tú no __________ (llevar) casco cuando tú __________ (caerse) , ¿verdad?" Yo le __________ (preguntar) al doctor: "¿Cómo sabe usted que yo no __________ (llevar) el casco? Y el doctor __________ (contestar): "No es difícil saberlo. ¡Me lo __________ (decir) la fractura que tienes en la cabeza!"

Before doing **Actividad 18** review the **ir a** + infinitive expressions (Chapter 2).

18 Eventos frustrados. Use the imperfect to describe what people were about to do and the preterite to tell why they couldn't.

▸ **Modelo:** *Ana / cenar (llegar / la visita)*
Ana iba a cenar cuando llegó la visita.

1. Nosotros / comprar tiquetes (acabarse / los tiquetes)
2. Algunas personas / salir de casa (sonar / el teléfono)
3. Tú / acostarse (empezar / el incendio)
4. El niño / cruzar la calle (pasar rápidamente / un auto)
5. La gente / abrir las ventanas (empezar a llover)

Answers to Actividad 18:
1. Nosotros íbamos a comprar tiquetes cuando se acabaron los tiquetes.
2. Algunas personas iban a salir de casa cuando sonó el teléfono.
3. Tú te ibas a acostar (ibas a acostarte) cuando empezó el incendio.
4. El niño iba a cruzar la calle cuando pasó rápidamente un auto.
5. La gente iba a abrir las ventanas cuando empezó a llover.

19 Testigo presencial *(Eyewitness).* Your classmates and you have just witnessed a traffic accident. The driver has disappeared and the police are interrogating the witnesses. Work in groups and answer the following questions for the police. Then, compare your testimony with other groups.

a. **Descripción de la persona**

1. ¿Era mujer o era hombre?
2. ¿Era alto/a, bajo/a, delgado/a?
3. ¿De qué color eran los ojos?
4. ¿Qué ropa llevaba?
5. ¿Estaba asustado el chofer?
6. ¿...?

b. **¿Dónde estabas y qué hacías cuando sucedió?**

▸ **Modelo:** *Yo estaba en la clase leyendo un libro cuando oí el choque (crash).*

20 ¿Qué dijeron? Work with a partner to retell what the persons said. Follow the model.

▸ **Modelo:** *Isabel / querer ir a Sevilla*
—¿Qué dijo Isabel?
—Isabel dijo que quería ir a Sevilla

1. Armando / querer ayudarles a Felipe y Adriana
2. Mi compañero/a de cuarto / ser difícil bailar salsa
3. Ustedes / no saber nada
4. Ellos / no poder usar la computadora
5. Adriana / tener miedo en Sevilla

Answers to Actividad 20:
1. dijo que quería...
2. dijo que era...
3. dijeron que no sabían...
4. dijeron que no podían...
5. dijo que tenía...

Lectura A

Introducción

In this selection, you'll learn about some popular sports in the Caribbean.

Reading strategy: Skimming for main ideas

By skimming titles and the first sentence of every paragraph, you can get a good idea about the content of the reading. There are usually three important parts to each paragraph:

1. **Topic:** The topic or theme can often be found by skimming the subtitles.
2. **Topic sentence:** The topic sentence can be found in the middle or at the end of each paragraph and states the main idea.
3. **Supporting details:** You must read the selection more closely to identify the details that support the main ideas. These can be facts about the topic or anecdotes to make the subject more interesting.

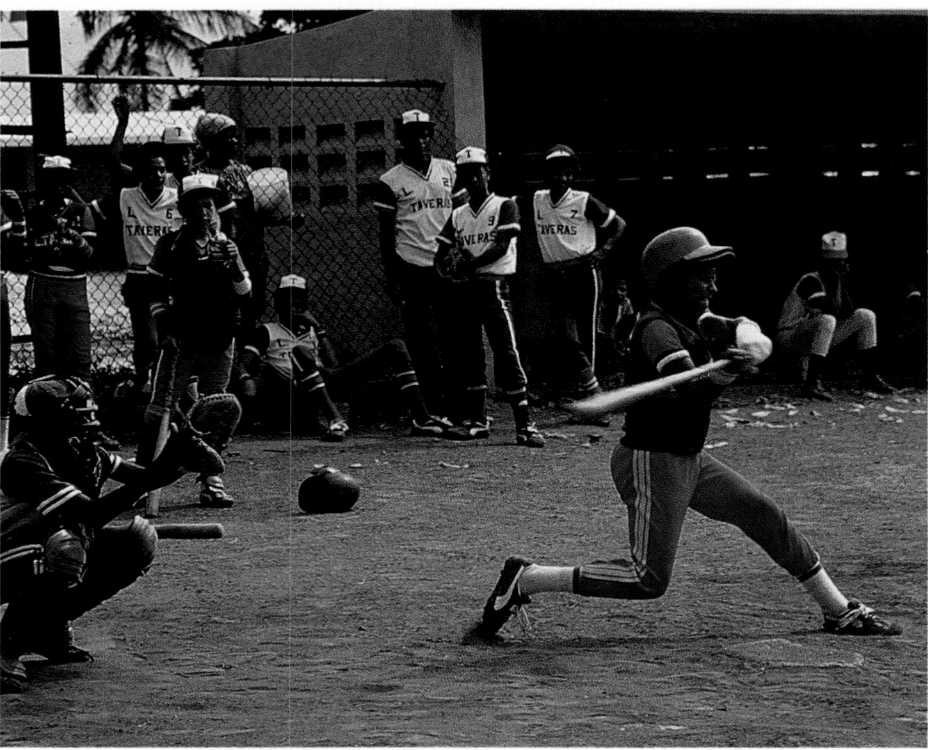

Los jóvenes jugando al béisbol en la República Dominicana.

Prelectura/postlectura

1 Without using a dictionary, read quickly the following selection about Caribbean sports. For each paragraph, identify and write the topic and topic sentence. Do not worry about the details.

2 ¿Qué más? Read the selection again in order to obtain additional information. Then, working in pairs, discuss the following questions.

1. ¿Cuál es la importancia en el Caribe de cada deporte discutido en la lectura?
2. ¿Cuál es el deporte más popular en tu región? ¿Quiénes lo practican? ¿Cuál es tu equipo preferido?
3. Compara tus preferencias deportivas con las de tus compañeros/as.

For **Actividad 3,** ask students to write this paragraph in the present tense.

3 Mis deportes favoritos. Write a paragraph about your favorite sports. Include answers to the following questions.

1. ¿Cuáles deportes practicas en las diferentes estaciones: en invierno, primavera, verano y otoño?
2. ¿Cuáles deportes prefieres solamente como espectador/a?

Algunos deportes caribeños°

Caribbean

El béisbol En los países de Cuba, Puerto Rico y la República Dominicana, el deporte nacional es el béisbol. Muchos caribeños lo practican desde la llegada° de los estadounidenses a las islas. Los chicos jóvenes juegan en las calles y en los parques y los partidos despiertan gran interés en la población. Muchos jugadores dominicanos, cubanoamericanos y puertorriqueños juegan en las ligas profesionales de los Estados Unidos y varios de ellos han tenido° grandes éxitos.° Cuba es el único país que por ahora prohibe la participación de cubanos en las ligas norteamericanas. Este deporte es popular también en las regiones caribeñas de Panamá y Colombia, donde también hay exitosos° equipos femeninos.

arrival

have had / successes

successful

Topic:
Topic Sentence:

El baloncesto Otro de los deportes populares en el Caribe y en gran parte de las regiones hispanas es el baloncesto. La televisón de los Estados Unidos tuvo mucha influencia en su introducción en las islas del Caribe.

Topic:
Topic Sentence:

El fútbol americano Los caribeños no juegan mucho este deporte, pero los partidos norteamericanos tienen espectadores en todo el mundo hispano porque se transmiten por los canales hispanos de televisión desde Miami. La gente de muchos países sabe los nombres de los equipos más populares de los Estados Unidos y es común encontrar a jóvenes que usan camisetas° y gorras° con los emblemas de equipos populares de fútbol americano.

You may wish to have students rewrite these sentences in the past, as a review of the imperfect.

T-shirts / caps

Topic:
Topic Sentence:

El fútbol Los juegos ceremoniales de los indígenas mayas y de los arauacos° de la zona caribeña fueron los precursores del fútbol. Ellos practicaban este juego con una pesada° pelota de caucho° y usaban la cintura° para mantener la pelota en el aire sin tocar el suelo.° Posteriormente,° este juego evolucionó hasta convertirse en el juego moderno que conocemos hoy, con millones de aficionados en todo el mundo.

Arawak Indians
heavy / rubber
waist / ground
Later

Topic:
Topic Sentence:

ETAPA B

Pistas y palabras

I. Discussing technology

El mundo tecnológico

Multimedia, televisión, CD y video

¿Computadora, televisor o centro de entretenimiento°? Es difícil decir, porque el TMP 5100 de Tatung desempeña° todas esas funciones. En esta compacta y polifacética° unidad se unen° la funcionalidad de una computadora Pentium de alto rendimiento° lista para multimedia, sintonizador° de televisión, CD-ROM 8X, tarjeta de sonido,°parlantes,° fax/módem y control remoto. Su interfase se ha simplificado para que los usuarios no familiarizados con la computadora puedan ver un CD presionando° los botones en el panel frontal o a través del° control remoto.

Precio: Información no disponible.°

entertainment center
performs
multifaceted / are combined
performance / synchronizer
sound card
speakers
by pressing
by means of
available

Correo electrónico° sin computadora

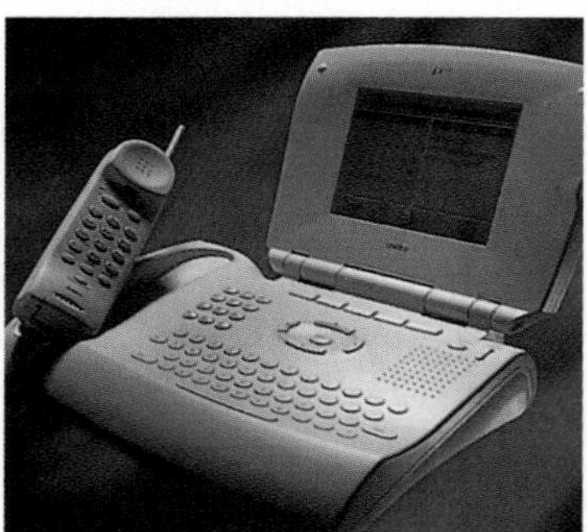

Las alternativas para aprovechar° las ventajas° de Internet sin necesidad de una computadora continúan proliferando. Probablemente estés familiarizado con WebTV y otras tecnologías que reciben Internet en la televisión, pero Axis de Uniden es uno de los primeros en hacerlo a través del teléfono. Axis combina un teléfono inalámbrico° de 900 Mhz, teclado,° módem y una pantalla° para gráficos y texto en un solo dispositivo.° La unidad° recibe los mensajes° a intervalos regulares durante el día y notifica al usuario.° Además de correo electrónico, también puedes tener acceso a servicios de noticias° en línea, precio de acciones° y todo tipo° de aplicaciones de Internet.

Precio: US$299-US$399

E-mail
to utilize / advantages
cordless / keyboard
screen / device
unit / messages
user
news / stock prices / all kinds

Palabras y expresiones útiles

la aplicación	*application*	el documento	*document*
el archivo	*computer file*	la impresora	*printer*
la ayuda	*help*	el mensaje	*message*
el botón	*button*	el programa	*program*
el directorio	*directory*	el ratón	*mouse*
el disco duro	*hard drive*	la red	*network*
abrir	*to open*	imprimir	*to print*
apagar	*to turn off*	mover (ue)	*to move*
archivar (guardar)	*to save*	prender (encender [ie])	*to turn on*
cerrar (ie)	*to close*	presionar (hacer clic, pulsar)	*to click with the mouse*
colgar (ue)	*to hang up*		

contestar	*to answer*	recibir	*to receive*
copiar	*to copy*	portátil	*portable*
enviar (mandar)	*to send*		

1 Cognados. Technical vocabulary has many cognates. Write a list of words from the ads on page 248 that are cognates to words in English. Work with a partner.

2 Preguntas. Which of the products on p. 248 can you use to do the following activities?

► **Modelo:** *recibir Internet por teléfono*
Para recibir Internet por teléfono, uso/prefiero/me gusta Axis.

1. mandarle un mensaje electrónico a un amigo
2. escribir una composición
3. buscar información en la red Internet
4. hacer una llamada por teléfono
5. jugar un juego en CD-ROM
6. mirar tu programa de televisión favorito
7. leer las noticias
8. ver las noticias
9. mandar o recibir un fax

Possible answers to Actividad 2:
1. Axis de Uniden y TMP 5100
2. TMP 5100
3. Axis de Uniden y TMP 5100
4. Axis de Uniden
5. TMP 5100
6. TMP 5100
7. Axis de Uniden
8. TMP 5100
9. TMP 5100

3 Combinaciones. Work with a partner to create as many sentences as possible by combining words from columns A, B, and C. Be sure to add any additional words you may need to create complete sentences about technology.

A	B	C
yo	prender	archivo
tú	mandar	párrafo
mis amigos	abrir	computadora
los profesores	cerrar	palabras
Ud.	buscar	mensaje
tú y yo	imprimir	programa
mi mamá	¿...?	documento
¿...?		¿...?

For **Actividad 3,** encourage students to write their sentences in the present. Then as homework, write the same sentences in the imperfect and the preterite. Minimum number of sentences: six per tense.

4 ¡Qué buena es la tecnología! Sometimes technology makes us work more than ever. You have just received a message from a friend, but you can't read the whole message. Complete the e-mail with the words provided.

mensaje	computadora	ayuda	impresora
programa	teléfono	tecnología	

¡Hola!

Hoy compré una nueva ◊*∞. Traté de instalar el *$∞¤< para mandarte un mensaje electrónico, pero dice que hay errores. La *$* tampoco funciona y no puedo imprimir este *$<*. Yo sé que soy nueva con la *&$v**∞, pero esto es ridículo. Por favor, necesito tu $*&Δ*. ¡Llámame, porque sé que por lo menos funciona mi *&∞!¤.

Tu amiga,

Leticia

Answers to Actividad 4:
1. computadora
2. programa
3. impresora
4. mensaje
5. tecnología
6. ayuda
7. teléfono

5 **La respuesta.** You cannot get in touch with Leticia because her telephone is busy. Write her an e-mail to answer her message (**Actividad 4**).

For **Enlace cultural** bring in pictures of Arecibo and Vieques and/or find sites for them using the various search engines on the World Wide Web.

ENLACE CULTURAL

El observatorio de Arecibo

Hay mucho interés en usar las nuevas tecnologías para aprender más sobre el mundo en que vivimos: las galaxias, las estrellas,° el sol, el agua, la tierra.° Para conocer más sobre el espacio, muchos astrónomos de todas partes del mundo van a Puerto Rico para utilizar el observatorio que está en Arecibo. Su radiotelescopio es enorme; tiene un diámetro de 400 metros, una superficie° de 16 hectáreas y se eleva a 185 metros sobre su plataforma. Con su ayuda, los científicos pueden medir° las radiaciones y determinar la composición química de los objetos estelares.°

La ciencia también ayuda a descubrir las causas de fenómenos que están cerca de la superficie terrestre,° más cerca de nosotros que las galaxias. Por ejemplo, en la Bahía° Fosforescente de Vieques, en Puerto Rico, ocurre un fenómeno nocturno muy dramático y hermoso: por la noche, aparecen° luces muy bonitas sobre el agua. Los científicos concluyeron que esta luz la emiten billones de criaturas microscópicas que viven en las aguas de la bahía.

stars
earth
surface
measure
stellar
earth
Bay
appear

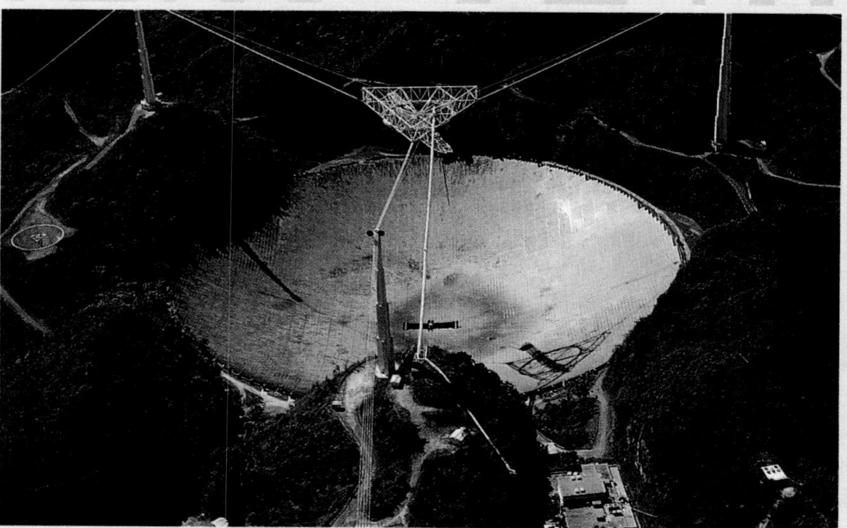

El observatorio de Arecibo en Puerto Rico.

Discusión en grupos

¿Hay observatorios astronómicos en la región donde vives? ¿Hay universidades o industrias que investigan temas científicos interesantes?

II. Talking about and looking for work

Buscando trabajo

INGENIERO DE SISTEMAS

Para **desarrollo**° tipo cliente servidor,° en Visual Basic y su aplicación en **INTERNET**.

Experiencia mínima requerida 2 años.

Enviar hoja de vida° con sueldo° deseado° a Av. 19 No. 104-09, Bogotá.

RECEPCIONISTAS

Estudios en secretariado, manejo de Word, Excel, mínimo 1 año de experiencia en **archivo**,° sistemas y recepción, edad máxima 30 años.
Enviar hoja de vida calle 45 No. 55A-05

Abogado(a) Administrador(a) de Empresas°

Necesita **fábrica líder°** de muebles para hospitales, etc., preferible con experiencia, que sea° ejecutivo(a), inteligente, **dedicado(a)** y con **aptitudes** industriales. Todo en una persona.

Citas: 7803046, 7802200.

Licenciados°

Requiere colegio con prestigio nacional, áreas inglés, matemáticas, educación física, psicopedagogía,° **experiencia manejo**° de alumnos. **Hoja de vida** Anunciador No. 2096, EL TIEMPO.

development / client server

résumé / salary / desired

filing

Companies

factory leader / Graduates who is

psychology of teaching

management

Palabras y expresiones útiles

el/la aspirante	*applicant*	la meta	*goal*
la calificación	*qualification, grade*	el negocio	*business*
la compañía	*company*	la responsabilidad	*responsibility*
el conocimiento	*knowledge*	el salario (sueldo)	*salary*
el desempleo	*unemployment*	la solicitud	*application*
el entrenamiento	*training*	el trabajo (puesto)	*work, position*
la entrevista	*interview*	despedir	*to lay off/fire*
la evaluación	*evaluation*	renunciar	*to quit (a job)*
la fábrica	*factory*	solicitar (un trabajo/ puesto)	*to apply (for a job)*
el hombre/ la mujer de negocios	*businessman/ businesswoman*	tiempo parcial	*part-time*
el horario de trabajo	*work schedule*	tiempo completo	*full-time*

6 **Requisitos.** Which of the classified ads offer or ask for the following?

1. La persona debe saber mucho sobre computadoras.
2. La persona necesita ser muy organizada.
3. La persona debe tener aptitudes industriales.
4. La persona debe tener experiencia con estudiantes.
5. La persona necesita saber gimnasia.
6. La persona tiene que saber escribir a máquina.
7. La persona debe tener experiencia en fábricas.

Answers to Actividad 6:
1. ingeniero de sistemas
2. recepcionista
3. abogado(a) administrador(a) de empresas
4. licenciados
5. licenciados
6. recepcionistas
7. abogado(a) administrador(a) de empresas

7 La solicitud. Complete this job application in Spanish.

Solicitud de empleo

Datos personales

Nombre: ______ Dirección: ______

Apellidos: ______ Ciudad: ______

Estado: ______ Código postal (*Zip*): ______

Teléfono y fax: ______

Correo electrónico: ______

Educación

Educación primaria: ______

Educación secundaria: ______

Universidad: ______

Otras instituciones: ______

Actividades, organizaciones, premios (*honors*): ______

______

Diploma o grado: ______

Empleos anteriores

Fechas:	Empresa:	Puesto:	Salario:	Supervisor/a:

Recomendaciones

Nombre:	Relación:	Dirección y teléfono:
1.		
2.		
3.		

8 Cuando era niño/a. Work with a partner to answer the following questions.

1. ¿Qué querías ser cuando eras niño/a? ¿Por qué?
2. ¿Qué querían ser tus hermanos/as?
3. ¿Cuántas veces cambiaste de opinión? ¿Cuándo? ¿Por qué?
4. ¿Qué quieres ser ahora? ¿Por qué?

9 Buscamos trabajo. The Spanish Department needs a student to help with office work. Write a job ad for this position.

Vistas y voces

I. Preparémonos

1 Anticipación. In pairs, answer these questions.

A. **1.** ¿Tienes computadora en tu casa? ¿De qué tipo es: de mesa o portátil? ¿Cuál prefieres? ¿Por qué?

2. ¿Crees que no tener computadora es una desventaja para la vida profesional moderna? ¿Crees que es una desventaja para la vida personal? ¿Por qué?

3. Si tu hermano/a, un/a primo/a o un/a gran amigo/a te pide ayuda para cometer un delito, ¿cómo reaccionas tú? ¿Por qué?

B. Review chapter opening photo 6B. Según tu opinión, ¿qué tiene Gafasnegras en la mano? ¿Qué va a hacer ella con ese aparato? ¿Qué crees que piensa Nayeli?

Para comprender mejor

cariñoso/a	*loving*	el parlante	*speaker*
cómodo/a	*comfortable*	la piedad	*mercy*
conforme	*according to*	el pleito	*fight*
la contraseña	*password*	el poder	*power*
desempeñar	*to perform*	predecible	*predictable*
la despedida	*farewell*	presumido/a	*conceited, arrogant*
detonar	*to detonate a bomb*	el secuestrador	*kidnapper*
la incertidumbre	*uncertainty*	se gana	*you win*
maltratar	*to mistreat*	se pierde	*you lose*

Correct order of video action shots: 1, 4, 3, 2

2 Secuencia. Put the video action shots in a logical order. Then, working in pairs, answer the following question: **¿Cómo pueden escaparse Nayeli, Adriana y Felipe del peligro?**

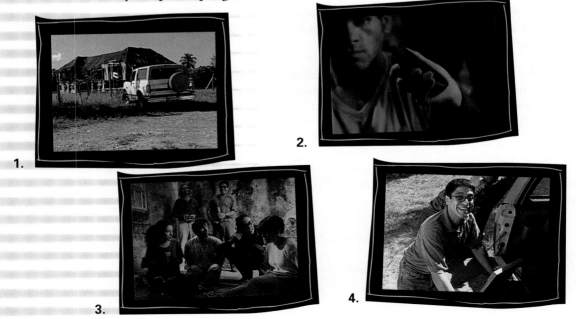

1.

2.

3.

4.

II. Miremos y escuchemos

3 Observaciones. While you view this episode, write the name of the person(s) associated with the following ideas.

1. Son prisioneros de Gafasnegras y los secuestradores. __________
2. Juega con la computadora de Felipe y Adriana. __________
3. Le grita al secuestrador Luis. __________
4. Tiene una bomba en las manos. __________
5. Describe a Nayeli como una mártir. __________
6. Tiene un control remoto para detonar la bomba. __________
7. Defiende a Adriana y Felipe diciendo que son inocentes. __________
8. Les deja la computadora a Adriana, Felipe y Nayeli. __________
9. No quiere dejarles la computadora con los prisioneros. __________
10. Detona la bomba. __________

Answers to Actividad 3:
1. Nayeli, Felipe y Adriana
2. Luis
3. Felipe
4. el primo de Luis
5. Gafasnegras
6. Gafasnegras
7. Nayeli
8. Gafasnegras
9. Luis
10. Gafasnegras

4 ¿Cómo están los personajes? Describe the reactions or emotions of different characters in this episode: el secuestrador Luis, Nayeli, Gafasnegras, Felipe.

III. Comentemos

5 Comprensión. Answer the following questions in groups.

1. ¿Quiénes están en el coche?
2. ¿Qué piensa doña Gafasnegras de Nayeli?
3. ¿Qué dice Nayeli de Felipe y Adriana? ¿Cómo se siente ella?
4. ¿Cómo se portan (behave) los secuestradores? ¿Qué piensas de ellos?
5. ¿Qué pasa al final de este episodio?

Answers to Actividad 5:
1. Adriana, Felipe, Nayeli, Gafasnegras, los secuestradores
2. Gasfasoscuras cree que Nayeli habla mucho y que es mártir.
3. Dice que Adriana y Felipe son inocentes y no deben morir. Se siente mal.
4. Son crueles. *Several answers are possible.*
5. *Answers will vary.*

6 Yo creo que... In pairs, discuss the fate of the jaguar twin by answering the following questions: ¿Dónde está el jaguar Yax-Balam en este momento? ¿Qué crees tú que le va a pasar al jaguar gemelo en el próximo episodio? ¿Lo va a conseguir doña Gafasnegras?

7 Análisis. Analyze the critical role of the computer by answering the following questions: ¿Qué importancia tiene la computadora en este episodio y durante los otros episodios del drama? ¿Cuáles son sus diferentes funciones? Work in groups of three.

8 Estoy/No estoy de acuerdo. Working in groups, compare your ideas with respect to the following statements of doña Gafasoscuras in this episode. Tell whether you are or are not in agreement and the reasons. Then, give examples, where possible.

1. "...qué maravilla es la tecnología..."
2. "...a los intelectuales les gusta saberlo todo...nunca están cómodos con las incertidumbres de la vida..."
3. "...La vida es una ruleta: a veces se gana y a veces se pierde..."

Lengua

I. Expressing reflexive actions

A. Reflexive verbs meaning *each other* and *to become*

Read this letter to the class dramatically with emphasis on the **nos.** Later on in this chapter you may wish to ask students for their advice, once they have learned the **ustedes** commands.

Como perros y gatos: Hace tres meses mi novio y yo decidimos casarnos.° Aunque tenemos planes de contraer matrimonio en un año, ambos° nos hemos dado cuenta° de que no paramos de pelear. Nos queremos° mucho, pero cuando peleamos, nos herimos° demasiado el uno al otro° y creo que eso afecta nuestra relación. ¿Cree que nos debemos casar? ¿Cómo cree que podemos evitar esas peleas?

—Julieta Santillana
Maracaibo, Venezuela

get married
both of us / we have realized
we love each other / we hurt
each other / one another

Reflexive verbs, as you have learned, are often used to express activities of daily routines. With reflexive verbs, the subject and the object of the sentence are the same; **yo me lavo.** Another use of the reflexive verbs happens when the subject is plural and the meaning is *each other.* **Nos queremos.** = *We love each other.* In this example, the verb is used in a *reciprocal* way. For emphasis and clarification, the expressions **el uno al otro**, **la una a la otra,** and **mutuamente** may be used. Note that **el uno al otro** is used for all male groups or mixed gender groups and **la una a la otra** is used for female groups.

Los prisioneros **se abrazan** y tratan de **consolarse el uno al otro.**	*The prisoners hug and try to comfort each other.*
Nosotros **nos escribimos** diariamente.	*We write to each other daily.*
Los dos deportistas **se respetan mutuamente.**	*The two athletes respect each other.*

Remind students about the personal **a** (Chapter 2) which is used with **otro/a** at the end of this expression.

1 **El uno al otro.** Summarize the action in each of the following sentences using a reflexive verb. Add expressions to clarify the meaning if needed.

▸ **Modelo:** *Juana mira a Raúl y él la mira a ella.*
Juana y Raúl se miran mutuamente or
Juana y Raúl se miran el uno al otro.

1. Fernando quiere mucho a Patricia y ella a él.
2. Nayeli respeta a Adriana y Adriana la respeta a ella.
3. Yo adoro a mi marido y él también a mí.
4. Felipe le escribe mensajes electrónicos a Armando y éste a Felipe.
5. Doña Gafasoscuras no entiende a Nayeli y ésta tampoco la entiende a ella.
6. Felipe no abraza a Adriana y ella tampoco lo abraza a él.
7. Usted no me conoce a mí y yo no la conozco a usted.

Answers to Actividad 1:
(Note: **Mutuamente** is an acceptable option for all.)
1. Fernando y Patricia se quieren mucho (el uno al otro).
2. Nayeli y Adriana se respetan (la una a la otra).
3. Mi marido y yo nos adoramos (el uno al otro).
4. Felipe y Armando se escriben mensajes electrónicos (el uno al otro).
5. Doña Gafasoscuras y Nayeli no se entienden (la una a la otra).
6. Felipe y Adriana no se abrazan (el uno al otro).
7. Usted y yo no nos conocemos (el uno al otro; la una a la otra).

Review stem-changing verbs in the present tense (Chapter 3) and also the **-ir** stem-changers in the preterite (Chapter 5). Point out that nonreflexive forms tend to take direct objects in which the object of the action is other than the subject.

B. Verbs used reflexively and nonreflexively

Many common verbs have reflexive and nonreflexive forms. Sometimes the meaning of the verb or of the sentence may change when the reflexive form of the verb is used. English versions of the Spanish reflexive verbs are either nonreflexive verbs or expressions with **to get** or **to become.**

Reflexive forms		**Nonreflexive forms**	
acostarse (ue)	*to go to bed, lie down*	acostar (ue)	*to put to bed*
alegrarse	*to become happy*	alegrar	*to make someone happy*
darse cuenta de	*to become aware of, notice*	dar	*to give*
despertarse (ie)	*to wake up*	despertar (ie)	*to wake someone up*
divertirse (ie)	*to have fun*	divertir (ie)	*to amuse someone*
dormirse (ue)	*to fall asleep*	dormir (ue)	*to sleep*
enamorarse de	*to fall in love with*	enamorar a	*to win someone's love*
enfermarse	*to get sick*	enfermar	*to make someone sick*
enojarse	*to get angry*	enojar	*to make someone angry*
equivocarse	*to be wrong/ mistaken*	equivocar	*to mistake*
irse	*to leave, go away*	ir	*to go*
levantarse	*to get up*	levantar	*to lift*
ponerse	*to put on; to become; to start doing something*	poner	*to put, place*
probarse (ue)	*to try on*	probar (ue)	*to taste, try*
quedarse	*to stay, remain behind*	quedar	*to remain*
sentarse (ie)	*to sit down*	sentar (ie)	*to seat someone*
sentirse (ie)	*to feel (well, bad, and so on)*	sentir (ie)	*to feel, sense, perceive*
vestirse (i)	*to get dressed*	vestir (i)	*to dress*

Answers to Actividad 2:

1. se despertó, Se levantó, se vistió, despertó, vistió
2. probé, me probé, me enamoré
3. me equivoqué, se puso, puso, se fue
4. me dormí, me quedé, sentí

2 **¿Reflexivo o no?** From the list to the left of each sentence, choose the reflexive or nonreflexive form of the verb to complete the sentence in the preterite. Work with a partner.

1. despertar(se) levantar(se) vestir(se) — Ricardo ________ muy temprano. ________ y ________. Después, ________ a los niños y los ________ con ropa adecuada para el clima.

2. enamorar(se) probar(se) — Estuve en Madrid cinco días. Allí ________ todas las tapas de un gran restaurante, visité los museos, ________ la mejor ropa en las tiendas y ________ del portero del hotel.

3.	equivocar(se) poner(se) ir(se)	Ayer __________ y abrí una carta que no era para mí. Ernesto __________ furioso y me dijo que nunca más iba a hablarme. Después, él __________ la carta en su maletín y __________ para su oficina.
4.	dormir(se) quedar(se) sentir(se)	Anoche __________ a las dos de la mañana y hoy __________ en cama hasta las doce del día. De pronto, __________ que había alguien en mi sala. ¡Era mi mamá que llegaba con mis regalos de cumpleaños!

3 **¿Qué hacen?** Look at the drawings and describe with a verb from the list on page 256 what the persons are doing. Add clarifying expressions if the situation is reciprocal.

Possible answers to Actividad 3:
1. La madre y el niño se besan.
2. Dos amigos se abrazan.
3. Una persona se enferma con un virus.
4. Dos payasos se ponen un sombrero.
5. Una niñita viste a su muñeca.
6. Alguien levanta una caja pesada.
7. Un payaso divierte a una niña.
8. Dos personas se enojan.

LENGUA EN ACCIÓN

Ponerse (to become), ponerse a... (to start...)

This verb is commonly used to express sudden changes of emotional and mental states or the onset of actions.

Verónica **se puso** furiosa cuando supo la verdad.	*Verónica became furious when she found out the truth.*
Ellos **se pusieron** tristes porque te fuiste.	*They became sad because you left.*
Nosotros **nos pusimos a** escribir inmediatamente.	*We started to write immediately.*

Before doing **Actividad 4,** have students give you a list of interesting Spanish adjectives and write them on the board.

4 **¿Cómo reaccionaron?** You and your friends have experienced many interesting situations in your lives. Working in pairs, ask each other how the person reacted to the situation described using the structures **ponerse** + adjective or **ponerse a** + infinitive. You may want to review the adjectives for describing people in earlier chapters. Look at the model for ideas.

► **Modelo:**

Situación	**Persona**	**Reacción**
Tuvo un accidente	Julia	Se puso a llorar.
Nos ganamos mil dólares	Nosotros	Nos pusimos muy contentos.

¿Cómo reaccionó Julia cuando tuvo un accidente?
Julia se puso a llorar.

¿Cómo reaccionaron ustedes cuando se ganaron mil dólares?
Nos pusimos muy contentos.

Situación	**Persona**	**Reacción**
1. Recibió el título de "Estudiante modelo".		
2. Sus padres le dieron un nuevo estéreo.		
3. Su mascota se murió.		
4. Sus amigos no fueron a su fiesta.		
5. Se ganó diez millones de dólares en la lotería.		
6. Vimos una película muy mala.		

II. Stressing the action and not the subject

Impersonal and passive se *constructions*

Los ovnis

VERÓNICA:	¡Qué cometa más hermoso! Su nombre es Hale Bopp. **Se ve** solamente una vez cada 2.400 años.	*What a beatiful comet. Its name is Hale Bopp. It is seen only once every 2400 years.*
RÓMULO:	¿Un cometa? Puede ser una visita extraterrestre ... ¿un ovni tal vez?	*A comet? It could be a visit from aliens . . . a UFO perhaps?*
VERÓNICA:	¡Qué tontería! Los ovnis no existen.	*What nonsense! UFOs don't exist.*
RÓMULO:	**Dicen** que los ovnis no existen, pero ¡yo creo que sí!	*It's said that they don't exist, but I believe they do!*
VERÓNICA:	¡Claro que no existen! **La gente dice** muchas tonterías.	*Of course they don't exist! People talk a lot of nonsense.*
RÓMULO:	Me estás llamando tonto... qué fresca eres. **Se dice** que los ovnis aparecen con mucha frecuencia en algunos sitios de la tierra.	*You are calling me silly . . . how fresh you are. It is said that UFOs often appear in some locations on earth.*
VERÓNICA:	No, esas cosas son alucinaciones. **Se ven** unas luces tontas en el cielo y luego **se opina** que son ovnis.	*No, those are hallucinations. A few silly lights in the sky are seen and people think they are UFOs.*
RÓMULO:	Bueno, está bien, me rindo. ¡Ese ovni es un cometa y los extraterrestres no existen!	*OK, I give up. That UFO is a comet and there are no aliens!*

Point out that even though **cometa** ends in an **a,** it is a masculine word. So is **planeta.**

The highlighted forms in the previous conversation are used to stress the action while letting the subject remain unknown or undefined. English uses several forms: *It's said, people say, they say, one says.* Spanish has several possible structures for expressing an action without naming a specific subject.

- Using **la gente** as the subject, as in English:

  La gente no sabe que Nayeli es inocente. — *People don't know that Nayeli is innocent.*

- Using the third person plural **(ellos) dicen:**

  Dicen que el jaguar tiene poderes mágicos. — *People say that the jaguar has magic powers.*

- Using a passive form with **se** (when using the passive form with **se,** the verb changes according to whether the passive subject is singular or plural):

  Se dice que Adriana está enamorada de Felipe. — *They say that Adriana is in love with Felipe.*

  Anoche **se vio un** ovni, pero anteanoche **se vieron dos.** — *A UFO was spotted last night, but two were seen the night before.*

5 **¿Dónde?** Work with a partner asking each other where people do the following things.

► **Modelo:** *hablar español / Colombia*
En Colombia se habla español.

1. fabricar computadoras / Japón
2. jugar al fútbol / el estadio
3. tocar la flauta andina / el Ecuador
4. esquiar / en el lago
5. vender los bates / tienda de deportes
6. bailar el tango / la Argentina
7. practicar el jai-alai / canchas deportivas

Answers to Actividad 5:

1. En el Japón se fabrican computadoras.
2. En el estadio se juega el fútbol.
3. En el Ecuador se toca la flauta andina.
4. En el lago se esquía.
5. En la tienda de deportes se venden los bates.
6. En la Argentina se baila el tango.
7. En las canchas deportivas se practica el jai-alai.

6 Los chismes. Work with a partner to find out whether the following things that you have heard are true. Follow the model.

▶ **Modelo:** *Los ovnis existen.*
—¿Existen los ovnis?
—Se dice que los ovnis existen, pero no lo creo or
—Dicen que los ovnis existen, pero no lo creo.

1. Madonna se casó.
2. Nuestro/a profesor/a se divorció.
3. Mi novio/a no me quiere.
4. Vamos a ganar mucho dinero.
5. Hay vida en la luna.
6. Tenemos examen mañana.
7. El mundo se va a acabar.
8. Julia Roberts ganó un Oscar.
9. Mi computadora no funciona.
10. ¿...?

7 ¡Trabajos seguros! You are the manager of a company and are making a list of the personnel and the things that are needed. Write complete sentences using the words provided.

▶ **Modelo:** *dos secretarias*
Se necesitan dos secretarias.

1. escritorios
2. cascos para los ingenieros
3. computadoras
4. sofá para la sala de espera
5. lámpara de escritorio
6. plantas verdes
7. contador
8. escritor técnico
9. cinco programadores
10. diseñador
11. dos supervisores
12. secretario

III. Giving instructions and making requests

Formal commands with usted and ustedes

¿Cómo funciona esta máquina?

You are learning how a new machine at school works and follow written instructions to do it.

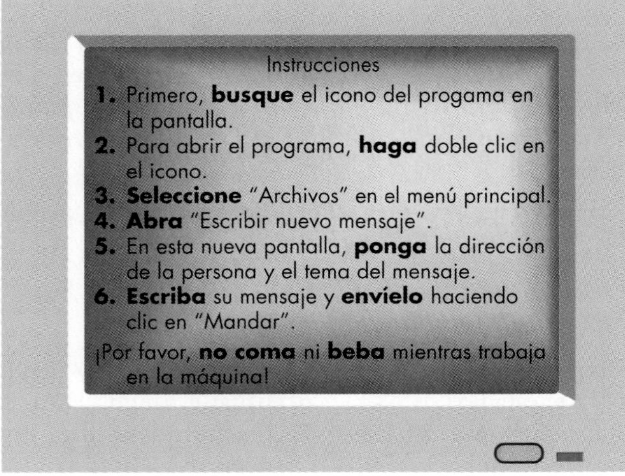

Instrucciones
1. Primero, busque el icono del progama en la pantalla.
2. Para abrir el programa, haga doble clic en el icono.
3. Seleccione "Archivos" en el menú principal.
4. Abra "Escribir nuevo mensaje".
5. En esta nueva pantalla, ponga la dirección de la persona y el tema del mensaje.
6. Escriba su mensaje y envíelo haciendo clic en "Mandar".
¡Por favor, no coma ni beba mientras trabaja en la máquina!

Look at the highlighted forms. What are the differences between these forms and other forms that you have learned in earlier chapters? What is the purpose of these forms in the instructions above? Do negative expressions have the same form as affirmative ones?

Commands for usted and ustedes	**-ar** verbs	**-er** and **-ir** verbs	
usted	seleccion**e** (Ud.) no seleccion**e** (Ud.)	com**a** (Ud.) no com**a** (Ud.)	escrib**a** (Ud.) no escrib**a** (Ud.)
ustedes	seleccion**en** (Uds.) no seleccion**en** (Uds.)	com**an** (Uds.) no com**an** (Uds.)	escrib**an** (Uds.) no escrib**an** (Uds.)

A. Regular verbs in the imperative

Commands, or imperative forms, are used to request something from people. The **usted** and **ustedes** forms are the same in affirmative and negative commands.

- To form the formal imperative, drop the **-o** of the first-person singular in the present tense and add **-e** for **-ar** verbs and **-a** to **-er** and **-ir** verbs. To form the plural, add **-en** and **-an** respectively.

8 **¿Qué le dices?** Imagine that you are giving a course in computers. Work with a partner reading aloud the to-do list that follows, converting each one of the instructions to formal commands in singular and plural forms.

Lista

1. Abrir el manual del estudiante.
2. Leer las instrucciones para encender la computadora.
3. Encender la computadora.
4. Escribir la contraseña (*password*).
5. Iniciar el programa de dibujo.
6. Pintar una ilustración para la composición de español.
7. Imprimir la ilustración en la impresora "Letras".
8. Terminar el programa.

Answers to Actividad 8:
1. Abra/Abran
2. Lea/Lean
3. Encienda/Enciendan
4. Escriba/Escriban
5. Inicie/Inicien
6. Pinte/Pinten
7. Imprima/Impriman
8. Termine/Terminen

9 **Está prohibido.** You have been asked to write the instructions for the employees in a company. Use the list below to tell the employees what they are not allowed to do. Work with a partner.

▸ **Modelo:** *Se prohibe fumar.*
Por favor, no fume.

1. Se prohibe beber junto a la computadora.
2. Se prohibe montar en bicicleta.
3. Se prohibe enviar mensajes ofensivos por correo electrónico.
4. Se prohibe hablar en la biblioteca.
5. Se prohibe consumir drogas.
6. Se prohibe dejar el auto en la calle.
7. Se prohibe correr en el edificio.

Answers to Actividad 9:
1. No beba(n)
2. No monte(n)
3. No envíe(n) (note the accent on the i)
4. No hable(n)
5. No consuma(n)
6. No deje(n)
7. No corra(n)

Ask students if they agree with the instructions

B. Stem-changing verbs in the imperative

Stem-changing verbs and verbs with orthographic changes in the present tense add the imperative endings to the present-tense stem of the first-person singular. Notice the orthographic changes necessary to keep the same sound for **-car**, **-gar** and **-zar** verbs, respectively.

Point out that the spelling changes in the first-person singular of the present tense indicative are the same in the imperative. The only additional spelling changes are with the **-car**, **-gar**, and **-zar** verbs and these are the same ones that occur in the **yo** form of the preterite (Chapter 4).

***yo* forms**	***usted/ustedes* commands**
apago	apa**gue**/n
busco	bus**que**/n
comienzo	com**ience**/n
conozco	cono**zca**/n
digo	di**ga**/n
hago	ha**ga**/n
pago	pa**gue**/n
pienso	**piense**/n
salgo	sal**ga**/n

Answers to Actividad 10:
1. Mantenga su habitación...
2. Pague el alquiler...
3. No haga ruido...
4. No salga...
5. Conozca las salidas...

After completing **Actividad 10**, have students express some of the *Do's* and *Don'ts* at their own school.

10 **¡Por favor!** Imagine that you are a landlord/landlady and are giving instructions to a new tenant about your house rules. Look at the list to create the commands, both affirmative and negative. Follow the model.

► **Modelo:** *Usted debe apagar las luces del jardín por la noche.*
Por favor, apague las luces del jardín por la noche.

1. Usted debe mantener su habitación limpia.
2. Usted siempre debe pagar el alquiler el primero de cada mes.
3. Usted no debe hacer ruido después de las diez de la noche.
4. Usted no debe salir por la puerta principal.
5. Usted debe conocer las salidas de emergencia.

Answers to Actividad 11:
1. comiencen
2. descansen
3. piensen
4. Conozcan

11 **Así son las cosas.** In the following selection, all the commands are missing. Read the story and tell the audience what this TV presenter wants them to do. Select the verbs from the list provided.

conocer descansar comenzar pensar

Público del canal veinte: ¡Ustedes son maravillosos! Por favor, _________ ustedes el programa con un aplauso para mi ayudante, Roberta Marín. Ahora, _________ ustedes muy cómodamente en sus asientos y _________ que van a participar en el mejor programa de la televisión latina. Bueno, y en este momento, voy a presentarles a un nuevo artista. ¡ _________ ustedes al mejor cantante de merengue del país! ¡Aquí está José Quintero! ¡Un aplauso para él!

C. Irregular verbs in the imperative

- Some verbs have irregular imperative forms.

Almost all of the verbs that do not end in an **-o** in the first-person singular of the indicative are irregular in the imperative.

	ir	**ser**	**estar**
usted	vaya	sea	esté
ustedes	vayan	sean	estén

- Subject pronouns follow the verb. It is possible to use subject pronouns with formal commands.

Vaya usted a las tres de la tarde, por favor.	*Go at three in the afternoon, please.*
Por favor, chicos, **sean ustedes** corteses.	*Please, children, be courteous.*

D. Position of subject and object pronouns in commands

Direct, indirect, and reflexive pronouns are attached at the end of an affirmative command. When the command is negative, the pronouns precede the command.

Escriba su mensaje y **envíelo** pulsando el botón.	*Write your message and send it by clicking on the button.*
No **se duerma** usted mientras trabaja aquí.	*Do not fall asleep while you work here.*
Escríbanos hoy mismo, pero **no nos pague** todavía.	*Write to us today, but don't pay us yet.*

12 Para nuestros visitantes. You are preparing a guest guide for a hotel and need to tell visitors what the hotel has to offer. Use the verbs in the list in the formal command form to attract guests to the hotel. Use each verb once.

visitar	comenzar	comprar	poner	nadar
sentarse	cenar	pagar	salir	venir

1. ...en nuestro restaurante Ricascosas, en la terraza
2. ...todas sus cuentas con cualquier tarjeta de crédito
3. ...en la piscina desde las ocho de la mañana hasta las nueve de la noche
4. ...los periódicos del día en nuestra recepción
5. ...en nuestras cómodas sillas y sofás a leer tranquilamente
6. ...las cartas en la oficina de correos del hotel
7. ...el día con un desayuno continental en su habitación
8. ...la ciudad en nuestros buses turísticos
9. ...a nuestra discoteca, la mejor de la ciudad
10. ...de su habitación a las tres de la tarde

Answers to Actividad 12:
1. Cenen
2. Paguen
3. Naden
4. Compren
5. Siéntense
6. Pongan
7. Comiencen
8. Visiten
9. Vengan
10. Salgan

13 Ésta es la tarea. You are organizing a celebration: enlist people to help you with several tasks. Working with a partner, tell each person what he/she has to do. Use formal commands and object pronouns. Follow the model.

► **Modelo:** *Don Roberto* *mandar las invitaciones*
Don Roberto, por favor, mándelas.

Lista de colaboradores	Lista de cosas por hacer
Adriana y Felipe, estudiantes	comprar las flores para adornar el salón
La profesora López	hacer la lista de invitados especiales
María Cecilia, profesora	seleccionar el menú para la cena
Tomás, futbolista	recibir las facturas y pagar las cuentas
Don Cipriano, entrenador	poner las mesas y tener listas las sillas

Possible answers to Actividad 13:
1. Adriana y Felipe, por favor, cómprenlas.
2. Profesora López, por favor, hágala.
3. María Cecilia, por favor, selecciónelo.
4. Tomás, por favor, recíbalas y páguelas.
5. Don Cipriano, por favor, póngalas y téngalas listas.

Before doing **Actividad 14**, point out that when the pronouns are attached to the affirmative commands an accent is written on the stressed syllable of the command itself. You may also wish to review double-object pronouns (Chapter 5).

Answers to Actividad 14:
1. La información, **désela** (usted) al director.
2. Los mensajes electrónicos, **mándeselos** (usted) a los clientes.
3. La sala de conferencias, **resérvenosla** (usted) para las tres p.m.
4. Los tiquetes para el Ecuador, **resérvemelos** (usted) a mí.
5. Los discos de la computadora, **véndaselos** (usted) a doña Rita.
6. Las cuentas, **págueselas** (usted) a las tiendas.
7. El auto, **mándenoslo** (usted) a la oficina central.
8. El problema, **explíqueselo** (usted) a don Armando.

Before doing **Actividad 15**, review placement of object pronouns (Chapter 5). **Answers:**
1. No se la dé.
2. No se los mande.
3. No nos la reserve.
4. No me los reserve.
5. No se los venda.
6. No se las pague.
7. No nos lo mande.
8. No se lo explique.

14 Ayudante ocupado. You are about to leave for a business trip. Work with a partner to tell your assistant the tasks he/she has to do. Follow the model, using formal commands and object pronouns.

► **Modelo:** *Las instrucciones se las envía usted al señor Morales.*
Las instrucciones, envíeselas al señor Morales.

1. La información se la da usted al director.
2. Los mensajes electrónicos se los manda usted a los clientes.
3. La sala de conferencias nos la reserva usted para las tres p.m.
4. Los tiquetes para el Ecuador me los reserva usted a mí.
5. Los discos de la computadora se los vende usted a doña Rita.
6. Las cuentas se las paga usted a las tiendas.
7. El auto nos lo manda usted a la oficina central.
8. El problema se lo explica usted a don Armando.

15 Ayudante desocupado. Based on **Actividad 14**, now tell your assistant not to do the things in the list.

16 Consejero. Choose one of the situations described below and tell your friend or friends what to do or not to do in each case. Use as many verbs as you can.

1. You sell computers in a store and are showing a client how to start to use a computer program. Give your client all the instructions.
2. You are organizing a sports tournament. Tell various people what they have to do regarding invitations, which sports are allowed, food for the visitors, selling the tickets, transportation, and so on.
3. You meet a tourist downtown and she asks you for directions to an important city landmark. Give her directions on how to get there with public transportation or driving her own car.
4. You are taking care of your neighbor's mischievous big dog. You usually address him with the **usted** form for fun because the dog looks so impressive. Tell him what to do and not to do while you are taking care of him.

Lectura B

Introducción

Today, computers and networks play an important role in students' professional and personal lives. Let's look at some facts about computers and the Internet.

Prelectura

1 Preguntas. Work with a partner to answer the following questions.

1. ¿Tienes tu propia computadora? ¿De qué marca es? ¿Cuánto te costó?
2. ¿Te gusta hacer las tareas en la computadora? ¿Por qué?
3. ¿Te gustan los juegos de computadoras? ¿Qué tipo de juegos?

4. ¿Utilizas tú la red Internet? ¿Para qué usas la red? ¿Usas la red en la escuela como parte de tus estudios o solamente para divertirte?
5. ¿Qué tipo de información buscas en Internet? ¿Cuáles son tus sitios preferidos?

Internet: La red mundial

En el mundo de las comunicaciones, ha habido° una explosión de nuevas tecnologías. La red mundial Internet y el sistema World Wide Web, o el Web, son dos nuevos e importantes recursos tecnológicos. Millones de computadoras están conectadas a Internet y los usuarios° pueden transmitir y recibir correo electrónico e información muy rápidamente. A los usuarios les gusta mucho el sistema Web porque este sistema presenta la información con textos atractivos, gráficos, animaciones, videos y sonidos. También es posible conversar por teléfono y tener videoconferencias con personas que están en otras partes del mundo. Actualmente,° la red Internet y el sistema Web tienen gran importancia económica para la venta y la compra de productos y servicios mundialmente.

there has been

users

Nowadays

Con el uso de las redes y con la gran variedad de programas para niños y adultos, la venta de computadoras aumenta continuamente. En 1995, por ejemplo, se vendieron más computadoras que televisores en el mundo y más teléfonos celulares que coches. Los niños de los Estados

Unidos e Inglaterra pasaron más tiempo usando las computadoras que mirando televisión. Actualmente, esta tendencia continúa en todas partes. El número de usuarios de Internet se ha duplicado° en los últimos diez años y sigue aumentando. La red la usan personas de todas las edades: desde niños pequeños que están aprendiendo a leer, hasta personas de mucha edad. Por ejemplo,° en España, más de 250.000 personas usaron la red Internet en 1997 en comparación con sólo 20.000 en 1996.

has doubled

For example

La mayoría de los materiales en Internet está actualmente en inglés, pero hay ya muchos sitios en español y los usuarios hispanohablantes aumentan cada vez más.

Las guías, los motores de búsqueda° y los catálogos de Internet facilitan el acceso a la información. Actualmente existen muchos de estos recursos como Yahoo, Alta Vista, Hot Bot, Excite, las Páginas Amarillas y las Páginas Blancas.

search engines

Un muchacho puertorriqueño trabajando en la computadora.

Postlectura

Answers to Actividad 2:
1. Se vendieron más computadoras.
2. Los usuarios son de todas las edades.
3. Les gusta la versatilidad del Internet y porque tienen acceso a la transmisión de voz, textos, gráficos, animaciones, datos, video y sonido.
4. En España hay más de 250.000 personas que usan la red Internet. El número de usuarios aumentó de 20.000 en 1996 a 250.000 en 1997.
5. Va a aumentar. Porque cada día hay más materiales en español.

2 Comprensión. Write answers to the following questions.

1. ¿Se vendieron más televisores o computadoras en el mundo, en 1995?
2. ¿Qué edad tienen los usuarios de Internet?
3. ¿Por qué les gustan a los usuarios la red Internet y el Web?
4. ¿Cuántos usuarios de Internet hay en España? ¿Cuánto aumentó el número de usuarios entre 1996 y 1997?
5. ¿Qué va a pasar con el número de usuarios hispanohablantes en el futuro? ¿Por qué?

3 Internet. In pairs, exchange information on the following questions.

1. ¿Qué catálogos, guías o motores de búsqueda usas tú para buscar información para tus trabajos de la universidad?
2. ¿Son difíciles de usar estos recursos de Internet?

4 La computadora y yo. Why is the computer important to you and your free time?

En resumen

I. Hablemos

1 *Una entrevista por radio.* You work as a news correspondent and have been asked to interview your favorite music or sports celebrity. Use some of the following questions to guide your interview. Ask at least ten questions about her or his achievements and background. Work with a partner. Be sure to use **usted** with the interviewee.

¿De dónde es Ud.?
¿Tocaba un instrumento/cantaba/hacía deportes cuando era joven?
¿Cuándo supo Ud. que quería ser deportista/cantante/músico/a profesional?
¿Cuándo fue su primer concierto/partido profesional?
¿...?

2 *¿Qué va a pasar?* In groups of three, act out the next scene of what happens to Adriana, Felipe, and Nayeli after Sunglasses leaves them. What do they say? What do they do? What will happen to them?

II. Investiguemos por Internet

Using Internet guides

Many Hispanic performers have their own Web pages, some of them with their own audio and video clips. You can find them through the Yellow and White Pages on the Internet, through Movie Guides, through the movie and music production companies or using Internet guides and catalogs.

3 *Mi artista preferido/a.* Work in groups in the classroom before you start your search. First, choose three Hispanic artists in any entertainment branch: TV, radio, film, music, or sports. You may also add a writer, a politician or a famous person in any social context. Then, make a list of at least six characteristics that you would like to find out about the three persons selected. For example, their age, what they do, if they are single or married, where they live, awards received, and so on. Use the name of the artist as the keyword to start your search. If you need more information about Hispanic artists in order to select the three names, you may start your search in the Yellow Pages in Spanish (**Páginas Amarillas**), in a specialized music, video or film guide or in an Internet guide like Yahoo.

Vocabulario informático	
archivos MIDI	*MIDI archives (digital music)*
audio digital	*digital audio*
efectos especiales	*special effects (F/X)*
efectos de sonido	*sound effects*
sonido digital	*digital sound*
video digital	*digital video, movies*

III. Escribamos

Writing strategy: Freewriting

One way to jump start the writing process is to practice freewriting. This is a good way to see what ideas you may have about a subject before organizing your writing. Here are some guidelines for generating these ideas.

1. Choose a topic that you are going to write about in Spanish—one of your own or one that has been assigned. Write it at the top of the page.
2. You may either sit in front of the computer, or write in longhand. A good strategy for working with the computer is to work with the computer screen turned off. This will avoid the temptation you may have to correct errors while writing.
3. Write about the idea in Spanish for five to ten minutes without stopping. For now, don't correct grammar, spelling, accents, or punctuation.
4. If you do not know the conjugation of a verb, write the infinitive.
5. If you do not know the Spanish word, write the word in English so you don't lose your train of thought.
6. If you can't think of the next word, write the last word over and over again until you have an idea.
7. After you are finished, read over your writing. Underline or highlight the important ideas and organize them as part of your outline.
8. Now you can begin to write your composition using these ideas.

Strategy in action

Turn to *Escribamos* in the Workbook to practice the strategy of freewriting.

4 Después de la entrevista. You have just had a great interview for the job of your dreams. Write a follow-up letter to the company to thank the person who interviewed you and to emphasize your interest in the job. Use freewriting techniques to start your letter. Be sure to include these elements in your final letter.

(Fecha)
(Dirección)
Estimado/a señor/a __________:
(Introducción)
(Experiencia)
(Despedida)
Atentamente,
(Nombre)

Assign **Actividad 5** as homework. Have students share their ideas electronically, if possible.

5 En resumen. Luis, the thug, is upset that Sunglasses didn't give him the computer. While he is in jail, he decides to complete his computer science studies and uses his own computer to write down his thoughts in an electronic diary that he keeps. Recount the events of the last episode from his point of view.

Música y baile

los audífonos	*headphones*
bailar	*to dance*
el/la bailarín/ina	*dancer*
la balada	*ballad*
la batería	*drum set*
el/la cantante	*singer*
cantar	*to sing*
el clarinete	*clarinet*
el conjunto	*band*
el disco compacto	*compact disc*
la flauta	*flute*
la grabadora (videograbadora)	*tape/video player/ recorder*
grabar	*to tape*
la guitarra	*guitar*
el merengue	*Caribbean rhythm*
la música	*music*
el piano	*piano*
el ritmo	*rhythm*
la salsa	*salsa music*
el saxofón	*saxophone*
el tambor	*drum*
tocar	*to play (an instrument)*
el trombón	*trombone*
la trompeta	*trumpet*
el violín	*violin*

Deportes

el/la aficionado/a	*fan*
el balón	*ball*
el bate	*bat*
la cancha	*court*
el/la deportista	*athlete, sports enthusiast*
el equipo	*team*
el/la espectador/a	*spectator*
el esquí	*ski*
ganar	*to win*
gozar	*to enjoy*
el/la jugador/a	*player*
el palo	*club*
el partido	*game*
patear	*to kick*
patinar	*to skate*
los patines	*skates*
la pelota	*ball*
perder	*to lose*
la pista	*rink (ice skating/hockey)*
la raqueta	*racket*
el uniforme	*uniform*

Tecnología

abrir	*to open (a document)*
apagar	*to turn off*
la aplicación	*application*
archivar (guardar)	*to save*
el archivo	*computer file*
la ayuda	*help*
el botón	*button*
cerrar (ie)	*to close (a document)*
colgar (ue)	*to hang up*
contestar	*to answer*
copiar	*to copy*
el directorio	*directory*
el disco duro	*hard drive*
el documento	*document*
enviar (mandar)	*to send*
hacer clic	*to click with the mouse*
la impresora	*printer*
imprimir	*to print*
el mensaje	*message*
mover (ue)	*to move*
prender (encender [ie])	*to turn on*
presionar (pulsar)	*to click on something on a computer screen*
el programa	*program*
el ratón	*mouse*
recibir	*to receive*
la red	*network*

Trabajo

el/la aspirante *applicant*
las calificaciones *qualifications*
la compañía *company*
el conocimiento *knowledge*
el desempleo *unemployment*
despedir (i) *to lay off, fire*
el entrenamiento *training*
la entrevista *interview*
la evaluación *evaluation*
la fábrica *factory*
el hombre/la mujer de negocios *businessman/ businesswoman*
el horario de trabajo *work schedule*
la meta *goal*
el negocio *business*
renunciar *to quit (a job)*
la responsabilidad *responsibility*
el salario (sueldo) *salary*
solicitar (un trabajo/ puesto) *to apply (for a job)*
la solicitud *application*
el trabajo (puesto) *work, position*
tiempo parcial *part-time*
tiempo completo *full-time*

Verbos reflexivos

acostarse (ue) *to go to bed, lie down*
alegrarse *to become happy*
darse cuenta de *to become aware of, notice*
despertarse (ie) *to wake up*
divertirse (ie) *to have fun, have a good time*
dormirse (ue) *to fall asleep*
enamorarse de *to fall in love*
enfermarse *to get sick*
enojarse *to get angry*
equivocarse *to make a mistake, be wrong*
irse *to leave, go away*
levantarse *to get up*
ponerse *to put on clothing; to become; to start doing something*
probarse (ue) *to try on*
quedarse *to stay, remain behind*
sentarse (ie) *to sit down*
sentirse (ie) *to feel (well, bad, and so on)*
vestirse (i) *to get dressed*

CAPÍTULO 7

LOCALIDAD: Ecuador

7A

¿Qué significa el sueño de Adriana?

7B

Adriana has a compelling dream, experiences the joining of two hemispheres with Felipe, and reveals the history of the disappearance of the Jaguar Twin.

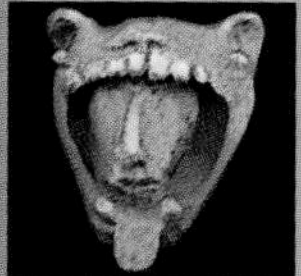

Vocabulary themes

- Talking about stores and shopping
- Shopping for clothes
- Talking about cars
- Asking for and giving directions
- Coping with traffic
- Describing the countryside

Language structures

- Describing past actions
- Describing actions in progress in the past
- Describing unplanned and unintentional occurrences
- Making comparisons of persons and things
- Expressing ideas that are subjective

Culture topics

- El vestido típico de Otavalo
- Fibras y textiles
- El nombre del Ecuador
- El salto Ángel

Readings

- El norte andino
- Rumiaya

Reading and writing strategies

- Tapping background knowledge
- Paraphrasing

Internet strategy

- Refining your Internet searches

ETAPA A

Ask students where they could buy **carne (carnicería), leche (lechería), pan (panadería). Floristería** is also used in many Hispanic countries.

Pistas y palabras

I. Talking about stores and shopping

En el centro comercial

- Note that many store names are made by adding **-ería** to the thing they sell.

1 ¿Dónde se compra? ¿En qué tipo de tienda puedes comprar los siguientes artículos?

1. aspirina
2. un traje de baño
3. perfume
4. maquillaje
5. una novela de amor
6. un cuaderno
7. una docena de rosas
8. un reloj
9. una corbata de seda

Answers to Actividad 1:

1. farmacia
2. Almacén Márquez
3. perfumería
4. Almacén Márquez, Boutique *La moda*
5. librería
6. papelería
7. florería
8. Almacén Márquez, joyería
9. Almacén Márquez, Boutique *La Moda*

2 Regalos. Tienes que comprar regalos para tu familia y para tus amigos. Haz una lista de dos amigos/as y de tres miembros de tu familia. Decide qué piensas comprar para cada persona, a qué tienda vas, y por qué. Trabaja con una pareja para hablar de tu lista.

	Nombre	Regalo	Tienda	Por qué
1.	________	________	________	________
2.	________	________	________	________
3.	________	________	________	________
4.	________	________	________	________
5.	________	________	________	________

ENLACE CULTURAL

El vestido típico de Otavalo

Los países hispanos tienen generalmente vestidos típicos nacionales o representativos de una región o de un grupo étnico. Normalmente, estos trajes tienen tradiciones de muchos años.

En Otavalo, las mujeres se visten con faldas de paño° oscuro, llamadas **anacos.** La blusa es blanca con bordados muy bonitos. Los collares tienen varias hileras de cuentas.° Muchos hombres llevan el pelo en una larga trenza.° Cuando hace mucho frío, los hombres usan *poncho* y las mujeres usan una **fachalina.**°

paño: cloth
cuentas: threads of beads
trenza: braid
fachalina: shawl

Hombres otavaleños en el mercado.

For **vestidos típicos** bring in pictures, stamps, dolls and/or items of clothing you may have acquired through your travels.

Discusión en grupos

1. Menciona un vestido típico que conozcas. ¿Quién lo usa? ¿Cuándo? ¿Cómo es?
2. ¿Tiene alguno de ustedes un vestido típico? ¿De qué región? ¿Cómo es?

II. Shopping for clothes

En el almacén

ROPA de HOMBRE
PROBADOR DE HOMBRES
ROPA de MUJER
PROBADOR DE MUJERES
¡OFERTA!
ASEO PERSONAL
descuento 20%
ACCESORIOS
chaquetas
pantalones
sacos
abrigos e impermeables
suéteres de lana
trajes
vestidos
camisas de algodón
blusas de seda
faldas y minifaldas
ropa interior
cosméticos
bufandas
guantes
perfume
talco
jabón
sombreros y gorras
botas de vaquero
bolsas
corbatas
cinturones de cuero
calcetines y medias
zapatos

Cut out pictures from Spanish-language magazines and have students identify the different items of clothing.

Palabras y expresiones útiles

el/la cliente	*customer*
el/la dependiente	*clerk*
el escaparate	*shop window, display case*
la ganga, oferta	*sale, discount*
la mancha	*stain*
el mostrador	*display case/counter*
el par	*pair*
el precio	*price*
el recibo	*receipt*
las sandalias	*sandals*
la sudadera	*sweat suit*
la talla	*size*
la venta	*sale*
los zapatos de tacón alto/bajo	*high-heeled, low-heeled shoes*
los zapatos de tenis	*sneakers*

devolver (ue)	*to return*	ir de compras	*to go shopping*
estar a cargo de	*to be in charge of*	llevar	*to wear*
estar de moda	*to be in style*	probar(se) (ue)	*to try on*

Claro que sí.	*Of course.*
¿Cómo me queda?	*How does it fit me?*
de cuadros	*plaid*
de lunares (puntos)	*polka dotted*
de manga corta/larga	*short/long-sleeved*
de rayas	*striped*
¿En qué le puedo ayudar?	*How can I help you?*
¿En qué puedo servirle?	*How can I help you?*
Está roto/a, sucio/a, manchado/a	*It's ripped/dirty/stained*
mediano/a	*medium*
pequeño/a	*small*
¿Puedo probarme el/la...?	*Can I try on the . . . ?*
Quiero cambiar(lo/la) por otro/a.	*I want to exchange (it) for another.*
Quiero que me devuelvan el dinero.	*I want you to return my money.*
Te/Le queda bien (mal, grande, pequeño/a, largo/a, corto/a, estrecho/a, flojo/a).	*It fits you well (poorly, big, small, long, short, tight, loose).*
Voy a llevar(me)...	*I'm going to take . . .*
Voy a probarme(lo/la).	*I'm going to try (it) on.*

3 **¿Qué piensas comprar?** ¿Qué ropa piensas comprar para las siguientes ocasiones? Haz una lista para cada una. Compárala con un/a compañero/a.

1. asistir a un partido de fútbol
2. ir a una discoteca nueva
3. ir a la fiesta de cumpleaños de tu novio/a
4. presentarte a tu primera entrevista de trabajo
5. ir a la playa
6. ir a esquiar
7. asistir a una boda muy elegante

Before doing **Actividad 3**, review colors, then ask students to describe what they are wearing today. **(¿Qué llevas hoy? ¿De qué color es?)**

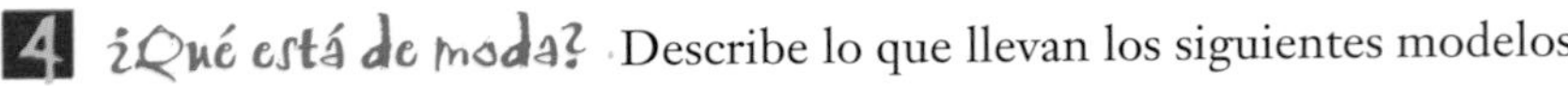

4 ¿Qué está de moda? Describe lo que llevan los siguientes modelos.

5 ¿Qué lleva? Trae una foto de un/a amigo/a o de una persona famosa a la clase y describe lo que lleva.

Before doing **Actividad 6**, tell students **talla** means *size.* Some equivalents of metric and U.S. sizes: Women: **shoes:** size **6** = ***36 metric*** and size **9** = ***40 metric***; **dresses and coats:** size **6** = ***34*** and size **16** = ***44***; **blouses:** size **8** = ***40*** and size **14** = ***46***. Men: **shoes:** size **8** = ***39 metric*** and size **12** = ***43 metric***; **suits:** size **38** = ***48*** and **48** = ***58***; **shirts:** size **15** = ***38*** and **17** = ***42***. After students do this exercise in pairs, ask each group key questions such as **¿Qué necesitaba tu cliente? ¿De qué color era?**

6 En la tienda. Estás en una tienda comprando ropa para una ocasión especial. Haz el papel de cliente y completa tu conversación con el/la dependiente.

DEPENDIENTE: Buenas tardes. ¿En qué le puedo servir?
CLIENTE: Buenas tardes. Voy a una fiesta este fin de semana y necesito __________.
DEPENDIENTE: ¿Es una ocasión formal o informal?
CLIENTE: __________.
DEPENDIENTE: ¡Ay qué bien, lo que usted busca está en oferta!
CLIENTE: ¡Qué suerte! Necesito la talla __________.
DEPENDIENTE: Pues tenemos una variedad. Hay en todas las tallas.
CLIENTE: ¿__________?
DEPENDIENTE: Sí, también hay en muchos colores: azul, verde, marrón, negro y gris.
CLIENTE: ¿__________?
DEPENDIENTE: Claro, Ud. puede llevar tres al probador.

Vas al probador y regresas.

CLIENTE: ¿__________?
DEPENDIENTE: No, creo que otro color le queda mejor.
CLIENTE: ¿__________?
DEPENDIENTE: Sí, ese color le queda muy bien.
CLIENTE: __________.
DEPENDIENTE: Con mucho gusto. Puede pagar Ud. en la caja (*register*).
CLIENTE: __________.

7 **Entre nosotros.** Trabaja con un/a compañero/a para crear un diálogo entre un dependiente de una tienda de ropa y un cliente que llega a última hora.

Have students do **Actividad 7** as homework to act out the next day in class as a 1-minute skit.

Cliente	Dependiente/a
Hoy estuviste de compras en una tienda de ropa. Cuando llegas a casa, te das cuenta de que la ropa tiene una mancha y no la puedes usar en la fiesta de esta noche. Decides regresar a la tienda para devolver las cosas o comprar algo diferente. Estás de muy mal humor y tienes mucha prisa porque ya es bastante tarde.	Trabajas en una tienda de ropa relativamente pequeña. Estás bastante cansado/a porque hoy fue un día muy largo. Faltan quince minutos para cerrar y en ese momento llega un/una cliente para cambiar una ropa que está manchada. Tu jefe/a se llevó las llaves de la caja y no puedes abrirla para atender al/a la cliente.

ENLACE CULTURAL

Fibras y textiles

En la época de los incas, la gente de las regiones frías de los Andes fabricaba su ropa de algodón o de lana de alpaca, de llama o de guanaco.° La lana de vicuña° era la más fina y estaba reservada para los monarcas incas, quienes usaban cada prenda° solamente una vez.

Unas alpacas en Bolivia.

guanaco and **vicuña:** *animals similar to the llama*

garment

En nuestra época moderna, después de la invención de las fibras sintéticas derivadas del petróleo como el nilón, el poliéster y el rayón, la importancia práctica de las fibras naturales es mucho menor. Actualmente, las fibras naturales como el algodón, la seda y la lana fina tienen un toque° de lujo° y muchas veces, un alto precio.

touch

luxury

Discusión en grupos

1. ¿De qué material es la ropa que llevan hoy tú y tus compañeros/as? ¿Qué materiales se usan para hacer la ropa de invierno? ¿Y la ropa de verano?
2. ¿Cuál es el material que prefieres para tu ropa? Describe la ropa que usabas cuando eras pequeño/a.
3. ¿Qué tipo de materiales naturales se vende en la región donde vives? ¿Hay diferencia de precio entre los materiales naturales y los materiales sintéticos?

VISTAS Y VOCES

I. Preparémonos

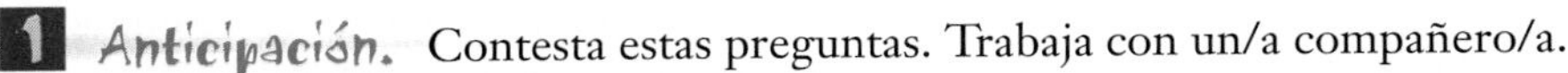

1 Anticipación. Contesta estas preguntas. Trabaja con un/a compañero/a.

A. **1.** Describe el caso de algún secuestro en tu región o en tu país. ¿A quién secuestraron? ¿Quién lo hizo? ¿Cómo sucedió? ¿Por qué?

2. ¿Quién te inspiró a estudiar tu especialización? ¿Cuándo? ¿Cómo?

3. Cuenta los detalles de la mejor sorpresa que tuviste el año pasado. ¿Cómo te afectó?

B. Mira la foto 7A en la página 271. ¿Quiénes están en la foto? ¿Qué hacen? ¿Qué crees que va a pasar ahora?

Para comprender mejor

a lo lejos	*at a distance*	empapado/a	*very wet*
a propósito	*by the way*	empujar	*to push*
atado/a	*tied*	fiel	*faithful*
el bordado	*embroidery*	el lío	*hassle*
burlarse de	*to make fun of*	llamativo/a	*attractive*
la cabaña	*shack*	lograr	*to achieve*
cobrar	*to charge*	Parece mentira.	*It seems unreal.*
la cubeta	*bucket*	quebrar	*to break*
cubierto/a	*covered*	el sudor	*sweat*
cubrir	*to cover*	vacío/a	*empty*
de veras	*really*	valiente	*brave*
desatar	*to untie*	la ventanita	*little window*

Before viewing this episode, describe the following relationships, writing them on the board: Don Gustavo (**amigo de Nayeli**); Doña Carmen (**la madrina de Nayeli**); Yax-Balam (**el jaguar gemelo robado**); Hun-Ahau (**el jaguar gemelo que doña Carmen tiene en Costa Rica**); Zulaya Piscomayo Curihual (**la señora de Otavalo**)

Correct order of video action shots: 4, 3, 2, 1

2 Secuencia. Estudia cada escena de video y contesta las siguientes preguntas. ¿Quién es el señor? ¿Es bueno o malo? ¿Qué relación tiene con Gafasnegras? ¿Qué importancia crees que él va a tener en los próximos episodios?

1.

2.

3.

4.

II. Miremos y escuchemos

3 **Mis observaciones.** Mientras miras y escuchas el episodio, escribe el nombre del personaje o de los personajes relacionado(s) con los siguientes eventos.

1. Llamó a don Gustavo por teléfono. ____________
2. Escuchó la historia del secuestro de Felipe y Adriana. ____________
3. Quebraron la ventanita con la computadora. ____________
4. Llamó a Gafasoscuras mientras vigilaba la casa de don Gustavo. ____________
5. Se fue a Costa Rica. ____________
6. Negociaron con un taxista para ir a Otavalo. ____________
7. Se asustó mucho con el sueño que tuvo. ____________

Answers to Actividad 3:
1. Nayeli
2. Don Gustavo
3. Felipe, Adriana y Nayeli
4. Miguel
5. Nayeli
6. Adriana y Felipe
7. Adriana

4 **¡Peligro!** ¿Quién crees que va a estar en más peligro? ¿Cómo?

III. Comentemos

5 **Comprensión.** Contesta las siguientes preguntas.
1. ¿A quién le cuentan Felipe y Adriana la historia del secuestro? ¿Dónde?
2. ¿Quién desató a Felipe? ¿Qué hizo Felipe con el detonador?
3. ¿Cómo se escaparon Nayeli, Adriana y Felipe de la cabaña?
4. Según Adriana, ¿quién inspiró a Nayeli a estudiar arqueología? ¿Adónde la llevaba en México? ¿Quién tiene el jaguar Hun-Ahau en su poder?
5. Nayeli le pidió a Gustavo que fuera a la oficina de correo expreso. ¿Por qué?
6. ¿Cómo se llama la persona que recogió el paquete? ¿De dónde es ella?
7. ¿Cuánto les va a cobrar el taxista a Felipe y Adriana por el viaje a Otavalo? ¿En dónde van a hacer una parada? ¿Cuántos días van a quedarse allí?
8. Describe a las personas y las cosas que observes en este episodio en el Ecuador. Después, compara la primera y la última vista geográfica del episodio.

Answers to Actividad 5:
1. a don Gustavo; en el Ecuador
2. Adriana; Lo cubrió con una cubeta vieja.
3. Quebraron la ventanita con la computadora y se escaparon.
4. Doña Carmen; Ella es la madrina de Nayeli. La llevaba al Museo de Antropología. Doña Carmen tiene a Hun-Ahau en su poder en su casa.
5. Para averiguar sobre un paquete que mandó un señor Covarrubias desde Sevilla.
6. Zulaya Piscomayo Curihual. Es de Otavalo.
7. trescientos mil sucres; en Mitad del Mundo; Adriana y Felipe no saben cuántos días van a quedarse en Mitad del Mundo.
8. *Answers will vary.*

6 **Miremos otra vez.** Arregla las escenas de video en la secuencia correcta.

7 **Yo creo que...** En grupos de tres, analicen el significado de dos afirmaciones de Nayeli que Adriana escucha en su sueño: "La fama no hace la felicidad", "Lo que verdaderamente importa son tus amigos y tu familia".

8 **Miguel.** Trabajando en parejas, discute las siguientes preguntas. ¿Quién es Miguel? ¿Cómo es? ¿Cuántos años crees que él tiene? ¿Qué está haciendo en este episodio? ¿Qué malas noticias le da a Gafasnegras?

Lengua

I. Describing past actions

Review of the preterite and the imperfect

In previous chapters, you learned the various uses of the preterite and imperfect to narrate in the past. Review Chapters 4 and 5 for the formation and uses of these commonly used past tenses. The following narration uses the preterite to tell a story in the past, while the imperfect describes the background or sets the stage for the actions. First, read it aloud. Then, working with a partner, underline the past tense verbs to determine the uses of the preterite and imperfect.

¡De perezoso° a héroe! El dramático día de Diego

lazy

Yo trabajo en el Almacén Rodríguez, de las cuatro de la tarde hasta las once de la noche. El jueves pasado fue un día horrible. Dejé el horario del tren en casa y perdí el tren de las tres y diez de la tarde. Tuve que esperar una hora por el siguiente tren. Cuando llegué al trabajo media hora tarde, el jefe estaba furioso. Traté de explicarle mi problema, pero él no tenía interés en escuchar excusas. Me dijo que yo era muy irresponsable, me criticó por ser perezoso y me hizo sentir muy mal.

Mi amiga Julia trabaja en el departamento de computadoras de la misma tienda, y yo soy dependiente en el departamento de música. Ese jueves por la tarde estuve muy ocupado,° con muchos clientes, y vendí bastantes artículos caros. Luego, a las nueve, Julia y yo salimos a cenar. Fuimos a nuestro restaurante ecuatoriano favorito. Comimos en una hora porque teníamos que regresar al trabajo.

busy

Assign **Actividad 1** as written homework as five sentences with space left for answers. Have students ask each other the questions in class (in groups of three or four), write out their answers, and then hand in both questions and answers.

Cuando regresamos al almacén, no había ni una estrella en el cielo. Eran las diez de la noche y todo estaba muy oscuro. Al acercarnos, vi a dos personas que salían de allí cargando máquinas pequeñas: eran una mujer alta, pelirroja, bien vestida y un hombre grande, de pelo oscuro y también muy elegante. A pesar de las apariencias, yo estaba seguro de que eran dos ladrones y de inmediato corrí hacia° ellos. Mientras tanto, Julia llamaba a los detectives de la tienda. Los guardias llegaron junto con la policía y se llevaron a los ladrones. ¡Fue un día muy dramático!

toward

1 **¿Qué pasó en la tienda?** Crea preguntas en el pasado sobre la historia de Diego y Julia. Pon atención al uso del pretérito y del imperfecto y usa palabras interogativas también.

2 **Situaciones.** Completa las siguientes narraciones con las formas apropiadas del pretérito y del imperfecto.

Answers to Actividad 2:

1. escribía
2. llamó
3. dijo
4. iba
5. conté
6. estaba
7. tenía
8. llegó
9. invitó
10. pude (stress the meaning of **pude** as *I wasn't able to and didn't,* a meaning clarified by the following sentence)
11. fui

La vida universitaria

Eran las ocho de la noche. Yo __________ (escribir) un trabajo de literatura latinoamericana en la computadora, cuando mi madre me __________ (llamar). Me __________ (decir) que ella __________ (ir) a visitarme a la universidad la semana siguiente. Yo le __________ (contar) que __________ (estar) muy ocupada y que __________ (tener) que presentar dos exámenes. A las nueve, mi compañero de cuarto __________ (llegar). Me __________ (invitar) a ir a una fiesta de la residencia. Yo no __________ (poder) resistir la tentación y __________ (ir) con él olvidando mis exámenes por completo.

En la tienda

Manolo __________ (necesitar) un traje y varios accesorios. Una tarde, él __________ (ir) a la tienda para comprárselos. Primero, se __________ (comprar) un traje negro muy elegante y después, __________ (seleccionar) una camisa blanca de seda muy cara. Finalmente, __________ (ir) al departamento de accesorios donde __________ (probarse) varios pares de botas de cuero. No le __________ (gustar) las botas y __________ (decidir) irse a casa. Cuando __________ (salir) de la tienda, __________ (estar) bastante cansado, pero muy contento.

1. necesitaba
2. fue
3. compró
4. seleccionó
5. fue
6. se probó
7. gustaron
8. decidió
9. salió
10. estaba

3 **¿Qué pasó?** Escribe un párrafo utilizando el pretérito y el imperfecto. Lee tu narración en grupos de tres. Después, comparen el uso de los dos tiempos verbales. (**Tema:** Una experiencia reciente en mi almacén favorito.)

II. Describing actions in progress in the past

Past progressive

¿Qué estaba haciendo la familia?	*What was the family doing?*
1. Yo **estaba hablando** por télefono con mi hermano Guillermo desde mi cuarto en la universidad.	*I was talking on the phone with my brother Bill from my room at the university.*
2. Mamá **estaba probándose** un vestido nuevo.	*Mom was trying on a new dress.*

3. Papá **estaba plantando** flores en el jardín. — *Dad was planting flowers in the garden.*
4. Abuela **estaba leyendo** una novela mexicana. — *Grandma was reading a Mexican novel.*
5. El gatito **estaba comiendo** en la cocina. — *The cat was eating in the kitchen.*
6. Guillermo **estaba escribiendo** un trabajo sobre la historia del Ecuador. — *Bill was writing a paper on the history of Ecuador.*

In order to make sure students know that the past progressive is a two-part verb tense, conjugate one verb (such as **leer** or **hablar**) completely, writing it out on the board.

- Review the formation and uses of the present progressive in Chapter 3, pages 126–127. Just as the present progressive describes what people are doing now (*I am walking. He is driving.*), the past progressive describes what people were doing at a particular time in the past (*We were running. They were watching television.*).

- The past progressive in Spanish is formed with the imperfect of **estar,** plus the present participle.

Adriana, Felipe y Nayeli **estaban luchando** por sus vidas.	*Adriana, Felipe and Nayeli were fighting for their lives.*
Raúl y yo **estábamos corriendo** en el parque.	*Raúl and I were running in the park.*
Ellos **estaban mirando** televisión.	*They were watching television.*
Yo **estaba durmiendo** una siesta.	*I was taking a nap.*
Tomás **estaba tomando** vino blanco.	*Tom was drinking white wine.*

- When used with the progressive, direct- and indirect-object pronouns follow the same placement patterns as reflexive pronouns. They may precede the conjugated form of **estar** or may be attached to the participle. When you add one or more pronouns to the participle, it is necessary to place a written accent over the stressed vowel.

Note the placement of the accent on **-ándo** and **-iéndo** when the pronoun is attached. This is also true when double-object pronouns and reflexive pronouns are appended to present participles.

Nos están llamando. Están llamándo**nos.**	*They are calling us.*
Nos estaban llamando. Estaban llamándo**nos.**	*They were calling us.*
Le estamos escribiendo una carta. Estamos escribiéndo**le** una carta.	*We are writing a letter to him.*
Le estábamos escribiendo una carta. Estábamos escribiéndo**le** una carta.	*We were writing a letter to him.*

Give students one to two minutes to write their answers to **Actividad 4** on a piece of scratch paper. Then check their answers orally, having student volunteers read out the entire correct sentence.

4 Comprensión. Selecciona la expresión más correcta para describir lo que estaban haciendo las personas.

1. En la perfumería, Margarita:
   a. estaban haciendo compras.
   b. está comiendo pan y queso.
   c. estaba comprando perfumes.

2. En la tienda de discos, Etelvina:
   a. está escribiendo cartas.
   b. estaban escuchando música.
   c. estaba comprando billetes para un concierto de música hip hop.
3. En el departamento de accesorios del Almacén Márquez, Felipe y Jorge:
   a. estaban mirando corbatas y camisas de algodón.
   b. estaba probándose botas de vaquero.
   c. estaban planeando un viaje al Perú.
4. En la florería, la dependiente:
   a. estábamos vendiendo papel.
   b. estaba arreglando flores.
   c. estaban comprando antibióticos.
5. En la farmacia, Carolina y yo:
   a. estábamos comparando los precios de diferentes marcas de aspirinas.
   b. estaban tomando un café.
   c. está comprando frutas y verduras.
6. En la tintorería, Feliciano y su hermano Toño:
   a. estaban llevando a lavar sus impermeables.
   b. estaba recogiendo sus abrigos.
   c. estaba llevando a lavar sus zapatos de tenis.

Answers to Actividad 4 (Note that both the verb form and the meaning must be correct):
1. c
2. c
3. a
4. b
5. a
6. a

5 ¡Qué gente tan ocupada! ¿Qué estaban haciendo ayer las siguientes personas cuando las llamó Pepe, un muchacho universitario de dieciocho años? Sigue el modelo.

▸ **Modelo:** *mi prima Estela / tomarse dos aspirinas*
Mi prima Estela estaba tomándose dos aspirinas.

1. mi abuelo / comer una naranja
2. la dependiente de la perfumería / arreglar los nuevos perfumes
3. mi profesora de física / preparar un experimento
4. el hombre que trabaja en la florería / vender flores para un funeral
5. mi compañero de cuarto del año pasado / planear un viaje a Uruguay
6. mi novia / hacer ejercicios
7. la doctora Vera / escribir una receta
8. mis amigos, Paco y Juana / ponerse los impermeables
9. el reportero del periódico *La nación* / escribir un artículo
10. mi perro / tomar una siesta

Answers to Actividad 5:
1. estaba comiendo
2. estaba arreglando
3. estaba preparando
4. estaba vendiendo
5. estaba planeando
6. estaba haciendo
7. estaba escribiendo
8. estaban poniéndose / se estaban poniendo
9. estaba escribiendo
10. estaba tomando

6 ¿Qué estabas haciendo...? Trabaja con un/a compañero/a. Haz preguntas sobre qué estaba haciendo en un momento determinado. Después de hacer la actividad oralmente, escribe las respuestas de tu compañero/a. Sigue el modelo.

▸ **Modelo:** *a las tres de la tarde*
—¿Qué estabas haciendo ayer, a las tres de la tarde?
—Estaba comiendo con amigos en la cafetería de la universidad.

1. ayer, a las once de la mañana
2. el 31 del diciembre pasado
3. esta mañana, a las seis
4. el sábado, a las once de la noche
5. la última vez que te llamó tu familia
6. anoche, a las siete
7. hoy, antes de la clase de español
8. cuando llegó tu compañero/a de cuarto
9. el jueves al mediodía
10. antes de ayer, a las dos de la mañana

III. Describing unplanned and unintentional occurrences

Before you have student volunteers read this dialogue aloud, illustrate unplanned occurrences by pretending that you are having a bad day. (1) Act very *agitated*; take out a piece of paper and while talking to students, rip it in half accidentally. Act *surprised* and say, **¡Se me rompió el papel!** (2) Then drop the papers and act *alarmed*, saying **¡Se me cayeron las hojas!** (3) Then look *startled*, look around, look inside your book bag, look *dismayed* and say **¡Se me olvidó el libro!** (4) Then look through your things again and look *really upset* and say, **¡Se me perdieron las llaves!** Have students restate what happened to you and write the sentences on the board. Look *innocent* and stress that you didn't break, drop, forget or lose those things. The *things* did it to you. Point out that when the items are plural, so is the verb.

Se for unplanned occurrences

Una noche de problemas y accidentes

RAQUEL: Marina, tuvimos una fiesta fabulosa. **Se te olvidó°** venir.
MARINA: Raquel, **no se me olvidó°** ir. **Se me perdieron°** las llaves del coche, las encontré tardísimo y cuando iba en camino para la fiesta, **se le acabó°** la gasolina al auto.
RAQUEL: ¡Ay, qué pena! La música fue excelente. Bailamos toda la noche. ¿Por qué no nos llamaste?
MARINA: Iba a llamar, pero después de tantos problemas, decidí regresar a casa.
RAQUEL: No sabíamos que tenías problemas. No **se nos ocurrió.°** Creíamos que estabas cansada, nada más. Lo siento mucho, Marina.
MARINA: Pues, quería pasar la noche bailando con ustedes, pero me puse a ver un video y me acosté temprano. ¿Pasó algo más en la fiesta?
RAQUEL: Sí, a Enrique **se le cayeron°** los lentes de contacto y pasó toda la noche bailando sin ver nada, a Juliana **se le rompieron°** los zapatos de tanto bailar y a mí **se me acabaron°** las energías al amanecer.°

You forgot
I didn't forget / I lost
ran out of
didn't occur to us
fell
broke
I ran out of / at dawn

- To indicate an unplanned or unintentional occurrence in English, we use expressions such as: *It slipped my mind*, *it got late*, or *it got lost in the mail.*
- Spanish frequently uses the following similar construction:
  se + indirect-object pronoun + verb in the third person + subject

Review briefly indirect-object pronouns (Chapter 4).

- The **indirect-object pronoun** is used because, in Spanish, this construction conveys the idea that the action happened *to* the person, rather than being *caused* by the person.
- The verbs on the next page are commonly used to indicate unplanned or unintentional occurrences.

acabar	*to finish*	perder	*to lose*
caer	*to fall*	quedar	*to remain, be left over*
ocurrir	*to occur*	romper	*to break*
olvidar	*to forget*		

7 ¿Qué hizo Josefa? Trabaja con un/a compañero/a. En la columna **Resultados** encuentras las cosas que hizo Josefa. Busca la razón de cada una en la columna **Razones.**

▸ **Modelo:** *Josefa no pudo comprar nada en la tienda.*
Se le olvidó el dinero.

Resultados

1. Decidió ir a México.
2. No tomó el tren a tiempo para llegar al trabajo.
3. Tenía los ojos muy rojos.
4. No pudo subir al avión para ir a España.
5. No fue posible entrar a su casa.

Razones

a. Se le olvidó el horario.
b. Se le perdió el pasaporte.
c. Se le ocurrió la idea de viajar a un país de habla española.
d. Se le perdieron las llaves de la casa.
e. Se le rompieron las gafas de sol.

Answers to Actividad 7:
1. c
2. a
3. e
4. b
5. d

8 ¡Qué mala suerte! Completa cada idea con la forma correcta del verbo.

▸ **Modelo:** *Se nos* __________ *las flores. (caer)*
Se nos cayeron las flores.

1. A Alberto se le __________ la mochila en la universidad. (perder)
2. Se me __________ mi blusa de algodón. (romper)
3. A Leticia y a Rafa se les __________ el impermeable. (olvidar)
4. ¡Se me __________ una idea maravillosa! (ocurrir)
5. Se nos __________ las bebidas. (acabar)
6. A Yayo se le __________ los calcetines favoritos. (romper)
7. Se me __________ las llaves de mi cuarto. (perder)
8. A María Luisa se le __________ ir al examen de biología. (olvidar)
9. Se me __________ un vaso de agua. (caer)
10. Se nos __________ la computadora. (romper)

Answers to Actividad 8:
1. perdió
2. rompió
3. olvidó
4. ocurrió
5. acabaron
6. rompieron
7. perdieron
8. olvidó
9. cayó
10. rompió

9 ¿Qué te pasó? Trabaja con un/a compañero/a contestando las siguientes preguntas sobre eventos que ocurrieron durante este año pasado.

1. ¿Se te perdió el traje de baño el verano pasado?
2. ¿A algún familiar se le olvidó tomar las medicinas?
3. ¿Se te rompió algo ayer en la cocina?
4. ¿Se te olvidó llevar el pasaporte al aeropuerto cuando ibas para Uruguay?
5. ¿Qué idea se te ocurrió hace poco?
6. ¿Se le rompió a tu amigo la sudadera nueva?
7. ¿Se te cayó algo recientemente?
8. ¿Se le rompió el reloj a tu compañero/a de cuarto?
9. ¿Se les perdieron a tus padres las llaves del auto el domingo?
10. ¿Se te olvidó el cumpleaños de tu mejor amigo/a?

After students have completed **Actividad 9**, have them report on two to three things that happened to their partner.

IV. Making comparisons of persons and things

A. Comparisons of inequality

Read the captions aloud while pointing to the appropriate illustrations. Note that the adjective agrees in gender and number with the noun that *precedes* it.

El auto rojo va **más** rápido **que** el auto azul.
El auto azul va **más** despacio **que** el auto rojo.

La casa es **menos** alta **que** el rascacielos.
El rascacielos es **más** alto **que** la casa.

La muchacha tiene **menos** dinero **que** el muchacho.
El muchacho tiene **más** dinero **que** la muchacha.

When referring to particular characteristics such as age, size, and appearance in order to compare persons or things that are unequal, Spanish uses the following structure:

más (*more*)/**menos** (*less*) + {adjective/adverb/noun} + **que** (*than*)

Which of the examples above shows a comparison of adjectives? Nouns? Adverbs?

Review the formation of adverbs (Chapter 3). To practice this construction, ask questions such as **¿Caminas lentamente? ¿Caminas más lentamente que tus amigos? ¿Hablas claramente? ¿Hablas más claramente que tus amigos?**

Comparison of adjectives

Here are some examples of adjective comparative formations:

Adriana dijo que Felipe era **más** bravo **que** un león.	*Adriana said that Felipe was braver than a lion.*
El Almacén Márquez es **mejor que** el Almacén Fernández.	*The Márquez Department Store is better than the Fernández Department Store.*
Nelia es **más alta que** su hermana Lupe, pero es **más baja que** su hermano Pepe.	*Nelia is taller than her sister Lupe, but shorter than her brother Pepe.*
Mi abuela es **mayor que** mi abuelo, pero **menor que** su hermana Paquita.	*My grandma is older than my grandpa, but younger than her sister Paquita.*

The following common adjectives have irregular comparative forms.

Adjective		Comparative form	
bueno	*good*	mejor(es)	*better*
malo	*bad*	peor(es)	*worse*
joven	*young*	menor(es)	*younger*
viejo	*old*	mayor(es)	*older*

Comparison of adverbs

Here are some examples of adverb comparisons:

Elena maneja **menos rápido que** Panchito. — *Elena drives less rapidly than Panchito.*

Erlina canta **mejor que** su hermano. — *Erlina sings better than her brother.*

Los atletas generalmente piensan **más** en la nutrición **que** otras personas. — *Athletes usually think more about nutrition than other people.*

The following common adverbs have *irregular* comparative forms.

Adverb		Comparative form	
bien	*well*	mejor	*better*
mal	*bad, ill*	peor	*worse*
mucho	*a lot*	más	*more*
poco	*a little*	menos	*less*

Assign **Actividad 10** as written homework to be checked in class and handed in. You may wish to have students write two sentences for each situation, one with **menos** and the other with **más**.

Comparison of nouns

Here are some examples of noun comparative formations.

Patricia tiene **más cosméticos que** Débora. — *Patricia has more cosmetics than Deborah.*

Londres tiene **menos restaurantes que** París. — *London has fewer restaurants than Paris.*

10 **¿Quién tiene más?** Escribe las comparaciones. Utiliza **más/menos que.** Sigue el modelo.

▸ **Modelo:** *El perfume* Amor *cuesta sesenta dólares. El perfume* Flor *cuesta ochenta dólares.*
El perfume Flor *cuesta más que el perfume* Amor.

1. En la universidad, Sonia tiene seis cursos. Abraham tiene ocho.
2. El coche *Divino* cuesta sesenta mil dólares. El coche *Elegante* cuesta setenta mil dólares.
3. La casa en que vive Eduardo tiene tres dormitorios. Pilar vive en una casa de cinco dormitorios.
4. En la familia de Anita hay nueve personas y en la familia de Carlos hay siete.
5. Para llegar al trabajo, Alberto viaja treinta y seis kilómetros. Fidel viaja veinte.

Answers to Actividad 10:

1. En la universidad, Abraham tiene más cursos que Sonia.
   En la universidad, Sonia tiene menos cursos que Abraham.
2. El coche *Elegante* cuesta más (dólares) que el coche *Divino.*
   El coche *Divino* cuesta menos (dólares) que el coche *Elegante.*
3. Pilar vive en una casa que tiene más dormitorios que la casa de Eduardo.
   Eduardo vive en una casa que tiene menos dormitorios que la casa de Pilar.
4. En la familia de Anita hay más personas que en la familia de Carlos.
   En la familia de Carlos hay menos personas que en la familia de Anita.
5. Para llegar al trabajo Alberto viaja más kilómetros que Fidel.
   Para llegar al trabajo Fidel viaja menos kilómetros que Alberto.

11 **¡Vamos a comparar!** Trabaja con un/a compañero/a. Compara las siguientes personas y cosas. Sigue el modelo. Utiliza los verbos **ser/estar/tener.**

▸ **Modelo:** *Nueva York / Boston (grande)*
Nueva York es más grande que Boston.

1. Guatemala / Argentina (pequeño)
2. metro / autobús (rápido)
3. Michael Jordan / Tiger Woods (bajo)
4. la computadora / la máquina de escribir (eficiente)
5. Newt Gingrich / Jesse Jackson (conservador)
6. mi casa / tu casa (lejos de la universidad)
7. un coche / un tren (cómodo)
8. una pequeña tienda de ropa / un almacén (personal)
9. Donald Trump / Bill Gates (dinero)
10. una rosa roja / una rosa amarilla (bonito)

12 **Más comparaciones.** Haz una encuesta (*survey*) en la clase. Pregúntales a tres compañeros/as sobre las cualidades de dos amigos/as. Compara a las dos personas usando adjetivos, adverbios y sustantivos. Preséntale los resultados al resto de la clase.

B. Superlatives: Going beyond the comparative

- To form the superlative, English adds *-est* to the adjective or uses expressions such as *the most* or *the least* with the adjective (*the most convenient*, *the greatest*, *the least expensive*, *the worst*).
- In Spanish, the definite article is used with **más** or **menos** with adjectives or adverbs. **Mejor** and **peor** are used with nouns and usually precede them. The superlative also requires the use of the preposition **de** to express *in* or *of*. The formulas are as follows:

definite article + **más/menos** + adjective + **de**
definite article + **mejor/peor** + noun + **de**

Stress the use of **de** in superlative constructions, especially in cases where English uses *in*: *The most intelligent girl in the class* = **la chica más inteligente de la clase.** In addition, in this construction when nouns are used along with adjectives, nouns come first, before the adjective (the opposite of English word order): the definite article + noun + **más/menos** + adjective + **de**.

Iván es **el más elegante de** los tíos Ríos.	*Ivan is the most elegant of the Ríos uncles.*
¿Cuál es **la mejor película de** este año?	*Which is the best movie of this year?*

13 **En mi opinión...** Contesta las preguntas usando la forma apropiada del superlativo.

1. ¿Cuál es el almacén más caro de tu región? ¿Qué vende?
2. ¿Cuál es el mejor coche de los Estados Unidos? ¿Por qué?
3. ¿Quién es la profesora más inteligente de tu universidad? Explica.
4. ¿Cuál fue la peor película que viste el año pasado? ¿En qué aspecto?
5. ¿Cuál es la música más popular de hoy? ¿Qué características tiene?

C. Comparisons of equality

When referring to particular characteristics in comparing persons or things that are equal, Spanish uses the structural formulas on page 289 for adjectives, adverbs, verbs, and nouns.

El muchacho es **tan alto como** la muchacha. La muchacha es **tan alta como** el muchacho.

La alumna canta **tan mal como** el alumno. El alumno canta **tan mal como** la alumna.

La niña tiene **tantos juguetes como** el niño. El niño tiene **tantos juguetes como** la niña.

- For comparison of adjectives:

  tan + adjective + **como** = *as* + adjective + *as*

  Miranda es **tan entusiasta como** Ina. *Miranda is as enthusiastic as Ina.*

- For comparison of adverbs:

  tan + adverb + **como** = *as* + adverb + *as*

  Clara toca la guitarra **tan bien como** Lisa. *Clara plays the guitar as well as Lisa.*

- For comparison of nouns:

  tanto/a/os/as + noun + **como** = *as much/many* + noun + *as*

  Teo tiene **tantas camisetas como** Samuel. *Teo has as many T-shirts as Samuel.*

  Notice that **tanto** agrees in number and gender with the noun that follows.

- For comparison of verbs:

  verb + **tanto** + como = *as much as*

  Enrique lee **tanto como** Luisa. *Enrique reads as much as Luisa.*

14 **¿Quiénes son? ¿Qué es?** Adivinen las personalidades o los eventos siguientes. Trabajen en parejas.

1. Es un actor tan famoso como Paul Newman y tan guapo como él. Fue estrella de las películas "Misión Imposible" y "Jerry Maguire". Gana tanto dinero como Arnold Schwarzenegger, pero es más jóven que él. ¿Quién es?
2. Más de doscientas personas murieron en este desastre. La explosión de este edificio federal fue el peor acto de terrorismo en territorio estadounidense y tan terrible como muchos desastres en otras partes del mundo. ¿Qué fue?
3. Esta mujer, originalmente de Albania, fue muy religiosa y siempre pensaba en los demás. Ayudó a los pobres más que muchas personas en el mundo. Fue tan buena como un ángel. ¿Quién fue?
4. No es tan famosa como el "Ratón Miguelito", pero es más bonita que el "Pato Donald". Tiene siete amigos que viven en el bosque.

Tell students not to worry about getting the right answers here. Have them use their imagination to see how close they can get to the people or events described here. Then give them the correct answers.

Answers to Actividad 14:

1. Tom Cruise
2. la destrucción del edificio federal de Oklahoma City
3. la Madre Teresa
4. Blancanieves (*Snow White*)

To save time you may wish to divide the class into five groups for **Actividad 15**, and assign each group one sentence to be presented to the entire class either orally or written on the board by a representative from each group.

15 Comprensión. Trabaja con un/a compañero/a. Crea comparaciones con las siguientes oraciones. Sigue el modelo.

▸ **Modelo:** *Nancy es muy inteligente. Su hermano Federico es muy inteligente también.*
Federico es tan inteligente como Nancy.

1. La casa de Antonio tiene siete cuartos. La casa de Guadalupe también tiene siete cuartos.
2. Las flores de la señora López son bonitas. Las flores del señor Pérez también son bonitas.
3. La Farmacia Robles prepara las medicinas muy bien. La Farmacia Sánchez también las prepara muy bien.
4. Jorge maneja rápidamente. Alicia también maneja rápidamente.
5. La Librería Cervantes tiene buenos libros. La Librería Cortázar también tiene buenos libros.

After students have finished their pair work, assign **Actividad 16** for written homework to be handed in at the next class, instructing students to make all comparisons of equality into comparisons of inequality and vice versa.

16 ¿Qué piensas tú? Trabaja con un/a compañero/a de clase. Lee las oraciones siguientes y di si estás de acuerdo o no. Si no estás de acuerdo, modifica la oración. Compara las opiniones tuyas con las de tu compañero/a.

1. El dinero es menos importante que el amor.
2. Hoy en día (*Nowadays*) los hombres tienen tanta ropa elegante como las mujeres.
3. Los estudiantes universitarios trabajan más que los profesores de la universidad.
4. En los Estados Unidos, el béisbol es tan importante como el fútbol americano.
5. La comida tailandesa es mejor que la comida italiana.
6. Es más fácil hablar con los amigos que con los padres.
7. Jugar al baloncesto es menos difícil que jugar al volibol.
8. Rosie O'Donnell es tan divertida como Janeane Garofalo.
9. En tu región, la primavera es más agradable que el otoño.
10. En California hay tan buenas universidades como en Massachusetts.

Lectura A

Introducción

In this chapter, Adriana and Felipe are in Otavalo, Ecuador, a very well-known town in the Andes, north of Quito. Most of its inhabitants belong to the Otavalo ethnic group. In this reading, you will learn some geographical facts about five Andean countries: Bolivia, Colombia, Ecuador, Perú, and Venezuela.

Reading strategy: Tapping background knowledge

When we read a text, our experiences and any previous knowledge of its topic will influence our interpretation and understanding of the text. The following activity will help you activate background knowledge you may have about Latin America.

1 ¿Qué sabes? Antes de leer, trabajen en grupos para repasar sus conocimientos sobre la geografía de la región.

Depending on the level and background of your students, you may wish to have students prepare their answers ahead of time before doing **Actividad 1** in groups.

1. Los países hispanos están en diferentes continentes. ¿Cuáles son estos continentes?
2. ¿Con qué mares u océanos limitan estos continentes?
3. ¿Cuáles son las capitales de estos cinco países: Bolivia, Colombia, Ecuador, Perú y Venezuela?
4. La topografía de estos cinco países es muy diversa. A ver si puedes mencionar una montaña importante que conozcas en alguno de ellos. Si recuerdas, menciona también una selva importante, un río y un desierto.
5. Menciona algunos mamíferos (*mammals*), aves, peces, reptiles o insectos que se encuentran en estos países.
6. En el mundo hispano, además del español, los habitantes hablan otros idiomas amerindios. ¿Conoces el nombre de alguno de estos idiomas autóctonos (*native*) de los cinco países mencionados?
7. Uno de estos cinco países no tiene costas. ¿Sabes cuál es?
8. Parte de Suramérica está en una zona tropical, pero no todas las regiones son calientes. ¿Recuerdas por qué?

El norte andino

Dramática vista de La Paz, Bolivia.

Bolivia Bolivia perdió su costa en una guerra° el siglo pasado y no tiene salida al mar. La cordillera° de los Andes forma en este país algunas de las cumbres° más altas de América; entre estas montañas está el Altiplano, donde se encuentra el famoso lago Titicaca y La Paz, la capital más alta del mundo (3.627 m.). El Altiplano se caracteriza por sus vientos helados°, su gran altitud y sus volcanes. En estas zonas montañosas viven las llamas, las alpacas y las vicuñas. Bolivia tiene siete y medio millones de habitantes y sus idiomas oficiales son el español, el quechua, el aimará y el tupiguaraní.

war
mountain range
summit, top
freezing

Panorama de Bogotá, Colombia.

Colombia Los Andes dividen el país en la región occidental° donde está Bogotá, la capital, y en la región oriental° donde están los Llanos° Orientales, en el límite° con Venezuela. El país limita con el Océano Atlántico al norte y el Pacífico al occidente.° Al sur, en el límite con con Perú y Brasil, está la selva° amazónica. Los variados climas del país permiten cultivar° muchos productos como el

western
eastern
Plains
border
west
jungle
grow

birds / majestic

café, el banano y gran cantidad de frutas; el país tiene además, una de las mayores variedades de aves° del mundo y el majestuoso° cóndor vive en sus montañas. Tiene casi cuarenta millones de habitantes y su idioma oficial es el español.

snow-capped mountains

belong

influenced

native American

Ecuador Su capital, Quito, está situada a casi tres mil metros de altura en la zona andina, donde hay bellos nevados° y volcanes activos como el Sangay, el Pichincha y el Cotopaxi. Las islas Galápagos, en el Océano Pacífico, pertenecen° al Ecuador y son famosas por su extraordinaria fauna. Los viajes de Darwin a estas islas influyeron° en sus teorías sobre la evolución de las especies. El grado de latitud cero cruza el país por el norte y le da su nombre a esta república andina de casi doce millones de habitantes. El español es el idioma oficial, pero también se hablan el quechua y otros idiomas amerindios.°

Vista de Quito, Ecuador.

mountain range

Incan

fearsome

Incan cultural heritage

Perú El Perú tiene veinticuatro millones de habitantes y su capital es Lima. En la sierra° peruana están Cuzco, la antigua capital del reino incaico,° y la misteriosa ciudad de Machu Picchu. El río Amazonas nace en la Sierra peruana con el nombre de Marañón. Este gran río es el habitat de las temibles° pirañas, de los hermosos delfines rosados y de las grandes anacondas.

Gente paseándose por la ciudad de Lima, Perú.

El Perú comparte la gran herencia cultural incaica° con Bolivia, el Ecuador, el sur de Colombia, y el norte de Argentina y Chile. Los idiomas oficiales son el español, el quechua y el aimará.

peak

height

stockbreeding

Venezuela Las sierras más importantes de Venezuela son Mérida y Perijá. Hay también montañas muy altas, como el pico° Bolívar, de 5.007 metros de altura.° Lleva este nombre en honor al libertador Simón Bolívar, quien nació en Caracas, la capital. La zona del lago Maracaibo, al noroeste, es caliente, húmeda y muy rica en petróleo. Al oeste, está la zona ganadera° de los Llanos que limita

Modernos edificios en Caracas, Venezuela.

con Colombia. En el sureste, las altas montañas y las mesetas forman hermosas cataratas,° como el salto° Ángel, la más alta del mundo (979 m.). Venezuela tiene casi veintidós millones de habitantes y su idioma oficial es el español.

waterfalls / waterfall

2 ¿Recuerdas ahora? Lee de nuevo las preguntas anteriores a la lectura y vuelve a contestarlas. Si es necesario, consulta los mapas del libro.

3 Geografía andina. Trabaja en grupos y contesta las siguientes preguntas sobre la lectura.

1. Di una característica de cada una de las capitales de los cinco países mencionados.
2. ¿Dónde están el Lago Maracaibo y el Lago Titicaca?
3. Compara el clima de las regiones del Lago Maracaibo y el del Lago Titicaca.
4. ¿Cuáles son las cataratas más altas del mundo? ¿Dónde están?
5. ¿Cuál es la capital más alta del mundo?
6. Menciona algunos idiomas que se hablan en Suramérica, además del español.
7. Clasifica los países de mayor a menor según el número de habitantes.
8. ¿Dónde están los volcanes Sangay y Pichincha?
9. ¿Qué otro nombre tiene el río Amazonas?
10. ¿Por qué es famosa la ciudad de Cuzco?
11. ¿Qué hombre famoso nació en Caracas?

Answers to Actividad 3:

1. La Paz, la capital más alta del mundo; Bogotá, está en la región occidental; Quito, está en la zona andina con bellos nevados y volcanes activos; Lima, capital actual; Cuzco, antigua capital; Caracas, donde nació Simón Bolívar.
2. Lago Maracaibo: Venezuela; Lago Titicaca: entre Bolivia y Perú.
3. Lago Maracaibo: caliente, húmedo; Lago Titicaca: vientos helados
4. Salto Ángel: Venezuela
5. La Paz
6. Quechua, aimará, tupiguaraní
7. Colombia, Perú, Venezuela, Ecuador, Bolivia
8. Ecuador
9. Marañón
10. Es la antigua capital del reino incaico
11. Simón Bolívar

4 ¿Es esto correcto? Trabaja en grupos. Las siguientes oraciones describen algo sobre un país. Señala cuáles oraciones son verdaderas y cuáles son falsas. Explica la razón.

1. Las playas de Bolivia son unas de las más famosas en Suramérica.
2. En la zona de Maracaibo, en el altiplano venezolano, hay gran cantidad de lagartos.
3. Los viajes de Darwin a las islas Galápagos influyeron mucho en sus teorías sobre la evolución de las especies.
4. El río Amazonas nace en las montañas peruanas.
5. La misteriosa ciudad de Machu Picchu fue la capital del reino incaico.

Answers to Actividad 4:

1. F—Perdió su costa en una guerra.
2. F—Es un lago.
3. V
4. V
5. F—Fue Cuzco.

5 ¿Quién sabe más? Trabajen en grupos de cuatro personas cada uno. Cada grupo escribe seis oraciones falsas o verdaderas sobre los países estudiados. Los otros grupos tienen un minuto para contestar si la oración es correcta o es falsa y por qué.

As a variation for **Actividad 5**, divide the class into five groups, one group per country.

6 Ropa para cada clima. En parejas, hagan una lista de la ropa que se necesita para estar en cada una de estas regiones:

- La Paz
- el Lago Maracaibo
- las islas Galápagos

ETAPA B

Pistas y palabras

I. Talking about cars

Necesitamos comprar un coche

Other words for *car horn* are **bocina** and **claxon.** Other words for *tire* are **goma** and **neumático.** Bring in a model or a picture of a car to illustrate car vocabulary.

—Mira mamá, los limpiaparabrisas funcionan muy bien. ¡Chas! ¡Chas!
—No juegues más con el coche. Sal de allí ahora mismo.
—No, mamá, ¡ven aquí! Ven a mirar el coche, ¡es muy bonito por dentro!

1. el baúl
2. el espejo retrovisor
3. el limpiaparabrisas
4. la llanta/rueda
5. las luces
6. el parabrisas
7. el pito
8. la placa
9. la puerta
10. el tanque de gasolina

—¡Abróchate el cinturón, mamá, que ya nos vamos de aquí!

1. el acelerador
2. el aire acondicionado
3. el apoyacabeza
4. el asiento
5. el asiento trasero
6. la bolsa de aire
7. el cinturón de seguridad
8. el freno
9. la guantera
10. el radio
11. el volante

Palabras y expresiones útiles

el aceite	*oil*	la gasolina	*gasoline*
el auto (automóvil, carro)	*car*	la licencia de manejar	*driver's license*
la batería (pila)	*battery*	la llanta pinchada	*flat tire*
el choque	*crash*	el motor	*motor*
el/la conductor/a	*driver*		
abrocharse (el cinturón)	*to buckle up (seatbelt)*	chocar	*to collide*
acelerar	*to accelerate*	conducir (manejar)	*to drive*
apagar	*to shut off*	dañar	*to injure; to damage*
arrancar	*to start*	pitar	*to beep the horn*

1 ¿Qué es? ¿A qué parte del coche se refiere cada una de estas oraciones?

1. El chofer se sienta allí.
2. Son absolutamente necesarios cuando llueve.
3. Se necesita para llamar la atención, ¡no para hacer ruido!
4. Los coches no pueden parar sin ellos.
5. Protege a los pasajeros en los accidentes.
6. Si tu coche no lo tiene, te va a dar mucho calor en el verano.
7. Allí pones tu pie y ¡el coche anda!
8. Se vende por litros en España y en muchas ciudades por galones.
9. Allí guardas papelitos y tal vez, ¡guantes!
10. Si dejas las luces encendidas muchas horas, se acaba.

Answers to Actividad 1:

1. el asiento
2. los limpiaparabrisas (**Limpiabrisas** is also used in many regions.)
3. el pito
4. los frenos
5. la bolsa de aire / el cinturón de seguridad
6. el aire acondicionado
7. el acelerador
8. la gasolina
9. la guantera
10. la batería

2 **¡Quiero comprar un Jaguar!** Contesta por escrito las preguntas para decidir qué tipo de auto te gustaría comprar.

1. ¿Qué clase de auto te gusta? ¿deportivo? ¿compacto? ¿económico? ¿de lujo (*luxury*)? ¿camioneta (*minivan*)? ¿camión? ¿Por qué?
2. ¿Qué color prefieres? ¿Por qué?
3. ¿Cuál es tu presupuesto?
4. ¿Qué características son esenciales en tu coche?
5. ¿Qué características son deseables pero no esenciales?

3 **¿Qué auto compramos?** Ahora vas a comprar un auto con un/a compañero/a. Comparen sus listas de la **Actividad 2** y decidan cuál de los dos autos piensan comprar y por qué.

4 **Presentación.** Trae una foto del auto de tus sueños y descríbelo.

You may wish to encourage students to use magazines, the World Wide Web or their own drawing skills for **Actividad 4**.

II. Asking for and giving directions

¿Dónde está?

Perdone la molestia, pero ¿me puede decir dónde está el museo?
Sí, señora, siga derecho por tres cuadras, pase por la catedral y doble a la izquierda. Está a tres cuadras a la derecha.

Tell students that **a la derecha/izquierda** is a shortened form of **a la mano derecha/a la mano izquierda,** which explains why these words are feminine. (You can also illustrate these expressions through hand gestures, pointing with your right hand and then with your left.) But remind them that **derecho** means *straight.*

Palabras y expresiones útiles

la dirección	*address*	la manzana (cuadra)	*street block*
la esquina	*corner*	el semáforo	*stoplight*
acelerar	*to accelerate*	estacionar	*to park*
bajar (por)	*to go down (a street)*	parar	*to stop*
cruzar	*to cross*	seguir derecho (recto)	*to go straight*
dar la vuelta	*to turn around*	subir (por)	*to go up (a street)*
doblar (a)	*to turn*	tener cuidado	*to be careful*

Cruce la calle.	*Cross the street.*
despacio	*slowly*
Doble a la derecha (izquierda).	*Turn to the right (left).*
Pase por…	*Pass by . . .*
Siga…	*Follow . . .*
¿Cómo llego a…?	*How do I get to . . . ?*
¿Me puede decir dónde está…?	*Can you tell me how to get to . . . ?*

5 ¿Cómo se llega a...? En parejas, practiquen dando instrucciones sobre cómo llegar a los lugares en el mapa. Mientras una persona da instrucciones, la otra las sigue en el mapa. Usen mandatos formales (**Ud.**).

¿Cómo se llega...

1. del museo al teatro?
2. del hotel al restaurante?
3. de la catedral al hotel?
4. de la escuela a la catedral?
5. de la biblioteca al museo?

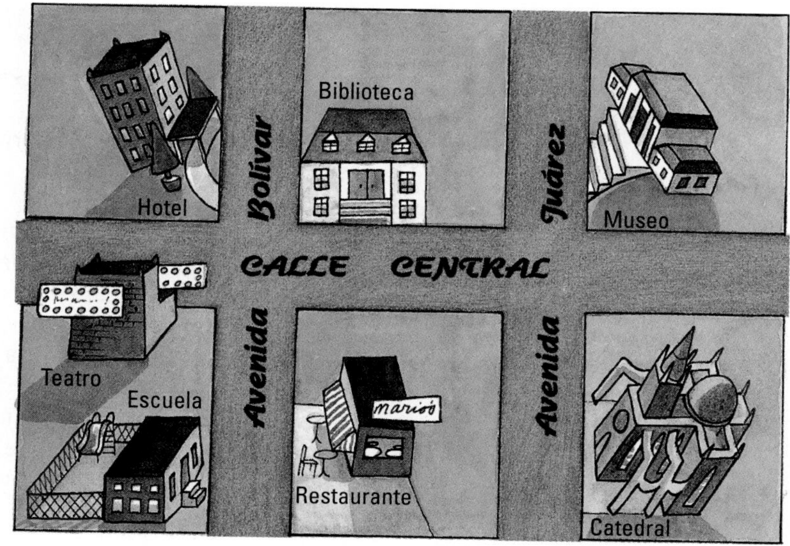

6 Ahora te toca a ti. Una persona visita tu universidad y necesita saber cómo llegar a los siguientes lugares desde la residencia estudiantil. Trabaja en parejas.

1. la cafetería
2. el edificio de la administración
3. la oficina del decano (*dean*)
4. la clase de español
5. la librería
6. la Facultad de Ciencias Naturales
7. la Facultad de Artes
8. la cancha de fútbol americano
9. el centro estudiantil
10. ¿...?

For **Actividad 6**, provide students with a copy of your campus map. At the end of the exercise have your students direct you with **a la derecha/izquierda; siga derecho** commands. You will probably wind up at your classroom door—at that point the exercise is over!

III. Managing in traffic

Las señales de tráfico

Alto/Pare **Ceder el paso** **Curva peligrosa** **Intersección** **Paso peatonal** **No estacionar/ No aparcar** **Escolares en la vía** **No hay paso** **No doblar** **En obras** **Derrumbe**

7 ¿Qué debes hacer? Indica dónde están generalmente estas señales y qué debes o qué no debes hacer cuando las ves.

See page 298 for possible answers.

▸ **Modelo:** *alto*
Debes parar el coche cuando ves la señal de "Alto" en las intersecciones.

1. intersección
2. paso peatonal
3. no hay paso
4. derrumbe
5. no doblar
6. curva peligrosa
7. en obras
8. no estacionar
9. escolares en la vía

Bring a globe to class to illustrate the meridians and the equator.

sphere

measure

measurement / concluded / flattened

ENLACE CULTURAL

El nombre del Ecuador

Mitad del mundo en el Ecuador.

En el siglo XVIII no se sabía si la tierra era una esfera° perfecta o no. Para saberlo, la Academia de Ciencias Francesa envió a un grupo de científicos a la colonia española Presidencia de Quito para medir° la circunferencia ecuatorial y la circunferencia del meridiano cero. Después de hacer la medida,° los científicos concluyeron° que la tierra era achatada° en los polos. Los especialistas usaron en su informe "las tierras del Ecuador" para referirse al sitio de la medida. Desde entonces, este nombre se volvió popular y posteriormente se adoptó como nombre oficial del país.

Discusión en grupos

1. ¿Cuál fue la conclusión de los científicos sobre la forma de la tierra?
2. ¿Por qué tiene el país el nombre de "Ecuador"?
3. ¿Qué hay en el sitio (0, 0) de la tierra?

Answers to Discusión en grupos:

1. La tierra era achatada en los polos.
2. Porque los científicos llamaban el sitio "las tierras del Ecuador".
3. Hay mucha agua. Está cerca de África.

IV. Describing the countryside

El paisaje y la naturaleza

Possible answers to Actividad 7:

1. Debes frenar si ves la señal **intersección.**
2. Debes parar si ves la señal **paso peatonal** y hay personas cruzando.
3. Debes parar y cambiar de dirección cuando ves la señal **no hay paso.**
4. Debes conducir con mucho cuidado cuando ves la señal **derrumbe.**
5. Debes seguir derecho cuando ves la señal **no doblar.**
6. Debes conducir lentamente cuando ves la señal **curva peligrosa.**
7. Debes conducir con cuidado cuando ves la señal **en obras.**
8. Debes buscar otro lugar cuando ves la señal **no estacionar.**
9. Debes parar si ves la señal **escolares en la vía** y hay estudiantes cruzando la calle.

Palabras y expresiones útiles

el arroyo	*stream*	la catarata	*waterfall*
el bosque	*forest*	la colina	*hill*
el campo	*countryside*	la costa	*coast*

la isla	*island*	el puerto	*port*
el lago	*lake*	la selva	*jungle*
el mar	*sea*	la selva tropical	*rainforest*
el océano	*ocean*	el valle	*valley*
la piedra	*stone*		

Assign **Actividad 8** as homework. Tell students they may need to use dictionaries.

Possible answers to Actividad 8:

1. nadar
2. tomar el sol
3. subir las montañas
4. correr
5. explorar
6. viajar en barco
7. caminar

8 Asociaciones. ¿Qué actividades se relacionan con los siguientes lugares?

1. el mar
2. la costa
3. las montañas
4. el campo
5. la selva
6. el lago
7. el bosque

Have students do **Actividad 9** as an in-class activity, using the knowledge they have and their imagination. You can do this singly or in groups of two to five. Note that at the end of this lesson there is a related activity (**Actividad 3**) using the Internet to find out information about different countries. You may wish to assign the countries to students or student groups at this point so that they can have about a week to prepare a two-minute talk on their country.

9 De vacaciones. Elige uno de estos lugares para tus vacaciones o elige otro lugar que te guste. Explica por qué prefieres ese lugar, qué hay para ver y qué actividades se pueden hacer allí.

Costa Rica	Bolivia	Colombia
Puerto Rico	España	Ecuador
México	Chile	¿...?

ENLACE CULTURAL

El salto Ángel

Las aguas del salto° Ángel, en el estado de Bolívar en Venezuela, caen desde 979 metros y producen un espectáculo impresionante. Ésta es la cascada más alta del mundo. Un piloto norteamericano, Jimmy Angel, la descubrió en 1935 cuando volaba sobre territorio venezolano. En segundo lugar en el mundo están las cataratas de Yosemite, en Califormia, con 739 metros de caída.° El salto Cuquenán, también en Venezuela, tiene 671 metros de caída y está en tercer lugar. En comparación, las cataratas° de Niágara, las más famosas del mundo, tienen una caída de solamente 61 metros.

salto: waterfall

Point out that there are several words for waterfall: **catarata, cascada.**

caída: fall, height

cataratas: waterfalls

Discusión en grupos

1. Mencionen cuatro cascadas importantes del mundo y por qué es importante cada una de ellas.
2. ¿Por qué creen que el salto Ángel tiene ese nombre?
3. ¿Hay cascadas en la región de ustedes? ¿Hay otro tipo de fenómeno natural interesante, como cañones (*canyons*), ríos grandes, lagos u otra cosa?
4. ¿Conocen alguna catarata famosa? ¿Cuál? ¿Dónde está? ¿Qué características tiene?

Answers to Discusión en grupos:

1. (a) El salto Ángel es la cascada más alta del mundo.
   (b) Las cataratas de Yosemite están en segundo lugar en altura.
   (c) El salto Cuquenán está en tercer lugar.
   (d) Las cataratas de Niágara son las más famosas.
2. por el apellido de Jimmy Angel
3. *Answers will vary.*
4. *Answers will vary.*

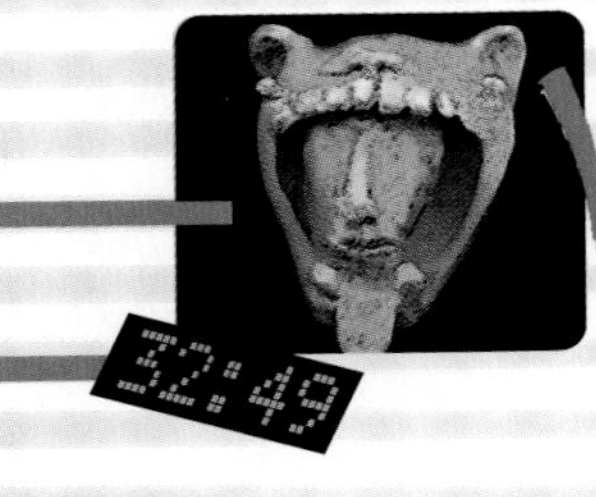

Vistas y voces

I. Preparémonos

1 Anticipación. Contesta las siguientes preguntas en parejas.

A. 1. Menciona algunos platos típicos de tu región. ¿Cuál es tu plato favorito?
2. Cuando estás de vacaciones con tu familia, ¿quién toma fotos? ¿Cuál es el motivo favorito en las fotos: las personas o los paisajes?
3. Describe un extraordinario lugar geográfico que te impresione como un paraíso. ¿Cómo es? ¿Dónde está? ¿Con quién vas allí? ¿Cómo te hace sentir?

B. Mira la foto 7B en la página 271. ¿Qué tipo de pájaro hay en la foto? ¿Dónde está y adónde va? ¿Quiénes lo miran? ¿Qué simboliza?

Para comprender mejor

a través de	*through*	desconocido/a	*unknown*
aconsejar	*to counsel*	devastador	*devastating*
aparentar	*to pretend*	enseguida	*right away*
apetecer	*to be appetizing*	evitar	*to avoid*
el barro	*clay*	fuera de serie	*outstanding*
colorado/a	*red*	el hecho	*deed*
contar con	*to count on*	el locro de queso	*potato soup*
culpable	*guilty*	el paraíso	*paradise*
darse cuenta de	*to realize*	rendirse	*to give in*
desaparecer	*to disappear*	tomar en cuenta	*to take into account*

2 Secuencia. Estudia las escenas de video y discute la siguiente pregunta con un/a compañero/a. ¿Qué va a pasar entre Gustavo y doña Gafasoscuras?

Possible answers to Actividad 3:
1. en el restaurante; Adriana, Felipe y don Gustavo comen comidas típicas y hablan.
2. en Mitad del Mundo; Adriana y Felipe son turistas, caminan, se tocan las manos entre los hemisferios, miran el paisaje y hablan mucho mientras el taxista cambia una llanta pinchada.
3. en el camino; Adriana y Felipe hacen una parada en una estación de gasolina. Beben agua y hablan del jaguar robado. Ven a mucha gente.
4. en el taxi; Adriana y Felipe miran las vistas de la naturaleza ecuatoriana y unos pájaros.

1.

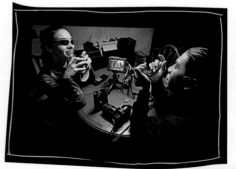

2.

3.

4.

II. Miremos y escuchemos

3 Mis observaciones. Mientras Adriana y Felipe buscan el jaguar, visitan diferentes lugares. Escribe las contestaciones a las siguientes preguntas: ¿Dónde están Felipe y Adriana y con quién? ¿Qué hacen? ¿Qué observan?

III. Comentemos

4 Comprensión. En grupos, contesten las siguientes preguntas.

1. ¿Cómo se llama el restaurante donde comen Adriana y Felipe?
2. ¿Qué piensa don Gustavo de los dos jóvenes?
3. ¿De qué están hechos los jaguares gemelos, según Adriana?
4. ¿Quién era Pacal y cuál es su relación con los jaguares?
5. ¿Cómo salieron los jaguares gemelos de la tumba de Pacal?
6. ¿Cómo y cuándo entra Nayeli en la historia de los jaguares?
7. ¿Con qué está mirando y escuchando doña Gafasoscuras su conversación?
8. ¿Dónde estudió Nayeli arqueología?
9. ¿Dónde está el códice maya más completo?
10. ¿Qué les dijo Nayeli sobre el jaguar a las autoridades en Dresden?
11. ¿Cuándo y dónde descubrió Nayeli el jaguar Hun-Ahau?
12. ¿Cómo se conocieron Nayeli y doña Carmen?
13. ¿Por qué tiene Nayeli que reunir a los jaguares gemelos? ¿Cuándo?
14. ¿Qué cosa extraordinaria siente Adriana en Mitad del Mundo?
15. ¿Cuáles eran los tres mundos de los mayas?
16. ¿Qué beben Adriana y Felipe en la estación de gasolina?
17. Imagínate que vas a sacar fotos de las vistas más extraordinarias de este episodio. Describe tres de ellas. ¿Qué elementos de la naturaleza hay en las fotos?

5 Turistas en el paraíso. Adriana compara Ecuador y la Mitad del Mundo con el paraíso. Resume toda la escena en que ella y Felipe se tocan los dedos entre los dos hemisferios del mundo. ¿Qué se dicen los dos jóvenes sobre el Ecuador, los dos hemisferios y los dos jaguares? En tu opinión, ¿cómo se sienten los dos sobre su misión de recuperar a Yax-Balam y sobre su relación personal? ¿Se besan? ¿Van a ser más que arqueólogos y turistas? ¿Por qué? Describe la música en este episodio—¿es lírica, aburrida, hipnótica, romántica, seria, nostálgica? ¿Te gusta?

6 Miremos otra vez. Después de mirar el episodio otra vez, arregla las escenas de video en la secuencia correcta.

7 En mi opinión. Adriana reflexiona y dice, "La vida es extraña, ¿no? A veces las coincidencias no parecen coincidencias". ¿Estás de acuerdo o no? Trabajen en grupos y den ejemplos concretos de la opinión de cada uno/a de ustedes.

8 Yo creo que... El 31 de agosto es muy importante en esta historia de los jaguares gemelos. Trabajando con un/a compañero/a, repasa las razones. Después, discutan las fechas importantes en sus vidas personales. ¿Cuáles son y por qué son importantes?

Answers to Actividad 4:
1. Se llama La choza.
2. Cree que Adriana y Felipe tienen cara de turistas inocentes.
3. Están hechos de barro.
4. Pacal era el gran rey de los mayas. Los jaguares fueron diseñados para acompañarlo a Xibalbá después de su muerte.
5. Unos ladrones precolombinos se los robaron.
6. En Dresdén, cuando Nayeli estudiaba el códice maya y encontró a Yax-Balam.
7. con una videocámara
8. Estudió en la UNAM, la universidad de México.
9. Está en una biblioteca de Dresden, Alemania.
10. Les dijo que pertenecía a México.
11. Nayeli descubrió el jaguar Hun-Ahau en 1990 en París.
12. Doña Carmen es la madrina de Nayeli y fue la mejor amiga de su madre, doña Estela.
13. para evitar desastres; para el 31 de agosto
14. Adriana siente que están a punto de recuperar al Yax-Balam, el jaguar perdido.
15. el cielo, la tierra y Xibalbá
16. agua
17. *Answers will vary.*

Correct order of video action shots: 3, 2, 1, 4

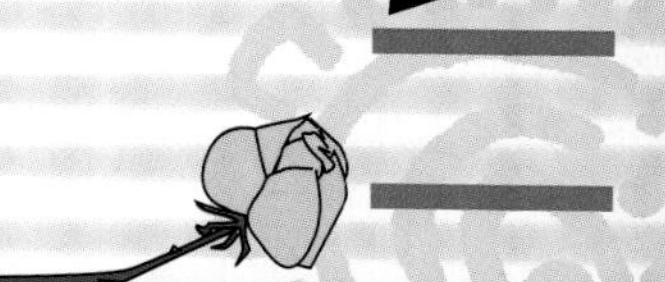

Lengua

Expressing ideas that are subjective

The present subjunctive forms for regular -ar, -er, and -ir verbs

There are two moods in Spanish, the *indicative*, which expresses actions that are definite, clear, factual events and outcomes; and the *subjunctive*, which expresses subjective feelings, emotions, wishes, doubts, or attitudes towards an event, or occurrence perceived as uncertain, unreal, or hypothetical.

Review the **usted** and **ustedes** commands from Chapter 6 and point out that their forms are identical to those of the present subjunctive.

- To form the present subjunctive of regular **-ar, -er,** and **-ir** verbs, drop the **-o** of the first person singular ending, then add the opposite endings (shown in the chart) to the remaining stem:

Verb	Present indicative	Subjunctive ending	Present subjunctive
comprar	**yo** compr**o**	**-e**	**yo** compr**e**
beber	beb**o**	**-a**	beb**a**
escribir	escrib**o**	**-a**	escrib**a**

Subject pronouns	comprar	beber	escribir
yo	compr**e**	beb**a**	escrib**a**
tú	compr**es**	beb**as**	escrib**as**
él/ella, Ud.	compr**e**	beb**a**	escrib**a**
nosotros/as	compr**emos**	beb**amos**	escrib**amos**
vosotros/as	compr**éis**	beb**áis**	escrib**áis**
ellos/ellas, Uds.	compr**en**	beb**an**	escrib**an**

- Note that the endings for **-er** and **-ir** verbs are identical.
- Because the subjunctive is formed from the first person singular, verbs that are irregular in the first person singular use that form as their base for all the subject pronoun endings. Study the following examples:

Verb	Present indicative	Subjunctive stem	Present subjunctive
decir	**yo** dig**o**	dig-	**yo** dig**a**
hacer	hag**o**	hag-	hag**a**
poner	pong**o**	pong-	pong**a**
traer	traig**o**	traig-	traig**a**
venir	veng**o**	veng-	veng**a**
ver	ve**o**	ve-	ve**a**
tocar	toc**o**	toc-	toqu**e***
pagar	pag**o**	pag-	pagu**e***
comenzar	comienz**o**	comienz-	comienc**e***

** Remember that some verbs have spelling changes. For verbs ending in **-car**, the **c** changes to **qu**; **-gar**, the **g** changes to **gu**; **-zar**, the **z** changes to **c** before **e**.*

1 Práctica. Trabaja con un/a compañero/a practicando las formas del subjuntivo de los siguientes verbos.

1. yo: comer, bailar, recibir
2. tú: regresar, traer, decidir
3. Ud: comprar, escribir, beber
4. nosotros: empezar, tocar, deber
5. ellos: llegar, aprender, hacer

Answers to Actividad 1:

1. coma, baile, reciba
2. regreses, traigas, decidas
3. compre, escriba, beba
4. empecemos, toquemos, debamos
5. lleguen, aprendan, hagan

2 Vamos a practicar. Cambia las formas del subjuntivo del plural al singular y del singular al plural.

▶ **Modelo:** *(yo) coma* *comamos*
(nosotros) hablemos *hable*

1. (él) baile
2. (yo) corra
3. (ella) escriba
4. (tú) toques
5. (usted) diga
6. (nosotros) escribamos
7. (ustedes) lleguen
8. (ellos) hagan
9. (nosotros) paguemos
10. (ellas) compren

First have students write their answers, then go around the class and drill them orally using these verbs and others from the lesson.

Answers to Actividad 2:

1. bailen
2. corramos
3. escriban
4. toquen / toquéis (Note: **Uds.** is plural of **tú** in Latin America.)
5. digan
6. escriba
7. llegue
8. haga
9. pague
10. compre

The present subjunctive forms for stem-changing verbs

- Verbs that end in **-ar** and **-er** have the same stem changes in the present subjunctive as in the present indicative.

pensar (e > ie)		**probar (o > ue)**	
piense	*pensemos*	pruebe	*probemos*
pienses	*penséis*	pruebes	*probéis*
piense	piensen	pruebe	prueben

perder (e > ie)		**volver (o > ue)**	
pierda	*perdamos*	vuelva	*volvamos*
pierdas	*perdáis*	vuelvas	*volváis*
pierde	pierdan	vuelva	vuelvan

- Present tense verbs that end in **-ir** have the stressed **e** changing to **i** and the unstressed **o** changing to **u** in the **nosotros** and **vosotros** forms. The other persons maintain the same stem-change patterns in the present subjunctive as in the present indicative.

mentir (e > ie)		**morir (o > ue)**	
mienta	*mintamos*	muera	*muramos*
mientas	*mintáis*	mueras	*muráis*
mienta	mientan	muera	mueran

First have students do **Actividad 3** as either an in-class written activity or as homework. Then drill orally adding stem-changing verbs such as **cerrar, volver, perder, morir.**

Answers to Actividad 3:
1. recomendemos, entendamos, sintamos
2. piensen/penséis, duerman/durmáis, pierdan/perdáis, prefieran/prefiráis (Note: **Uds.** is plural of **tú** in Latin America.)
3. quieran, pidan, empiecen
4. empiece, sirva, siga
5. duerma, encuentre, repita

3 Práctica. Con un/a compañero/a, practica las formas del subjuntivo.

¿Cuál es el plural del subjuntivo de los siguientes verbos?
1. yo: recomiende, entienda, sienta
2. tú: pienses, duermas, pierdas, prefieras
3. ella: quiera, pida, empiece

¿Cuál es el singular del subjuntivo de los siguientes verbos?

4. nosotros: empecemos, sirvamos, sigamos
5. ellos: duerman, encuentren, repitan

The present subjunctive forms of irregular verbs

In Spanish, these verbs have irregular subjunctive forms in the present.

dar	estar	haber	ir	saber	ser
dé*	esté	haya	vaya	sepa	sea
des	estés	hayas	vayas	sepas	seas
dé	esté	haya	vaya	sepa	sea
demos	estemos	hayamos	vayamos	sepamos	seamos
deis	estéis	hayáis	vayáis	sepáis	seáis
den	estén	hayan	vayan	sepan	sean

** Note that **dé** in the subjunctive carries an accent to distinguish it from the preposition **de**.*

Answers to Actividad 4:
1. dé, vaya, sepa
2. seas, estés, des
3. haya, dé, vaya
4. estemos, seamos, demos
5. den, estén, vayan

4 Práctica. Practica las formas del subjuntivo de los siguientes verbos con un/a compañero/a.

1. yo: dar, ir, saber
2. tú: ser, estar, dar
3. Ud.: haber, dar, ir
4. nosotros: estar, ser, dar
5. ellos: dar, estar, ir

Uses of the present subjunctive: Expressions of volition

Estudios y entretenimiento

RITA: Nico, hay una excursión a las montañas. Quiero que me **acompañes.** Salimos el viernes a la cinco de la tarde. ¿Quieres ir?

NICO: Quiero, pero no debo ir porque tengo que estudiar para el examen de cálculo. Si es posible, prefiero que **te quedes** aquí y que me **ayudes** a estudiar. ¿Puedes?

RITA: Nico, te aconsejo° que **dejes** de estudiar tanto. Es importante que **cambies** de ambiente.° Te recomiendo que **tomes** un fin de semana libre.

advise
atmosphere

NICO: Tienes razón, Rita. Voy a ir, pero te pido que **volvamos** temprano el domingo. ¿De acuerdo?

RITA: Está bien. Quiero que **te diviertas** un poco, pero también que **tengas** buenos resultados en tu examen.

- There are two main ways to tell people that we want them to do something.

Direct commands (imperative)	
Doble Ud. a la derecha.	*Turn to the right.*

Subjunctive construction	
Quiero que Ud. doble a la derecha.	*I want you to turn to the right.*

- Notice that to use the subjunctive, we use two subjects in two different clauses: the main clause, and the subordinate clause. The verb of the subordinate clause must be in the subjunctive mood if the first verb expresses volition.
- The typical structure for the subjunctive mood is as follows:

Main clause +	**que** +	Subordinate clause (with verb in the subjunctive)
Quiero	que	**Ud. doble a la derecha.**

** Note that the subjunctive is used when there is a change of subject signalled by* ***que****.*

Point out that when there is no change of subject, the main verb is followed by an infinitive (no **que**) as in English: **Quiero estudiar.** (*I want to study.*)

- In the conversation above, identify the verbs of volition that signal use of the subjunctive mood (the verbs in boldface). What do these verbs have in common?

Here are some important verbs of volition, some of which you already know.

aconsejar	*to advise*	preferir (ie)	*to prefer*
desear	*to want*	querer (ie)	*to want*
mandar	*to order*	recomendar (ie)	*to recommend*
necesitar	*to need*	rogar (ue)	*to beg, plead*
pedir (i)	*to request, ask for*	sugerir	*to suggest*

- The verb of the main clause may also be an impersonal phrase such as *it's necessary*, *it's essential*, and so on, but the verb in the subordinate clause must be in the subjunctive mood.

When the entire sentence is impersonal (no change of subject), the expression is followed by the infinitive: **Es importante estudiar** = *It is important to study.*

Es importante que **estudies.**	*It's important that you study.*
Es urgente que **compres** zapatos nuevos.	*It's urgent that you buy new shoes.*

Here are some common expressions of volition, some of which you already know.

Es importante...	*It's important . . .*	Es esencial...	*It's essential . . .*
Es preciso...	*It's necessary . . .*	Es preferible...	*It's preferable . . .*
Es necesario...	*It's necessary . . .*	Es urgente...	*It's urgent . . .*

Note that when the subject of the subjunctive clause is not explicitly stated it can often be found in the indirect object preceding the main verb: **Te ruego que estudies.** (The **te** lets you know that the subject of **estudiar** is **tú.**)

Answers to Actividad 5:

1. compres
2. seas
3. ahorres
4. ayude
5. lleve
6. manejes
7. conduzca
8. se especialice
9. ganemos
10. guste

5 Escenas de la vida. Completa los siguientes dialoguitos con las formas correctas del subjuntivo:

PANCHO: Te ruego que me ________ (comprar) un coche convertible importado.
PAPÁ: Te aconsejo que ________ (ser) independiente y que ________ (ahorrar) dinero para comprar tu propio coche.

SRA. RÍOS: Necesito que Ud. me ________ (ayudar) a seleccionar dos vestidos.
DEPENDIENTE: Señora, el vestido azul de seda le queda bien. Le recomiendo que se lo ________ (llevar).

LILIANA: Estás bebida (*drunk*). Miguel y yo te rogamos que no ________ (manejar).
EMILIA: Tienen razón. Prefiero que uno de ustedes ________ (conducir) mi coche.

PROFESOR: Le aconsejo que ________ (especializarse) en economía en su futura carrera.
ESTUDIANTE: ¡Sí, sí! Es bueno que mis compañeros y yo ________ (ganar) mucho dinero, pero también es importante que nos ________ (gustar) nuestra profesión.

After students have completed **Actividad 6** have one to two students per group write their sentences on the board. Go over the sentences with the entire class. You may wish to have each group create an overhead collectively which can be then shown to the entire class for correction and comment.

6 Consejos. Algunas personas piden que les des consejos en las situaciones siguientes. Trabaja con un/a compañero/a en esta actividad con los verbos **aconsejar, recomendar** y **sugerir.** Usa el subjuntivo en la frase subordinada.

► **Modelo:** —*Quiero ir al cine, pero tengo que pagar las cuentas del mes y no tengo mucho dinero. ¿Qué me aconsejas?*
—*Te aconsejo que pagues las cuentas primero y que vayas al cine otro día.*

1. Tengo dos invitaciones—una para ir a un concierto con mis amigos y otra para salir a cenar con mi familia. ¿Qué me aconsejas tú que haga yo?
2. Pablo quiere romper (*to break up*) con su novia. Ella lo quiere mucho, pero Pablo está enamorado de otra muchacha. ¿Qué le sugieres a él que haga?
3. Mi compañera de cuarto escucha música toda la noche y yo no puedo dormir. ¿Qué me aconsejas que le diga yo?
4. Había tres amigos en mi cuarto y desapareció mi reloj de oro. ¿Debo preguntarles si alguno de ellos tiene mi reloj o no debo hacerlo? ¿Qué me aconsejas que haga?
5. Toda mi ropa está sucia y mañana tengo una entrevista para un trabajo. ¿Qué es necesario que yo haga?
6. Nuestros primos están aquí de visita. ¿Adónde nos recomiendas que los llevemos?
7. La semana que viene es el santo de mi tía, una señora mayor. ¿Qué me sugieres que le regale?
8. Acabo de conseguir un buen trabajo en el Banco Central. ¿Qué marca de coche recomiendas que me compre?
9. Nos ganamos la lotería y queremos ir de vacaciones a un país hispano. ¿Adónde nos aconsejas que vayamos y qué recomiendas que veamos?
10. A Ina le duele la cabeza. ¿Qué recomiendas que ella haga?

7 **Tengo que contarte algo.** Escribe una lista de diez consejos para amigos/as, profesores/as, parientes y personas profesionales. Compara tu lista con la lista de un/a compañero/a de clase. Selecciona diez consejos de las dos listas y preséntalos a la clase.

Lectura B

Introducción

The Ecuadorian legend that you are about to read tells the story of a shepherd boy who tended llamas and who became the soul of a rock, Rumiaya. This spirit is the watchman of a small lake in the Limpiopungo plains at the foot of the Cotopaxi, a majestic snow-covered volcano in Ecuador. The God of the Cotopaxi allows Rumiaya to become human again and tell his story when a traveler, wandering the plains, shows interest in the lonely stone.

In **quechua**, the Inca language spoken in Bolivia, Ecuador, and Perú, **rumi** means *stone* or *rock*, **aya** means *spirit* or *soul*. Limpiopungo is the combination of the Spanish adjective **limpio**, *clean*, and the quechua noun **pungo**, *plains*.

Prelectura

1 **Las leyendas.** Legends have some facts based on events or actions that may be true, but they also contain fantastic elements, many times involving magical characters or circumstances. Discuss with the members of your group one or two legends you know. You might talk about, for example, a haunted house or place, a person that lived many years ago or a mysterious event that has triggered your curiosity.

2 **Los pastores.** With a partner, discuss what you know about shepherds. How would you define their work? What kind of animals do they care for? Why was their work very important earlier, in the United States? Why is their work still important in many regions of the world? Who are the modern shepherds today?

Rumiaya

Limpiopungo es una planicie° junto al Cotopaxi, el gran volcán nevado° del Ecuador. En este valle hay un hermoso lago de aguas limpias y cristalinas. Junto a este hermoso lago hay una piedra que parece un vigía.° Las personas que van a este lugar dicen que, a veces, el alma° de esta piedra, Rumiaya, sale de ella para contar su historia. Esto solamente sucede cuando los viajeros tienen mucho interés en la gran piedra, como los viajeros que llegan a la planicie esta noche. Ellos miran la piedra intensamente. De pronto, Rumiaya sale de la piedra; lleva un

plain / snow-capped

watchman / soul

El gran volcán Cotopaxi, cubierto de nieve.

Assign the reading to be done as homework so that students are prepared to answer the questions in **Actividad 3.**

grueso° poncho de lana de llama, zamarros° y un gorro muy abrigado° para protegerse del frío. Los ojos negros le brillan como cristales. Deslumbra° con su mirada a los viajeros y empieza a hablar:

heavy / chaps covering pants / warm
Dazzles

—Me llamo Rumiaya, el alma de la piedra. Vivo en la roca. Esta noche es especial y puedo contar mi historia. Hace mucho tiempo, solamente las llamas y los nativos del Cotopaxi vivíamos aquí. Yo era un pastorcito de llamas y cuando amanecía,° sacaba° las llamas a pastar° por la mañana. Me sentaba en la orilla° de la laguna y me ponía a mirar sus tranquilas y hermosas aguas durante muchas horas sin cansarme.

at dawn / I took out / graze
edge

Un día, cuando miraba embelesado° la laguna, una de las pequeñas llamas se acercó mucho y cayó al agua.

spellbound

Sin dudarlo ni un momento, entré a la laguna para salvarla, pero empecé a hundirme.° No pude salir y me hundí hasta que todo se volvió oscuro. Un terrible frío me llenó el cuerpo. Yo ya no era de esta vida.

to sink

De pronto, el gran dios de la montaña vino hacia mí y yo le dije:

—¡Gran dios de la montaña, creo que voy a morir! ¿Qué va a hacer mi alma sin mi amada° laguna? Si muero, ¡déjame junto a ella!

beloved

Con voz de viento, el gran dios de la montaña me dijo:

—Voy a concederte° tu deseo. Vas a estar eternamente junto al agua en forma de roca, pero como quieres tanto a la laguna, tú mereces° que tu historia se conozca. Desde ahora° vas a ser Rumiaya, el alma de la piedra. Cuando alguien demuestre° interés por ti, puedes tomar la forma humana y contar tu historia.

grant
deserve
From now on
shows

Misteriosamente, como viene, Rumiaya desaparece en la noche, dejando un aire de melancolía.

Answers to Actividad 3:

1. Rumiaya. El alma de una piedra. Lleva un poncho, zamarros y gorro. Tiene ojos negros. Toma forma humana cuando hay personas interesadas en la roca.

Postlectura

3 Personajes y eventos. Trabaja en grupos y discute las siguientes preguntas.

1. Identifica a los personajes de la leyenda. ¿Quiénes son? Descríbelos.
2. ¿Quién narra la historia de Rumiaya?
3. ¿Cómo era la ropa del pastorcillo cuando salió de la piedra?
4. Según la ropa que lleva, ¿cómo es el clima en la planicie? ¿Quién vive allí?
5. ¿Por qué se cayó a la laguna una de las pequeñas llamas?
6. ¿Encontró el pastorcillo a la llama?
7. ¿Cómo era la voz del gran dios de la montaña?
8. ¿En qué convirtió el dios de la montaña al pastorcillo?
9. ¿Cuándo puede contar Rumiaya su historia?

4 Suciopungo. Escribe la forma del imperfecto o del pretérito en esta corta historia.

La planicie __________ (ser) hermosa, pero __________ (estar) llena de basura. Los viajeros que __________ (pasar) por allí no __________ (preocuparse) ni de la ecología ni de las plantas y animales que __________ (vivir) en ella. Un día, el rey de aquel país __________ (prohibir) tirar papeles y restos de comida en la planicie porque él __________ (querer) conservarla limpia. Desde ese día, el rey __________ (empezar) a castigar personalmente a todos los infractores (*offenders*) hasta que Suciopungo __________ (convertirse) en Limpiopungo.

5 Mis deseos son órdenes. Usa la forma correcta del subjuntivo para las órdenes del rey. Elige el verbo correcto de la lista de infinitivos.

enseñar	hacer	ser	tirar
estar	saber	obedecer	cuidar

1. No quiero que la planicie __________ sucia y ordeno que nadie __________ basura en ella.
2. Quiero que mi reino __________ el más limpio del mundo.
3. Espero que todos los habitantes __________ mis órdenes y siempre __________ lo que yo digo.
4. Quiero que todos los habitantes __________ que siempre voy a castigar a los infractores.
5. Quiero que los padres y los profesores les __________ buenas costumbres a los niños.
6. Es necesario que todos nosotros __________ la naturaleza.

6 Fantasía y realidad. Trabaja en grupos de dos personas. Una persona de cada grupo hace una lista de los eventos que parecen ser reales en la historia de Rumiaya; la otra persona hace una lista de los eventos que no son o no parecen ser reales. Discutan las razones de cada uno/a para clasificar los eventos como reales o irreales.

7 Mi propia leyenda. Escribe en español una corta leyenda sobre un tema de tu región, del campo o de la ciudad. Incluye elementos de la realidad y de la fantasía.

Los viajeros. Miran la piedra con interés.
Las llamas. Rumiaya era su pastor. Una llama se cayó al agua.
Los nativos del Cotopaxi. Viven con Rumiaya y sus llamas en el campo.
El gran dios de la montaña (volcán) convierte a Rumiaya en el alma de una roca.
2. Rumiaya
3. Llevaba un poncho grueso de lana de llama, zamarros y gorro.
4. Hace frío. Allí viven llamas y los nativos del Cotopaxi.
5. Miraba la laguna.
6. No. Se hundió.
7. Tenía voz de viento.
8. en el alma de una roca
9. cuando las personas lo miran con interés

Assign **Actividad 4** as homework. Go over orally in class. Discuss the meaning of the story. Is the ending happy or sad? Why?
1. era
2. estaba
3. pasaban
4. se preocupaban
5. vivían
6. prohibió
7. quería
8. empezó
9. se convirtió

Answers to Actividad 5:
1. esté / tire
2. sea
3. obedezcan / hagan
4. sepan
5. enseñen
6. cuidemos

After students have finished **Actividad 6**, divide the board into two sections and have students give you the **fantasía** elements for one section and the **realidad** for the other. Write them down and discuss items of interest.
Assign **Actividad 7** as written homework. Before returning the legends, read a few of the most interesting ones to the class. Discuss the **realidad** and **fantasía** in the students' legends.

En resumen

I. Hablemos

1 Contrastes. Lee la lectura de la Etapa A (página 291) y haz una comparación entre dos de esos países. Trabaja con una pareja y preséntenle sus observaciones a la clase.

2 ¡Se escaparon! Luis, el programador de computadoras, descubre que Adriana, Felipe y Nayeli no murieron en la explosión. Él habla con su primo de cómo se escaparon. Inventa una conversación entre ellos. Trabaja con una pareja.

II. Investiguemos por Internet

Refining your Internet searches

One of the advantages of using the Internet is that information is usually updated regularly. This is very useful when you need time-sensitive data for your projects or writing assignments. In this chapter, you will work on gathering up-to-date information about one of the five Hispanic countries that you have read about in this chapter: Bolivia, Colombia, Ecuador, Perú, and Venezuela. There are many Web sites with information about countries in the world. The educational institution or your community library may have a license for an on-line encyclopedia. Ask your librarian about it. There are two Internet sites that you may want to visit when searching for current facts about Hispanic countries. One is The Latin American Network Information Service (LANIC) at the University of Texas at Austin (http://lanic.utexas.edu/) and the on-line World Factbook published by the The Central Intelligence Agency (http://www.odci.gov/cia/). Look at this site for the CIA publications when you have reached their home page.

Actividad 3
Be sure to allow sufficient time for students to gather the information for **Actividad 3**. Assign countries at least one week in advance of when students will present to class. A good time to do this is in conjunction with **Actividad 9 De vacaciones** on page 299 of this lesson.

3 Un país hispano. In this activity, you will gather information about one Hispanic country. You will then present the information to the class. Before you start, make a list of at least six facts that you would like to present to your class. For example, current population, area of the country, currency, main cities, popular touristic sites, and so on. If you find interesting photos, include them also. Use the words in your list to refine your search. For example, if you have chosen **Bolivia**, you may want to use one or more keywords to refine your search. For example, if you want to know more about its population, you may start your search by writing: **Bolivia** *and* **población.** Check the Help section of your browser to structure your searches in the most efficient way, or look for help on the Houghton Mifflin Web site.

Vocabulario informático	
delimitar la búsqueda	*refine the search*

III. Escribamos

Writing strategy: Paraphrasing

One good way to check your comprehension of something you have heard, seen, or read, is to paraphrase. When you paraphrase, you put information and ideas in your own words. This is a good way to practice new language structures and reinforce new vocabulary without quoting a source directly.

Examples: (Taken from the final reading of this chapter)

Original:
Limpiopungo es una planicie junto al Cotopaxi, el gran volcán nevado del Ecuador.

Paraphrase:
Limpiopungo es un lugar en Ecuador que está al lado de un volcán que se llama Cotopaxi.

Original:
Junto a este hermoso lago hay una piedra que parece un vigía.

Paraphrase:
Una piedra grande está cuidando el lago.

Strategy in action

Turn to *Escribamos* in the Workbook to practice the writing strategy of paraphrasing.

4 **Limpiopungo.** En tus propias palabras, escribe un resumen de tres párrafos de la leyenda de Limpiopungo.

5 **El sueño de Adriana.** Vuelve a ver el video donde Nayeli aparece en el sueño de Adriana. Escribe un resumen del sueño con tus propias palabras.

Vocabulario

Tiendas

el almacén	*department store*	**la librería**	*bookstore*
la boutique	*boutique*	**la papelería**	*stationery store*
los discos	*records*	**la perfumería**	*perfume store*
la farmacia	*pharmacy*	**la tintorería**	*dry cleaner*
la florería	*florist*	**la zapatería**	*shoe store*
la joyería	*jewelry store*		

Ropa

el abrigo	*coat*	**el perfume**	*perfume*
los accessorios	*accessories*	**la ropa de hombre**	*menswear*
el aseo personal	*personal items*	**la ropa de mujer**	*womenswear*
la blusa de seda	*silk blouse*	**la ropa interior**	*underwear*
la bolsa	*purse*	**el saco**	*blazer, suit jacket (for men)*
las botas de vaquero	*cowboy boots*	**las sandalias**	*sandals*
la bufanda	*scarf*	**el sombrero**	*hat*
los calcetines	*socks*	**la sudadera**	*sweat suit*
la camisa de algodón	*cotton shirt*	**el suéter de lana**	*wool sweater*
la chaqueta	*jacket*	**el talco**	*powder*
el cinturón de cuero	*leather belt*	**el traje**	*suit*
la corbata	*necktie*	**el vestido**	*dress*
la falda	*skirt*	**los zapatos**	*shoes*
la gorra	*cap*	**los zapatos de tacón alto/bajo**	*high-heeled/low-heeled shoes*
el guante	*glove*	**los zapatos de tenis**	*sneakers*
el impermeable	*raincoat*		
las medias	*stockings*		
la minifalda	*miniskirt*		

De compras en el almacén

el/la cliente	*customer*	**el jabón**	*soap*
los cosméticos	*cosmetics*	**la mancha**	*stain*
de cuadros	*plaid*	**mediano/a**	*medium*
de lunares (puntos)	*polka dotted*	**el mostrador**	*display case/counter*
de manga corta (larga)	*short- (long-) sleeved*	**la oferta**	*sale, discount*
de rayas	*striped*	**el par**	*pair*
el/la dependiente	*clerk*	**pequeño/a**	*small*
el descuento	*discount*	**el precio**	*price*
devolver (ue)	*to return*	**el probador de hombres**	*men's dressing room*
el escaparate	*shop window, display case*	**el probador de mujeres**	*women's dressing room*
estar a cargo de	*to be in charge of*	**el recibo**	*receipt*
estar de moda	*to be in style*	**la talla**	*size*
la ganga	*sale, discount*	**la venta**	*sale*
ir de compras	*to go shopping*		

Claro que sí.	*Of course*
¿Cómo me queda?	*How does it fit me?*
¿En qué puedo servirle?	*How can I help you?*
¿En qué le puedo ayudar?	*How can I help you?*
Está roto/a, sucio/a, manchado/a.	*It's ripped/dirty/stained.*
¿Puedo probarme el...?	*Can I try on the . . .?*
Quiero cambiarlo/la por otro/a.	*I want to exchange it for another.*
Quiero que me devuelvan el dinero.	*I want you to return my money.*
Te/Le queda bien, mal, grande, pequeño/a, largo/a, corto/a, estrecho/a, flojo/a.	*It fits you well, poorly, big, small, long, short, tight, loose.*
Voy a llevarme...	*I'm going to take . . .*
Voy a probármelo/la.	*I'm going to try it on.*

Coches, carros y automóviles

abrocharse el cinturón	*to buckle up (seatbelt)*
el aceite	*oil*
el acelerador	*gas pedal*
acelerar	*to accelerate*
el aire acondicionado	*air conditioning*
apagar	*to shut off*
el apoyacabeza	*headrest*
arrancar	*to start*
el asiento	*seat*
el asiento trasero	*rear seat*
el auto (automóvil, carro)	*car*
la batería (pila)	*battery*
el baúl	*trunk*
la bolsa de aire	*air bag*
chocar	*to collide, crash*
el choque	*crash*
el cinturón de seguridad	*seatbelt*
conducir (manejar)	*to drive*
el/la conductor/a	*driver*
dañar	*to injure; to damage*
el espejo retrovisor	*rear view mirror*
el freno	*brake*
la gasolina	*gasoline*
la guantera	*glove box*
la licencia de manejar	*driver's license*
el limpiaparabrisas	*windshield wipers*
la llanta (rueda)	*tire*
la llanta pinchada	*flat tire*
las luces	*headlights*
el motor	*motor*
el parabrisas	*windshield*
pitar	*to beep the horn*
el pito	*horn*
la placa	*license plate*
la puerta	*door*
el radio	*radio*
el tanque de gasolina	*gas tank*
el volante	*steering wheel*

¿Dónde está?

¿Cómo llego a...?	*How do I get to . . . ?*
Cruce la calle.	*Cross the street.*
Doble/Dé la vuelta a la derecha/izquierda.	*Turn right/left.*
Está a ... cuadras.	*It's . . . blocks from here.*
¿Me puede decir dónde está...?	*Can you tell me where . . . is?*
Pase por ...	*Go/Pass by . . .*
Perdone la molestia.	*I beg your pardon.*
Siga derecho (recto) ...	*Continue straight . . .*

Señales de tráfico

Alto (Pare)	*Stop*	**No doblar**	*Do not turn*
Ceder el paso	*Yield*	**No estacionar (No aparcar)**	*No parking*
Curva peligrosa	*Dangerous curve*	**No hay paso**	*Do not enter*
Derrumbe	*Falling rock*	**Paso peatonal**	*Pedestrian crossing*
En obras	*Construction*	**Suba por...**	*Go up . . .*
Escolares en la vía	*Student crossing*		
Intersección	*intersection*		

A manejar

acelerar	*to accelerate*	**la esquina**	*corner*
bajar por	*to go down (a street)*	**estacionar**	*to park*
cruzar	*to cross*	**la manzana (cuadra)**	*street block*
dar la vuelta	*to turn around*	**parar**	*to stop*
despacio	*slowly*	**seguir derecho (recto)**	*to go straight*
la dirección	*address*	**el semáforo**	*stoplight*
doblar a la derecha/ izquierda	*to turn left/right*	**subir por**	*to go up (a street)*
		tener cuidado	*to be careful*

Paisaje y naturaleza

el altiplano	*high plateau, altiplano*	**la montaña**	*mountain*
el arroyo	*stream*	**nevado/a**	*snow-capped*
el bosque	*forest*	**el océano**	*ocean*
el campo	*countryside*	**la piedra**	*stone*
las cataratas	*waterfalls*	**el puerto**	*port*
la colina	*hill*	**el río**	*river*
la costa	*coast*	**la selva**	*jungle*
la isla	*island*	**la selva tropical**	*rainforest*
el lago	*lake*	**el valle**	*valley*
la llanura (planicie)	*plains*	**el volcán**	*volcano*
el mar	*sea*		

Verbos

aconsejar	*to advise*	**hacérsele a uno tarde**	*to become late*
caer	*to fall*	**mandar**	*to order*
Es esencial...	*It's essential . . .*	**ocurrir**	*to occur*
Es importante...	*It's important . . .*	**olvidar**	*to forget*
Es necesario...	*It's necessary . . .*	**quedar**	*to remain, be left over*
Es preciso...	*It's necessary . . .*	**rogar (ue)**	*to beg, plead*
Es preferible...	*It's preferable . . .*	**romper**	*to break*
Es urgente...	*It's urgent . . .*	**sugerir (ie)**	*to suggest*

CAPÍTULO 8

LOCALIDAD: Ecuador

8A

¿Qué plan secreto tiene Zulaya?

8B

Sunglasses is about to grab the Jaguar Twin in Otavalo. However, Zulaya deftly devises other plans.

Vocabulary themes

- Talking about food and nutrition
- Talking about health and exercise
- Making an appointment with a doctor
- Talking about money
- Buying jewelry and merchandise in a marketplace

Language structures

- Expressing emotions and wishes
- Expressing doubt or certainty
- Talking about the unknown
- Talking about persons and things
- Describing actions

Culture topics

- Alimentos y remedios naturales
- El cacao, una moneda valiosa
- Los mercados y el arte del regateo

Readings

- Comidas ideales
- Los países del Cono Sur

Reading and writing strategies

- Comparing and contrasting
- Using visual organizers

Internet strategy

- Formulating a query

ETAPA A

Pistas y palabras

I. Talking about food and nutrition

A. La pirámide de la alimentación°

food pyramid
to maintain ourselves / healthy
shows
foods
to eat / quantity / upper

Mantener una **dieta** balanceada es importante para **conservarnos° sanos.° La pirámide de la alimentación** nos **muestra°** los productos recomendados en cada grupo de **alimentos.°** En la base de la pirámide están los alimentos que debemos **consumir°** en mayor **cantidad°** y en la parte superior,° están los alimentos que solamente debemos consumir en cantidades mínimas.

Bring in these food items either as real food or as pictures from magazines.

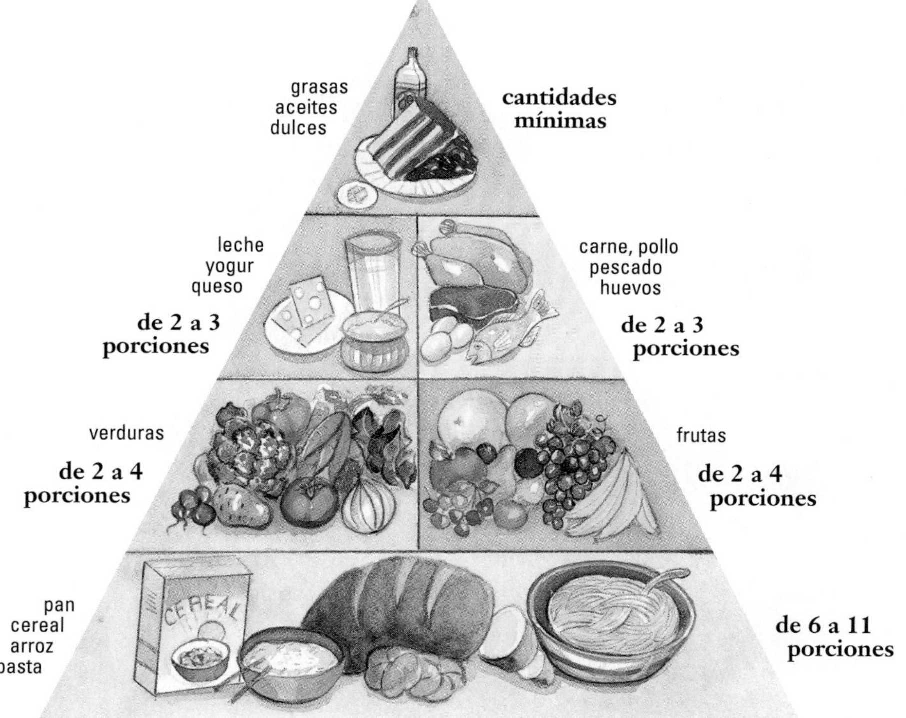

B. Las porciones

level
maintains
pregnant / nutritious

El número recomendado de **porciones** depende de cuántas **calorías** necesite la persona **diariamente**. Las calorías **dependen**, a su vez, del nivel° de actividad que **mantenga°** la persona, de su edad, de su sexo y de sus circunstancias. Por ejemplo, una persona muy **sedentaria** necesita menos calorías que una persona **activa**, las personas jóvenes consumen, por lo general, más calorías que las personas ancianas y las mujeres **embarazadas°** deben mantener una dieta **nutritiva°** con mucho calcio. Las personas que sufren de alergias o de alguna insuficiencia **física** pueden necesitar dietas especiales.

Palabras y expresiones útiles

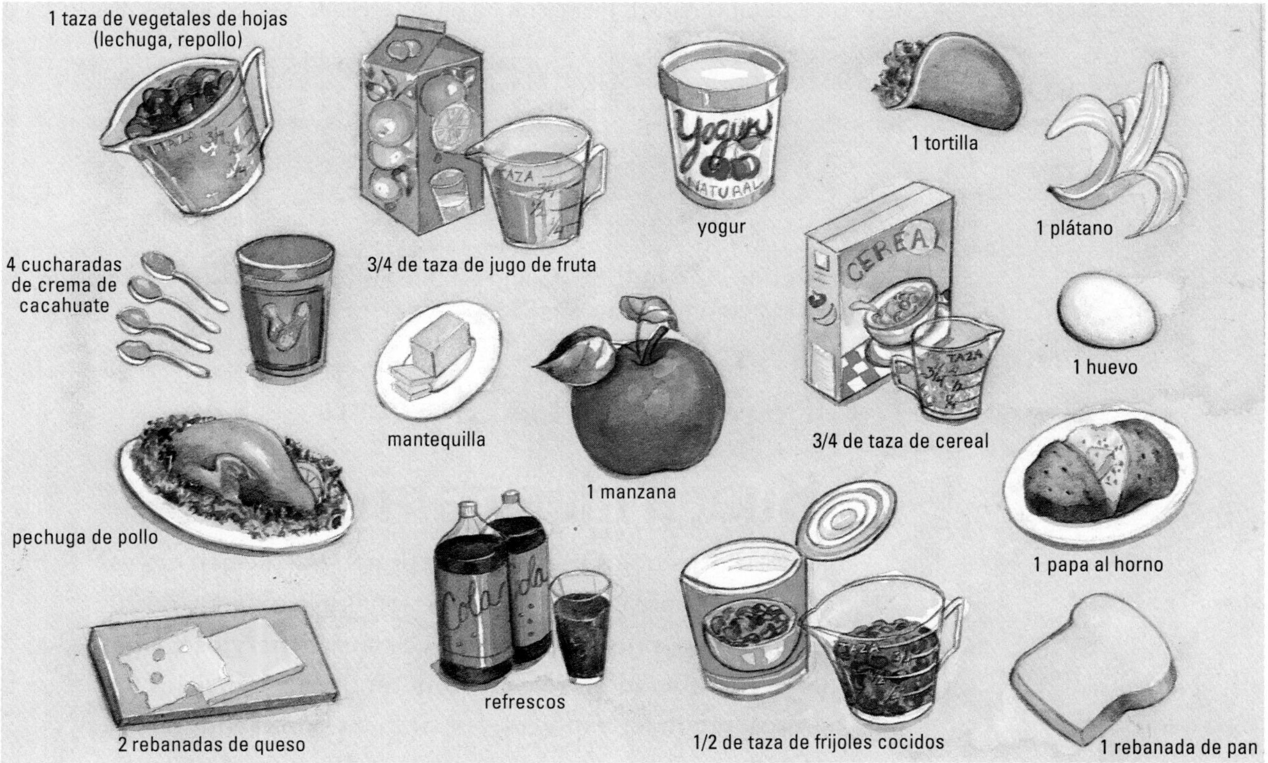

1 taza de vegetales de hojas (lechuga, repollo)
3/4 de taza de jugo de fruta
yogur
1 tortilla
1 plátano
4 cucharadas de crema de cacahuate
mantequilla
1 manzana
3/4 de taza de cereal
1 huevo
pechuga de pollo
refrescos
1 papa al horno
2 rebanadas de queso
1/2 de taza de frijoles cocidos
1 rebanada de pan

1 **Ponlas en su grupo.** Pon las comidas de la lista en el grupo de alimentos que les corresponde en la pirámide. Trabaja en parejas.

2 **¿Comes una dieta balanceada?** Haz una lista de lo que comiste ayer. Compárala con la de una pareja. Hablen de lo que necesitan hacer para mantener una dieta balanceada.

3 **Encuesta.** Hazles una encuesta a cinco compañeros/as sobre sus hábitos alimenticios (*eating habits*). Después , clasifica cada uno de estos alimentos en el sitio que le corresponde en la pirámide.

1. ¿Qué bebes cuando tienes sed? ¿Cuál es tu bebida favorita?
2. ¿Bebes alcohol? ¿Cuántas veces por semana? ¿Cuándo?
3. ¿Cuál es la fruta que más te gusta? ¿Cuál es la fruta que menos te gusta? ¿Por qué?
4. ¿Cuál es la verdura que más te gusta? ¿Cuál es la verdura que menos te gusta? ¿Por qué?
5. ¿Cuál es tu comida favorita? ¿Por qué?
6. ¿Cuál es la comida que menos te gusta? ¿Por qué?
7. ¿Cuántos vasos de agua tomas al día?
8. ¿Qué comes cuando tienes hambre entre las comidas?

Haz un resumen de la información que conseguiste. Dale un reportaje a la clase.

Review food vocabulary from Lesson 3 before doing the **Actividades 1–5.**

Peanut butter is also called **manteca de maní** in some countries.

Another word for *diet* is **régimen.** You may wish to teach the expression **estar a dieta** *(to be on a diet)* and **perder/ganar peso** *(lose/gain weight).* Keep the discussion positive and be sensitive to all students.

Variation to **Actividad 4:** Have students plan an unbalanced meal with a variety of foods.

4 **Planeando el menú.** Tienes que planear la comida de una semana para la cafetería de tu universidad. Planea un menú balanceado para todos los días.

Menú diario				
lunes	martes	miércoles	jueves	viernes

5 **Para todas las edades.** ¿Cómo cambiarías (*would you change*) este menú para niños de siete a nueve años? ¿Para personas mayores?

II. Talking about health and exercise

Buena idea para el estrés

Más de 150 estudios psicológicos afirman que el **ejercicio** es un **antídoto** para el **estrés**.° Tres sesiones a la semana, de 20 o 30 minutos, no sólo le calman la **tensión nerviosa**, sino que la **mantienen en forma**.° Una tanda° de ejercicios vigorosos, según los expertos, aumenta las ondas alfa° de **relajación**, emitidas por el **cerebro**.° Además, reduce la tensión muscular y aviva° el ritmo del **corazón**.° "Usted se siente **relajada**,° pero muy despierta. Esto hace que pueda resolver mejor sus problemas", dice David Holmes, psicólogo de la Universidad de Kansas (Estados Unidos).

stress

stay in shape / set

alpha waves

emitted by the brain

intensifies / heart

relaxed

6 **Preguntas personales.** Contesta las preguntas.

1. ¿Qué cosas causan el estrés?
2. ¿Qué hace la gente para reducir el estrés en su vida?
3. ¿Qué síntomas tienes cuando sientes mucho estrés?
4. ¿Qué tipo de ejercicio haces? ¿Cuántas veces por semana?
5. ¿Qué síntomas tienes cuando tienes gripe (*flu*)?
6. ¿Vas al médico cuando estás enfermo/a? ¿Qué te recomienda generalmente?
7. ¿Cuántas horas duermes cada noche?
8. ¿Cuántas horas duermes la noche antes de tomar un examen?

In some countries, **gripa** is also used.

7 **Un plan para una vida sana.** Haz una lista de cinco cosas que te causan estrés. Con una pareja, haz un plan para aliviar el estrés en tu vida. Preséntale el plan a la clase.

For **Actividad 7**, remind students that **sana** (*healthy*) is a false friend. *Sane* = **cuerdo/a.**

III. Making an appointment with a doctor

Una cita° con la médica

appointment

At this point review the **cognados falsos** section in Chapter 1. In the dialogue, point out that **atender** is another false friend and that *to attend* = **asistir.**

RECEPCIONISTA: Buenos días. Oficina de la doctora Medina.
SR. JARAMILLO: Buenos días. Habla el Sr. Jaramillo.
RECEPCIONISTA: ¿En qué le puedo ayudar, Sr. Jaramillo?
SR. JARAMILLO: Mi hija Claudia **se torció°** el **tobillo°** y es necesario que la doctora Medina la vea hoy. — *twisted / ankle*
RECEPCIONISTA: ¿La niña puede caminar?
SR. JARAMILLO: No, no puede. Parece que tiene el tobillo **fracturado.°** — *broken*
RECEPCIONISTA: Entonces lo mejor es que la lleve a **la sala de emergencia°** inmediatamente para tomarle una **radiografía.°** — *emergency room* / *X-Ray*
SR. JARAMILLO: ¿Y la doctora Medina no puede atenderla?
RECEPCIONISTA: No, lo siento. La doctora Medina está ahora en el hospital atendiendo a otros **pacientes.°** Cuando usted llegue al hospital, pida por favor, que le llamen a la doctora Medina. Ella puede **atender°** a la niña allí. — *patients* / *take care of*
SR. JARAMILLO: Muchas gracias, señorita.
RECEPCIONISTA: No hay de qué. **¡Ojalá°** que la niña **se mejore°** pronto! — *I hope / gets better*

Palabras y expresiones útiles

el antibiótico	*antibiotic*	la lengua	*tongue*
la aspirina	*aspirin*	el músculo	*muscle*
la cápsula	*capsule*	el oído	*ear*
el catarro	*cold*	la píldora (pastilla)	*pill*
el/la curandero/a	*healer*	la presión sanguínea	*blood pressure*
la enfermedad	*illness*	la prueba	*test, exam*
el examen físico	*physical exam*	la receta	*prescription*
la fractura	*fracture*	el remedio	*remedy*
la gripe	*flu*	la sangre	*blood*
el hueso	*bone*	el síntoma	*symptom*
la infección	*infection*	la tableta	*tablet*
la inyección	*injection*	el yeso	*cast*
el jarabe	*syrup*		

Point out that **oreja** = *outer ear.* **Mareado** (*seasick*) is interesting with its derivation from the word **mar. Embarazada** is another false friend (*to be embarrassed* = **estar avergonzado/a**).

aliviar	*to alleviate/ease (pain or symptoms)*	respirar	*to breathe*
aliviarse	*to get better*	romper(se) (el brazo)	*to break (one's arm)*
cuidarse	*to take care of oneself*	sacar la lengua	*to stick out one's tongue*
curar	*to cure*		
doler (ue)	*to hurt*	sangrar	*to bleed*
enfermarse	*to get sick*	ser alérgico/a a... (tener alergia a...)	*to be allergic to . . .*
estornudar	*to sneeze*		
evitar	*to avoid*	toser	*to cough*
hacer una cita	*to make an appointment*	vomitar	*to vomit*

Expresiones con *estar*		Expresiones con *tener*	
estar embarazada	*to be pregnant*	tener apetito	*to have an appetite*
estar mareado/a	*to be dizzy*	tener buena/mala salud	*to be in good/bad health*
estar resfriado/a	*to have a cold*	tener catarro/resfrío	*to have a cold*
		tener dolor	*to have pain*
		tener escalofríos	*to shiver, have a chill*
		tener gripe	*to have the flu*
		tener náuseas	*to be nauseous*

After students have completed **Actividad 8,** act out a few situations and ask for advice. Act sick from having eaten some of the bad foods mentioned in the nutrition section.

8 ¿Qué recomienda el médico? ¿Qué recomienda un/a médico/a en estas circunstancias? Trabajen en parejas e inventen recomendaciones para los siguientes síntomas. Comiencen sus recomendaciones con una de las frases siguientes.

Recomiendo que	Es importante que
Prefiero que	Es urgente que
Es mejor que	Sugiero que
Le pido que	Es bueno que

1. No tengo mucho apetito.
2. Me torcí el brazo.
3. Tengo fiebre y náuseas.
4. Me duele el estómago.
5. Estoy mareado/a y tengo dolor de cabeza.
6. Tengo catarro y no puedo respirar.
7. Me duele la cabeza.
8. Fui a un concierto anoche y me torcí la pierna.
9. ¿...?

9 En la consulta del médico. En parejas, hagan el papel de médico/a y paciente. Discutan los síntomas y las recomendaciones para mejorarse.

10 Remedios caseros. *(Home remedies).* Haz una lista de cinco remedios caseros que conoces para curar dolores o enfermedades, por ejemplo: **sopa de pollo para un catarro**. Con una pareja compara tu lista y habla de los beneficios de estos remedios tradicionales en comparación con las medicinas modernas.

ENLACE CULTURAL

Alimentos y remedios naturales

Buena salud y buena nutrición son importantes para el bienestar° diario. Los habitantes nativos de América tuvieron muchos recursos naturales para obtener las dos cosas. Entre los productos de la tierra, conocemos bien el maíz, las papas y los cereales° la quinoa° y el amaranto.° Muchas plantas medicinales conocidas por esas comunidades se usan para fabricar medicinas o cosméticos o también como modelos para sintetizarlos químicamente. Por ejemplo, el aloe o penca sávila° y los bálsamos° de Perú y Tolú para cremas; la yerba mate°, el guaraná° y la cafeína para bebidas; la quinina para medicinas y bebidas; la enzima papaína° de la papaya para ablandar° las carnes; el girasol rojo, la valeriana° y el tilo° en la medicina alternativa y la capsaicina° de los chiles para cremas contra la artritis.

Go to your local food store and bring in some of these items. Other sources of information: Internet and magazines.

well being

grains / quinoa plant / amaranth

aloe vera / balms

mate tea herb / healing plant

papaya enzyme

to tenderize / echinacea; flowering plant used as sedative / lime tree / medicinal pepper substance

Discusión en grupos

1. ¿Es efectiva la medicina alternativa? ¿Puede reemplazar la medicina tradicional?
2. Mencionen tres productos medicinales, industriales o cosméticos que conocen en forma natural o sintética.

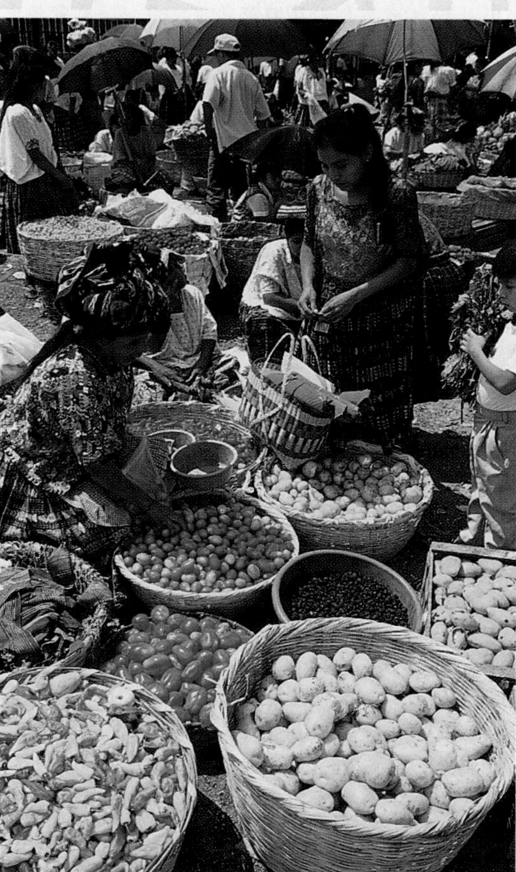

Vendiendo chiles, tomates, papas y diferentes vegetales en el mercado de Cobán, Guatemala.

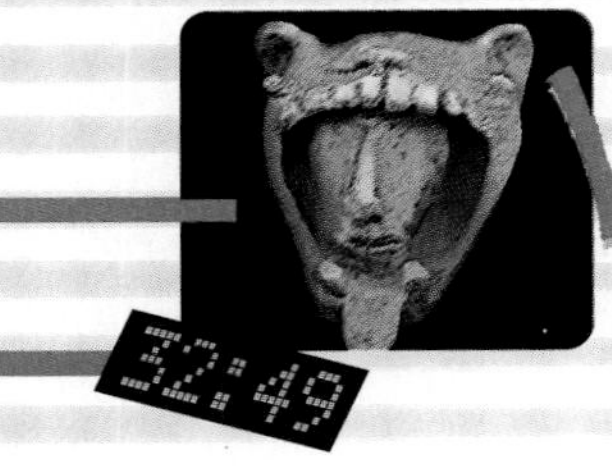

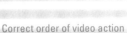

VISTAS Y VOCES

I. Preparémonos

1 Anticipación. Con un/a compañero/a, contesta las siguientes preguntas.

A. **1.** Si quieres esconder algún objeto, ¿dónde lo pones? ¿Qué escondes?
2. Describe algún mercado al aire libre en tu región. ¿Dónde está, en la ciudad o en el campo? ¿Qué venden? ¿Qué compras tú allí?
3. ¿Siempre dices la verdad? Explica.

B. Mira la foto 8A en la página 315. ¿Quién es esta mujer y qué está haciendo?

Para comprender mejor

al aire libre	*open air*	el logro	*accomplishment*
la altura	*height*	mareado/a	*nauseous, dizzy*
el amanecer	*sunrise, dawn*	la nube	*cloud*
el arbusto	*bush*	la piedra	*stone*
la bolsa	*bag*	poderoso/a	*powerful*
el cielo	*heaven, sky*	el quechua	*Quechua language*
cumplir	*to fulfill*	silvestre	*wild*
el/la curandero/a	*healer*	el soroche	*altitude sickness*
engañar	*to deceive*	el tejido	*weaving*
envolver	*to wrap*	la tierra	*earth*
forjar	*to forge, to shape*	la vela	*candle*
el hogar	*home*	el/la vendedor/a	*salesperson*

2 Secuencia. Estudia cada una de las cuatro escenas de video.

Correct order of video action shots: 4, 2, 1, 3

1.

2.

3.

4.

II. Miremos y escuchemos

3 Mis observaciones. Mientras miras el episodio, escribe el nombre del personaje (o personajes) asociado(s) con las siguientes actividades.

1. Tiene(n) a Yax-Balam en las manos. __________
2. Habla(n) con Zulaya en su tienda. __________
3. Camina(n) por el mercado en Otavalo. __________
4. Se siente(n) mal y tiene(n) un sueño. __________
5. Un pájaro blanco vuela enfrente de su cara. __________
6. Despierta(n) a Adriana. __________
7. Habla(n) con Felipe y Adriana sobre el soroche. __________
8. Va(n) a la casa de la curandera. __________
9. Habla(n) en quechua y cura(n) a Adriana. __________
10. Pregunta(n) por Zulaya. __________

Answers to Actividad 3:

1. Zulaya
2. un señor (Mario)
3. Adriana y Felipe
4. Adriana
5. Nayeli
6. Felipe
7. un curandero
8. Felipe y Adriana
9. doña Remedios
10. Gafasoscuras

III. Comentemos

4 Comprensión. Con un/a compañero/a, contesta las siguientes preguntas.

1. Describe a Zulaya. ¿Qué tiene en las manos?
2. ¿Con quién habla Zulaya en la tienda? ¿Sobre qué?
3. ¿Qué envuelve y pone Zulaya en dos bolsas idénticas mientras habla con Mario?
4. ¿Cómo se siente Adriana? ¿Qué tiene?
5. Cuando está dormida, Adriana tiene un sueño en que Nayeli le dice que el jaguar va a ser su guía en la vida. También le describe otras tres guías de la vida. Una es la verdad. ¿Cuáles son las otras dos?
6. Cuando se despierta Adriana, ¿adónde van ella y Felipe?
7. ¿Quién es doña Remedios? ¿Qué tiene dentro y fuera de la casa?
8. Según doña Remedios, ¿por qué está enferma Adriana?
9. ¿Cuándo se despierta el jaguar, según doña Remedios?
10. ¿Qué dice ella sobre simplificar la vida? ¿Por qué?
11. ¿Qué les pregunta Gafasnegras a los vendedores del mercado?

Answers to Actividad 4:

1. Es una señora mayor; es morena, de pelo corto. Tiene más o menos cincuenta años. Tiene a Yax-Balam en las manos.
2. Zulaya habla con su amigo Mario de devolver a Yax-Balam a México.
3. Zulaya envuelve a Yax-Balam y una piedra del mismo tamaño que el jaguar.
4. Adriana se siente mal y está mareada. Tiene náuseas y tal vez soroche.
5. Las otras dos guías son la justicia y el honor.
6. Van a ver a doña Remedios.
7. Doña Remedios es la curandera del pueblo. Su casa tiene muchas flores y plantas.
8. Su corazón y su intelecto están en guerra.
9. Se despierta al amanecer.
10. Adriana debe simplificar su vida para que pueda ver lo que la naturaleza le muestra.
11. Pregunta si conocen a Zulaya Piscomayo Curihual y dónde está.

5 Guías de la vida. En este episodio, Adriana sueña que Nayeli le habla. La madrina le dice, "El que no sabe su historia no puede forjar su destino". Trabajando con un/a compañero/a, discute esta idea con respecto a la historia de los jaguares y a tu vida del pasado y del futuro.

6 Miremos otra vez. Después de mirar el episodio otra vez, organiza las escenas de video en la secuencia correcta. Después, compara la cura que le hace doña Remedios a Adriana con el tipo de tratamiento que recibes tú cuando estás enfermo/a.

7 Somos artistas. En grupos de cuatro, creen un cartel representando las vistas y voces del mercado de Otavalo. Describan los detalles de cuatro escenas: el panorama del mercado de Otavalo; unos tejidos típicos; una tienda de ropa y objetos; la gente que está en el mercado. Después, comparen su interpretación artística con otros grupos.

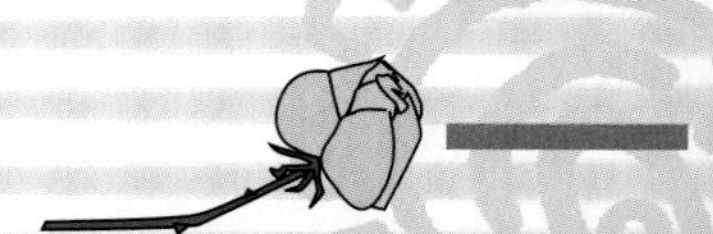

Lengua

I. Expressing emotions and wishes

More uses of the present subjunctive

Salud eterna

ESTER: Estoy contenta de que **vengamos** mucho al Centro de Salud. Es importante que **cuidemos** nuestra salud.

ADÁN: Sí, mi amor, me alegro de que **hagamos** los ejercicios juntos.

ESTER: Lamento° que nuestros hijos Pepe y Marina no **participen** en estas actividades. A veces, me preocupa° que Pepe no **practique** ningún deporte y que Marina **sea** tan sedentaria. Ojalá° **cambien** su estilo de vida. Siempre están ocupados, viven con mucho estrés y no tienen tiempo para hacer ejercicio.

ADÁN: Estoy de acuerdo.° Temo° que **tengan** problemas de salud en el futuro.

ESTER: Querido, no me sorprende° que los médicos **digan** que el ejercicio reduce el estrés. Me encanta hacer ejercicio.

I regret

it worries me

I hope

I agree / I'm afraid

it doesn't surprise me

Look at the verbs in the subjunctive. What infinitives do they come from? Underline the expression in the main clause that requires the use of the subjunctive. What do these expressions have in common? Why do you think that the subjunctive is needed in each case?

- Remember that for the subjunctive to be needed, the structure usually looks like this.

Main clause	que	Subordinate clause
verb (subject 1)	que	verb (subject 2)

- It is not only the structure that causes the subjunctive to be used, but what the verb in the main clause expresses.
- In Spanish, when expressing emotions such as happiness, sadness, fear, anger, regret, shame, dislikes, sorrow, pleasure, joy, hope, and the like in the main clause, the subjunctive is used in the subordinate clause. Notice that emotion can be expressed personally or impersonally.

Personally	
Lamento que Marta y Luis no hagan ejercicio.	*I regret that Marta and Luis don't exercise.*

Impersonally

Es una lástima que Marta y Luis no hagan ejercicio. — *It is a pity that Marta and Luis don't exercise.*

- When there is only one subject, the structure changes and the infinitive is used.

  Lamento no tener un trabajo. — *I regret not having a job.*

- Common verbs and impersonal expressions used to express emotion are:

alegrarse	*to be happy*	es una lástima	*it's a shame*
enojarse	*to be angry*	esperar	*to hope*
es bueno	*it's good*	estar contento/a de	*to be happy*
es extraño	*it's strange*	lamentar	*to lament, regret, be sorry*
es malo	*it's bad*	molestar	*to bother*
es mejor	*it's better*	sentir (ie)	*to be sorry, lament, regret*
es peor	*it's worse*	sorprender	*to surprise*
es ridículo	*it's ridiculous*	temer	*to fear, be afraid of*
es terrible	*it's terrible*	tener miedo (de)	*to be afraid of*

Have students work in small groups to prepare five sentences with change of subject and five without. Have them read their sentences with great emotion to help solidify this grammar point.

LENGUA EN ACCIÓN

Ojalá para expresar esperanza

The Moors were in Spain from 711 to 1492 and there is much Arabic influence in the Spanish language. **Ojalá** is an Arabic word which means *God (Allah) willing,* and expresses the equivalent in Spanish of *I/Let's hope.* It only has one form and is always followed by the subjunctive.

Ojalá (que) nos sirvan frutas para el postre. — *I hope that they serve us fruit for dessert.*

It is also used on its own as an exclamation:

—¿Nos van a servir frutas para el postre? — *Are they going to serve us fruit for dessert?*
—¡Ojalá! — *Let's hope so!*

At this point you may wish to show pictures of the Alhambra (mentioned in Chapter 4) and point out that many words begining with **al-** are of Arabic origin (**álgebra, alfombra, alquimia,** and so on).

1 ***Comprensión.*** Completa las siguientes ideas con la forma correcta del subjuntivo de los verbos en paréntesis.

1. No me gusta que mi compañero de cuarto __________ (fumar).
2. Esperamos que Gualterio no __________ (tener) gripe.
3. El médico lamenta que sus pacientes no __________ (seguir) sus consejos.
4. Mi amiga Alicia está contenta de que sus dos hijas __________ (comer) alimentos variados.
5. Es una lástima que hoy __________ (hacer) mal tiempo para la fiesta.
6. Ojalá que papá no __________ (enojarse) con nosotros por llegar tarde esta noche.

Answers to Actividad 1:
1. fume
2. tenga
3. sigan
4. coman
5. haga
6. se enoje

7. sirva
8. preste
9. se muera
10. guste

7. Me gusta que la cafetería _________ (servir) mejor comida que el año pasado.
8. Irene se alegra de que su primo le _________ (prestar) equipo para hacer ejercicios.
9. Adelina tiene miedo de que su hermano mayor _________ (morirse) del SIDA (*AIDS*).
10. A Marco Antonio le sorprende que nos _________ (gustar) la comida italiana.

Answers to Actividad 2:

1. se alegran / sea
2. lamenta / fume
3. enseñe
4. sorprende / planeen
5. sentimos / tenga
6. espera / estudien / hagan
7. se gane / nos lleve
8. molesta / tomen
9. estamos / sea

2 Episodios de la vida. Varias personas expresan sus emociones sobre los siguientes episodios de la vida. Reemplaza los verbos entre paréntesis con la forma correcta del presente (indicativo o subjuntivo). Sigue el modelo.

► **Modelo:** *yo (esperar) que Paco (comer) menos grasa*
Yo espero que Paco coma menos grasa.

1. mis tíos (alegrarse) de que Adán (ser) tan saludable
2. Mauro (lamentar) que su esposa todavía (fumar) cigarros
3. ojalá que mi novio me (enseñar) buena nutrición
4. no nos (sorprender) que Teresa y Javier (planear) hacer un crucero por el Caribe
5. nosotros (sentir) que Guillermo (tener) SIDA
6. el profesor Ramírez (esperar) que sus estudiantes (estudiar) mucho para el examen de sociología y que (hacer) los ejercicios
7. ojalá mamá (ganarse) la lotería y (llevarnos) de vacaciones a la Argentina
8. me (molestar) que José y Miguel (tomar) tanta cerveza
9. nosotros (estar) contentos de que el agua (ser) tan buena para la salud

Answers to Actividad 3:

1. a. trabajen
1. b. haya
2. a. esté
2. b. hable
3. a. exageren
3. b. beba
4. a. haya
4. b. nos preocupemos; vivamos
5. a. haga
5. b. gaste; use

3 Reacciones. Primero, escribe la forma correcta del subjuntivo en cada frase de la derecha. Después, trabaja con un/a compañero/a. Cada persona selecciona la afirmación con la que está de acuerdo y explica por qué.

Declaración	Reacciones ¿a o b? ¿Por qué?
1. El costo de la educación universitaria es demasiado alto.	a. Es mejor que los estudiantes _________ (trabajar) antes de ir a la universidad. b. Me molesta que no _________ (haber) educación gratis para todos.
2. Muchos estadounidenses piensan seguir una dieta balanceada.	a. Me alegro de que la gente _________ (estar) consciente de la buena nutrición. b. No me gusta que la gente _________ (hablar) tanto de la dieta.
3. Beber mucho alcohol es un problema serio en la sociedad.	a. Es extraño que algunas personas _________ (exagerar) el problema del alcohol. b. Temo que la gente _________ (beber) mucho alcohol.

4. Tener una mente sana en un cuerpo sano es una buena filosofía.	a. Estoy contento/a de que ________ (haber) más énfasis en lo que comemos todos los días. b. Es ridículo que nosotros ________ (preocuparse) tanto de la salud. Es mejor que nosotros ________ (vivir) día a día.
5. Un coche es una necesidad esencial de la vida.	a. Es bueno que el coche nos ________ (hacer) la vida más fácil. b. Es absurdo que la gente ________ (gastar) tanto tiempo viajando en coche y que no ________ (usar) el transporte público.

II. Expressing doubt or certainty

More uses of the subjunctive

En el restaurante *Mar azul*

CÉSAR: Norma va a ir con nosotros al restaurante *Mar azul*, pero no creo que Iván **vaya** porque le tiene alergia al pescado.

LILI: No, no es cierto que Iván le **tenga** alergia al pescado, es que no le gusta. Además, no importa, pues allí también sirven buena carne. ¿Crees que Iván no **coma** carne tampoco?

CÉSAR: Creo que le **encanta** la carne. Pero, tenemos que llamar al restaurante porque dudo que **esté** abierto hoy, lunes.

LILI: No te preocupes, ya llamé. Es cierto que *Mar azul* **está** abierto y podemos salir en media hora. ¡Tengo muchísimas ganas de comer langosta fresca!

Lili

César

Notice which verbs are in the subjunctive and which are not. Underline the expression in the main clause that requires the use of the subjunctive in the subordinate clause. What do these expressions have in common? Why do you think that the subjunctive is needed in each case? Find other examples that use the indicative. What do these expressions have in common that do not require the use of the subjunctive?

Expressions of doubt, uncertainty, denial, and disbelief

In Spanish, when expressing doubt, uncertainty, denial, and disbelief in the main clause, the subjunctive is used in the subordinate clause.

- Common verbs and impersonal expressions expressing doubt, denial, and disbelief are:

Using these expressions, have students create original sentences to be read to the class in a tone of doubt and denial.

dudar	*to doubt*	no es cierto	*it's not certain*
es dudoso	*it's doubtful*	no es verdad	*it's not true*
es imposible	*it's impossible*	no estar seguro	*to be unsure*
negar (ie)	*to deny*	no pensar (ie)	*not to think*
no creer	*not to believe*		

- **Dudar** takes the subjunctive whether the subject in the subordinate clause is different or the same.

Moncho duda que él pueda jugar al golf hoy.	*Moncho doubts he can play golf today.*
Moncho duda que su hermano pueda jugar al golf hoy.	*Moncho doubts that his brother can play golf today.*

LENGUA EN ACCIÓN

Quizás y tal vez: Usos especiales del subjuntivo

Both **quizás** and **tal vez** mean *perhaps* and are followed by the subjunctive when the speaker intends to express doubt or uncertainty. **Que** is omitted.

Quizás yo prepare una comida de pollo esta noche.	*Perhaps I'll prepare a chicken meal tonight.*
Tal vez llueva mañana.	*Perhaps it will rain tomorrow.*

Expressions of belief or certainty

In Spanish, when expressing belief or certainty, certain verbs and verb expressions use the indicative.

Es cierto que Raúl tiene diabetes.	*It's true that Raul has diabetes.*
Creo que en el futuro vamos a encontrar una cura para el SIDA.	*I believe that in the future, we are going to find a cure for AIDS.*

- Common verbs and impersonal expressions expressing belief or certainty are:

To practice this point, original sentences should be stated emphatically, with certainty, unless they are questions.

creer	*to think*	es cierto	*it's certain, true*
opinar	*to think, have an opinion*	es evidente	*it's evident*
pensar	*to think*	es verdad	*it's true*

- When **creer**, **opinar**, and **pensar** are used to ask a question, the subjunctive is often used.

Dra. Medina, ¿piensa Ud. que yo tenga gripe?	*Dr. Medina, do you think that I have the flu?*
¿Cree Ud. que mi hijo se mejore pronto?	*Do you think that my son will get better soon?*

4 Momentos de la vida. Completa los diálogos con el subjuntivo o el indicativo.

Sami está en la oficina de la doctora Colón, una psicóloga excelente.

SAMI: Es verdad que yo no __________ (sentirse) muy bien. Estoy triste.
DRA. COLÓN: Todos tenemos momentos bajos en la vida. Sami, no niego que tú __________ (estar) deprimido. Es importante que tú __________ (hablar) de tus problemas.
SAMI: Gracias, doctora, creo que Ud. me __________ (poder) ayudar.

Ernesto y Amanda están en el restaurante Comida rápida.

ERNESTO: No creo que nosotros __________ (deber) comer un almuerzo con mucha grasa, pero dudo que tú __________ (seguir) mis consejos. Recuerda: nunca es demasiado pronto para pensar en la nutrición.
AMANDA: No niego que las papas fritas __________ (ser) malas para la salud y es cierto que la ensalada __________ (contribuir) a la buena nutrición; pero, es imposible que la gente __________ (comer) solamente ensaladas y verduras. Es muy aburrido.
ERNESTO: Es verdad que nosotros __________ (deber) tener una dieta balanceada. Vamos a pedir ensalada y hamburguesas, ¿de acuerdo?

Gregorio y Adelita, dos novios se declaran su amor y amistad.

GREGORIO: Adelita, es verdad que me __________ (querer). ¿No?
ADELITA: Corazón, es cierto que te __________ (adorar) y es verdad que __________ (querer) vivir el resto de mi vida contigo.
GREGORIO: Es evidente que nosotros __________ (ir) a ser muy felices, ¿no crees?
ADELITA: Opino que tú y yo nos __________ (respetar) mucho y no somos solamente novios sino también muy buenos amigos.

Answers to Actividad 4:
1. me siento
2. estés
3. hables
4. puede
5. debamos
6. sigas
7. son
8. contribuye
9. coma
10. debemos
11. quieres
12. adoro
13. quiero
14. vamos
15. respetamos

5 ¿Es verdad? Tú no estás de acuerdo con tu amigo sobre sus opiniones. Usa expresiones verbales como **no es verdad, niego que, dudo que, no creo que,** and so on, para expresar las opiniones contrarias. Sigue el modelo.

▸ **Modelo:** *Costa Rica es más grande que Perú.*
No es verdad que Costa Rica sea más grande que Perú.

1. Las aspirinas son buenas para el dolor de garganta.
2. Una computadora IBM funciona mejor que una computadora Macintosh.
3. Hay muchos buenos restaurantes en esta ciudad.
4. Es importante hacer ejercicios todos los días.
5. La comida de nuestra cafetería no tiene mucha grasa.
6. El mejor coche del país es el Honda.
7. La gente debe comer una dieta balanceada.
8. A todos los médicos les gusta operar a las cinco de la mañana.
9. Los estudiantes universitarios se visten elegantemente.

Answers to Actividad 5:
The verbs will be changed to the following subjunctive forms:
1. sean
2. funcione
3. haya
4. sea
5. no tenga
6. sea
7. deba
8. guste
9. se vistan

6 Verdades y dudas. Escríbele un correo electrónico a tu prima, contándole las cosas que sabes y las dudas que tengas. Incluye diez ideas sobre la vida académica, social, familiar y profesional, utilizando las expresiones de duda, negación y certeza (*certainty*).

Lectura A

Introducción

In this chapter you have learned about food and nutrition. The reading that follows describes six important products in a healthy diet. The reading was published by the magazine *Vanidades Continental* in its section about health and nutrition.

Reading strategy: Comparing and contrasting

The six products presented in this reading are different in many respects, but also have some similarities. Before reading, do the activities that follow. This kind of comparing and contrasting will prepare you for the reading's content and will enable you to compare the foods presented.

1 Preferencias. Trabaja en parejas. Pregúntale a tu compañero/a si los productos de la lista le gustan mucho, poco o nada. Sigue el modelo.

▸ **Modelo:** *—¿Cuánto te gusta el arroz: mucho, poco o nada?*
—A mí, el arroz me gusta...

Productos

1. arroz
2. bróculi
3. huevos
4. yogur
5. banano
6. chocolate

2 Todo es relativo. Trabaja en parejas. Basándote en las respuestas de tu compañero/a, compara sus preferencias por los productos. Sigue el modelo.

▸ **Modelo:** *A ti te gusta el arroz más que/menos que/tanto como el yogur.*

3 Muy saludable. Discute con tu compañero/a cuál de los seis productos es más o menos saludable. Sigue el modelo.

▸ **Modelo:** *Yo creo que el banano es menos saludable que el yogur. ¿Qué crees tú?* or
Yo creo que el banano es más saludable que el yogur. ¿Qué crees tú?
Yo creo que el banano es tan saludable como el yogur. ¿Qué crees tú?

Answers to Actividad 4:
1. V
2. V
3. F—Relaja los nervios.
4. F—Contienen 22% menos.
5. V
6. V
7. V (Point out that **bróculi** is also spelled **brócoli**.)
8. F—Tiene más de la mitad del calcio requerido diariamente.
9. F—Es un alimento básico del 50% de la población mundial.
10. V

4 ¿Verdadero o falso? Después de leer la lectura, trabajen en parejas y discutan si las oraciones siguientes son falsas o verdaderas. Corrijan las oraciones falsas.

1. Comer banano da buen humor.
2. El yogur contiene bacilos vivos.
3. Consumir chocolate pone nerviosa a la gente.
4. Los huevos contienen más colesterol de lo que se creía.
5. El chocolate contiene proteínas.
6. Los huevos mantienen los músculos en forma.
7. El bróculi protege contra el cáncer.
8. El yogur no tiene mucho calcio.
9. Casi nadie come arroz en el mundo.
10. El banano es un alimento muy versátil.

Comidas ideales

Estos seis alimentos básicos son como el A B C de la nutrición. No sólo revitalizan, sino que contienen vitaminas y minerales esenciales para el organismo. Inclúyalos a menudo en su alimentación diaria... ¡y su cuerpo y su mente, se lo agradecerán!° *will thank you*

Arroz

¿Por qué comerlo? Porque es un carbohidrato complejo que posee los ocho aminoácidos esenciales y sólo contiene 90 calorías por cada media taza.° *cup*

¿Comida fácil? Sí. Hierva una taza de agua y agregue° media taza de arroz. Baje a fuego lento. Cocine 20 minutos. ¡Y ya está! *add*

¿Versátil? Puede hacer mil combinaciones con arroz: paellas, arroz con pollo, etc. Con él no se aburrirá.° *will not get bored*

¿Poderes mágicos? ¡Es nada menos que el alimento básico del 50% de la población mundial!

Bróculi

¿Por qué comerlo? Porque una taza es rica en vitaminas A y C, contiene 3 gramos de proteínas y sólo 28 calorías.

¿Comida fácil? Sin duda. Si quiere, cómalo crudo,° pero si lo prefiere cocinado, póngalo unos 2 o 3 minutos en el microondas, o hágalo al vapor° y agréguele limón. *raw* / *steam it*

¿Versátil? Por supuesto. Combínelo con arroz, con queso derretido, pollo... ¡y hasta con yerbas aromáticas!

¿Poderes mágicos? Contiene elementos que pueden ofrecer protección contra el cáncer.

Huevos

¿Por qué comerlos? Porque contienen un promedio de 6 gramos de proteína, con sólo 75 calorías y 5 gramos de grasa. En cuanto al colesterol, los huevos tienen 22 por ciento menos colesterol de lo que se creía.

¿Comida fácil? ¿Qué no puede hacerse con ellos?

¿Versátil? Ya sea pasados por agua, en tortillas, revoltillos° o hervidos, se adaptan a todo lo que quiera. *scrambled*

¿Poderes mágicos? Los humildes° huevos, cargados de proteínas, proporcionan energía y ayudan a mantener en forma los músculos. *humble*

Yogur

¿Por qué comerlo? Porque una taza de yogur tiene 100 calorías, y proporciona° más de la mitad del calcio requerido diariamente. *supplies*

¿Comida fácil? Se compra ya hecho,° y se ingiere a cualquier hora. ¡Muy sabroso con frutas naturales! *ready made*

¿Versátil? Sí. Puede usarlo como sustituto de aceites y grasas en muchos platos.

¿Poderes mágicos? Los bacilos° vivos del yogur protegen contra infecciones y la lactosa ayuda a hacer buenas digestiones. *bacilli*

Banano

¿Por qué comerlo? Porque con sólo 100 calorías es rico en fibra y potasio. También por su alto nivel de carbohidratos.

¿Comida fácil? La más fácil (y una de las menos costosas). Cómalo como la naturaleza lo hizo o, si quiere, puede cocinarlos.

¿Versátil? Los caribeños saben hasta qué punto.° Comen los bananos fritos, asados, hervidos, horneados°... *degree* / *baked*

¿Poderes mágicos? Tienen aminoácidos que brindan° energía y dan buen humor. *provide*

Chocolate

¿Por qué comerlo? Una barra chica de chocolate puede contener riboflavina, hierro, calcio y proteínas. ¿En cuanto a calorías? 220.

¿Comida fácil? Sin duda.

¿Versátil? Se convierte en ricos dulces y postres. Para evitar las calorías, puede optar por cocoa y mezclarla con leche descremada.° *skim*

¿Poderes mágicos? El chocolate contiene una mezcla de cafeína y magnesio, parecida a la de ciertos calmantes, que relaja los nervios y da energías.

5 **¿Qué es?** Contesta las siguientes preguntas sobre la lectura.

1. ¿Quién te va a agradecer que comas estos seis alimentos básicos?
2. ¿Es necesario comer estos alimentos diariamente?
3. ¿Cuál de estos alimentos contiene mucha fibra?
4. Según tu opinión, ¿son los seis alimentos comidas fáciles? ¿Cuál es la más fácil?
5. ¿Son realmente mágicos los poderes de estos alimentos?

6 **Categorías.** Trabajen en grupos. Cada grupo elige dos alimentos para comparar sus calorías y su versatilidad. Luego, cada grupo escribe las comparaciones y las presenta a la clase. Miren el modelo para sacar ideas.

▸ **Modelo:** *El arroz tiene menos calorías que el chocolate, pero ambos productos son muy versátiles.*
El yogur es bastante versátil y tiene tan pocas calorías como el banano.

Alimento	Número de calorías	Muy versátil	Poco versátil
Arroz			
Huevos			
Bróculi			
Yogur			
Banano			
Chocolate			

7 **Recomendaciones.** Trabaja con un/a compañero/a y menciona por lo menos diez recomendaciones sobre los seis productos de la lista anterior. Comienza las oraciones con: **es importante, es necesario, es conveniente, es bueno, es mejor, es peor, es malo.** Sigue el modelo.

▸ **Modelo:** *No es bueno que consumas mucho chocolate.*
Es conveniente que incluyas yogur en tu dieta.

8 **Una dieta balanceada.** Imagínate que tú eres especialista en nutrición. Trabaja en parejas y dale a tu compañero/a algunas recomendaciones para tener una dieta balanceada. Sigue el modelo.

▸ **Modelo:** *comer diariamente de seis a ocho raciones de pan, cereal, arroz o pasta*
—¿Qué es necesario hacer para tener una dieta balanceada?
—Para tener una dieta balanceada es necesario que comas de seis a ocho raciones de pan, cereal, arroz o pasta.

1. incluir diariamente cantidades mínimas de grasas en las comidas
2. consumir un mínimo de dos raciones de leche, yogur o queso por día
3. comer diariamente dos o tres porciones de carne, pollo, pescado o huevos
4. comer entre dos y cuatro porciones de frutas
5. no usar mucha mantequilla en las comidas diarias
6. beber mucha agua diariamente
7. no abusar del azúcar y los dulces

9 **Mis alimentos básicos.** Según tus gustos y las tradiciones de tu familia elige tres alimentos básicos que sean importantes para consumir a menudo (*often*) en la alimentación diaria. Describe por qué es importante consumir el producto, si es una comida fácil y versátil y si tiene poderes mágicos. Preséntale tu selección a la clase.

ETAPA B

Pistas y palabras

I. Talking about money

A. En la casa de cambio

Note that in the last sentence of the dialogue the subjunctive is used after **que,** with the meaning *I hope that,* a use analogous to **ojalá**.

—Buenas tardes, a sus órdenes.
—Buenas tardes. Quisiera cambiar unos **cheques de viajero**° en dólares por **moneda en efectivo**.° ¿A cuánto está el cambio hoy?
—Está a 5.100 sucres por dólar.
—Bueno, a ver... ¿Me puede Ud. **cambiar**° un cheque de cuarenta dólares, por favor?
—Claro que sí, con mucho gusto. **Endóselo**° aquí, por favor.
—Ya está, aquí lo tiene.
—Gracias. ¿Desea usted algo más?
—Sí, por favor, necesito mandar un **giro postal**° al Ecuador. ¿Ofrecen ustedes ese servicio?
—No, lo siento, pero puedo venderle un **cheque certificado** y usted personalmente lo **envía**° **por correo.**
—Y ¿cuánto **cobran**° ustedes por el cheque certificado?
—**La tasa de cambio**° es un poco más favorable y la **comisión** nuestra por el cheque no es muy alta.
—Está bien, entonces, deme Ud. un cheque certificado de ciento cincuenta dólares.
—¿Cómo lo quiere pagar?
—Con tarjeta de crédito.°
—Muy bien. Aquí tiene usted su dinero en efectivo y su cheque certificado. **Revíselos**° por favor, antes de salir.
—A ver... Bien, parece que todo está en orden. Muchas gracias. Adiós.
—Adiós. Que esté usted muy bien.

travelers' checks
cash
exchange
Endorse it
money order
send
charge
rate of exchange
credit card
Check them

Palabras y expresiones útiles

el billete	*bill*	la cuenta de ahorros	*savings account*
la caja	*cashier*	la firma	*signature*
la caja fuerte	*safe*	el gasto	*expense*
el/la cajero/a	*cashier*	el préstamo	*loan*
el cambio	*exchange, change*	el presupuesto	*budget*
la cuenta corriente	*checking account*	el promedio	*average*
ahorrar	*to save*	pedir prestado	*to borrow*
depositar (dinero)	*to deposit (money)*	prestar	*to lend*
firmar	*to sign*	sacar (retirar) dinero	*to withdraw money*

¿Cuánto vale? (¿Cuánto cuesta?) *How much does it cost?*

1 **¿Cuánto es?** Tienes dinero y quieres cambiarlo por moneda de otro país. Completa la tabla y escribe cuánto dinero vas a recibir. (Pista: Primero tienes que cambiar las cantidades a dólares estadounidenses para calcularlo.)

▸ **Modelo:** *Si tienes 100 nuevos pesos mexicanos y quieres comprar pesetas lo calculas así:*
100 nuevos pesos (100 / 8,5150) = $11,74 dólares americanos X 151,150 pesetas = 1.775 pesetas.

B. Tasas de cambio

País	Moneda nacional	Tasa de cambio por dólar
Estados Unidos	Dólar	1
Europa	Euro	1,1070
Chile	Peso	453,40
México	Nuevo peso	8,5150
España	Peseta	151,150
Venezuela	Bolívar	535,510

For the latest exchange rates, use the Internet or call your local bank. Bring in any coins and/or bills you may have from the Hispanic world.

Moneda que quieres cambiar	Moneda que quieres comprar	Cantidad que recibes en la nueva moneda
24 dólares americanos	Euro	
777 nuevos pesos mexicanos	bolívares venezolanos	
1.000 pesetas españolas	nuevos pesos mexicanos	
300 pesos chilenos	dólares americanos	
550 Euro	pesetas españolas	
250 bolívares venezolanos	pesos chilenos	
79 dólares americanos	nuevos pesos mexicanos	

Remember that Spanish uses a decimal point where English uses a comma, and vice versa.

2 El presupuesto. Haz un presupuesto semanal para las siguientes categorías de gastos.

Alquiler y servicios: agua, luz, teléfono...	Comida	Entretenimiento (*Entertainment*)
Bebidas	Transporte	Misceláneos
	Ropa	

3 Presupuestos mensuales. Compara tus gastos con los gastos de tres o cuatro compañeros/as. Calcula el promedio mensual para cada persona y para todo el grupo. Preséntalo a la clase.

For **Actividad 3,** assign one group per country. Have students first do the budget in dollars and then convert it. You may or may not wish to permit the use of calculators.

4 En el banco. Estás en el banco y tienes que abrir una cuenta de ahorros y comprar un cheque certificado. Crea una conversación entre el/la dependiente del banco y tú.

ENLACE CULTURAL

El cacao, una moneda valiosa

Un señor cortando frutas de cacao en México.

Los mayas y los aztecas usaban los granos° de cacao como moneda para comprar otros alimentos o productos de lujo. El intercambio de productos fue muy importante para crear un comercio activo que ayudó al desarrollo de la agricultura, las artes y la arquitectura de estas civilizaciones.

Como alimento, los aztecas consumían el cacao sin azúcar y lo llamaban **xocoatl**.° Actualmente, lo que nosotros llamamos chocolate es la pasta de cacao mezclada° con leche, azúcar y vainilla.

beans

bitter water

mixed

Discusión en grupos

Unos jóvenes españoles tomando churros con chocolate.

1. ¿Qué productos que contienen cacao consumen ustedes regularmente? ¿Cuál es el producto preferido?
2. ¿Cómo les gusta a cada uno de ustedes beber el chocolate? ¿caliente o frío? ¿con crema o con leche? ¿con azúcar y con vainilla?
3. ¿Les gusta intercambiar productos entre ustedes? Por ejemplo, ¿discos, lápices,...?

II. Buying jewelry and merchandise in a marketplace

De compras en el mercado

Adriana and Felipe are about to visit a typical marketplace in Otavalo, Ecuador. Here is a preview of some items and customs that you will see in this episode.

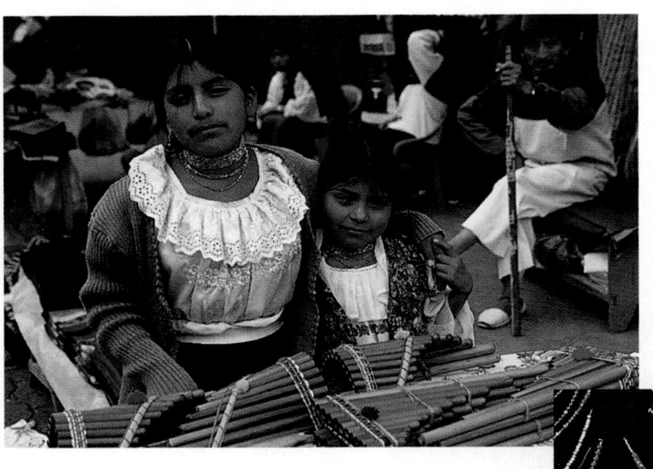

◄ ***Dos muchachas ecuatorianas vendiendo instrumentos musicales en Otavalo.***

▼ ***Artesanías y joyas típicas de plata y de oro en el mercado de Otavalo.***

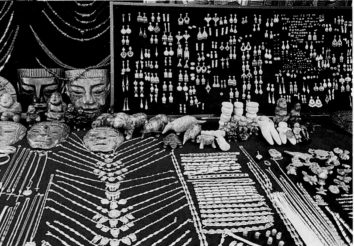

Bring in jewelry and/or pictures of jewelry.

Palabras y expresiones útiles

el anillo	*ring*	el pendiente	*pendant, earring*
los aretes	*earrings*	la perla	*pearl*
las artesanías	*folk art*	la piedra	*stone*
la cadena	*chain*	la plata	*silver*
el cobre	*copper*	el prendedor	*brooch*
el collar	*necklace*	la pulsera	*bracelet*
el diamante	*diamond*	el quilate	*karat*
la esmeralda	*emerald*	el reloj	*watch*
las joyas	*jewelry*	el tapete	*rug, small carpet, tapestry*
la/s joya/s de fantasía	*costume jewelry*	el tapiz	*tapestry*
el oro	*gold*	la turquesa	*turquoise*

regatear — *to bargain*

5 **¿Qué llevan?** Haz una lista de las joyas que llevan tus compañeros/as de clase.

6 **Comprando regalos.** Estás de vacaciones y tienes que comprar regalos para las personas de la lista. Describe las joyas que vas a comprar para cada una de ellas y por qué.

1. tu hermano/a
2. tu mejor amigo
3. tu mejor amiga
4. tu novio/a
5. tu madre
6. tu padre
7. una sobrina de quince años
8. tu hermano de diez años

7 **Regateando.** Estás en el mercado comprando las joyas, pero todos los vendedores te dan precios diferentes. Crea una conversación con un/una vendedor/a. Tú regateas para obtener el mejor precio. (Lee el *Enlace cultural* para más información sobre el regateo.)

ENLACE CULTURAL

Los mercados y el arte del regateo

El regateo es el arte de negociar un precio más bajo cuando un comprador quiere comprar algo. En los mercados artesanales° y en las tiendas pequeñas de España y América Latina todavía es usual regatear por el precio. En los mercados de las ciudades pequeñas, como Otavalo, y cuando se compran productos de vendedores ambulantes,° también es costumbre pedir rebaja° en el precio.

craft
street vendors
discount

De compras en el mercado al aire libre de Otavalo.

Discusión en grupos

1. ¿Es posible regatear en la región donde ustedes viven?
2. ¿Qué estrategias conocen ustedes para pedir rebajas?

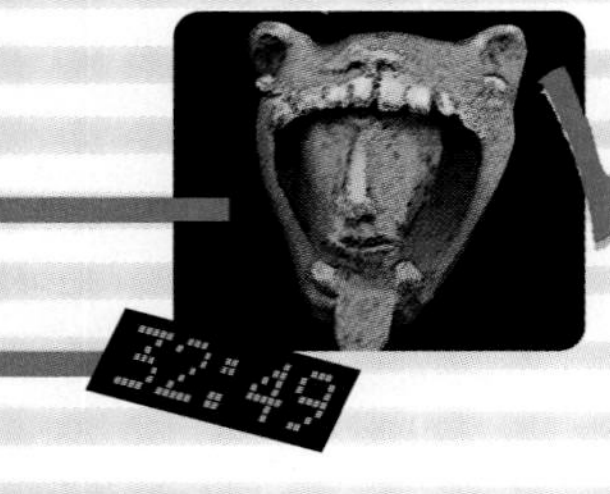

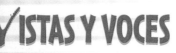

Vistas y voces

I. Preparémonos

1 Anticipación. Con un/a compañero/a, contesta las siguientes preguntas.

A. **1.** ¿Qué prefieres en los tejidos: muchas formas diferentes, colores muy fuertes, diseños geométricos, personas, animales, escenas de la naturaleza?
2. ¿Cuál es tu hora preferida del día? ¿y tu libro favorito? ¿Por qué?
3. ¿Tuviste buena o mala suerte el año pasado? Da un ejemplo.
4. Describe los tejidos típicos de tu región. ¿Dónde los venden? ¿Tienes uno?

B. Mira la foto 8B en la página 315. ¿Qué hay en la bolsa que Zulaya le da a Gafasnegras? Explica el posible plan secreto de Zulaya.

Answers to Actividad 4:
1. Están en Otavalo en la calle del mercado. Están contentos.
2. Adriana se siente mejor. Doña Remedios le dio un té para curarla.
3. Están mirando un tejido. Tiene un amanecer grande, casas, el cielo, la tierra, unas nubes, unas piedras.
4. La tienda es de Zulaya. Ella lleva una blusa blanca de Otavalo con un bordado de diferentes colores, una falda negra. Adriana quiere ver el tejido del amanecer.

Para comprender mejor

a través de	*through*	la oveja	*sheep*
asegurar	*to assure*	la pieza	*piece*
de ninguna manera	*in no way*	principal	*main*
desempeñar un papel	*to play a role*	la puerta de atrás	*back door*
		reír	*to laugh*
¡Diablos!	*Darn!*	el siglo	*century*
¡Dios mío!	*My Goodness!*	vigilar	*to watch*
la magia	*magic*	¡Ya lo verán!	*You/They'll see!*
el/la mensajero/a	*messenger*		

2 Secuencia. En parejas, háganse preguntas sobre lo que sucede en cada escena de video. Después, organicen las escenas en un orden lógico.

1.

2.

3.

4.

Correct order of video action shots: 3, 4, 2, 1

II. Miremos y escuchemos

3 Mis observaciones. Mientras miras el episodio, escribe tus observaciones sobre Adriana. ¿Qué objetos o cosas le afectan más en este episodio y le hacen reflexionar sobre los jaguares? ¿Con quién está cuando ve estas cosas y cómo actúa? ¿Qué revelan sus acciones y reacciones sobre su personalidad?

III. Comentemos

4 Comprensión. En grupos, contesten las siguientes preguntas.

1. ¿Dónde están Felipe y Adriana? ¿Cómo están?
2. ¿Cómo se siente Adriana? ¿Qué le dio doña Remedios para curarla?
3. ¿Qué están mirando Adriana y Felipe? Descríbelo.
4. ¿De quién es la tienda? ¿Qué ropa lleva esta persona? ¿Qué dice Adriana que quiere ver?
5. ¿Qué libro ve Adriana en la tienda? ¿Es una coincidencia? ¿Qué le fascina a Zulaya?
6. ¿Cómo termina el libro y cuál es la fecha importante para reunir a los dos gemelos en México? ¿Por qué?
7. Cuando Adriana le da a Zulaya la información confidencial sobre Yax-Balam, ¿dónde pone Zulaya la mano?
8. ¿Qué les da Zulaya a Adriana y Felipe?
9. ¿Por cuál puerta salen Adriana y Felipe? ¿Por qué?
10. ¿Ve Gafasnegras a Adriana y Felipe?¿Qué le da Zulaya a doña Gafasnegras? ¿Qué esconde Zulaya?
11. ¿Qué tipo de animales pasan por el camino? ¿Por qué están corriendo Adriana y Felipe? ¿Qué hay dentro del paquete que tiene Adriana?
12. ¿De qué está segura Adriana? ¿Qué siente Adriana al tocar el jaguar? ¿Les trae buena o mala suerte Yax-Balam?¿Qué hacen los dos jóvenes con Yax-Balam? ¿Se ríe mucho o poco Adriana?
13. ¿Qué encuentra doña Gafasnegras en su paquete? ¿Dónde está ella? ¿Qué dice ella sobre la suerte en ese momento?

5 El plan secreto de Zulaya. Resume el plan secreto de Zulaya para devolver a Yax-Balam a México. ¿Con quién habla Zulaya? ¿Qué hace con el jaguar para protegerlo? ¿Qué características personales tiene ella? ¿Qué piensas tú de ella?

6 Miremos otra vez. Después de mirar el episodio otra vez, arregla las escenas de video en la secuencia correcta.

7 Mi análisis. ¿A qué se refiere Gafasnegras al final del episodio cuando dice "El que ríe de último, ¡ríe mejor!" ¿Crees que tiene razón? Explica tus ideas. Habla con un/a compañero/a.

8 Puedo sentir la magia. En este episodio, Adriana siente la magia del jaguar. ¿Qué objeto, libro, tejido o cosa que tú conozcas te da la sensación de magia? ¿Qué es? ¿Cómo es? Por ejemplo, algo de una persona muy especial, de un lugar romántico, de tu familia, de un/a amigo/a, de un viaje inolvidable, una foto especial. Conversa en parejas.

5. Ve el libro de Nayeli sobre Yax-Balam y Hun-Ahau. Sí, es una coincidencia. A Zulaya le fascinan los objetos de arte precolombino y el misterio de las piezas perdidas.
6. Los gemelos siguen separados. El treinta y uno de agosto es la muerte de Pacal y los gemelos Yax-Balam y Hun-Ahau tienen que acompañar a Pacal a Xibalbá.
7. Zulaya pone la mano sobre una bolsa.
8. Zulaya les da una bolsa a Adriana y a Felipe.
9. Salen por la puerta de atrás porque Gafasnegras llega a la tienda.
10. Gafasnegras no ve a Adriana y Felipe. Zulaya le da una bolsa a doña Gafasnegras. Parece idéntica a la que ella le dio a Felipe y Adriana. Zulaya esconde el libro de Nayeli.
11. Son ovejas. Están corriendo para escaparse de Gafasnegras. Adriana tiene el jaguar auténtico, Yax-Balam está en la bolsa.
12. Adriana está segura de que es el jaguar auténtico. Adriana siente la magia de los siglos en sus manos. Cree que Yax-Balam les trae buena suerte. Los dos jóvenes tienen a Yax-Balam entre sus dos manos. Se ríe mucho.
13. Gafasnegras encuentra una piedra en su paquete. Ella dice que la suerte le volvió la espalda otra vez. (= tiene mala suerte)

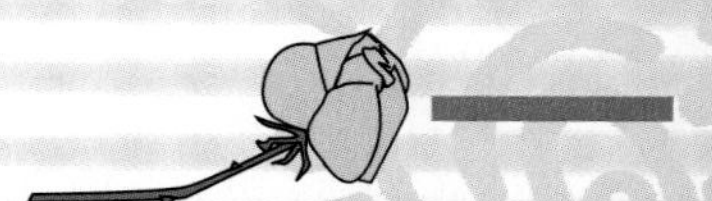

Lengua

I. Talking about the unknown

The subjunctive with adjective clauses

Memorando

Para: Doña Rosario Domínguez
De: Elsa Samaranch
Fecha: 30 de septiembre

El propósito de este memorando es darle una lista de lo que necesito en mi nueva oficina.

1. Necesito una computadora que **pueda** conectarse con la red Internet a alta velocidad. La que tengo actualmente es demasiado lenta.
2. Como usted sabe, es necesario seguir buscando un buen secretario o secretaria para mi departamento. Debe ser una persona que **sepa** manejar muy bien las redes y las bases de datos.
3. Necesito una nueva enciclopedia electrónica que **tenga** todos los datos sobre nuestros mercados en España y América Latina.
4. Es muy importante modernizar nuestra impresora. Vamos a buscar una máquina que **sea** mucho más rápida que la que tenemos.

Le ruego que se comunique conmigo cuando tome usted su decisión sobre lo que necesito. Gracias.

Look at all of the phrases above that use the subjunctive. How do these verb phrases differ from the ones that have been previously presented? What do they have in common?

- In Spanish, when expressing something in the subordinate clause that refers to an indefinite, non-existent, or unknown person or thing, the subjunctive mood is used.

Quiero una dieta que **incluya** los cuatro grupos de alimentos.	*I am looking for a diet that includes the four food groups.*
Necesitamos un secretario que **sepa** inglés y español.	*We need a secretary who knows both English and Spanish.*
No hay nadie que **tenga** el cuerpo perfecto.	*There is not anyone who has a perfect body.*

- When expressing something in the subordinate clause that refers to a definite or existent person or thing, the indicative mood is used.

Yo sigo la dieta *Buena Salud*, que me gusta mucho.	*I'm following the* Good Health *diet, which I like a lot.*
Mi esposo busca el nuevo teléfono celular de AT&T que tiene su sobrina.	*My husband is looking for the new AT&T cell phone that his niece has.*
Necesito al cardiólogo Rivas que atiende pacientes a domicilio.	*I need cardiologist Rivas who makes home visits.*

For further clarification of this point, take the subjunctive sentences of the previous section and make them definite: **Quiero *la* dieta que *incluye;* Necesitamos *el* secretario que *sabe; Hay alguien* que *tiene...***

1 Estoy buscando apartamento. Completa las siguientes ideas sobre el apartamento que estás buscando.

1. Busco un apartamento que __________ (ser) grande.
2. Necesito una cocina en la que yo __________ (poder) atender a mis invitados.
3. Necesito un balcón que __________ (tener) espacio para poner mis plantas.
4. Busco un condominio donde __________ (poder) tener mis gatos.
5. En el comedor, necesito una lámpara que __________ (dar) mucha luz.
6. Quiero que el cuarto de baño __________ (estar) cerca de mi alcoba.
7. Quiero que la cocina __________ (tener) horno microondas.

Answers to Actividad 1:
1. sea
2. pueda
3. tenga
4. pueda
5. dé
6. esté
7. tenga

2 ¿Qué necesita usted? ¿Cómo quieres que sean estas personas y cosas? Usa el subjuntivo y sigue el modelo. Usa verbos como **quiero, necesito, busco.**

▸ **Modelo:** *un médico*
Busco un médico que cure las alergias.

1. un profesor
2. un dentista
3. un restaurante
4. una computadora
5. una médica
6. una película
7. un banco
8. un presidente
9. un coche

3 Un sueño posible. Acabas de ganarte la lotería y tienes muchísimo dinero. ¿Qué quieres de la vida? Escribe un párrafo sobre tus preferencias y tus sueños. Compara tu texto con el de un/a compañero/a.

II. Talking about persons and things

Selected uses of the definite article

Look at the uses of the definite article in the postcard. When is it used? When is it omitted?

El volcán Chimborazo en las montañas de los Andes en Ecuador.

Queridísimo Teo:

*Ya estoy en **el** Ecuador. **Las** montañas son magníficas y **los** nevados son hermosos. Sigo **la** misma rutina todos los días: A **las** seis de **la** mañana me levanto, me lavo **el** pelo con champú de hierbas naturales, me pongo **el** suéter de lana, desayuno y voy **al** trabajo. Estoy muy contenta trabajando con **el** doctor Curihual, **el** famoso arqueólogo. ¡Uso **el** español todos los días!*

Te quiero con todo el corazón

Abrazos[1] y besitos[2] de tu novia,

Carolina

[1]hugs; [2]kisses

Uses of the definite article

- With parts of the body

Me torcí **el** tobillo.	*I sprained my ankle.*
Me lavo **el** pelo con champú de hierbas naturales.	*I wash my hair with herbal shampoo.*

- With clothing and other personal articles

Review reflexives from Chapter 6. *Bathing suits* is singular in Spanish because each person wears only one suit.

Elena se puso **el** reloj de plata y perlas.	*Elena put on her silver and pearl watch.*
Las muchachas se pusieron **el** traje de baño.	*The girls put on their bathing suits.*

- Before abstract nouns and nouns used in a general sense

El dinero es esencial en **la** vida.	*Money is essential in life.*
No me gusta **el** café.	*I do not like coffee.*

- With the time of day, days of the week, and to indicate *on*

Son **las** nueve de la noche.	*It's nine p.m.*
Los Burgos salen **el** domingo.	*The Burgos are leaving on Sunday.*

- When referring to or talking about people who have titles, except for **don/doña***

La doctora Orozco es de Texas.	*Doctor Orozco is from Texas.*
Doña Delia Domínguez es encantadora.	*Doña Delia Domínguez is charming.*
El presidente tiene muchas responsabilidades.	*The President has many responsibilities.*

- With the names of languages, except when they follow **de**, **en**, or forms of **hablar, practicar, estudiar, aprender,** and **entender**

Para el año 2050, **el** español va a ser la lengua extranjera más hablada de los Estados Unidos.	*By the year 2050, Spanish will be the most widely spoken world language in the United States.*
¿Sabes hablar español?	*Do you know how to speak Spanish?*
Solamente sé contar en español.	*I know only how to count in Spanish.*

- With certain countries or states**

la Argentina	**la** India
el Brasil	**el** Japón
el Canadá	**el** Paraguay
el Ecuador	**el** Perú
los Estados Unidos	**la** República Dominicana
la Florida	**el** Uruguay

* *Notice that you do not use a definite article when addressing someone directly:* **Doctor Orozco, ¿de dónde es usted?**

** *Note that the use of the article varies with many of these countries.*

4 *Las rutinas.* Escribe la forma correcta del artículo, si es necesario.

1. ¿Qué champú usas cuando te lavas __________ pelo? ¿Y qué jabón usas cuando te lavas__________ cara?
2. En el accidente, ¿te rompiste __________ brazo izquierdo o __________ rodilla derecha?
3. __________ japonés es una lengua muy bonita; también me encanta __________ español.
4. __________ amor y __________ verdad son cosas importantes en la vida. __________ dinero es menos importante.
5. Sandra se probó __________ camiseta nueva y __________ pantalones de lana.
6. __________ profesor Márquez enseña mejor que __________ profesora Benítez.
7. Debes lavarte __________ dientes después de cada comida.
8. Fuimos al cine __________ viernes a __________ diez de la noche.
9. Yo no bebo __________ cerveza; me gustan más __________ vino blanco chileno y __________ ron (*rum*) puertorriqueño.
10. __________ amistad es un elemento necesario en la vida.

Answers to Actividad 4:
1. el / la
2. el / la
3. El / el
4. El / la / El
5. la / los
6. El / la
7. los
8. el / las
9. — / el / el
10. La

5 *Composición.* Escribe un párrafo sobre tus preferencias personales en joyas, ropa y diversiones. Presta atención especial al uso de los artículos. Después, pregunta a un/a compañero/a cuáles son sus preferencias personales.

III. Describing actions

Infinitives used with prepositions

En el banco

TONI: **Antes de** depositar dinero, siempre averiguo mi saldo (*balance*). Si tengo dinero suficiente en mi cuenta corriente, entonces deposito el dinero en la cuenta de ahorros.

BETO: Pues yo también, pero **en vez de** ir personalmente al banco, siempre hago los depósitos electrónicamente. Todos los jueves, **al** recibir mi cheque, voy al cajero automático *(ATM machine)* o uso mi computadora **para** hacer los depósitos.

TONI: Yo casi siempre voy personalmente al banco **para** depositar mi dinero y **al salir** del banco, reviso muy bien todos los recibos.

BETO: Claro, eso es muy importante. Yo siempre reviso mis papeles **antes de** hacer los depósitos y **después de** hacerlos.

Beto **Toni**

Look at the examples above and identify when infinitives are used in these sentences. What kind of word do they generally follow? Where do pronouns go when an infinitive is used?

- Where English uses preposition + present participle to express the idea of doing something *(before running/after eating/instead of flying)*, Spanish utilizes preposition + infinitive (**antes de correr/después de comer/en vez de volar).**
- **Al** + infinitive means *upon* or *on* or *when* + verb.

Al llegar, cené con la familia.	*Upon arriving, I ate supper with the family.* *When I arrived, I ate supper with the family.*
Al salir de clase por la mañana, siempre vamos a almorzar en la cafetería.	*After leaving my classes in the morning, we always have lunch in the cafeteria.*

- Review the prepositions on page 157 before doing the following activities.

6 ¿Antes o después? Trabaja con un/a compañero/a y contesta las preguntas con **antes** o **después.** Sigue el modelo.

▸ **Modelo:** —*¿Cuándo empezaste tu dieta? (después de...)*
—*Empecé mi dieta después de comerme mi última galleta de chocolate.*

1. ¿Cuándo miraste la televisión ayer? (antes...)
2. ¿Cuándo fuiste de compras a las tiendas de ropa la semana pasada? (después de...)
3. ¿Cuándo prefieres estudiar? (antes de...)
4. ¿Cuándo vas al banco? (después de...)
5. ¿Cuándo tomaste cerveza el sábado? (antes de...)
6. ¿Cuándo escribiste el correo electrónico anoche? (después de...)
7. ¿Cuándo asistes a tus clases de español? (antes de...)
8. ¿Cuándo comes en tu restaurante favorito? (después de...)
9. ¿Cuándo tomaste las vacaciones el año pasado? (antes de...)

Answers to Actividad 7:
1. a. antes de / después de / en vez de
1. b. antes de / después de / en vez de
1. c. antes de / después de / en vez de
2. a. antes de / después de / en vez de
2. b. antes de / después de / hasta / en vez de
2. c. al, antes de / después de
3. a. antes de / en vez de
3. b. después de
3. c. antes de / en vez de
4. a. en vez de
4. b. antes de / después de / en vez de
4. c. antes de / después de
5. a. antes de / después de / en vez de
5. b. antes de / después de / en vez de
5. c. al / después de

7 Mis preferencias. Completa las frases con las preposiciones apropiadas (*appropriate*). Después, trabaja con un/a compañero/a, contestando cuáles son las preferencias de cada uno/a.

al   antes de   después de   hasta   en vez de

1. Prefiero comer...
   a. __________ bailar en la discoteca.
   b. __________ dormir.
   c. __________ ir al cine.
2. Ayer tenía ganas de jugar al volibol...
   a. __________ estudiar para mi examen.
   b. __________ cenar.
   c. __________ terminar las clases.
3. El año pasado pasé el segundo semestre viajando por el Ecuador...
   a. __________ decidir en qué quería especializarme.
   b. __________ estudiar el primer semestre en los Estados Unidos.
   c. __________ quedarme aquí en los Estados Unidos.
4. Cuando yo era joven, me gustaba ir a la playa en el verano...
   a. __________ sufrir el calor de la ciudad todo el verano.
   b. __________ viajar con mi familia.
   c. __________ pasar el resto de las vacaciones en un campamento de verano.

5. Mañana voy al cine con mi novio/a...
   a. __________ escribir mi trabajo para la clase de antropología.
   b. __________ hacer mi experimento de laboratorio para el curso de química.
   c. __________ terminar de jugar al tenis con el equipo universitario.

8 Planes y preferencias. Utilizando las preposiciones (**antes de, después de, en vez de, hasta, al**) con diferentes infinitivos, escribe una lista de diez actividades académicas, sociales y personales. Compara tu lista con la de un/a compañero/a.

Lectura B

Introducción

With the exception of Paraguay and Uruguay, all South American countries are Andean countries, but to different degrees. As you have learned, Bolivia, Ecuador, and Peru have large Andean regions. Colombia's Andes are located only in its western territory, while one branch of the Andes enters Venezuela on its border with Colombia. In this chapter, you will read about Argentina, Chile, Paraguay, and Uruguay. These four countries are usually called the **Cono Sur**, the Southern Cone, because of their location.

Prelectura

1 Más o menos que. Forma comparaciones con la información de las siguientes oraciones. Sigue el modelo.

Before doing **Actividad 1**, review comparisons, Chapter 7.

▸ **Modelo:** *La cordillera de los Andes tiene 7.242 metros de longitud y la cordillera del Himalaya tiene 2.500 metros de longitud.*
La cordillera de los Andes es más larga que la cordillera del Himalaya. or
La cordillera del Himalaya es menos larga que la cordillera de los Andes. or
La cordillera del Himalaya no es tan larga como la cordillera de los Andes.

1. Las Montañas Rocosas miden 6.400 metros de longitud y la cordillera de los Andes mide 7.242 metros.
2. El volcán Popocatepetl de México es muy activo. El volcán Cotopaxi del Ecuador no es muy activo.
3. América del Norte tiene 23.477.00 km^2 de superficie. América del Sur tiene 30.271.000 km^2.

2 Tanto como. Crea comparaciones basándote en los datos que se describen a continuación.

▸ **Modelo:** *En América del Sur y América del Norte hay grandes cordilleras.*
Tanto en América del Sur como en América del Norte hay grandes cordilleras.

1. En América del Norte hay volcanes y en América Central también.
2. Colombia y Venezuela tienen costas en el Mar Caribe.
3. En Chile y Argentina hay montañas altísimas.
4. En Uruguay y Paraguay hay estaciones de invierno y de verano.
5. Buenos Aires y Bogotá son ciudades muy grandes.
6. Chile y Argentina están en el Cono Sur.

Answers to Actividad 2:
1. Tanto en América del Norte como en América Central hay volcanes.
2. Tanto Colombia como Venezuela tienen costas en el Mar Caribe.
3. Tanto en Chile como en Argentina hay montañas altísimas.
4. Tanto en Uruguay como en Paraguay hay estaciones de invierno y de verano.
5. Tanto Buenos Aires como Bogotá son muy grandes.
6. Tanto Chile como Argentina están en el Cono Sur.

Los países del Cono Sur

La Avenida 9 de Julio de Buenos Aires, Argentina.

Argentina La Argentina tiene 35 millones de habitantes. Casi 8 millones viven en Buenos Aires, la capital, que está situada en la cuenca° del gran Río de la Plata. El Aconcagua es la montaña más alta del hemisferio (6.959 m.) y en sus valles se cultivan uvas° y se fabrica vino de gran calidad. En las llanuras de las Pampas se cultivan cereales y se cría ganado° para la exportación de carne de excelente calidad. El **churrasco**° argentino es conocido en todo el mundo. La meseta° de la Patagonia, de clima seco y ventoso,° desciende hacia la costa, donde hay importantes reservas de petróleo. Argentina comparte con Bolivia y Paraguay la región subtropical del Chaco. Con Chile comparte la Isla Grande, en la Tierra del Fuego. Argentina considera propias las Islas Malvinas.° El idioma oficial del país es el español, pero también se hablan el arauaco, el guaraní y el quechua.

basin
grapes
cattle
Argentinean barbecue
plain
windy
Falkland Islands

Chile La República de Chile tiene 14 millones de habitantes; 5 millones viven en su capital, Santiago. El país es una estrecha faja° de tierra en el suroeste de América del Sur, entre el Océano Pacífico y los Andes, donde las montañas llegan a más de 6 mil metros de altura. Al norte está el Atacama, uno de los desiertos más secos del mundo. El país tiene muchas islas, entre ellas, la extraordinaria isla de Pascua, donde se encuentran enormes cabezas de piedra. Chile produce gran cantidad de pescado, frutas y vinos; es un importante exportador de cobre,° y tiene extensas reservas de petróleo y salitre.° Puerto Montt en Chile y Mendoza en Argentina son dos importantes sitios para deportes de invierno. El español es el idioma oficial del país y se hablan también mapuche, quechua y aimará.

Santiago, la ciudad capital de Chile.

narrow strip
copper
salt residue

Paraguay En Paraguay hay 5 millones de habitantes. De ellos, más de un millón viven en el área metropolitana de la capital, Asunción; y el resto de la población vive en los fértiles valles del Oriente. El país no es montañoso ni tiene costas, pero sus ríos Paraná y Paraguay le dan salida al mar. Al occidente está la fértil llanura° del Chaco que comparte con Argentina. Los lagos paraguayos son famosos por su belleza, en especial el lago Ypacaraí, un gran atractivo turístico. Paraguay es el mayor exportador de energía eléctrica° en América Latina y posee la central hidroeléctrica más potente del mundo en la represa° de Itaipú. Es también un gran productor de soya y de algodón. Sus productos de cuero° son de excelente calidad. El español y el guaraní son sus idiomas oficiales.

Plaza de los Héroes, Asunción, Paraguay.

plain

electrical energy

dam

leather

Uruguay En la República del Uruguay viven más de 3 millones de personas y casi la mitad de ellas residen en Montevideo, la capital. Uruguay es un país pequeño y sólo Surinam es menor que él. No hay montañas, solamente existen las **cuchillas**, que son ondulaciones° entre 200 y 500 metros de altura. Su clima es templado y sus playas tienen un gran atractivo turístico durante el verano, en especial el balneario° de Punta del Este. El estuario° del Río de la Plata y el litoral° atlántico son las zonas geográficas más importantes del país. Uruguay es un país casi solamente de emigrantes; la hermosa ciudad de Colonia Sacramento, representa la herencia arquitectónica de origen español y portugués. El país produce textiles de alta calidad, lanas, cueros y cereales. El idioma oficial del país es el español.

rolling hills

resort, spa

estuary / coast

La plaza de la Independencia en Montevideo, Uruguay.

Postlectura

Answers to Actividad 3:
1. F Están en Uruguay.
2. V
3. F La Argentina tiene más habitantes.
4. F Le da salida a Paraguay.
5. V
6. V
7. F Uruguay es más pequeño.
8. F Está en la Argentina.
9. V

3 ¿Verdadero o falso? Trabaja en grupos. Las siguientes oraciones describen algo sobre un país. Señala cuáles oraciones son verdaderas y cuáles son falsas. Explica la razón.

1. En la Patagonia hay hermosas playas turísticas.
2. El Paraguay no tiene problemas de energía eléctrica.
3. La Argentina tiene tantos habitantes como Chile.
4. El río Paraná le da salida al mar a Uruguay.
5. El quechua se habla tanto en Argentina como en Chile.
6. Argentina y Paraguay comparten la región del Chaco.
7. El Uruguay es un país tan grande como Chile.
8. La montaña más alta de Suramérica está en Venezuela.
9. En Puerto Montt se puede esquiar en julio y agosto.

Answers to Actividad 4:
1. Buenos Aires: 8 millones de personas
   Santiago: 5 millones
   Asunción:1 millón
   Montevideo: 3 millones
2. Paraguay
3. Chaco: subtropical y fértil
   Pampas: más seco; cultivan cereales y tienen ganado
4. El Aconcagua
5. Buenos Aires
6. español y guaraní
7. Es uno de los desiertos más secos del mundo. Está en el norte de Chile.
8. a la Argentina
9. *The Falklands,* por su historia con Gran Bretaña

4 Geografía del Cono Sur. Trabaja en grupos y contesta las siguientes preguntas sobre la lectura.

1. Da una característica de cada una de las capitales de los cuatro países mencionados.
2. ¿Dónde está el Lago Ypacaraí?
3. Compara el clima de las regiones del Chaco y de las Pampas.
4. ¿Cuál es la cumbre más alta del hemisferio?
5. ¿Cuál es la capital más grande del Cono Sur?
6. ¿Cuáles son los idiomas oficiales de Paraguay?
7. ¿Qué es el Atacama? ¿Dónde está?
8. Según la Argentina, ¿a qué país pertenecen las islas Malvinas?
9. ¿Sabes qué otro nombre tienen las Islas Malvinas? ¿Por qué?

Answers to Actividad 5:
Argentina: Buenos Aires; español; Aconcagua, Pampas, el Chaco, las Malvinas; 35 millones; vino, ganado, petróleo
Chile: Santiago; español; Los Andes, el Atacama, Isla de Pascua, Puerto Montt; 14 millones; pescado, frutas, vino, cobre, petróleo, salitre
Paraguay: Asunción; español y guaraní; el Oriente, ríos Paraná y Paraguay, llanura del Chaco, Lago Ypacaraí, la represa de Itaipú; 5 millones; energía eléctrica, soya, algodón, cuero
Uruguay: Montevideo; español; las cuchillas, el balneario de Punta del Este, el litoral atlántico; 3 millones; textiles, lanas, cueros, cereales

5 Comparemos. Llena la tabla con datos importantes sobre los países del Cono Sur.

	Argentina	Chile	Paraguay	Uruguay
Capital				
Lengua oficial				
Montañas, valles, etc.				
Población				
Productos importantes				

6 De dos en dos. Trabajen en grupos. Basándose en la tabla de la **Actividad 5**, cada grupo elige dos países para comparar y presenta la comparación a la clase.

7 ¿Quién sabe más? Trabajen en grupos. Cada grupo escribe cuatro oraciones falsas o verdaderas sobre los países estudiados. Intercambien las oraciones con otro grupo. Cada grupo tiene un minuto para contestar si la oración es verdadera o es falsa y por qué.

8 Mis regiones favoritas. Trabaja en grupos de dos o tres personas. Cada grupo compara dos regiones de los Estados Unidos y le presenta la comparación a la clase.

En resumen

I. Hablemos

1 Una dieta sana. En parejas, hagan el papel de nutricionista y paciente. Primero, el/la paciente le presenta al/a la nutricionista la dieta que sigue actualmente. Después, el/la nutricionista compone una dieta balanceada para el/la paciente.

2 Medicina tradicional y moderna. En parejas, hagan el papel de un/a médico/a moderno/a y la curandera del video. Discutan el mejor tratamiento para curar a Adriana de una gripe muy fuerte con fiebre y tos.

II. Investiguemos por Internet

Formulating a query

The information available on the Internet is vast, and many times the results of your search may be too broad. In these cases, you need to enhance your search in order to reduce the number of search results and to be able to find the information that is relevant for your purposes. Refer to your browser's instructions to formulate your query. It is important to be specific and to include as many keywords in your query as possible. Your browser may require that you write these keywords using a "+" sign before or after the specific word or words you are looking for, or that you connect them with "AND." For example "**+ chocolate + historia**" or "**chocolate** AND **historia.**" You can also refine your search by excluding words that you don't want in your search, for example "**+ chocolate – historia + productos.**" If you need help, you can find it on the Houghton Mifflin Web site.

Vocabulario informático			
la consulta	*query*	formular una consulta / una búsqueda	*to formulate a query*

3 Té, chocolate, café y mate. Work in groups. Each group selects one of these four beverages. Your objective is to find (a) five facts about the history of the product, and (b) the name of a dish or a popular beverage based on the product and its ingredients. All groups will present their results to the class. Using only the name of the beverage will give you too many search results. Make your search more specific by adding to it one of the following keywords: **historia, productos, exportación, bebida(s).** You may also find other synonyms for tea and herbal teas like **tisana, infusión, agua aromática.** If you decide to do your search starting with the Hispanic countries, remember that many Hispanic countries export coffee (mainly Colombia and Costa Rica). **Cacao** is originally from Mexico, but is also exported by Ecuador and the Dominican Republic. Tea is popular in many countries, mainly in the **Cono Sur** countries, where also **mate** is the most typical beverage.

Expansion for Actividad 3: Another product from Central and South America is bananas. In supermarkets the banana sticker often tells where the fruit comes from (Costa Rica, Honduras, Mexico, Ecuador, and so on). Bring in some banana stickers to class and have students do a word search on the net under keywords **banana, banano, plátano, guineo.** Explain that in some countries **banana** is masculine, and in others, feminine.

III. Escribamos

Writing strategy: Using visual organizers (Venn Diagrams)

One way to visually organize your ideas when comparing or contrasting two or more items is by creating a Venn Diagram. Begin by listing the things that are unique to the items in the outer rings of the circle. Then list the things that the items have in common in the center, where the circles overlap. Below is a sample of a Venn Diagram that has been done to compare shopping centers with Hispanic market places.

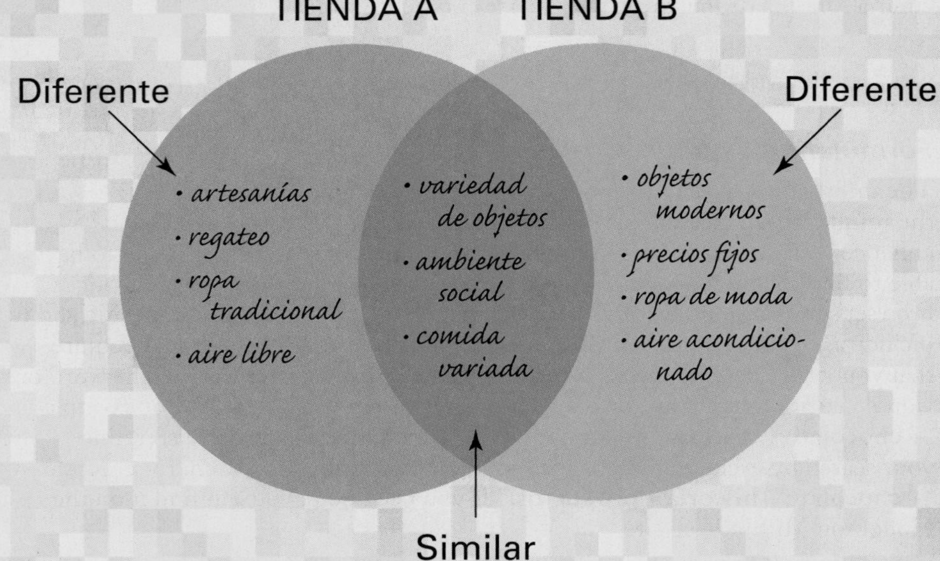

Strategy in action

Turn to *Escribamos* in the Workbook to practice the writing strategy of using visual organizers.

4 **Anuncios.** Compara dos tiendas de tu ciudad usando un diagrama de Venn. Después, escribe, para cada tienda, un anuncio comercial que refleje sus productos o servicios.

5 **Personajes.** Haz una comparación entre Zulaya y doña Gafasoscuras usando un diagrama de Venn. Después escribe una composición comparando a las dos personas.

Nutrición

activo/a	*active*
al horno	*baked*
el alimento	*food*
el antídoto	*antidote*
el arroz	*rice*
la caloría	*calorie*
la cantidad	*quantity*
el cereal	*cereal*
el cerebro	*brain*
cocido/a	*cooked*
conservarse	*to maintain oneself*
consumir	*to consume*
el corazón	*heart*
la crema de cacahuate	*peanut butter*
diariamente	*daily*
la dieta	*diet*
los dulces	*sweets*
el ejercicio	*exercise*
embarazada	*pregnant*
el estrés	*stress*
físico/a	*physical*
los frijoles	*beans*
la grasa	*fat*
mantenerse en forma	*to stay in shape*
nutritivo/a	*nutritious*
la pasta	*pasta*
la pechuga	*breast (of an animal)*
la pirámide de la alimentación	*food pyramid*
el plátano/banano	*banana*
la porción	*portion*
la rebanada	*slice*
la relajación	*relaxation*
relajado/a	*relaxed*
el repollo	*cabbage*
sano/a	*healthy*
sedentario/a	*sedentary*
la tensión nerviosa	*nervous tension*
los vegetales	*vegetables*
el yogur	*yogurt*

Salud

(See p. 319.)

Expresiones de emoción

alegrarse	*to be happy*
enojarse	*to be angry*
es bueno	*it's good*
es extraño	*it's strange*
es malo	*it's bad*
es mejor	*it's better*
es peor	*it's worse*
es ridículo	*it's ridiculous*
es terrible	*it's terrible*
es una lástima	*it's a shame*
esperar	*to hope*
estar contento/a de	*to be happy*
lamentar	*to lament, regret, be sorry*
molestar	*to bother*
sentir (ie)	*to be sorry, lament, regret*
sorprender	*to surprise*
temer	*to fear, be afraid of*
tener miedo de	*to be afraid of*

Expresiones de duda

dudar	*to doubt*
es dudoso	*it's doubtful*
es imposible	*it's impossible*
negar (ie)	*to deny*
no creer	*not to believe*
no es cierto	*it's not certain, true*
no es verdad	*it's not true*
no estar seguro	*to be unsure*
no pensar (ie)	*not to think*
quizás	*maybe, perhaps*
tal vez	*maybe, perhaps*

Expresiones de certidumbre (certainty)

creer	*to think*
es cierto	*it's certain, true*
es evidente	*it's evident*
es verdad	*it's true*
no negar (ie)	*not to deny*
opinar	*to think, have an opinion*
pensar (ie)	*to think*

Dinero

ahorrar	*to save*
el billete	*bill*
la caja	*cashier*
la caja fuerte	*safe*
el/la cajero/a	*cashier*
cambiar	*to exchange*
el cambio	*exchange, change*
el cheque certificado	*certified check*
los cheques de viajero	*travelers' checks*
cobrar	*to charge*
la comisión	*commission*
la cuenta corriente	*checking account*
la cuenta de ahorros	*savings account*
depositar (dinero)	*to deposit (money)*
endosar	*to endorse*
enviar	*to send*
la firma	*signature*
firmar	*to sign*
el gasto	*expense*
el giro postal	*money order*
la moneda en efectivo	*cash*
pedir prestado	*to borrow*
por correo	*by mail*
el préstamo	*loan*
prestar	*to lend*
el presupuesto	*budget*
el promedio	*average*
revisar	*to check, examine*
sacar (retirar) dinero	*to withdraw money*
la tasa de cambio	*rate of exchange*
¿Cuánto vale? (¿Cuánto cuesta?)	*How much does it cost?*

En el mercado

el anillo	*ring*
los aretes	*earrings*
las artesanías	*folk art*
la cadena	*chain*
el cobre	*copper*
el collar	*necklace*
el diamante	*diamond*
la esmeralda	*emerald*
la/s joya/s de fantasía	*costume jewelery*
las joyas	*jewelry*
el oro	*gold*
el pendiente	*pendant, earring*
la perla	*pearl*
la piedra	*stone*
la plata	*silver*
el prendedor	*brooch*
la pulsera	*bracelet*
el quilate	*karat*
regatear	*to bargain*
el reloj	*watch*
el tapete	*rug, small carpet, tapestry*
el tapiz	*tapestry*
la turquesa	*turquoise*

CAPÍTULO 9

LOCALIDAD: Costa Rica

9A

¿Tiene Armando la solución?

9B

Nayeli, Felipe, and Adriana are reunited at doña Carmen's ranch in Costa Rica when suddenly an ominous surprise interrupts their happiness.

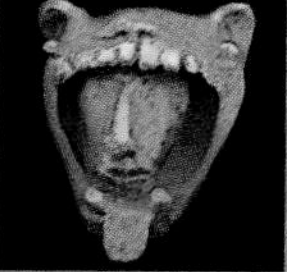

Vocabulary themes

- Talking about household chores and furnishings
- Talking about the kitchen and cooking
- Talking about animals and plants
- Discussing environmental issues

Language structures

- Expressing impending actions
- Substituting for persons, places, and things
- Making requests and giving orders
- Talking about the past
- Expressing feelings about the past
- Expressing resultant conditions

Culture topics

- La hamaca
- Utensilios tradicionales
- El maíz, una planta multifacética
- Los parques nacionales

Readings

- Así cualquiera cocina
- Un apartamento al estilo Shakira
- Árboles con historia—El último dragón

Reading and writing strategies

- Identifying descriptions of existing and non-existing objects and persons
- Creating a point of view

Internet strategy

- Searching for images

ETAPA A

Pistas y palabras

TV can be either **televisor** or **televisión.**
Review room vocabulary from Chapters 1 and 2.

I. Talking about household chores and furnishings

Los muebles y quehaceres de la casa

a. El hijo aspira la alfombra.
b. La hija sacude los muebles.
c. El padre hace la cama.
d. La madre barre el piso.
e. La niña saca la basura.
f. La abuela lava los platos.

Palabras y expresiones útiles

la lavadora	*washing machine*	los quehaceres	*chores*
la plancha	*iron*	la secadora	*clothes dryer*
cocinar	*to cook*	planchar la ropa	*to iron clothes*
lavar la ropa	*to wash clothes*	secar la ropa	*to dry clothes*
ordenar el cuarto	*to clean the room*		

1 **¿Recuerdas?** ¿Cómo se llaman los cuartos de la casa? ¿Cómo se llaman los otros muebles del dibujo? Con una pareja repasen el vocabulario de los cuartos y muebles.

For **Actividad 1,** bring in doll-house furniture or pictures from magazines and have the class identify them.

2 **Asociaciones.** ¿Qué mueble u otra parte de la casa asocias con las siguientes acciones o cosas?

1. agua
2. piso
3. libro
4. ropa
5. dormir
6. sentarse
7. ventana
8. descansar

Possible answers to Actividad 2:
1. lavabo, llave, grifo
2. alfombra
3. mesita, escritorio, estantería
4. aparador
5. cama
6. sillón, silla, sofá
7. cortinas
8. sofá, cama

3 **¿Quién hace qué?** Di quién hace los quehaceres en tu casa. Compara la lista con la de una pareja. ¿Cuáles son las responsabilidades del padre? ¿de la madre? ¿de los hijos?

4 **Buscan una casa que...** Trabajas para una compañía de bienes raíces (*real estate*) y tienes que buscarles vivienda a cinco clientes que tienen gustos y necesidades diferentes. Mira la lista de tus clientes y describe el apartamento o casa más apropiado para cada uno. Incluye también los muebles para cada vivienda. Sigue el modelo y recuerda usar el subjuntivo.

▶ **Modelo:** *La profesora de francés necesita una casa que tenga una habitación, una oficina y un baño. Es necesario que la oficina tenga...*

Nombre	Número de personas	Necesidades y gustos
1. La profesora de francés	1	Le gusta leer. No necesita mucho espacio. Tiene muy poco dinero.
2. La familia Suárez	6	Los cuatro hijos son muy activos. La familia necesita mucho espacio. Todos tienen que salir temprano y tienen que bañarse antes de las 7.00 a.m.
3. La familia Burgos	5	Hay dos hijos mayores. A todos les gusta ver televisión y leer. La madre del señor Burgos vive con ellos y le encanta cocinar.
4. Niki y Patricio	2	Niki es escritora y trabaja en casa. A Patricio le gustan los deportes. Es una pareja con mucho dinero.
5. El señor Martín	4	El señor Martín tiene dos perros y un gato. Le gusta trabajar en el jardín y leer antes de dormirse.

5 **Tu casa.** Haz un plano (*diagram*) de tu casa o apartamento. Incluye los cuartos y los muebles que hay en cada uno. Usa las preposiciones de lugar (ver página 157 en capítulo 4) como **encima de, al lado de, enfrente de,** etc.

Look up *hammocks* (**hamacas**) on the WWW.

ENLACE CULTURAL

La hamaca

Se cree que la hamaca tuvo su origen en las regiones del Caribe, donde hay hábiles tejedores° y donde se usan muy pocos muebles en las casas. Actualmente, la hamaca es tan popular que existe en multitud de variedades. Muchas regiones tienen su propio estilo de hamacas, por ejemplo los **chinchorros** del Caribe colombiano y venezolano, los cuales son de macramé o de crochet, con boleros° por los lados.

Las hamacas son excelentes para mecerse,° para dormir en el campo a salvo de° reptiles y otros animales o simplemente para descansar. ¡Pero es muy importante colgar° la hamaca en un sitio seguro!

skilled weavers

folds

to swing
safe from
to hang

Discusión en grupos

1. ¿Creen ustedes que la hamaca es un mueble? Escriban tres razones en pro y tres en contra de llamar mueble a la hamaca.
2. ¿Cuál creen ustedes que es el mejor lugar para colgar (*hang*) una hamaca?
3. En español existe el verbo "hamacarse". ¿Qué hace una persona que "se hamaca"?
4. ¿Por qué creen que es práctico dormir en una hamaca en las selvas tropicales?

La gente descansando en las hamacas, en la Playa del Carmen de México.

II. Talking about the kitchen and cooking

Cosas en la cocina

el congelador
el gabinete, la estantería
la licuadora
el procesador de comidas
la batidora
la tostadora
el mostrador
el microondas (el micro)
el fregadero
la olla
la cafetera
la sartén
la estufa
el/la refrigerador/a
el lavaplatos
el horno
el asador

Palabras y expresiones útiles

Bring in these items in the form of toys, items from your own kitchen, or pictures from magazines.

la cucharada	*tablespoonful*
la cucharadita	*teaspoonful*
el utensilio	*utensil, tool*

añadir (agregar)	*to add*	freír (i)	*to fry*
batir	*to whip, beat*	hervir (ie)	*to boil*
calentar (ie)	*to heat*	hornear	*to bake*
cocinar	*to cook*	mezclar	*to mix*
congelar	*to freeze*	moler (ue)	*to grind*
cortar	*to cut*	picar	*to chop*
enfriar	*to cool*	revolver (ue)	*to turn*

asado/a	*broiled*
caliente	*hot*
frito/a	*fried*

Possible answers to Actividad 6:
1. la tostadora
2. la olla
3. el microondas
4. el lavaplatos
5. la cafetera
6. el gabinete, la estantería
7. la cocina, la estufa, el microondas

6 El lugar perfecto. Identifica dónde se ponen las siguientes cosas.

1. El pan se pone en ________.
2. La sopa de pollo se prepara en ________.
3. La comida se calienta rápidamente en ________.
4. Los platos sucios se ponen en ________.
5. El café se prepara en ________.
6. Los platos se guardan en ________.
7. La comida se cocina en ________.

Before doing **Actividad 7**, review food vocabulary, Chapters 3 and 8. Answers will vary.

7 ¿Para qué se usa? ¿Qué comidas se pueden preparar con los siguientes utensilios?

1. el asador
2. el horno
3. el microondas
4. la batidora
5. el procesador de comida
6. la sartén
7. la olla
8. la licuadora

Possible answers to Actividad 8:
1. huevos, mantequilla, cocinar en una sartén
2. carne picada cocinada en una sartén, con pan, lechuga, salsa de tomate, cebollas
3. lechuga, aceite, vinagre, champiñones, tomates
4. huevos, leche, espinacas, mantequilla, cocinados en una sartén especial
5. pan, jamón, queso, mostaza y mayonesa

8 El gran chef. Tu hermano menor te pregunta cómo preparar las siguientes cosas. Dile qué ingredientes tiene cada comida y cómo se hace.

1. huevos fritos
2. hamburguesas
3. ensalada
4. omelette
5. sandwich de jamón y queso

9 Querida Cristina. Lee la carta que escribió un señor a la revista *Cristina* para pedir consejos. Contéstale la carta al señor y dale tres consejos para resolver su problema.

FOBIA A LA COCINA

Hace tres años que tengo una novia maravillosa. Tenemos planes de casarnos pero tengo miedo de que nuestro matrimonio fracase (*will fail*) porque ella me ha confesado que no le gusta la cocina y que no sabe ni freír un huevo. A mí me encanta comer y estoy acostumbrado a la buena sazón (*tasty cooking*) de mi madre. Yo la amo profundamente y no quiero que por esto nuestra relación termine. ¿Qué puedo hacer?

ENLACE CULTURAL

Utensilios tradicionales

Una olla de barro.

La olla de barro°

En muchos países hispanos, los frijoles, los garbanzos° y las sopas de varios tipos se hacían y se servían tradicionalmente en ollas de barro. Todavía se hace así en muchas partes.

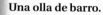

clay pot

chick peas

Bring in any special cooking utensils you may have collected in your travels.

La piedra de moler

La piedra de moler es un mortero grande que se usa para triturar° los alimentos antes de preparar las comidas. Esta piedra existe en muchas versiones en diferentes países de América y se usa para triturar el maíz, las hierbas u otros alimentos. En México existen dos tipos de morteros: el **molcajete** para las hierbas y el **metate** para el maíz.

to grind

Una señora mexicana cocinando en el comal.

El molinillo

Para batir bien el chocolate se usa en muchas partes un palito de madera° con una bolita dentada° en un extremo. En México se llama **molinillo,** en Colombia se llama **bolinillo.**

wooden stick

toothed with sharp points

Preparando el chocolate en Tizimín, en Yucatán, México.

La paila

La paila° puede ser de muchas formas y materiales. La paila mexicana se llama **comal;** es un disco grande y plano, de barro o de metal. La **paellera** española es una paila grande y poco honda,° muy práctica para cocinar y servir la paella.°

large pan

deep

rice with seafood, meat, chicken

Una paella española preparada en Barcelona.

Discusión en grupos

1. ¿Se usan las ollas de barro en la región de ustedes, por ejemplo en la cocina, en el jardín o como adorno?
2. ¿Existe en sus familias o en su región un plato tradicional que requiera utensilios especiales para prepararlo o para servirlo? ¿Cómo es ese utensilio?
3. La barbacoa (*grill*) es muy popular en los Estados Unidos. ¿Qué tipo de utensilios usan ustedes en su región para la barbacoa? ¿Se usa gas o carbón?
4. ¿Qué utensilio de cocina se usa modernamente en vez de la piedra de moler?

The word *barbecue* originally came from the Spanish **barbacoa,** a word adapted from the original inhabitants of the Caribbean.

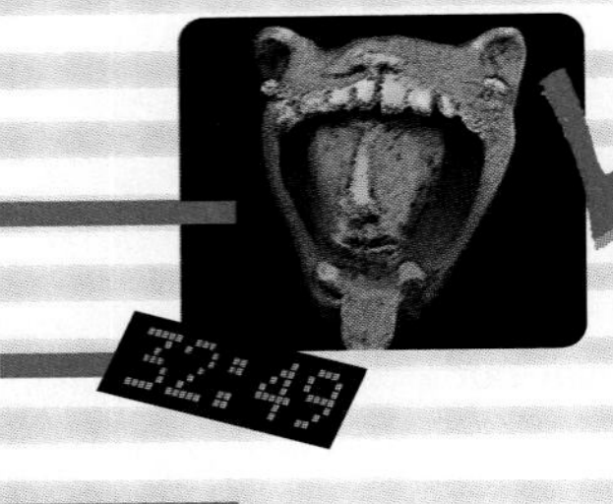

VISTAS Y VOCES

I. Preparémonos

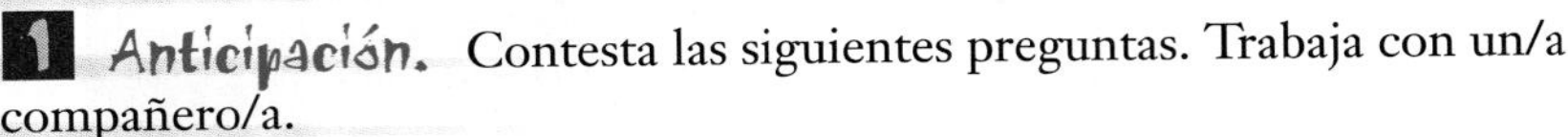

1 Anticipación. Contesta las siguientes preguntas. Trabaja con un/a compañero/a.

A. 1. ¿Tienes padrino, madrina o una persona especial que tú quieres como a un miembro de tu familia? ¿Cómo es esa persona? ¿Dónde vive y qué hace? ¿Cuándo la ves?
2. Describe un episodio en que un/a amigo/a te traicionó. ¿Qué pasó? ¿Dónde? ¿Cuándo? ¿Son ustedes amigos/as ahora o no?
3. ¿Qué cosas se pueden hacer con el dinero? ¿Cometerías un crimen por el dinero? ¿Por qué?

B. Mira la foto 9A en la página 353. Según tu opinión, ¿quién es esta persona? ¿Qué relación tiene con Nayeli? Explica.

Para comprender mejor

a punto de	*about to*	la madrina	*godmother*
el/la ahijado/a	*godson/ goddaughter*	la maldad	*evil*
así	*like that*	merecer	*to deserve*
conforme a	*in accordance with*	ni la menor idea	*not even the least idea*
cumplir	*to fulfill*	el/la pintor/a	*painter*
demasiado	*too much*	quizás	*perhaps*
en cuanto	*as soon as*	reunido/a	*reunited*
en cuanto a	*in relationship to*	si no fuera por ti	*if it weren't for you*
enterarse de	*to learn*	tanto	*so much*
la felicidad	*happiness*	tapar	*to cover*
la finca	*farm*	traicionar	*to betray*
fuera de	*out of*	un rato	*a little while*
hondo/a	*deep*	la valentía	*bravery*
el/la jardinero/a	*gardener*		

2 Secuencia. Después de estudiar cada escena de video, inventa una conversación entre los dos pintores. ¿Qué dicen sobre los jaguares gemelos? Después, organiza las escenas en un orden lógico. Trabaja en parejas.

Order of video action shots: 4, 2, 1, 3

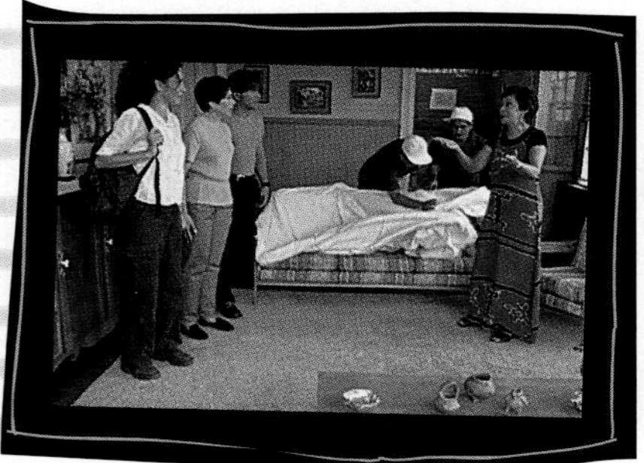
1.

2.

3.

4.

II. Miremos y escuchemos

3 Mis observaciones. Mientras miras y escuchas el episodio, describe una acción y la actitud de los siguientes personajes. Escribe tus observaciones.

Nayeli doña Carmen Armando Zulaya Adriana Felipe

4 ¡Juntos otra vez! ¿Cómo son los jaguares gemelos? Descríbelos.

III. Comentemos

5 Comprensión. En grupos, contesta las siguientes preguntas.

1. ¿A dónde llega Nayeli? ¿Cómo se siente Nayeli al llegar allí? ¿Qué ve Nayeli en el mueble?
2. ¿Qué le cansa a Nayeli?
3. ¿Dónde y cuándo conoció Nayeli a Armando? Según Nayeli, ¿qué les hizo Armando a Adriana y Felipe y de qué acusó a Nayeli?
4. ¿Cómo reacciona doña Carmen a lo que le dice Nayeli?
5. ¿Dónde está Armando? ¿Qué le dice Armando a Zulaya y qué le contesta ella? ¿Qué comenta Zulaya sobre el dinero?
6. ¿Cómo llegan Adriana y Felipe a la finca? ¿Qué llevan allí?
7. ¿Quiénes más están en la sala de doña Carmen? ¿Qué están haciendo allí?
8. ¿Cómo reacciona Nayeli al ver a Felipe, Adriana y Yax-Balam?
9. ¿A quién le da a Yax-Balam Adriana? ¿Qué pone Nayeli en el mueble de la sala y con quién? ¿Qué dice Adriana en ese momento?
10. ¿Qué comenta Nayeli sobre México?
11. ¿Qué cosa le da un muchacho a Nayeli? ¿Dónde la pone?
12. ¿Qué sucede al final de la escena?

6 Miremos otra vez. Después de mirar el episodio otra vez, arregla las escenas de video en la secuencia correcta. Escribe dos frases, explicando cada una.

7 El dilema de Armando. Resume la conversación entre Zulaya y Armando.

8 Nuestra opinión. En grupos de tres, expliquen el significado de lo que Felipe le dice a Adriana. Luego, intercambien las respuestas con otro grupo y compárenlas.

"Te lo mereces todo, Adriana, la felicidad, el triunfo, todo. Si no fuera por ti, quién sabe dónde estarían los jaguares. ¡Con tu tenacidad y tu valentía, vas a salvar a todo México!"

Answers to Actividad 5:

1. Llega a la finca de doña Carmen en Costa Rica. Se siente feliz. Ve al jaguar Hun-Ahau.
2. Le cansa siempre estar en guardia.
3. Nayeli conoció a Armando en la universidad en México (UNAM) cuando eran estudiantes. Armando mandó a Adriana y Felipe a la aventura peligrosa de buscar a Nayeli y al jaguar. También Nayeli cree que él es culpable de acusar a Nayeli de robar al jaguar Yax-Balam.
4. Le dice que quizás Nayeli no sepa todo y que tiene que controlar su imaginación.
5. Armando está en México. Él le dice a Zulaya que va a mandar a una persona a recoger el jaguar. Zulaya le contesta que le dio el paquete con el jaguar a la representante de Armando. A ella no le interesa el dinero.
6. Llegan a la finca en coche. Llevan el jaguar, Yax-Balam.
7. Unos pintores están en la sala. Están tapando el sofá.
8. Nayeli está muy emocionada.
9. Adriana se lo da a Nayeli. Nayeli pone a Yax-Balam en el mueble con Hun-Ahau. Adriana dice, "Misión más o menos cumplida."
10. Nayeli comenta, "México lindo y querido, estás a punto de florecer."
11. Le da una rosa amarilla. Nayeli la pone en el mueble.
12. Adriana y Felipe bailan al final del episodio.

32:51

Lengua

I. Expressing impending actions

Present subjunctive or indicative after adverbial conjunctions

¿Quién va a hacer la cena?

YOLANDA: **Antes de que**° me vaya para mi clase de biología, tenemos que discutir quién va a preparar la cena esta noche.

RITA: Pues yo no puedo. Voy a ir de compras **después de** que mi novio y yo salgamos del trabajo.

FELIPE: Y yo tengo que hacer tareas para la clase de francés y no puedo regresar a casa **hasta que**° las termine. ¿A qué hora es la cena?

RITA: ¿La cena? Vamos a cenar **cuando** tú llegues a casa y la prepares. ¡Hoy es tu turno!°

FELIPE: Vaya, vaya°, y ¿por qué es mi turno?

YOLANDA: Por una razón muy sencilla. Rita preparó la cena ayer, anteayer me tocó a mí y hoy, todos queremos cenar **tan pronto como**° lleguemos a casa.

Before
until
it's your turn!
Well, I never!
as soon as

In Spanish, some adverbial conjunctions always take the subjunctive. These conjunctions indicate intent, purpose, or condition.

Conjunctions always followed by subjunctive	
a fin (de) que	*in order that*
a menos que	*unless*
antes (de) que	*before*
con tal (de) que	*provided that*
en caso (de) que	*in case*
para que	*so that*
sin que	*without*

In Spanish, other adverbials take either the indicative or the subjunctive, depending on the meaning of the sentence as to which is used.

- If the action is customary or habitual, the present indicative is used.

Some keywords that indicate habitual action are **siempre, generalmente,** and **todos los días.**

Cuando José **recibe** su salario cada mes, sale a cenar con sus amigos.	*When José receives his salary each month, he eats dinner with his friends.*
Tan pronto como José **recibe** su salario se pone muy contento.	*As soon as José receives his salary, he becomes very happy.*

- If the action has already taken place and can be described with certainty, a past indicative tense is used.

Cuando José **recibió** su salario, se puso muy contento.	*When José received his salary, he became very happy.*
Tan pronto como José **recibió** su salario se lo gastó todo en viajes.	*As soon as José received his salary, he spent it all on trips.*

- When an activity has not yet taken place, the present subjunctive is used.

Cuando José **reciba** su salario va a gastárselo todo en viajes.	*Whenever José receives his salary, he is going to spend it all on trips.*
Tan pronto como yo **ahorre** suficiente dinero, voy a comprarme un coche importado.	*As soon as I save enough money, I am going to buy an imported car.*

Conjunctions followed by subjunctive or indicative	
aunque	*although*
cuando	*when*
después (de) que	*after*
en cuanto	*as soon as*
hasta que	*until*
luego que	*as soon as*
mientras que	*as long as*
tan pronto como	*as soon as*

When the subject is the same in the two sentences, the following prepositions are used with an infinitive:

Conjunctions followed by an infinitive	
antes de	*before*
después de	*after*
para	*in order to*
sin	*without*

Antes de recibir mi salario, no puedo planear mis vacaciones.	*Before receiving my salary, I cannot plan my vacation.*
Después de estudiar, voy a salir a divertirme.	*After studying, I'm going to go out to have fun.*

Answers to Actividad 1:
1. b
2. b
3. a
4. a
5. b

1 Responsabilidades. Trabaja con una pareja. Determinen si lo que hace la familia de Felipe es habitual (indicativo) o son acciones futuras (subjuntivo). Seleccionen la posibilidad correcta.

1. Cada jueves, Felipe prepara la cena para la familia en cuanto...
   a. llegue a casa de sus clases.
   b. llega a casa de sus clases.
2. Paquita, la hermana de Felipe, siempre le ayuda en la cocina cuando...
   a. pueda.
   b. puede.
3. Paquita piensa alquilar su propio apartamento, pero no puede hasta que...
   a. ahorre el dinero.
   b. ahorra el dinero.
4. Su mamá va a comprar nuevos muebles para la alcoba tan pronto como...
   a. haya rebajas en las tiendas.
   b. hay rebajas en las tiendas.
5. Su papá trabaja cerca de la tienda de comestibles y generalmente compra los comestibles después de que...
   a. termine de trabajar.
   b. termina de trabajar.

Answers to Actividad 2:
1. lleguen
2. vengan
3. se vayan
4. saque
5. pague
6. dé

2 Planes. Diego y Marianela están haciendo los planes para una fiesta que van a tener. Completa cada frase con la forma correcta del verbo entre paréntesis.

DIEGO: Tenemos que limpiar la casa antes de que __________ (llegar) los invitados.

MARIANELA: Claro, hay que limpiarla antes de que __________ (venir) los invitados, pero también tan pronto como __________ (irse) los invitados tenemos que limpiar toda la casa de nuevo.

DIEGO: Carlos va a comprar los refrescos después de que él __________ (sacar) dinero del banco.

MARIANELA: Diego, por ahora, yo no te puedo dar dinero. Te lo doy tan pronto como el jefe me __________ (pagar) el salario este viernes. ¿Está bien?

DIEGO: No hay ningún problema, Marianela. No necesito el dinero ahora mismo (*right now*). No tienes que pagarme nada hasta que tu jefe te __________ (dar) tu salario.

Answers to Actividad 3:
1. llegue a casa
2. recibamos
3. lleguen
4. se levante
5. tenga

3 Ayer y mañana. Escríbele un correo electrónico a tu primo/a, describiéndole lo que tú ya hiciste y lo que van a hacer tú y tus compañeros de apartamento. Sigue el modelo.

► **Modelo:** *El verano pasado, tan pronto como tuve el dinero, alquilé una cabaña en la playa con mis amigos.*
El mes que viene, tan pronto como...
El mes que viene, tan pronto como tenga dinero, voy a alquilar una cabaña en la playa con mis amigos.

1. Anoche cuando llegué a casa, me preparé una bebida de frutas en mi batidora.
   Mañana, cuando...

2. En cuanto recibimos nuestros salarios el mes pasado, pagamos las cuentas de teléfono, gas y electricidad.
   Este mes, en cuanto...
3. Ayer no cenamos hasta que todos llegaron de la universidad.
   Hoy, no vamos a cenar hasta que...
4. Yayo se duchó esta mañana tan pronto como se levantó.
   Mañana, Yayo va a ducharse tan pronto como...
5. El año pasado, cuando recibí dinero de mi abuela, me compré un coche jaguar.
   Esta semana, cuando...

II. Substituting for persons, places, and things

Review of pronouns

Retirado is also used for *retired.* **Jubilado** is etymologically associated with *jubilation* and *joyousness* and reflects the fact that in many Hispanic countries old age is respected and is a happy time in a person's life.

¡Nueva vida!

LOLA: Ahora que tú y yo estamos jubilados,° es bueno no tener que cuidar una casa enorme. Nos podemos acostar tarde y también podemos levantarnos cuando queramos, sin preocuparnos de ir al trabajo. ¡Me encanta nuestro nuevo apartamento!

retired

PEPE: A mí también me gusta mucho. El apartamento es bastante grande y tiene aparatos muy eficientes como el microondas y el aire acondicionado central. Pero, todavía podemos mejorar las cosas: el televisor es viejo y tenemos que reemplazarlo° con uno de pantalla° grande y sonido estereofónico. ¿No te parece buena idea?

replace it / screen

LOLA: Me parece muy buena idea, pero si vamos a cambiar el televisor, me gustaría cambiar todos los electrodomésticos° también.

electrical appliances

PEPE: Entonces, además de la televisión, compremos un nuevo equipo de sonido y ¡un nuevo mueble para ponerlo todo!

Working with a partner, identify the types of pronouns in the dialogue between Lola and Pepe. Refer to the chart, if necessary.

Pronombres

Sujeto	Complemento directo	Complemento indirecto	Reflexivo	Preposicionales
yo	me	me	me	mí
tú	te	te	te	ti
usted	lo/la	le	se	usted
él	lo	le	se	él
ella	la	le	se	ella
nosotros/as	nos	nos	nos	nosotros/as
vosotros/as	vos	os	os	vosotros/as
ustedes	los/las	les	se	ustedes
ellos	los	les	se	ellos
ellas	las	les	se	ellas

Pronouns are important substitutes for people, places, or things. As you do the following activities, refer to specific uses of pronouns you have already covered: subjects (**sujetos,** Chapter 1); direct objects (**complementos directos,** Chapter 4); indirect objects (**complementos indirectos,** Chapter 4); reflexives (**reflexivos,** Chapter 3); prepositional pronouns (**preposiciones,** Chapter 4).

Answers to Actividad 4:
1. Sí, yo también lo tengo que conseguir.
   Sí, yo también tengo que conseguirlo.
2. Sí, yo también los necesito del mismo color.
3. Sí, yo también las prefiero azules para la sala.
4. Sí, yo también los quiero para mi alcoba.
5. Sí, yo también insisto en que los hijos lo tengan.

Before doing **Actividad 5,** point out that some answers are in the past and others are in the present.

Answers to Actividad 5:
1. yo te las compré
2. se me olvidó comprártela
3. nosotros ya la sacamos
4. yo te los lavo hoy
5. nosotras los sacudimos
6. yo no te lo quiero organizar; yo no quiero organizártelo
7. yo lo lavé esta tarde con él
8. yo no se lo traje a ustedes
9. yo ya lo bañé
10. nosotras no se/te la guardamos después de usarla

4 Amueblando la casa. La familia Ordóñez (mamá, papá y sus hijos Tina, Lili y Serafín) va a comprar nuevos muebles para su casa. ¿Cuáles son sus preferencias? Substituye los substantivos por los pronombres de complemento directo en cada frase. Sigue el modelo.

▸ **Modelo:** MAMÁ: *Prefiero una alfombra de lana.*
TÚ: *Sí, yo también la prefiero.*

1. TINA: Tenemos que conseguir *un microondas.*
2. MAMÁ: Necesitamos *un refrigerador y una estufa* del mismo color.
3. SERAFÍN: Papá prefiere *las dos sillas azules* para la sala.
4. LILI: Yo quiero *un tapete y una balanza* para mi alcoba.
5. PAPÁ: Insisto en que los hijos tengan *un televisor.*

5 Diálogos diarios. Trabaja con una pareja. Haz las preguntas usando los pronombres necesarios y cambiando los verbos. Sigue el modelo.

▸ **Modelo:** —*¿Me prestas tu coche, papá?*
—*Sí, hijo, te lo presto.*

1. —¿Me compraste nuevas cortinas, mamá?
   —Sí, hija, _________.
2. —¿Se te olvidó comprarme la lámpara, primo?
   —No, prima, no _________.
3. —Hijos, ¿ya sacaron la basura?
   —Sí, papá, _________.
4. —¿Me lavas los platos hoy?
   —Sí, mi amor, _________.

5. —¿Sacudieron los muebles, sobrinas?
   —Sí, tía, __________.
6. —¿Quieres organizar mi armario, mamita?
   —No, hija, __________.
7. —¿Lavaste el auto esta tarde con tu papá, hijo?
   —Sí, mamá, __________.
8. —¿Nos trajiste un estéreo nuevo para nosotros, papá?
   —No, hijos, __________.
9. —¿Ya bañaste al perrito, nieta?
   —Sí, abuelita __________.
10. —¿Me guardaron la licuadora después de usarla, hijas?
    —No, mamá, __________.

6 Preguntas personales. Hazles cinco preguntas a tres compañeros/as de clase sobre su casa o apartamento, utilizando las diferentes clases de pronombres de la tabla.

III. Making requests and giving orders

Familiar commands

Linda **María**

Un regalo inesperado°

LINDA: **Oye,°** **despiértate,°** María; tengo algo que mostrarte.°
MARÍA: Estoy cansada. **No me hables.°** **Déjame** en paz.°
LINDA: Pero, **escúchame,°** quiero que veas mi nuevo coche.
MARÍA: **Vete°** de aquí. Necesito dormir... **Espérate.°** **¡Ven** acá!° ¿Qué coche? ¿Cuándo te lo compraste?

unexpected
Listen / wake up / show you
Don't talk to me / Leave me alone. / listen to me
Get out / Wait. / Come here!

In Chapter 6, you learned the formation and uses of the formal **Ud./Uds.** commands. From this dialogue, what can you observe about the formation of the **tú** command forms as well as pronoun placement in the affirmative and in the negative?

A. The *tú* affirmative commands

In Spanish, the *affirmative familiar* commands do not use the subjunctive forms.

- To form the *affirmative familiar* command for **tú,** use the third person singular of the present tense:

Regular verb	Present indicative	*Tú* affirmative command
cantar	canta	canta tú
beber	bebe	bebe tú
escribir	escribe	escribe tú
recordar	recuerda	recuerda tú
entender	entiende	entiende tú
oír	oye	oye tú
volver	vuelve	vuelve tú
pedir	pide	pide tú

- The following verbs have irregular forms for the **tú** affirmative command:

Verb	*Tú* affirmative command	Verb	*Tú* affirmative command
ir	ve	salir	sal
ser	sé	tener	ten
poner	pon	hacer	haz
venir	ven	decir	di

This was presented with **usted** commands in Chapter 6.

- Direct, indirect, and reflexive pronouns are attached to the end of an affirmative familiar command, just as they are with affirmative formal commands. When attaching pronouns to a command, an accent must be written if the stress falls on the third or fourth syllable from the end of the word.

¡Di**me** que sí, por favor!	*Say yes to me, please!*
¡Esos son mis libros, por favor, dá**melos!**	*Those are my books, please, give them to me!*
Quiero ese coche. ¡Cómpra**melo,** por favor!	*I want that car. Buy it for me, please!*

B. The *tú* negative commands

In Spanish, the *negative familiar* commands for **tú** are the same as the subjunctive forms, which you learned in Chapter 7.

Regular or irregular verb	*Tú* negative command
bailar	no bailes
beber	no bebas
conducir	no conduzcas
correr	no corras
decir	no digas

(chart continues on page 369)

Regular or irregular verb	*Tú* negative command
ir	no vayas
ser	no seas
volver	no vuelvas

- When the command is negative, all reflexive, direct-, and indirect-object pronouns precede the command forms, as they do with formal commands.

¡Por favor, no **les digas** nada a mis padres!	*Please, don't tell my parents anything!*
¿Ves esta llave? ¡Nunca **se la des** a nadie!	*Do you see this key? Never give it to anyone!*
No **te pongas** esa chaqueta hoy.	*Don't put on that jacket today.*

- When the subject **tú** is used, it follows the command form.

Contesta tú, Marina, te toca a ti. *You answer, Marina, it's your turn.*

7 Instrucciones. Vamos a repasar las instrucciones para utilizar la nueva computadora que compraste. Cambia los mandatos formales por los mandatos familiares en estas instrucciones para enviar correo electrónico. Haz otros cambios necesarios. Sigue el modelo.

► **Modelo:** *Primero, busque el icono del progama en la pantalla* (screen).
Primero, busca el icono del programa en la pantalla.

1. Para abrir el programa, **haga** doble clic en el icono.
2. **Seleccione** "Archivos" en el menú principal.
3. **Abra** "Escribir nuevo mensaje".
4. En esta nueva pantalla, **ponga** la dirección de la persona y el tema del mensaje.
5. **Escriba** un mensaje y **envíelo** pulsando el botón "Mandar".
6. ¡Por favor, no **coma** ni **beba** mientras trabaja en la máquina!

Answers to Actividad 7:
1. haz
2. Selecciona
3. Abre
4. pon
5. Escribe; envíalo
6. comas, bebas (Note that students also have to change last verb to **trabajas**.)

8 ¡Los próximos cincuenta años! Dale consejos a otro/a amigo/a de tu misma edad para tener una vida sana. Sigue el modelo.

► **Modelo:** ___*Come*___ *(comer) mucho pescado*

1. __________ (no comer) mucha carne roja.
2. __________ (cambiar) la rutina.
3. __________ (salir) de casa y __________ (caminar) todos los días.
4. __________ (hacer) ejercicios en el gimnasio con un/a amigo/a.
5. __________ (escuchar) música y __________ (leer) revistas en tu sillón favorito.
6. __________ (comer) ensalada y __________ (no beber) mucho alcohol.
7. __________ (leer) el periódico en el patio.
8. __________(preparar) una bebida de frutas en el procesador.

Answers to Actividad 8:
1. No comas
2. Cambia
3. Sal, camina
4. Haz
5. Escucha, lee
6. Come, no bebas
7. Lee
8. Prepara

9 Oye, amigo/a. Escribe diez consejos para vivir bien en la casa, en la escuela y en tu grupo social. Léeselos a tus compañeros/as de clase y compara las ideas.

Lectura A

Introducción

The following two readings are excerpts of two articles published by *Vanidades Continental*, a popular magazine read by millions of readers in Spain, Latin America, and the United States. This magazine publishes articles about current events, famous people, film, video, fashion, decorating, and other themes.

Play a song from one of Shakira's albums and/or find her Web site. Bring in pictures from home magazines of different kinds of kitchens, living rooms, and dining rooms to review furniture vocabulary and discuss styles of homes.

Reading strategy: Identifying descriptions of existing and nonexisting objects and persons

In the first of the two readings presented, you will read the description of an ideal kitchen and the important things to keep in mind when you decide to create one yourself. In this case, note that the subjunctive is used to describe the characteristics of this ideal kitchen. The second reading is an excerpt of an interview with Shakira, a famous young Colombian singer and composer. Here you will read a short description of two rooms in Shakira's apartment. Note that the indicative is used as the rooms described are actual, existing rooms in her apartment.

Before you read, do the following activities to review the uses of the indicative and the subjunctive when describing people and things. If necessary, review this structure in the *Lengua* section of Chapter 8, Etapa B.

Answers to Actividad 1:
1. tiene
2. hay
3. pueden
4. hay

1 La cocina ideal. Las siguientes frases describen algunas características de la cocina ideal. Escribe las frases de nuevo, describiendo una cocina real. Sigue el modelo.

▶ **Modelo:** *La cocina ideal es una cocina que sea cómoda.*
La cocina de mi casa es muy pequeña.

1. La cocina ideal es una cocina que tenga espacio suficiente para moverse.
2. La cocina ideal es una cocina en la que haya espacio para todos los electrodomésticos.
3. La cocina ideal es una cocina en la que los niños puedan abrir el refrigerador sin ayuda.
4. La cocina ideal es una cocina en la que haya suficientes estanterías para todo.

Answers to Actividad 2:
1. me gustan
2. son
3. son, sirven
4. es
5. armonizan

2 Pasos necesarios. Éstas son las instrucciones del artículo para tener una cocina perfecta. Relata para un/a amigo/a qué haces para amueblar tu cocina. Sigue el modelo.

▶ **Modelo:** *Seleccione objetos que no sean impersonales.*
Yo siempre selecciono objetos que no son impersonales.

1. Seleccione los materiales que más le gusten.
2. Seleccione materiales que sean fáciles de mantener.
3. Seleccione objetos que sean útiles y que sirvan de adorno en la cocina.
4. Seleccione un piso que sea fácil de limpiar.
5. Seleccione materiales que armonicen con el resto de la casa.

3 *Asociaciones.* Relaciona cada palabra de la columna A con la palabra más adecuada de la columna B. Crea una frase con cada selección.

A	B
higiene diaria	amplio
estantes y armarios	orden en la cocina
decoración	comida fresca
espacio	comidas rápidas
horno microondas	agua y jabón
refrigerador	colores

Answers to Actividad 3:
1. higiene diaria: agua y jabón
2. estantes y armarios: orden en la cocina
3. decoración: colores
4. espacio: amplio
5. horno microondas: comidas rápidas
6. refrigerador: comida fresca

Así cualquiera cocina

Lo primero que tiene que ser una cocina es funcional, es decir, que le resulte cómoda, que usted tenga suficiente espacio para moverse, que los equipos electrodomésticos estén colocados° de modo que no le estorben° en su uso, que los niños puedan abrir el refrigerador sin crear problemas, y que haya suficientes estanterías altas para colocar aquellos productos que deben quedar fuera de su alcance.°

placed / *be in the way* / *out of their reach*

Pero que sea funcional no quiere decir que sea impersonal, fría o que recuerde a un quirófano.° Seleccione los materiales que más le gusten, sin perder de vista su facilidad para el mantenimiento y la higiene diaria. No renuncie a tener a la vista° aquellos utensilios que, más que elementos en la cocina, pueden convertirse en parte integral de la decoración como son las ollas de cobre° y de barro cocido° o vidriado° con las que puede hasta hacer una colección.

operating room / *visible* / *copper / baked clay / glazed*

"La cocina. Organizada, espaciosa, clara, funcional y, además, agradable y acogedora.° Según el estilo que más le guste, ponga en su cocina muebles de hierro y piso de mármol, o decore este ambiente con ultramodernas piezas de acero.°"

cozy / *steel*

El piso es otro elemento importante a la hora de "armar" su cocina. Escoja el material que sea fácil de mantener, de limpiar, y que también armonice° con el estilo del resto de la casa. Para un ambiente más clásico, el mármol° será° la elección perfecta.

is in harmony / *marble / will be*

Remind students that these questions refer to the reading "Así cualquiera cocina."

Answers to Actividad 4:
1. **V**
2. **F**—No tienen que ser impersonales.
3. **F**—Pueden convertirse en una parte integral de la decoración.
4. **V**
5. **F**—Es importante que sean fáciles de mantener.
6. **V**
7. **F**—Es para un ambiente clásico.
8. **V**

4 ¿Verdadero o falso? Contesta si las siguientes frases sobre la cocina ideal son verdaderas o falsas. Si son falsas, corrígelas.

1. La cocina ideal debe tener mucho espacio.
2. Las cocinas funcionales son muy impersonales.
3. No es bueno tener los utensilios a la vista.
4. Las ollas de cobre sirven como objetos de decoración.
5. No importa que los materiales no sean fáciles de mantener.
6. La cocina debe armonizar con el resto de la casa.
7. El mármol es el material perfecto para cualquier cocina.
8. Es posible hacer una colección con las ollas de la cocina ideal.

5 La cocina de mi casa. Discutan en grupos cómo era la cocina de sus casas cuando eran jóvenes y cómo es la cocina del sitio donde ahora viven. Si viven en una residencia estudiantil, ¿con quién comparten la cocina?

Un apartamento al estilo Shakira

El salón principal, sala y comedor son originales, muy a su estilo, una bellísima mesa, un cuadro de la Virgen de Guadalupe y un sofá napoleónico, marcan un fuerte contraste con una platanera° caribe, a lo cual nos dice Shakira con una sonrisa:° "Este es el toque° de mi tierra, Barranquilla. El resto de la decoración lo hacen artesanías de Colombia y de todos los países del mundo que he tenido° oportunidad de conocer; además, me gustan las cosas hechas artesanalmente, donde prime° lo auténtico, lo artístico".

Su habitación es amplia, sencilla. Su cama de cedro,° con trabajo artesanal en el espaldar.° Pequeños girasoles° incrustados reflejan su gusto juvenil, casi infantil. Muñecos de felpa° y una vela° en forma de girasol que le regaló a "su princesita" el gran amor de su vida, una conocida figura que espera dar a conocer su nombre con bombos y platillos° en el momento oportuno. Por ahora vive su amor de fantasía... de adolescencia. Sobre el amor tiene su punto de vista que prefiere expresarlo a través de sus canciones.

"En su templo-estudio se nota la decoración *pop* muy juvenil, pues Shakira ha puesto en el suelo un tapiz de Elvis Presley y las patas° de la mesa simulan unos tenis."

banana tree
smile / touch
I have had
predominate
cedar
head piece / sunflowers
Stuffed animals / candle
with a lot of hype
legs

6 Así es su apartamento. Describe las cosas que hay en el apartamento de Shakira. Sigue el modelo.

► **Modelo:** *A Shakira le gustan las cosas originales.*
En su apartamento hay objetos muy originales.

1. A Shakira le gustan los sofás napoleónicos.
2. A Shakira le gustan las artesanías de colores.
3. A Shakira le gustan las cosas auténticas.
4. A Shakira le gustan los objetos artísticos.
5. A Shakira le gustan los girasoles.

7 El apartamento de Shakira. Contesta las preguntas sobre la lectura.

1. ¿Cómo prefiere Shakira expresar su amor?
2. El novio de Shakira tiene un nombre especial para ella. ¿Cuál es?
3. ¿Dónde tiene Shakira unos muñecos de felpa?
4. Describe dos objetos de su sala que tienen mucho contraste entre ellos.
5. Describe la cama de Shakira.
6. Describe la sala y el comedor de Shakira.
7. ¿Qué símbolo religioso tiene la cantante en su apartamento?

Answers to Actividad 7:
1. a través de sus canciones
2. "princesita"
3. en su habitación (dormitorio)
4. un cuadro de la Virgen de Guadalupe y una platanera caribe
5. Es de cedro, con trabajo artesanal en el espaldar.
6. Son muy originales con cosas tradicionales y modernas de muchas partes del mundo.
7. un cuadro de la Virgen de Guadalupe

8 ¿Cómo quiere Shakira que sea su cocina? Crea frases completas integrando los adjetivos de la lista.

► **Modelo:** *Ella quiere que en su apartamento haya cosas originales.*

original	funcional	bello	artesanal
juvenil	de cedro	natural	caribe

9 Cada cual con sus gustos. Carlos y Nubia piensan casarse y van a comprar muebles y adornos para la sala de su futura casa. Lee la descripción de los gustos de cada uno de ellos. Con una pareja, crea un diálogo entre Carlos y Nubia sobre la compra de los muebles.

Carlos	Nubia
Pienso que es importante que los muebles tengan personalidad. Por ejemplo, los muebles antiguos de mi abuela son hermosos y quiero que haya muebles así en mi futuro apartamento. No me gustan mucho los objetos de metal para adornar la casa. Prefiero las cerámicas y las maderas. Definitivamente, no me gustan los colores fuertes ni los objetos brillantes.	Mi sala ideal debe tener objetos modernos, que reflejen la época de avances tecnológicos y nuevos inventos. Me encantan las lámparas de bronce, las esculturas de acero y las mesas de cristal. Claro que también me gustan los muebles con historia, pero solamente si me recuerdan a una persona querida o un evento importante en mi vida.

ETAPA B

For *A. Los animales del mundo,* bring in pictures of various animals and any stuffed animals (**animales de peluche; animales de felpa**) you may have. Review common animals such as **perros** and **gatos.**

Pistas y palabras

I. Talking about animals and plants

Some animal proverbs to discuss literal and figurative meanings:
—No se deje dar gato por liebre.
—En boca cerrada no entran moscas.
—Perro que bien ladra, su comida gana.
—Más vale pájaro en mano que cien volando.

A. Los animales del mundo

Los mamíferos

Los pájaros

Los reptiles

B. Las plantas del mundo

Las plantas

The carnation is the official flower of Spain.

Possible answers to Actividad 1:
1. vaca, caballo, cabra, pato; margaritas, girasoles
2. culebra, lagarto; violetas
3. burro, caballo, cabra, cerdo, gallina, gallo, pavo; maíz
4. perro, gato, perico
5. ballena, delfín
6. cabra, león, llama, oso, tigre, cóndor; violeta
7. rata, ratón, paloma; caléndulas
8. jaguar, mono, tigre, perico, anaconda, caimán, culebra

1 ¿Dónde viven? Di qué animales y plantas hay en los siguientes lugares.

1. el campo
2. el desierto
3. la finca (*farm*)
4. el apartamento
5. el mar
6. las montañas
7. la ciudad
8. las selvas tropicales

2 Asociaciones. ¿Qué animales se asocian con las siguientes características?

1. lento/a
2. inteligente
3. perezoso/a
4. rápido/a
5. estúpido/a
6. hermoso/a
7. elegante
8. sucio/a
9. peligroso/a

3 Ponlos en su grupo. Pon las plantas en categorías. Agrúpalas por color, estación, comestibles (*edible*), o no comestibles. Trabaja con un/a compañero/a.

4 Animales en peligro. Hagan una lista de animales que están en peligro de extinción. Expliquen por qué están en peligro y qué se puede hacer para protegerlos. Trabajen en grupos.

ENLACE CULTURAL

El maíz°, una planta multifacética

El maíz, originario de América, es una planta de gran importancia a lo largo y ancho° del continente americano. Existen muchos tipos de maíz: blanco, amarillo, colorado° y de granos° oscuros, casi azules o negros. En Suramérica, existe una variedad de maíz de granos grandes llamada **choclo.** Es muy popular comer choclo asado con mantequilla. En México, el **elote,** es decir, la mazorca° de maíz entera, también se come asado, con mantequilla.

corn / *throughout all* / *red* / *kernels* / *corn on the cob*

Diferentes variedades de maíz de Latinoamérica.

Ahora, como antes, la dieta de muchas regiones contiene productos basados en el maíz: sopas, salsas, postres, tamales° y tortillas (**arepas** en Colombia y Venezuela). Las tortillas y arepas se consumen tanto como el pan en los Estados Unidos y Europa. Con maíz se preparan también bebidas refrescantes y bebidas alcohólicas como la **chicha.** Un plato italiano muy popular, **la polenta,** también es de maíz.

filled corn husk

As many of the flowers in **Actividad 3** come in different colors, bring in pictures or real flowers to show students. Your local grocery store may sell edible flowers. Be sure students are creative with their categories, which can range from (dis)likes, size, smell, cost, and so on.

Discusión en grupos

1. ¿Existen en la región de ustedes comidas especiales que usen el maíz como ingrediente?
2. ¿Qué platos de maíz hay en restaurantes mexicanos o TexMex?
3. ¿Les gustan a ustedes las tostaditas (*chips*) de maíz azul?
4. ¿Qué productos de maíz se venden en los supermercados de tu ciudad?
5. ¿Conocen ustedes recetas de platos que contengan maíz?

II. Discussing environmental issues

Consejos ecológicos

A muchos nos preocupa **el deterioro del planeta** y las **consecuencias** de nuestras desiguales° relaciones con la **naturaleza.** Pero gran parte de la gente considera que no puede hacer nada o que los problemas son tan grandes que se escapan de sus manos. Nada más falso.

unequal

Existen innumerables cosas que podemos hacer día a día para ayudar a **conservar el planeta** y llevar una **existencia** más **armoniosa** con la naturaleza. No se trata de° una lucha a muerte° entre **tecnología** y naturaleza, entre el hombre y las demás° **especies.**° Tomando consciencia° de nuestra **responsabilidad ecológica,** podemos aprender a coexistir adecuadamente° con el medio ambiente.° Lo único° que se requiere en muchas ocasiones es una pequeña modificación en nuestro **comportamiento.**° No debemos dejar° de hacer o usar las cosas que nos gustan o nos son cómodas. Tan sólo° debemos hacerlas de una manera más ecológica.

It isn't about / fight to the death / the remaining / species / Being aware
adequately / environment / The only thing
behavior / stop
only

Usa tu propia° taza...

Lleva un vaso o taza a la oficina y úsalo para beber agua o café. Así no **producirás**° **basura**° cada vez que tengas sed. Piensa en la **pila**° de vasos **desechados**° que acumulas al año y la cantidad de basura que se evita° si tú y tus compañeros de trabajo usan su propia taza.

own
you won't produce
garbage
pile / discarded
you would eliminate

¿Quieres salvar el mundo?

Empieza por **ahorrar**° **papel.**

El papel es producido de fibra vegetal procesada que se obtiene **explotando**° **los bosques**° del mundo.

Toda hoja° tiene dos caras.° **Reusándolas** y escribiendo o imprimiendo en su reverso, reduces tu **consumo**° de papel. Al reducir tu consumo, reduces la presión sobre los bosques y la cantidad de basura.

save
exploiting
forests
sheet of paper / sides
consumption

¡Apágalo!°

Apaga un bombillo° o la computadora, impresora, máquina de escribir° o cualquier otro aparato eléctrico que no estés usando. **La energía** consumida por estos equipos° se produce quemando° **combustible**° caro, que **contamina** el medio ambiente o explotando nuestros **recursos hidroeléctricos naturales** limitados y cada vez más **escasos.**°

Turn it off!
lightbulb
typewriter
instruments / burning
fuel
scarce

Answers to Actividad 5:
1. **F**—Puede hacer mucho.
2. **V**
3. **F**—Es necesaria una pequeña modificación.
4. **F**—Sí, puede coexistir.
5. **F**—Es mejor usar un vaso o una taza por todo el año.
6. **V**
7. **F**—La energía que usan daña el ambiente.
8. **F**—Son limitados.
9. **F**—Contaminan.
10. **V**

5 ¿Verdadero o falso? Di si las siguientes oraciones de la lectura son verdaderas (**V**) o falsas (**F**). Si son falsas, corrígelas.

1. Una sola persona no puede hacer nada para resolver los problemas ecológicos.
2. Se puede vivir en armonía con la naturaleza.
3. Debemos modificar nuestras vidas modernas por completo.
4. La tecnología no puede coexistir con una naturaleza limpia.
5. Debemos usar muchas tazas de plástico.
6. Debemos ahorrar papel.
7. No es necesario que apaguemos los aparatos eléctricos cuando no se usan.
8. Nuestros recursos hidroeléctricos son ilimitados.
9. Los combustibles no contaminan ni el aire ni el agua.
10. Todo el mundo tiene responsabilidades ecológicas.

6 ¿Qué más podemos hacer? Haz una lista de cinco cosas que se pueden hacer para ayudar a conservar el planeta.

7 El papel. ¿Cómo se pueden reusar las hojas de papel? Haz una lista con una pareja. Usa tu imaginación.

8 A escribir. ¿Cuál es el problema ecológico que más te preocupa? ¿Por qué? ¿Cómo se puede resolver?

ENLACE CULTURAL

Los parques nacionales

El Parque Nacional Braulio Carrillo en Costa Rica tiene una catarata impresionante.

Los Estados Unidos establecieron el primer parque nacional del mundo en 1872 para proteger el ecosistema del parque Yellowstone. Desde entonces y con el crecimiento de las ciudades, estos parques son más y más importantes para proteger la naturaleza y mantener el equilibrio ecológico del planeta. Por esta razón, los gobiernos de muchos países, apoyados° por las organizaciones internacionales como la UNESCO,° han establecido parques naturales para proteger la fauna y la flora locales.

En los países hispanos hay numerosos parques nacionales, muchos de ellos declarados por la UNESCO sitios Patrimonio de la Humanidad.°

supported

United Nations Educational, Scientific, and Cultural Organization

Human Heritage sites

Discusión en grupos

1. ¿Hay regiones o ciudades protegidas en tu estado? ¿Conocen alguna de ellas?
2. ¿Qué plantas o animales están protegidos en los parques nacionales del país?
3. ¿Se puede acampar (*go camping*) en esos parques?

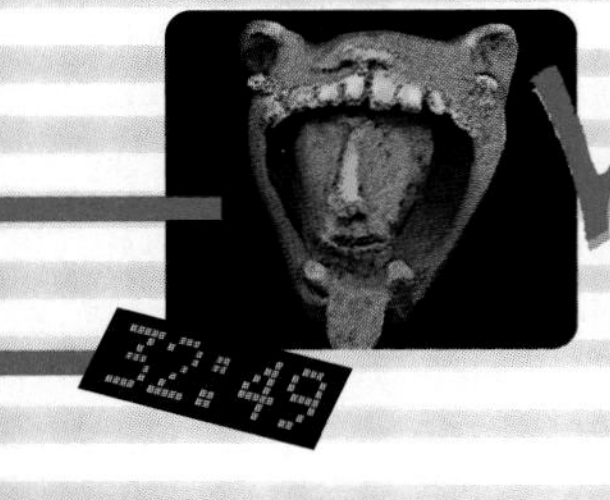

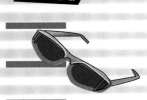

VISTAS Y VOCES

I. Preparémonos

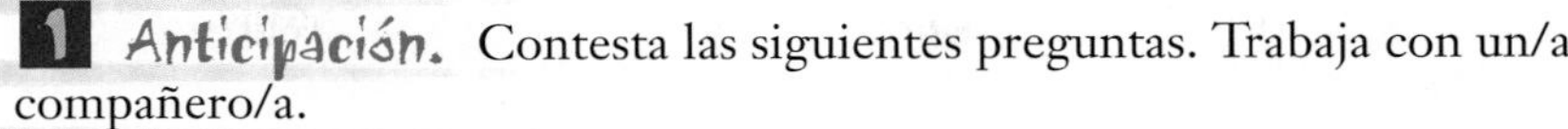

1 Anticipación. Contesta las siguientes preguntas. Trabaja con un/a compañero/a.

A. 1. ¿Qué característica geográfica predomina en tu región: los bosques, las montañas, los ríos, los lagos, los volcanes?

2. ¿De qué colores son el pájaro y la flor que representan tu estado? ¿Son bonitos?

3. ¿Prefieres vivir en el campo o en la ciudad? ¿Por qué? Menciona una buena característica de los dos lugares.

B. Mira la foto 9B en la página 353. ¿Qué están haciendo los pintores en la casa de doña Carmen? ¿Por qué?

Para comprender mejor

apagar	*to turn off, go off*	fiel	*loyal*
asombrado/a	*astonished*	fingir	*to fake*
astuto/a	*sharp*	incómodo/a	*uncomfortable*
atreverse	*to dare*	infundado/a	*unfounded*
la caminata	*walk*	involucrado/a	*involved*
comprobar	*to prove*	la mariposa	*butterfly*
devolver	*to return*	la palanca	*lever*
disculpar	*to forgive*	por encima de	*above*
el ejército	*army*	la prueba	*proof*
en seguida	*right away*	la riqueza	*wealth*
engañado/a	*deceived*	sabroso/a	*delicious*
expuesto/a	*exposed*	suplicar	*to beg*
fallar	*to fail*	el zorro	*fox*
la fe	*faith*		

2 Secuencia. Estudia cada escena de video y contesta la siguiente pregunta. ¿Por qué está tan serio todo el mundo? Después, arregla las escenas en un orden lógico.

Order of video action shots: 2, 3, 4, 1

1.

2.

3.

4.

II. Miremos y escuchemos

3 Mis observaciones. Mientras miras, escribe descripciones de la flora y la fauna que observes en Costa Rica. ¿De qué colores y formas son?

III. Comentemos

4 Comprensión. Contesta las siguientes preguntas.

1. ¿Con qué compara Adriana la gran diversidad biológica de Costa Rica? ¿Qué dice Adriana sobre las mariposas de Costa Rica?
2. ¿Qué comparación hace Felipe entre los pájaros de Costa Rica y la gente?
3. ¿Sabe Adriana por qué se siente incómoda en la presencia de doña Carmen?
4. ¿Qué relación hay entre doña Carmen y Nayeli?
5. ¿Qué opina Felipe de la imaginación de Adriana? ¿Qué quiere hacer ella?
6. ¿Qué están haciendo los pintores en la casa de doña Carmen?
7. ¿Cómo reacciona Nayeli cuando Adriana le cuenta sus sospechas sobre doña Carmen? ¿Tiene pruebas?
8. Según Adriana, ¿cómo se explican los jeroglíficos mayas en las piezas que se encuentran en Costa Rica? ¿Qué pasa al final de esta escena?

5 ¿Y tú qué piensas? Imagínate que en este episodio el pájaro azul y anaranjado puede hablar. ¿Qué dice sobre doña Carmen? ¿Es una persona de confianza?

6 Miremos otra vez. Después de mirar el episodio otra vez, arregla las escenas de video en la secuencia correcta y narra brevemente el contenido del episodio.

7 ¿Qué animal eres? Adriana compara a Felipe con un perro fiel. Él la compara a ella con un zorro astuto. Describan las características positivas de estos dos animales. ¿Con qué animal se identifican ustedes? ¿Por qué?

8 En nuestra opinión. En grupos de tres, discutan las siguientes opiniones de Adriana y Felipe. Cuando terminen, intercambien y comparen las respuestas con otro grupo.

ADRIANA: "...es urgente que conservemos la riqueza natural de los bosques."
FELIPE: "¿En este siglo cómo puede un país funcionar sin ejército?"

Answers to Actividad 4:
1. Adriana la compara con un paraíso de novela. Dice que cinco por ciento de las mariposas conocidas en el mundo se encuentran en Costa Rica.
2. Felipe dice que la gente es conservadora en comparación con los colores de los pájaros.
3. No. Es una intuición.
4. Es madrina de Nayeli.
5. Felipe cree que Adriana está nerviosa y cansada y su imaginación está trabajando horas extras. Adriana quiere hablar con Nayeli y contarle sus dudas sobre doña Carmen.
6. Están mirando la palanca que controla la electricidad de la casa.
7. Nayeli está asombrada, ofendida y furiosa. Adriana no tiene pruebas.
8. Había ladrones precolombinos. Se apagan las luces.

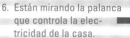

Lengua

I. Talking about the past

Formation of the present perfect tense

Mario　　　　　Tomás

Mario ha tenido un buen día.

TOMÁS: ¿Qué **has hecho**° hoy, Mario? — *have you done*

MARIO: **He tenido**° un día muy bueno. **He trabajado**° en mi proyecto sobre el medio ambiente, **he ido**° a la tienda de comestibles y **he cocinado**° una cena muy sabrosa para mi novia. — *I have had / I have worked*; *I have gone / I have cooked*

TOMÁS: ¿Qué estás celebrando?

MARIO: Esta noche vamos a celebrar nuestro aniversario. Tú sabes que **hemos sido**° novios por dos años. — *we have been*

TOMÁS: Hombre, ¿y cuándo van a casarse?

MARIO: Pues **hemos decidido**° casarnos el próximo verano. **Ya hemos comprado**° una finca que tiene muchos animales, flores y jardines. — *we have decided*; *We have already bought*

TOMÁS: ¡Qué bien, felicidades a ti y a Verónica!

The present perfect tense has two parts—the present indicative of the verb **haber** and the past participle. Here are the present indicative forms of the auxiliary verb **haber.**

Present indicative of *haber*

haber			
yo	he	nosotros/as	hemos
tú	has	vosotros/as	habéis
él/ella, Ud.	ha	ellos/ellas, Uds.	han

Point out that **ser** and **ir**, which are usually irregular, have regular past participles, **sido** and **ido.**

The past participle is formed by eliminating the **-ar, -er** or **-ir** of the infinitive and adding the following endings: **-ado** for **-ar** verbs and **-ido** for **-er** and **-ir** verbs.

Regular verbs: Past participle of		
***-ar* verbs**	***-er* verbs**	***-ir* verbs**
bailar	comer	recibir
bail**ado** (*danced*)	com**ido** (*eaten*)	recib**ido** (*received*)

- The following verbs have irregular past participles.

Irregular participles

Infinitive	Past participle	English
abrir	**abierto**	*open*
cubrir	**cubierto**	*covered*
decir	**dicho**	*said, told*
descubrir	**descubierto**	*discovered*
hacer	**hecho**	*made, done*
escribir	**escrito**	*written*
morir	**muerto**	*died, dead*
poner	**puesto**	*put, placed*
resolver	**resuelto**	*resolved*
romper	**roto**	*broken, torn*
ver	**visto**	*seen*
volver	**vuelto**	*returned*

- You must write an accent over the **i** of the **-ido** ending for those **-er** and **-ir** verbs whose stems end in a vowel.

Infinitive	Stem	Past participle	English
creer	cre-	creído	*believed*
leer	le-	leído	*read*
oír	o-	oído	*heard*
traer	tra-	traído	*brought*

The present perfect tense *(el pretérito perfecto)*

	hablar	querer	venir
yo	**he** hablado	**he** querido	**he** venido
tú	**has** hablado	**has** querido	**has** venido
él/ella, usted	**ha** hablado	**ha** querido	**ha** venido
nosotros/nosotras	**hemos** hablado	**hemos** querido	**hemos** venido
vosotros/vosotras	**habéis** hablado	**habéis** querido	**habéis** venido
ellos/ellas, ustedes	**han** hablado	**han** querido	**han** venido

- Note that in Spanish the present perfect is called **el pretérito perfecto.**

- Direct, indirect, and reflexive pronouns come before the conjugated form of **haber.** No word can can ever come between the auxiliary verb **haber** and the perfect participle.

Pepe ha visto a Maribel en la celebración. Pepe **la** ha visto.	*Pepe has seen Maribel at the celebration. Pepe has seen her.*
La profesora **me** ha escrito muchos mensajes electrónicos.	*The teacher has written me many e-mails.*
La hija de don Antonio **se** ha ido para la universidad.	*Don Antonio's daughter has left for the university.*

To stress placement of pronouns for the present perfect, tell students that these pronouns go *right before the verb* and that negatives, as in other compound tenses, go *before* the pronouns: **Nadie me ha visto.**

1 **¿Sueño o realidad?** ¿Es posible salvar el planeta? En la clase de ciencias, los estudiantes hablan de lo que se ha hecho para proteger el planeta.

▸ **Modelo:** *(nosotros / descubrir) nuevas maneras de conservar energía.*
Nosotros hemos descubierto nuevas maneras de conservar energía.

Este año ...

1. (las compañías de coches / producir) menos coches.
2. (el gobierno / limpiar) los ríos y los océanos.
3. (los ecologistas / proteger) a los animales en peligro de extinción.
4. (nosotros / examinar) la cuestión de los desperdicios nucleares.
5. (los pueblos / publicar) guías para conservar el uso del agua.
6. (los estudiantes / escribir) en la computadora en vez de cortar árboles para hacer papel.
7. (los restaurantes de comida rápida / eliminar) casi todos los productos hechos de plástico.
8. (mi universidad / usar) menos aire acondicionado y menos petróleo (*fuel*).
9. (mi familia / apagar) las luces al salir de los cuartos.
10. (yo ¿...?)

Answers to Actividad 1:
1. han producido
2. ha limpiado
3. han protegido
4. hemos examinado
5. han publicado
6. han escrito
7. han eliminado
8. ha usado
9. ha apagado
10. he ¿...?

2 **Parque Nacional Salvaelplaneta.** Antonio Bello ha ido al Parque Nacional Salvaelplaneta en el Zoológico Bellafauna. Cuenta qué ha hecho Antonio y qué animales y plantas ha visto. Utiliza una expresión de la columna A y una expresión de la columna B. Haz todos los cambios necesarios. Sigue el modelo.

▸ **Modelo:** *Antonio ha visto tortugas.*
Antonio ha bebido agua natural.

A	B
ver	monos
tocar	jirafa
observar	elefante
dar de comer a (*feed*)	agua natural
comprar tarjetas postales de	tortuga
sacar fotografías de	cocodrilo
mirar un documental sobre	serpiente
caminar entre	árboles
beber	flores
jugar con	plantas
admirar	

3 Ciudadanos responsables. Escribe una composición de dos párrafos. En el primer párrafo, describe lo que hiciste el año pasado para proteger o mejorar el medio ambiente (pretérito). En el segundo párrafo describe lo que has hecho este semestre (pretérito perfecto).

II. Expressing feelings about the past

Present perfect subjunctive

Un planeta en peligro

LILIA: Es terrible que nosotros **hayamos contaminado** el aire con tantos productos químicos.
INÉS: Y a mí no me gusta que las grandes compañías **hayan producido** tantos coches.
LILIA: A mí tampoco. Es triste que el gobierno no **haya aprobado** leyes más estrictas para proteger el medio ambiente.
INÉS: Estoy de acuerdo.
LILIA: También es una lástima que los desperdicios° nucleares **hayan ensuciado**° los ríos.
INÉS: Tenemos que seguir luchando por la naturaleza.

waste / have soiled

The irregular past participles for the present perfect also apply to the present perfect subjunctive.

When the idea in the main clause requires the subjunctive, and the time frame of the subordinate clause requires the present perfect, the *present perfect subjunctive* appears in the subordinate clause. The present perfect subjunctive is formed with the present subjunctive of the auxiliary verb **haber** + the *past participle* of the verb. Following are the forms for **haber.**

Present subjunctive of *haber*

haber			
yo	haya	nosotros/as	hayamos
tú	hayas	vosotros/as	hayáis
él/ella, Ud.	haya	ellos/ellas, Uds.	hayan

The present perfect subjunctive

yo	**haya** conservado
tú	**hayas** requerido
él/ella, Ud.	**haya** coexistido
nosotros/nosotras	**hayamos** abierto
vosotros/vosotras	**hayáis** hecho
ellos/ellas, Uds.	**hayan** producido

4 La contaminación: mi compañera de planeta. Un grupo de amigos da sus opiniones sobre el tema de la contaminación en la vida contemporánea. Completa cada frase con la forma correcta del pretérito perfecto del subjuntivo. Sigue el modelo.

▸ **Modelo:** *Es bueno que las autoridades hayan limpiado (limpiar) el agua contaminada en las ciudades.*

1. No es verdad que todos los países __________ (solucionar) los problemas de la contaminación del medio ambiente.
2. Es una lástima que los coches __________ (ser) causa de la contaminación del aire.
3. Temo que el número de águilas __________ (reducirse) este año.
4. Ojalá que no __________ (morirse) muchos peces este año en las aguas contaminadas.
5. Es bueno que el gobierno de los Estados Unidos __________ (darse cuenta) de (*realize*) la urgencia de proteger los animales.
6. Estoy contento que los jóvenes __________ (utilizar) menos agua en la ducha.
7. Es bueno que los parques nacionales __________ (preservar) las flores y los bosques en peligro de extinción.
8. Me alegro que recientemente los ecólogos __________ (preocuparse) por los animales marinos como el delfín y la ballena (*whale*).

Answers to Actividad 4:
1. hayan solucionado
2. hayan sido
3. se haya reducido
4. se hayan muerto
5. se haya dado cuenta
6. hayan utilizado
7. hayan preservado
8. se hayan preocupado

5 (No) Estoy de acuerdo. En parejas, determinen si están o no están de acuerdo con las opiniones expresadas en la actividad anterior. Expliquen por qué.

6 Soy director/a. Imagínate que tú eres el/la director/a de la Oficina de Protección del Medio Ambiente de tu país. Escribe un reportaje de dos párrafos cortos sobre los problemas más urgentes (párrafo uno) y las soluciones para esos problemas (párrafo dos).

III. Expressing resultant conditions

Estar and past participle

El artículo de Tino

TINO: Tengo que escribir un trabajo sobre la ecología. ¿Está **abierto**° el Jardín Botánico? Quiero estudiar las flores y plantas **transplantadas**° de otros estados.

open
transplanted

closed / open

brought

published

based / research

ROSA: No, hoy está **cerrado**° porque es lunes, pero está **abierto**° los otros días de la semana. El zoológico sí está abierto hoy, tal vez puedes empezar con los animales **traídos**° de otras regiones.

TINO: Sí, voy a empezar el trabajo hablando sobre los animales. Según un artículo **publicado**° en la revista *La naturaleza*, muchos de ellos están en peligro de extinción.

ROSA: Sí, y la información está **basada**° en trabajos de investigación° de mucha gente. Cuando escribas el artículo, ¡dame una copia para leerlo!

- In Spanish, it is possible to use past participles as adjectives. Like all adjectives in Spanish, they must agree in number and gender with the noun they modify.

La **información está basada** en investigaciones. *The information is based on research.*

- However, when they are used as part of a perfect tense, they do not change to reflect gender and number.

Tino **ha basado** su artículo en investigaciones. *Tino has based his article on research.*

Answers to Actividad 7:
1. están sobrepobladas
2. está contaminado
3. está destruída
4. está deforestado
5. están agotados

7 Problemas serios. Usa el participio como adjetivo para describir los problemas mencionados. Después, numera estos problemas en orden de importancia. Explica las razones de tu elección. Trabaja en parejas para comparar las opiniones.

▸ **Modelo:** *el aire (contaminar)*
El aire está contaminado.

1. las ciudades (sobrepoblar) (*overpopulated*)
2. el océano (contaminar)
3. la capa de ozono (destruir)
4. el Amazonas (deforestar)
5. los recursos naturales (agotar) (*exhausted*)

Answers to Actividad 8:
1. Ya están cerradas.
2. Ya está publicado.
3. Ya están construídas.
4. Ya están protegidos; Ya están hechos.
5. Ya están investigadas.
6. Ya está preparado.
7. Ya está comprado; Ya está escrito.

8 Quiero saber. Un estudiante, un poco distraído, pregunta sobre algunas acciones en pro de la conservación del medio ambiente. Tú le contestas diciéndole que ya todo está hecho usando el participio como adjetivo. Sigue el modelo y recuerda cambiar el género y el número.

▸ **Modelo:** *—¿Nadie va a escribir una carta de protesta contra la contaminación?*
—Ya está escrita.

1. ¿Nadie va a cerrar las playas contaminadas de nuestra ciudad?
2. ¿Nadie va a publicar el libro de Jacques Cousteau sobre la contaminación del mar?
3. ¿Nadie va a construir nuevas instalaciones para los osos pandas?
4. ¿Nadie va a hacer planes para proteger el delfín y el manatí?
5. ¿Nadie va a investigar las consecuencias negativas del cigarrillo?
6. ¿Nadie va a preparar el informe sobre nuestra campaña (*campaign*) ecológica?
7. ¿Nadie va a comprar el papel para escribir nuestro informe?

9 **Y tú, ¿qué crees?** Contesta por escrito las siguientes preguntas sobre el medio ambiente.

1. ¿Qué se debe hacer para conservar energía?
2. ¿Cuál es la solución para usar menos gasolina?
3. ¿Qué debemos hacer para que las grandes compañías sean más responsables?
4. ¿Cómo debemos vivir para reducir la explotación de los recursos naturales?

Lectura B

Introducción

This reading presents the story of a very old Dragon tree in the town of Icod de los Vinos, on the island of Tenerife, one of the Spanish Canary Islands. Dragon trees live very long lives and grow to be very tall. Their leaves are sword-shaped and bluish-green. These trees are numerous in the tropics and also grow in California. The very tall and famous Dragon tree from Tenerife is one of the oldest trees ever known.

Prelectura

1 **El reino vegetal.** Discute con un/a compañero/a las siguientes afirmaciones. ¿Son verdaderas? ¿Son importantes?

1. Las plantas son seres vivos y sienten dolor cuando las cortamos.
2. Los árboles cuidan nuestra atmósfera y debemos cuidarlos.
3. Hay plantas que viven mucho más que nosotros, los humanos.
4. Debemos vivir en armonía con la naturaleza.

2 **Naturaleza sana.** Completa las siguientes afirmaciones con palabras de la lista. Compara tus respuestas con las de un/a compañero/a.

▸ **Modelo:** *Quiero vivir en una ciudad que tenga* <u>*áreas verdes*</u>.

áreas verdes	mucho tiempo	basura	sano
naturaleza	agradables	flores	muerta

1. Debemos cuidar los árboles para que vivan __________.
2. Una ciudad sin áreas verdes es una ciudad __________.
3. Quiero que en mi casa siempre haya __________.
4. No me gusta que en las ciudades haya __________ por las calles.
5. Es muy triste que la gente no cuide la __________.
6. Las selvas y los bosques son nuestra garantía para que la tierra sea un planeta __________.
7. Es importante que nuestras ciudades sean lugares__________ para vivir.

Answers to Actividad 2:
1. mucho tiempo
2. muerta
3. flores
4. basura
5. naturaleza
6. sano
7. agradables

Árboles con historia—El último dragón

El dragón de Tenerife es el patriarca vegetal de España. Prácticamente no hay nada en Icod de los Vinos, una pequeña ciudad tenerifeña° de 21.000 habitantes, que no utilice el reclamo publicitario del árbol más antiguo y más grueso° de España para promocionarse.°

in Tenerife
thick
promote itself

La monstruosa figura de este abuelo vegetal, con un peso de 144 toneladas y que puede tener nada menos que 3.500 años de existencia, es la primera seña° de identidad de los icodenses,° y su principal atractivo turístico. Unas 6.000 personas acuden diariamente a contemplarlo, a fotografiarse y a asombrarse° de la monstruosa monumentalidad del drago.° La razón quizás esté en lo que Anastasio González oyó decir a su madre y ésta a la suya, que el Drago de Tenerife "es el padre de todos los dragos de Canarias".

sign / from Icod
to take shade
Dragon tree

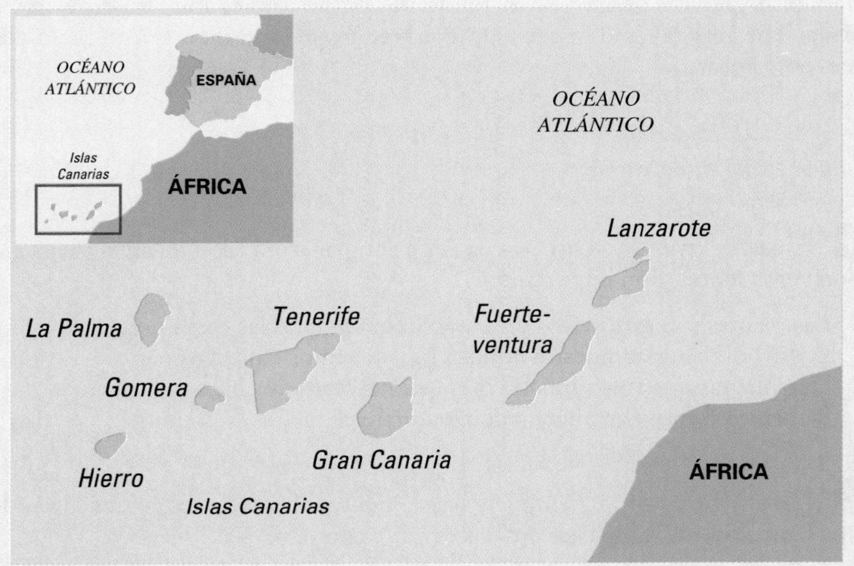

Según Domingo Lorenzo, un perito° agrícola que contrataron como "médico particular" del drago, "el árbol se quedó agotado° tras la espectacular floración° de 1995 y todavía no se ha recuperado del todo". Y no es para menos,° pues las flores aumentaron su peso en 2.7 toneladas, de donde nacieron docenas de miles de semillas. Un trabajoso parto° múltiple que, según su cuidador, es el mejor síntoma de su buena salud. De hecho,° hacía más de 50 años que no se conocía

expert
exhausted
bloom
And it's no wonder
delivery, birth
In fact

El Drago de Icod.

una floración así. Y nuevamente se cumplió la tradición, pues estos árboles siempre han sido utilizados en Canarias como auténticos barómetros biológicos. Si florecen por el sur, el invierno será° lluvioso en la costa; si lo hacen por el norte, sólo en la montaña, y si es por todo el árbol, las lluvias serán generalizadas. La floración estival° del Drago de Icod anunció el final de uno de los peores períodos de sequía° que se han conocido en Tenerife. Recientemente, la carretera se ha desviado° y el drago ya tiene su jardín propio, aunque° no sin polémica, pues un alto muro impide su visión de cerca, por lo que a partir de ahora hay que pagar para verlo.

will be

summer

drought

has detoured

although

Ficha técnica

• *Nombre popular*	el Drago de Icod
• *Nombre científico*	Dracaena draco
• *Localidad*	Icod de los Vinos (en Santa Cruz de Tenerife, en las Islas Canarias)
• *Edad aproximada*	3.500 años
• *Altura*	18 metros
• *Perímetro (a 1,50 metros)*	16,14 metros
• *Mejor época para verlo*	todo el año

Postlectura

Answers to Actividad 3:

1. dragón
2. con el dinero de los turistas
3. Tienen un médico particular: Domingo Lorenzo.
4. 3.500 años
5. monstruoso, vegetal, agotado, antiguo, grueso
6. Se quedó agotado.
7. Predicen el clima de las varias regiones. Dicen que sí.
8. Es el principal atractivo turístico. Hay un muro que impide su visión de cerca.
9. de todos los dragos de Canarias
10. 6.000. Lo fotografian y se quedan asombradas de la monumentalidad del drago.
11. Por la espectacular floración (y producción de semillas) de 1995.
12. tinerfeños, icodenses.

3 El drago milenario. Contesta las preguntas sobre la lectura.

1. La gente usa el nombre de un animal para el árbol. ¿Cuál es ese nombre?
2. ¿Cómo se pagan los gastos para mantener bien al drago de Tenerife?
3. ¿Cómo cuidan la salud del viejo drago?
4. ¿Qué edad tiene este "abuelo vegetal"?
5. Menciona cinco adjetivos usados en la lectura para describir el árbol.
6. ¿Qué le sucedió al drago con la última floración?
7. ¿Qué predicen (*predict*) las floraciones del árbol? ¿Son ciertas?
8. ¿Por qué hay que pagar ahora para ver el árbol?
9. ¿De quién es padre este árbol?
10. ¿Cuántas personas van a ver el árbol diariamente? ¿Qué hacen allí?
11. ¿Cómo se sabe que el árbol tiene buena salud?
12. ¿Como se llaman las personas que son de Tenerife? ¿Y las personas de Icod?

4 La ecología. Discute uno de los siguientes temas en grupos de tres o cuatro estudiantes.

1. ¿Conocen algún árbol tan viejo o más viejo que el drago?
2. ¿Conocen algún árbol tan grande o más grande que el drago?
3. ¿Por qué es importante proteger los árboles?
4. ¿Crees que el uso de la computadora puede resultar en que usemos menos papel?
5. ¿Son importantes los árboles para el clima de la tierra?
6. ¿Existe en tu región una flor, un árbol o una planta característica de la zona?
7. En muchos países de América Latina, la flor nacional es la orquídea. ¿Existe una flor nacional de los Estados Unidos?
8. ¿Qué animal se asocia con tu estado? ¿Es un animal protegido? ¿Está en peligro de extinción?
9. ¿Qué animal se asocia con los Estados Unidos? ¿Cómo es y dónde se encuentra?
10. ¿Qué ave se asocia generalmente con las montañas de los Andes? ¿Cómo es? ¿Está en peligro de extinción?

5 Mi parque nacional preferido. Escribe en español un corto ensayo (un párrafo) sobre un parque nacional que conozcas o sobre un parque nacional de tu región o de tu estado. Menciona las plantas y los animales principales que existen allí.

6 Mi planta preferida. Escribe un corto ensayo en español sobre un árbol que te guste mucho, sobre una flor hermosa que te guste o sobre alguna otra planta importante para ti.

7 Mi animal preferido. ¿Tienes una mascota? Si la tienes, escribe un corto ensayo en español sobre tu animalito. Si no tienes mascota, escribe sobre un animal que te guste mucho. ¿Cómo es? ¿Dónde vive?

En resumen

I. Hablemos

1 Un plan ecológico. Eres miembro de una organización ecológica de la universidad. Haz una lista de algunos problemas ecológicos de la universidad y discute un plan para resolverlos. Trabaja en grupos de tres o cuatro.

2 Vendo muebles a doña Carmen. Tu eres director/a de la "Galería de Muebles" en los Estados Unidos. Doña Carmen te llama porque ella quiere comprar otros muebles para su casa. Con una pareja, inventen una conversación entre tú (el/la director/a) y doña Carmen sobre los tipos y colores de los muebles, los precios y el transporte.

II. Investiguemos por Internet

Searching for images

The Internet is an important broadcasting medium. Many international organizations use it to inform and educate people about global problems that can affect the quality of life in our communities and on our planet. In this chapter, you will concentrate on searching for images to illustrate your project. Search engines on the Web allow searching for images directly in any document. For example, if you are looking for pictures of the Galápagos Islands in Ecuador, you can formulate your search in this way: **galapagos:image.** However, images may have been indexed by other names, so if you don't get satisfactory results, use keywords as you have done in other chapters. Refer also to your browser's "help" section for hints on how to search for images or to this book's Web site.

Vocabulario informático

imagen digital	*digital image*
indexar	*to index*

3 El patrimonio de la humanidad. Work in groups and select one of the following tasks.

1. Present to the class a Hispanic site or city that UNESCO (**http://www.unesco.org**) has declared World Heritage (*patrimonio de la humanidad*). These sites are listed in UNESCO's World Heritage List, published by their World Heritage Program.
2. Select a plant or an animal that you know is in danger of extinction (*en peligro de extinción*) and look for information about it.

III. Escribamos

Writing strategy: Creating a point of view

An important consideration when writing is to think about who is telling the story. By determining with whose voice the story is told, you can create different ways to view your topic.

Through whose eyes is the story of "El último dragón" told? How would the story change if it were told through the tree itself? the eyes of a tourist? a lumberjack? a small child? a ninety-year-old grandmother? the tree's flowers?

Strategy in action

Turn to *Escribamos* in the Workbook to practice the writing strategy of creating a point of view.

4 Otro punto de vista. Escribe la historía de *El último dragón* con un punto de vista diferente. Usa uno de los puntos de vista mencionados en la estrategia.

5 Según Zulaya. Escribe la historia del jaguar en Ecuador desde el punto de vista de Zulaya. Incluye su decisión de dárselo a Adriana y darle la piedra a doña Gafasoscuras.

Vocabulario

En la casa

la almohada	*pillow*
el aparador	*bureau*
la aspiradora	*vacuum cleaner*
aspirar la alfombra	*to vacuum the carpet*
la balanza	*scale*
barrer el piso	*to sweep the floor*
cocinar	*to cook*
la cómoda	*chest of drawers*
las cortinas	*curtains*
la escoba	*broom*
el espejo	*mirror*
hacer la cama	*to make the bed*
el inodoro (sanitario)	*toilet*
el lavabo (lavamanos)	*sink*
la lavadora	*washing machine*
lavar la ropa	*to wash clothes*
lavar los platos	*to wash dishes*
la llave (el grifo)	*faucet*
la mesa	*table*
la mesita	*coffee table*
la mesita de noche	*night stand*
ordenar el cuarto	*to clean the room*
el papel sanitario (papel higiénico)	*toilet paper*
el pasillo	*hall*
la plancha	*iron*
planchar la ropa	*to iron clothes*
sacar la basura	*to take out the garbage*
sacudir los muebles	*to dust the furniture*
el secador de pelo	*hair dryer*
la secadora	*clothes dryer*
secar la ropa	*to dry clothes*
el sofá	*sofa*
el televisor/ la televisión	*television set*

En la cocina

añadir (agregar)	*to add*	**hervir (ie)**	*to boil*
asado/a	*broiled*	**hornear**	*to bake*
el asador	*broiler*	**el horno**	*oven*
la batidora	*mixer*	**el lavaplatos**	*dishwasher*
batir	*to whip, beat*	**la licuadora**	*blender*
la cafetera	*coffee maker*	**mezclar**	*to mix*
calentar (ie)	*to heat*	**el microondas (el micro)**	*microwave oven*
caliente	*hot*	**moler (ue)**	*to grind*
cocinar	*to cook*	**el mostrador**	*counter*
el congelador	*freezer*	**la olla**	*pot*
congelar	*to freeze*	**picar**	*to chop*
cortar	*to cut*	**el procesador de comidas**	*food processor*
la cucharada	*tablespoonful*	**el/la refrigerador/a**	*refrigerator*
la cucharadita	*teaspoonful*	**revolver (ue)**	*to turn*
enfriar	*to cool*	**la sartén**	*frying pan*
la estufa	*stove*	**la tostadora**	*toaster*
el fregadero	*sink*	**el utensilio**	*utensil, tool*
freír (i)	*to fry*		
frito/a	*fried*		
el gabinete, la estantería	*cabinet*		

Conjunciones

a fin (de) que	*in order that*	**hasta que**	*until*
a menos que	*unless*	**luego que**	*as soon as*
antes (de) que	*before*	**mientras que**	*as long as*
con tal (de) que	*provided that*	**para (que)**	*in order to, so (that)*
cuando	*when*	**sin (que)**	*without*
después (de) que	*after*	**tan pronto como**	*as soon as*
en caso (de) que	*in case*		
en cuanto	*as soon as*		

Animales

el águila *(f.)*	*eagle*	**el flamenco**	*flamingo*
la anaconda	*anaconda*	**la gallina**	*hen*
la ardilla	*squirrel*	**el gallo**	*rooster*
el armadillo	*armadillo*	**la iguana**	*iguana*
la ballena	*whale*	**el jaguar**	*jaguar*
el burro	*donkey*	**la jirafa**	*giraffe*
el caballo	*horse*	**el lagarto (la lagartija)**	*lizard*
la cabra	*goat*	**el león**	*lion*
el caimán	*cayman, alligator*	**la llama**	*llama*
el cerdo (cochino, puerco)	*pig*	**el lobo**	*wolf*
el cóndor	*condor*	**el mamífero**	*mammal*
el delfín	*dolphin*	**el mono**	*monkey*
el elefante	*elephant*	**el oso**	*bear*
		la oveja	*sheep*

el pájaro	*bird*	**el ratón**	*mouse*
la paloma	*pigeon, dove*	**el reptil**	*reptile*
el pato	*duck*	**el tigre**	*tiger*
el pavo	*turkey*	**la víbora (culebra, serpiente)**	*snake*
el perico	*parrot*	**el zorro**	*fox*
el pingüino	*penguin*		
la rata	*rat*		

Plantas y flores

la caléndula	*marigold*	**la parra**	*grapevine*
el clavel	*carnation*	**la petunia**	*petunia*
el girasol	*sunflower*	**la rosa**	*rose*
el maíz	*corn*	**el tulipán**	*tulip*
la margarita	*daisy*	**la violeta**	*violet*

Ecología

ahorrar papel	*to save paper*	**la especie**	*species*
armonioso/a	*harmonious*	**la existencia**	*existence*
la basura	*garbage*	**explotar**	*to exploit*
el bombillo	*lightbulb*	**el medio ambiente**	*environment*
el bosque	*forest*	**la naturaleza**	*nature*
el combustible	*fuel*	**la pila**	*pile*
el comportamiento	*behavior*	**el planeta**	*planet*
la consecuencia	*consequence*	**los recursos hidroeléctricos naturales**	*natural hydroelectric resources*
conservar	*to save, conserve*	**la responsabilidad ecológica**	*ecological responsibility*
el consumo	*consumption*	**reusar**	*to reuse*
contaminar	*to contaminate*	**salvar**	*to save*
desechado/a	*discarded*	**la tecnología**	*technology*
el deterioro	*deterioration*		
la energía	*energy*		
escaso/a	*scarce*		

LOCALIDAD:
Costa Rica

10A

¿Qué pasa con doña Carmen?

10B

Tension builds as Adriana confesses her suspicions to Felipe and Nayeli. After the lights suddenly go out at dinner, disaster strikes and the truth is revealed.

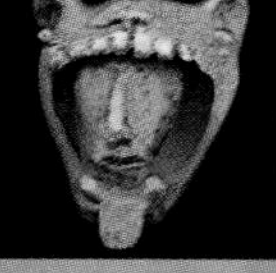

Vocabulary themes
- Commemorating holidays and celebrations
- Talking about traditions and beliefs
- Talking about art and artists
- Talking about crafts and folk art

Language structures
- Expressing wishes, opinions, and beliefs
- Indicating subjective emotions and attitudes in the past
- Talking about prior events
- Clarifying and specifying references to persons and things
- Asking questions
- Expressing opposing opinions

Culture Topics
- El carnaval
- La Nochevieja
- El muralismo
- Arte ambulante

Readings
- El rostro mestizo de la Navidad en América
- Arte y artesanía

Reading and writing strategies
- Identifying the thesis and the arguments in a text
- Summarizing

Internet strategy
- Using bookmarks

ETAPA A

Pistas y palabras

I. Commemorating holidays and celebrations

Fiestas y celebraciones

La **conmemoración** de **eventos históricos o religiosos,** los **homenajes** (*homages, tributes*) a personas importantes y la celebración de fechas significativas tienen expresiones sociales de muchos tipos, por ejemplo:

- Declarar el día como **fiesta nacional o regional**
- **Celebrar** una **ceremonia religiosa o cívica**
- Organizar un **desfile** (*parade*) por las calles de la ciudad
- Hacer **festivales** y fiestas populares o familiares
- Hacer **exhibiciones públicas**
- Publicar un libro sobre el tema o **en honor de** una persona o evento
- Poner en un lugar público **una placa** que explique el evento, **una estatua, un mural** o alguna otra **obra de arte** (*work of art*)
- **Componer** (*compose*) una canción o **un himno**

Seville, Spain, is famous for its Holy Week Processions. Bring in cultural material from books (James Mitchener's *Iberia,* for example) and the WWW.

Semana Santa, Antigua, Guatemala.

La Semana Santa

La Semana Santa es una celebración católica que honra la vida de Jesucristo, su pasión, muerte y resurrección. En los países hispanos hay ceremonias y **ritos** religiosos durante esa semana.

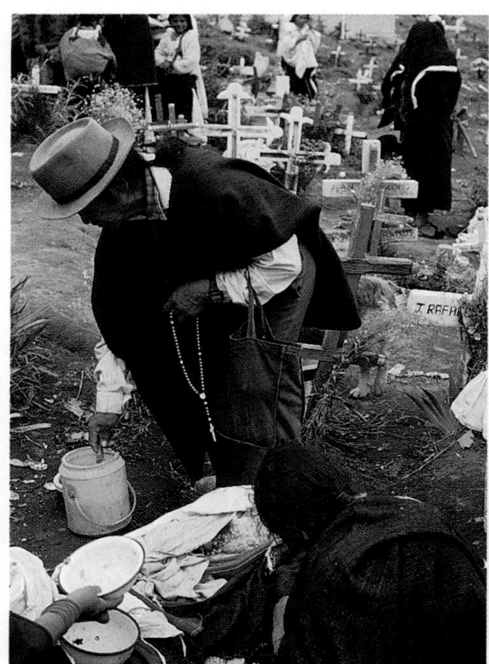

Día de los Muertos en Otavalo, Ecuador.

El Día de los Muertos

En el Día de los Muertos se honran las almas (*souls*) de los antepasados y se reza (*pray*) por las ánimas (*spirits*) que buscan el descanso eterno. En algunos países hispanos, esta fiesta se llama el Día de las Ánimas. En México, Ecuador y Perú, esta fiesta adquiere (*acquires*) colorido (*style*) **folclórico.**

El Día Nacional

En casi todos los países hispanos, el Día Nacional, o Día de la Independencia, se celebra con desfiles y ceremonias civiles o militares.

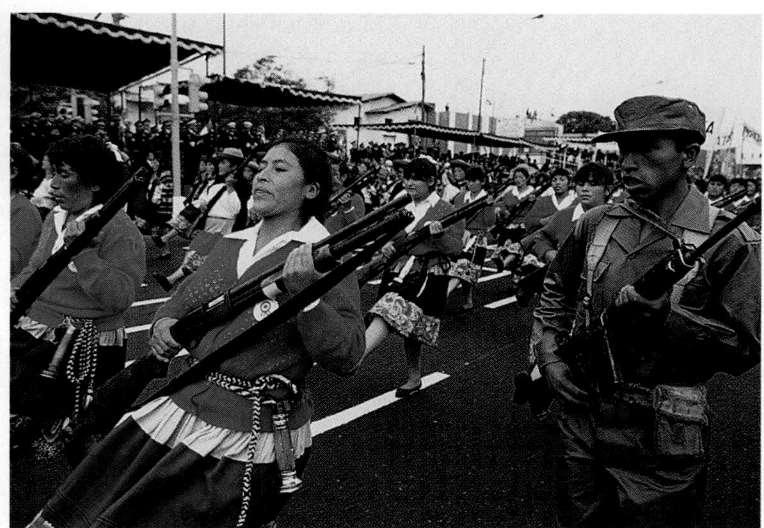

Desfile del Día Nacional en Lima, Perú.

Palabras y expresiones útiles

la bandera	*flag*	el folclor	*folklore*
la broma	*trick*	los fuegos artificiales	*fireworks*
el concierto	*concert*	la guerra	*war*
el desfile	*parade*	la máscara	*mask*
el disfraz	*costume*	la participación	*participation*
el espectáculo	*show, spectacle*		
actuar	*to act*		
participar	*to participate*		
auténtico/a	*authentic*	folclórico/a	*folkloric*
bello/a	*beautiful*	magnífico/a	*magnificent*
entretenido/a	*entertaining*		

In some Spanish-speaking countries it is also customary to celebrate a person's **día del santo** in addition to his or her birthday (**cumpleaños**).

1 **Fiestas importantes.** Haz una lista de las fiestas que celebras durante el año. Incluye fiestas familiares (cumpleaños y aniversarios), fiestas universitarias (la graduación) o fiestas nacionales y regionales. Compara tu lista con la lista de un/a compañero/a y conversa sobre cómo se celebran las fiestas que has seleccionado.

2 **El Día de la Independencia.** Describe qué hacías para celebrar el Día de la Independencia cuando eras niño/a. Compáralo con lo que haces ahora.

ENLACE CULTURAL

El Carnaval

Disfraces en el Carnaval de Barranquilla, Colombia.

El Carnaval tiene su origen en las fiestas que se han celebrado por siglos, en las regiones católicas europeas durante los cuatro días anteriores a la Cuaresma.° Estas fiestas no tienen actualmente° carácter religioso, sino que son celebraciones, con bailes, música, comidas deliciosas, disfraces y frecuentemente, con desfiles por las calles. El Carnaval termina el martes, víspera° de la Cuaresma, la cual comienza el Miércoles de Ceniza.° El Carnaval se celebra de diferentes maneras en algunas ciudades y pueblos de los países hispanos, pero tienen una cosa en común: es una época de fiestas populares.

Lent

currently

day before

Ash Wednesday

Discusión en grupos

1. ¿Dónde se celebra el Carnaval en los Estados Unidos?
2. ¿Se celebran fiestas en tu región para recordar un evento histórico o en honor de una persona famosa? ¿Hay comidas especiales y desfiles por las calles?
3. ¿Conocen ustedes los días nacionales de otros países? ¿Cómo se celebran?
4. ¿Cómo se celebran los cumpleaños en la familia de cada uno/a de ustedes?

II. Talking about traditions and beliefs

A. Tradiciones y creencias

En todas las culturas se han desarrollado° ritos y ceremonias para **prevenir catástrofes** y **males,°** para **pedir favores especiales** y para **conmemorar** eventos importantes. Muchas ceremonias religiosas estaban relacionadas con el deseo de **aplacar a los dioses°** para que ellos protegieran° a la población, a los animales y los alimentos.° También podían celebrarse para alejar° a **los malos espíritus** que causaban enfermedades y males.

developed · *evil* · *placate the gods* · *would protect / foods* · *dispel*

Actualmente, los festivales no religiosos pueden tener muchas razones para celebrarse, por ejemplo para **honrar°** a una persona, para **recordar un hecho histórico,°** y modernamente, por motivos comerciales y económicos.

honor · *historic event*

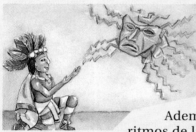

La adoración al sol Los incas **adoraban** al dios Sol° o Inti, que controlaba los **fenómenos** de la naturaleza, como la lluvia y las cosechas.° Además creían que él tenía poder sobre los ritmos de la vida como **los nacimientos,°** las enfermedades y la muerte. Para los aztecas, el dios Sol también era **poderoso°** y le ofrecían **sacrificios.**

sun god · *crops* · *births* · *powerful*

El conejito de Pascua° En las épocas precristianas, se celebraba la renovación de la naturaleza al llegar la primavera. En esas celebraciones se pedía **la fertilidad** de la tierra y de los animales para que no faltaran° alimentos en el invierno. Los huevos y los conejitos de Pascua son antiguos **símbolos** de fertilidad.

Easter bunny · *lack*

Celebrando el modernismo El progreso, el desarrollo tecnológico e industrial y los **logros°** de la humanidad son el centro de muchas celebraciones en nuestra época. Las grandes **exposiciones mundiales** y los **juegos olímpicos** son dos ejemplos del deseo de **festejar°** estos logros.

achievements · *celebrate*

Pabellón en la Exposición de Sevilla.

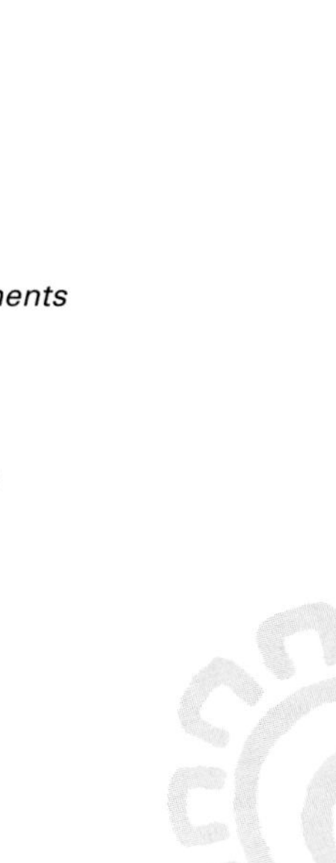

B. Algunos días de fiesta

Enero
1° Día de Año Nuevo
6 Día de los Reyes Magos

Febrero
14 Día de San Valentín
Carnaval (Semana anterior al Miércoles de Ceniza—*Ash Wednesday*)

Marzo
Semana Santa (Fecha variable)
Domingo de Pascua (Fecha variable)

Abril
1° Día de los Inocentes (EE.UU., Europa)

Mayo
1° Día del Trabajo (Países hispanos)
5 Día de la Batalla de Puebla (México)

Julio
4 Día de la Independencia (EE.UU.)

Octubre
12 Día de la Raza
31 Día de las brujas

Noviembre
1° Fiesta de Todos los Santos
2 Día de los Muertos
Día de Acción de Gracias (Fecha variable)

Diciembre
Hanukkah (Fecha variable)
Kwanza (Fecha variable)
25 Navidad
28 Día de los Inocentes (Países hispanos)
31 Nochevieja
Ramadán (Países islámicos/fecha variable)

3 Asociaciones. ¿Qué fiestas asocias con las siguientes cosas?

1. el verano
2. un árbol verde
3. un picnic
4. un corazón rojo
5. la nieve
6. la bandera
7. la primavera
8. el invierno
9. un desfile
10. un regalo
11. un disfraz

4 Preguntas. Contesta las preguntas según la lectura y tus experiencias propias.

1. ¿Por qué se desarrollaron ritos en las culturas antiguas?
2. ¿Con qué se relacionaban muchas ceremonias religiosas?
3. ¿Por qué adoraban los incas el sol? ¿Y los aztecas?
4. ¿Qué significaba antes el conejito de Pascua? ¿Qué significa para ti?
5. ¿Qué importancia tienen los juegos olímpicos? ¿Dónde comenzaron? ¿Por qué?
6. ¿Celebras el nuevo año? ¿Cómo lo celebras? ¿Con quién?
7. ¿Cómo celebras el día de San Valentín?

5 El Día de los Inocentes. ¿Le has hecho bromas a alguien el Día de los Inocentes? ¿A quién? ¿Qué broma le hiciste y cómo reaccionó la persona? ¿Alguien te ha hecho bromas a ti? ¿Quién? Describe las bromas y cómo reaccionaste tú.

Answers to Actividad 4:
1. para prevenir catástrofes y males, para pedir favores especiales y para conmemorar eventos importantes
2. Con el deseo de aplacar a los dioses para recibir su protección.
3. Porque los incas creían que el sol controlaba los fenómenos de la naturaleza y los ritmos de la vida. Para los aztecas era poderoso y le ofrecían sacrificios.
4. Fertilidad. (*Answers will vary.*)
5. Representan los logros de la sociedad moderna. Comenzaron en Grecia para celebrar los logros mundiales y promover la paz.
6. *Answers will vary.*
7. *Answers will vary.*

In most countries **el Día de los Inocentes** is celebrated on December 28. After the first person falls for the joke the other says **inocente,** the way we say *April fools* in English.

ENLACE CULTURAL

La Nochevieja

A medianoche, la gente en España come doce uvas para celebrar el Año Nuevo.

El 31 de diciembre, la Nochevieja, es el momento de hacer los propósitos° para el año nuevo. Tal vez queramos ser más ordenados, mejores estudiantes, personas más amables y simpáticas, comer alimentos nutritivos, no ser chismosos,° tratar bien a los amigos, etc. Estos son objetivos que quizás podamos lograr con esfuerzo° y voluntad.° Sin embargo, el futuro es desconocido° y para ayudarse en los propósitos y prevenir cualquier mal, en algunas partes se recurre° a rituales para recibir el nuevo año. Por ejemplo, en España y otros países hispanos se acostumbra comer doce uvas, una por cada campanada° del reloj a las doce de la noche. En otras partes, como en Colombia, es buena suerte entrar al Año Nuevo llevando ropa interior amarilla y comiéndose las doce uvas de medianoche.

resolutions

gossipy

effort / will

unknown

to turn to

stroke

Discusión en grupos

1. ¿Existen en la región de ustedes ceremonias o rituales para recibir el año nuevo?
2. ¿Es útil hacer propósitos de año nuevo? ¿Por qué?
3. ¿Qué creencias conocen para llamar la buena suerte? ¿Y qué creencias conocen para evitar la mala suerte?
4. Realicen una encuesta a todos los miembros del grupo con estas tres preguntas: ¿Existe la buena suerte? ¿Existe la mala suerte? ¿Es necesaria la suerte para tener éxito? Preséntenle los resultados a la clase.

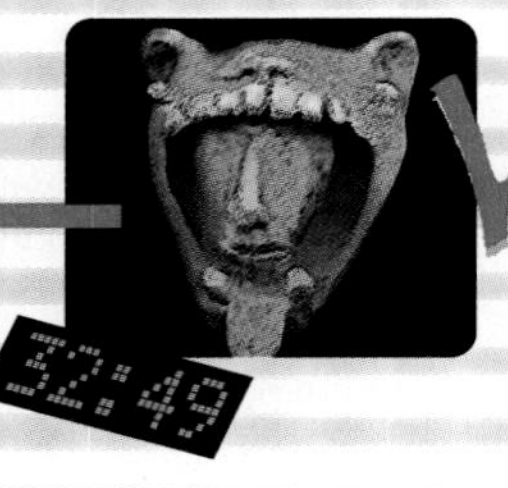

Vistas y voces

I. Preparémonos

1 Anticipación. Contesta las siguientes preguntas. Trabaja con un/a compañero/a.

A. **1.** ¿Qué haces cuando se corta la luz en tu casa?
2. Menciona una situación que te cause angustia. ¿Qué haces para calmarte?
3. ¿Cómo proteges tu apartamento o casa contra los robos?
B. Mira la foto 10A en la página 395. ¿De qué habla doña Carmen?

Para comprender mejor

a menudo	*often*	la falla	*failure*
alterarse	*to get upset*	la incomodidad	*inconvenience*
la anfitriona	*host*	la indirecta	*heavy hint*
la angustia	*anxiety*	ingenioso/a	*clever*
comprensivo/a	*understanding*	inquietarse	*to get worked up*
desconcertar	*to take aback*	Tranquilízate.	*Calm down.*
la disculpa	*apology*	se fue la luz/	*the light(s)*
en seguida	*right away*	se cortó la luz	*went out*

2 Secuencia. Estudia cada escena de video y contesta las siguientes preguntas. ¿Qué les ha pasado a los jaguares gemelos? Según tu opinión, ¿que está pensando Nayeli? ¿De qué crees que están hablando Adriana y Felipe?

1.

2.

Order of video action shots: Answers may vary.

3.

4.

II. Miremos y escuchemos

3 **Mis observaciones.** Mientras miras y escuchas el episodio, indica si las siguientes frases son **verdaderas** o **falsas**. Corrige las frases falsas.

1. ______ En la finca se corta la luz.
2. ______ Adriana no se altera cuando se corta la luz.
3. ______ Las fallas eléctricas son normales en esta zona de Costa Rica.
4. ______ Cuando se corta la luz, doña Carmen permanece en la habitación.
5. ______ Felipe va a examinar el generador.
6. ______ La casa de doña Carmen es vieja.
7. ______ Los jaguares gemelos desaparecen.
8. ______ Según Nayeli, Zulaya se robó los jaguares.
9. ______ Nayeli trata de calmarlos a todos.
10. ______ La casa de doña Carmen está vigilada con videocámaras.

Answers to Actividad 3:
1. **V**
2. **F**—Adriana se altera.
3. **V**
4. **F**—Doña Carmen sale del comedor cuando se corta la luz.
5. **F**—Felipe permanece en el comedor.
6. **V**
7. **V**
8. **F**—Nayeli piensa que Armando se robó los jaguares.
9. **V**
10. **V**

III. Comentemos

4 **Comprensión.** Trabajando en grupos, contesta las siguientes preguntas.

1. ¿Quiénes están en el comedor en esta escena?
2. ¿Qué pasa con la luz? ¿Cómo reacciona Adriana?
3. ¿Quién no está en el comedor?
4. ¿Están Felipe y Nayeli preocupados con la falla eléctrica?
5. ¿Quién sale de la casa de doña Carmen? ¿Dónde estuvo doña Carmen? ¿Cuántas veces por mes se corta la electricidad?
6. ¿Qué descubren al pasar a la sala? Según Nayeli, ¿quién se robó los jaguares gemelos?
7. ¿Qué usa doña Carmen para vigilar la finca?
8. Al final de este episodio, ¿cómo reaccionan Adriana y Nayeli?

Answers to Actividad 4:
1. Nayeli, doña Carmen, Felipe y Adriana están en el comedor.
2. Se corta la luz. Adriana llama a Felipe. Ella se altera y está inquieta.
3. Doña Carmen no está.
4. No están preocupados sobre la falla eléctrica.
5. No sabemos. Dice que fue a examinar el generador. La electricidad se corta dos o tres veces por mes.
6. Descubren que los jaguares gemelos no están. Armando se robó los jaguares gemelos, según Nayeli.
7. Usa videocámaras.
8. Adriana está furiosa (indignada). Nayeli parece muy preocupada.

5 **La ahijada.** Describe la actitud de Nayeli hacia (*toward*) doña Carmen en este episodio. ¿Todavía tiene confianza en su madrina? ¿Por qué? ¿Cómo se siente ella al empezar y al terminar el episodio? Explica.

6 **Miremos otra vez.** Después de mirar el episodio otra vez, arregla las escenas de video en la secuencia correcta y narra la acción.

7 **Robo.** ¿Para dónde crees que va el ladrón de los jaguares gemelos? ¿Qué deja en el mueble en lugar de los gemelos? ¿Para quién trabaja? ¿Es Gafasnegras? Trabaja en parejas.

8 **Yo opino que...** En grupos de tres, analicen el significado de los siguientes comentarios. ¿Quiénes los dicen? Digan si están de acuerdo o no dando ejemplos del video y de la vida. Luego, intercambien las respuestas con otro grupo y compárenlas.

1. "Los ladrones son muy ingeniosos."
2. "No digas nada hasta que no sepas la verdad. Es muy fácil sacar conclusiones erróneas."

Lengua

I. Expressing wishes, opinions, and beliefs

Review of the present subjunctive

Before you do the activities in this section, review the formation and uses of the present subjunctive in chapters 7, 8, and 9. Then, complete the following activities with a partner. Review the following examples of verbs or expressions that require use of the subjunctive.

- Verbs of volition

  Quiero que todos **celebremos** el Carnaval. — *I want us all to celebrate carnival.*

- Verbs of emotion

  Rafa **se alegra** de que todos **participen** en el festival. — *Rafa is happy that all are participating in the festival.*

- Unknown facts

  Estamos buscando un concierto de música que no **sea** muy caro. — *We are looking for a music concert that is not very expensive.*

- Impersonal expressions

  Es magnífico que **haya** festivales populares en Puerto Rico. — *It's magnificent that there are popular festivals in Puerto Rico.*

- Conjunctions

  Vamos a la celebración **después de que** Paco **llegue.** — *We're going to the celebration after Paco arrives.*

Answers to Actividad 1:
1. acompañe
2. pase / gaste
3. haga
4. participe
5. cante
6. siga / pierda
7. tenga

1 Los abuelos dan consejos. Martina nos cuenta lo que su abuelita Adela quiere que ella haga. Completa lo que dice Martina.

1. Mi abuelita Adela me dice que la _________ (acompañar) a la iglesia donde tienen conciertos de música muy entretenidos.
2. Ella insiste en que yo _________ (pasar) más tiempo en casa practicando las lecciones de música. Ni ella ni mis padres permiten que yo _________ (gastar) tiempo en diversiones.
3. Ella y mi abuelo dicen que me _________ (hacer) cantante de ópera como mi tía Juana.
4. Mi abuela me aconseja que no _________ (participar) en los espectáculos de música popular para no arruinar mi voz.
5. Mi abuelo dice que es posible que yo _________ (cantar) con el famoso cantante Plácido Domingo.
6. Mi abuela teme que yo no _________ (seguir) sus consejos y que _________ (perder) muchas y muy buenas oportunidades profesionales.
7. Mis abuelos me quieren mucho y esperan que yo _________ (tener) éxito con mi carrera.

2 **Los primos.** Sara y Enrique hablan sobre la manera de celebrar el Día Nacional en su país y su ciudad. Selecciona la forma correcta del subjuntivo o del indicativo, según el contexto.

SARA: Me parece una buena idea que (honramos / honremos) a las personas que han muerto luchando en la guerra.

ENRIQUE: Sí, debemos honrarlas por su esfuerzo y espero que mi prima Melania (canta / cante) durante la ceremonia conmemorativa de mañana.

SARA: Pues dudo que ella (quiere / quiera) cantar. Estoy segura de que (prefiere / prefiera) tocar la guitarra y que le va a pedir a Roberto que (canta / cante).

ENRIQUE: Es posible, pero cuando la (vemos / veamos), voy a rogarle que (cante / canta) junto con Roberto.

SARA: Espero que te (escucha / escuche), pero no estoy segura de que (hace / haga) lo que le pides.

Answers to Actividad 2:
1. honremos
2. cante
3. quiera; prefiere; cante
4. veamos; cante
5. escuche; haga

3 **Mis opiniones.** Utiliza las expresiones verbales siguientes para expresar por escrito tu opinión (positiva o negativa) sobre los hechos de la lista. Recuerda usar el presente de subjuntivo. Cuando termines, compara tus frases con las de un/a compañero/a.

es absurdo	es bueno	es fantástico	es lógico
es malo	es maravilloso	es terrible	es triste
es ridículo	es importante	no es cierto	no es mentira

▸ **Modelo:** *Los deportistas famosos hacen comerciales de ropa cara.*
Es malo / No es malo que los deportistas famosos hagan comerciales de ropa cara.

1. Algunas personas famosas tienen casas enormes.
2. Hay actores que fuman en las películas.
3. Varias ciudades tienen desfiles populares.
4. Durante el verano hay espectáculos al aire libre.
5. Muchos atletas hacen comerciales de cereales y vitaminas.
6. Ciertos actores de televisión y cine son muy excéntricos.
7. Algunos cantantes cancelan sus conciertos.
8. Muchas personalidades del cine usan drogas y alcohol.
9. Muchos actores ayudan a los enfermos de SIDA y cáncer.
10. Muchos pueblos conmemoran a las personas que han muerto defendiendo su país.

Require students to use at least six different expressions.

Answers to Actividad 3:
1. tengan
2. haya / fumen
3. tengan
4. haya
5. hagan
6. sean
7. cancelen
8. usen
9. ayuden
10. conmemoren

II. Indicating subjective emotions and attitudes in the past

The past subjunctive (imperfecto de subjuntivo)

"El presidente les **pidió** a los ciudadanos que **honraran** a los héroes muertos en las guerras y que **asistieran** a las ceremonias que se van a celebrar mañana."	*The president asked citizens to honor heroes who died in war and to attend ceremonies that are going to be celebrated tomorrow.*
"El presidente de la Asociación de Veteranos **recomendó** que las ceremonias se **celebraran** en todos los pueblos y ciudades."	*The president of the Veteran's Association recommended that the ceremonies be celebrated in all towns and cities.*
"La policía les **recordó** a todos que no **bebieran** alcohol ni **condujeran** sus coches en estado de ebriedad."	*The police reminded everyone not to drink alcohol nor drive their cars under the influence.*

The past subjunctive (imperfect subjunctive)

You have already studied the imperfect and preterite tenses in the indicative. In Spanish, there is one simple past tense in the subjunctive mood—the imperfect subjunctive—which is used in the same way as the present subjunctive, but refers to circumstances, events and situations of the past. Remember that, as in the present subjunctive, the main clause verb determines whether the subordinate clause verb is in the subjunctive mood.

- To form the past subjunctive of both regular and irregular verbs, eliminate the **-ron** of the *third person plural* of the *preterite* tense and add the following endings. To review the forms of the preterite, refer to Chapters 4 and 5.

festejar	tener	pedir
festej**ara**	tuvi**era**	pidi**era**
festej**aras**	tuvi**eras**	pidi**eras**
festej**ara**	tuvi**era**	pidi**era**
festej**áramos**	tuvi**éramos**	pidi**éramos**
festej**arais**	tuvi**erais**	pidi**erais**
festej**aran**	tuvi**eran**	pidi**eran**

Note that there is an accent on the **nosotros** forms of these verbs, but no accents on the **vosotros** forms.

- Note that verbs that are irregular in the preterite are also irregular in the past subjunctive.
- Alternative forms for the imperfect subjunctive are **-se, -ses, -se, -semos, -seis, -sen** added to the third person plural of the preterite after eliminating the indicative ending **-ron.**

These alternate forms tend to be used mostly in literary, written Spanish, and are more common in Spain than in Latin America.

4 **Práctica.** Indica las formas del imperfecto de subjuntivo.

1. yo: conmemorar, volver, servir
2. tú: desfilar, entender, recibir
3. él: bailar, comprender, decir
4. nosotros: honrar, poner, mentir
5. Uds.: actuar, tener, seguir

Answers to Actividad 4:
1. conmemorara, volviera, sirviera
2. desfilaras, entendieras, recibieras
3. bailara, comprendiera, dijera
4. honráramos, pusiéramos, mintiéramos
5. actuaran, tuvieran, siguieran

5 **Celebrando con la familia.** En voz alta, lee el siguiente párrafo sobre las celebraciones de días de fiesta de la familia de Nelson. Utiliza el imperfecto del subjuntivo de los verbos entre paréntesis.

Mis padres querían que todos nosotros (celebrar) juntos los días de fiesta nacionales y por eso se pusieron contentos de que (venir) los abuelos desde Venezuela para estar con nosotros. Mi hermana Lola quería que nosotros (participar) en el desfile del pueblo y que (salir) a cenar después de mirar el desfile. Pero Tito, mi hermano, prefirió que nos (quedar) en casa después del desfile para mirar los espectáculos de la noche por televisión. Tito también insistió en que nosotros (invitar) a sus compañeros de la universidad a cenar en casa con nosotros.

Answers to Actividad 5:
1. celebráramos
2. vinieran
3. participáramos
4. saliéramos
5. quedáramos
6. invitáramos

6 **Un mes de muchas órdenes.** Eres Tere, una cantante y actriz de treinta y dos años. Escribe un correo electrónico de ocho frases a tu amigo Carlos en Chile, contándole lo que tu agente te pidió que hicieras el mes pasado. Utiliza estos verbos en el pasado.

querer	preferir	ser importante	sugerir
pedir	insistir	decir	temer

► **Modelo:** *Mi agente sugirió que descansara mucho.*

III. Talking about prior events

A. Past perfect indicative (pluscuamperfecto)

¿No habías estado allí?

ANDRÉS: ¿Dónde pasaste las vacaciones?

TANIA: Fui a Panamá porque ya **había viajado**° por otros países hispanos y quería conocerlo.

had traveled

ANDRÉS: Ah, yo creía que tú ya **habías estado** allí. ¿Con quién fuiste?

TANIA: No, yo nunca **había ido**° a Panamá. Fui con mi primo Mario. Él ya me **había acompañado**° antes a Costa Rica.

had gone
had accompanied

ANDRÉS: ¿Y qué te gustó más?

TANIA: Me gustó mucho el festival folclórico de Panamá. Mario nunca **había asistido**° y a él también le encantó.

had attended

Pluscuamperfecto

Refer students to Chapter 9 to refresh their memories on regular and irregular past participles.

- The past perfect indicative tense (or pluperfect) is formed with the imperfect tense of the auxiliary verb **haber** in combination with the past participle of the verb that indicates the action: **había viajado, habías asistido, habíamos escrito.**
- In English, the equivalent is the past perfect tense (I *had traveled*, you *had attended*, we *had written*, she *had asked me for them*, I *had already dressed*).
- Direct- and indirect-object pronouns, as well as reflexive pronouns, come before the conjugated form of **haber** in the past perfect tense: **Ella me los había pedido.** (or) **Ya me había vestido.**

	comprar	**leer**	**recibir**
yo	**había** comprado	**había** leído	**había** recibido
tú	**habías** comprado	**habías** leído	**habías** recibido
él/ella, Ud.	**había** comprado	**había** leído	**había** recibido
nosotros/as	**habíamos** comprado	**habíamos** leído	**habíamos** recibido
vosotros/as	**habíais** comprado	**habíais** leído	**habíais** recibido
ellos/ellas, Uds.	**habían** comprado	**habían** leído	**habían** recibido

7 ¿Qué había pasado antes? Francisco llegó muy tarde a la fiesta de celebración del cuatro de julio. Utiliza el pluscuamperfecto para relatar qué había pasado antes de que llegara Francisco.

1. La banda _________ (tocar) por tres horas.
2. Algunas parejas _________ (bailar) mucho.
3. Muchos invitados _________ (comer) aperitivos y _________ (beber) cerveza y vino.
4. Un grupo musical _________ (cantar) canciones nacionales típicas.
5. Todos nosotros _________ (divertirse) muchísimo.
6. La comida _________ (terminarse), y Francisco no pudo comer.

Answers to Actividad 7:
1. había tocado
2. habían bailado
3. habían comido / habían bebido
4. había cantado
5. nos habíamos divertido
6. se había terminado

8 ¿Qué dijo Rosana? Explica cómo celebraron el año nuevo las siguientes personas, según lo que te contó Rosana. Usa la forma correcta del pluscuamperfecto. Después, compara tus frases con las frases de un/a compañero/a.

► Modelo: *Lucía (bailar) con Roberto*
Rosana me contó que Lucía había bailado con Roberto toda la noche.

1. Mi mamá (comer) doce uvas
2. Mis tíos (mirar) la celebración en la tele
3. Mi compañero/a de cuarto (ir) a una fiesta muy divertida
4. El/La presidente de la universidad (asistir) a una ceremonia académica

Answers to Actividad 8:
1. había comido
2. habían mirado
3. había ido
4. había asistido

9 Las distintas épocas de mi vida. Indica cinco actividades que ya habías hecho antes de matricularte en la universidad (cuando tenías tres, seis, nueve, doce, quince y dieciséis años, por ejemplo). Utiliza el pluscuamperfecto y sigue el modelo. Puedes seleccionar diferentes edades.

► **Modelo:** *un año / caminar*
Cuando yo tenía un año, ya había aprendido a caminar.

B. Past perfect subjunctive (Pluscuamperfecto de subjuntivo)

- As with the present perfect subjunctive, when the idea in the main clause requires use of the subjunctive, the *past perfect subjunctive* appears in the subordinate clause. It is used when the action indicated occurred prior to the one expressed in the main clause.
- The past perfect subjunctive is formed with the imperfect subjunctive of the auxiliary verb **haber** + the *past participle* of the verb. Following are the forms for **haber.**

Review the present perfect subjunctive, which is presented in Chapter 9.

Imperfect subjunctive of *haber*

haber			
yo	**hubiera**	nosotros/nosotras	**hubiéramos**
tú	**hubieras**	vosotros/vosotras	**hubierais**
él/ella, usted	**hubiera**	ellos/ellas, ustedes	**hubieran**

The past perfect subjunctive (pluscuamperfecto de subjuntivo)

yo	**hubiera** celebrado
tú	**hubieras** creído
él/ella, usted	**hubiera** vuelto
nosotros/nosotras	**hubiéramos** ido
vosotros/vosotras	**hubierais** recordado
ellos/ellas, ustedes	**hubieran** confesado

Answers to Actividad 10:

1. me alegré, hubiéramos tenido, hubiéramos venido
2. Fue, hubiera podido
3. fue, me gustó, se hubieran puesto
4. me sentí, hubieran tocado, fue, hubiera llovido
5. importó, hubiera llovido, me encantó, nos hubiéramos divertido

10 Después del desfile. Fuiste a un desfile con tus amigos/as donde había muchos estudiantes de la escuela. Después del desfile, todos hablan del evento. Cambia todos los verbos al tiempo pasado, utilizando el pluscuamperfecto de subjuntivo cuando sea necesario.

MARICARMEN: **Me alegro** de que no **hayamos tenido** clases y de que **hayamos venido** a celebrar el día de fiesta juntos.

GERÓNIMO: **Es** un honor que la orquesta de nuestra escuela **haya podido** marchar en el desfile.

JOSEFINA: Sí, no solamente eso **es** bueno, sino también **me gusta** que los compañeros **se hayan puesto** sus trajes regionales.

GERÓNIMO: ¡Qué buena costumbre! **Me siento** contento de que **hayan tocado** instrumentos tradicionales. Pero **es** una lástima que **haya llovido.**

MARICARMEN: ¡No, no **importa** que **haya llovido!** **Me encanta** que **nos hayamos divertido** tanto.

Gerónimo Maricarmen Josefina

11 Las preferencias de los padres. Con una pareja, describe cinco actividades que hiciste en el pasado y si les gustaron o no a tus padres. Sigue el modelo. Emplea el pluscuamperfecto de subjuntivo y el vocabulario de este capítulo.

▶ **Modelo:** *tocar la trompeta en la fiesta de graduación*
A mis padres les gustó que yo hubiera tocado la trompeta en la fiesta de graduación.

1. ir al desfile y a los bailes populares en el Carnaval
2. participar en el coro (*chorus*) que cantó para el presidente del país
3. repartir comida para las familias pobres de mi barrio
4. conducir el auto principal en el desfile del 1° de mayo
5. divertirse hasta el amanecer para celebrar el Año Nuevo

Answers to Actividad 11:
1. hubiera ido
2. hubiera participado
3. hubiera repartido
4. hubiera conducido
5. me hubiera divertido

After students have finished, have them make up original sentences following the pattern in **Actividad 11.**

12 Me arrepiento de todo. Imagínate que tienes noventa y cinco años y estás escribiendo tus memorias. Allí dices que te arrepientes (*regret*) de haber hecho diez cosas en tu vida. Usa **ojalá** y el pluscuamperfecto de subjuntivo para describirlas. Explica también por qué te arrepientes de ellas. Sigue el modelo.

▶ **Modelo:** *Ojalá que yo no hubiera roto el antiguo plato de cerámica de mi mamá cuando era niño/a.*

Lectura A

Introducción

The following reading presents a particular interpretation of certain beliefs of some pre-Columbian cultures about the human embodiment or incarnation of God. These beliefs, which may be considered similar to those of the Christian faith, are presented by the writer to argue that dissimilar cultures may still share some similar religious beliefs.

Reading strategy: Identifying the thesis and the arguments in a text

The text that you will read is an expository reading. In this type of text, the author presents a thesis (main idea) in an explicit or implicit way and presents arguments or facts (supporting ideas) to sustain it. In this reading, the thesis is explicit and is stated at the beginning of the text. This way of presenting the thesis first and then the supporting arguments is called *deductive.* Can you identify the thesis of this reading as well as the arguments presented to support it?

1 Palabras clave. Las palabras subrayadas (*underlined*) ayudan a comprender la lectura. Estúdialas y consulta el diccionario si lo necesitas.

1. Los padres conciben a sus hijos.
2. Engendrar un hijo es procrear una nueva generación.
3. Doncella era la palabra que se usaba antes en español para describir a una chica joven y virgen.
4. Los prodigios son eventos o cosas que contradicen las leyes de la naturaleza.

2 *La tesis.* En la lectura, la tesis del autor está explícita. Lee la frase siguiente e identifica los dos componentes de la tesis: la causa y el efecto.

Tesis: "El prodigio (*wonder*) de una concepción milagrosa estaba tan profundamente arraigado a (*rooted in*) sus culturas, que la aceptación del ritual de la Navidad cristiana fue natural."

3 *Busca el ejemplo.* Las frases siguientes son algunos ejemplos que usa la autora para apoyar (*support*) su tesis. Léelas y consulta el diccionario para asegurarte de que las entiendes bien.

1. Los incas contaban la historia de Cauillaca, una hermosa doncella que, sin saberlo, había concebido un hijo.
2. La madre de Huitzilopochtli, el dios azteca de la guerra, lo engendró cuando ella guardó en su pecho unas plumas de pájaro que había encontrado.
3. Una muchacha concibió a Goranchacha, el héroe de la cultura muisca de Colombia, cuando ella se expuso a los rayos del sol.
4. Los aztecas tenían un templo en el Cerro de Tepeyac, dedicado a Tonantzin, "la madre de los dioses". Ella se les aparecía a los indígenas como una jovencita y les contaba cosas secretas.

EL ROSTRO MESTIZO DE LA NAVIDAD EN AMÉRICA

Antes de que los españoles llegaran a América, los indígenas tenían entre sus experiencias religiosas la imagen sorprendente de madres vírgenes. El prodigio de una concepción milagrosa estaba tan profundamente arraigado a sus culturas, que la aceptación del ritual de la Navidad cristiana fue natural.

Los incas contaban la historia de Cauillaca, una hermosa doncella que sin saberlo, había concebido un hijo de Viracocha, el dios creador, simplemente al comer una fruta que éste había hecho caer a la tierra tras° convertirse en pájaro.

Huitzilopochtli, el dios guerrero de los aztecas, fue engendrado° cuando su madre guardó en el pecho las hermosas plumas que había hallado° al barrer el suelo de un templo sagrado.

Y entre los muiscas°, el gran héroe, Goranchacha, fue concebido por una muchacha que se expuso° a los rayos del sol en las alturas de una montaña. Después del nacimiento, ella permaneció virgen.

En todas estas tradiciones se honraba a la mujer como mediadora entre los hombres y la divinidad. Por ejemplo, la virgen morena de Guadalupe, cuya festividad es hoy en día una de las celebraciones más importantes de diciembre, se apareció al indio Juan Diego, apenas diez años después de la caída° de Tenochtitlán. Apareció precisamente en el Cerro de Tepeyac donde antes había un templo dedicado a Tonantzin, "Madre de los dioses". Según el fraile Torquemada, ella se presentaba a los indígenas "en figura de una jovencita, y les revelaba cosas secretas."

after

conceived / fall

found

Colombian civilization

was exposed

4 Comprensión. Trabaja en grupos y contesta las siguientes preguntas sobre la lectura.

1. ¿Qué imagen de la madre contribuyó para que algunos indígenas de América aceptaran la Navidad cristiana?
2. ¿Con quién tuvo un hijo Cauillaca?
3. ¿Quién se convirtió en pájaro?
4. ¿Cómo se convirtió el sol en padre de Goranchacha?
5. ¿Cuál es el papel que muchas religiones le asignan a la mujer ante la divinidad?
6. ¿Quién era Tonantzin? ¿Dónde se aparecía a los indígenas?
7. ¿Qué decía el fraile Torquemada sobre la figura de Tonantzin?

Answers to Actividad 4:
1. la madre virgen
2. Viracocha
3. Viracocha
4. Una muchacha se expuso a los rayos del sol.
5. mediadora entre los hombres y la divinidad
6. madre de los dioses / En el Cerro de Tepeyac
7. que tenía figura de jovencita y revelaba secretos

5 Las cosas son así. Trabaja en grupos. Completa los argumentos presentados en la lectura con la forma correcta del imperfecto de subjuntivo.

▸ **Modelo:** *Fue fácil que las poblaciones americanas (aceptar) el ritual de Navidad.*
Fue fácil que las poblaciones americanas aceptaran el ritual de Navidad.

1. No era cierto que todas esas culturas (honrar) a la mujer como mediadora.
2. Fue un prodigio que la virgen morena de Guadalupe (aparecerse) al indio Juan Diego.
3. No era extraño que Cauillaca no (saber) que había concebido un hijo.
4. Fue natural que las culturas amerindias (aceptar) el ritual de Navidad.

Answers to Actividad 5:
1. honraran
2. se apareciera
3. supiera
4. aceptaran

6 Tema, tesis y argumentos. Repite, con tus propias palabras, el tema de la lectura, la tesis y dos argumentos presentados por la autora. ¿Cuál es tu opinión de la tesis de la autora? Compara tus ideas con las de tus compañeros/as.

7 Una creencia. Trabaja en grupos de dos o tres personas. Cada grupo escribe una corta leyenda que conozcan sobre el origen de una persona legendaria, sobre un sitio especial, una ciudad o algún objeto interesante.

For **Actividad 7,** the person, place, or thing can be imaginary. Encourage students to be creative. Make up names and bring in pictures or drawings to illustrate the sources.

ETAPA B

Pistas y palabras

I. Talking about art and artists

la pintura

la escultura

la cerámica

el dibujo

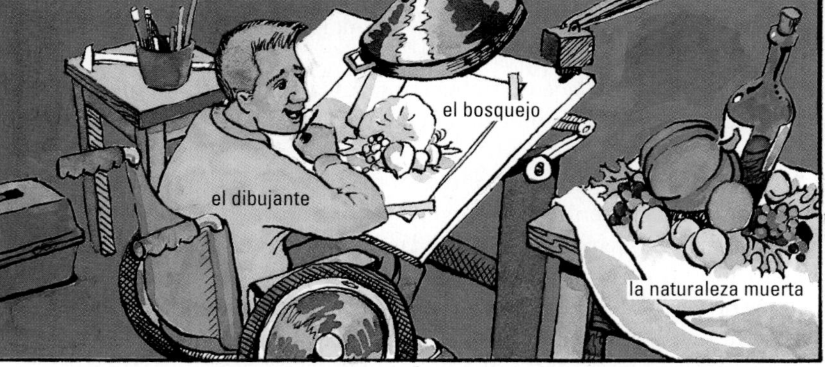

El estudio de arte

Palabras y expresiones útiles

la acuarela	*watercolor*	el detalle	*detail*
la arquitectura	*architecture*	la dimensión	*dimension*
el arte clásico	*classic art*	la figura	*figure*
el arte contemporáneo	*contemporary art*	la forma	*form*
el arte moderno	*modern art*	la fotografía	*photograph*
el/la artista	*artist*	el/la fotógrafo/a	*photographer*
el autorretrato	*self-portrait*	la ilustración	*illustration*
la cámara	*camera*	el/la modelo	*model*
los colores primarios	*primary colors*	el mosaico	*mosaic*
los colores secundarios	*secondary colors*	el museo	*museum*
la composición	*composition*	los neutros	*neutrals*
el contraste	*contrast*	la pintura al óleo	*oil paint*
el cuadro	*painting; square*	la textura	*texture*

colgar (ue)	*to hang*
construir	*to construct, build*
crear	*to create*
dibujar	*to draw*
diseñar	*to design*
mostrar (ue)	*to show*
pintar	*to paint*
sacar (tomar) fotos	*to take photos*

abstracto/a	*abstract*	en color/es	*(in) color*
claro/a	*light*	oscuro/a	*dark*
en blanco y negro	*black and white*		

LENGUA EN ACCIÓN

Movimientos artísticos

Most artistic periods are described in English with the suffix *-ism.* The corresponding Spanish term ends in **-ismo.** For example:

Modernism = **modernismo**
Impressionism = **impresionismo**

The artist who created art within this period is described in English with the suffix *-ist.* The corresponding Spanish term ends in **-ista.** Note that the ending is the same whether the artist is male or female.

modernist = **el/la modernista**
impressionist = **el/la impresionista**

What do you think the Spanish terms for the following might be?

cubism, cubist, realism, realist, surrealism, surrealist, expressionism, expressionist, romanticism, romanticist

1 Preguntas personales. Contesta las preguntas.

1. ¿Qué tipo de arte te gusta más? ¿Por qué?
2. ¿Quién es tu artista favorito/a? ¿De dónde es? ¿Qué tipo de arte hace?
3. ¿Te gusta ir a museos? ¿Por qué? ¿Por qué no?
4. ¿Conoces a algunos artistas hispanos? ¿Cuáles? ¿De dónde son? Describe sus obras.

Before doing **Actividad 2**, show students several paintings and give brief biographies of the following artists: Diego Rivera, Siqueiros, Orozco, Xul Solar, Frida Kahlo, Marisol. You may also wish to tell students about Spanish artists such as Velázquez, El Greco, Goya, and Picasso. Use art books, postcards, and/or the WWW.

2 Arte moderno. ¿Qué piensas de estas obras artísticas? En grupos, contesta las preguntas y describe cada cuadro.

A

1. ¿Qué colores usa el artista?
2. ¿Cuáles son las formas dominantes del cuadro?
3. ¿Qué símbolos reconoces? ¿Qué relación tienen con el tema del cuadro?
4. Según tu opinión, ¿tiene el artista una visión positiva del mundo? ¿Por qué?

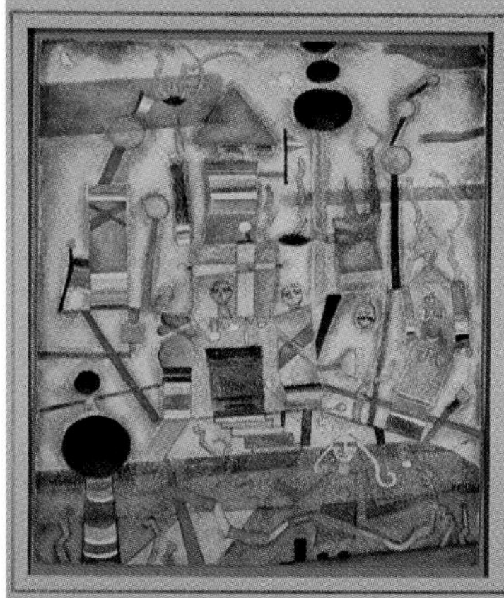

"Patria B", Xul Solar.

B

1. ¿Es el cuadro serio o divertido? ¿Qué elementos expresan esa emoción?
2. ¿Qué diferencia hay entre las "dos" Fridas del cuadro?
3. ¿Qué elementos comunes tienen las dos Fridas?
4. ¿Por qué crees que los corazones son visibles?
5. ¿Qué te dice este autorretrato de Frida Kahlo sobre ella?

"Las dos Fridas", Frida Kahlo (1939).

C

1. ¿Cómo es la familia? ¿Es rica, pobre, feliz o infeliz? ¿Cómo lo sabes?
2. Describe a cada miembro de esta familia. ¿Dónde está el padre?

3. ¿Por qué crees que la artista usa la escultura para expresar este motivo?
4. Describe los colores.

Marisol (Marisol Escobar), "The Family" (1962). Painted wood and other materials in three sections, overall, 6'10⅝" x 65½" x 15½" (209.8 x 166.3 x 39.3 cm). The Museum of Modern Art, New York. Advisory Committee Fund. Photograph © 1998 The Museum of Modern Art, New York.

3 Preséntala. En una revista o libro de arte, escoge una foto de una obra de arte que te guste. Tráela a la clase y descríbela.

ENLACE CULTURAL

El muralismo

El muralismo fue un movimiento de renovación en el arte latinoamericano a principios del siglo XX. Apareció en México y se extendió por casi todos los países hispanos, en especial, en los que hay un alto porcentaje de población indígena, como Bolivia y Ecuador. Los murales tienen generalmente grandes dimensiones y sus motivos centrales representan eventos históricos o elementos de la identidad nacional, muchas veces con aspectos indígenas. Los principales muralistas mexicanos fueron Diego Rivera, David Alfaro Siqueiros y José Clemente Orozco. En el Ecuador, se ha destacado Osvaldo Guayasamín; en Bolivia, Miguel Alandia Pantoja y en Colombia, Pedro Nel Gómez.

"El Mercado de Tenochtitlán", pintura de Diego Rivera.

Osvaldo Guayasamín en su casa museo, en Quito.

Discusión en grupos

1. ¿Hay decoraciones especiales en edificios, parques o casas en su pueblo? Descríbanlas.
2. ¿Hay murales en la región de ustedes? ¿Conoce alguno de ustedes murales en otros estados? ¿Cómo son y qué representan?
3. ¿Son los grafitis una expresión artística? ¿Son las pinturas de las cavernas (*caves*) expresiones artísticas de nuestros antepasados?

II. Talking about crafts and folk art

Objetos artesanales

Nature stores often carry **alebrijes** in the U.S. If you own one, bring it in. Ask students if they have seen **alebrijes**. Where? What animals? This is a good opportunity to review the animal vocabulary in Chapter 9.

Alebrijes

En Oaxaca se hacen **artesanías** como estas **figuritas** de madera **pintadas a mano.** Son muy populares entre los **coleccionistas,** y además se consideran como talismanes de la **buena suerte.** Hay alebrijes en forma de unicornios, jirafas, iguanas, jaguares, armadillos, etc.

Alebrijes en forma de jaguar, Oaxaca, México.

Ojo de Dios

Muchos símbolos indígenas fueron destruidos durante la colonización española de América, pero el Ojo de Dios **ha permanecido** (*has remained*) desde entonces porque tiene forma de **cruz** (*cross*). En muchas partes se usa como talismán porque se cree que **trae** buena suerte.

Chica mexicana con un "Ojo de Dios" en la mano.

Réplicas precolombinas

En Colombia **se fabrican** actualmente **réplicas** de objetos precolombinos **de oro**. Estas **piezas** se usan como joyas, como decoración en las casas o como **adornos** de bolsos y **correas** (*belts*).

Una máscara precolombina, Museo de Oro, Bogotá.

If you own any "Toledo Gold," be sure to bring it to class along with a copy of El Greco's famous painting of Toledo. Point out the location of Toledo on the map in the front of this book.

El damasquinado

En la ciudad española de Toledo, **hábiles artesanos** trabajan con la técnica del damasquinado, es decir, la decoración de metales preciosos. Allí se fabrican hermosos objetos como el que vemos en la foto, con adornos **dorados** de hermosos diseños de influencia árabe.

Artesano toledano.

4 Clasificación de los objetos artesanales. Trabaja con un/a compañero/a y construye una tabla sobre los cuatro objetos artesanales descritos (*described*) arriba.

	Alebrijes	Ojo de Dios	Réplicas pre-colombinas	Objetos de Toledo
origen				
material				
uso				
colores				
¿...?				

5 Artesanías personales. Diseña un objeto artesanal que represente la historia de tus antepasados (*ancestors*). Puede ser real o imaginario. Dibújalo y describe su historia incluyendo qué es, para qué se usa, y con qué material se hace.

For **Actividad 5,** be sensitive to the fact that some of your students may not wish to talk about their heritage. Encourage them to be creative and use their imagination.

ENLACE CULTURAL

Arte ambulante

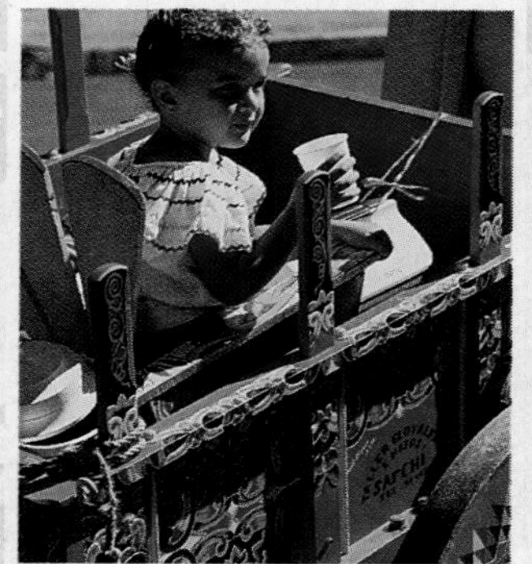

Carreta costarricense.

En muchos países hispanos podemos ver autobuses y vehículos totalmente cubiertos con dibujos de colores. Estos adornos representan motivos importantes para su dueño como un hermoso paisaje o su santo preferido. Hasta los años sesenta, este tipo de buses eran frecuentes como transporte público en Colombia; actualmente sólo se ven en regiones rurales o durante festivales folclóricos. Lo mismo ha sucedido con las bellas carretas° pintadas de Costa Rica: alguna vez fueron un medio de transporte y ahora se han convertido en uno de los símbolos importantes de la identidad costarricense. Los buses pintados colombianos, llamados generalmente "buses de escalera"° y las carretas costarricenses se venden ahora como recuerdos turísticos.

wagons

ladder

Discusión en grupos

1. ¿Existen vehículos decorados en su región? Piensen, por ejemplo, en los colores o dibujos especiales que algunas personas usan en sus autos o motocicletas.
2. ¿Conocen otras expresiones del arte popular en su estado o país?
3. ¿Qué decoración prefiere cada uno de ustedes para su auto, moto o bicicleta?

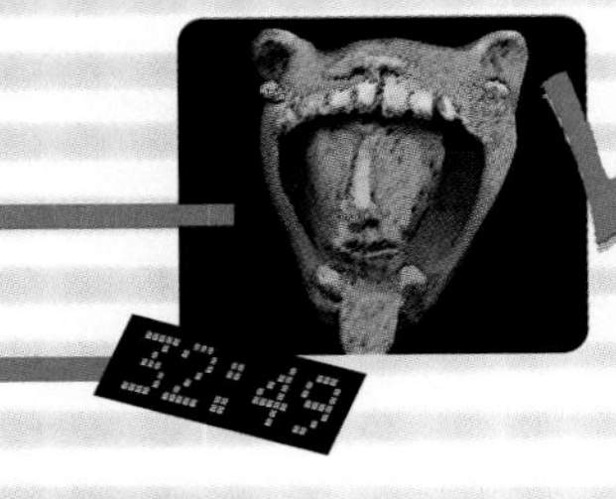

VISTAS Y VOCES

I. Preparémonos

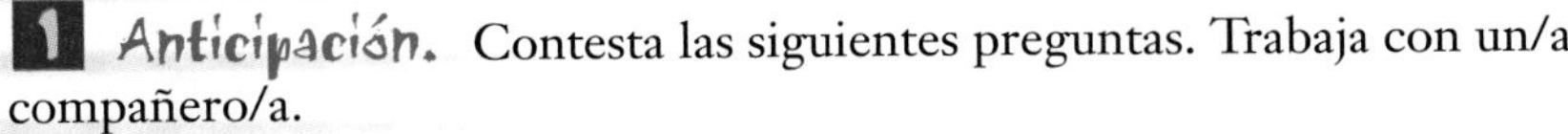

1 Anticipación. Contesta las siguientes preguntas. Trabaja con un/a compañero/a.

A. **1.** Cuando tienes sospechas sobre las acciones de un/a amigo/a, ¿se las dices directamente o hablas con otra persona primero? ¿Por qué? Da un ejemplo.
2. ¿Qué mensaje delicado o alarmante has recibido tú (o alguien de tu familia o un/a amigo/a) en el contestador telefónico?
3. Describe tú una misión peligrosa o difícil que tú hiciste el semestre pasado. ¿Qué plan seguiste tú para cumplirla?

B. Mira la foto 10B en la página 395. ¿Qué dicen Nayeli y Adriana sobre doña Carmen?

Para comprender mejor

alargar	*to lengthen*	el halago	*praise*
alejar	*to keep away*	el hogar	*home*
alterado/a	*upset*	incomprensivo/a	*unsympathetic*
confiar	*to trust*	inquietante	*disturbing*
correr el riesgo	*to run the risk*	por qué diablos	*why in the world*
deshecho/a	*shattered*	por su propia cuenta	*on her/his own*
¡Dios mío santo!	*Good grief!*	el rastro	*trace*
duro/a	*hard*	regañar	*to scold*
el engaño	*deceit*	el/la testigo	*witness*
Está en contra nuestra.	*He/She is against us.*	la traición	*betrayal*
la fuerza	*strength*	ya	*already; now*
el golpe	*blow*	el contestador automático	*answering machine*
gordo/a	*serious; heavy*		
la grabadora	*tape recorder/ answering machine*		

2 Secuencia. Estudia cada escena de video y contesta las siguientes preguntas. ¿Quién es Armando? ¿Qué interés tiene en los héroes gemelos? ¿Es lógico tener confianza en él o tener sospechas de él? Explica. Después, arregla las escenas en un orden lógico.

Order of video action shots: 2, 1, 3, 4

1.

2.

3.

4.

II. Miremos y escuchemos

3 Mis observaciones. Mientras miras y escuchas el episodio, escribe las reacciones y emociones que Nayeli tiene durante este episodio. ¿Qué pasa y cómo se siente Nayeli hacia doña Carmen, Adriana, Armando y Felipe?

III. Comentemos

4 Comprensión. Contesta las siguientes preguntas.

1. ¿A quién le pregunta Adriana en dónde están los jaguares gemelos?
2. ¿Quién quiere llamar a la policía?
3. ¿Con quiénes quiere hablar primero doña Carmen?
4. ¿En qué están todos de acuerdo?
5. ¿Quién deja un mensaje telefónico en el contestador automático de doña Carmen?
6. ¿Quiénes escuchan el mensaje primero?
7. ¿Cuál es el "problema gordo" que menciona Armando en su mensaje?
8. ¿Quién es Mariluz Gorrostiaga? ¿Qué hizo ella? ¿Dónde está?
9. ¿Cómo reacciona Nayeli cuando escucha el mensaje telefónico?
10. ¿Qué plan tiene Nayeli para recuperar a los gemelos?
11. ¿A quién llama doña Carmen?
12. Al final del episodio, ¿tiene doña Carmen confianza en Armando? ¿Por qué?

5 El camino del jaguar. ¿Crees tú que los héroes gemelos van a llegar a México a tiempo para el treinta y uno de agosto y en buenas condiciones? Explica.

6 Miremos otra vez. Después de mirar el episodio otra vez, arregla las escenas de video en la secuencia correcta y narra la acción.

7 El engaño. Nayeli habla sobre el engaño y la traición. ¿Quién(es) engaña(n) a quién(es)? ¿Cómo? ¿Cuál es el resultado? ¿Por qué?

8 En mi opinión... En grupos de tres, identifiquen a los personajes que dicen las siguientes frases. Luego, digan si están o no de acuerdo y por qué. Finalmente, intercambien y comparen las respuestas con otro grupo.

"...es importante que no actuemos sin pensar."
"El futuro de México depende de nosotros."
"No confíes en nadie, confía sólo en tu intuición."

Answers to Actividad 4:

1. Pregunta a doña Carmen.
2. Adriana quiere llamar a la policía.
3. Ella quiere hablar con los vecinos y con los pintores.
4. En recuperar a los jaguares gemelos.
5. Armando deja un mensaje en el contestador automático.
6. Nayeli, Felipe y Adriana.
7. Gafasnegras tiene los gemelos y está en San Antonio.
8. Gafasnegras. Se robó a los gemelos. Ella está en San Antonio.
9. Está deshecha. (alterada)
10. Felipe y Nayeli van a ir a San antonio y Nayeli va a México.
11. Ella llama a Armando.
12. Ella no tiene confianza en Armando porque cree que Armando la engañó.

Lengua

I. Clarifying and specifying references to persons and things

Relative pronouns

Gente

JUAN: Compré unas joyas de oro **que** le voy a mandar a mi hija.

ANA: Tengo un primo **a quien**° le voy a mandar un CD-ROM sobre Latinoamérica.

to whom

JUAN: ¿El primo **del cual** me hablaste ayer? ¿Va a viajar a algún país hispano?

ANA: No, pero **lo que**° le encanta es relajarse de noche explorando las civilizaciones precolombinas a través de la tecnología.

the thing that

Relative pronouns are used in Spanish to combine two sentences that have a noun or pronoun in common. The main relative pronouns in English are *that*, *which*, and *who/whom*, all of which are sometimes omitted. In Spanish, they must be used.

- **Que** refers to things as well as people *(that, which, who)*.

Compré una pequeña vasija **que** debo mandar a mi hija.	*I bought a small bowl that (which) I should send to my daughter.*
Tengo un primo **que** es escultor.	*I have a cousin who is a sculptor.*

- **Quien/quienes** refers only to people (*who/whom*) and is used after prepositions and the personal **a.**

Maricarmen Hernández es la médica **a quien** consulto cuando me siento enfermo.	*Maricarmen Hernandez is the doctor whom I consult when I feel sick.*

Éste es el dependiente **con quien** hablé para conseguir una tarjeta de crédito. — *This is the clerk with whom I spoke to get a credit card.*

- **Lo que** refers to an idea or a previous situation (*what, that which*).

A Papá no le gustó **lo que** le pintó el artista. — *Dad did not like what the artist painted for him.*

Lo que necesito es una pulsera de diamantes y esmeraldas. — *What I need is a diamond and emerald bracelet.*

Stress that **lo que** is "neuter" in gender (neither masculine nor feminine) and refers to a whole idea. This contrasts with the more specific **el/la/los/las que** and **cual/es** which occur later in this chapter.

- When **cual** or **cuales** is used to refer to a noun, it has an article that agrees in gender and number with the noun.

El artista **del cual** te hablé es joven. — *The artist about whom I talked to you is young.*

La pintora **a la cual** le dieron el premio es paraguaya. — *The artist to whom the prize was awarded is from Paraguay.*

1 Comprensión. Conecta lógicamente las siguientes ideas con el pronombre relativo **que.**

▸ **Modelo:** *Laura es una buena artista. Sabe mucho sobre la pintura al óleo.*
Laura es una buena artista que sabe mucho sobre la pintura al óleo.

1. Dana tiene un dibujo. El dibujo es nuevo.
2. Me regalaron una escultura. La escultura es de bronce.
3. Tengo un bosquejo. El bosquejo representa una naturaleza muerta.
4. ¿Dónde está la arcilla? Compré la arcilla ayer.
5. Le di a Carmen una ilustración. La ilustración es muy bonita.

Answers to Actividad 1:
1. Dana tiene un dibujo que es nuevo.
2. Me regalaron una escultura que es de bronce.
3. Tengo un bosquejo que representa una naturaleza muerta.
4. ¿Dónde está la arcilla que compré ayer?
5. Le di a Carmen una ilustración que es muy bonita.

2 En la tienda. Irene va a la tienda para comprar un regalo de bodas para su prima. Completa las frases con las formas correctas de los pronombres relativos **que, quien** y **lo que**.

IRENE: Me llamo Irene Gómez y quisiera ver al dependiente con _________ hablé esta mañana sobre regalos de cerámica.
DEPENDIENTE: Ah, sí, fui yo _________ hablé con usted, señorita.
IRENE: Mi prima registró aquí la lista de regalos para su boda porque le encantaron los platos mexicanos _________ ella compró.
DEPENDIENTE: Me alegro de que le hayan gustado los platos.
IRENE: Ahora, _________ quiero hacer es regalarle seis vasos y tazas del mismo diseño, por favor.
DEPENDIENTE: Claro que sí. ¿Cómo quiere pagar?
IRENE: Quiero pagar con un cheque, pero la chequera es nueva y tengo cheques _________ no tienen mi dirección actual. ¿Aprueba usted el cheque?
DEPENDIENTE: Llamaré a mi supervisora para que ella apruebe su cheque.
IRENE: Gracias.

Answers to actividad 2:
1. quien
2. quien
3. que
4. lo que
5. que

3 Opiniones. Hazles una entrevista a tus compañeros/as sobre sus preferencias. Todas las respuestas deben hacerse con frases completas y usar **que, quien, quienes** o **lo que.**

1. ¿Qué día de fiesta te gusta más a ti? ¿Por qué? ¿y a tu hermano/a?
2. ¿Qué festival de tu región atrae (*attracts*) el mayor número de personas? ¿Cómo participas tú en él y cómo es?
3. ¿Qué región de tu país tiene más celebraciones? ¿Qué tipos de celebraciones son?
4. ¿Qué evento deportivo de tu región atrae más publico?

II. Asking questions

Differentiating between qué and cuál

Arquitectura

PROFESORA: ¿**Cuál** es una de las catedrales más importantes del mundo hispano moderno? ¿**Qué** características tiene?

ESTUDIANTE 1: La catedral que diseñó el arquitecto Antonio Gaudí en Barcelona es muy famosa. Es muy grande y moderna. ¿**Qué** piensa Ud. de ella?

PROFESORA: Pienso que Gaudí fue un innovador. ¿**Cuáles** son otras de las obras artísticas de Gaudí y en **qué** año las diseñó?

ESTUDIANTE 2: Gaudí diseñó otros edificios y parques muy hermosos, también; creo que lo hizo después de que diseñó la catedral de Barcelona.

In Spanish, the equivalents of the English interrogatives *what* and *which* are expressed in two ways, with different meanings, depending on the context.

Uses of *qué*

- When you want to request a definition or an explanation, use **qué** as the subject of the verb. It translates as *what* and carries an accent.

¿**Qué** es el cubismo? — *What is Cubism?*

Uses of *cuál*

- When you ask for a choice among a selection of several possibilities, **cuál/cuáles** is used as the subject of a verb and can be translated as *what* or *which*.

¿**Cuál** de estas pinturas prefieres? — *Which painting do you prefer?*
¿**Cuáles** de esos dibujos te gustan? — *Which of those drawings do you like?*

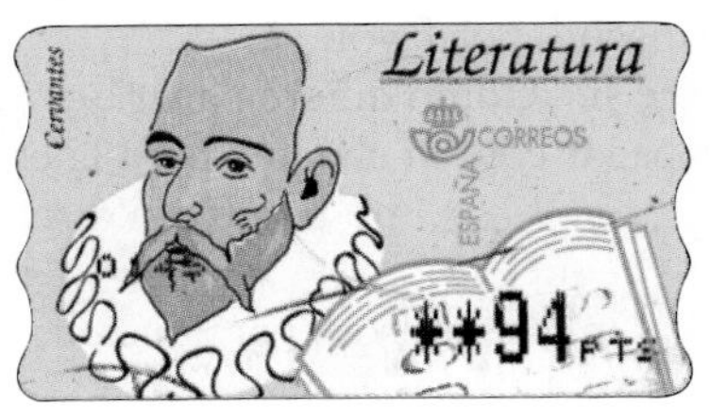

4 **Dime tu opinión.** Una pareja está en un museo en Sudamérica. Completa el diálogo que tienen Rosa y Luis con las formas apropiadas de **qué** o **cuál.**

ROSA: ¿ __________ de todas las pinturas te gusta más en esta sala?
LUIS: No sé __________ es mi favorita. Todas tienen colores muy vivos y agradables. ¿ __________ prefieres tú, mi amor?
ROSA: Me encanta todo el arte, pero me pregunto, ¿ __________ simbolizan los diseños geométricos?
LUIS: No tengo ni idea. ¿ __________ representan los colores en estas pinturas? No estoy seguro de que esto sea arte.

Answers to Actividad 4:
1. Cuál
2. cuál
3. Cuál
4. Qué
5. Qué

III. Expressing opposing opinions

Pero and sino

Festivales

PEPITO: Me gustó el festival de mayo, **pero**° me cansé mucho bailando.
ROLANDO: Yo no bailé, **sino**° que canté con el grupo folclórico panameño. Me dio muchísima satisfacción hacerlo.

° *but*
° *rather, on the contrary*

In Spanish, *but* is expressed in two ways, with different meanings. When you have two clauses and the second contradicts the meaning in the first, you use **sino** to mean *rather* or *on the contrary*. No me gusta el café, **sino** el chocolate. (*I do not like coffee, rather I prefer chocolate.*) In most other instances, **pero** is used to express *but*. Traté de llamarlo, **pero** no estaba en casa. (*I tried to call him, but he was not at home.*)

Often, in these types of sentences, **sino** is preceded by a negative clause and **pero** by a positive.

5 En la tienda de artesanías. Oneka y Cassandra están en la tienda de artesanías, donde están comprando regalos para llevar a sus familias y amigos. Tienen diferentes opiniones. Completen el diálogo con las formas correctas de **pero** o **sino.**

Answers to Actividad 5:
1. pero
2. sino
3. pero
4. pero
5. sino

Objetos frágiles

ONEKA: A mi hermano y a mi cuñada les encantan los platos de cerámica, ________ son muy delicados para llevar en el avión.

CASSANDRA: Yo no voy a comprar objetos frágiles, ________ tejidos. Es mejor porque los tejidos se pueden llevar sin problemas.

ONEKA: Tienes razón, ________ estas vasijas son perfectas para mi nueva cocina.

CASSANDRA: Se me ocurre una idea fantástica: compras los platos y las vasijas, ________ no las llevas en la mano, ________ que las mandas por correo.

6 No estoy de acuerdo. Usando el vocabulario del capítulo y el modelo de la actividad anterior, escribe un cuentito con opiniones opuestas, con **sino** y **pero.**

Lectura B

Introducción

The following reading presents some thoughts about arts and crafts in general and specifically about art in Hispanic countries.

Prelectura

1 El arte. El museo principal de tu ciudad va a hacer una exposición de los cuadros preferidos de varias personas de la comunidad. Trabaja en grupos y pregúntales a tus compañeros/as qué cuadro/s le prestarían al museo.

Arte y artesanía

Con el encuentro de América, Europa y África, la estética hispanoamericana adquirió° una identidad multifacética. Desde el siglo XV hasta fines del siglo XVIII, la herencia° española influyó en el desarrollo° del arte, la arquitectura y las artesanías en los países hispanos. Posteriormente, las culturas autóctonas,° la presencia de culturas africanas, y las características geográficas e históricas de cada país, enriquecieron° y le dieron identidad propia a las expresiones artísticas locales.

acquired
heritage
development
native
enriched

A finales del siglo XIX y a principios del siglo XX, con la independencia y formación de las nuevas repúblicas americanas, se intensificó el cultivo de las artes nacionales en los diferentes países. En la pintura, la escultura y la música, aparecieron movimientos artísticos con sello° nacionalista, como lo fue el muralismo mexicano.

hallmark

En este momento, florecieron° también las artesanías nacionales y aumentó° su aprecio como expresión de la identidad nacional y de las culturas regionales. Cada región tiene actualmente artesanías típicas como

bloomed
increased

"Albañil"
Este cuadro del pintor mexicano, Diego Rivera, es una obra artística muy expresiva.

"Composición con pájaro"
Este cuadro del pintor mexicano, José Obregón, es una obra de arte de estilo abstracto.

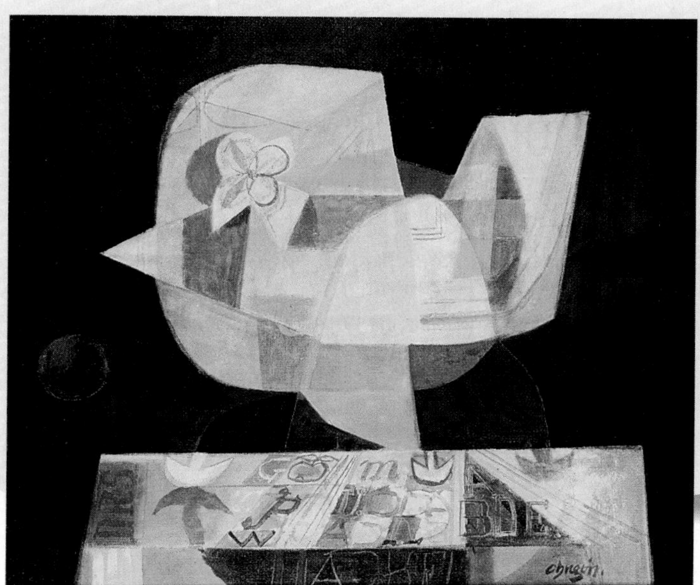

miniatures

muebles de madera, tapetes, exquisitas miniaturas,° telas, ropa, hamacas e infinidad de hermosos objetos que expresan el espíritu nacional y regional de sus gentes.

"La granja"
En este cuadro, César López, un pintor folclórico colombiano, expresa su visión de una escena en el campo.

Postlectura

2 Tesis. ¿Cuál te parece que es la tesis de la lectura? Selecciona el párrafo que la contiene.

3 Argumentos. Menciona dos argumentos que apoyan (*support*) esta tesis.

Answers to Actividad 4:
1. **V**
2. **V**
3. **F**—El muralismo apareció en México.
4. **V**
5. **F**—Las nuevas repúblicas lograron su independencia a finales del siglo XIX y a principios del siglo XX.
6. **V**
7. **V**
8. **V**

4 ¿Verdadero o falso? Determina cuáles de estas afirmaciones son verdaderas y cuáles son falsas, según lo que dice la lectura. Corrige las falsas.

1. La estética hispanoamericana tiene una identidad multifacética.
2. Las artesanías representan la identidad nacional.
3. El muralismo fue un movimiento artístico español.
4. Cada país tiene su propia identidad artística.
5. Las nuevas repúblicas americanas lograron su independencia a finales del siglo XV.
6. Después de la independencia, cada región desarrolló su identidad nacional con sus artesanías.
7. El arte hispanoamericano también tiene influencia de culturas africanas.
8. En algunas regiones, las hamacas son también artesanías.

5 A escribir. Según tu opinión, ¿existe diferencia entre el arte que ves en las galerías de arte de tu ciudad y las artesanías locales? ¿Cuáles son esas diferencias?

En resumen

I. Hablemos

1 Planeando una fiesta. En grupos de tres, planeen una gran fiesta para su universidad. Hagan una lista de lo que hay que hacer para organizar un desfile, un baile y una exposición de arte. Usen algunas de las siguientes frases en sus listas:

Es importante que…
Es bueno que…
Quiero/Queremos que…
…antes de que…
…tan pronto como…

2 A San Antonio. Adriana y Felipe hacen un plan mientras viajan a San Antonio para recuperar al jaguar. Discute con un/a compañero/a las cuatro cosas más importantes que deben hacer. ¿Adónde deben ir? ¿Con quién deben hablar?, etc.

II. Investiguemos por Internet

Using bookmarks

As you have learned, Internet guides provide a vast amount of information classified by theme. However, classifications may be different from one Internet guide to another. When you are looking for information in several Web sites and you would like to compare them, you may want to use bookmarks to access the sites easily. You may also use the list that your browser keeps of recent visited sites. This list is accessible from the upper menu in your browser.

Vocabulario informático	
el separador (indicador, sitio favorito)	*bookmark*

3 ¡Carnaval! Work in groups and search for at least three carnival celebrations in the Hispanic world. Report to the class where and when each carnival is, and the reason it is celebrated. Does it have its own name? If there are pictures of the celebration, select at least one picture and describe it to the class. Mention also whether people use costumes in each one of the carnivals you are describing.

III. Escribamos

Writing strategy: Summarizing

A summary is a version of something that you have read or seen that contains only the most important information and leaves out much of the detail. Once you have identified the main idea and supporting detail, you can connect these ideas in paragraph form. Unlike paraphrasing, a summary intends to condense the material and present it in a straightforward way.

Review the following strategies to prepare for writing a summary.

Providing supporting detail (Chapter 3)
Taking notes in the margin (Chapter 4)
Paraphrasing (Chapter 7)

Strategy in action

Turn to *Escribamos* in the Workbook to practice the writing strategy of summarizing.

4 **Resumen.** Escribe un resumen de una de las lecturas en este capítulo. Compara tu composición con un/a compañero/a.

5 **¿Qué pasó en Costa Rica?** Escribe un resumen de los cuatro episodios del video que están videofilmados en Costa Rica. Compara tu composición con la de un/a compañero/a.

Vocabulario

Fiestas y celebraciones

actuar	*to act*
adorar	*to adore*
aplacar a los dioses	*to placate the gods*
auténtico/a	*authentic*
la bandera	*flag*
bello/a	*beautiful*
la broma	*trick*
el buen/mal espíritu	*good/bad spirit*
la catástrofe	*catastrophe*
celebrar	*to celebrate*
la ceremonia	*ceremony*
componer	*to compose*
el concierto	*concert*
el conejito de Pascua	*Easter bunny*
la conmemoración	*commemoration*
conmemorar	*to commemorate*
el desfile	*parade*
el disfraz	*costume*
en honor de	*in honor of*
entretenido/a	*entertaining*
el espectáculo	*spectacle*
la estatua	*statue*
el evento	*event*
la exhibición, exposición	*exhibition*
la exposición mundial	*world's fair*
el fenómeno	*phenomenon*
la fertilidad	*fertility*
festejar	*to celebrate*
el festival	*festival*
la fiesta	*party*
el folclor	*folklore*
folclórico/a	*folkloric*
los fuegos artificiales	*fireworks*
la guerra	*war*
histórico/a	*historic*
el himno	*hymn*
el homenaje	*hommage*
honrar	*to honor*
los juegos olímpicos	*olympic games*
el logro	*achievement*

magnífico/a	*magnificent*	**la placa**	*plaque*
los males	*evils, harmful things*	**poderoso/a**	*powerful*
la máscara	*mask*	**prevenir**	*to prevent*
el mural	*mural*	**público/a**	*public*
el nacimiento	*birth*	**recordar un hecho histórico**	*to remember a historic event*
nacional	*national*	**regional**	*regional*
la obra de arte	*work of art*	**religioso/a**	*religious*
la participación	*participation*	**el rito**	*ritual*
participar	*to participate*	**el sacrificio**	*sacrifice*
pedir favores especiales	*to ask for special favors*	**el símbolo**	*symbol*

Arte, artesanías y artistas

abstracto/a	*abstract*	**la dimensión**	*dimension*
la acuarela	*watercolor*	**diseñar**	*to design*
el adorno	*decoration*	**dorado/a**	*golden*
a mano	*by hand*	**en blanco y negro**	*black and white*
la arcilla, el barro	*clay*	**en color/es**	*color*
la arquitectura	*architecture*	**el/la escultor/a**	*sculptor*
el arte clásico	*classic art*	**la escultura**	*sculpture*
el arte contemporáneo	*contemporary art*	**fabricarse**	*to manufacture*
el arte moderno	*modern art*	**la figura (figuritas)**	*figure (small figures)*
la artesanía	*crafts*	**la forma**	*form*
artesano/a	*artisan*	**la fotografía**	*photograph*
el/la artista	*artist*	**el/la fotógrafo/a**	*photographer*
el autorretrato	*self-portrait*	**hábil**	*skillful*
el barro	*clay*	**el horno**	*kiln*
el bosquejo	*sketch*	**la ilustración**	*illustration*
el bronce	*bronze*	**la madera**	*wood*
la cámara	*camera*	**el marco**	*frame*
la cerámica	*ceramics*	**el mármol**	*marble*
claro/a	*light*	**el/la modelo**	*model*
el/la coleccionista	*collector*	**el mosaico**	*mosaic*
colgar (ue)	*to hang*	**mostrar (ue)**	*to show*
los colores primarios	*primary colors*	**el museo**	*museum*
los colores secundarios	*secondary colors*	**la naturaleza muerta**	*still life*
la composición	*composition*	**los neutros**	*neutrals*
construir	*to construct, build*	**oscuro/a**	*dark*
el contraste	*contrast*	**el paisaje**	*landscape*
la correa	*belt*	**la paleta**	*palette*
crear	*to create*	**permanecer**	*to remain*
la cruz	*cross*	**la pieza**	*piece*
la cruz de oro	*cross made of gold*	**el pincel**	*brush*
el cuadro	*square, painting*	**pintado/a**	*painted*
el detalle	*detail*	**pintar**	*to paint*
el/la dibujante	*drawer, illustrator*	**el/la pintor/a**	*painter*
dibujar	*to draw*	**la pintura**	*painting*
el dibujo	*drawing*	**la pintura al óleo**	*oil paint*

la réplica	*replica*
el retrato	*portrait*
la rueda	*wheel*
sacar (tomar) fotos	*to take photos*
la textura	*texture*
traer buena suerte	*to bring good luck*
la vasija	*bowl, pot*

Algunos días de fiesta

Carnaval	*Carnival (celebration just before Ash Wednesday)*
Día de Acción de Gracias	*Thanksgiving*
Día de Año Nuevo	*New Year's Day*
Día de las Brujas	*Halloween*
Día de San Valentín	*Valentine's Day*
Día de la Batalla de Puebla (cinco de mayo)	*The Battle of Puebla*
Día de la Independencia	*Independence Day*
Día de la Raza	*Ancestor's Day, Columbus Day*
Día de los Muertos	*Day of the Dead*
Día de los Inocentes	*April Fool's Day*
Día de los Reyes Magos	*Three Kings' Day*
Día del Trabajo	*Labor Day*
Domingo de Pascua	*Easter Sunday*
Fiesta de todos los Santos	*All Saints' Day*
Hanukkah	*Hanukkah*
Kwanza	*Kwanza*
Miércoles de Ceniza	*Ash Wednesday*
Navidad	*Christmas*
Nochevieja	*New Year's Eve*
Semana Santa	*Holy Week*
Ramadán	*Ramadan*

CAPÍTULO 11

LOCALIDAD: Texas

11A

11B

¿Qué quiere el Sr. Guzmán?

Time is running out for Adriana and Felipe. They must help Nayeli reunite the Hero Twins Yax-Balam and Hun-Ahau on August 31. We follow them on their search for Sunglasses, but they meet someone unexpected along the way.

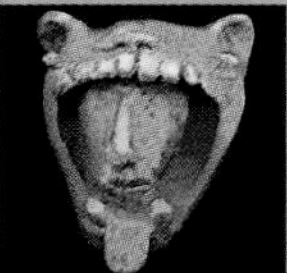

Vocabulary themes
- Talking about societal problems
- Reacting to societal issues
- Evaluating and discussing films
- Discussing television and the media

Language structures
- Expressing the future
- Expressing conjecture
- Expressing possible conditions
- Expressing what you would do
- Speculating about the past
- Expressing hypothetical actions and situations in the past

Culture topics
- La peste del siglo XX
- La clonación: Dilema moderno
- El cine hispano
- La televisión hispana

Readings
- ¡Miedos del milenio!
- Ídolos mexicanos

Reading and writing strategies
- Distinguishing facts and opinions
- Narrowing a topic

Internet strategy
- Searching for related words

ETAPA A

Pistas y palabras

I. Talking about societal problems

Jóvenes de fin de siglo

La **juventud** de hoy es una **generación** preocupada por su futuro. Para ellos, la **incertidumbre**° está presente como nunca antes, pero, la **muerte** no está entre sus **angustias**° principales. Sin embargo, el **SIDA**° y las drogas sí están entre sus preocupaciones. Además, estos jóvenes modernos tienen consciencia social y han **aumentado**° sus demandas de educación, **empleo,**° **servicios de salud,** espacios de expresión cultural y **representación política.**

Antes de casarse, los jóvenes del país piensan en estudiar y **obtener**° un empleo, pero en México, el trabajo se ha **convertido en**° un sueño más difícil de **alcanzar**° que el amor.

Diversos estudios indican que, en la **población** joven, la crisis ha propiciado° un aumento en el número de **suicidios, actos delictivos,**° **consumo**° de drogas y alcohol, **embarazos**° no deseados y **enfermedades sicológicas.**

uncertainty / obtain, get

turned into
worries / to reach
AIDS

has led to

increased / delinquent / consumption / employment / pregnancies

SIDA stands for "Síndrome de inmunodeficiencia adquirida." Note that the letters are the same for AIDS but changed, anagram-style. Although the words in translation are cognates, the syntax forces a change in their order. This is a good opportunity to remind students that adjectives come after nouns in Spanish.

Palabras y expresiones útiles

la adicción	*addiction*
el/la adolescente	*adolescent*
las armas	*weapons*
el asesinato	*assassination, murder*
el/la asesino/a	*murderer*
la cárcel (prisión)	*prison*
el consejo	*advice*
el crimen	*crime*
la cura	*cure*
la delincuencia	*delinquency*
la depresión	*depression*
el/la detective	*detective*
la drogadicción	*drug addiction*
el logro	*achievement*
el/la policía	*police officer*
la policía	*police force*
la pobreza	*poverty*
el programa educativo	*educational program*
el programa de prevención contra el SIDA	*AIDS prevention program*
el programa social	*social program*
el robo	*robbery*
la solución	*solution*
el sueldo mínimo	*minimum wage*
la terapia	*therapy*
el/la trabajador/a social	*social worker*
el tráfico de drogas	*drug trafficking*
la vigilancia del vecindario	*neighborhood watch*

arrestar	*to arrest*
asesinar	*to assassinate, murder*
encarcelar	*to imprison*
fracasar	*to fail*
lograr	*to achieve; to obtain*
matar	*to kill*
(no) tener éxito	*to (not) be successful*
triunfar	*to succeed*

1 **¿Verdadero o falso?** Di si las siguientes frases son verdaderas o falsas según la lectura. Si son falsas, corrígelas.

1. Los jóvenes de México están preocupados por el futuro.
2. La muerte está entre sus angustias principales.
3. La educación es importante para los jóvenes mexicanos.
4. Los jóvenes piensan obtener un empleo después de casarse.
5. Es difícil encontrar empleo.
6. El consumo de drogas ha aumentado.

Answers to Actividad 1:
1. V
2. F—La incertidumbre está entre sus angustias principales.
3. V
4. F—Piensan obtener un empleo antes de casarse.
5. V
6. V

2 **Titulares.** Eres reportero/a para el periódico de tu pueblo. Escribe frases completas para presentar los artículos que tienen estos titulares.

▸ **Modelo:** *tráfico de drogas*
Los Estados Unidos anuncian un nuevo plan para eliminar el tráfico de drogas.

1. el consumo de alcohol
2. los problemas ecológicos
3. la pobreza
4. el SIDA
5. los actos delictivos
6. las enfermedades sicológicas
7. el desempleo
8. el asesinato
9. ¿...?

Answers to Actividad 2:
Answers will vary. Encourage students to be imaginative and use the names of a variety of countries in their headlines.

3 **Soluciones.** En grupos, creen soluciones posibles para tres problemas sociales en la **Actividad 2.** La lista siguiente tiene algunas soluciones posibles.

más policías
más trabajos
aumentar los impuestos sobre el alcohol
aumentar el sueldo mínimo
¿...?

4 **A escribir.** Escribe una composición de dos párrafos sobre uno de los problemas sociales y algunas soluciones. Usa la siguiente organización para tu composición.

Problema
Causas
Soluciones

Further information in Spanish on AIDS can be found on the WWW via a search under the word SIDA, Sida, or sida.

ENLACE CULTURAL

La peste del siglo XX

El SIDA (síndrome de inmunodeficiencia adquirida) se detectó por primera vez en 1981. El virus que causa la enfermedad se llama virus de inmunodeficiencia humana (VIH) y fue identificado en 1986. Desde entonces, muchos enfermos dedican su tiempo a informarnos sobre cómo es vivir con esta enfermedad. Éste es el testimonio de Laura:

"Cuando termino de hablar, la gente se asombra,° nadie cree que yo sea° VIH positiva, me imaginan flaca, llena de manchas...°

Creo que después de contarles mi vida no ven a Laura—VIH sino a Laura, y eso depende de la manera de dar el testimonio. Yo no lo doy para inspirar lástima° sino para decirles que uno puede vivir con el virus. En una conferencia me encontré con un amigo de la infancia. Nos dio un susto° tremendo. Se me acercó° y me preguntó qué hacía allí y le dije que hacía parte de la conferencia. Cuando me tocó° hablar fue horrible. Lo primero que dije es que había alguien entre el público que me conocía, que posiblemente se iba a asombrar por lo que iba a contar, pero que no me iba a callar,° que esperaba que tomara consciencia y que recordara los viejos tiempos.

Cuando finalicé mi historia este amigo estaba llorando y yo también. Se me acercó, me abrazó y me dijo que podía contar con° él hoy, mañana y siempre. Me dio gracias porque estaba dando mi vida por la de ellos, para que se protegieran... A través del VIH me di cuenta de que tengo amigos, aunque conozco a gente seropositiva° que ha sido muy rechazada."°

are astonished / am
spots
pity
scare
He approached me
it was my turn
be quiet
count on
HIV-positive / rejected

Discusión en grupos

1. ¿Qué razones tiene Laura para dar su testimonio?
2. ¿Crees que tener SIDA o VIH es un estigma? ¿Por qué?
3. ¿Conoces a alguna persona o grupo de personas que sean rechazados por tener una enfermedad o un problema físico?
4. ¿Crees que una persona que tenga SIDA debe contárselo a su jefe? ¿A sus familiares? ¿A sus amigos? ¿Por qué?

II. Reacting to societal issues

Una encuesta nacional

En México, se hizo una encuesta a quinientos jóvenes entre los trece y los veinticuatro años sobre los problemas a los que ellos se enfrentan (*confront*) en el futuro. Aquí hay algunas de sus respuestas.

AUTOESTIMA° *self-esteem*

¿Te sientes con capacidad para resolver todos tus problemas?

Frecuencia	Edad 13 a 17 años	18 a 24 años	Promedio
	Porcentaje	Porcentaje	Porcentaje
Siempre	22	35	29
Casi siempre	47	53	50
A veces	29	12	20
Casi nunca	2	–	1

¿Qué tan triunfador° te sientes? *successful*

Frecuencia	Sexo Hombres	Mujeres	Promedio Hombres y mujeres
	Porcentaje	Porcentaje	Porcentaje
Mucho	32	49	40
Algo	48	47	48
Poco	15	3	9
Nada	2	1	1

¿Te gusta tu aspecto físico?

Frecuencia	Sexo Hombres	Mujeres	Promedio Hombres y mujeres
	Porcentaje	Porcentaje	Porcentaje
Mucho	25	25	25
Algo	62	53	57,5
Poco	8	11	9,5
Nada	5	11	8

ADICCIONES

¿Acostumbras tomar alcohol?

Frecuencia	Sexo Hombres	Mujeres	Promedio Hombres y mujeres
	Porcentaje	Porcentaje	Porcentaje
Sí	55	35	45
No	45	65	55

¿Conoces directamente a alguien que tenga problemas con...?

	Porcentaje Sí	Porcentaje No
su forma de beber	68	32
el consumo de drogas	63	37

5 **Opiniones.** Contesta las preguntas de la encuesta. En grupos, recojan la información y calculen el porcentaje de respuestas en la clase. Comparen sus opiniones con las de los jóvenes mexicanos.

Save the lists provided in **Actividad 6** and then re-introduce them later in this chapter once students know the future tense. Ask students what people will think of their objects one hundred years from now.

6 **El futuro.** Aunque hay muchos problemas sociales, también hay muchas cosas buenas. Haz una lista de diez objetos representantivos de nuestra época que tú pondrías (*you would put*) en una cápsula del tiempo para abrir en el futuro. **Cosas para considerar:** eventos importantes, música, comida, tecnología, vestido, cosas personales y comunicaciones.

7 **En grupos.** Trabajen en grupos de tres. Comparen sus listas personales de la **Actividad 6** y elijan diez objetos de sus listas. Preséntenle su lista a la clase y expliquen por qué escogieron finalmente esos diez objetos.

ENLACE CULTURAL

La clonación: Dilema moderno

La ovejita Dolly.

En 1997, nació la ovejita° Dolly, el clon de una oveja adulta. Antes de Dolly, solamente se habían clonado animales muy pequeños y muy jóvenes. Este experimento comprobó que, en el futuro, las técnicas de clonación van a hacer posible la creación de copias idénticas de animales muy grandes, y aún clones de seres humanos.

sheep

Actualmente, los científicos también pueden modificar la estructura genética de una especie, introduciendo genes de otras especies. Los animales creados de esta manera son animales transgénicos,° es decir, que tienen genes de varias especies. Por ejemplo, los ingenieros genéticos pueden crear animales con genes humanos para producir proteínas y tejidos° útiles en la lucha contra enfermedades graves. Y, por supuesto,° estos animales transgénicos, también se pueden clonar.

Actualmente (*at the present moment*) is a false cognate.

transgenic

synthetic tissues
of course

Discusión en grupos

1. ¿Conoce alguno de ustedes un par de gemelos/as? ¿Se visten igual? ¿Están en el mismo colegio? ¿Andan siempre juntos/as?
2. ¿Creen que prohibir la clonación de seres humanos impida el progreso de la ciencia?
3. ¿Pueden la clonación y las técnicas transgénicas ser problemas graves en el futuro?

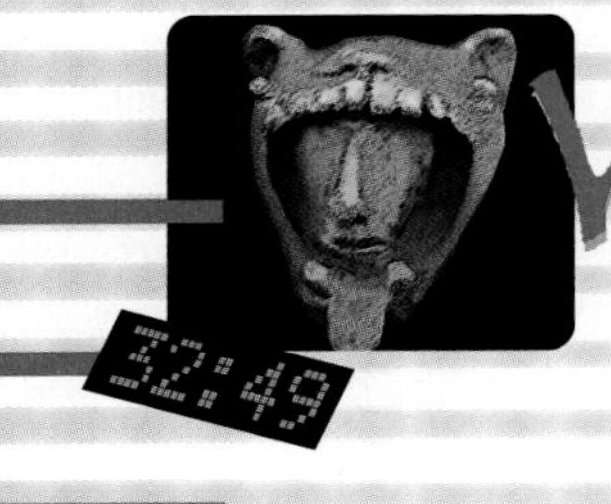

VISTAS Y VOCES

I. Preparémonos

1 Anticipación. Contesta estas preguntas con un/a compañero/a.

A. **1.** ¿Describe a tu mejor amigo/a. ¿Qué le importa en la vida?
2. Todos cometemos errores, ¿verdad? ¿Qué tipo de errores cometes tú?
3. Describe dos acciones que haces por tu universidad. ¿Por qué?

B. Mira la foto 11A en la página 433. ¿Quién es este señor? ¿Cuántos años tiene? ¿Qué hace? ¿Es bueno o malo? ¿Qué relación tiene con doña Gafasnegras?

Para comprender mejor

el anticuario	*antique store/dealer*	el/la dueño/a	*owner*
apuntar	*to jot down*	en busca de	*in search of*
caer en la trampa	*to fall in the trap*	encargado/a	*in charge of*
la casualidad	*coincidence*	esbelto/a	*slender*
el/la coleccionista	*collector*	la esperanza	*hope*
colgar	*to hang*	hace poco	*a little while ago*
el compadre	*dear friend*	la mitad	*half*
cuanto antes	*as soon as possible*	la patria	*country*
de acuerdo	*agreed*	por si acaso	*just in case*

2 Secuencia. Arregla cada escena en un orden lógico.

1. 

2. 

3. 

4. 

Order of video action shots: 4, 2, 3, 1

II. Miremos y escuchemos

3 Mis observaciones. Mientras miras, escribe tres características o emociones que muestren los siguientes personajes.

contento/a	alterado/a	determinado/a	listo/a
triste	patriótico/a	sincero/a	nervioso/a
preocupado/a	frustrado/a	deprimido/a	fiel
cariñoso/a	sorprendido/a	arrogante	fuerte

1. Adriana
2. Felipe
3. Gafasnegras
4. Raúl
5. el dueño del anticuario

III. Comentemos

4 Comprensión. Contesta las siguientes preguntas.

1. ¿Dónde están Adriana y Felipe? ¿A quién buscan ellos en este episodio?
2. ¿Cómo saben los anticuarios de San Antonio algo sobre los jaguares gemelos?
3. ¿Qué buscan Adriana y Felipe en la guía telefónica?
4. ¿Cuántos teléfonos hay en el apartamento de Adriana? ¿Dónde?
5. ¿Por qué va Gafasnegras a *ese* anticuario en San Antonio?
6. ¿Qué le dice el dueño del anticuario a Gafasnegras sobre los gemelos?
7. ¿Qué le pide Gafasnegras al dueño?
8. ¿Estará el coleccionista en su oficina hoy? ¿Por qué?
9. Después de que sale Gafasnegras del anticuario, ¿a quién llama el dueño? ¿Qué le dice?
10. Al leer el periódico, ¿qué anuncio ve Felipe? ¿Qué deciden hacer él y Adriana?
11. ¿Con quién se encuentra Adriana enfrente de su apartamento? ¿Qué le muestra?
12. ¿Qué le cuenta Adriana al dueño del anticuario? ¿Qué le aconseja él a ella?
13. ¿Cómo calma el anticuario a Adriana?

5 Somos detectives. Pónganse en el lugar de Adriana y Felipe. ¿Qué van a hacer ustedes para encontrar a los héroes gemelos y devolverlos a México? ¿Dónde? ¿Cómo?

6 Miremos otra vez. Después de mirar el episodio otra vez, arregla las escenas de video en la secuencia correcta.

7 La gran trampa. Imagina que tú estás trabajando para Raúl y el anticuario. Inventa un anuncio de periódico para engañar a doña Gafasoscuras y hacerle caer en una trampa para que no se quede con los gemelos. Trabaja con un/a compañero/a y léele el anuncio a la clase.

8 ¿Cómo desaparecieron? Escribe un corto resumen sobre la desaparición de los gemelos, desde la perspectiva del anticuario, cuando él ha hablado con Adriana.

Answers to Actividad 4:

1. Están en el apartamento de Adriana y su amiga en San Antonio. Ellos buscan a Gafasnegras.
2. Tienen que saber porque hay noticias en la televisión.
3. a los anticuarios de San Antonio
4. Hay dos teléfonos, uno en la sala y uno en la cocina.
5. porque ese anticuario es el único experto en esas piezas en San Antonio
6. Él le dice que no se especializa en las piezas como los gemelos.
7. Le pide el número de teléfono del coleccionista.
8. Sí, porque es sábado.
9. Llama a Raúl. Le dice que Gafasnegras cayó en la trampa.
10. Ve un anuncio que habla del "arte precolombino." Adriana va a ver al anticuario, y Felipe sigue con las llamadas.
11. Se encuentra con Patricia, su compañera de cuarto. Le muestra el periódico.
12. Adriana le cuenta que ella y Felipe son estudiantes de arqueología y que están buscando objetos de arte maya (a los gemelos). Él le aconseja que hable con Raúl que es realmente agente de las autoridades mexicanas, y no coleccionista de arte.
13. Le dice que Raúl tiene todo bajo control.

Lengua

I. Expressing the future

The future tense

¿Qué quiere hacer Sonia?

SONIA: Tío Efraín, pronto **tendré** que° elegir una especialización y creo que ya sé cuál **será.**° — *will have to* / *will be*

EFRAÍN: **¿Estudiarás**° para ser psicóloga o **harás**° algo diferente? — *Will you study / will you do*

SONIA: Algo un poco diferente, tío Efraín. Pienso estudiar trabajo social. **Ayudaré**° a los jóvenes que tengan problemas con drogas y alcohol. — *I will help*

EFRAÍN: Muy bien sobrina, ¿y cuándo **vas a terminar** tu pregrado?

SONIA: **Termino** pronto, tío. **Me matriculo** para hacer la maestría en un año.

EFRAÍN: Te felicito, Sonia, estoy seguro de que **vas a tener** mucho éxito.

In Spanish, there are three different ways to express the future.

- **ir a** + infinitive (*to be going to*)
- present indicative (*will*)
- future tense (*will*)

Find examples of each of these forms in the conversation above.

- Most verbs in Spanish are regular in the future. The infinitive is used as the stem for regular verbs. To form the *future* indicative, add the future endings to the stem, as shown in the chart on page 442.

Infinitive	Subject	Stem	Ending	Future tense
consumir	yo	consumir-	**é**	consumir**é**
creer	tú	creer-	**ás**	creer**ás**
dar	usted	dar-	**á**	dar**á**
ignorar	él	ignorar-	**á**	ignorar**á**
ir	ella	ir-	**á**	ir**á**
perder	nosotros/as	perder-	**emos**	perder**emos**
recibir	vosotros/as	recibir-	**éis**	recibir**éis**
recordar	ustedes	recordar-	**án**	recordar**án**
resolver	ellos	resolver-	**án**	resolver**án**
sentir	ellas	sentir-	**án**	sentir**án**

- Very few verbs have irregular stems. To form their *future indicative*, add the future endings to the following stems.

Infinitive	Stem	*Yo* form of the future tense
caber	cabr-	**cabré**
decir	dir-	**diré**
hacer	har-	**haré**
poder	podr-	**podré**
poner	pondr-	**pondré**
querer	querr-	**querré**
saber	sabr-	**sabré**
salir	saldr-	**saldré**
tener	tendr-	**tendré**
valer (*to be worth*)	valdr-	**valdré**
venir	vendr-	**vendré**

- Note that the future of **hay**, the impersonal form of **haber**, is **habrá.**

LENGUA EN ACCIÓN

Para expresar el futuro

There are several important time expressions that signal future actions or situations.

- The adjective **este/a** preceding the noun may be used to indicate future.

Esta noche nos quedaremos en casa en vez de cenar en un restaurante. — *Tonight we'll stay at home instead of eating supper in a restaurant.*

- With **semana, mes, año,** use the expressions **que viene** and **entrante** (*upcoming*) following the noun, or the adjective **próximo/a** (*next*) preceding or following the noun.

El **próximo mes**/El **mes próximo** Nancita hará un programa de radio. — *Next month Nancita will do a radio program.*

El **año que viene** voy a escribir una gran novela.	*Next year, I am going to write a great novel.*
La **semana entrante,** Gloria Estefan dará un concierto en México.	*Next week Gloria Estefan will give a concert in Mexico.*

Other expressions used with the future tense:

esta mañana	*this morning*	mañana	*tomorrow*
esta tarde	*this afternoon/ evening*	pasado mañana	*day after tomorrow*
		más tarde	*later*
esta noche	*tonight*	después	*afterwards*

1 **¿Qué pasará?** Paco reflexiona sobre algunos hechos futuros importantes. Completa las siguientes frases con la forma correcta del futuro.

1. La semana que viene, mi compañero de cuarto y yo __________ (empezar) un centro para ayudar a los drogadictos de la comunidad.
2. El consumo de alcohol __________ (causar) muchos accidentes en las carreteras.
3. Mis hermanas no __________ (fumar) cigarrillos.
4. Miles de hombres y mujeres __________ (enfermarse) del SIDA este año.
5. La semana entrante, los estudiantes de mi escuela __________ (aprender) mucho sobre problemas ecológicos.

Answers to Actividad 1:
1. empezaremos
2. causará
3. fumarán
4. se enfermarán
5. aprenderán

2 **¿Qué será será?** Tú y tus compañeros de pregrado hablan sobre lo que harán después de la graduación. Pon en futuro los verbos que están entre paréntesis en la forma de **tú.** Cuando termines, hazle las preguntas a un/a compañero/a.

▸ **Modelo:** *¿En qué región __________ (vivir)?*
¿En qué región vivirás?

1. ¿__________ (hacer) un máster o un doctorado antes de empezar a trabajar?
2. ¿Qué profesión __________ (tener)? ¿__________ (ganar) más o menos de cien mil dólares al año?
3. ¿__________ (preocuparse) por los problemas sociales y económicos de los jóvenes?
4. ¿__________ (usar) transporte público para llegar al trabajo? ¿Qué marca de coche __________ (preferir)?
5. ¿__________ (alquilar) o __________ (comprar) tu apartamento o casa?
6. ¿__________ (fumar) o no? ¿__________ (consumir) alcohol o no?
7. ¿Cuántas semanas de vacaciones __________ (tomar)? ¿Adónde __________ (viajar) y con quién?
8. ¿__________ (casarse) antes de cumplir los treinta años? ¿__________ (tener) hijos? ¿Por qué?

Answers to Actividad 2:
1. Harás
2. tendrás / Ganarás
3. Te preocuparás
4. Usarás / preferirás
5. Alquilarás / comprarás
6. Fumarás / Consumirás
7. tomarás / viajarás
8. Te casarás / Tendrás

3 ¿Qué opinas tú? Muchas cosas pueden suceder en nuestra sociedad durante los próximos diez años. Indica si estás de acuerdo con estas afirmaciones. Trabaja con un/a compañero/a y explica tus razones.

1. El número de suicidios entre los jóvenes aumentará.
2. La gente tendrá más educación.
3. Habrá menos casos de SIDA en el país.
4. Los jóvenes conseguirán trabajo muy fácilmente.
5. El gobierno prohibirá la venta de cigarrillos en todo el país.
6. Habrá más contaminación en las ciudades.
7. La pobreza y el hambre disminuirán en todo el mundo.
8. Descubrirán nuevas medicinas para curar las enfermedades mentales.

4 Predicciones. Escribe una composición sobre la situación de uno de estos problemas sociales en el año 2.020: (a) el consumo de alcohol y drogas, (b) la cura definitiva del SIDA, (c) el costo de la educación universitaria, (d) la delincuencia en el país o (e) la contaminación ambiental.

II. Expressing conjecture

The future of probability

¿Dónde estará Luzmila?°

ANA: Luzmila no ha llegado y estoy preocupada. ¿Qué hora **será**?°
FEDERICO: No sé. **Serán**° las tres de la tarde.
ANA: ¿**Aparecerá** Luzmila° pronto o no?
FEDERICO: ¿Dónde **estará**?° Espero que llegue pronto.
ANA: Ojalá lo haga.

Where can Luzmila be?
I wonder what time it is.
It must be (it's probably)
I wonder whether Luzmila will appear / Where can she be?

The future may be used to express *probability*, when there is doubt or questioning about a present action or situation. The equivalent in English can be *probably*, *I/We wonder*, *It must be . . .*

5 Las preocupaciones de los mayores. Los señores Pérez tienen cincuenta años y se preguntan cómo serán las cosas cuando ellos tengan ochenta años. Usa el futuro para expresar probabilidad.

1. ¿Cuál _________ (ser) el porcentaje de suicidios entre los ancianos?
2. ¿_________ (haber) buena atención médica para los mayores?
3. ¿_________ (pagar, nosotros) mucho por nuestro seguro médico?
4. ¿_________ (eliminar) el gobierno la pobreza en que viven muchos ancianos?
5. ¿Dónde _________ (vivir, nosotros)? ¿_________ (vender) nuestra casa?
6. ¿_________ (viajar, nosotros) de vez en cuando para conocer nuevos lugares?
7. ¿_________ (sufrir, nosotros) de alguna enfermedad grave?
8. ¿_________ (querer) cuidarnos nuestros hijos cuando lo necesitemos?

Answers to Actividad 5:
1. será
2. Habrá
3. Pagaremos
4. Eliminará
5. viviremos / Venderemos
6. Viajaremos
7. Sufriremos
8. Querrán

6 ¿Qué estarán haciendo? Las personas de la lista son importantes en tu vida actual. ¿Dónde estarán estas personas dentro de veinte años? ¿Qué estarán haciendo? ¿Serán todavía parte de tu vida?

mi hermano/a	mi madre	mi mejor amigo/a
mi compañero/a de cuarto	mi novio/a	mis tíos

7 El destino. Escribe diez preguntas sobre cómo podrá ser tu vida académica, social y personal dentro de diez años. Sigue el modelo.

▸ **Modelo:** *¿Seré feliz en mi profesión?*

III. Expressing possible conditions

Si clauses using the present tense

La ecología es asunto de todos

ETEL: **Si terminas** tu libro de historia, vamos al cine esta noche para ver *El Amazonas está en peligro.*

GLORIA: ¡Qué buena idea! Voy a invitar a mi novio, **si no te importa.** Su especialización es la ecología.

ETEL: Muy bien. **Si tienes** el periódico allí, mira el horario de las películas, por favor.

GLORIA: Con mucho gusto. **Si termina** temprano, tendremos tiempo para ir a la exposición de arte sobre el bosque tropical.

As in the dialogue above, in an *if clause*, when you wish to indicate a present action or situation that is possible or likely to occur, you use the present indicative. The verb in the other clause (the result clause) is generally in the present or future tense or is a command.

Si estudias, esta noche **iremos** al cine.	*If you study, we will go to the movies tonight.*
Si quieres conservarte sano **¡no fumes!**	*If you want to be healthy, don't smoke!*

- Notice that an *if* clause sentence can begin with either the result clause or with the *if* clause.

Si vamos al cine temprano, **tendremos** tiempo para cenar después.	*If we go to the movies early, we'll have time to eat afterwards.*
Tendremos tiempo para cenar después, **si vamos** al cine temprano.	*We'll have time to eat afterwards, if we go to the movies early.*

8 Condiciones. Escoge una frase de cada una de las dos columnas para expresar una condición y un resultado. Puedes empezar con la frase de la columna A o de la columna B.

A	B
1. si tengo tiempo hoy	a. grabaremos el programa
2. si salimos muy temprano	b. yo tampoco los saludo a ellos
3. si sale Sammy Sosa en Univisión	c. voy a estudiar toda la noche
4. si a las 8 a.m. estoy durmiendo	d. debes estudiar mucho
5. si hay muchos autos en la ciudad	e. iré al cine
6. si quieres obtener buenas notas	f. ¡despiértame, por favor!
7. si mis amigos no me saludan	g. habrá mucha contaminación
8. si tengo examen mañana	h. no perderemos el tren

Answers to Actividad 9:
1. veo, dormiré (duermo)
2. tenemos, escucharemos (escuchamos)

9 Nuestras rutinas. Algunas amigas están tomando refrescos en su club de tenis y están hablando de varios temas. Completa su conversación con el presente del indicativo o del futuro.

1. Si yo _________ (ver) una película de horror hoy, no _________ (dormir) bien esta noche.
2. Si mi esposo y yo _________ (tener) tiempo esta noche, _________ (escuchar) las noticias económicas en la radio.

3. Si mi hija no _________ (hacer) su tarea el viernes, no _________ (poder) ir al Museo de Ciencias este sábado.
4. En mi familia, si los chicos _________ (quedarse) en casa los fines de semana, _________ (hacer) ejercicios para mantenerse en buena forma.
5. Nosotros _________ (cambiar) la compañía de cable si _________ (haber) un aumento de precio.
6. Si nosotros _________ (participar) en el programa sobre el SIDA que ofrecen en el colegio, _________ (aprender) mucho.
7. Mi esposo _________ (recibir) una pensión, si _________ (perder) su trabajo.
8. Si a todos nosotros nos _________ (gustar) los burritos, _________ (almorzar) en el cafecito mexicano.

3. hace, podrá (puede)
4. se quedan, harán (hacen)
5. cambiaremos (cambiamos), hay
6. participamos, aprenderemos (aprendemos)
7. recibirá (recibe), pierde
8. gustan, almorzaremos (almorzamos)

10 **Si esto sucede…** Tú y tus compañeros/as de apartamento hablan sobre lo que van a hacer cuando sucedan los eventos de la lista siguiente. Trabaja con un/a compañero/a y explica qué haces o qué vas a hacer en estas situaciones.

1. Si estoy deprimido/a…
2. Si hay una epidemia de SIDA en mi ciudad…
3. Si no tengo dinero para mi educación…
4. Si mi novio/a no me quiere…
5. Si mi mejor amigo/a se enoja...
6. Si hay gente que necesita mi ayuda...
7. Si mi prima tiene bulimia...
8. Si alguien me insulta…

Lectura A

Introducción

The author talks about the many things that have frightened people during the ages. He thinks that fright itself is probably the most human—and animal—of feelings and compares how people in the 21st century have different things to worry about than they did a thousand years ago, in the Middle Ages.

Reading strategy: Distinguishing facts from opinions
Informational texts contain descriptions of facts, situations, or events. News and historical descriptions are informational texts. These texts are not necessarily impartial and the writer may seek to influence readers in a certain way by using strategies such as: giving examples that support his or her ideas, using quotes, introducing doubt or making strong assertions. In order to read this type of text, the reader needs to distinguish facts from opinions and get familiar with the devices used by writers to influence their readers.

1 Le tengo miedo al futuro. Trabaja con un/a compañero/a y discute tres cosas que te dan miedo cuando piensas en tu futuro. Luego, discute las tres cosas que deben temer más tu comunidad o tu país en los próximos cinco años.

2 Los miedos de mis abuelos. Escoge, según tu opinión, tres cosas que les daban miedo a tus abuelos. Cuando termines, discute con un/a compañero/a cuáles cosas les dan miedo a las personas modernas también. Ponlas en orden de importancia y compáralas. Puedes usar las palabras de la lista o añadir otras ideas.

las enfermedades	la discriminación
el hambre	los problemas económicos
los terremotos	la violencia
la guerra	la incertidumbre

¡Miedos del milenio!

Si no le temes a Dios, ¡témele a la peste!° Si no le tienes miedo a la bomba atómica, ¡témele al SIDA! Los miedos de ayer y de hoy son una muestra° de que esas sensaciones también tienen historia y están sometidas° a procesos culturales, religiosos y políticos. Ahora, en el segundo milenio,° podemos preguntarnos cuáles son los miedos más característicos del hombre contemporáneo. Y ayudados, por ejemplo,

plague
sample
bound
millennium

por el historiador francés, Georges Duby, comparemos algunas de las angustias° del año dos mil con las del año mil.

Tal vez lo más humano (y también lo más animal) es el miedo. El más antiguo de los miedos es, quizás, el miedo a lo desconocido° y de él nacen múltiples terrores. Sin embargo, ha habido otras cosas peores aguardando° al hombre.

El hombre de hoy está lleno de inquietudes° y preguntas y, la mayoría de las veces, sus miedos difieren de los de hace mil años, aunque se pueden encontrar similitudes entre unos y otros, como el miedo a la miseria,° a las catástrofes naturales y a las enfermedades. A pesar de los avances tecnológicos y los descubrimientos científicos, el hombre contemporáneo está sometido° a nuevos desamparos.°

Tal vez los miedos de hoy son más agudos que los del medioevo,° como el miedo a la desaparición del género humano, a la destrucción de la naturaleza, a una catástrofe nuclear, a una nueva guerra mundial.

Con todo, el miedo puede ser una especie de estimulador de búsquedas° espirituales y de vuelos imaginativos. Por lo demás, a la persona que tiene miedo, todavía no se le ha acabado° el mundo. ¡Qué nervios!°

anxieties
the unknown
awaiting
worries
poverty
is subjected to / troubles
Middle Ages
searches
has not ended/ How frightening!

3 Comprensión. Trabaja en grupos y contesta las preguntas sobre la lectura.

1. ¿Qué épocas compara el autor del texto?
2. ¿Cuál es el miedo más humano de todos?
3. ¿Qué miedos tenía la gente a partir del año mil?
4. Según el autor, ¿de qué condiciones tiene miedo el hombre moderno?
5. Cuando el autor dice que los miedos de hoy son más agudos que los del pasado, ¿qué ejemplos da?

Answers to Actividad 3:
1. Compara la época contemporánea con la Edad Media.
2. El miedo a lo desconocido.
3. Tenía miedo al más allá, a las epidemias, al hambre, al futuro.
4. El miedo a la miseria, a las catástrofes naturales y a las enfermedades.
5. El miedo a la desaparición del género humano, a la destrucción de la naturaleza, a una catástrofe nuclear, a una nueva guerra mundial.

4 Estrategias. Trabaja con un/a compañero/a. Busca frases del texto para ilustrar estas estrategias que usa el autor.

1. dar ejemplos
2. mencionar a expertos
3. comparar épocas

5 Opinión. Trabaja con un/a compañero/a. Analicen esta frase del autor y discutan por qué contiene un pensamiento positivo sobre el miedo.

A la persona que tiene miedo, todavía no se le ha acabado el mundo.

6 Así lo he entendido yo. Repite, con tus propias palabras, el tema de la lectura. Expone claramente cuál es la idea principal del autor del texto.

ETAPA B

Pistas y palabras

I. Evaluating and discussing films

El cine

★★★★★ Excelente
★★★★ Muy buena
★★★ Buena
★★ ¡Humm!
★ No vaya... ¡Dios lo ayude!...

estrenos°

premiering

El retrato de una dama°

lady

Con Nicole Kidman, John Malkovich y Barbara Hershey
Dirección: Jane Campion

★★★★★
Exquisita. Está basada en una novela de Henry James, la que **trata de**° una joven americana que vive en la Europa del **siglo** pasado. Cuando ella **rechaza**° una propuesta° matrimonial, se ve envuelta° en el malvado° acoso° a que la somete° una extraña pareja de amantes.° Obtuvo dos **nominaciones** de la *Academia* y **se destaca**° el magistral regreso de la **realizadora**° de *La lección de piano*. Es un regalo a los ojos. Una de estas **películas** que **aparecen** muy **de vez en cuando**° y que no hay que dejarla pasar.
Consejo: Vaya a verla. Es cine del mejor.

deals with
rejects
proposal / involved with / creator / bad / pursuit / subjects
lovers / from time to time
stands out

El regreso del Jedi

Con Harrison Ford, Mark Hamill y Carrie Fisher
Dirección: Richard Marquand

★★★
Se acaba la trilogía. En esta última parte, los **acontecimientos**° se **suceden** con mayor tranquilidad. Ya develado° el misterio de Darth Vader (uno de los mejores **villanos**° de todos los tiempos) con su hijo y la Princesa Leia, los realizadores pusieron **el foco**° en la creación de **efectos especiales** de última generación. Como en las otras, las imágenes y el **sonido** han sido recreados usando el original. Fanáticos,° ¡no **se desesperen!**° G. Lucas, su realizador, está preparando las partes 1, 2 y 3 para delicia° de todos.
Consejo: Las tres **merecen**° verse.

events
revealed
villains
Fans / do not despair
focus
delight
deserve

Palabras y expresiones útiles

el actor	*actor*	el guión	*script*
la actriz	*actress*	el largometraje	*feature film*
la actuación	*acting*	la narración	*narration*
la animación	*animation*	el ocio	*free time*
el argumento	*plot*	la pantalla	*screen*
la cadena/el canal	*channel*	el papel	*role*
la cartelera de cine	*movie programming*	el personaje (principal, secundario)	*(main, secondary) character*
la crítica	*criticism*	el/la protagonista	*main character*
la entrada	*ticket*	la reseña	*critique, review*
la escena	*scene*	la secuencia	*sequence*
la estrella de cine	*movie star*	la sinopsis	*synopsis*
el estreno	*premiere*		

criticar	*to criticize*
hacer el papel	*to play a role*
presentar (pasar) una película	*to show a movie*

cómico/a	*funny (adj.)*	de horror	*horror (adj.)*
de acción	*action (adj.)*	de suspenso	*thriller (adj.)*
de amor	*love (adj.)*	de misterio	*mystery (adj.)*
de ciencia ficción	*science fiction (adj.)*	de vaqueros	*western (adj.)*

1 Asociaciones. ¿Cuál de las dos películas mencionadas se relaciona con estos temas?

1. extraterrestres
2. amor
3. villanos
4. OVNIs
5. siglo XIX
6. novios
7. acción
8. efectos especiales
9. historia

2 Preguntas personales. Trabaja en parejas y contesta las preguntas.

1. ¿Te gusta ir al cine? ¿Por qué?
2. ¿Qué tipo de películas te gustan? ¿de amor? ¿cómicas? ¿de horror? ¿...?
3. ¿Quién es tu actor favorito? ¿Por qué? ¿Cómo es?
4. ¿Quién es tu actriz favorita? ¿Por qué? ¿Cómo es?
5. ¿Cuál es tu película favorita? Describe su tema y menciona quiénes actúan en ella.
6. ¿Cómo seleccionas una película cuando quieres ir al cine? ¿leyendo las reseñas? ¿escuchando las opiniones de amigos? ¿viendo los anuncios comerciales en la televisión?

Many films have homepages on the WWW.

3 Las películas de hoy. Escoge una de las películas que hay esta semana en los cines y haz un resumen o una reseña de ella. Preséntale tu trabajo a la clase.

ENLACE CULTURAL

El cine hispano

Rosie Pérez, una actriz puertorriqueña en EE.UU.

Argentina y México se consideran como las dos potencias del cine latinoamericano. Argentina abrió su primera sala de cine en 1900 y ya en 1922 empezó a producir sus propias películas. Los motivos principales de esas producciones eran los musicales, el cine de humor y los melodramas. En México se empezaron a producir películas propias en 1910 y desde entonces, el cine mexicano y sus estrellas han sido enormemente populares en el mundo hispano.

Desde los años 80, España se ha unido a estos dos países como uno de los más importantes productores de cine de habla hispana.° En los Estados Unidos la presencia de los artistas hispanos es cada vez mayor.

° *Spanish-speaking*

Discusión en grupos

1. ¿Qué actrices o actores hispanos conocen ustedes? ¿En qué películas han actuado?
2. ¿Cuáles son las películas hispanas que más les gustan? Si no han visto ninguna, pueden hablar sobre la película norteamericana que más les ha gustado.
3. ¿Cuál es la película más popular del momento en la región de ustedes?
4. Hagan una pequeña encuesta entre los/las compañeros/as sobre cuáles son los tipos de películas preferidas: por ejemplo, películas de humor, de horror, de acción, de aventura, de vaqueros (*cowboys*), de amor u otras. (Refiéranse a la lista de la página 451.)
5. ¿Cuáles son las dos actrices y los dos actores estadounidenses más dramáticos hoy en día? ¿Y los más cómicos? Describan otras tres características de cada uno/a de ellos/as.

II. Discussing television and the media

La televisión

Show the news report about Nayeli from the Chapter 2 video.

Adictos a la tele

Los niños argentinos ven un promedio de cuatro horas de televisión por día—según investigaciones de la Fundación Televisión Educativa—y estos **datos** son **elevados**° y **preocupantes**,° ya que, según los investigadores, el sesenta por ciento de los programas *audiovisuales producidos* por los Estados Unidos, y que se ven en todo el mundo, tienen un *contenido violento.*

high / worrisome

- La fiebre por la música latina no acaba... HTV°—la primera cadena de **cable** de música latina a **nivel** mundial°—acaba de **lanzar**° el show *Videohits.* Este **programa semanal** de media hora presentará los videos musicales más **exitosos.**°

Hispano Televisión
global / launch
successful

- Univisión se ha puesto las pilas° con su nueva **programación matinal.**° El programa "Despierta América" encanta con su variedad y "Mayte" con su personalidad.

charged their batteries
morning

- Los **televidentes**° de Latinoamérica y el Caribe estarán más tranquilos para la temporada de huracanes° que **se avecina**° pues **cuentan con**° la cadena de información metereológica por cable *The Weather Channel* (**El canal del Tiempo**) en español, la cual ha **anunciado** a Eduardo Ruiz como presidente de la operación en español.

TV viewers
hurricanes / are approaching
count on

Palabras y expresiones útiles

el/la anunciador/a — *announcer*
la cadena — *channel*
la columna — *column*
el/la comentador/a — *commentator*
la crónica — *chronicle*
el documental — *documentary*
la emisora — *broadcasting station*
el entretenimiento — *entertainment*
el/la locutor/a — *announcer*
las noticias — *news*
el noticiero — *news program*
el ocio — *free time*
el/la periodista — *journalist*
la prensa — *press*
el/la presentador/a — *presenter*
el/la reportero/a — *reporter*
la telenovela — *soap opera*
la televisión (cadena) de cable — *cable TV*

emitir (transmitir) — *to transmit (a TV, radio program)*
televisar — *to televise*

dramático/a — *dramatic*
de investigación — *investigative*

4 **¿En qué canal está?** Menciona los programas de televisión que ves en las siguientes ocasiones.

1. Quieres escuchar música nueva.
2. Te gusta cocinar.
3. Quieres saber si necesitas paraguas.
4. Tienes ganas de reírte.
5. Estás triste y quieres ver algo emocionante.
6. Te interesa oír las noticias del día.
7. Hay un partido de fútbol hoy.
8. Quieres escuchar algo en español.

5 **Adictos a la tele.** Trabajen en grupos y hagan una encuesta entre todos con estas dos preguntas: (a) ¿Cuántas horas pasas viendo la televisión diariamente? y (b) ¿Cuáles son tus tres programas favoritos? Calculen el promedio de horas diarias para el grupo y la lista de programas favoritos. Preséntenle los resultados a la clase.

6 **A escribir.** Escribe una breve composición sobre cómo la violencia en la televisión afecta a los niños y a los jóvenes.

ENLACE CULTURAL

La televisión hispana

Todos los países hispanos tienen excelentes canales de televisión y muchos programas se transmiten por la televisión de cable a todo el mundo hispano, desde España hasta el Cono Sur. También en los Estados Unidos hay programas en español muy populares, por ejemplo el show de "Cristina" y "Sábado Gigante" de Don Francisco.

Las telenovelas más populares se distribuyen a todos los países hispanos y millones de personas disfrutan de las intrigas y el romance de estas series de televisión. Países como México, Colombia, Venezuela y Argentina son grandes productores de populares telenovelas.

Cristina.

Don Francisco.

Discusión en grupos

1. ¿Qué canales hispanos se transmiten por la televisión de cable de tu región?
2. ¿Qué tipo de programas de televisión son los más populares entre ustedes?
3. ¿Cuál es el canal favorito de todos/as los/las chicos/as del grupo?
4. ¿Existe un canal de televisión en su escuela o universidad? ¿Qué programas transmite?

Vistas y voces

I. Preparémonos

1 Anticipación. Contesta estas preguntas. Trabaja con un/a compañero/a.

A. **1.** ¿En quién tienes tú total confianza? ¿Por qué? ¿Cómo es esa persona?
2. ¿Qué experiencia ha sido la más fácil o difícil de tu vida? Descríbela.
3. ¿Te importa lo que otras personas piensen de ti? Explica.
4. ¿Qué deporte prefieres mirar, el fútbol, el tenis, el golf? ¿Por qué?

B. Mira la foto 11B en la página 433. Adriana parece muy alterada en presencia del hombre del anillo raro. ¿Quién es? ¿Qué hace?

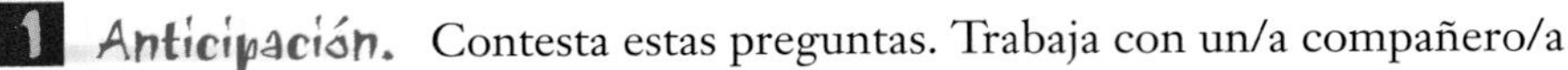

Para comprender mejor

aclarar	*to clear up*	Las Canarias	*The Canary Islands (restaurant on the Riverwalk)*
agradecer	*to thank*	Mansión del Río	*River Mansion (café on the Riverwalk)*
alcanzar	*to accomplish*	el medio	*means*
el anonimato	*anonymity*	Paseo del Río	*Riverwalk (in San Antonio)*
ansioso/a	*anxious*	la pesadilla	*nightmare*
el asunto	*matter*	probar	*to prove*
atrapar	*to trap*	el puente	*bridge*
la cárcel (prisión)	*jail*	recorrer	*to tour*
el corto plazo	*short notice*	tirar	*to throw*
desafiar	*to challenge*		
devolver	*to return*		
las esposas	*handcuffs*		
estar a cargo de	*to be in charge of*		
golpear	*to hit*		

2 Secuencia. Estudia las escenas de video y comenta las preguntas con un/a compañero/a. ¿Qué le ha pasado a doña Gafasnegras? ¿Qué tiene que ver la pelota de fútbol con ella y los jaguares gemelos? Usa la imaginación.

1.

2.

Correct order of video action shots: 1, 4, 3, 2

3.

4.

Answers to Actividad 4:
1. En un restaurante al aire libre, en San Antonio. Hay flores y plantas, una fuente, algunas personas, mesas y sillas.
2. Trabaja para I.L.E.Y.A.N., una asociación dedicada a la recuperación de objetos maya. Es director. Nayeli la fundó. Adriana está alterada. La piedra es verde.
3. Se llama Mariluz Gorrostiaga Hinojosa.
4. No hay tiempo para llamar a las autoridades. También creen que Nayeli es culpable de robar los jaguares.
5. Hay treinta personas en el barco, más o menos.
6. Una pelota de fútbol. Tiene aproximadamente veinte años. Hace mucho sol.
7. Raúl está en un coche. Ellos tienen micrófonos.
8. Felipe le golpea la cabeza a Gafasnegras con la pelota de fútbol. Se le caen las gafas negras.
9. Le ofrece una suma de dinero atractiva que él no acepta. Le pone las esposas.
10. la bolsa con los jaguares gemelos

II. Miremos y escuchemos

3 Observaciones. Mientras Nayeli va a México, otros eventos ocurren en San Antonio en un restaurante del Paseo del Río y en un puente. Escribe quién(es) participa(n), y qué hace(n) y nota(n) en cada lugar.

III. Comentemos

4 Comprensión. En grupos, contesten las siguientes preguntas.

1. Describe el lugar dónde se encuentran Adriana y Raúl.
2. ¿Para cuál organización trabaja Raúl? ¿En qué capacidad? ¿Quién la fundó? ¿Cómo reacciona Adriana al ver el anillo de Raúl? De qué color es la piedra?
3. ¿Cómo se llama Gafasnegras realmente?
4. ¿Por qué no quiere Raúl pedirle ayuda a las autoridades?
5. ¿Aproximadamente cuántas personas hay en el barco que pasa?
6. ¿Qué tiene en la mano el chico de la camisa azul? ¿Cuántos años tiene, crees tú? ¿Qué tiempo hace?
7. Felipe y Adriana están en dos lados del puente esperando a Gafasnegras. ¿Dónde está Raúl? ¿Qué aparato usan los tres?
8. ¿Qué hace Felipe cuando Gafasnegras trata de tirar la bolsa con los gemelos al río? ¿Qué se le cae a ella?
9. ¿Qué le ofrece Gafasnegras a Raúl? ¿Acepta él? ¿Qué le pone a Gafasnegras?
10. ¿Qué recoge Adriana del puente y se la da a Raúl?

5 Miremos otra vez. Después de mirar el episodio otra vez, arregla las escenas de video en la secuencia correcta. Después, narra la acción.

6 ¡Felipe el futbolista! ¿Qué tiene que ver la pelota de fútbol con Gafasnegras y los jaguares gemelos? ¿Qué tipo de ¡¡¡GOL!!! marca Felipe en esta escena? ¿Cómo se siente él?

7 Análisis, análisis. En grupos, conversen sobre la relación que tienen las dos afirmaciones siguientes con la historia de los jaguares. ¿Quién las dice y qué revelan sobre la personalidad de cada personaje? ¿Cómo son estas afirmaciones pertinentes en la vida de cada uno/a de ustedes?

"El dinero no me importa." "El fin justifica los medios."

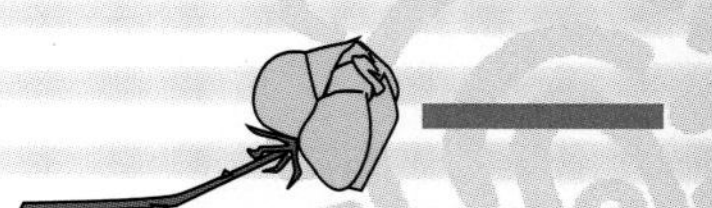

Lengua

I. Expressing what you would do

The conditional tense

Forms of the conditional

¿Qué querrías° hacer hoy?

CARLOS: Necesito un cambio. ¿**Te gustaría**° ir al cine, mi amor?
IRENE: No, gracias, querido. **Preferiría**° mirar una película portuguesa en la televisión.
CARLOS: ¡Qué buena idea! **Me encantaría**° practicar mi portugués. Nos quedaremos en casa.

would you like
Would you like
I would prefer
I would love

Most verbs in Spanish are regular in the conditional. The English equivalent of this tense is *would* or *could* plus the *verb: would/could + speak, eat, write*, and so on. To form the *conditional* tense of regular verbs, add these conditional endings to the stem. As with the future tense, the conditional stem for regular verbs is the infinitive.

Infinitive	Subject	Stem	Ending	Conditional tense
anunciar	yo	anunciar-	**-ía**	anunciar**ía**
aumentar	tú	aumentar-	**-ías**	aumentar**ías**
contar	él	contar-	**-ía**	contar**ía**
correr	ella	correr-	**-ía**	correr**ía**
escribir	usted	escribir-	**-ía**	escribir**ía**
estar	nosotros/as	estar-	**-íamos**	estar**íamos**
lanzar	vosotros/as	lanzar-	**-íais**	lanzar**íais**
pedir	ellos	pedir-	**-ían**	pedir**ían**
ver	ellas	ver-	**-ían**	ver**ían**
volver	ustedes	volver-	**-ían**	volver**ían**

As with the future, few verbs are irregular in the conditional tense. These irregular verbs share the same stems as the future tense.

Infinitive	Stem	*Yo* form of the conditional tense
caber	cabr-	**cabría**
decir	dir-	**diría**
hacer	har-	**haría**
poder	podr-	**podría**
poner	pondr-	**pondría**
querer	querr-	**querría**
saber	sabr-	**sabría**
salir	saldr-	**saldría**
tener	tendr-	**tendría**
venir	vendr-	**vendría**
valer (*to be worth*)	valdr-	**valdría**

- Note that **hay,** the impersonal form of **haber** becomes **habría** in the conditional.

Additional uses of the conditional tense

- The conditional tense is often used as an expression of politeness.

¿**Podrías** ayudarme con mi reportaje esta noche? — *Could you (Would you) help me with my report tonight?*
Me **gustaría,** pero pienso ir al cine esta noche. Quizás mañana te pueda ayudar. — *I would like to, but I'm planning on going to the movies tonight. Perhaps I can help you tomorrow.*

Be sure students do not confuse the conditional *would* with the *would* meaning *used to* that takes the imperfect tense: **Cuando yo era niña yo jugaba todos los días:** *When I was young I would (used to) play every day.*

- The conditional is also used to report past speech. This occurs when a sentence of this kind contains two clauses. The conditional is used in the subordinate clause to express what actions would have occurred.

Pensé que **iríamos** al cine esta noche. — *I thought we would go to the movies tonight.*
Me gustaría, pero no sabía que **tendría** que terminar este reportaje para mañana. — *I would like to, but I didn't know that I would have to finish this report by tomorrow.*

1 **Soy crítico/a de cine.** Tú sueñas con ser crítico/a de cine. Explica qué harías en ese caso. Trabaja con un/a compañero/a.

1. (Leer) el guión original antes de ver la película.
2. (Evaluar) la relación entre el guión y la película.
3. (Juzgar) la interpretación de los actores y las actrices.
4. (Describir) el impacto de la historia cinematográfica y de la actuación de los artistas.
5. (Caracterizar) los efectos especiales que haya usado el director.
6. (Analizar) los temas de la película.
7. (Determinar) los mensajes de la película para el público.
8. (Calificar) la dirección de la película.
9. (Escribir) una reseña para la prensa y la televisión.
10. (Presentar) la reseña en el noticiero de televisión.

Answers to Actividad 1:

1. Leería
2. Evaluaría
3. Juzgaría
4. Describiría
5. Caracterizaría
6. Analizaría
7. Determinaría
8. Calificaría
9. Escribiría
10. Presentaría

2 Actividades. Utiliza el condicional para describir lo que harían las personas de la lista en determinados lugares. Sigue el modelo.

▸ **Modelo:** *en casa / mi hermano/a*
En casa, mi hermano miraría la televisión.

1. en el campo / mis primas Sonia y Penélope
2. en casa / mi papá
3. en el laboratorio de computadoras / mis compañeros/as de clase
4. en el museo / mi novio/a y yo
5. en la videoteca del centro / mis hermanas
6. en la biblioteca / tú
7. en el laboratorio de ciencias de la universidad / la profesora de química
8. en el gimnasio / yo
9. en el banco / mi padre
10. en su trabajo en el banco / mi mamá

Answers to Actividad 3:
1. dijo / iríamos
2. informaron / presentarían
3. me imaginé / sería
4. Fue / cambiaría
5. contó / escribiría
6. dijo / habría
7. Creí / sería
8. dijeron / ganarían

3 ¿Qué haríamos? Cambia las frases del presente al pasado. Pon el primer verbo en el pretérito y el segundo en el condicional. Sigue el modelo.

▸ **Modelo:** *Creo que hoy habrá un buen noticiero.*
Creí que hoy habría un buen noticiero.

1. Paco me dice que iremos al cine mañana.
2. Teresa y Marianela nos informan que presentarán la película a las siete.
3. Me imagino que mi programa favorito será hoy.
4. Es evidente que el director cambiará el guión de la película.
5. Manuel me cuenta que escribirá una reseña de la última película de Pedro Almodóvar.
6. Mi profesora de drama nos dice que no habrá clase la semana próxima.
7. Creo que la nueva telenovela será un éxito.
8. En las noticias dicen que los artistas hispanos ganarán muchos premios.

4 Soy reportero/a. Trabaja en parejas. Haz una lista de preguntas para entrevistar a un/a artista de cine que acaba de terminar una película con mucho éxito. Usa el condicional de los verbos de la lista para crear preguntas sobre su vida profesional, social y personal.

▸ **Modelo:** *¿En qué tipos de películas actuaría Ud.?*
¿Cómo manejaría Ud. una carrera y una familia?

casarse
comprar
vestirse
tener
ayudar
ganar
vivir
viajar
hacer

II. Speculating about the past

The conditional of probability

En la oficina del periódico

TINA: ¿Dónde **estaría** Roberta° anoche? Parece que no durmió nada. **Iría**° a la discoteca con Fernando... ¿no crees?

INDALECIO: No, no lo creo. **Se quedaría**° en casa trabajando. Ella tenía que terminar muchas reseñas para la edición de hoy.

I wonder where Roberta was
She probably went
She probably stayed

The conditional may be used to express *probability* when there is doubt or questioning about a past action or situation. The equivalent in English can be *probably, I/We wonder* plus the past tense.

5 Las probabilidades. Tus amigos te invitaron al cine pero tú no fuiste porque estabas enfermo/a. Tu hermano menor te está haciendo preguntas sobre lo que tus amigos hicieron y tienes que adivinar las respuestas. Usa el condicional de probabilidad.

▸ **Modelo:** —*¿A qué hora salieron?*
—*Saldrían a las siete de la noche.*

1. ¿Qué película vieron tus amigos?
2. ¿Dónde presentaron la película?
3. ¿Quiénes fueron al cine?
4. ¿Comieron palomitas de maíz (*popcorn*)?
5. ¿Se divirtieron mucho?
6. ¿Fueron a un restaurante después del cine?
7. ¿A qué hora llegaron a casa?

Answers to Actividad 5:
1. verían
2. presentarían
3. irían
4. comerían
5. se divertirían
6. Irían
7. llegarían

Remind students that the **al** + *infinitive* construction translates as *upon* + *-ing.*

6 Posibles reacciones. ¿Qué harías o dirías tú en las siguientes situaciones? Usa diferentes verbos en el condicional para cada situación.

▸ **Modelo:** *al ganar la lotería*
Yo compraría una nueva casa para mis padres y empezaría una emisora de televisión en español.

1. al recibir una llamada telefónica de un productor de cine para darte un contrato
2. al saber que tu mejor amigo/a es la nueva estrella en la telenovela "Las horas de nuestras vidas"
3. al aceptar un trabajo como reportero/a para la revista de adolescentes "Tele-para-ti"
4. al conocer a Chayanne
5. al conseguir cuatro entradas como televidentes para un programa de MTV
6. al ver mucha violencia en la televisión durante una semana
7. al convertirte en director/a de un programa de noticias en la televisión
8. al ir a Hollywood por una semana con todos los gastos pagados

III. Expressing hypothetical actions and situations in the past

Si clauses (contrary-to-fact situations)

¿Qué harías...?

CARMELITA: **Si yo ganara**° la lotería, **compraría** mi propio estudio de televisión.
JUANCHO: **Si tuviera**° dos millones de dólares, **viajaría** por todo el mundo mirando obras de arte.

If I won
If I had

Review the use of simple *if* clauses with the present and future indicative, in Etapa A, p. 446.

- To express a contrary-to-fact (hypothetical) situation, use a **si**-clause followed by the past subjunctive. The main clause is in the conditional tense.

Si **fuéramos** artistas, **seríamos** famosos. — *If we were artists, we would be famous.*

To help students gain a basic understanding of the sequence of tenses with these clauses, write these three sample sentences on the board: (1) **Si tengo tiempo, como/comeré.** (2) **Si tuviera tiempo, comería.** (3) **Si hubiera tenido tiempo, habría comido.** Review meanings in English.

7 Suposiciones. Cambia los verbos del presente a las formas correctas del pasado para formar situaciones hipotéticas.

▸ **Modelo:** *Si Luz tiene tiempo, va al cine.*
Si Luz tuviera tiempo iría al cine.

1. Si Jorge invita a Ángela al teatro, ella irá con él.
2. Si funciona mi nueva computadora, escribo un trabajo para la clase de drama.
3. Si Tomás necesita una impresora, sus padres se la compran.
4. Si hacemos ejercicios y comemos bien, estaremos en buena forma.
5. Si tengo tiempo, reciclo mis cajas de cartón para ayudar a proteger el medio ambiente.
6. Si Elena y Patricia visitan Perú, conocerán a Machu Picchu.
7. Si mi esposo y yo compramos una videograbadora, los hijos la usarán demasiado.
8. Si fumo muchos cigarrillos, moriré joven.
9. Si hay escasez de agua, mi familia se baña solamente tres o cuatro veces a la semana.
10. Si se prohiben los programas violentos, habrá menos crímenes.

Answers to Actividad 7:

1. invitara / iría
2. funcionara / escribiría
3. necesitara / comprarían
4. hiciéramos / comiéramos / estaríamos
5. tuviera / reciclaría
6. visitaran / conocerían
7. compráramos / usarían
8. fumara / moriría
9. hubiera / se bañaría
10. prohibieran / habría

8 ¿Qué harías? Contesta las preguntas creando oraciones hipotéticas con el subjuntivo y el condicional. Trabaja con un/a compañero/a. Preséntenle las respuestas a la clase.

1. ¿Qué harías si tuvieras un accidente en el coche de tus padres?
2. ¿A quién invitarías si tus padres te regalaran tres entradas para el programa de Oprah?
3. ¿Cómo reaccionarías si te ofrecieran un trabajo en una planta nuclear?
4. ¿A qué persona famosa quisieras conocer y qué le dirías si la conocieras?
5. ¿Qué harías si no estudiaras en la universidad?
6. ¿Adónde viajarías si tuvieras un año libre y el dinero no fuera un obstáculo?
7. Si pudieras convertirte en un animal, ¿cuál sería y por qué?
8. Si tus padres te dieran un teléfono celular, ¿cómo lo utilizarías?
9. Si tu primo de dieciocho años tuviera SIDA, ¿qué le dirías?
10. ¿Qué harías si fueras presidente/a de tu país?

9 *A escribir.* ¿Qué harías si pudieras hacer tu propia película? Escribe un párrafo de diez oraciones para completar esta idea. Describe el tema, a quién contratarías, dónde filmarías, para qué público sería la película, cuánto costaría,...

▸ **Modelo:** *Si yo fuera director/a, haría una película (de amor). La película sería sobre...*
Yo contrataría a...

Lectura B

Introducción

This text focuses on two of the most famous Mexican singers and actors of the twentieth century. They are still in the limelight, more than forty years after their deaths. They have become legends, not only in Mexico, but in the entire Hispanic world, where their films and songs are as popular as when they were alive.

Prelectura

1 *Ídolo popular.* Elige un/a artista de cine, televisión o un/a cantante que te guste mucho. Basándote en tus conocimientos sobre esa persona, elige las frases que más te gusten para expresar tu opinión sobre él/ella. Haz frases completas siguiendo el modelo.

▸ **Modelo:** *Es un ídolo en todo el mundo hispano.*
Jimmy Smits es un ídolo en todo el mundo hispano.

Es un ídolo en todo el mundo.
Es completamente original.
No hay nadie igual.
Me gusta su manera de actuar/cantar.
Sus interpretaciones son de alta calidad.
Me encanta, es mi artista favorito/a.
Tiene un estilo especial.
Le gusta a todo el mundo.
Ya es una leyenda.
Es incomparable.
Es el/la artista más popular del momento.
No hay nadie como él/ella.

Answers to Actividad 2:
1. discos
2. ídolos
3. olvidar
4. popularidad
5. imaginación
6. inolvidables

2 *Artistas famosos.* Llena los espacios en blanco con una palabra de la lista.

ídolos	popularidad	inolvidables
olvidar	discos	imaginación

1. Los __________ de los dos artistas mexicanos continúan teniendo mucha popularidad.
2. Ambos artistas siguen siendo __________ del cine y de la música.
3. El pueblo mexicano nunca podrá __________ a estos artistas.
4. Tienen tanta __________ como los artistas modernos.
5. Ellos supieron interpretar la __________ popular mexicana.
6. Estos artistas son dos figuras de estilos __________.

3 *Mejor que nadie.* Trabaja con un/a compañero/a y comenta quién es el/la artista de cine más famoso/a de este año. ¿Cuántos premios ha ganado esta persona? ¿Qué películas conocidas ha hecho? ¿Creen ustedes que este/a artista pasará a la historia del cine y que el público lo/la recordará aún después de su muerte?

For information on Jorge Negrete, Pedro Infante, and María Félix, go to the WWW and search under their names.

ídolos MEXICANOS

Aunque hace casi 40 años que ambos desaparecieron, Jorge Negrete y Pedro Infante siguen siendo ídolos del cine y de la música, y gozan de° tanta aceptación en el público como muchos actores del presente e incluso más; sus filmes y discos continúan teniendo la misma popularidad de su época. Las figuras de estos dos actores se han convertido en símbolos imperecederos;° el pueblo nunca podrá olvidarlos porque representan lo más genuino y mejor de ellos.

Completamente originales, cada uno en su estilo, ellos supieron representar al pueblo mexicano con simpatía y arte, llevando este mensaje a todos los rincones° del mundo donde se entendía el idioma español. Como ídolos de la época moderna, las figuras de estos dos astros° están rodeadas° no sólo de la admiración por su oficio de cantantes y actores, sino por las leyendas de sus propias vidas. Todavía la historia de las dos esposas en el funeral de Pedro sigue causando tanto interés como el cuento del famoso collar° que Jorge le regaló a María Félix y que, a su muerte, se convirtió en objeto de controversia. Pero por encima de todos estos dimes y diretes,° por encima de la leyenda que envuelve° a quienes supieron dar rienda suelta° a la imaginación popular, está la calidad de las interpretaciones° que ellos nos dejaron en sus discos y películas.

enjoy

immortal

corners

stars / surrounded

necklace
gossip
surrounds / give free rein
performances

JORGE NEGRETE Y PEDRO INFANTE: DOS FIGURAS Y DOS ESTILOS INOLVIDABLES

Postlectura

Answers to Actividad 4:
1. Jorge Negrete y Pedro Infante
2. Fueron actores y cantantes.
3. Hace unos cuarenta años.
4. Sí.
5. Representan lo más genuino y lo mejor del pueblo.
6. El collar que Pedro le regaló a María Félix se convirtió en objeto de controversia cuando ella murió.
7. La gente habla de las dos esposas de Pedro Infante.
8. Puede ver sus películas y escuchar sus discos hoy en día.

Answers to Actividad 5:
1. fuera / sería
2. pudiera / sería
3. tuviera / podría
4. cantara / se venderían
5. ganara / me pagarían
6. lograra / sabría

4 Comprensión. Trabajen en grupos y contesten las siguientes preguntas sobre la lectura.

1. ¿Cómo se llaman los dos artistas mexicanos de los que habla el texto?
2. ¿Qué hacían estos dos artistas?
3. ¿Cuántos años hace que murieron?
4. ¿Se venden los discos que ellos grabaron hace muchos años?
5. ¿Por qué siguen siendo populares?
6. ¿Qué dicen las leyendas sobre un collar? ¿Quién se lo regaló a quién?
7. ¿De qué esposas habla la gente todavía?
8. ¿Por qué el pueblo mexicano nunca podrá olvidarlos?

5 Si yo fuera... Estás soñando despierto/a *(daydreaming)* con la fama y la riqueza que tendrías si fueras famoso/a. Crea frases para expresar tus sueños. Sigue el modelo.

► **Modelo:** *(ser) canciones originales / mis discos (venderse) por todo el mundo*
Si mis canciones fueran originales, mis discos se venderían por todo el mundo.

1. (ser) artista de calidad / yo (ser) un ídolo popular
2. (poder) tocar la guitarra / yo (ser) el mejor guitarrista del mundo
3. (tener) una voz hermosa / yo (poder) dar conciertos con Pavarotti y Mariah Carey
4. (cantar) canciones de calidad / mis discos (venderse) en todo el mundo
5. (ganar) un Oscar / los directores de cine (pagarme) sumas astronómicas
6. (lograr) fama y fortuna / todo el mundo (saber) mi nombre

6 Crítico/a de cine y música. Después de leer la lectura, describe con tus propias palabras en español cuál es la opinión del autor sobre estos dos artistas.

7 ¡Es indispensable! La tecnología moderna ha revolucionado el cine y la música. Si tu fueras un/a artista de música, ¿qué tipo de artista serías? ¿Cómo sería tu carrera profesional?

8 Ésta es mi historia. Basándote en los datos de la lectura, crea una historia sobre ti, como artista de cine o de televisión, tal como la contaría alguien cincuenta años después de tu muerte.

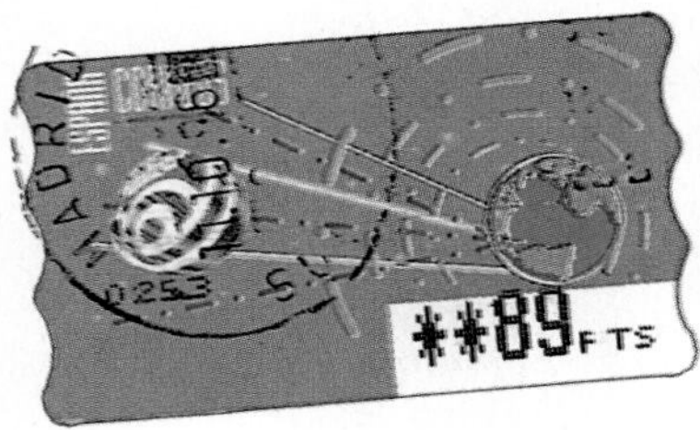

En resumen

I. Hablemos

1 **Crítico/a de televisión.** Trabajen en parejas y escriban una reseña de un programa de televisión para el periódico de la escuela. Preséntenle su reseña a la clase.

Have students make their own three- to five-minute video programs on this subject.

2 **En la tele.** En grupos de tres o cuatro, organicen un programa de opinión con algunos de los personajes del video. Escojan un/a presentador/a y definan un papel para cada uno/a de los miembros del grupo. El tema del programa es: Los robos de objetos arqueológicos y cómo prevenirlos.

II. Investiguemos por Internet

Searching for related words

Sometimes you may want to search for information using variations of the same keyword. Imagine that you are looking for information about film and you are not sure whether you should use **cine, cines,** or **cinematógrafo** as your keyword. In this case, you may formulate your query by replacing the parts of the words that are different with a symbol, such as an asterisk. In this way, by writing **cine***, you will be looking for the three words at the same time and your search engine will display all documents containing **cine, cines,** or **cinematógrafo.** In addition to the vocabulary in this chapter, you may want to access the topics **entretenimiento** and **ocio** in Internet Guides in Spanish, or use them as keywords. Refine your search by using several keywords as you have learned before by adding **cine***, **telenovela, película,** and so on to these words. Work with your partners creating concrete and useful queries! Refer to your search engine's "help" mode or to Houghton Mifflin's Web site for more ideas.

Vocabulario informático			
el comodín	*wild card*	el asterisco	*asterisk*

3 **Cartelera de cine.** Work in groups and select one of these activities: (a) Look for a TV program in Spanish in the United States or in a Hispanic country. (b) Look for one interesting movie in Spanish and present it to the class. (c) Look for the current movies being presented in your area and create a one-week program of movies for a friend visiting from Mexico.

Present your results to the class. Include the keywords that you used, where you found the information and how you got to that Web site.

III. Escribamos

Writing strategy: Narrowing a topic

The secret of writing a compelling paragraph is to choose a topic that is focused. If the topic is very broad, there is too much information to cover adequately. It may be necessary to narrow your topic several times before it is focused enough for a clear, concise paragraph.

Here is an example of a topic that has been narrowed down several times.

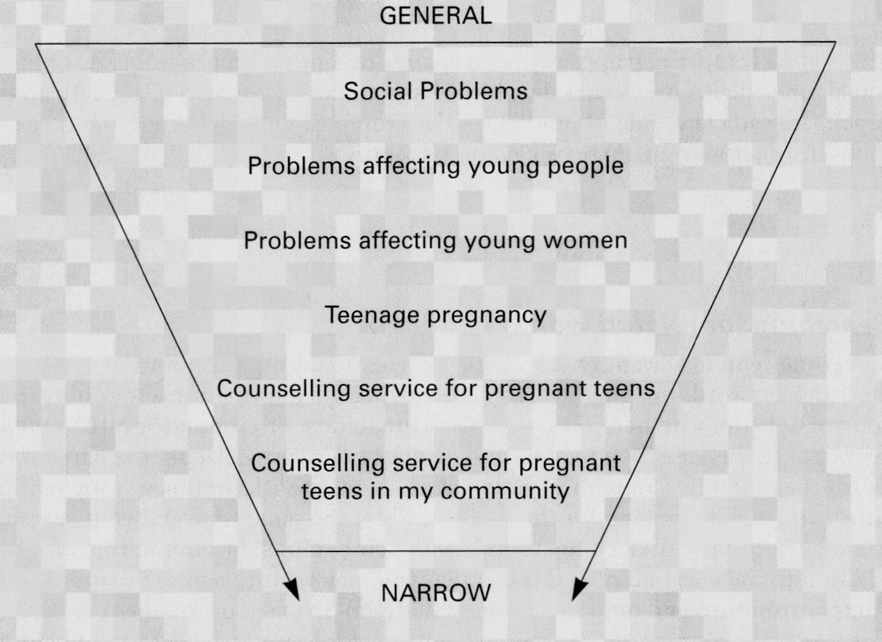

Strategy in action

Turn to *Escribamos* in the Workbook to practice the writing strategy of narrowing a topic.

4 Problemas del futuro. Si no resolvemos los problemas sociales de hoy, habrá muchos problemas en el futuro. Escoge un tema y escribe tus predicciones de lo que pasará.

5 ¿Qué pasará? Predice (*Predict*) lo que le pasará a tu personaje favorito del video "Caminos del jaguar" dentro de diez años.

Vocabulario

Problemas sociales

el acto delictivo	*delinquent act*
la adicción	*addiction*
el/la adolescente	*adolescent*
alcanzar	*to reach*
la angustia	*worry*
las armas	*weapons*
arrestar	*to arrest*
asesinar	*to assassinate, murder*
el asesinato	*assassination, murder*
el/la asesino/a	*murderer*
aumentar	*to increase*
la cárcel (prisión)	*prison*
el consejo	*advice*
el consumo	*consumption*
convertir	*to convert*
el crimen	*crime*
la cura	*cure*
la delincuencia	*delinquency*
la depresión	*depression*
el/la detective	*detective*
la drogadicción	*drug addiction*
el embarazo	*pregnancy*
el empleo	*employment*
encarcelar	*to imprison*
la enfermedad sicológica	*psychological illness*
fracasar	*to fail*
la generación	*generation*
la incertidumbre	*uncertainty*
la juventud	*youth*
lograr	*to achieve, to obtain*
el logro	*achievement*
matar	*to kill*
la muerte	*death*
obtener	*to obtain*
la población	*population*
la pobreza	*poverty*
el/la policía	*police officer*
la policía	*police force*
el programa de prevención contra el SIDA	*AIDS prevention program*
el programa educativo	*educational program*
el programa social	*social program*
la representación política	*political representation*
el robo	*robbery*
los servicios de salud	*health services*
el SIDA	*AIDS*
la solución	*solution*
el sueldo mínimo	*minimum wage*
el suicidio	*suicide*
tener éxito	*to be successful*
la terapia	*therapy*
el/la trabajador/a social	*social worker*
el tráfico de drogas	*drug trafficking*
triunfar	*to succeed*
la vigilancia del vecindario	*neighborhood watch*

El cine

el acontecimiento	*event*
el actor	*actor*
la actriz	*actress*
la actuación	*acting*
la animación	*animation*
aparecer	*to appear*
el argumento	*plot*
la cartelera de cine	*movie programming*
cómico/a	*funny (adj.)*
la crítica	*criticism*
criticar	*to criticize*
de acción	*action (adj.)*
de amor	*love (adj.)*
de ciencia ficción	*science fiction (adj.)*

de horror *horror (adj.)*
de misterio *mystery (adj.)*
de suspenso *thriller (adj.)*
de vaqueros *western (adj.)*
de vez en cuando *from time to time*
desesperar *to despair*
los efectos especiales *special effects*
la entrada *ticket*
la escena *scene*
la estrella de cine *movie star*
el estreno *premiere*
el foco *focus*
el guión *script*
hacer el papel *to play a role*
el largo metraje *feature film*
merecer *to deserve*
la narración *narration*
la nominación *nomination*
la pantalla *screen*
el papel *role*
la película *movie*
el personaje (principal, secundario) *(main, secondary) character*
presentar (pasar) una película *to show a movie*
el/la protagonista *main character*
el/la realizador/a *creator*
rechazar *to reject*
la reseña *critique*
la secuencia *sequence*
el siglo *century*
la sinopsis *synopsis*
el sonido *sound*
suceder *to occur*
tratar de *to deal with, be about*
el/la villano/a *villain*

La televisión

el/la anunciador/a *announcer*
anunciar *to announce*
audiovisual *audiovisual*
avecinar(se) *to come near, come close*
el cable *cable*
la cadena/el canal *channel*
la columna *column*
el/la comentador/a *commentator*
el contenido *content*
la crónica *chronicle*
los datos *data*
el documental *documentary*
dramático/a *dramatic*
elevado/a *high*
la emisora *broadcasting station*
emitir (transmitir) *to transmit (a TV, radio program)*
el entretenimiento *entertainment*
de investigación *investigative*
el/la locutor/a *announcer*
el nivel *level*
las noticias *news*
el noticiero *news program*
el ocio *free time*
el/la periodista *journalist*
la prensa *press*
preocupante *worrisome*
el/la presentador/a *presenter*
producido/a por *produced by*
el programa semanal *weekly program*
la programación matinal *morning programming*
el/la reportero/a *reporter*
la telenovela *soap opera*
el/la televidente *TV viewer*
televisar *to televise*
la televisión (cadena) de cable *cable TV*
violento/a *violent*
la videoteca *videostore*

CAPÍTULO 12

LOCALIDAD: Texas, Puerto Rico, Ecuador, Costa Rica, México

12A

12B

Armando and all of his cohorts finally get what they deserve. So do Adriana, Felipe, and Nayeli. And of course, Yax-Balam and Hun-Ahau.

¿Qué es I.L.E.Y.A.N.?

Vocabulary themes

- Talking about ancient civilizations
- Talking about the Aztecs and the Incas
- Discussing the history of Hispanics in the United States
- Talking about the Hispanic population in the United States

Language structures

- Narrating in the present and the past
- Retelling and reporting
- Talking about abstract ideas
- Questioning and requesting

Culture topics

- Artes y ciencias
- Ecos del pasado
- Semblanzas latinas
- Lenguas en contacto

Readings

- Héroes mayas
- ¡BRAVO a los hispanos!

Reading and writing strategies

- Taking notes in a chart
- Editing your own work

Internet strategy

- Using synonyms and word combinations

ETAPA A

Pistas y palabras

I. Talking about ancient civilizations

Culturas precolombinas

Have students find out more about these cultures from the WWW.

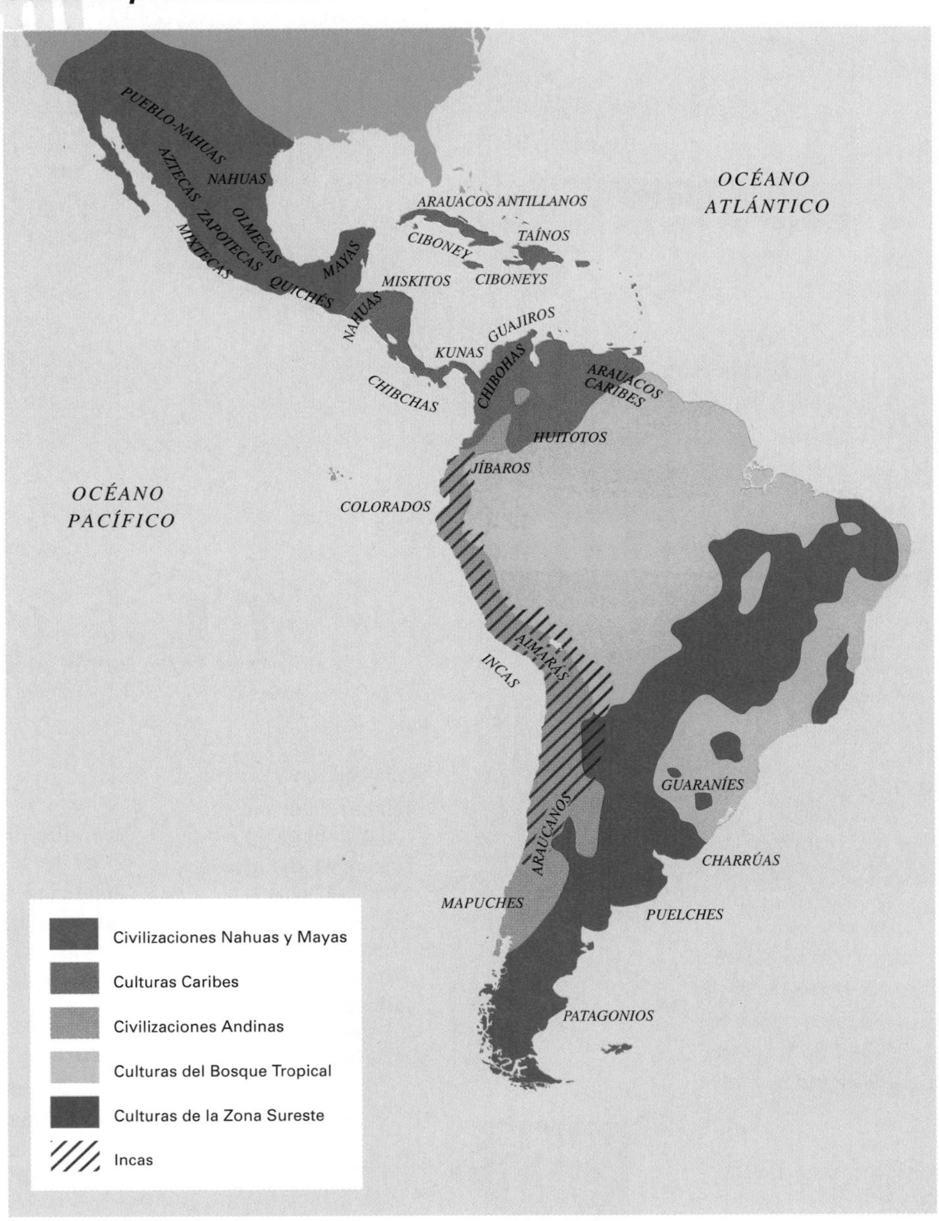

Las culturas que **poblaban**° el territorio americano, tanto al norte como al sur, eran numerosas y probablemente llegaron al continente desde Siberia, a través de Alaska. También hay teorías que afirman que varios grupos llegaron a través del Océano Pacífico. Tal vez nunca sepamos con seguridad cuándo llegaron y cuántas culturas había en el continente. **Sin embargo**,° conocemos muchas de ellas, grandes y pequeñas, a través de relatos° históricos y de **investigaciones arqueológicas.** El nivel° de **desarrollo**° de estos **pueblos** iba desde el más elemental hasta el más sofisticado. En el territorio hispano de hoy, se han identificado numerosos **grupos culturales.** Entre ellos, los siguientes:

populated

Nonetheless
reports
level / development

A. *Las civilizaciones nahuas y mayas.* Se extendieron por gran parte del territorio centroamericano, por el norte de México y por el suroeste norteamericano. Entre los grupos más importantes de estas regiones están los aztecas, los quichés, los mixtecas, los zapotecas, los olmecas y los indios pueblo.

B. *Las culturas caribes.* A este grupo pertenecen muchos pueblos de Centroamérica, el norte y el oeste de Colombia, el oeste de Venezuela y de las islas de las Antillas. A estas culturas pertenecen los indios kunas de Panamá y los **desaparecidos** indios taínos y arauacos de las islas caribeñas.

C. *Civilizaciones andinas.* En el sur de Colombia, en Bolivia, Ecuador, Chile, Perú y parte de Argentina hay grupos muy numerosos. Entre las culturas de estas regiones están los descendientes de las importantes culturas incas (o quechuas) y la cultura aimará. Actualmente existen muchos grupos indígenas andinos, como el de los otavaleños, en Ecuador. En el sur de la zona andina vivieron los araucanos. Actualmente, los indios mapuches de Chile mantienen vivos su cultura y su idioma.

D. *Culturas del bosque tropical.* Algunas de estas culturas son los colorados y los jíbaros de Ecuador y Brasil, y los huitotos de Colombia.

E. *Culturas de la zona sureste.* Entre estas culturas, están los patagonios, los charrúas, los puelches y los guaraníes. El guaraní es idioma oficial en Paraguay.

1 **Comprensión.** Contesta las preguntas según la lectura.

1. ¿De dónde vinieron las culturas que poblaban el territorio americano?
2. ¿Cuántos grupos culturales había?
3. ¿Qué grupo vivía en el territorio que ahora es parte de los Estados Unidos?
4. ¿Qué grupos vivían en el territorio que ahora es México? ¿Colombia? ¿Chile? ¿Puerto Rico? ¿Bolivia? ¿Perú?
5. Menciona algunas de las culturas amerindias de Suramérica.
6. ¿Dónde vivían los incas y los aztecas?
7. ¿Dónde viven actualmente los mapuches? ¿los colorados?

2 **Lazos (connections) con el presente.** Mira las cinco zonas culturales del mapa de la página 472. Menciona los países modernos que están en cada zona y dos ciudades en cada uno de estos países. Trabaja con un/a compañero/a. Consulta también los mapas de América Latina, que se encuentran al principio y al final del libro.

Answers to Actividad 1:
1. probablemente desde Siberia, a través de Alaska y el Océano Pacífico
2. Tal vez nunca lo sepamos.
3. pueblo
4. México: culturas nahuas-mayas, quichés
   Colombia: culturas caribes, andinas, del bosque tropical
   Chile: mapuches
   Puerto Rico: taínos, arauacos
   Bolivia: culturas andinas, descendientes de los incas, quechuas, aimarás
   Perú: culturas andinas
5. otavaleños, mapuches, colorados, misquitos, jíbaros, huitotos
6. Los incas vivían en el sur de Colombia, noroeste de Bolivia, Ecuador, Perú, norte de Chile y Argentina. Los aztecas vivían en la zona central de México, en Yucatán y en Guatemala.
7. Mapuches: Chile
   Colorados: Ecuador

ENLACE CULTURAL

Artes y ciencias

La expresión artística de las culturas amerindias tomó infinidad de formas, tanto en la fabricación de objetos de uso diario como en la de objetos ornamentales y en el desarrollo de la ciencia.

Orfebres

Los orfebres son las personas que fabrican objetos de oro. La elaboración de delicados objetos de oro fue un arte practicado por varios grupos amerindios de México, Colombia, Costa Rica, Ecuador y Panamá.

Alfareros

Los alfareros son las personas que fabrican objetos de cerámica. Las hermosas obras de cerámica de la cultura mochica demuestran la habilidad de sus alfareros.

Astrónomos

El calendario azteca ilustra la habilidad de los artesanos y los profundos conocimientos que tenía esta cultura sobre la posición y el movimiento de los astros.

Artesanos

La labor manual se ha mantenido por generaciones en muchas regiones de América Latina. Un ejemplo es el sombrero que vemos aquí.

Discusión en grupos

1. ¿Qué lugar de su ciudad conservarían ustedes para las próximas generaciones: una plaza, un parque, un barrio, un edificio?
2. Entre los objetos hechos a mano en su región, ¿cuáles son los más populares y los más costosos? ¿Quiénes los fabrican? ¿Son parte de alguna tradición?
3. Mencionen tres razones por las que la arqueología es tan importante para conocer nuestro pasado.

II. Talking about the Aztecs and the Incas

Dos grandes civilizaciones: Los aztecas y los incas

Dos de las civilizaciones más **desarrolladas**° en el siglo XV, al empezar la **exploración** y la **conquista** españolas, fueron la azteca y la inca.

developed

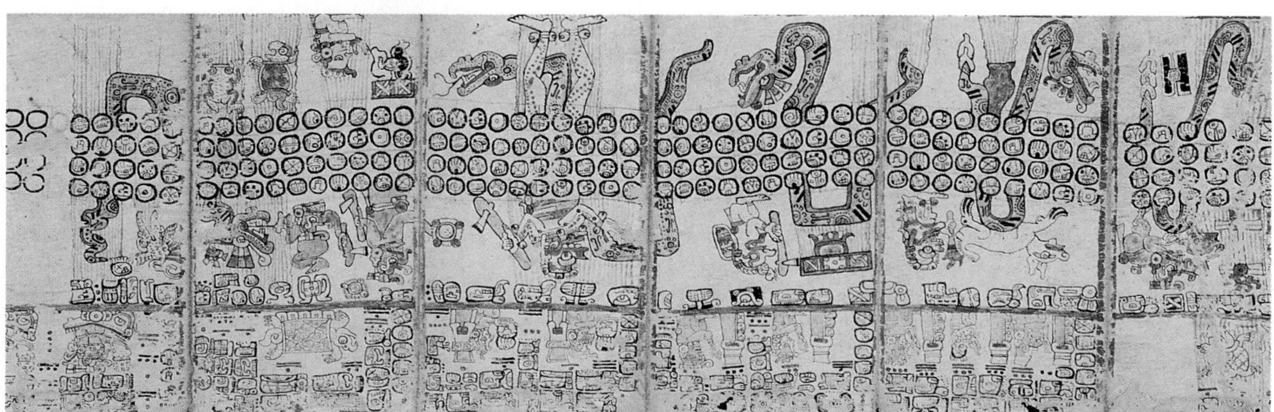

Escritura jeroglífica en un códice

Los aztecas

Los aztecas pertenecían al grupo **étnico**° y **lingüístico**° de los *nahuas*, grandes **astrónomos, estadistas**° y **constructores.**° Su imperio fue extenso y poderoso hasta que llegó Hernán Cortés, el explorador y conquistador español. A principios del siglo XV, Cortés **venció**° a Moctezuma, el emperador azteca, y en las **ruinas** de Tenochtitlán, la capital del imperio, **fundó**° la Ciudad de México.

ethnic / linguistic
statesmen / builders
defeated
founded

Uno de los grandes logros de las culturas de esta zona fue el uso de la **escritura**,° que podemos ver hoy en los **códices**, llenos de hermosos jeroglíficos. Actualmente, los **descendientes** de los nahuas, **además de**° **desempeñar**° **oficios**° y profesiones modernas, **cultivan la tierra** y son **hábiles**° **tejedores**° de lana y algodón.

writing
in addition to / performing
occupations / skillful / weavers

Los incas

En el sur, el imperio de los incas **se distinguió**° por su admirable organización y por sus conocimientos de astronomía. Los incas construyeron **imponentes**° ciudades de piedra y tenían una red° de más de veinte mil kilómetros de caminos que comunicaban a los 12 millones de habitantes del imperio. Entre las ciudades de piedra están Cuzco, la antigua capital del imperio incaico, y Machu Picchu, las **ruinas** de una ciudad que permaneció **perdida**° por muchos siglos.° Cuzco es la ciudad que lleva más tiempo **habitada**° en Suramérica. Fue fundada en el año 1100 y ha sido reconstruida° varias veces después de guerras y **terremotos.**° Cuzco ha sido declarada° por la UNESCO como una ciudad del patrimonio mundial.

was distinguished
imposing
network
lost
centuries / inhabited
has been reconstructed
earthquakes / has been declared

Machu Picchu

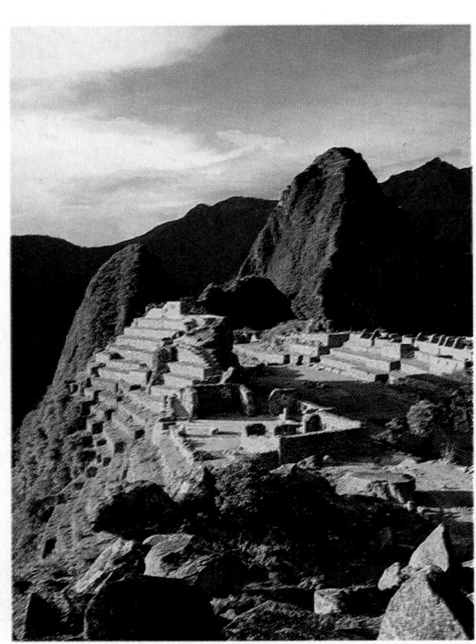

El imperio inca duró hasta 1527, cuando el explorador y conquistador español Francisco Pizarro venció° a Atahualpa, el emperador, en la batalla de Cajamarca. Sin embargo,° hubo muchas rebeliones y el último emperador, Túpac Amaru, fue ejecutado° en 1572.

conquered

Nevertheless

executed

Los descendientes de los incas siguen hablando su idioma nativo, el quechua, y participan activamente en las sociedades a las que pertenecen en Bolivia, Ecuador, Perú, al sur de Colombia, y el norte de Chile y Argentina.

Cuzco is also spelled Cusco.

3 Comprensión. Contesta las preguntas según esta lectura.

1. ¿Quiénes fueron Hernán Cortés? ¿Moctezuma? ¿Francisco Pizarro? ¿Atahualpa? ¿Túpac Amaru?
2. ¿Cuándo venció Cortés a los aztecas? ¿Qué hizo después?
3. ¿Cuándo venció Pizarro a los incas? ¿Dónde?
4. Menciona algunos de los logros de los aztecas y de los incas.
5. ¿Para qué construyeron caminos los incas?
6. ¿Cuántas personas vivían en el imperio inca?
7. ¿Por qué es importante la ciudad de Cuzco?
8. ¿Qué idioma hablaban los incas?

Answers to Actividad 3:

1. Hernán Cortés: explorador y conquistador español
   Moctezuma: emperador azteca
   Francisco Pizarro: explorador y conquistador español
   Atahualpa: emperador inca
   Túpac Amaru: emperador inca
2. A principios del siglo XV. Fundó la ciudad de México en las ruinas de Tenochtitlán.
3. En 1527, en la batalla de Cajamarca.
4. Aztecas: astrónomos, estadistas, constructores, uso de la escritura (jeroglíficos), hábiles tejedores.
5. Para comunicación entre los habitantes.
6. 12 millones
7. Fue fundada en 1100 y fue declarada por la UNESCO como una ciudad del patrimonio mundial.
8. quechua

4 Azteca o inca. Trabaja con un/a compañero/a. Comenten si las cosas de esta lista están relacionadas con los aztecas, los incas, o con las dos culturas.

1. caminos
2. ciudades de piedra
3. la astronomía
4. códices
5. Tenochtitlán
6. estadistas
7. el uso de la escritura
8. conquistadores españoles

Answers to Actividad 4:

1. incas
2. incas
3. aztecas, incas
4. aztecas
5. aztecas
6. aztecas
7. aztecas
8. aztecas, incas

5 Ciudades perdidas. ¿Cómo fue posible que la ciudad de Machu Picchu hubiera estado perdida por tantos siglos? ¿Por qué nadie la había encontrado antes? Trabaja con un/a compañero/a y menciona cuatro razones que expliquen este hecho.

ENLACE CULTURAL

Ecos del pasado

La rueda° y la pelota son dos inventos aparentemente muy sencillos, pero que han tenido mucha importancia para nuestra vida moderna.

wheel

El juego de pelota de los mayas

Este juego maya influyó en la creación de juegos de pelota modernos. La pelota que usaban los mayas era de hule° y podía rebotar.° En el siglo XV, en Europa solamente se usaban pelotas de madera y no se conocían las pelotas que rebotaban.

rubber / bounce

La rueda y los números

Las culturas amerindias conocían la rueda, pero nunca la usaron ni para el transporte ni en objetos útiles en la vida diaria. Sin embargo, sabemos que por ejemplo los mayas, dominaban conceptos complejos como el cero y el movimiento de los astros.°

stars

Discusión en grupos

1. Mencionen algunos juegos de pelota modernos en los que es absolutamente necesario usar una pelota que rebote. ¿En qué juegos se usan pelotas que no rebotan?
2. Si ustedes tuvieran que elegir solamente un invento del siglo XX, ¿cuál sería y por qué?

Answers to Discusión en grupos:

1. pelotas que rebotan: tenis, básquetbol, ping-pong (pinpón), volibol.
   pelotas que no rebotan: golf, croquet, billar, juego de bolos (boliche)
2. *Answers will vary.*

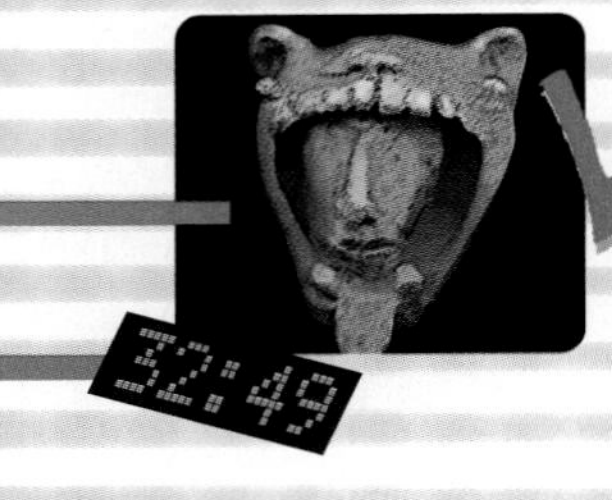

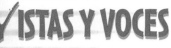

VISTAS Y VOCES

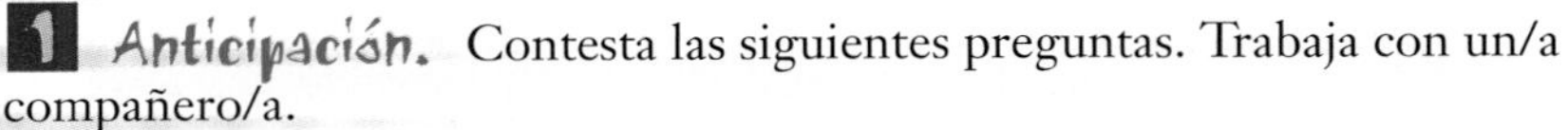

I. Preparémonos

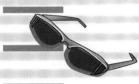

1 Anticipación. Contesta las siguientes preguntas. Trabaja con un/a compañero/a.

A. 1. Reflexionando sobre tu pasado, ¿qué eventos te parecen los más importantes para la vida contemporánea? ¿Hay circunstancias que te compliquen la vida actualmente?

2. ¿Qué personas tienen autoridad sobre ti y tu vida actual? ¿Qué te piden que hagas o no hagas?

3. ¿Qué simbolizan las flores para ti? ¿En qué ocasiones recibes y das flores?

4. En pocas palabras, ¿cuál es tu filosofía de la vida? Por ejemplo, la vida es para disfrutarla; la vida es para trabajar y tener éxito; el dinero es la primera prioridad; el honor personal es un objetivo; una vida sin misión no es vida. ¿Qué crees tú?

B. Mira la foto 12A en la página 471. ¿Quién es el hombre arrestado? ¿Por qué?

Para comprender mejor

advertir	*to warn*	hacer caso	*to pay attention*
arrestar	*to arrest*	el hecho	*deed, act*
el cacao	*chocolate*	irreprochable	*untouchable*
capaz	*capable*	meter	*to put (in)*
la comisaría	*police station*	no quedarle remedio a alguien	*to have no choice*
comprometido/a	*compromised*	salir limpio	*to be cleared of blame*
corregido/a	*corrected*	si me lo propongo	*if I put my mind to it*
empalagar	*to smother with sweetness*	sumamente	*very, extremely*
en fila	*single file*	valioso/a	*valuable*
las esposas	*handcuffs*		
fuera de serie	*exceptional*		

2 Secuencia. Estudia las escenas de video y comenta con un/a compañero/a por qué los personajes arrestados en este episodio son algunos de "Los Malos".

Video action shots (in order of arrests): 2, 1, 3, 4

1.

2.

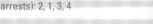

3.

4.

II. Miremos y escuchemos

3 Mis observaciones. Mientras miras el video, escribe los nombres de las personas arrestadas, en qué país, y la reacción que tengan.

III. Comentemos

4 Comprensión. Trabajen en grupos y contesten las siguientes preguntas.

1. ¿En dónde pone Raúl a doña Gafasoscuras? ¿Qué le pasa al coche?
2. ¿Qué les pasa a los primos ladrones? ¿Son solteros los dos?
3. ¿Qué reconoce el primo casado? ¿Qué siente el primo Luis y qué pregunta sobre la vida en la cárcel?
4. ¿Qué le dice Armando de Landa al detective?
5. ¿Admite doña Carmen que ella es culpable de robar a los jaguares gemelos?
6. ¿Por qué están preocupados los ladrones/pintores de la casa de doña Carmen?
7. ¿Qué flor le da Felipe a Adriana? ¿Cómo llama Adriana a Felipe y él a ella?
8. Al hablar del bien y del mal, ¿qué dice Felipe del bien? ¿A qué deporte puede referirse su comentario?
9. ¿Qué regalo le ofrece Adriana a Felipe? ¿Qué le dice sobre los mayas y el chocolate? ¿Qué dice Felipe sobre el chocolate y Adriana? ¿Se lo comen?
10. ¿Cómo están los dos al final de la escena?

5 Los ciclos de la vida. Raúl reflexiona y dice, "Todo tiene un fin. Todo cumple un ciclo: la vida, la muerte, el bien y el mal, es inevitable". ¿Cuál es el fin del ciclo con respecto a la historia de los jaguares? Trabajen en parejas.

6 Miremos otra vez. Arregla las escenas del video en el orden correcto.

7 ¿Y usted, doña Carmen? Inventa un diálogo entre Nayeli y doña Carmen antes de que la policía la arreste. ¿Qué le pregunta la ahijada y cómo le responde la madrina sobre los jaguares gemelos, y sobre la relación personal entre las dos mujeres? Trabaja en parejas.

8 En mi opinión. Trabajen en grupos e identifiquen a los personajes que dicen estas afirmaciones. Comenten si están de acuerdo o no con cada una de ellas y por qué.

"No hay nada que yo no pueda hacer si me lo propongo".
"En este mundo sólo cuentan los hechos".
"Las apariencias engañan".
"El dinero todo lo arregla".
"No todo se puede comprar".

Answers to Actividad 4:

1. La pone en el coche. El coche se mueve mucho.
2. Los primos están en la estación de policía, con esposas en las manos. El primo de pelo largo es casado.
3. Reconoce que el robo fue un error. El primo Luis siente que su carrera de programador esté en la basura y pregunta si hay computadoras en la cárcel.
4. Armando dice que es inocente y que el dinero lo arregla todo.
5. No, ella dice que los cargos son falsos y que tiene el mejor abogado del país.
6. Porque no tienen abogado.
7. Le da una rosa blanca. Adriana llama "Hun-Ahau" a Felipe y él la llama "Yax-Balam".
8. Dice, "Otro punto para el bien". Puede referirse al fútbol.
9. Adriana le ofrece chocolates a Felipe. Adriana le dice que para los mayas, el cacao era muy valioso. Felipe le responde, "El chocolate es dulce, pero no tan dulce como tú".
10. Están contentos.

Lengua

I. Narrating in the present and the past: Sequence of tenses

A. Present and present perfect subjunctive in subordinate clauses

¡Conozcamos a nuestros antepasados!

MAMÁ: Adelina, **es** una lástima que todavía no **hayas visitado** el Perú, donde nacieron tus abuelos y bisabuelos. ¿No puedes ir con Carmelo como parte de la excursión a Suramérica?

ADELINA: Sí, estoy segura de que podremos incluir el Perú en nuestro itinerario. Le **diré** a Carmelo que **viajemos** al país de mis antepasados.

MAMÁ: Claro, **dile** que te **acompañe** allí. Lo pasarán muy bien.

ADELINA: Por supuesto, le **pediré** que **subamos** hasta las ruinas de Machu Picchu en tren y que después **visitemos** la antigua ciudad de Cuzco.

MAMÁ: ¡Será una excursión maravillosa!

- When narrating in Spanish, and the subjunctive is needed in the subordinate clause, it is important to coordinate the sequence of tenses of the main and the subordinate clauses. You have learned these sequences of tenses in the sections of the textbook dealing with the subjunctive. (See pages 384, 409, and 463.)

  Can you identify in the dialog the verb tenses used in each main clause and its subordinate clause?

- The following is a summary of the possible sequence of tenses when the subjunctive is needed in the subordinate clause and the verb of the main clause is in the present, in the future, or is a command.

Before doing this activity, direct students to the box on p. 482, on the "Special uses of the present perfect."

Main clause verb Indicative	Subordinate clause verb Subjunctive
1. present 2. future 3. command	present subjunctive present perfect subjunctive

1. Main clause with the present

Yo **quiero** que **visites** Tenochtitlán conmigo.	*I want you to visit Tenochtitlan with me.*
Es maravilloso que nosotros **hayamos visitado** Cuzco.	*It's wonderful that we have visited Cuzco.*

2. Main clause with the future

Será imposible que **subamos** hasta Machu Picchu a pie.	*It will be impossible for us to climb up to Machu Picchu by foot.*
¿Podrá ser cierto que doña Carmen **haya mentido** todo el tiempo?	*Can it be possible that doña Carmen has lied all the time?*

3. Main clause with a command

Pídeles a tus amigos que **lean** el Popol Vuh.	*Ask your friends to read the Popol Vuh.*
¡Alégrate de que todo se **haya aclarado!**	*Be happy that all has been cleared up!*

1 **Historia.** Elige la forma correcta del verbo en las frases que siguen. Si tienes dudas, revisa el diálogo y los ejemplos anteriores. Trabaja con un/a compañero/a.

Answers to Actividad 1:
1. b
2. b
3. a
4. c
5. a
6. c

1. Es bueno que _________ una película sobre la civilización de los incas, los mayas y los aztecas.
a. hacen b. hayan hecho c. han hecho

2. Es una lástima que tanta gente indígena _________ exterminada por conquistadores y enfermedades.
a. fue b. haya sido c. fueron

3. Tío, dígales a mis primos que me _________ a visitar las pirámides en México.
a. acompañen b. acompañaron c. acompañaran

4. Buscaremos un restaurante que _________ mole poblano mexicano.
a. sirve b. sirviera c. sirva

5. Pídeles a los profesores que te _________ cómo se leen los jeroglíficos mayas.
a. expliquen b. explicaran c. explican

6. Es maravilloso que muchos arqueólogos _________ las culturas de Suramérica y Centroamérica.
a. estudiaron b. estudian c. estudien

2 **Todos me dan sugerencias.** Eres estudiante de maestría en arqueología y vas a pasar el año viviendo en Latinoamérica e investigando las civilizaciones antiguas. Escribe las sugerencias que te dan tu familia, tus amigos y tu profesor/a. Incluye información que has aprendido en esta lección sobre los diferentes grupos hispanos. Completa cada oración con una idea original en el presente de subjuntivo.

1. Mis padres quieren que yo...
2. Mi novio me pide que yo...
3. Mi profesor/a de inglés me sugiere que yo...
4. Mi hermano insiste en que yo...
5. Mis abuelos prefieren que yo...
6. Mi compañera de cuarto desea que yo...
7. Mi mejor amigo/a me pide que yo...

LENGUA EN ACCIÓN

Special uses of the present perfect

- When the main sentence is in the present perfect and the subordinate clause requires the subjunctive, the subordinate verb can be in the present or in the present perfect subjunctive. The content of the sentence will determine which of the two tenses of the subjunctive will render the intended meaning.

La profesora nos **ha pedido** que **escribamos** una composición sobre los mayas.	*The teacher has asked us to write a composition about the Mayans.*
Ha sido un milagro que Nayeli **haya podido** comprobar su inocencia.	*It has been a miracle that Nayeli has been able to prove her innocence.*

Answers to Actividad 3:
1. b
2. a
3. b
4. b
5. a
6. a

3 Eventos. Trabaja con un/a compañero/a y completa estas oraciones con el verbo correcto.

1. Los profesores nos han pedido que ________ estas frases con el verbo correcto.
   a. completamos b. completemos
2. Todo el año hemos estado muy satisfechos de que ________ aprender tanto sobre las civilizaciones precolombinas.
   a. hayamos podido b. podamos
3. Todos mis amigos me han pedido que los ________ a mis fiestas.
   a. haya invitado b. invite
4. ¡Nos ha gustado mucho que todos nosotros ________ español tan bien este semestre!
   a. hemos aprendido b. hayamos aprendido
5. A mis padres no les ha preocupado mucho que yo, además de estudiar, ________ a todas las fiestas de mi universidad. ¡Todas mis notas son muy buenas!
   a. haya ido b. he ido
6. Es importante que ________ más sobre nuestra historia.
   a. sepamos b. sabemos

B. Imperfect and past perfect subjunctive in subordinate clauses

Mi tía y yo

Mi tía Penélope **quería** que yo **fuera** con ella a la tienda de ropa mexicana porque allí tenían una venta enorme, pero yo le **dije** que por favor, **cambiara** el plan. Le **pedí** que en vez de ir a comprar ropa, **fuéramos** a comprar discos y a cenar en su restaurante favorito. Me pareció muy bien combinar las compras con la invitación a mi tía Penélope porque mi mamá también me **había sugerido** que **invitara** a mi tía a comer en su restaurante favorito para celebrar su cumpleaños. Mi tía no quería cambiar de planes, pero para convencerla, le expliqué que **era necesario** que yo **comprara** buenos discos de música latinoamericana para mi fiesta de graduación. Por fin, mi tía aceptó la invitación y fuimos tanto a cenar como a comprar discos.

- When narrating events in the past and the subjunctive is needed in the subordinate clause, you need to coordinate the sequence of tenses of the main and the subordinate clauses. You have learned these sequences of tenses in the sections of the textbook dealing with the subjunctive (pages 384, 409, 463). Can you identify in the dialog the verb tenses used in each main clause and its subordinate clause?
- The following is a summary of the possible sequence of tenses when the subjunctive is needed in the subordinate clause and the verb of the main clause is in the preterite, the imperfect, the conditional, or the past perfect.

Main clause verb Indicative	Subordinate clause verb Subjunctive
1. preterite 2. imperfect 3. conditional 4. past perfect	imperfect subjunctive past perfect subjunctive

1. Main clause with the preterite

Mis profesores me **dijeron** que **leyera** sobre la historia antigua.	*My teachers told me to read about ancient history.*
Nos **gustó** mucho que tú **hubieras asistido** a la conferencia sobre Cuzco.	*We were very pleased that you had attended the lecture about Cuzco.*

2. Main clause with the imperfect

Nayeli **deseaba** que todos sus estudiantes **fueran** excelentes.	*Nayeli wanted all her students to be excellent.*
No **era** muy probable que Armando **hubiera sido** culpable del robo.	*It wasn't very likely that Armando had been responsible for the theft.*

3. Main clause with the conditional

Sería muy bueno que todos **cuidáramos** nuestro patrimonio cultural.	*It would be great if we all took care of our cultural heritage.*
Tendríamos paz en el mundo si todos **hubiéramos sido** más generosos.	*We would have peace in the world if we all had been more generous.*

4. Main clause with the past perfect

Antes del descubrimiento de Machu Picchu, nadie **había sospechado** que **hubiera** ciudades perdidas en los Andes.	*Before the discovery of Machu Picchu, nobody had suspected that there were lost cities in the Andes.*
Adriana le dijo a Felipe que le **había encantado** que los jaguares finalmente **hubieran llegado** a México.	*Adriana told Felipe that she was delighted that the jaguars had finally arrived in Mexico.*

Answers to Actividad 4:
1. c
2. b
3. b
4. b
5. a
6. c

4 Las culturas de Latinoamérica. Escoge la forma correcta del verbo para completar cada frase.

1. Fue admirable que las antiguas culturas amerindias __________ tanto a la civilización mundial.
   a. contribuyeron b. contribuyan c. contribuyeran
2. Mis compañeros de clase habían sugerido que nosotros __________ a un concierto de música andina.
   a. asistamos b. asistiéramos c. hayamos asistido
3. Sería importante que __________ más investigación sobre el papel de las mujeres y los hombres en las civilizaciones antiguas.
   a. se haya hecho b. se hiciera c. se hubiera hecho
4. Todavía tendríamos los libros mayas si Armando de Landa no los __________.
   a. ha destruido b. hubiera destruido c. haya destruido
5. Fue muy importante que los arqueólogos __________ los jeroglíficos mayas.
   a. pudieran descifrar b. puedan descifrar c. pudieron descifrar
6. Mis padres querían que yo __________ español.
   a. estudié b. estudiaría c. estudiara

5 Todos te dieron sugerencias. Escribe las sugerencias que los padres, amigos y el/la profesor/a le dieron a tu amiga.

1. Sus padres querían que ella...
2. Su novio le dijo que ella...
3. Su profesor/a de inglés le había sugerido que ella...
4. Su hermano insistió en que ella...
5. Sus abuelos preferirían que ella...
6. Su compañera de cuarto deseó que ella...
7. Su mejor amigo/a le había pedido que ella...

Before doing **Actividad 6**, review contrary to fact **si**-clauses from Chapter 11. Here the sequence of tenses rule applies except the indicative/subjunctive order is reversed, as the **si**-clause comes first.

Answers to Actividad 6:
1. permitiera / iría
2. terminara / llevaría
3. pudiera / iríamos
4. saliera / podríamos
5. vinieran / invitaríamos

6 Si tengo tiempo. Tu familia y tú tienen ganas de hacer muchas actividades. Crea frases hipotéticas usando estas ideas. Sigue el modelo.

► **Modelo:** *Si tengo tiempo, voy a Chichén Itzá.*
Si tuviera tiempo, iría a Chichén Itzá.

1. Si mamá me permite, iré de viaje por las ruinas de Centroamérica.
2. Si termino con mi laboratorio de biología antes de las seis, te llevo al recital de poesía nahuatl.
3. Si mi hermana puede conseguir entradas, vamos al concierto de música peruana.
4. Si papá sale del trabajo temprano, podemos ver el documental sobre las ruinas de Tikal.
5. Si mis tíos vienen de Venezuela, los invitamos a ver la obra teatral sobre la vida de los mayas.

LENGUA EN ACCIÓN

Special uses of the imperfect and past perfect subjunctive

- The imperfect subjunctive or the past perfect subjunctive may also be used in the subordinate clause when the main clause has a verb in the present or the present perfect (see I. Narrating in the present p. 480). The only condition here is that the event described in the subordinate clause must have happened before the one described in the main clause.

Siento mucho que tus amigos no te **invitaran** a la excursión por el Ecuador.	*I am very sorry that your friends didn't invite you to the excursion in Ecuador.*
Cuando **leo** el Popol Vuh me parece muy interesante que los mayas nunca **hubieran usado** la rueda.	*When I read the Popol Vuh, it seems very interesting to me that the Mayans had never used the wheel.*
Ha sido muy triste que te **hubieras ido** sin despedirte de mí.	*It has been very sad that you (had) left without saying good-bye to me.*

7 **Así sucedieron las cosas.** Dos amigos hablan sobre varios incidentes históricos. Completa las frases con uno de los verbos de la lista.

hubieran quemado	descubrieran	tuvieran
fueran	hubiera encontrado	hubiera preguntado

1. No me gusta que el profesor nos __________ tantas cosas difíciles en el examen de historia latinoamericana.
2. Es una desgracia que __________ casi todos los códices de los mayas.
3. Me ha sorprendido mucho que nadie __________ antes a Machu Picchu.
4. Nos impresiona que los incas __________ tantos conocimientos de astronomía.
5. Es importante que los arqueólogos __________ el significado de la escritura maya.
6. ¿Es posible que los incas __________ tan buenos astrónomos como los mayas?

Answers to Actividad 7:
1. hubiera preguntado
2. hubieran quemado
3. hubiera encontrado
4. tuvieran
5. descubrieran
6. fueran

II. Retelling and reporting

Passive voice

Las casas de las civilizaciones antiguas

designed / *altar* / *done*

Las casas aztecas **fueron diseñadas**° con un patio interior, una cocina y un pequeño santuario° para los dioses.

Las casas incas **fueron construidas** de adobe o piedra, pero la mayoría de las casas aztecas y mayas **fueron hechas** de adobe. Los trabajos domésticos **eran realizados**° por las mujeres aztecas, incas y mayas.

- In conversational Spanish, you have already learned two separate constructions to convey the passive voice, stressing the action and not the subject of an event (Chapter 6, p. 258).

Se construyó una pirámide. / **Se construyeron** pirámides.	*A pyramid was built. / Pyramids were built.*
Construyeron pirámides.	*They built pyramids.*

- In Spanish, as in English, the pure passive voice is formed with the verb **ser** + past participle.

En el siglo XV muchas ciudades **fueron construidas** en Latinoamérica.	*In the fifteenth century, many cities were built in Latin America.*
El significado de los astros **era interpretado** por los sacerdotes aztecas e incas.	*The meaning of the stars was interpreted by the Aztec and Incan priests.*

- The preposition **por** is used to indicate by whom the action was/is done.

La ciudad de Cuzco **fue fundada** por los incas en el siglo XI.	*The city of Cuzco was founded by the Incas in the eleventh century.*
Los mensajes de los incas **eran llevados** por los chasquis, los mensajeros incas.	*The messages of the Incas used to be carried by the chasquis, the Incan messengers.*

- The past participle must agree in gender and in number with the subject of the sentence.

Las pirámides de Chichén Itzá **fueron construidas** por el pueblo tolteca.	*The Chichén Itzá pyramids were built by the Toltecs.*
El libro original del Popol Vuh **fue escrito** por los Maya Quichés de Guatemala. **Fue copiado** y después traducido al español por el sacerdote Francisco Jiménez en el siglo XVI.	*The original Popol Vuh was written by the Quiche Maya of Guatemala. It was copied and then translated into Spanish by the priest Francisco Jiménez in the sixteenth century.*

- The verb **ser** may be used in any tense according to the context.

Las pirámides aztecas **han sido** visitadas por millones de turistas.	*The Aztec pyramids have been visited by millions of tourists.*
En la época de los incas, las ciudades siempre **eran construidas** de piedra.	*In the times of the Incas, the cities were always built of stone.*
Es posible que Machu Picchu **haya sido construida** como ciudad sagrada.	*It is possible that Machu Picchu has been built as a sacred city.*

LENGUA EN ACCIÓN

Uses of the passive voice

- In written Spanish, the passive voice with the verb **ser** + *past participle* is most often used in newspapers, magazines, and formal writing. It is also very frequently used to establish past events and facts. For this reason, the preterite may be more common than the imperfect.
- Remember that many common passive expressions in English use *to be + participle* while Spanish prefers **se** + *third person* of the verb. Note that the verb agrees in number with the noun. Following is a list of some of these expressions. Review Chapter 6 (p. 258) for more examples.

Aquí se habla español.	*Spanish is spoken here.*
Se venden apartamentos.	*Apartments for sale (are sold).*
Se prohibe fumar.	*Smoking is forbidden. (No smoking.)*
Se sirve comida portuguesa.	*Portuguese food is served.*
Se cambian cheques.	*Checks (are) cashed.*
Se hacen llaves aquí.	*Keys (are) made here.*

8 **Un vistazo (glimpse) al pasado.** Completa cada frase en el pasado con la voz pasiva. Usa el pretérito del verbo **ser** en todas las frases.

1. El calendario azteca __________ ____________________ (crear) hace muchos siglos.
2. Las hierbas __________ ____________________ (usar) como medicinas por diferentes grupos indígenas.
3. El chicle __________ ____________________ (producir) por los aztecas.
4. Varios animales __________ ____________________ (ofrecer) a los dioses en algunas ceremonias religiosas.
5. Las herramientas (*tools*) __________ ____________________ (fabricar) de piedra y hueso (*bone*).
6. En algunas regiones, el chile __________ ____________________ (utilizar) como especie en las comidas.
7. El quetzal __________ ____________________ (considerar) como un ave hermosa.
8. La astronomía __________ ____________________ (estudiar) por los mayas.
9. Machu Picchu __________ ____________________ (construir) por los incas.
10. El sol y la luna __________ ____________________ (adorar) por los pueblos precolombinos.
11. El uso del cero __________ ____________________ (comprender) por los mayas.
12. La escritura __________ ____________________ (representar) por jeroglíficos (*hieroglyphics*).

Answers to Actividad 8:
Before doing **Actividad 8,** review regular and irregular past participles, p. 382.

1. fue creado
2. fueron usadas
3. fue producido
4. fueron ofrecidos
5. fueron fabricadas
6. fue utilizado
7. fue considerado
8. fue estudiada
9. fue construido
10. fueron adorados
11. fue comprendido
12. fue representada

Answers to Actividad 9:

1. Los bellos objetos de cerámica fueron fabricados por los mochicas.
2. El maíz era molido por las mujeres.
3. Los bonitos tejidos con...fueron hechos por los nazcas.
4. Las pirámides precolombinas eran consideradas (como) lugares sagrados por la gente.
5. Los sacrificios humanos fueron realizados por los aztecas, los mayas y los incas.
6. El juego de pelota fue practicado por diferentes grupos indígenas.
7. El oro y otros metales fueron usados por los artesanos en objetos...
8. Las ceremonias religiosas eran celebradas por los sacerdotes.
9. El maíz fue cultivado por muchos grupos indígenas.
10. El chocolate amargo fue usado como bebida sagrada por los aztecas.

9 Datos del pasado. Paquita está estudiando en el Perú y le cuenta a su familia sobre algunas características de las culturas precolombinas. Trabajen en parejas y cambien los verbos a la voz pasiva. Usen el pretérito cuando el verbo esté en pretérito y el imperfecto cuando la frase esté en imperfecto. Sigan el modelo.

► **Modelo:** *En varias ceremonias religiosas la gente tocaba las flautas.*
En varias ceremonias religiosas las flautas ***eran tocadas*** *por la gente.*

1. Los mochicas fabricaron bellos objetos de cerámica.
2. Las mujeres molían (*ground*) el maíz.
3. Los nazcas hicieron bonitos tejidos con formas geométricas y con imágenes de animales y personas.
4. La gente consideraba las pirámides precolombinas como lugares sagrados.
5. Los aztecas, los mayas y los incas realizaron sacrificios humanos.
6. Diferentes grupos indígenas practicaron el juego de pelota.
7. Los artesanos usaron el oro y otros metales en objetos decorativos y religiosos.
8. Los sacerdotes celebraban las ceremonias religiosas.
9. Muchos grupos indígenas cultivaron el maíz.
10. Los aztecas usaron el chocolate amargo como bebida sagrada.

10 Bienvenidos/as a mi tierra. Escribe una guía turística—para tus amigos que vienen del Paraguay—describiendo un sitio arqueológico importante de tu región. Toma las siguientes preguntas como guías e incluye oraciones en voz pasiva.

1. ¿Cómo se llama el sitio? ¿Qué características tiene?
2. ¿Por quién fue construido? ¿Cómo vivían los habitantes allí? ¿Qué hacían?
3. ¿Qué animales había? ¿Qué papel tenían estos animales?
4. ¿Por quién fue descubierto el sitio?
5. ¿Por quiénes es visitado el sitio? ¿Por cuántas personas? ¿En qué estaciones del año?

Lectura A

Introducción

The second part of Popol Vuh, the sacred book of the Mayas, narrates how the Mayan Hero Twins overpowered the frightening Lords of the Mayan underworld, Xibalbá, a parallel world beneath ours, with plants, animals, and people. The version of the Popol Vuh that we know today is a Spanish translation of an old Quiche Maya book done by the Jesuit Francisco Jiménez. Side-by-side with the Spanish text, the translator included a transcript of the original Quiche Maya language, which probably was an interpretation of a lost Mayan codex. The classical Mayan names of the Hero Twins, Hun-Ahau and Yax-Balam, are transcribed in the Popol Vuh as Hunahpú and Ixbalamqué.

Reading strategy: Taking notes in a chart

When reading a passage with sequential events or with names that are unusual or not easy to remember, it is important to keep track of the who, what, where, and why of the narration.

To prepare yourself for the reading, create a chart like the following and fill in the information in your own words as you read the story of the twins. Because the characters do more than one thing, it is a good idea to number their actions in chronological order. The first one is done for you.

¿Quién/es?	¿Qué hizo/ hicieron?	¿Dónde?	¿Por qué?	¿Cuándo?
Hun-Camé y Vucub-Camé	1. Mataron a los padres de los gemelos.	1. Xibalbá	1. Porque no pudieron ganar los juegos de pelota.	¿...?

Héroes mayas

En el Popol Vuh, el libro sagrado° de los mayas, se cuenta la historia de Hunahpú° y de Ixbalamqué,° los grandes héroes gemelos que vencieron° a los señores° de Xibalbá, Hun°-Camé y Vucub°-Camé.

sacred
Lord One / Little Jaguar
defeated / lords, gods / Death One / Death Seven

Hunahpú e Ixbalamqué eran hijos de otro famoso gemelo maya, Hun-Hunahpú. El hermano gemelo de Hun-Hunahpú se llamaba Vucub-Hunahpú y ambos eran los mejores jugadores de pelota del mundo de la superficie. Los señores de Xibalbá los invitaron a jugar pelota en Xibalbá, pero los mataron porque no pudieron ganar los juegos de pelota en Xibalbá ni cumplir con las pruebas imposibles que les pusieron. A Vucub-Hunahpú lo enterraron° en la plaza de juego de pelota de Xibalbá y la cabeza de Hun-Hunahpú la colgaron° en un árbol de calabazas.°

Ixquic,° la madre de los Héroes Gemelos, quedó embarazada cuando se acercó para coger° una calabaza y la cabeza de Hun-Hunahpú le escupió° en la palma de la mano. Como los señores de Xibalbá querían matarla, Ixquic tuvo que escapar a casa de Ixmucané,° la madre de Hun-Hunahpú y Vucub-Hunahpú. Allí nacieron Hunahpú e Ixbalamqué. Con los años, estos gemelos llegaron a ser grandes jugadores de pelota. Sin embargo, el ruido de su juego enfureció a Hun-Camé y Vucub-Camé, quienes decidieron matarlos invitándolos a jugar pelota en Xibalbá, tal como lo habían hecho con su padre y su tío.

Al llegar a Xibalbá, Hunahpú e Ixbalamqué descubrieron los trucos° de los dioses del mal con la ayuda de varios animales y pasaron todas las pruebas en las que su padre y su tío habían fracasado:° pudieron fumarse un cigarro sin fuego, quemar una antorcha° sin gastarla;° sobrevivir en las casas de la oscuridad,° del frío, de las navajas,° y de los murciélagos;° pudieron recoger flores de diversos tipos sin moverse de un solo sitio y, por último, pudieron vencer° la misma muerte. De esta manera, no solamente ganaron el juego de pelota, sino que destruyeron a los señores de Xibalbá y se convirtieron en dioses auténticos con forma de astros en el firmamento.°

buried
hung
calabash (hard pumpkin-like fruit)
Blood Woman
to take / spat
Daykeeper and Grandmother of Light
tricks
failed
torch / using it up
darkness / knives / bats
conquer
sky

Answers to Actividad 2:

1. Estaba en el mundo subterráneo. Era un mundo paralelo al nuestro y los señores malos de Xibalbá vivían allí.
2. El padre y el tío de los Héroes Gemelos. Señores de Xibalbá, vencidos por los héroes.
3. "Hun" = **uno**; "Vucub" = **siete**.
4. Se enojaron porque hacían mucho ruido mientras jugaban a la pelota.
5. Ixmucané. Recibió a Ixquic, madre de los Héroes gemelos.
6. Porque los señores de Xibalbá querían matarla.
7. Les gustaba jugar a la pelota.
8. Se fumaron un cigarro sin fuego, quemaron una antorcha sin gastarla, sobrevivieron en lugares peligrosos, recogieron flores sin moverse y vencieron la muerte.
9. En dioses con forma de astro.

1 La familia de los Héroes. Haz un árbol geneológico de la familia de los héroes gemelos.

2 Personajes y eventos. Usa tus apuntes para contestar las preguntas.

1. ¿Dónde estaba Xibalbá? ¿Qué era y quién vivía allí?
2. ¿Quiénes eran Hun-Hunahpú y Vacub-Hunahpú? ¿Y Hun-Camé y Vucub-Camé?
3. ¿Qué significan las palabras **Hun** y **Vucub,** según la lectura?
4. ¿Por qué se enojaron los señores de Xibalbá con Hunahpú e Ixbalamqué?
5. ¿Cómo se llamaba la abuela de los Héroes Gemelos? ¿A quién recibió ella en su casa?
6. ¿Por qué tuvo que huir Ixquic de Xibalbá?
7. ¿Qué les gustaba hacer a los gemelos Hunahpú e Ixbalamqué?
8. ¿Qué cosas imposibles pudieron hacer con éxito Hunahpú e Ixbalamqué?
9. ¿En qué se convirtieron Hunahpú e Ixbalamqué después de vencer a los dioses de Xibalbá?

3 Inventa un mito. Ahora que las estatuas de los gemelos están juntas en el museo en México, pueden tener más aventuras. Inventa otro mito de los Héroes Gemelos en el tiempo contemporáneo.

ETAPA B

Pistas y palabras

I. Discussing the history of Hispanics in the United States

Los hispanos en los Estados Unidos

El español como lengua común

La **identidad** hispana es el resultado del **encuentro** de las culturas amerindias con la cultura española, varias culturas africanas y otras europeas, desde el siglo XV hasta el siglo XIX. **A partir del**° siglo XX, las naciones recién formadas han ido consolidando su propia identidad. No se puede hablar, entonces, de una sola identidad hispana ni de una sola **raza,**° pero sí de un elemento común en todas las regiones: el español. El uso del español como lengua **común** es también lo que **une**° a la comunidad hispana de los Estados Unidos.

Starting from
race
unites

Los territorios españoles en América del Norte

La presencia hispana en los Estados Unidos no es solamente un fenómeno moderno, pues parte del **territorio** del país fue de la corona° española. Entre los siglos XV y XVII se fundaron muchas **poblaciones** españolas al norte y al sur del Río Grande y fueron incluídas en el Virreinato de la Nueva España, el que en 1784, comprendía° gran parte de los territorios de América del Norte, toda América Central y las Antillas.

crown
made up

La Guerra de 1847

Desde el siglo XVIII, hubo muchos cambios en la soberanía de estos territorios hasta llegar a la división política actual.° El último cambio ocurrió con la

current

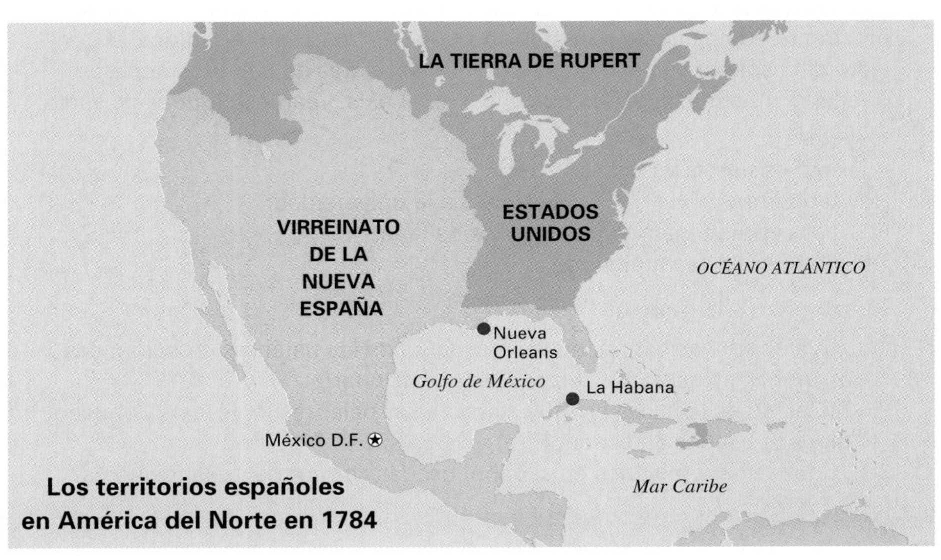

Los territorios españoles en América del Norte en 1784

Guerra de 1847, cuando más de 1.300.000 kilómetros cuadrados del territorio mexicano pasaron a los Estados Unidos. Esta área incluye los estados actuales de Arizona, Nevada, Utah, Texas, California, Nuevo México y la parte occidental° de Colorado.

western

Answers to Actividad 1:
1. Es el resultado del encuentro de las culturas amerindias con la cultura española, varias culturas africanas y otras europeas desde el siglo XV hasta el siglo XIX.
2. el español
3. En el siglo XV
4. Mucho del suroeste.
5. Arizona, Nevada, Utah, Texas, California, Nuevo México y la parte occidental de Colorado.

1 Comprensión. Contesta las preguntas según la lectura.

1. ¿Qué es la identidad hispana?
2. ¿Cuál es el elemento común que unifica las regiones hispanas?
3. ¿Cuándo comenzó la presencia hispana en los Estados Unidos?
4. ¿Cuánto territorio de los Estados Unidos era de México antes del 1847?
5. ¿Qué estados de los Estados Unidos de hoy eran parte de la Nueva España?

2 Cronología. Completa esta línea cronológica con los datos de la lectura.

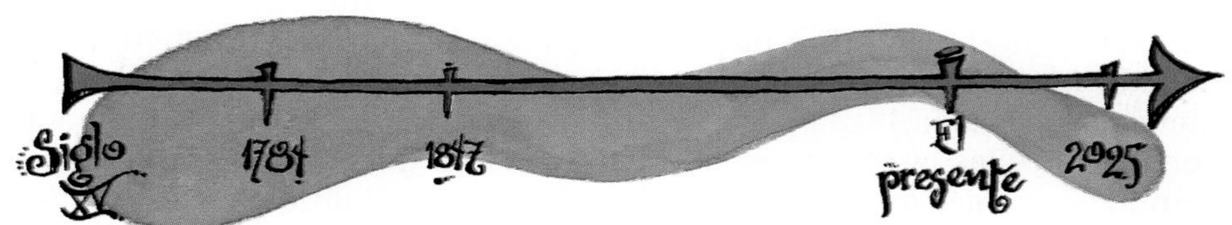

Some answers to Actividad 3: Arizona, Florida, Texas (Tejas), Nuevo México, Colorado, California, Nevada, Amarillo, Lima, Madrid, Boca Ratón, San Francisco, San Diego, Loma Linda, Plano, El Paso, San Antonio.

3 La influencia hispana en la lengua. En los Estados Unidos hay muchos nombres de sitios y ciudades que proceden del español. Hagan una lista de los que conozcan y sobre el posible significado de cada uno.

▸ **Modelos:** *Los Ángeles* = The Angels *Nevada* = Snowland, Snowfall

ENLACE CULTURAL

Lenguas en contacto

Cuando dos o más lenguas están en contacto constante una con otra, los préstamos° de palabras son muy comunes. En los Estados Unidos, el contacto del español con el inglés ha creado variantes de palabras inglesas que usan muchos hispanos que viven en el país. Veamos algunas de estas palabras:

borrowing

Ayer me pusieron un **ticket**.
Hoy tengo que enviar las **aplicaciones** a la universidad.
En nuestra sala tenemos una **carpeta** de lana.
Te llamo **para atrás** más tarde.

Discusión en grupos

1. ¿Cuáles son las expresiones en español de las palabras mencionadas arriba? Si es necesario, consulten el diccionario.
2. En las áreas técnicas es muy común usar palabras inglesas. ¿Conocen algunas usadas en español?
3. ¿Conocen expresiones en español usadas comunmente en el inglés?

II. Talking about the Hispanic population in the United States

La población hispana en los Estados Unidos

En 1995, el 74% de todos los hispanos vivía en cinco estados: California, Texas, Nueva York, Florida e Illinois. Solamente en California, vivían 9 millones de ellos, la concentración de hispanos más alta del país, la mayoría de ellos de origen mexicano. Los hispanos de Nueva York son de muchas procedencias, pero los puertorriqueños son uno de los grupos más numerosos. En la Florida, la mayor parte son cubanos llegados a la península en los años 60, después de la Revolución cubana, y en los años 80, cuando hubo una fuga masiva de la isla.

En los próximos 25 años, la población total de los Estados Unidos incrementará en 72 millones de personas. De este número, 32 millones (44%) serán de origen hispano y vivirán en los cinco estados mencionados anteriormente. California seguirá siendo el estado más populoso de la nación en el año 2.025, y también seguirá teniendo el mayor número de hispanos: 21 millones que representarán el 36% del total de los hispanos estadounidenses. El segundo estado más numeroso será Texas, el que también será el segundo en población hispana con 10 millones de ellos, es decir, el 17%. En tercer lugar estará la Florida, con 4,9 millones, luego Nueva York con 4,3 millones y por último Illinois con 2,3 millones. Habrá muchos hispanos viviendo en otros estados, también. *U.S. Census Bureau, 1996*

4 Comprensión. Contesta las preguntas.

1. ¿En qué estado vive la mayoría de los mexicanoamericanos? ¿Por qué?
2. ¿En qué estado vive la mayoría de los puertorriqueños?
3. ¿En qué estado vive la mayoría de los cubanos? ¿Por qué?
4. ¿Qué estado va a tener el mayor número de hispanos en el futuro?
5. Calcula el total de hispanos en el año 2.025.

5 La influencia hispana. Completa el siguiente cuadro con la influencia que diferentes grupos de hispanos han tenido en la lengua, la comida, los deportes y la música en los EE.UU. Añade otras categorías a tu gusto.

Grupo	Lengua	Comida	Música	Deportes

Answers to Actividad 4:

1. California. California y Texas están cerca de México. La Florida está cerca de Cuba. Nueva York e Illinois tienen ciudades grandes que atraen a la gente y a sus familiares.
2. Nueva York.
3. La Florida. Está cerca de Cuba.
4. California.
5. 58,3 millones. Note: **incrementará** indicates a *total increase* in population.

Play some of Gloria Estefan's songs in Spanish.

role

ENLACE CULTURAL

Semblanzas latinas

Andy Garcia.

Andrés Arturo García Méndez nació en Cuba el 12 de abril de 1956 y llegó a los Estados Unidos con sus padres en 1961. Ha participado en muchas películas de éxito y es muy buen actor. Andy tiene tres hijos y se considera muy cubano.

Gloria María Fajardo nació en Cuba el primero de septiembre de 1957 y llegó a los Estados Unidos antes de cumplir los dos años de edad. Gloria ha cantado y tocado la guitarra desde niña, pero su carrera profesional se inició en el grupo *Miami Sound Machine,* dirigido por su marido Emilio Estefan. La artista tiene dos hijos, Nayib, nacido en 1980, y Emily Marie, nacida en 1994.

Gloria Estefan.

Jackie Guerra nació en California de padres mexicanos. Mientras estudiaba ciencias políticas, participó en un concurso de artistas aficionados y lo ganó. En ese momento decidió ser humorista y ese mismo año le ofrecieron un programa propio de televisión: *First Time Out.* En la película de la vida de Selena hizo el papel° de Suzette, la hermana de la cantante. Actualmente, Jackie tiene muchos planes para el futuro y le llueven las ofertas.

Discusión en grupos

1. ¿Qué diferencias y semejanzas hay entre estos tres artistas hispanos?
2. ¿Han visto la actuación de alguno de ellos?
3. ¿Conoce alguno de ustedes la biografía de otro/a artista hispano/a? Si no conocen a otros artistas hispanos, hablen sobre el/la artista más conocido/a del momento.

Jackie Guerra.

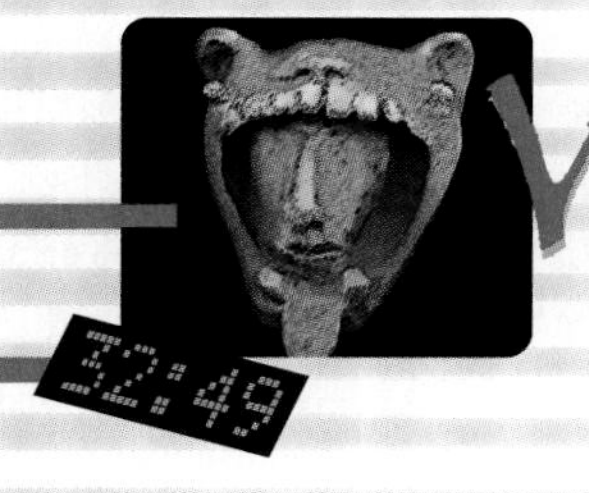

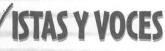

VISTAS Y VOCES

I. Preparémonos

1 Anticipación. Trabajen en parejas y contesten las siguientes preguntas.

A. **1.** Describe una catástrofe que haya tenido tu país recientemente.
2. ¿De dónde son tus antepasados? ¿Qué sueños tenían? ¿Cuál es uno de tus sueños?
3. ¿Quiénes son un héroe y una heroína de tu país? ¿Cómo son? ¿Cuáles son sus hazañanas (*heroic deed*)?
4. ¿Qué planes, circunstancias o personas pueden cambiar el futuro y la prosperidad de tu país? ¿Qué piensas hacer por tu país en el futuro?

B. Mira la foto 12B en la página 471. ¿Por qué está la señora desconocida con Adriana y Nayeli? ¿Qué crees que dice el papelito que tiene en la mano?

Para comprender mejor

al revés	*backwards*	el hallazgo	*find*
la alegría	*joy*	idear	*to make a plan*
el/la antepasado/a	*ancestor*	inexplicable	*unexplainable*
averiguar	*to find out*	el peligro	*danger*
de veras	*really*	presentar	*to introduce*
descorazonar	*to discourage*	pues	*well*
la deuda	*debt*	la respuesta	*answer*
el/la diputado/a	*deputy*	suponer	*to guess*
el espejo	*mirror*	el/la televidente	*TV viewer*
fortalecer	*to fortify*	el titular	*headline*
el halago	*praise*	yucateco/a	*from the Yucatan*

2 Secuencia. Estudia las escenas de video y comenta cómo crees que va a terminar la historia. Trabaja con un/a compañero/a.

1.

Order of video action shots: 1, 4, 3, 2

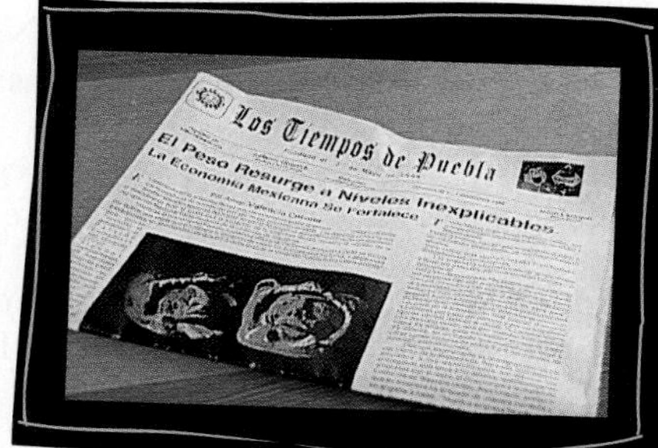

2.

3.

4.

II. Miremos y escuchemos

3 Mis observaciones. Escribe lo que pasa en este episodio entre Nayeli y Adriana; entre Felipe y Adriana; entre Raúl y Nayeli y entre los gemelos.

III. Comentemos

4 Comprensión. En grupos, contesten las siguientes preguntas.

1. ¿Dónde están Nayeli, Felipe y Adriana? ¿Está lloviendo? ¿Quién presenta a Nayeli? ¿Qué dice? ¿Qué tiene Adriana en las manos?
2. ¿Cuál era el sueño de Nayeli, Adriana y Felipe? ¿ De qué fue acusada Nayeli y por qué? En realidad, ¿quién era el criminal? ¿Cuál fue el gran plan de Armando?
3. ¿Cómo explica Nayeli su papel en el descubrimiento de los gemelos? ¿Qué dice Adriana sobre los antepasados? ¿De qué más habla?
4. Adriana le cuenta a Felipe su sueño de conseguir algo. ¿Qué es?
5. ¿Qué significa I.L.E.Y.A.N.? ¿y al revés?
6. ¿Qué le da Raúl a Nayeli? ¿Qué simboliza, según Raúl? ¿Cómo está ella?
7. ¿De qué es la foto que Raúl le muestra a Nayeli? ¿Qué pasa entre ellos?
8. ¿Cómo se llama el periódico? ¿Quién lo lee? ¿Qué dicen los titulares?

5 Una flor y chocolates. Analiza la relación entre Felipe y Adriana. En tu opinión, ¿qué siente Felipe por Adriana y ella por él? ¿Cómo han cambiado desde el principio de la historia? ¿Van a estar juntos en cinco años? Explica. ¿Por qué son dos de *Los Buenos* de "Caminos del jaguar"?

6 Miremos otra vez. Arregla las escenas en el orden correcto. Después discute esta pregunta: Si tuvieras un/a gemelo/a, ¿cómo sería?

7 Abuelita, ¿qué piensas tú? Nayeli tiene otro sueño en el que Abuelita le habla brevemente sobre lo que ha pasado los últimos dos episodios. ¿Qué le dice?

8 La gran cuestión. Adriana pregunta, "¿Cómo es posible integrar la paz y la alegría a la vida?" Contéstale, con referencia a tu escuela, tu país y al mundo.

9 Desde el corazón... Imagina que los héroes gemelos conversan sobre su vida como hermanos, sobre Adriana, Felipe y Nayeli y sobre sus aventuras. Trabajando en parejas, ponte en el lugar de Yax-Balam o Hun-Ahau y escribe un diálogo desde su perspectiva. Usa el título "¡Somos héroes gemelos!"

Yo, Yax-Balam, héroe gemelo...

Yo, Hun-Ahau, héroe gemelo...

Answers to Actividad 4:

1. Están en una plaza en México. No, no está lloviendo; hace mucho sol; hace buen tiempo. El señor diputado la presenta. Dice que sin Nayeli, los jaguares gemelos todavía estarían en manos de criminales. Adriana tiene a Yax-Balam y Hun-Ahau en las manos.
2. Su sueño era devolver a los héroes gemelos a su propio hogar, a México y a la tumba de Pacal. Nayeli fue acusada de robar a los gemelos porque ella fue la última en ver a Yax-Balam antes de que desapareciera. El verdadero criminal fue Armando. Su plan fue robar a Yax-Balam en su ruta de México a Sevilla.
3. Dice que los gemelos querían reunirse y ella sólo era su vehículo. Adriana dice que todo tiene su ciclo. También dice, "Tenemos que escuchar a nuestros antepasados". Habla de escuchar el corazón, no solamente el intelecto.
4. Adriana quiere conseguir la paz universal.
5. Instituto para Localizar Elementos Yucatecos y Arte Nacional. Al revés deletrea "N.A.Y.E.L.I."
6. Le da una rosa blanca. Raúl le dice a Nayeli que simboliza el espejo de su sinceridad. Nayeli está triste por la traición de su madrina, doña Carmen.
7. De una pieza que van a recuperar como su próximo proyecto. Se besan.
8. *Los Tiempos de Puebla* es el nombre del periódico. Esperanza lee el periódico. El titular dice, "El peso resurge a niveles inexplicables. La economía mexicana se fortalece."

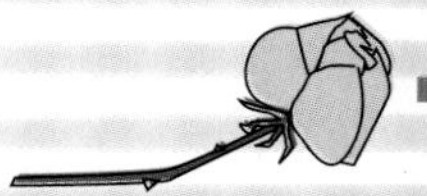

Lengua

I. Talking about abstract ideas

Lo + adjective

Lo mejor y lo peor

CLAUDIA: Fui al cine y vi *Como agua para chocolate.* Me encantó.
ISABEL: La he visto. **Lo mejor**° fue cuando Tita cocinó esa cena maravillosa para Pedro.
CLAUDIA: Tienes razón y **lo más horrible**° fue cuando se murió Roberto.
ISABEL: Bueno, sí, pero **lo peor de todo**° ocurrió con la muerte de Pedro.

The best part
the most horrible part
the worst part of all

- You can use **lo** + the masculine singular of the *adjective* to form a noun expression. In this case, the expression does not refer to any one noun but rather describes abstract qualities or general characteristics.

lo bueno	*the good thing/aspect/part*
lo más increíble	*the most incredible thing/aspect/part*
lo menos difícil	*the least difficult thing/aspect/part*
lo romántico	*the romantic thing/aspect/part*

LENGUA EN ACCIÓN

Special use of lo

- Often **lo** is used to take the place of an adjective or noun or to refer to a total idea that has already been stated:

¿Eres latina? Sí, **lo** soy.	*Are you Latina? Yes, I am.*
¿Es Humberto arqueólogo?	*Is Humberto an archaeologist?*
No, no **lo** es. Es antropólogo.	*No, he is not. He is an anthropologist.*
¿Son los hispanos la minoría más grande de este país? Sí, **lo** son.	*Are Hispanics the largest minority in this country? Yes, they are.*

1 **Entrevista.** Haz las siguientes preguntas sobre diferentes aspectos de la vida. Escribe lo que te dicen tus compañeros/as.

1. ¿Qué es lo bueno de hablar diferentes lenguas?
2. ¿Qué será lo mejor de la vejez?
3. ¿Qué es lo bueno de hacer ejercicio?
4. ¿Qué es lo más importante de la libertad?
5. ¿Qué fue lo más relevante de la década pasada?
6. ¿Qué es lo frustrante de la vida académica?
7. ¿Qué es lo peor de la adolescencia?
8. ¿Qué será lo más interesante de visitar otros países?

9. ¿Qué ha sido lo más divertido de tu vida hasta ahora?
10. ¿Qué es lo más triste de la sociedad hoy en día?
11. ¿Qué es lo más terrible del racismo?
12. ¿Qué es lo más motivante en tu vida?

2 **Los opuestos.** Indica lo positivo y lo negativo de las siguientes cosas.

1. tu cuarto
2. la televisión
3. las cuatro estaciones del año
4. las ciudades grandes
5. el campo
6. la playa
7. un apartamento
8. una casa vieja
9. el trabajo
10. tu escuela
11. la red Internet
12. tu personalidad

II. Questioning and requesting

Differentiating between pedir and preguntar

Lo necesito.

PATRICIO: ¿Puedo **pedirte** un favor? Necesito que me prestes cincuenta dólares. No quiero que me **preguntes** por qué.

MARUJA: Está bien, Patricio. No te preocupes. Te voy a dar un cheque ahora mismo y no voy a preguntarte nada.

PATRICIO: Gracias, y si se me olvida darte el dinero, **pídemelo.**°

° ask me for it

In Spanish there are two verbs that are used to indicate *ask*, but each has a different meaning.

- The verb **pedir** means *to ask for*, or *to request something from someone.* **Pedir** is also used to order food or drink.

Las autoridades le **piden** más detalles a Nayeli.	*The authorities ask Nayeli for more details.*
Adriana **pide** chocolate para Felipe.	*Adriana requests chocolate for Felipe.*

- The verb **preguntar** means to ask a question. It is used to obtain information about someone or something. **Preguntar por** means to to inquire about someone.

Raúl le **pregunta** a Nayeli qué va a hacer ahora.	*Raúl asks Nayeli what she is going to do now.*
Nayeli **pregunta por** doña Carmen.	*Nayeli asks about doña Carmen.*

3 Tengo los mejores padres del mundo. Completa el párrafo con la forma correcta de **pedir** o **preguntar** en el tiempo presente.

Pancho quiere aprender más sobre sus raíces hispanas. Les __________ permiso a sus padres para hacer un viaje por el suroeste de los Estados Unidos. Le __________ a su mamá si puede utilizar su coche. Ella le dice que sí, pero le __________ que no maneje rápido y que revise el aceite con frecuencia. Su papá le __________ si necesita dinero. También le __________ si quiere usar su videocámara. Pancho le contesta que sí, y además le __________ su cámara fotográfica. Su papá le __________ que no deje las máquinas en el coche. Pancho promete hacer todo lo que le __________ sus padres y se va muy contento.

Answers to Actividad 3:
1. pide
2. pregunta
3. pide
4. pregunta
5. pregunta
6. pide
7. pide
8. piden

4 Quiero ir de vacaciones. Usando la forma apropiada de **pedir** o **preguntar,** escribe lo que debes decir en las siguientes circunstancias.

1. Tienes ganas de ir a Miami durante las vacaciones, pero no tienes suficiente dinero.
2. Quieres llamar a una compañera de clase para que te acompañe, pero no sabes su número telefónico.
3. Necesitas saber los precios de los vuelos a la Florida.
4. Deseas reservar habitaciones en el Hotel Caribe en la zona cubana de Miami, pero no sabes en qué calle está.
5. Después de hacer las reservaciones en el hotel, quieres saber si hay un restaurante nicaragüense cerca de allí.
6. Te encuentras con dos amigas de la universidad y quieres saber cómo están y qué planes tienen.

Lectura B

Introducción

The BRAVO awards were created to recognize the talents of the increasing number of Hispanics in the entertainment industry. This article from the magazine *Cristina* lists the recipients of this award in 1996.

Write down names of famous Hispanic celebrities on index cards. On separate cards, write down the description of each celebrity. Distribute one name and one description card to each student and then have students find the cards that match personality and description. When all matches have been made, have each student report on his or her celebrity.

Prelectura

1 Hispanos famosos. Con una pareja, haz un lista de hispanos famosos en las áreas del arte, cine, música, deportes y política.

Arte	Cine	Música	Deportes	Política

Bring in current articles on the **Premios Bravo** for comparison and for updating information.

stars
shine
awarding

Fue una noche llena de estrellas°... Y el Concilio Nacional de la Raza (NCLR, por sus siglas en inglés), hizo que brillaran° más que nunca al entregar° los *Premios Bravo 1996* a los artistas hispanos más talentosos del cine y la televisión en inglés.

presentation

awarded

En la ceremonia de entrega° de premios, celebrada en el Teatro Wiltern de Los Angeles, la prestigiosa organización hispana premió° a los artistas que a través de su carrera han representado dignamente y de una manera positiva la cultura latina.

La gran gala de premios fue conducida por Giselle Fernández, conductora del noticiero *Access Hollywood* y por el actor comediante Cheech Marín. La premiación estuvo muy concurrida° y contó con la presencia de casi todo el firmamento de estrellas latinas que están triunfando en Hollywood.

Raúl Yzaguirre, presidente de NCLR, reconoció la labor de los artistas e hizo un llamado para que continúen conquistando triunfos en el cine y la TV de USA. "Hemos recorrido mucho camino° y hemos cambiado la imagen de los latinos en Hollywood, pero todavía nos falta mucho por recorrer", dijo Yzaguirre.

We have come a long way

had a large audience

winners

¡Bravo por los ganadores!°

Cine

Actriz y actor sobresalientes
Elizabeth Peña, *Lone Star*
Edward James Olmos, *Caught*

Televisión

Lauren Vélez, *New York Undercover*
Michael DeLorenzo, *New York Undercover, NYPD Blue (ABC)*

Programa sobresaliente
Gloria Estefan: *The Evolution Tour – Life in Miami (HBO)*

Actuación sobresaliente en comedia
Liz Torres, *The John Larroquette Show*

Actuación masculina sobresaliente en *show*
Raúl Rodríguez, *Latino Laugh Festival*

Actuación femenina sobresaliente en *show*
Gloria Estefan, *The Evolution Tour – Life in Miami (HBO)*

Actuación sobresaliente en TV y cine
Edward James Olmos, *Larry McMurtry Streets of Laredo*

Actor y actriz sobresalientes en TV *(en papel crossover)*
Teresa Saldaña, *The Commish*
Jimmy Smits, *NYPD Blue*

Documental sobresaliente
Intimate Portrait, Gloria Estefan

Programa para niños y jóvenes
Sesame Street

Premios especiales
Película sobresaliente
Lone Star

Contribución a la música en cine y TV
Los Lobos

Homenaje especial
Freddy Prinze

Galardón por servicio a la comunidad
Latino Communication Center

Postlectura

2 Entrega de premios. Contesta las preguntas según la lectura.

1. ¿Cuál es el nombre de los premios?
2. ¿Dónde se celebró la entrega de premios?
3. ¿Qué artistas condujeron la ceremonia?
4. ¿Qué cultura han representado los artistas que recibieron premios?
5. ¿Asistieron muchas personas a la entrega de premios?
6. ¿De qué imagen habla Raúl Yzaguirre?
7. ¿Quién ganó premio por un documental?
8. ¿Qué programa para niños y jóvenes ganó premio?
9. ¿Qué asociación ganó premio por servicio a la comunidad?
10. Menciona a cinco artistas ganadores de premios del año pasado y en qué los ganaron.

Answers to Actividad 2:
1. Premios Bravo
2. En el teatro Wiltern de Los Angeles
3. Giselle Fernández y Cheech Marín
4. Latina
5. Sí
6. La de los latinos en Hollywood
7. Gloria Estefan
8. Sesame Street
9. Latino Communication Center
10. *Answers will vary.*

3 Artistas concretos. Usa la tabla de la **Actividad 1** y llénala con nombres de artistas mencionados/as en la lectura. Comenta tu selección con otro/a compañero/a.

4 Reportero/a de moda. Eres reportero/a de moda para un periódico. Describe lo que lleva cada uno/a de los artistas a la fiesta de los premios Bravo.

5 A escribir. Los jueces te eligieron para presentar el premio a uno/a de los actores/actrices que escogiste. Escribe una presentación interesante para esa persona.

En resumen

I. Hablemos

1 Historia personal. Hazle una entrevista a una persona hispanohablante o a alguien que tenga aquí un pariente de otro país. Averigua la historia de su familia y pregúntale sobre su experiencia en los Estados Unidos. Preséntale la historia de esa persona a la clase.

2 Predicciones. ¿Qué les pasará a los personajes del video? Trabajen en grupos. Escojan dos personajes del video y describan cómo será su vida en cinco años. ¿Qué harán? ¿Por qué? ¿Tendrán otras aventuras? Preséntenle sus ideas a la clase.

II. Investiguemos por Internet

Using synonyms and word combinations

You have learned ways of specifying and delimiting your search to obtain better results when looking for information. Now that you have learned more Spanish vocabulary, you may want to try another technique for specifying your search, based on using keywords that are synonyms or several words with related meaning. In this chapter you will be looking for articles about ancient civilizations in the Americas. Refer to your browser's help on how to formulate your query. Usually, synonyms or combinations of related words are listed in a search query by separating the different words with commas, for example: **civilización, cultura, pueblo** or **Machu Picchu, ruinas, incas, Perú.** This technique is very useful when you are using names in your search and these names are the same in English and Spanish. Including one word in Spanish will increase your probabilities of obtaining documents in Spanish and not only in English. Evaluate the results of your search and if needed, refine it with the techniques that you have learned before.

Vocabulario informático	
la combinación de palabras	*word combination*
las palabras relacionadas	*related words*
el sinónimo	*synonym*

3 Civilizaciones, pueblos y culturas. Your task is to find out to what the names in the list below are related. You already know some of them, some of them you may not know—yet. Work in groups and answer the following questions: What do these names refer to? a culture? a site? both? Write a short description and present your results to the class. These are related words and phrases that you can use in your search with any of the names in the list: **civilización, cultura, pueblo, ruina, ruinas, imperio, imperios, capital, códice, "imperio inca", "ciudad perdida", "ruinas antiguas"** and so on. Remember to write quotation marks with phrases. You also will have to write quotation marks if the name in the list has more than one word. The first related word is given in the list.

Palabra clave	Palabra relacionada 1	Palabra relacionada 2	Palabra relacionada 3
1. Acueducto de Segovia	España		
2. Altamira	España	cueva	
3. Chichén Itzá	México		
4. Monte Albán	México		
5. Nazca	Perú		
6. Sacsahuamán	Perú		
7. San Agustín	Colombia		
8. Tairona	Colombia		
9. Tiahuanaco	Bolivia		
10. Tikal	Guatemala		

IV. Escribamos

Writing strategy: Editing your own work

An important, yet often overlooked, step in writing is to edit your own work. It is important to focus on content and organization as well as on form. Use this "self editing" checklist as a guide to editing your own writing. It can also be used as a guideline for peer editing.

A. Focus on content: Ask yourself these questions:

- ❒ *Is the topic interesting?*
- ❒ *Is the main idea clearly expressed?*
- ❒ *Does the supporting detail enhance the main idea?*
- ❒ *Is the order of sentences and ideas logical and easy to follow?*
- ❒ *Does the conclusion summarize my ideas?*

B. Focus on form: Check the following:

- ❒ *gender of nouns*
- ❒ *subject/verb agreement*
- ❒ *noun/adjective agreement*
- ❒ *word order within the entire sentence*
- ❒ *word order within each phrase*
- ❒ *new vocabulary*
- ❒ *influences of English idioms on Spanish*
- ❒ *spelling and capitalization*
- ❒ *punctuation*
- ❒ *use of accents*

After editing your work, remember to focus on appearance. If the composition is handwritten, be sure that it is legible and that you write on every other line. If it is computer-generated, be sure to print it out double-spaced.

Answers to Actividad 5: Encourage students to be creative. They can add new characters to their story. Suggest that they choose famous characters in the news and media, historical characters and even characters from your own campus and class to mix in with the video characters.

Strategy in action

Turn to *Escribamos* in the Workbook to practice the writing strategy of editing your own work.

4 ¿País bilingüe o monolingüe? Escribe una composición con razones en pro o en contra de tener un país monolingüe, bilingüe o multilingüe.

5 La siguiente misión de I.L.E.Y.A.N. Al final del video, Raúl habla con Nayeli de otra misión para recuperar objetos arqueológicos perdidos. Inventa su siguiente aventura y escribe lo que pasará con Nayeli y Raúl.

Vocabulario

Culturas y civilizaciones

además de	*in addition to*
la astronomía	*astronomy*
el/la astrónomo/a	*astronomer*
el códice	*manuscript, codex*
la conquista	*conquest*
el/la constructor/a	*builder*
cultivar	*to cultivate*
desaparecido/a	*disappeared*
desarrollado/a	*developed*
el desarrollo	*development*
el/la descendiente	*descendant*
desempeñar	*to perform*
distinguir	*to distinguish*
la escritura	*writing*
el/la estadista	*statesman/ stateswoman*
étnico/a	*ethnic*
la exploración	*exploration*
fundar	*to found*
el grupo cultural	*cultural group*
hábil	*skillful*
habitado/a	*inhabited*
imponente	*imposing*
la invención	*invention*
las investigaciones arqueológicas	*archaeological research*
lingüístico/a	*linguistic*
el oficio	*occupation*
perdido/a	*lost*
pertenecer	*to belong to*
poblado/a	*populated*
poblar	*to populate*
el pueblo	*town*
las ruinas	*ruins*
sin embargo	*nonetheless*
el/la tejedor/a	*weaver*
el terremoto	*earthquake*
la tierra	*earth, land*
vencer	*to conquer*
la zona central	*central zone*

La identidad hispana en los Estados Unidos

a partir de	*starting from*
común	*common*
el encuentro	*encounter*
la identidad	*identity*
la minoría	*minority*
la población	*population*
la raza	*race*
el territorio	*territory*
unir	*to unite*

Reference Section

Appendix A: Verb charts

REGULAR VERBS

Simple tenses

Infinitive	Past participle Present participle	Indicative: Present	Indicative: Imperfect	Indicative: Preterite	Indicative: Future	Indicative: Conditional	Subjunctive: Present	Subjunctive: Imperfect*
cantar *to sing*	cantado cantando	canto cantas canta cantamos cantáis cantan	cantaba cantabas cantaba cantábamos cantábais cantaban	canté cantaste cantó cantamos cantasteis cantaron	cantaré cantarás cantará cantaremos cantaréis cantarán	cantaría cantarías cantaría cantaríamos cantaríais cantarían	cante cantes cante cantemos cantéis canten	cantara cantaras cantara cantáramos cantarais cantaran
correr *to run*	corrido corriendo	corro corres corre corremos corréis corren	corría corrías corría corríamos corríais corrían	corrí corriste corrió corrimos corristeis corrieron	correré correrás correrá correremos correréis correrán	correría correrías correría correríamos correríais correrían	corra corras corra corramos corráis corran	corriera corrieras corriera corriéramos corrierais corrieran
subir *to go up,* *to climb up*	subido subiendo	subo subes sube subimos subís suben	subía subías subía subíamos subíais subían	subí subiste subió subimos subisteis subieron	subiré subirás subirá subiremos subiréis subirán	subiría subirías subiría subiríamos subiríais subirían	suba subas suba subamos subáis suban	subiera subieras subiera subiéramos subierais subieran

*In addition to this form, another one is less frequently used for all regular and irregular verbs: **cantase, cantases, cantase, cantásemos, cantaseis, cantasen; corriese, corrieses, corriese, corriésemos, corrieseis, corriesen; viviese, vivieses, viviese, viviésemos, vivieseis, viviesen.**

Commands

Person	Affirmative	Negative	Affirmative	Negative	Affirmative	Negative
tú	canta	no cantes	corre	no corras	sube	no subas
usted	cante	no cante	corra	no corra	suba	no suba
ustedes	canten	no canten	corran	no corran	suban	no suban
nosotros	cantemos	no cantemos	corramos	no corramos	subamos	no subamos
vosotros	cantad	no cantéis	corred	no corráis	subid	no subáis

Stem-changing verbs: -ar *and* -er *groups*

		Indicative	Subjunctive	Commands		Other *-ar* and *-er* stem-changing verbs
Type of change in the verb stem	**Subject**	**Present**	**Present**	**Affirmative**	**Negative**	
	yo	**pienso**	**piense**	—	—	atravesar *to go through, to cross*; cerrar *to close*;
-ar verbs	tú	**piensas**	**pienses**	**piensa**	no **pienses**	despertarse *to wake up;* empezar *to start*;
e > ie	él/ella, Ud.	**piensa**	**piense**	**piense**	no **piense**	negar *to deny*; sentarse *to sit down.*
	nosotros/as	pensamos	pensemos	pensemos	no pensemos	
pensar *to think*	vosotros/as	pensáis	penséis	pensad	no penséis	nevar *to snow* is only conjugated in the third
	ellos/as, Uds.	**piensan**	**piensen**	**piensen**	no **piensen**	person singular.
	yo	**cuento**	**cuente**	—	—	acordarse *to remember;* acostar(se) *to go to bed;*
-ar verbs	tú	**cuentas**	**cuentes**	**cuenta**	no **cuentes**	almorzar *to have lunch;* colgar *to hang;* costar
o > ue	él/ella, Ud.	**cuenta**	**cuente**	**cuente**	no **cuente**	*to cost;* demostrar *to demonstrate, to show;*
	nosotros/as	contamos	contemos	contemos	no contemos	encontrar *to find;* mostrar *to show;* probar
contar *to count,*	vosotros/as	contáis	contéis	contad	no contéis	*to prove, to taste;* recordar *to remember.*
to tell	ellos/as, Uds.	**cuentan**	**cuenten**	**cuenten**	no **cuenten**	
	yo	**entiendo**	**entienda**	—		encender *to light, to turn on;* extender *to stretch;*
-er verbs	tú	**entiendes**	**entiendas**	**entiende**	no **entiendas**	perder *to lose.*
e > ie	él/ella, Ud.	**entiende**	**entienda**	**entienda**	no **entienda**	
	nosotros/as	entendemos	entendamos	entendamos	no entendamos	
entender *to under-*	vosotros/as	entendéis	entendáis	entended	no entendáis	
stand	ellos/as, Uds.	**entienden**	**entiendan**	**entiendan**	no **entiendan**	
	yo	**vuelvo**	**vuelva**	—	—	mover *to move;* torcer *to twist.*
-er verbs	tú	**vuelves**	**vuelvas**	**vuelve**	no **vuelvas**	llover *to rain* is only conjugated in the third
o > ue	él/ella, Ud.	**vuelve**	**vuelva**	**vuelva**	no **vuelva**	person singular.
	nosotros/as	volvemos	volvamos	volvamos	no volvamos	
volver *to return*	vosotros/as	volvéis	volváis	volved	no volváis	
	ellos/as, Uds.	**vuelven**	**vuelvan**	**vuelvan**	no **vuelvan**	

Stem-changing verbs: -ir *verbs*

Group I

Type of change in the verb stem	Subject	Indicative: Present	Indicative: Preterite	Subjunctive: Present	Subjunctive: Imperfect	Commands: Affirmative	Commands: Negative
-ir verbs	yo	**siento**	sentí	**sienta**	**sintiera**	—	—
e > ie or **i**	tú	**sientes**	sentiste	**sientas**	**sintieras**	**siente**	no **sientas**
Infinitive:	él/ella, Ud.	**siente**	**sintió**	**sienta**	**sintiera**	**sienta**	no **sienta**
sentir *to feel*	nosotros/as	sentimos	sentimos	**sintamos**	**sintiéramos**	**sintamos**	no **sintamos**
Present participle:	vosotros/as	sentís	sentisteis	**sintáis**	**sintierais**	sentid	no **sintáis**
sintiendo	ellos/as, Uds.	**sienten**	**sintieron**	**sientan**	**sintieran**	**sientan**	no **sientan**
-ir verbs	yo	**duermo**	dormí	**duerma**	**durmiera**	—	—
o > ue or **o > u**	tú	**duermes**	dormiste	**duermas**	**durmieras**	**duerme**	no **duermas**
Infinitive:	él/ella, Ud.	**duerme**	**durmió**	**duerma**	**durmiera**	**duerma**	no **duerma**
dormir *to sleep*	nosotros/as	dormimos	dormimos	**durmamos**	**durmiéramos**	**durmamos**	no **durmamos**
Present participle:	vosotros/as	dormís	dormisteis	**durmáis**	**durmierais**	dormid	no **durmáis**
durmiendo	ellos/as, Uds.	**duermen**	**durmieron**	**duerman**	**durmieran**	**duerman**	no **duerman**

Other similar verbs: advertir *to warn;* arrepentirse *to repent;* consentir *to consent, to pamper;* convertir(se) *to turn into;* divertir(se) *to amuse (oneself);* herir *to hurt, to wound*; mentir *to lie;* morir *to die;* preferir *to prefer;* referir *to refer;* sugerir *to suggest.*

Group II

Type of change in the verb stem	Subject	Indicative: Present	Indicative: Preterite	Subjunctive: Present	Subjunctive: Imperfect	Commands: Affirmative	Commands: Negative
-ir verbs	yo	**pido**	pedí	**pida**	**pidiera**	—	—
e > i	tú	**pides**	pediste	**pidas**	**pidieras**	**pide**	no **pidas**
Infinitive: pedir *to*	él/ella, Ud.	**pide**	**pidió**	**pida**	**pidiera**	**pida**	no **pida**
ask for, to request	nosotros/as	pedimos	pedimos	**pidamos**	**pidiéramos**	**pidamos**	no **pidamos**
Present participle:	vosotros/as	pedís	pedisteis	**pidáis**	**pedierais**	pedid	no **pidáis**
pidiendo	ellos/as, Uds.	**piden**	**pidieron**	**pidan**	**pidieran**	**pidan**	no **pidan**

Other similar verbs: competir *to compete;* despedir(se) *to say good-bye;* elegir *to choose;* impedir *to prevent;* perseguir *to chase;* repetir *to repeat;* seguir *to follow;* servir *to serve;* vestir(se) *to dress, to get dressed.*

Verbs with spelling changes

	Verb type	Ending	Change	Verbs with similar spelling changes
1	bus**car** *to look for*	**-car**	• Preterite: yo bus**qué** • Present subjunctive: bus**que**, bus**ques**, bus**que**, bus**quemos**, bus**quéis**, bus**quen**	comunicar, explicar, indicar, sacar, pescar
2	cono**cer** *to know*	**-cer** or **-cir**	• Present indicative: cono**zco**, conoces, conoce, and so on • Present subjunctive: cono**zca**, cono**zcas**, cono**zca**, cono**zcamos**, cono**zcáis**, cono**zcan**	nacer, obedecer, ofrecer, parecer, pertenecer, reconocer, conducir, traducir
3	ven**cer** *to win*	**-cer** or **-cir**	• Present indicative: ven**zo**, vences, vence, and so on • Present subjunctive: ven**za**, ven**zas**, ven**za**, ven**zamos**, ven**záis**, ven**zan**	convencer, torcer *to twist*
4	**leer** *to read*	**-eer**	• Preterite: leyó, leyeron • Imperfect subjunctive: leyera, leyeras, leyera, leyéramos, leyerais, leyeran • Present participle: leyendo	creer, poseer *to own*
5	lle**gar** *to arrive*	**-gar**	• Preterite: lle**gué** • Present subjunctive: lle**gue**, lle**gues**, lle**gue**, lle**guemos**, lle**guéis**, lle**guen**	colgar, navegar, negar, pagar, rogar, jugar
6	coger *to take*	**-ger** or **-gir**	• Present indicative: co**jo** • Present subjunctive: co**ja**, co**jas**, co**ja**, co**jamos**, co**jáis**, co**jan**	escoger, proteger, recoger, corregir, dirigir, elegir, exigir
7	se**guir** *to follow*	**-guir**	• Present indicative: si**go** • Present subjunctive: si**ga**, si**gas**, si**ga**, si**gamos**, si**gáis**, si**gan**	conseguir, distinguir, perseguir
8	**huir** *to flee*	**-uir**	• Present indicative: huyo, huyes, huye, huimos, huís, huyen • Preterite: huí, huiste, huyó, huimos, huisteis, huyeron • Present subjunctive: huya, huyas, huya, huyamos, huyáis, huyan • Imperfect subjunctive: huyera, huyeras, huyera, huyéramos, huyerais, huyeran • Present participle: huyendo • Commands: huye tú, huya usted, huyan ustedes, huíd vosotros, huyamos nosotros no huyas tú, no huya usted, no huyan ustedes, no huyamos nosotros, no huyáis vosotros	concluir, contribuir, construir, destruir, disminuir, distribuir, excluir, influir, instruir, restituir, substituir
9	abra**zar** *to embrace*	**-zar**	• Preterite: abra**cé**, abrazaste, abrazó, and so on • Present subjunctive: abra**ce**, abra**ces**, abra**ce**, abra**cemos**, abra**céis**, abra**cen**	alcanzar, almorzar, comenzar, empezar, gozar, rezar

Verbs that need a written accent

	Verb type	Ending	Change	Verbs with similar spelling changes
1	son**reír** *to smile*	**-eír**	See p. 519 for a complete conjugation of these verbs.	freír
2	env**iar** *to send*	**-iar**	• Present indicative: envío, envías, envía, enviamos, enviáis, envían • Present subjunctive: envíe, envíes, envíe, enviemos, enviéis, envíen	ampliar, criar, desviar, enfriar, guiar, variar
3	contin**uar** *to continue*	**-uar**	• Present indicative: continúo, continúas, continúa, continuamos, continuáis, continúan • Present subjunctive: continúe, continúes, continúe, continuemos, continuéis, continúen	acentuar, efectuar, exceptuar, graduar, habituar, insinuar, situar

Compound tenses

Indicative					Subjunctive	
Present perfect	**Past perfect**	**Preterite perfect**	**Future perfect**	**Conditional perfect**	**Present perfect**	**Past perfect**
he	**había**	**hube**	**habré**	**habría**	**haya**	**hubiera**
has	**habías**	**hubiste**	**habrás**	**habrías**	**hayas**	**hubieras**
ha cantado	**había** cantado	**hubo** cantado	**habrá** cantado	**habría** cantado	**haya** cantado	**hubiera** cantado
hemos corrido	**habíamos** corrido	**hubimos** corrido	**habremos** corrido	**habríamos** corrido	**hayamos** corrido	**hubiéramos** corrido
habéis vivido	**habíais** vivido	**hubisteis** vivido	**habréis** vivido	**habríais** vivido	**hayáis** vivido	**hubierais** vivido
han	**habían**	**hubieron**	**habrán**	**habrían**	**hayan**	**hubieran**

REFLEXIVE VERBS

Regular and irregular reflexive verbs: Position of the reflexive pronouns in the simple tenses

Example 1: *lavarse*

			Indicative					Subjunctive	
Infinitive	**Present participle**	**Reflexive pronouns**	**Present**	**Imperfect**	**Preterite**	**Future**	**Conditional**	**Present**	**Imperfect**
lavar**se**	lavándo**me**	**me**	lavo	lavaba	lavé	lavaré	lavaría	lave	lavara
to wash	lavándo**te**	**te**	lavas	lavabas	lavaste	lavarás	lavarías	laves	lavaras
oneself	lavándo**se**	**se**	lava	lavaba	lavó	lavará	lavaría	lave	lavara
	lavándo**nos**	**nos**	lavamos	lavábamos	lavamos	lavaremos	lavaríamos	lavemos	laváramos
	lavándo**os**	**os**	laváis	lavabais	lavasteis	lavaréis	lavaríais	lavéis	lavarais
	lavándo**se**	**se**	lavan	lavaban	lavaron	lavarán	lavarían	laven	lavaran

Example 2: *ponerse*

			Indicative					Subjunctive	
Infinitive	**Present participle**	**Reflexive pronouns**	**Present**	**Imperfect**	**Preterite**	**Future**	**Conditional**	**Present**	**Imperfect**
	poniéndo**me**	**me**	pongo	ponía	puse	pondré	pondría	ponga	pusiera
	poniéndo**te**	**te**	pones	ponías	pusiste	pondrás	pondrías	pongas	pusieras
poner**se**	poniéndo**se**	**se**	pone	ponía	puso	pondrá	pondría	ponga	pusiera
to put on,	poniéndo**nos**	**nos**	ponemos	poníamos	pusimos	pondremos	pondríamos	pongamos	pusiéramos
get (sad,	poniéndo**os**	**os**	ponéis	poníais	pusisteis	pondréis	pondríais	pongáis	pusierais
happy, etc.)	poniéndo**se**	**se**	ponen	ponían	pusieron	pondrán	pondrían	pongan	pusieran

Example 3: *vestirse*

			Indicative					Subjunctive	
Infinitive	**Present participle**	**Reflexive pronouns**	**Present**	**Imperfect**	**Preterite**	**Future**	**Conditional**	**Present**	**Imperfect**
	vistiéndo**me**	**me**	visto	vestía	vestí	vestiré	vestiría	vista	vistiera
	vistiéndo**te**	**te**	vistes	vestías	vestiste	vestirás	vestirías	vistas	vistieras
vestir**se**	vistiéndo**se**	**se**	viste	vestía	vistió	vestirá	vestiría	vista	vistiera
to get	vistiéndo**nos**	**nos**	vestimos	vestíamos	vestimos	vestiremos	vestiríamos	vistamos	vistiéramos
dressed	vistiéndo**os**	**os**	vestís	vestíais	vestisteis	vestiréis	vestiríais	vistáis	vistierais
	vistiéndo**se**	**se**	visten	vestían	vistieron	vestirán	vestirían	vistan	vistieran

Regular and irregular reflexive verbs: Position of the reflexive pronouns with commands

Person	Affirmative	Negative	Affirmative	Negative	Affirmative	Negative
tú	láva**te**	no **te** laves	pon**te**	no **te** pongas	víste**te**	no **te** vistas
usted	láve**se**	no **se** lave	pónga**se**	no **se** ponga	vísta**se**	no **se** vista
ustedes	láven**se**	no **se** laven	póngan**se**	no **se** pongan	vístan**se**	no **se** vistan
nosotros	lavémo**nos**	no **nos** lavemos	pongámo**nos**	no **nos** pongamos	vistámo**nos**	no **nos** vistamos
vosotros	lava**os**	no **os** lavéis	pone**os**	no **os** pongáis	vestí**os**	no **os** vistáis

IRREGULAR VERBS

Andar, caber, caer

Infinitive	Past participle / Present participle	Indicative: Present	Indicative: Imperfect	Indicative: Preterite	Indicative: Future	Indicative: Conditional	Subjunctive: Present	Subjunctive: Imperfect
and**ar**	and**ado**	ando	andaba	**anduve**	andaré	andaría	ande	**anduviera**
to walk;	and**ando**	andas	andabas	**anduviste**	andarás	andarías	andes	**anduvieras**
to go		anda	andaba	**anduvo**	andará	andaría	ande	**anduviera**
		andamos	andábamos	**anduvimos**	andaremos	andaríamos	andemos	**anduviéramos**
		andáis	andabais	**anduvisteis**	andaréis	andaríais	andéis	**anduvierais**
		andan	andaban	**anduvieron**	andarán	andarían	anden	**anduvieran**
cab**er**	cab**ido**	**quepo**	cabía	**cupe**	**cabré**	**cabría**	**quepa**	**cupiera**
to fit; to	cab**iendo**	cabes	cabías	**cupiste**	**cabrás**	**cabrías**	**quepas**	**cupieras**
have enough		cabe	cabía	**cupo**	**cabrá**	**cabría**	**quepa**	**cupiera**
space		cabemos	cabíamos	**cupimos**	**cabremos**	**cabríamos**	**quepamos**	**cupiéramos**
		cabéis	cabíais	**cupisteis**	**cabréis**	**cabríais**	**quepáis**	**cupierais**
		caben	cabían	**cupieron**	**cabrán**	**cabrían**	**quepan**	**cupieran**
ca**er**	ca**ído**	**caigo**	caía	caí	caeré	caería	**caiga**	**cayera**
to fall	ca**yendo**	caes	caías	caíste	caerás	caerías	**caigas**	**cayeras**
		cae	caía	**cayó**	caerá	caería	**caiga**	**cayera**
		caemos	caíamos	caímos	caeremos	caeríamos	**caigamos**	**cayéramos**
		caéis	caíais	caísteis	caeréis	caeríais	**caigáis**	**cayerais**
		caen	caían	**cayeron**	caerán	caerían	**caigan**	**cayeran**

Commands

	andar		caber		caer	
Person	Affirmative	Negative	Affirmative	Negative	Affirmative	Negative
tú	anda	no andes	cabe	no **quepas**	cae	no **caigas**
usted	ande	no ande	**quepa**	no **quepa**	**caiga**	no **caiga**
ustedes	anden	no anden	**quepan**	no **quepan**	**caigan**	no **caigan**
nosotros	andemos	no andemos	**quepamos**	no **quepamos**	**caigamos**	no **caigamos**
vosotros	andad	no andéis	cabed	no **quepáis**	caed	no **caigáis**

Dar, decir, estar

		Indicative					Subjunctive	
Infinitive	**Past participle** **Present participle**	**Present**	**Imperfect**	**Preterite**	**Future**	**Conditional**	**Present**	**Imperfect**
dar *to give*	da**do** da**ndo**	**doy** das da damos dais dan	daba dabas daba dábamos dabais daban	**di** **diste** **dio** **dimos** **disteis** **dieron**	daré darás dará daremos daréis darán	daría darías daría daríamos daríais darían	**dé** **des** **dé** **demos** **deis** **den**	**diera** **dieras** **diera** **diéramos** **dierais** **dieran**
decir *to say, tell*	**dicho** **diciendo**	**digo** **dices** **dice** decimos decís **dicen**	decía decías decía decíamos decíais decían	**dije** **dijiste** **dijo** **dijimos** **dijisteis** **dijeron**	**diré** **dirás** **dirá** **diremos** **diréis** **dirán**	**diría** **dirías** **diría** **diríamos** **diríais** **dirían**	**diga** **digas** **diga** **digamos** **digáis** **digan**	**dijera** **dijeras** **dijera** **dijéramos** **dijerais** **dijeran**
estar *to be*	esta**do** esta**ndo**	**estoy** **estás** **está** estamos estáis **están**	estaba estabas estaba estábamos estabais estaban	**estuve** **estuviste** **estuvo** **estuvimos** **estuvisteis** **estuvieron**	estaré estarás estará estaremos estaréis estarán	estaría estarías estaría estaríamos estaríais estarían	**esté** **estés** **esté** **estemos** **estéis** **estén**	**estuviera** **estuvieras** **estuviera** **estuviéramos** **estuvierais** **estuvieran**

Commands

	dar		decir		estar	
Person	**Affirmative**	**Negative**	**Affirmative**	**Negative**	**Affirmative**	**Negative**
tú	da	no **des**	**di**	no **digas**	**está**	no **estés**
usted	**dé**	no **dé**	**diga**	no **diga**	**esté**	no **esté**
ustedes	**den**	no **den**	**digan**	no **digan**	**estén**	no **estén**
nosotros	**demos**	no **demos**	**digamos**	no **digamos**	**estemos**	no **estemos**
vosotros	dad	no **deis**	decid	no **digáis**	**estad**	no **estéis**

*Haber**, *hacer, ir*

Infinitive	Past participle / Present participle	Indicative: Present	Indicative: Imperfect	Indicative: Preterite	Indicative: Future	Indicative: Conditional	Subjunctive: Present	Subjunctive: Imperfect
haber	habido	he	había	hube	habré	habría	haya	hubiera
to have	habiendo	has	habías	hubiste	habrás	habrías	hayas	hubieras
		ha	había	hubo	habrá	habría	haya	hubiera
		hemos	habíamos	hubimos	habremos	habríamos	hayamos	hubiéramos
		habéis	habíais	hubisteis	habréis	habríais	hayáis	hubierais
		han	habían	hubieron	habrán	habrían	hayan	hubieran
hacer	hecho	hago	hacía	hice	haré	haría	haga	hiciera
to do	haciendo	haces	hacías	hiciste	harás	harías	hagas	hicieras
		hace	hacía	hizo	hará	haría	haga	hiciera
		hacemos	hacíamos	hicimos	haremos	haríamos	hagamos	hiciéramos
		hacéis	hacíais	hicisteis	haréis	haríais	hagáis	hicierais
		hacen	hacían	hicieron	harán	harían	hagan	hicieran
ir	ido	voy	iba	fui	iré	iría	vaya	fuera
to go	yendo	vas	ibas	fuiste	irás	irías	vayas	fueras
		va	iba	fue	irá	iría	vaya	fuera
		vamos	íbamos	fuimos	iremos	iríamos	vayamos	fuéramos
		vais	ibais	fuisteis	iréis	iríais	vayáis	fuerais
		van	iban	fueron	irán	irían	vayan	fueran

Commands

Person	hacer: Affirmative	hacer: Negative	ir: Affirmative	ir: Negative
tú	haz	no hagas	ve	no vayas
usted	haga	no haga	vaya	no vaya
ustedes	hagan	no hagan	vayan	no vayan
nosotros	hagamos	no hagamos	vamos	no vayamos
vosotros	haced	no hagáis	id	no vayáis

*Note: The imperative of **haber** is not used.

Jugar, oír, oler

		Indicative					Subjunctive	
Infinitive	**Past participle Present participle**	**Present**	**Imperfect**	**Preterite**	**Future**	**Conditional**	**Present**	**Imperfect**
jugar *to play*	jug**ado** jug**ando**	**juego**	jugaba	**jugué**	jugaré	jugaría	**juegue**	jugara
		juegas	jugabas	jugaste	jugarás	jugarías	**juegues**	jugaras
		juega	jugaba	jugó	jugará	jugaría	**juegue**	jugara
		jugamos	jugábamos	jugamos	jugaremos	jugaríamos	**juguemos**	jugáramos
		jugáis	jugabais	jugasteis	jugaréis	jugaríais	**juguéis**	jugarais
		juegan	jugaban	jugaron	jugarán	jugarían	**jueguen**	jugaran
oír *to hear,* *to listen*	**oído** **oyendo**	**oigo**	oía	oí	oiré	oiría	**oiga**	**oyera**
		oyes	oías	oíste	oirás	oirías	**oigas**	**oyeras**
		oye	oía	**oyó**	oirá	oiría	**oiga**	**oyera**
		oímos	oíamos	oímos	oiremos	oiríamos	**oigamos**	**oyéramos**
		oís	oíais	oísteis	oiréis	oiríais	**oigáis**	**oyerais**
		oyen	oían	**oyeron**	oirán	oirían	**oigan**	**oyeran**
oler *to smell*	ol**ido** ol**iendo**	**huelo**	olía	olí	oleré	olería	**huela**	oliera
		hueles	olías	oliste	olerás	olerías	**huelas**	olieras
		huele	olía	olió	olerá	olería	**huela**	oliera
		olemos	olíamos	olimos	oleremos	oleríamos	olamos	oliéramos
		oléis	olíais	olisteis	oleréis	oleríais	oláis	olierais
		huelen	olían	olieron	olerán	olerían	**huelan**	olieran

Commands

	jugar		oír		oler	
Person	**Affirmative**	**Negative**	**Affirmative**	**Negative**	**Affirmative**	**Negative**
tú	**juega**	no **juegues**	**oye**	no **oigas**	**huele**	no **huelas**
usted	**juegue**	no **juegue**	**oiga**	no **oiga**	**huela**	no **huela**
ustedes	**jueguen**	no **jueguen**	**oigan**	no **oigan**	**huelan**	no **huelan**
nosotros	**juguemos**	no **juguemos**	**oigamos**	no **oigamos**	olamos	no olamos
vosotros	jugad	no **juguéis**	**oíd**	no **oigáis**	oled	no oláis

Poder, poner, querer

		Indicative					Subjunctive	
Infinitive	**Past participle Present participle**	**Present**	**Imperfect**	**Preterite**	**Future**	**Conditional**	**Present**	**Imperfect**
pod**er** *to be able to, can*	pod**ido** pud**iendo**	**puedo** **puedes** **puede** podemos podéis **pueden**	podía podías podía podíamos podíais podían	**pude** **pudiste** **pudo** **pudimos** **pudisteis** **pudieron**	**podré** **podrás** **podrá** **podremos** **podréis** **podrán**	**podría** **podrías** **podría** **podríamos** **podríais** **podrían**	**pueda** **puedas** **pueda** podamos podáis **puedan**	**pudiera** **pudieras** **pudiera** **pudiéramos** **pudierais** **pudieran**
pon**er** *to put*	**puesto** pon**iendo**	**pongo** pones pone ponemos ponéis ponen	ponía ponías ponía poníamos poníais ponían	**puse** **pusiste** **puso** **pusimos** **pusisteis** **pusieron**	**pondré** **pondrás** **pondrá** **pondremos** **pondréis** **pondrán**	**pondría** **pondrías** **pondría** **pondríamos** **pondríais** **pondrían**	**ponga** **pongas** **ponga** **pongamos** **pongáis** **pongan**	**pusiera** **pusieras** **pusiera** **pusiéramos** **pusierais** **pusieran**
quer**er** *to want, wish; to love*	quer**ido** quer**iendo**	**quiero** **quieres** **quiere** queremos queréis **quieren**	quería querías quería queríamos queríais querían	**quise** **quisiste** **quiso** **quisimos** **quisisteis** **quisieron**	**querré** **querrás** **querrá** **querremos** **querréis** **querrán**	**querría** **querrías** **querría** **querríamos** **querríais** **querrían**	**quiera** **quieras** **quiera** queramos queráis **quieran**	**quisiera** **quisieras** **quisiera** **quisiéramos** **quisierais** **quisieran**

Commands

	poner		querer	
Person	**Affirmative**	**Negative**	**Affirmative**	**Negative**
tú usted ustedes nosotros vosotros	**pon** **ponga** **pongan** **pongamos** poned	no **pongas** no **ponga** no **pongan** no **pongamos** no **pongáis**	**quiere** **quiera** **quieran** queramos quered	no **quieras** no **quiera** no **quieran** no queramos no queráis

*The imperative of **poder** is used very infrequently.

Saber, salir, ser

		Indicative					Subjunctive	
Infinitive	**Past participle Present participle**	**Present**	**Imperfect**	**Preterite**	**Future**	**Conditional**	**Present**	**Imperfect**
saber *to know*	sabido sabiendo	sé sabes sabe sabemos sabéis saben	sabía sabías sabía sabíamos sabíais sabían	supe supiste supo supimos supisteis supieron	sabré sabrás sabrá sabremos sabréis sabrian	sabría sabrías sabría sabríamos sabríais sabrían	sepa sepas sepa sepamos sepáis sepan	supiera supieras supiera supiéramos supierais supieran
salir *to go out,* *to leave*	salido saliendo	salgo sales sale salimos salís salen	salía salías salía salíamos salíais salían	salí saliste salió salimos salisteis salieron	saldré saldrás saldrá saldremos saldréis saldrán	saldría saldrías saldría saldríamos saldríais saldrían	salga salgas salga salgamos salgáis salgan	saliera salieras saliera saliéramos salierais salieran
ser *to be*	sido siendo	soy eres es somos sois son	era eras era éramos erais eran	fui fuiste fue fuimos fuisteis fueron	seré serás será seremos seréis serán	sería serías sería seríamos seríais serían	sea seas sea seamos seáis sean	fuera fueras fuera fuéramos fuerais fueran

Commands

	saber		salir		ser	
Person	**Affirmative**	**Negative**	**Affirmative**	**Negative**	**Affirmative**	**Negative**
tú	sabe	no sepas	sal	no salgas	sé	no seas
usted	sepa	no sepa	salga	no salga	sea	no sea
ustedes	sepan	no sepan	salgan	no salgan	sean	no sean
nosotros	sepamos	no sepamos	salgamos	no salgamos	seamos	no seamos
vosotros	sabed	no sepáis	salid	no salgáis	sed	no seáis

Sonreír, tener, traer*

Infinitive	Past participle Present participle	Indicative: Present	Indicative: Imperfect	Indicative: Preterite	Indicative: Future	Indicative: Conditional	Subjunctive: Present	Subjunctive: Imperfect
sonreír *to smile*	sonreído sonriendo	sonrío sonríes sonríe sonreímos sonreís sonríen	sonreía sonreías sonreía sonreíamos sonreíais sonreían	sonreí sonreíste sonrió sonreímos sonreísteis sonrieron	sonreiré sonreirás sonreirá sonreiremos sonreiréis sonreirán	sonreiría sonreirías sonreiría sonreiríamos sonreiríais sonreirían	sonría sonrías sonría sonriamos sonriáis sonrían	sonriera sonrieras sonriera sonriéramos sonrierais sonrieran
tener* *to have*	tenido teniendo	tengo tienes tiene tenemos tenéis tienen	tenía tenías tenía teníamos teníais tenían	tuve tuviste tuvo tuvimos tuvisteis tuvieron	tendré tendrás tendrá tendremos tendréis tendrán	tendría tendrías tendría tendríamos tendríais tendrían	tenga tengas tenga tengamos tengáis tengan	tuviera tuvieras tuviera tuviéramos tuvierais tuvieran
traer *to bring*	traído trayendo	traigo traes trae traemos traéis traen	traía traías traía traíamos traíais traían	traje trajiste trajo trajimos trajisteis trajeron	traeré traerás traerá traeremos traeréis traerán	traería traerías traería traeríamos traeríais traerían	traiga traigas traiga traigamos traigáis traigan	trajera trajeras trajera trajéramos trajerais trajeran

Commands

Person	sonreír: Affirmative	sonreír: Negative	tener: Affirmative	tener: Negative	traer: Affirmative	traer: Negative
tú	sonríe	no sonrías	ten	no tengas	trae	no traigas
usted	sonría	no sonría	tenga	no tenga	traiga	no traiga
ustedes	sonrían	no sonrían	tengan	no tengan	traigan	no traigan
nosotros	sonríamos	no sonríamos	tengamos	no tengamos	traigamos	no traigamos
vosotros	sonreíd	no sonriáis	tened	no tengáis	traed	no traigáis

*Many verbs ending in **-tener** are conjugated like this verb: **contener, detener, entretener(se), mantener, obtener, retener.**
Similar verbs to **tener: entretener(se), detener, obtener.** See reflexive verb conjugation on page 511.

Valer, venir, ver*

Infinitive	Past participle Present participle	Indicative: Present	Indicative: Imperfect	Indicative: Preterite	Indicative: Future	Indicative: Conditional	Subjunctive: Present	Subjunctive: Imperfect
val**er** *to be worth*	val**ido** val**iendo**	**valgo**	valía	valí	**valdré**	**valdría**	**valga**	valiera
		vales	valías	valiste	**valdrás**	**valdrías**	**valgas**	valieras
		vale	valía	valió	**valdrá**	**valdría**	**valga**	valiera
		valemos	valíamos	valimos	**valdremos**	**valdríamos**	**valgamos**	valiéramos
		valéis	valíais	valisteis	**valdréis**	**valdríais**	**valgáis**	valierais
		valen	valían	valieron	**valdrán**	**valdrían**	**valgan**	valieran
ven**ir*** *to come*	ven**ido** v**i**n**iendo**	**vengo**	venía	**vine**	**vendré**	**vendría**	**venga**	**viniera**
		vienes	venías	**viniste**	**vendrás**	**vendrías**	**vengas**	**vinieras**
		viene	venía	**vino**	**vendrá**	**vendría**	**venga**	**viniera**
		venimos	veníamos	**vinimos**	**vendremos**	**vendríamos**	**vengamos**	**viniéramos**
		venís	veníais	**vinisteis**	**vendréis**	**vendríais**	**vengáis**	**vinierais**
		vienen	venían	**vinieron**	**vendrán**	**vendrían**	**vengan**	**vinieran**
v**er** *to see*	**visto** **viendo**	**veo**	**veía**	vi	veré	vería	**vea**	viera
		ves	**veías**	viste	verás	verías	**veas**	vieras
		ve	**veía**	vio	verá	vería	**vea**	viera
		vemos	**veíamos**	vimos	veremos	veríamos	**veamos**	viéramos
		veis	**veíais**	visteis	veréis	veríais	**veáis**	vierais
		ven	**veían**	vieron	verán	verían	**vean**	vieran

Commands

Person	valer: Affirmative	valer: Negative	venir: Affirmative	venir: Negative	ver: Affirmative	ver: Negative
tú	vale	no **valgas**	**ven**	no **vengas**	**ve**	no **veas**
usted	**valga**	no **valga**	**venga**	no **venga**	**vea**	no **vea**
ustedes	**valgan**	no **valgan**	**vengan**	no **vengan**	**vean**	no **vean**
nosotros	**valgamos**	no **valgamos**	**vengamos**	no **vengamos**	**veamos**	no **veamos**
vosotros	valed	no **valgáis**	venid	no **vengáis**	**ved**	no **veáis**

*Similar verb to **venir: prevenir**

Appendix B: Prefixes and suffixes

PREFIXES

Prefix	Meaning and use	Example	English
ante-	*before*	antenoche, antepasado	*last night, ancestor*
des-	*lack of a quality*	desatento/a, desafortunado/a	*inattentive, unfortunate*
en-/em-	*used to form verbs*	envejecer, emparejar	*to get old, to pair/to match*
ex-	*previous; used with professions or roles*	el expresidente, el exmarido	*ex-president, ex-husband*
in-/im-	*lack of*	inconveniente, imperfecto/a	*inconvenient, imperfect*
infra-	*below a standard*	infrahumano/a	*subhuman*
mega-	*large, 1,000*	el megáfono, el megavatio	*megaphone, megawatt*
micro-	*small , 1/100*	el microondas, el microgramo	*microwave, microgram*
multi-	*many*	multicolor, multimedia	*multicolor, multimedia*
post-/pos-	*after*	posponer, postoperatorio	*postpone, postoperative*
pre-	*before*	predecir, el precontrato	*to predict, pre-contract*
super-	*high degree of a quality*	superbuen/a, el superhombre	*extra good, superman*
ultra-	*beyond, more than*	ultramoderno/a	*ultramodern*
vice-	*second*	el vicepresidente	*vice president*

SUFFIXES

Suffix	Meaning and use	Example	English
-a/-o	*most common feminine and masculine endings of nouns and adjectives*	el secretario, la secretaria	*male secretary, female secretary*
-able	*able to; used in adjectives*	adorable, criticable, pasable	*adorable, criticizable, passable*
-ado, -ido	*past participle endings*	he hablado, he comido	*I have spoken, I have eaten*
-ado/a, -ido/a	*ending of the past participle used as adjective*	está cansado/a, está vencido/a	*he/she is tired; he/she is defeated*
-ancia	*feminine noun ending*	la ambulancia, la importancia	*ambulance, importance*
-ano/a	*most common ending of adjectives of nationality*	cubano/a, colombiano/a, venezolano/a	*Cuban, Colombian, Venezuelan*
-ante	*ending of adjectives formed from verbs*	abundante, fascinante, interesante	*abundant, fascinating, interesting*
-ario	*collection*	el diario, el cuestionario, el diccionario, el horario,	*diary, questionnaire, dictionary, schedule*
-ción	*feminine noun ending*	la canción, la estación, la opción, la situación	*song, station, option, situation*
-dad	*feminine noun ending*	la ciudad, la vanidad	*city, vanity*
-eño/a	*ending of some adjectives of nationality*	madrileño/a, panameño/a	*from Madrid, from Panama*

Suffix	Meaning and use	Example	English
-ense	*ending of some adjectives of nationality*	costarricense, estadounidense	*from Costa Rica, from the United States*
-ería	*shop, store*	la cafetería, la lechería, la joyería, la panadería	*cafeteria, milk store, jewelry store, bakery*
-ísimo/a	*extremely; used with adjectives*	buenísimo/a, riquísimo/a	*extremely/very, very good/delicious*
-ista	*feminine or masculine ending; describes profession, skill or a specific quality*	el/la capitalista, el/la lingüista, el/la optimista, el/la dentista	*capitalist, linguist, optimist, dentist*
-ito/a	*diminutive ending*	Pedrito, Juanita, la casita, amarillito	*little Pedro, little Juana, little house, yellowish (a little yellow)*
-mente	*ending of some adverbs*	actualmente, claramente	*presently, clearly*
-or/a	*person or thing that does something; used with professions, machines and so on*	el/la autor/a, el/la editor/a, el/la computador/a, el detector	*author, publisher, computer, detector*
-s, -es	*plural ending of nouns and adjectives*	los secretarios, las secretarias, fáciles	*secretaries, easy*
-tad	*feminine noun ending*	la libertad, la voluntad	*freedom, will*

Appendix C: Classroom expressions

Mandatos plurales (ustedes)	*Mandatos singulares (usted)*	*Mandatos singulares (tú)*	*Commands*
Abran el libro.	Abra el libro.	Abre el libro.	*Open your book(s).*
Aprendan el vocabulario.	Aprenda el vocabulario.	Aprende el vocabulario.	*Learn the vocabulary.*
Cierren el libro.	Cierre el libro.	Cierra el libro.	*Close your book(s).*
Escriban la tarea.	Escriba la tarea.	Escribe la tarea.	*Write the homework.*
Escuchen.	Escuche.	Escucha.	*Listen.*
Estudien la lección.	Estudie la lección.	Estudia la lección.	*Study the lesson.*
Hagan el ejercicio.	Haga el ejercicio.	Haz el ejercicio.	*Do the exercise.*
Lean la lectura.	Lea la lectura.	Lee la lectura.	*Read the passage.*
Levanten la mano.	Levante la mano.	Levanta la mano.	*Raise your hand(s).*
Repasen la gramática.	Repase la gramática.	Repasa la gramática.	*Review the grammar.*
Repitan.	Repita.	Repite.	*Repeat.*
Siéntense.	Siéntese.	Siéntate.	*Sit down.*
Sigan.	Siga.	Sigue.	*Continue.*
Tomen asiento.	Tome asiento.	Toma asiento.	*Have a seat.*
Vayan a la pizarra.	Vaya a la pizarra.	Ve a la pizarra.	*Go to the board.*

Spanish-English Vocabulary

This vocabulary includes most of the active vocabulary presented in the chapters. (Some exceptions are many numbers, some names of cities and countries, and some obvious cognates.) The list also includes many receptive words found throughout the chapters. The definitions are limited to the context in which the words are used in this book. Active words are followed by a number that indicates the chapter in which the word appears as an active item; the abbreviation **P** refers to the **Capítulo preliminar**.

The following abbreviations are used:

adj.	adjective	*Lat. Am.*	Latin American
adv.	adverb	*m.*	masculine
f.	feminine	*Mex.*	Mexican
inf.	infinitive	*pl.*	plural
lang.	language		

A

a to, for, 4; **~ bordo** on board, 4; **~ cargo de** in charge of, 7, 11; **~ fin (de) que** in order that, 9; **~ la derecha** on/to the right, 4; **~ la izquierda** on/to the left, 4; **~ la vez** at the same time, 3; **~ la vista** visible, handy, 9; **~ lo largo y ancho** throughout, 9; **~ lo lejos** at a distance, 7; **~ mano** by hand, 10; **~ menos que** unless, 9; **~ menudo** often, 5, 10; **~ partir de** starting from, 12; **~ pie** on foot, 3; **~ propósito** by the way, 7; **~ punto de** about to, 9; **~ quien** to whom, 10; **~ salvo de** safe from, 9; **~ solas** alone, 2; **~ sus órdenes** at your service, 3; **~ través de** by means of, 6; through, 7, 8; **~ veces** sometimes, at times, 3
abierto/a open, 9
ablandar to tenderize, 8
abogado/a *(m., f.)* lawyer, 5
abrazo hug, 5
abrigado/a warm, 7
abrigo *(m.)* coat, 2
abril *(m.)* April, 1
abrir to open, 1; (a document), 6
abrocharse (el cinturón) to buckle up, 7
abstracto/a abstract, 10
abuelo/a *(m., f.)* grandfather/grandmother, 1, 5
aburrido/a boring, 1
acabar to finish, 1; **~ de** to have just done or completed an action, 1
acampar to go camping, 9
accesorios *(m. pl.)* accessories, 7
accidentado/a rough, 3
acciones *(f. pl.)* stock, 6
aceite *(m.)* oil, 7; **~ de oliva** olive oil, 3
acelerador *(m.)* gas pedal, 7
acelerar to accelerate, 7
acercar(se) to approach, 11
achatado/a flattened, 7
ácido/a sour, 3
aclarar to clear up, 11
aconsejar to advise, counsel, 7
acontecimiento *(m.)* event, 11
acostar (ue) to put to bed, 3
acostarse (ue) to go to bed, lie down, 3, 6
actividad *(f.)* activity, 1
activo/a active, 8
acto delictivo *(m.)* delinquent act, 11
actor *(m.)* actor, 11
actriz *(f.)* actress, 11
actuación *(f.)* acting, 11
actual current, 12
actualmente today, 5; nowadays, 6; currently, 10
actuar to act, 10
acuarela *(f.)* watercolor, 10
adecuadamente adequately, 9
además de besides, 3; in addition to, 12
adicción *(f.)* addiction, 11
adivinar to guess, 5
adjetivo *(m.)* adjective, 5
administrador/a de hogar *(m., f.)* household manager, 5
adolescencia *(f.)* adolescence, 5
adolescente *(m., f.)* adolescent, 11
adorar to adore, 10
adorno *(m.)* decoration, 10
adquirir (ie) to acquire, 6
aduana *(f.)* customs, 5
aduanero/a *(m., f.)* customs agent, 5
adulto/a adult, 5; **ser ~** to be an adult, 5
advertir (ie) to warn, 12
aeromozo/a *(m., f.)* flight attendant, 5
aeropuerto *(m.)* airport, 2
afeitarse to shave, 3
aficionado/a *(m., f.)* fan, 6
afuera de outside of, 6
agente de viajes *(m., f.)* travel agent, 5
agosto August, 1
agotar to exhaust, 9
agradable pleasant, 1
agradecer (zc) to thank, 4, 11
agregar to add, 8, 9
aguardar to wait, 11
aguas termales *(f. pl.)* hot springs, 5
águila (el) *(f.)* eagle, 9
ahijado/a *(m., f.)* godson/goddaughter, 9
ahora now, 3; **~ mismo** at this very moment, right now, 3
ahorrar to save, 8
aire *(m.)* air, **~ acondicionado** *(m.)* air conditioning, 7; **al ~ libre** outside, 4, 8
ajá uh-huh, 5
al a + el
alargar to lengthen, 10
albóndiga *(f.)* meatball, 3
alcanzar to reach, accomplish, 11
alcoba *(f.)* bedroom, 2
alegrar to make someone happy, 6
alegrarse to be(come) happy, 5, 8
alegre happy, 2
alegría *(f.)* happiness, 5; joy, 12
alejar to keep away; to dispel, 10
alemán *(m.)* German language, 1
alemán/ana German, P
alfombra *(f.)* rug, 1
algo something, anything, 3
alguien someone, somebody, 3
algún, alguno/a some, 3
alimento *(m.)* food, 8
aliviado/a relieved, 2
aliviar to alleviate, ease pain or symptoms, 8
aliviarse to get better, 8
alivio *(m.)* relief; **¡qué ~!** what a relief!, 4

allá over there, 3
allí there, 3
alma (el) *(f.)* soul, 7
almacén *(m.)* department store, 7
almohada *(f.)* pillow, 9
almorzar (ue) to have lunch, 3
almuerzo *(m.)* lunch, 3
alojarse to stay (in a hotel), 3
alquilar to rent, 1; **~ videos** to rent videos, 1
alquiler *(m.)* rent, 2
alterado/a upset, 2, 10
alterarse to get upset, 10
altiplano *(m.)* high plain, plateau, 7
¡Alto! Stop!, 7
alto/a tall, 1
altura *(f.)* level, 3; height, 7
alumno/a *(m., f.)* pupil, student, 1
ama de casa (el) *(f.)* housewife, 5
amable nice, friendly, 1
amanecer *(m.)* dawn, 8
amante *(m., f.)* lover, 10
amargo/a bitter, 3
amarillo/a yellow, 1
ambiente *(m.)* atmosphere, 6
ambos/as both, 6
amigo/a *(m., f.)* friend, 1, 5; **estar con amigos** to be with friends, 1
ampliación *(f.)* expansion, 3
amplio/a big, 2
anaranjado/a orange, 1
anatomía *(f.)* anatomy, 1
ancho/a wide; **de ancho** in width, 5
andar to walk, ride, 1; to go, 5
andén *(m.)* train platform, 4
anfitrión/ona *(m., f.)* host/hostess, 10
angustia *(f.)* anxiety, 10, 11
anillo *(m.)* ring, 8
ánima (el) *(f.)* spirit, 10
animación *(f.)* animation, 11
anoche last night, 4
anonimato *(m.)* anonymity, 11
ansioso/a anxious, 11
anteanoche the night before last, 4
anteayer the day before yesterday, 4
antepasado/a *(m., f.)* ancestor, 12
antes de before, 4; **~ que** before, 9
antibiótico *(m.)* antibiotic, 8
anticuario *(m.)* antique store/dealer, 11
antídoto *(m.)* antidote, 8
antipático/a unfriendly, 1
antorcha *(f.)* torch, 12
antropología *(f.)* anthropology, 1
anunciador/a *(m., f.)* announcer, 11
anunciar to announce, 11
añadir to add, 9
año *(m.)* year; **el ~ pasado** last year, 4; **tener ... años** to be . . . years old, 2
apagar to turn off, 6, 9; to shut off, 7, 9; to go off, 9
aparador *(m.)* bureau, 9
aparcamiento *(m.)* parking, 3
aparcar to park; **no ~** no parking, 7
aparecer (zc) to appear, 5, 11
aparentar to pretend, 7
apartamento *(m.)* apartment, 2
apetecer (zc) to be appetizing, 7
apio *(m.)* celery, 3
aplacar (a los dioses) to placate (the gods), 10
aplicación *(f.)* application, 6
apoyacabeza *(m.)* headrest, 7
apoyar to support, 9
aprender to learn, 1
aprovechar to utilize, 6
apuesta *(f.)* bet, 5
apuntar to sign up, 11
aquel/aquella that, 3
aquél/aquélla that one, 3
aquellos/as those, 3
aquéllos/as those, 3
aquí here, 3
árbol *(m.)* tree, 6
arbusto *(m.)* bush, 8
archivar to save, 6
archivo *(m.)* archive, document collection, 4; computer file, 6; file, 6
archivos MIDI *(m.)* MIDI archives (digital music), 6
arcilla *(f.)* clay, 10
ardilla *(f.)* squirrel, 9
aretes *(m. pl.)* earrings, 8
argentino/a Argentinean, P
argumento *(m.)* plot, 11
armario *(m.)* closet, 2
armas *(f. pl.)* weapons, 11
armonioso/a harmonious, 9
arqueología *(f.)* archaeology, 1
arquitecto/a *(m., f.)* architect, 5
arquitectura *(f.)* architecture, 10
arrancar to start (a car), 7
arrecife *(m.)* reef, 5
arreglado/a arranged, 5
arreglar to fix, 5
arrestar to arrest, 11, 12
arriba de up, on top of, above, 4
arrimarse to come near/close, 11
arrogante arrogant, 1
arroyo *(m.)* stream, 7
arroz *(m.)* rice, 8
arte *(m.)* art, 1; **~ clásico** classic art, 10; **~ contemporáneo** contemporary art, 10; **~ moderno** modern art, 10
artesanal *(adj.)* craft, 8
artesanía *(f.)* crafts, 10
artesanías *(f. pl.)* folk art, 8
artesano/a *(m., f.)* artisan, 10
artista *(m., f.)* artist, 1, 5, 10
asado/a broiled, 9
asador *(m.)* broiler, 9
ascensor *(m.)* elevator, 3
asegurar to assure, 8
aseo personal *(m.)* personal items, 7
asesinar to assassinate, murder, 11
asesinato *(m.)* assassination, murder, 11
asesino/a *(m., f.)* murderer, 11
así like that, 9
asiento *(m.)* seat, 4, 7; **~ trasero** rear seat, 7
asistir a to attend (a class), 1
asombrado/a astonished, 9
asombrarse to be astonished, 11
aspiradora *(f.)* vacuum cleaner, 9
aspirante *(m., f.)* applicant, 6
aspirar (la alfombra) to vacuum (the carpet), 9
aspirina *(f.)* aspirin, 8
asterisco *(m.)* asterisk, 11
astro *(m.)* star, 11
astrónomo/a *(m., f.)* astronomer, 12
astuto/a sharp, clever, 9
asunto *(m.)* affair, 4; matter, 11
asustado/a frightened, 4
atado/a tied, 7
atender (ie) to pay attention to, 1; to take care of, 8
aterrizar to land, 5
atleta *(m., f.)* athlete, 5
átomo *(m.)* atom, 1
atraer to attract, 10
atrapar to trap, 11
atrasado/a delayed; **estar ~** to be late, 4, 5
atreverse to dare, 9
audífonos *(m. pl.)* headphones, 6
audio digital *(m.)* digital audio, 6
aumentar to increase, 11
aunque although, 5
auténtico/a authentic, 10
auto(móvil) *(m.)* car, 7
autobús *(m.)* bus, 3
autóctono/a native, 7
autopista *(f.)* expressway, 3
autorretrato *(m.)* self-portrait, 10
autovía *(f.)* highway, 3
ave (el) *(f.)* bird, 7
avecinar(se) to come near/close, 11
averiguar to find out, 4, 11, 12
avión *(m.)* plane, 3
avisar to let (someone) know, 4
avivar to intensify, 8
¡Ay! Ouch!, Ow!, 6
ayer yesterday, 4
ayuda *(f.)* help, 6; **~ financiera** financial aid, 8
ayudar to help, 1; **¿En qué le puedo ~?** How can/may I help you?, 3, 4, 7
azafrán *(m.)* saffron, 3
azúcar *(m., f.)* sugar, 3
azul blue, 1
azulejos *(m. pl.)* tiles, 2

bacilo *(m.)* bacillus, 8
bahía *(f.)* bay, 6
bailar to dance, 1, 6

bailarín/ina *(m., f.)* dancer, 6
bajar (de) to get down (from), 4
bajar por to go down (a street), 7
bajo under, 4; **~ los cielos** in the world, 5
bajo/a short, 1
balada *(f.)* ballad, 6
balanza *(f.)* scale, 9
balcón *(m.)* balcony, 2
ballena *(f.)* whale, 9
balneario *(m.)* resort, spa, 8
balón *(m.)* beachball, 5; ball, 6
baloncesto *(m.)* basketball, 6
bálsamo *(m.)* balm, 8
banano *(m.)* banana, 8
banco *(m.)* bank, 2
bandera *(f.)* flag, 10
bandido/a *(m., f.)* thug, 5
bañarse to take a bath, 3
bañera *(f.)* bathtub, 2
barato/a inexpensive, 2
barbacoa *(f.)* grill, 9
barco *(m.)* boat, 3; ship, 4
barrer (el piso) to sweep (the floor), 9
barro *(m.)* clay, 10; **~ cocido/vidriado** baked/glazed clay, 9
barroco/a Baroque, 2
basado/a based, 9
básquetbol *(m.)* basketball, 6
basura *(f.)* garbage, 9
basurero *(m.)* waste basket, 1
bate *(m.)* bat, 6
batería *(f.)* drum set, 6; battery, 7
batidora *(f.)* mixer, 9
batir to whip, beat, 9
baúl *(m.)* trunk, 7
bebé *(m., f.)* baby boy/girl, 5
beber to drink, 1
bebida *(f.)* drink, 3
bebido/a drunk, 7
béisbol *(m.)* baseball, 6
belleza *(f.)* beauty, 5
bellísimo/a very pretty, 5
bello/a beautiful, 10
beneficios tributarios *(m. pl.)* tax benefits, 6
besar to kiss, 4
besitos *(m. pl.)* kisses, 8
biblioteca *(f.)* library, 2
bicicleta *(f.)* bike, 3
billete *(m.)* ticket, 4; bill, 8
biología *(f.)* biology, 1
bisabuelo/a *(m., f.)* great grandfather/great grandmother, 5
bizcocho *(m.)* cake, 3
blanco/a white, 1
blusa *(f.)* blouse, 7; **~ de seda** silk blouse, 7
boca *(f.)* mouth, 5
boda *(f.)* wedding, 3
boleto *(m.)* ticket, 4
bolígrafo *(m.)* pen, 1
boliviano/a Bolivian, P
bollo *(m.)* hard roll, 3
bolsa *(f.)* purse, 7; bag, 8; **~ de aire** air bag, 7
bombero/a *(m., f.)* fire fighter, 5
bombillo *(m.)* lightbulb, 9
bordado *(m.)* embroidery, 7
borde *(m.)* border, 3
borracho/a drunk, 2
borrador *(m.)* eraser, 1
bosque *(m.)* forest, 7, 9; **~ pluvioso** rainforest, 6
bosquejo *(m.)* sketch, 10
botas *(f. pl.)* boots, 2; **~ de vaquero** cowboy boots, 7
botón *(m.)* button, 6
botones *(m.)* bellhop, 3
boxeo *(m.)* boxing, 6
brasileño/a Brazilian, P
brazo *(m.)* arm, 5
brillar to shine, 12
brindar to provide, 8
bróculi (*also* brócoli) *(m.)* broccoli, 8
broma *(f.)* joke, 2; trick, 10
bronce *(m.)* bronze, 10
broncearse to get a tan, 5
bucear to go skindiving, snorkeling, 5
¡Buen viaje! Have a nice trip!, 4
bueno/a good, 1, 7; **es bueno** it's good, 8
bufanda *(f.)* scarf, 2, 7
burlarse (de) to make fun of, 7
burro *(m.)* donkey, 9
buscador Internet *(m.)* search engine, 2
buscar to look for, search, 1; **~ conchas** to look for shells, 5
búsqueda *(f.)* search, 1
buzón *(m.)* mailbox, 3

C

caballo *(m.)* horse, 9
cabaña *(f.)* shack, 7
cabeza *(f.)* head, 5, 6
cable *(m.)* cable, 11
cabra *(f.)* goat, 9
cabrito *(m.)* goat, 3
cacao *(m.)* chocolate, 12
cada each, 4
cadáver *(m.)* cadaver, corpse, 1
cadena *(f.)* chain, 8; channel, 11
cadera *(f.)* hip, 6
caer to fall, 7; **~ bien/mal** to like/dislike (a person), 4; **~ en la trampa** to fall in the trap, 11; **no me cae nada mal** he's OK, 4
caerse to fall, 6
café *(m.)* *(color)* brown, 1; café, 2; coffee, 3
cafetera *(f.)* coffee maker, 9
caída *(f.)* fall, 10
caimán *(m.)* cayman, alligator, 9
caja *(f.)* cashier, 8; **~ fuerte** safe, 8
cajero/a *(m., f.)* cashier, 8; **~ automático** *(m.)* ATM machine, 8
calabaza *(f.)* calabash, 12
calamar *(m.)* squid, 3
calcetines *(m.)* socks, 7
calculadora *(f.)* calculator, 1
calefacción *(f.)* heat, 2
calendario *(m.)* calendar, 1
caléndula *(f.)* marigold, 9
calentar (ie) to heat, 9
caliente hot, 9
calificaciones *(f. pl.)* qualifications, grades, 6
calificar to name, 6
callarse to be quiet, 11
calmado/a calm, 2
cálmate relax, calm down, 3
calor *(m.)* heat; **hace (mucho/un poco de) ~** it's (very/a litle) hot, 2; **tener ~** to be hot; 2
caloría *(f.)* calorie, 8
cama *(f.)* bed, 1, 3
cámara *(f.)* camera, 10
camarero/a *(m., f.)* waitperson, 3
camarón *(m.)* shrimp *(Lat. Am.)*, 3
cambiar to exchange, 8
cambio *(m.)* change, 8; **~ de moneda** *(m.)* money exchange, 3; **en ~** on the other hand, 3
caminar to walk, 1
caminata *(f.)* walk, 9
camino *(m.)* way, 2
camioneta *(f.)* minivan, 7
camisa *(f.)* shirt, 7; **~ de algodón** cotton shirt, 7
camiseta *(f.)* T-shirt, 6
campanada *(f.)* stroke, 10
campaña *(f.)* campaign, 9
campo *(m.)* countryside, 7
canadiense *(m., f.)* Canadian, P
canal *(m.)* channel, 11
Canarias *(f. pl.)* the Canary Islands, restaurant on the Riverwalk, 11
canario *(m.)* canary, 5
cancha *(f.)* court, field, 6; **~ de tenis** tennis court, 2
cangrejo *(m.)* crab, 3
cansado/a tired, 2
cantante *(m., f.)* singer, 6
cantar to sing, 1, 6
cantidad *(f.)* quantity, 1, 8
cañón *(m.)* canyon, 7
capaz capable, 12
capilla *(f.)* chapel, 2
cápsula *(f.)* capsule, 8
cara *(f.)* face, 3, 5; side, 9
cárcel *(f.)* prison, jail, 11
caribeño/a from the Caribbean, 6
cariñoso/a loving, 6
Carnaval *(m.)* carnival, 10
carne *(f.)* meat, 3; **~ de vaca (res)** beef, 3
carnicería *(f.)* meat market, 3
caro/a expensive, 2

carpeta *(f.)* folder, 1
carpintero/a *(m., f.)* carpenter, 5
carreta *(f.)* wagon, 10
carretera *(f.)* road, 7; **~ de doble calzada** divided highway, 7
carro *(m.)* car, 7
carta *(f.)* menu, 3; letter, 1
cartel *(m.)* poster, 1
cartelera de cine *(f.)* movie programming, 11
cartera *(f.)* wallet, 1
cartero/a *(m., f.)* mail carrier, 5
casa *(f.)* house, 2
casado/a married, 5; **estar ~** to be married, 5
casarse (con) to get married, 5
cascada *(f.)* waterfall, 5
casco *(m.)* helmet, 6
casualidad *(f.)* coincidence, 11
catalán/ana Catalan, 4
catarata *(f.)* waterfall, 7
catarro *(m.)* cold, 8; **tener ~** to have a cold, 8
catástrofe *(f.)* catastrophe, 10
catorce fourteen, 1
caucho *(m.)* rubber, 6
caverna *(f.)* cave, 10
cebolla *(f.)* onion, 3
Ceder el paso Yield, 7
cedro *(m.)* cedar, 9
celebrar to celebrate, 10
celos *(m. pl.)* jealousy, 5; **tener ~** to be jealous, 5
cena *(f.)* dinner, 3
cenar to have dinner, 3
ceniza *(f.)* ash, 10
centro *(m.)* center; **~ comercial** shopping district, 2; **~ de entretenimiento** entertainment center, 6; **en el ~** in the center, 3
cepillarse to brush, 3
cerámica *(f.)* ceramics, 10
cerca de close to, near, 4
cerdo *(m.)* pig, 9
cerebro *(m.)* brain, 8
ceremonia *(f.)* ceremony, 10
cero zero, 1
cerrado/a closed, 3
cerrar (ie) to close, 3, 6
certeza *(f.)* certainty, 8
cerveza *(f.)* beer, 3
chaqueta *(f.)* jacket, 2, 7
cheque certificado *(m.)* certified check, 8
cheques de viajero *(m. pl.)* travelers' checks, 3, 8
chico/a *(m., f.)* boy/girl, 1; child, young person, 5
chileno/a Chilean, P
chino *(m.)* Chinese language, 1
chino/a Chinese, P
chocar to wreck, 7
choque *(m.)* crash, 7
chuleta de puerco *(f.)* pork chop, 3
churrasco *(m.)* barbecue, 8
cibernauta *(m., f.)* cyberspace surfer, 3
ciclismo *(m.)* biking, 6
cielo *(m.)* heaven, sky, 8
cien(to) one hundred, 1, 3
ciencias *(f. pl.)* sciences, 1; **~ médicas** medical sciences, 1; **~ naturales** natural sciences, 1; **~ políticas** political science, 1; **~ sociales** social sciences, 1
ciento uno one hundred and one, 3
cierto true, certain, 8; **es ~** it's certain, true, 8; **no es ~** it's not certain, true, 8
cima *(f.)* top, 4
cinco five, 1
cincuenta fifty, 1
cine *(m.)* movie theater, 2
cintura *(f.)* waist, 6
cinturón *(m.)* belt; **~ de cuero** leather belt, 7; **~ de seguridad** seatbelt, 7
cita *(f.)* appointment, 8
ciudad *(f.)* city, 2
clarinete *(m.)* clarinet, 6
claro/a light, 10; **claro que sí** of course, 7
clase *(f.)* class, 1; **~ turística** coach class, 5
clavel *(m.)* carnation, 9
cliente *(m., f.)* shopper, 3; customer, 7
clima *(m.)* climate, 1; **tener buen/mal ~** to have a good/bad climate, 2
cobrar to charge, 7, 8
cobre *(m.)* copper, 8
coche *(m.)* car, 3
cochino *(m.)* pig, 9
cocido/a cooked, 8
cocina *(f.)* kitchen, 2; cooking, cuisine, 3
cocinar to cook, 9
cocinero/a *(m., f.)* cook, chef, 5
códice *(m.)* manuscript, codex, 2, 12
código *(m.)* code; **~ personal** password, 6; **~ postal** zip code, 6
coger to take, 12
coleccionista *(m., f.)* collector, 10, 11
colgar (ue) to hang up, 6; to hang, 10, 11
colina *(f.)* hill, 7
collar *(m.)* necklace, 8
colocar to place, 9
colombiano/a Colombian, P
colorado/a red, 7
colores *(m. pl.)* colors; **~ primarios** primary colors, 10; **~ secundarios** secondary colors, 10
colorido *(m.)* style, 10
columna *(f.)* column, 11
combinación (de palabras) *(f.)* (word) combination, 12
combustible *(m.)* fuel, 9
comedor *(m.)* dining room, 2
comentador/a *(m., f.)* commentator, 11
comenzar (ie) to begin, 3
comer to eat, 1
cometa *(m.)* comet, 6
cómico/a funny, 1, 11
comida *(f.)* food, meal, 3
comisaría *(f.)* police station, 12
comisión *(f.)* comission, 8
cómo no of course, P
¿Cómo? What?, 1; **~ me queda?** How does it fit me?, 7; **~ quiere Ud. pagar?** How do you want to pay?, 3; **~ se dice...?** How do you say. . . ?, P
cómoda *(f.)* chest of drawers, 9
comodidad *(f.)* comfort, 6
comodín *(m.)* wild card, 11
compadre *(m.)* buddy, 11
compañero/a *(m., f.)* companion, mate; **~ de clase** classmate, 1; **~ de cuarto** roommate, 1
compañía *(f.)* company, 6
compartir to share, 5
componer to compose, 10
comportamiento *(m.)* behavior, 9
composición *(f.)* composition, 10
comprar to buy, 1
comprender to understand, 1; to make up (comprise), 12
comprensivo/a understanding, 10
comprobar (ue) to prove, 9
comprometido/a compromised, 12; engaged
computadora *(f.)* computer, 1
común common, 12
con with, 1, 4; **~ bombos y platillos** with a lot of hype, 9; **~ cheques de viajero** with travelers' checks, 3; **~ desayuno** with breakfast, 3; **~ media pensión** with breakfast and lunch, 3; **~ permiso** excuse me, P; **~ tal (de) que** provided that, 9; **~ tarjeta de crédito** with a credit card, 3
concentrarse to concentrate, 5
concierto *(m.)* concert, 10
concluir to conclude, 7
concurrido/a crowded; **estar muy ~** to have a large audience, 12
concurso *(m.)* contest, 5
condiciones del tiempo *(f. pl.)* weather conditions, 2
cóndor *(m.)* condor, 9
conducir to drive, 2, 7
conductor/a *(m., f.)* driver, 7
conejito de Pascua *(m.)* Easter bunny, 10
conejo *(m.)* rabbit, 5
confiar to trust, 10
confirmación *(f.)* confirmation, 3; **Aquí tengo mi ~** Here is my confirmation, 3
conforme a according to, 6; in accordance with, 9
congelador *(m.)* freezer, 9
congelar to freeze, 9
congreso *(m.)* conference, 3
conjugar to conjugate, 3
conjunto *(m.)* band, 6
conmemoración *(f.)* commemoration, 10
conmemorar to commemorate, 10

conmigo with me, 4
conocer (zc) to know, be familiar with, 2
conocimiento *(m.)* knowledge, 6
conquista *(f.)* conquest, 12
coreano/a Korean, P
consecuencias *(f. pl.)* consequences, 9
conseguir (i) to get, obtain, 3
consejero/a *(m., f.)* counselor, 5
consejo *(m.)* advice, 11
conserje *(m., f.)* concierge, 3
conservar to save, conserve, 9
conservarse to maintain oneself, 8
consolar (ue) to comfort, 6
constructor/a *(m., f.)* builder, 12
construir to construct, build, 10
consulta *(f.)* query, 8
consumir to consume, 8
consumo *(m.)* consumption, 9, 11
contador/a *(m., f.)* accountant, 5
contaminar to contaminate, 9
contar (ue) to count, 3, 4, 5; **~ con** to count on, 7
contenido *(m.)* content, 11
contento/a content, happy, 2; **estar ~ de** to be happy, 8
contestador automático *(m.)* answering machine, 10
contestar to answer, 4, 6
contigo with you, 4
contra against, 3
contraseña *(f.)* password, 6
contraste *(m.)* contrast, 10
conveniente convenient, 1
convertir (ie, i) to convert, 11
copa *(f.)* wine glass, 3
copiar to copy, 6
corazón *(m.)* heart, 8
corbata *(f.)* necktie, 7
cordillera *(f.)* mountain range, 7
coro *(m.)* chorus, 10
corona *(f.)* crown, 12
correa *(f.)* belt, 10
corregido/a corrected, 12
correo *(m.)* post office, 2; **~ electrónico** *(m.)* E-mail, 6; **por ~** by mail, 8
correr to run, 1; **~ el riesgo** to run the risk, 10
cortar to cut, 9
cortinas *(f. pl.)* curtains, 9
corto/a short, 1; **corto plazo** short notice, 11
cosméticos *(m.)* cosmetics, 7
costa *(f.)* coast, 7
costar (ue) to cost, 3
costarricense *(m., f.)* Costa Rican, P
costumbre *(f.)* custom, 3
crear to create, 10
crecer to grow (a person), 5
creer to believe, 1; to think, 8
creído believed, 9
crema de cacahuate *(f.)* peanut butter, 8
criado/a *(m., f.)* servant, maid, 5; *(adj.)* raised, 6
crimen *(m.)* crime, 11
crítica *(f.)* criticism, 11
criticar to criticize, 11
crónica *(f.)* chronicle, 11
Cruce la calle Cross the street, 7
crudo/a raw, 8
cruz *(f.)* cross, 10
cruzado/a crossed, 5
cruzar to cross, 7
cuaderno *(m.)* notebook, 1
cuadra *(f.)* street block, 7; **está a ... cuadras** it's . . . blocks from here, 7
cuadrado/a square, 4
cuadro *(m.)* square, painting, 10; **de cuadros** plaid, 7
¿cuál(es)? what?, which?, 1, 10
cuando when, 9
¿cuándo? when?, 1
¿cuánto? how much?, 1; **~ cuesta?** how much is it?, 4; **~ cuesta...?** how much does. . . cost?, 3; **~ es?** how much is it?, 4; **~ vale?** how much does it cost?, 8
cuanto/a as much as; **cuanto antes** as soon as possible, 11; **en cuanto** as soon as, 9; **en cuanto a** regarding, 3; in relationship to, 9
¿cuántos/as? how many?, 1
cuarenta forty, 1
Cuaresma *(f.)* Lent, 10
cuarteto *(m.)* quartet, 6
cuarto *(m.)* quarter hour, 1; room, 2; **~ de baño** bathroom, 2
cuarto/a fourth, 4
cuatro four, 1
cuatrocientos four hundred, 3
cubano/a Cuban, P
cubanoamericano/a Cuban American, P
cubeta *(f.)* bucket, 7
cubierto/a covered, 7, 9
cubrir to cover, 7
cuchara *(f.)* spoon, 3
cucharada *(f.)* tablespoonful, 9
cucharadita *(f.)* teaspoonful, 9
cucharita *(f.)* teaspoon, 3
cuchillo *(m.)* knife, 1
cuenca *(f.)* river basin, 8
cuenta *(f.)* check, bill, 3; **~ corriente** checking account, 8; **~ de ahorros** savings account, 8
cuento *(m.)* story, 5
cuero *(m.)* leather, 8
cuidado *(m.)* care; **tener ~** to be careful, 7
cuidar to take care of, 4
cuidarse to take care of oneself, 8
culebra *(f.)* snake, 9
culpa *(f.)* fault, **no es ~ tuya** it's not your fault, 3
culpable guilty, 7
cultivar to cultivate, 12
cumbre *(f.)* summit, top, 7
cumpleaños *(m.)* birthday, 1
cumplir to fulfill, 8, 9
cuñado/a *(m., f.)* brother-/sister-in-law, 5
cura *(f.)* cure, 11
curandero/a *(m., f.)* healer, 8
curar to cure, 8
Curva peligrosa Dangerous curve, 7

dañar to injure; to damage, 7
dar to give, 4; **~ la vuelta** to turn around, 7; **~ un paseo** to take a walk, 1
darse cuenta de to become aware of, notice, 6; to realize, 7
datos *(m. pl.)* data, 11
de of, 1; from, 4; **~ acción** action (*adj.*), 11; **~ acuerdo** agreed, 11; **~ al lado** next door, 5; **~ amor** love (*adj.*), 11; **~ alta velocidad** high speed, 4; **~ ancho** in width, 5; **~ ciencia ficción** science fiction (*adj.*), 11; **~ cuadros** plaid, 7; **~ dónde** from where, 1; **~ habla española** Spanish-speaking; **~ habla hispana** Spanish-speaking, 11; **~ hecho** in fact, 9; **~ horror** horror (*adj.*), 11; **~ ida y vuelta** round trip, 4; **~ investigación** investigative, 11; **~ la mañana/tarde/noche** in the morning/afternoon/night, 1; **~ largo** in length, 5; **~ lunares/puntos** polka dotted, 7; **~ manga corta/larga** short/long-sleeved, 7; **~ misterio** mystery (*adj.*), 11; **~ moda** in style, 7; **~ nada** you're welcome, P; **~ ninguna manera** in no way, 8; **~ oro** made of gold, 10; **~ rayas** striped, 7; **~ repente** suddenly, 5; **~ suspenso** thriller (*adj.*), 11; **~ todos modos** anyway, 4; **~ una vez** once and for all, 5; **~ vaqueros** western (*adj.*), 11; **~ veras** really, 4, 7, 12; **~ vez en cuando** from time to time, 11
¿de quién(es)? whose?, 2
debajo de underneath, below, 4
deber to ought to; to owe, 1; should, 2
debido a because of, 3
decano/a *(m., f.)* dean, 7
decidir to decide, 1
décimo tenth, 4
decir (i) to say, tell, 3; **¿Qué quiere ~ ... ?** What does . . . mean?, P
dedicarse to dedicate, devote oneself, 5
dedo *(m.)* finger/toe, 5
deficiente not acceptable, 3
dejar to leave (behind), 3; **~ de hacer** to stop doing, 9
delante de in front of, 4
delfín *(m.)* dolphin, 9
delgado/a thin, 1
delicia *(f.)* delight, 11
delimitar (la búsqueda) to refine, limit (the search), 7
delincuencia *(f.)* delinquency, 11
demás remaining, 9
demasiado too much, 9

demora *(f.)* delay, 4
dentado/a toothed, 9
dentista *(m., f.)* dentist, 5
dentro de inside of, 4
depender (de) to depend (on), 2
dependiente dependent, 1; *(m., f.)* store clerk, 3, 7
deportista *(m., f.)* athlete, sports enthusiast, 6
depositar (dinero) to deposit (money), 8
depresión *(f.)* depression, 11
deprimido/a depressed, 2
derecha *(f.)* right-hand; **a la ~** on/to the right, 4
Derrumbe Falling Rock, 7
desafiar to challenge, 11
desagradable unpleasant, 1
desamparo *(m.)* trouble, 11
desaparecer (zc) to disappear, 7
desaparecido/a disappeared, 12
desarrollado/a developed, 12
desarrollo *(m.)* development, 12
desatar to untie, 7
desayunar to have breakfast, 3
desayuno *(m.)* breakfast, 3
descendiente *(m., f.)* descendant, 12
descomponerse to break, 5
desconcertar (ie) to take aback, 10
desconocido/a unknown, 5, 7
descorazonar to discourage, 12
descremado/a skim (milk), 8
describir to describe, 1
descrito/a described, 10
descubierto/a discovered, 9
descubrir to discover, 1
descuento *(m.)* discount, 7
desde from, since, 4; **~ aquí** from here, 3
deseado/a desired, 6
desear to wish for, 1; to want, 3
desechado/a discarded, 9
desempeñar to play a part, 6; to perform, 12; **~ un papel** to play a role, 8
desempleo *(m.)* unemployment, 6
desesperación *(f.)* desperation, 5
desesperarse to despair, 11
desfile *(m.)* parade, 10
desgraciadamente unfortunately, 4
deshacerse de to get rid of, 4
deshecho/a shattered, 10
desigual uneven, 9
desilusionado/a disappointed, 2
deslumbrar to dazzle, 7
desorganizado/a disorganized, 1
despacio slowly, 7
despedida *(f.)* farewell, 6
despedir (i, i) to lay off/fire, 6
despedirse (i, i) to say good-bye, 5
despegar to take off, 5
despejado clear (weather); **está ~** it's clear, 2
desperdicios *(m. pl.)* waste, 9
despertar (ie) to wake someone up, 6
despertarse (ie) to wake up, 3, 6
después after, 3; afterwards, 4; **~ de** after, 4; **~ (de) que** after, 9
destacarse to stand out, 11
desviarse to detour, 9
detalle *(m.)* detail, 10
deterioro *(m.)* deterioration, 9
detonar to detonate (a bomb), 6
detrás de behind, 4
deuda *(f.)* debt, 12
devastador/a devastating, 7
devolver (ue) to return, 7, 9, 11
día *(m.)* day, 1; **~ de Año Nuevo** New Year's Day, 10; **~ de las Brujas** Halloween, 10; **~ de los Inocentes** April Fool's Day, 10; **~ de San Valentín** Valentine's Day, 10; **~ del Trabajo** Labor Day, 10
¡Diablos! Darn!, 8
diamante *(m.)* diamond, 8
diariamente daily, 8
dibujante *(m., f.)* drawer, illustrator, 10
dibujar to draw, 10
dibujo *(m.)* drawing, 10
dicho said, told, 9
diciembre *(m.)* December, 1
diecinueve nineteen, 1
dieciocho eighteen, 1
dieciséis sixteen, 1
diecisiete seventeen, 1
diente *(m.)* tooth, 3, 5
dieta *(f.)* diet, 8
diez ten, 1
difícil difficult, 1
dimensión *(f.)* dimension, 10
dimes y diretes *(m. pl.)* gossip, 11
dinero *(m.)* money, 3
diputado/a deputy, 12
¡Dios mío! My goodness!, 3, 8; **~ santo!** Good grief!, 10
dirección *(f.)* address, 3, 7
directorio *(m.)* directory, 6
disco *(m.)* record, 7; **~ compacto** compact disc, 6; **~ duro** hard drive, 6
discoteca *(f.)* discotheque, 2
disculpa *(f.)* pardon, 10
disculpar to forgive, 9
diseñar to design, 10
diseñado/a designed, 2
diseño *(m.)* design, 6
disfraz *(m.)* costume, 10
disfrutar to enjoy, 3
disponible available, 6
dispositivo *(m.)* device, 6
distinguir to distinguish, 12
divertido/a enjoyable, 1
divertir (ie, i) to amuse someone, 6
divertirse (ie, i) to enjoy oneself, 3; to have fun, have a good time, 6
divorciado/a divorced, 5; **estar ~** to be divorced, 5
doblar to turn, 7; **no ~** do not turn, 7
doble double, 3; **~ a la derecha/izquierda** turn to the right/left, 7
doce twelve, 1
doctor/a *(m., f.)* doctor, 5
documental *(m.)* documentary, 11
documento *(m.)* document, 6
doler (ue) to hurt, 8
dolor *(m.)* pain, 5; **tener ~** to have pain, 8
domicilio *(m.)* dwelling, 4
domingo *(m.)* Sunday, 1
dominicano/a Dominican, 5
dominio Internet *(m.)* Internet domain, 4
doncella *(f.)* young virgin, 10
¿dónde? where?, 1
dorado/a golden, 10
dormir (ue) to sleep, 3
dormirse (ue) to fall asleep, 3, 6
dormitorio *(m.)* bedroom, 2
dos two, 1
doscientos two hundred, 3
drago *(m.)* dragon tree, 9
dramático/a dramatic, 11
drogadicción *(f.)* drug addiction, 11
ducha *(f.)* shower, 2
ducharse to take a shower, 3
dudar to doubt, 8
dudoso doubtful, 8; **es ~** it's doubtful, 8
dueño/a *(m., f.)* owner, 2, 11
dulce sweet, 3
dulces *(m. pl.)* sweets, 8
duplicarse to double, 6
durante during, 4
duro/a tough, 3; hard, 10

e and, 1
ecuatoriano/a Ecuadorian, P
economía *(f.)* economics, 1
económico/a economical, 4
edad *(f.)* age, 4; **~ adulta** adulthood, 5
edificio *(m.)* building, 2
editor/a *(m., f.)* editor, 5
efectos *(m. pl.)* effects; **~ de sonido** sound effects, 6; **~ especiales** special effects (F/X), 6, 11
egoísta egotistic, 1
ejecutar to execute, 12
ejemplo *(m.)* example; **por ~** for example, 6
ejercicio *(m.)* exercise, 8
ejército *(m.)* army, 9
el the, 1; **el cual** who, 10
elección *(f.)* election, 1
eléctrico/a electric, 8
electricista *(m., f.)* electrician, 5
electrodoméstico *(m.)* electric appliance, 9
elefante *(m.)* elephant, 9
elegante elegant, 1
elegir (i, i) to choose, 4
elevado/a high, 11

embarazada pregnant, 8; **estar ~** to be pregnant, 8
embarazo *(m.)* pregnancy, 11
emigración *(f.)* immigration, 5
emisora *(f.)* broadcasting station, 11
emitir transmit a TV/radio program, 11
emocional emotional, 1
empacar to pack, 1
empalagar to smother with sweetness, 12
empapado/a very wet, 7
empezar (ie) to begin, 3
empleado/a *(m., f.)* employee, 5
empleo *(m.)* employment, 11
empresa *(f.)* company, 6
empujar to push, 7
en in, on, at, 4; **~ blanco y negro** in black and white, 10; **~ busca de** in search of, 11; **~ cambio** on the other hand, 3; **~ caso (de) que** in case that, 9; **~ color(es)** in color, 10; **~ contra** against, 10; **~ cuanto** as soon as, 9; **~ cuanto a** regarding, 3; in relationship to, 9; **~ el centro** in the center, 3; **~ estado de ebriedad** under the influence, 10; **~ este momento** at this moment, 3; **~ fila** single file, 12; **~ grupos** in groups, P; **~ honor de** in honor of, 10; **~ obras** (under) construction, 7; **~ parejas** in pairs, P; **~ punto** exactly on the hour, 1; **~ seguida** right away, 3, 4, 7, 9, 10; **~ uso** in use, 2
enamorado/a in love, 2; **estar ~** to be in love, 5
enamorar to win someone's love, 6
enamorarse (de) to fall in love (with), 5, 6
encantador/a charming, 4
encantar to delight, enchant, like very much, 4
encarcelar to imprison, 11
encargado/a de in charge of, 11
encender (ie) to turn on, 6
encima on top of, 4; **~ de** above, on top of, over, on, 4; **por ~** above, 9
encontrar (ue) to find, 2, 3
encuentro *(m.)* encounter, 12
encuesta *(f.)* survey, 7
endosar to endorse, 8
energía *(f.)* energy, 9
enero *(m.)* January, 1
enfermar to make someone sick, 6
enfermarse to get sick, 6, 8
enfermedad *(f.)* illness, 8; **~ sicológica** psychological illness, 11
enfermero/a *(m., f.)* nurse, 5
enfermo/a sick, 2
enfrentar to confront, 11
enfrente de right in front of, across, 4
enfriar to cool, 9
engañado/a deceived, 9
engañar to betray, 6; to deceive, 8
engaño *(m.)* deceit, 10; deception, 12
engendrado/a conceived, 10
enlace *(m.)* link, 3
enojado/a angry, 2
enojar to make someone angry, 6
enojarse to get angry, 6; to be angry, 8
enlazar to connect, 3
ensalada *(f.)* salad, 3
ensayo *(m.)* essay, 5
enseguida right away, 3, 4, 7, 9, 10
ensuciar to soil, 9
entender (ie) to understand, 3
enterarse de to learn (find out about), 9
entonces then, 3
entorno *(m.)* area, 3
entrada *(f.)* entree, 3; ticket, 11
entrante upcoming, 11
entre between, among, 4
entrega *(f.)* presentation, 12
entregar to award, 12
entremés *(m.)* appetizer, 3
entrenamiento *(m.)* training, 6
entretenido/a entertaining, 10
entretenimiento *(m.)* entertainment, 8, 11
entrevista *(f.)* interview, 6
entusiasmado/a enthusiastic, 2
enviar to send, 6, 8
envidioso/a greedy, 1
envolver (ue) to wrap, 8
equipo *(m.)* team, 6; instrument, 9
equivaler to equal, 3
equivocar to mistake, 6
equivocarse to be mistaken/wrong, 6
es it is, 1
esbelto/a slender, 11
escala *(f.)* layover, 5
escalera *(f.)* ladder, 10; staircase, 1
escalofríos *(m. pl.)* shivers; **tener ~** to shiver, have a chill, 8
escaparate *(m.)* window display, 7
escaso/a scarce, 9
escena *(f.)* scene, 11
escoba *(f.)* broom, 9
Escolares en la vía Student crossing, 7
esconder to hide, 4
escribir to write, 1; **~ a mano** to write by hand, 2; **~ a máquina** to type, 2; **~ cartas** to write letters, 1; **~ en la computadora** to write on the computer, 2
escrito/a written, 9
escritor/a *(m., f.)* writer, 2
escritorio *(m.)* desk, 1
escritura *(f.)* writing, 12
escuchar to listen to, 1
escultor/a *(m., f.)* sculptor, 5, 10
escultura *(f.)* sculpture, 10
escupir to spit, 12
ese/a that, 3
ése/ésa that one, 3
esencial essential, 7; **es ~** it's essential, 7
esfera *(f.)* sphere, 7
esfuerzo *(m.)* effort, 10
esmeralda *(f.)* emerald, 8
eso sí que está claro that's clear, 3
esos/as those, 3
ésos/ésas those, 3
espalda *(f.)* back, 5
espaldar *(m.)* headboard, 9
español *(m.)* Spanish language, 1
español/a Spanish, P
espantoso/a frightening, 4
especialidad *(f.)* specialty, 3
especialización *(f.)* major, 1
especie *(f.)* species, 9
espectáculo *(m.)* spectacle, 10
espectador/a *(m., f.)* spectator, 6
espejo *(m.)* mirror, 9, 12; **~ retrovisor** *(m.)* rearview mirror, 7
esperanza *(f.)* hope, 11
esperar to wait, 2; to hope, 8
espíritu *(m.)* spirit, 10; **buen/mal ~** good/bad spirit, 10
esposa *(f.)* wife, 5
esposas *(f. pl.)* handcuffs, 11, 12
esposo *(m.)* husband, 5
esquí *(m.)* ski, skiing, 6
esquina *(f.)* corner, 7
está it is, 2; **~ a ... cuadras** it's. . .blocks from here, 7; **~ bien, está bien** OK, OK, 3; **~ despejado** it's clear, 2; **~ en contra nuestra** is against us, 10; **~ manchado/a** it's stained, 7; **~ nublado** it's cloudy, 2; **~ roto/a** it's ripped, broken, 7; **~ sucio/a** it's dirty, 7
estable stable, 1
estación *(f.)* season, 1; station, 2; **~ de tren** *(f.)* train station, 2; **¿En qué ~ estamos?** What season is it?, 1
estacionar to park, 7; **no ~** no parking, 7
estadía *(f.)* stay, 5
estadio *(m.)* stadium, 2
estado libre asociado *(m.)* free associated state, 5
estadounidense *(adj.)* U.S. , P, 5
estante *(m.)* bookshelf, 1
estantería *(f.)* cabinet, 9
estar to be, 2; **~ a tiempo** to be on time, 4, 5; **~ a cargo de** to be in charge of, 7, 11; **~ a punto de** to be about to, 4; **~ atrasado/a** to be late, 4, 5; **~ casado/a** to be married, 5; **~ con amigos** to be with friends, 1; **~ contento/a de** to be happy, 8; **~ de acuerdo** to agree, 4; **~ de moda** to be in style, 7; **~ de vacaciones** to be on vacation, 4; **~ divorciado/a** to be divorced, 5; **~ embarazada** to be pregnant, 8; **~ en contra** to be against, 10; **~ en peligro** to be in danger, 2; **~ enamorado/a** to be in love, 5; **~ listo/a** to be ready, 3; **~ mareado/a** to be dizzy, 8; **~ muerto/a de hambre** to be starving, famished, 3; **~ muy concurrido/a** to have a large audience, 12; **~ resfriado/a** to have a cold, 8; **~ separado/a** to be separated, 5
estatua *(f.)* statue, 10

estatura *(f.)* height, 3
este *(m.)* east, 4
este/a this, 3
éste/ésta this one, 3
estelar stellar, 6
estival summer, 9
estómago *(m.)* stomach, 5
estorbar to be in the way, 9
estornudar to sneeze, 8
estos/as these, 3
éstos/éstas these, 3
estrecho/a tight, 7; narrow, 8
estrella *(f.)* star, 6; **~ de cine** movie star, 11
estreno *(m.)* premiere, 11
estrés *(m.)* stress, 8
estuario *(m.)* estuary, 8
estuco *(m.)* stucco, 2
estudiante *(m., f.)* student, 1; **~ de maestría** master's degree student, 1; **~ de pregrado** undergraduate student, 1
estudiar to study, 1
estufa *(f.)* stove, 9
estúpido/a stupid, 1
étnico/a ethnic, 12
evaluación *(f.)* evaluation, 6
evento *(m.)* event, 10
evidente evident, 1; **es ~** it's evident, 8
evitar to avoid, 7, 8; to eliminate, 9
examen físico *(m.)* physical, 8
excelente excellent, 1
excursión *(f.)* tour, 4
exhibición *(f.)* exhibition, 10
existencia *(f.)* existence, 9
éxito *(m.)* success, 6; **tener ~** to be successful, 11
exitoso/a successful, 6
explicar to explain, 4
exploración *(f.)* exploration, 12
explotar to exploit, 9
exponer to expose, 10
exposición mundial *(f.)* world's fair, 10
expresión idiomática *(f.)* idiomatic expression, 5
expuesto/a exposed, 9
extranjero/a foreign, 3
extraño/a strange, 6; **es ~** it's strange, 8
extrovertido/a outgoing, 1

fábrica *(f.)* factory, 6
fabricar(se) to manufacture, 10
fachalina *(f.)* shawl, 7
fácilmente easily, 3
facturar el equipaje to check in luggage, 5
facultad *(f.)* school (in a university), 1
faja *(f.)* strip, 8
falda *(f.)* skirt, 7
falla *(f.)* failure, 10
fallar to fail, 9
falso/a false, 4
faltar to lack, need; to be left (to do), 4
familia *(f.)* family, 5
familiar family *(adj.)*, 4
fanesca quiteña *(f.)* typical stew from Quito, 7
farmacéutico/a *(m., f.)* pharmacist, 5
farmacia *(f.)* pharmacy, 7
fascinante fascinating, 1
fascinar to fascinate, 4
favor *(m.)* favor; **por ~** please, P
fe *(f.)* faith, 9
febrero *(m.)* February, 1
fecha *(f.)* date, 1; **¿Qué ~ es hoy?** What is today's date?, 1
felicidad *(f.)* happiness, 9
¡Feliz viaje! Have a nice trip!, 4
fenómeno *(m.)* phenomenon, 10
feo/a ugly, 1
ferrocarril *(m.)* train, 3
ferroviario/a *(adj.)* train, 3
fertilidad *(f.)* fertility, 10
festejar to celebrate, 10
ficha *(f.)* piece, 5
fiel faithful, 7; loyal, 9
fiesta *(f.)* party, 10; **~ de todos los Santos** All Saints' Day, 10
figura *(f.)* figure, 10
figurita *(f.)* small figure, 10
filosofía *(f.)* philosophy, 1
fin *(m.)* end; **por ~** finally, 3, 5
finalmente finally, 5
finca *(f.)* farm, 9
fingir to fake, 9
firma *(f.)* signature, 8
firmamento *(m.)* sky, 12
firmar to sign, 8
física *(f.)* physics, 1
físico/a physical, 8
fisiología *(f.)* physiology, 1
flamenco *(m.)* flamingo, 9
flauta *(f.)* flute, 6
flojo/a lazy, 1; loose, 7
floración *(f.)* bloom, 9
florecer (zc) to bloom, 10
florería *(f.)* florist, 7
florero *(m.)* flower vase, 1
foco *(m.)* focus, 11
folclor *(m.)* folklore, 10
folclórico/a folkloric, 10
folleto *(m.)* brochure, 4
forjar to forge, 8
forma *(f.)* form, 10
fórmula *(f.)* formula, 1
formular (una consulta/búsqueda) to formulate (a query), 8
fortalecer (zc) to fortify, 12
foto(grafía) *(f.)* photograph, 1, 10
fotógrafo/a *(m., f.)* photographer, 5, 10
fracasar to fail, 11
fractura *(f.)* fracture, 8
fracturado/a fractured, 8
francés *(m.)* French language, 1
francés/esa French, P
fregadero *(m.)* sink, 9
freír (i) to fry, 9
freno *(m.)* brake, 7
fresco *(m.)* cool air; **hace ~** it's cool, 2
frijoles *(m. pl.)* beans, 8
frío *(m.)* coldness; **hace (mucho/un poco de) ~** it's (very/a little) cold, 2; **tener ~** to be cold, 2
frito/a fried, 9
frondoso/a lush, 3
fruta *(f.)* fruit, 3
frutería *(f.)* fruit stand, 3
fuegos artificiales *(m. pl.)* fireworks, 10
fuera (de) outside (of), 4; (out) of, 9; **~ de serie** outstanding, 7, 12; **~ de (su) alcance** out of (their) reach, 9
fuerte hard, 5
fuerza *(f.)* strength, 10
fumar to smoke; **no ~** no smoking, 3, 4
fundar to found, 12
furia *(f.)* wrath, 6
fútbol *(m.)* soccer, 6; **~ americano** football, 6
futbolista *(m., f.)* soccer player, 1

gabinete *(m.)* cabinet, 9
gafas negras/oscuras/de sol *(f. pl.)* sunglasses, 2
gallego/a Gallician, 4
galleta *(f.)* cookie, 3
gallina *(f.)* hen, 9
gallo *(m.)* rooster, 9
gamba *(f.)* shrimp *(Spain)*, 3
ganadero/a stockbreeding, 7
ganado *(m.)* cattle, 8
ganador/a *(m., f.)* winner, 12
ganar to win, 6
ganga *(f.)* sale, discount, 7
garbanzos *(m. pl.)* chickpeas, 9
gasolina *(f.)* gasoline, 7
gastar to use up, 12
gasto *(m.)* expense, 8
gato/a *(m., f.)* cat, 5
gemelo/a *(m., f.)* twin, 1, 11
generación *(f.)* generation, 11
generalmente generally, 5
generoso/a generous, 1
gente *(f.)* people, 1
gerente *(m., f.)* manager, 5
gimnasia *(f.)* gymnastics, 6
girasol *(m.)* sunflower, 9; **~ rojo** echinacea, 8
giro postal *(m.)* money order, 8
gol *(m.)* goal, 4
golpe *(m.)* blow, 10
golpear to hit, 11
gordito/a fat, 1

gordo/a fat, 1; serious, heavy (problem), 10
gorra *(f.)* cap, 2, 7
gozar (de) to enjoy, 4, 6
grabadora *(f.)* tape recorder, 6, 10
grabar to tape, 6
gracia *(f.)* flourish, grace, 5
gracias *(f. pl.)* thanks, P
grado (centígrado/Celsio) *(m.)* degree (centigrade/Celsius), 2
grande big, large, 1; older, 1
grano *(m.)* bean, 8; kernel, 9
grasa *(f.)* fat, grease, 8
gratuito/a free, 3
grifo *(m.)* faucet, 5
gripe *(f.)* flu, 8; **tener ~** to have the flu, 8
gris gray, 1
grupo *(m.)* group; **~ cultural** *(m.)* cultural group, 12; **en grupos** in groups, P
guantera *(f.)* glove box, 7
guantes *(m. pl.)* gloves, 2, 6, 7
guapo/a handsome, good-looking, 1
guardado/a hidden, 5
guardar to save, 6
guatemalteco/a Guatemalan, P
guayaba *(f.)* guava, 5
guerra *(f.)* war, 10
guía *(m., f.)* tour guide, 4; **~** *(f.)* guide book, 4; **~ Internet** *(f.)* Internet Guide, 2, 5
guión *(m.)* script, 11
guiso *(m.)* stew, 5
guitarra *(f.)* guitar, 6
gustar to like, 4
gusto *(m.)* pleasure; **el ~ es mío** the pleasure is mine, P; **¡qué gusto!** What a pleasure!, 4

H

hábil skillful, 10, 12
hábilmente easily, 6
habitación *(f.)* room, 3
habitado/a inhabited, 12
hábitos alimenticios *(m. pl.)* eating habits, 8
hablar to speak, 1
hace; **~ buen/mal tiempo** the weather is good/bad, 2; **~ (mucho/un poco de) calor** it's (very/a little) hot, 2; **~ fresco** it's cool, 2; **~ (mucho/un poco de) frío** it's (very/a little) cold, 2; **~ poco** a little while ago, 11; **~ sol** it's sunny, 2; **~ (mucho) viento** it's (very) windy, 2
hacer to do; to make, 2; **~ caso** to pay attention, 12; **~ castillos de arena** to build sand castles, 5; **~ clic** to click with a mouse, 6; **~ cola** to wait in line, 5; **~ daño a alguien** to harm someone, 6; **~ ejercicio** to exercise, 1; **~ el papel** to play a role, 11; **~ esquí acuático** to go water skiing, 5; **~ la cama** to make the bed, 9; **~ surfing** to surf, 5; **~ un picnic** to have a picnic, 5; **~ una cita** to make an appointment, 8; **~ una llamada de larga distancia** to make a long distance phone call, 3; **~ una llamada por cobrar** to make a collect call, 3
hacerse + *profession* to become + *profession*, 5; **hacérsele tarde a uno** to become late, 7
hacia toward, 4
halago *(m.)* praise, 10, 12
hallazgo *(m.)* find, 12
hambre (el) *(f.)* hunger, 3; **tener (mucha) ~** to be (very) hungry, 2, 3; **¡qué ~!** I'm very hungry!, 3
hasta until, 4; **~ la vista** until we meet again, P; **~ que** until, 9
hay there is, there are, 1
hecho *(m.)* deed, act, 7, 12; made, done, 9; **de ~** in fact, 9
helado *(m.)* ice cream, 3
helado/a freezing, 7
hallar to find, 10
herencia *(f.)* heritage, 5, 7
herir (ie, i) to hurt, 6
hermanastro/a *(m., f.)* stepbrother/sister
hermano/a *(m., f.)* brother/sister, 1, 5
hervir (ie, i) to boil, 9
hijastro/a *(m., f.)* stepson/daughter
hijo/a *(m., f.)* son/daughter, 5
hileras (de cuentas) *(f. pl.)* rows (of beads), 7
himno *(m.)* hymn, 10
historia *(f.)* history, 1
histórico/a historic, 10
hogar *(m.)* hearth, 8; home, 10
hoja *(f.)* leaf; **~ de vida** résumé, 6; **~ de papel** sheet of paper, 9
hombre *(m.)* man, 1; **~ de negocios** businessman, 6
homenaje *(m.)* hommage, 10
hondo/a deep, 9
hondureño/a Honduran, P
honesto/a honest, 1
honrar to honor, 10
hora *(f.)* hour; **¿Qué ~ es?** What time is it?, 1
horario *(m.)* schedule, 4; **~ de trabajo** work schedule, 6
hornear to bake, 9
horno *(m.)* oven, 9; kiln, 10; **al ~** baked, 8
horrible horrible, 1; **lo más ~** the most horrible part, 12
hospedarse to stay in a hotel, 3
hoy en día today, 5; nowadays, 7
hueso *(m.)* bone, 8
huésped *(m., f.)* guest, 3
huevo *(m.)* egg, 3
hule *(m.)* rubber, 12
humilde humble, 8

I

idea *(f.)* idea; **ni ~** I haven't got a clue, 4; **ni la menor ~** not even the least idea, 9
idealista idealistic, 1
idear to make a plan, 12
identidad *(f.)* identity, 12
idioma *(m.)* language, 1
iglesia *(f.)* church, 1
ilegal illegal, 4
ilustración *(f.)* illustration, 10
imagen digital *(f.)* digital image, 9
impacientemente impatiently, 3
imperdonable unforgiveable, 3
imperecedero/a immortal, 11
imperfecto/a imperfect, 1
imperio *(m.)* empire, 12
impermeable *(m.)* raincoat, 2, 7
imponente imposing, 12
importante important, 1; **es ~** it's important, 7
importar to matter, be of concern, 4
imposible impossible; **es ~** it's impossible, 8
impresionante impressive, 6
impresora *(f.)* printer, 1, 6
imprimir to print, 1, 6
impuesto *(m.)* tax, 4
inalámbrico/a cordless, 6
incaico/a Incan, 7
incertidumbre *(f.)* uncertainty, 6, 11
incomodidad *(f.)* inconvenience, 10
incómodo/a uncomfortable, 9
incomprensivo/a unsympathetic, 10
inconveniente inconvenient, 1
indexar to index, 9
indicador *(m.)* bookmark, 10
indígena indigenous, 5
indirecta *(f.)* heavy hint, 10
inexplicable unexplainable, 12
infección *(f.)* infection, 8
influir to influence, 7
infractor/a *(m., f.)* offender, 7
infundado/a unfounded, 9
ingeniería *(f.)* engineering, 1
ingeniero/a *(m., f.)* engineer, 5
ingenioso/a clever, 10
inglés *(m.)* English language, 1
inglés/esa English, P
injusto/a unfair, 6
inodoro *(m.)* toilet, 9
inolvidable unforgettable, 2
inquietante disturbing, 10
inquietarse to get worked up, 10
inquietud *(f.)* worry, 11
inquilino/a *(m., f.)* tenant, 2
insoportable unbearable, 3
insuficiente insufficient, 1

inteligente intelligent, 1
interesante interesting, 1
interesar to interest, be of interest, 4
internacional international, 1
internauta *(m., f.)* Internet surfer, 3
interpretación *(f.)* performance, 11
intersección intersection, 7
introvertido/a timid, 1
invención *(f.)* invention, 12
inversión *(f.)* investment, 3
investigación *(f.)* research, 9; **periodismo de ~** *(m.)* investigative journalism, 11
investigaciones arqueológicas *(f. pl.)* archaeological research, 12
investigar to research, 1
invierno *(m.)* winter, 2
involucrado/a involved, 9
involucrar to involve, 6
inyección *(f.)* injection, 8
ir to go, 2; **~ a** *(+ inf.)* going to, 2; **~ de compras** to go shopping, 5, 7; **~ de pesca** to fish, 5; **~ de vacaciones** to go on vacation, 4; **~ con destino a** to leave/depart with destination to, 4
irreprochable untouchable, 12
irse to go away, leave, 3, 6; **~ de vacaciones** to go on vacation, 4
isla *(f.)* island, 4, 7
italiano *(m.)* Italian language, 1
italiano/a Italian, P
itinerario *(m.)* itinerary, 4
izquierda *(f.)* left-hand; **a la~** on/to the left

J

jabón *(m.)* soap, 7
jamás never, 3
japonés *(m.)* Japanese language, 1
japonés/esa Japanese, P
jarabe *(m.)* syrup, 8
jardín *(m.)* garden, 2
jardinero/a *(m., f.)* gardener, 5, 9
jarra *(f.)* pitcher, 3
jefe/a *(m., f.)* leader, boss, 5
jeroglíficos *(m. pl.)* hieroglyphics, 12
jirafa *(f.)* giraffe, 9
joven young, 1, 7; *(m., f.)* young person, 4
joyas *(f. pl.)* jewelry, 8; **~ de fantasía** costume jewelry, 8
joyería *(f.)* jewelry store, 7
jubilado/a retired, 9
judío/a Jewish, 4
Juegos Olímpicos *(m.)* Olympic Games, 10
jueves *(m.)* Thursday, 1
jugador/a *(m., f.)* player, 6
jugar (ue) a + *sport* to play + *sport*, 1
jugo *(m.)* juice *(Lat. Am.)*, 3
julio *(m.)* July, 1
junio *(m.)* June, 1
junto a side-to-side with, close to, 4
jurar to swear, 6
juventud *(f.)* youth, 11

L

laboratorio *(m.)* laboratory, 1
lado *(m.)* side; **al ~ de** beside, to/on the side of, 4
ladrar to bark, 5
ladrillo *(m.)* brick, 2
ladrón/ona *(m., f.)* thief, 4
lagarto *(m.)* lizard, 9
lagartija *(f.)* lizard, 9
lago *(m.)* lake, 7
lágrima *(f.)* tear, 5
lamentar to lament, regret, be sorry, 8
lámpara *(f.)* lamp, 1
langosta *(f.)* lobster, 3
lanzar to launch, 11
lápiz *(m.)* pencil, 1
largo/a long, 1; **a lo largo y ancho** throughout, 9; **de largo** in length, 5
largometraje *(m.)* feature film, 11
lástima *(f.)* pity, 11; **es una ~** it's a shame, pity, 8; **¡qué ~!** What a pity! too bad!, 1
lavabo *(m.)* (kitchen) sink, 9
lavadora *(f.)* washing machine, 9
lavamanos *(m.)* (bathroom) sink, 9
lavaplatos *(m.)* dishwasher, 9
lavar to wash, 1; **~ la ropa** to wash the clothes, 9; **~ los platos** to wash the dishes, 9
lavarse to get washed, 3
lazo *(m.)* connection, 12
lección *(f.)* lesson, 1
leche *(f.)* milk, 3
lechón asado *(m.)* roast pig, 5
lechuga *(f.)* lettuce, 3
legumbre *(f.)* vegetable, 3
leer to read, 1
leído/a read, 9
lejos (de) far from, 4; **a lo lejos** at a distance, 7
lengua *(f.)* language, 1; tongue, 8
lente *(m.)* lens, 5
lento/a slow, 1
león *(m.)* lion, 9
levantar to lift, 1
levantarse to get up, 3, 6
libertad *(f.)* liberty, 1
libra *(f.)* pound, 3
libre free, 4
librería *(f.)* bookstore, 2, 7
libro *(m.)* book, 1
licencia de manejar *(f.)* driver's license, 7
licuadora *(f.)* blender, 9
líder *(m., f.)* leader, 6
ligero/a light, 3
limitar to limit, 2
límite *(m.)* border, 7
limpiaparabrisas *(m. pl.)* windshield wipers, 7
lingüística *(f.)* linguistics, 1
lingüístico/a linguistic, 12
lío *(m.)* trouble, 3; hassle, 7
listo/a intelligent, sharp, clever, 1; ready, 2; **estar ~** to be ready, 3
literatura *(f.)* literature, 1
litoral *(m.)* coast, 8
llamar to call, 1; **~ la atención** to attract attention, 8
llamativo/a attractive, 7
llanta *(f.)* tire, 7; **~ pinchada** flat tire, 7
llano *(m.)* plain, 7
llanura *(f.)* plains, 7
llave *(f.)* key, 1, 3; faucet, 9
llegada *(f.)* arrival, 4
llegar to arrive, 1; **~ a tiempo** to arrive on time, 4; **~ atrasado/a** to arrive late, 4; **al ~** upon arriving, 5
llevar to carry; to wear, 1
llevarse to take, get; **~ bien** to get along, 5; **voy a llevarme...** I'm going to take . . . , 7
llover (ue) to rain, 3
llovizna (mucho/un poco) it's drizzling (a lot/a little), 2
llueve (mucho/un poco) it's raining (a lot/a little), 2
lluvia *(f.)* rain, 5
lo *neuter pronoun*, 12; **~ más horrible** the most horrible part, 12; **~ mejor** the best part, 12; **~ peor de todo** the worst part of all, 12; **~ que** which, 4; what, that which, 10; **~ siento** I'm sorry, 3, 4; **~ único** the only thing, 9
lobo *(m.)* wolf, 9
locro *(m.)* soup *(Ecuador)*; **~ de papa** *(m.)* potato soup, 7; **~ de queso** *(m.)* potato soup with avocado and cheese, 7
locutor/a *(m., f.)* announcer, 11
lograr to achieve, 7, 11; to obtain, 11
logro *(m.)* achievement, 8, 10, 11
Londres London, 4
longitud *(f.)* length, 3
luces *(f. pl.)* headlights, 7
lucrativo/a profitable, 4
luego later, 3; then, 3, 5; **~ que** as soon as, 9
lugar *(m.)* place, 2
lujo *(m.)* luxury, 7
lunes *(m.)* Monday, 1
luz *(f.)* light, 1

M

madera *(f.)* wood, 10
madrastra *(f.)* stepmother
madre *(f.)* mother, 1, 5
madrina *(f.)* godmother, 9

mágico/a magic, 6
magnífico/a magnificent, 10
maíz *(m.)* corn, 9
majestuoso/a majestic, 7
maldad *(f.)* evil, 9
males *(m. pl.)* evil, 10
maleta *(f.)* suitcase, 3
maletero/a *(m., f.)* porter, 4
maletín *(m.)* briefcase, 1
mallorquín/ina Mallorcan, 4
malo/a bad, 1, 7; **es malo** it's bad, 8
maltratar to mistreat, 6
mamífero *(m.)* mammal, 7
mancha *(f.)* stain, 7; spot, 11
manchado/a stained, 7; **está ~** it's stained, 7
mandar to send, 1, 4, 6; to order, 7
mandarina *(f.)* tangerine, 3
manejar to drive, 7
manejo *(m.)* management, 6
manga *(f.)* sleeve, 7; **de ~ corta/larga** short/long-sleeved, 7
mano *(f.)* hand, 1, 3, 5; **a ~** by hand, 10
Mansión del Río River Mansion, café on the Riverwalk, 11
mantener to maintain, 8
mantenerse ~ en forma to stay in shape, 8
mantequilla *(f.)* butter, 8
manzana *(f.)* apple, 3; street block, 7
mañana *(f.)* morning, 1; **por la ~** in the morning, 1
mapa *(m.)* map, 1
maquillarse to put on makeup, 3
máquina de escribir *(f.)* typewriter, 9
maquinaria *(f.)* equipment, 6
mar *(m.)* sea, ocean, 7
maravilla *(f.)* wonder, 2
marco *(m.)* frame, 10
mareado/a dizzy, 8; **estar ~** to be dizzy, 8
mareo *(m.)* dizziness, 8
margarita *(f.)* daisy, 9
marido *(m.)* husband, 5
mariposa *(f.)* butterfly, 9
mármol *(m.)* marble, 10
marrón brown, 1
martes *(m.)* Tuesday, 1
marzo *(m.)* March, 1
más and, 1; more, plus, 7
masaje terapéutico *(m.)* therapeutic massage, 4
máscara *(f.)* mask, 10
matar to kill, 11
matemáticas *(f. pl.)* mathematics, 1
materia *(f.)* academic subject, 1
matriculado/a registered, 3
máximo/a highest, 7
mayo *(m.)* May, 1
mayor older, 1, 7; **ser ~** to be older, 5
mazorca *(f.)* corn on the cob, 9
me falta (el tenedor) the (fork) is missing, 3
me gusta(n) I like, 1
me gustaría... I would like . . . , 3
mecánico/a *(m., f.)* mechanic, 5
mecerse (zc) to swing, 9
media *(f.)* half (hour), 1; average, 6
mediano/a medium, 7
medianoche *(f.)* midnight, 1
medias *(f. pl.)* stockings, 7
médico/a *(m., f.)* doctor, 5
medida *(f.)* measurement, 7
medio *(m.)* means, 11; **~ ambiente** environment, 9
medio/a average, 2
mediodía *(m.)* noon, 1
medioevo *(m.)* Middle Ages, 11
medir (i) to measure, 6, 7
megavatio *(m.)* megawatt, 3
mejor better, 3; **es ~** it's better, 8; **lo ~** the best part, 12
mejora *(f.)* improvement, 3
mejorarse to get better, 8
mellizo/a *(m., f.)* twin, 11
menor younger, 7; **ser ~** to be younger, 5
menos less, minus, 1; **a ~ que** unless, 9; **no es para ~** it's no wonder, 9
mensaje *(m.)* message, 6
mensajero/a *(m., f.)* messenger, 8
mentir (ie, i) to lie, 12
mentiroso/a liar, 1
menú *(m.)* menu, 3
mercado *(m.)* market, 2
mercancía *(f.)* merchandise, 3
merecer (zc) to deserve, 9, 11
merengue *(m.)* Caribbean rhythm, 6
mes *(m.)* month; **el ~ pasado** last month, 4; **¿En qué ~ estamos?** What month is it?, 1
mesa *(f.)* table, 1, 9
mesita *(f.)* coffee table, 9; **~ de noche** night stand, 9
meta *(f.)* goal, 6
meter to put (in), 12
metro *(m.)* subway, 3
mexicano/a Mexican, P
mexicanoamericano/a Mexican American, P
mezcla *(f.)* mix, 5
mezclar to mix, 9
mezquita *(f.)* mosque, 4
micro(ondas) *(m.)* microwave oven, 9
miedo *(m.)* fear, **tener ~** to be afraid (of), 2
mientras while, 4; **~ que** as long as, 9
miércoles *(m.)* Wednesday, 1
mil *(m.)* (one) thousand, 3
milenio *(m.)* millennium, 11
millón *(m.)* million, 3
miniatura *(f.)* miniature, 10
minifalda *(f.)* miniskirt, 7
mínimo/a lowest, 7
minoría *(f.)* minority, 12
mirar to look at, 1
misa *(f.)* mass, 5
mitad *(f.)* half, 11
mochila *(f.)* bookbag, backpack, 1
modelo *(m., f.)* model, 10
moderno/a modern, 1
moler (ue) to grind, 9
molestar to bother, annoy, 4, 8
mondongo *(m.)* tripe, 5
moneda en efectivo *(f.)* cash, 8
mono *(m.)* monkey, 9
montaña *(f.)* mountain, 7
montar to go, ride; **~ a caballo** to go horseback riding, 5; **~ en bicicleta** to go bicycling, 5
monumento *(m.)* monument, 2
morado/a purple, 1
morder (ue) to bite, 5
moreno/a dark-complexioned, 1
morir (ue) to die, 3
moros *(m. pl.)* Moors, 3
mosaico *(m.)* mosaic, 10
mosca *(f.)* fly, 3
mostrador *(m.)* counter, 5, 7, 9; display case, 7
mostrar (ue) to show, 3, 10
moto(cicleta) *(f.)* motorcycle, 3
motor *(m.)* motor, 7; **~ de búsqueda** search engine, 2
mover (ue) to move, 6
muchacho/a *(m., f.)* boy/girl, 5
muerte *(f.)* death, 3, 11
muerto/a dead, 9; **estar ~ de hambre** to be starving, famished, 3
muestra *(f.)* sample, 11
mujer *(f.)* woman, 1; **~ de negocios** businesswoman, 6
muñeco de felpa *(m.)* stuffed animal, 9
murciélago *(m.)* bat, 12
músculo *(m.)* muscle, 8
museo *(m.)* museum, 2, 10
música *(f.)* music, 6
músico/a *(m., f.)* musician, 5
musulmán/ana Muslim, 4
muy very, 1

N

nacer (zc) to be born, 5
nacimiento *(m.)* birth, 10
nacional national, 10
nada nothing, 3; **de ~** you're welcome, P
nadar to swim, 5
nadie nobody, 1, 3
naranja *(f.)* orange, 3
nariz *(f.)* nose, 5
narración *(f.)* narration, 11
natación *(f.)* swimming, 6
naturaleza *(f.)* nature, 3, 9; **~ muerta** still life, 10
náuseas *(f. pl.)* nausea; **tener ~** to be nauseous, 8

navaja *(f.)* knife, 12
navegador *(m.)* browser, 1
navegar to travel by boat; **~ en velero** to go sailing, 5; **~ por Internet** to surf the Internet/Web, 1
Navidad *(f.)* Christmas, 10
naviero/a shipping, 3
necesario/a necessary, 7; **es ~** it's necessary, 7
necesitar to need, 1
negar (ie) to deny, 8
negocio *(m.)* business, 4, 6
neoyorquino/a *(adj.)* New York, 6
nervios *(m. pl.)* nerves; **¡qué ~!** how frightening!, 11
nervioso/a nervous, 2
neutros *(m. pl.)* neutrals, 10
nevado/a snow-capped, 7
nevar (ie) to snow, 3
ni (... ni) neither . . . (nor), 3; **~ idea** I haven't got a clue, 4; **~ la menor idea** not even the least idea, 9
nicaragüense *(m., f.)* Nicaraguan, P
nieto/a *(m., f.)* grandson/granddaughter, 5
nieva (mucho/un poco) it's snowing (a lot/a little), 2
niñez *(f.)* childhood, 5
ningún, ninguno/a no one, nobody, none, 3
niño/a *(m., f.)* child, 1; baby/toddler, 5
nivel *(m.)* level, 8, 11
no no, 1; **~ sé** I don't know, P
noche *(f.)* night, 1; **por/en la ~** in the night, 1
Nochebuena *(f.)* Christmas Eve, 10
Nochevieja *(f.)* New Year's Eve, 10
nocturno/a nightly, 4
nominación *(f.)* nomination, 11
noreste *(m.)* northeast, 4
noroeste *(m.)* northwest, 4
norte *(m.)* north, 4
nota *(f.)* note, 2
noticias *(f. pl.)* news, 11
noticiero *(m.)* news program, 11
novecientos nine hundred, 3
novela *(f.)* novel, 5
noveno/a ninth, 4
noventa ninety, 1
noviazgo *(m.)* courtship, 3
noviembre *(m.)* November, 1
novio/a *(m., f.)* boyfriend/girlfriend, 1
nube *(f.)* cloud, 8
nublado cloudy, 2; **está ~** it's cloudy, 2
nuera *(f.)* daughter-in-law, 5
nuestro/a(s) our, 2
nueve nine, 1
nuevo/a new, 1
número *(m.)* number, 1
nunca never, 3
nutritivo/a nutritious, 8

O

o... o either . . . or, 3
obra de arte *(f.)* work of art, 10
obtener to obtain, 11
occidental western, 7
océano *(m.)* ocean, 7
ochenta eighty, 1
ocho eight, 1
ochocientos eight hundred, 3
ocio *(m.)* free time, 11
octavo/a eighth, 4
octubre *(m.)* October, 1
ocupado/a busy, 7
ocurrir to occur, 7
oeste *(m.)* west, 4
oferta *(f.)* sale, discount, 7
oficina *(f.)* office, 2
oficio *(m.)* occupation, 12
ofrecer (zc) to offer, 4
oído *(m.)* inner ear, 8; heard, 9
ojalá I hope, let's hope, 8
ojo *(m.)* eye, 5
ola *(f.)* wave, 6
olla *(f.)* pot, 9
olvidar to forget, 7
olvídelo forget it, 4
once eleven, 1
onda alfa *(f.)* alpha wave, 8
ondulaciones *(f. pl.)* rolling hills, 8
ónice *(m.)* onyx, 2
onza *(f.)* ounce, 3
opinar to think, have an opinion, 8
oportunista opportunistic, 1
optimista optimistic, 1
ordenar (el cuarto) to clean (the room), 9
oreja *(f.)* ear, 5
organizado/a organized, 1
oriental eastern, 7
orilla *(f.)* shore, 4; edge, 7
oro *(m.)* gold, 8; **de ~** made of gold, 10
orografía *(f.)* contour, 3
oscuridad *(f.)* darkness, 12
oscuro/a dark, 10
oso *(m.)* bear, 9
ostra *(f.)* oyster, 3
otoño *(m.)* autumn, 2
otros/as other; **otras veces** other times, 5
oveja *(f.)* sheep, 9
OVNI *(m.)* UFO, 6
oxígeno *(m.)* oxygen, 1
¡Oye! Listen!, Hey!, 4

P

paciente *(adj.)* patient, 1; *(m., f.)* patient, 8
padrastro *(m.)* stepfather
padre *(m.)* father, 1, 5
padres *(m. pl.)* parents, 5
pagar to pay, 1; **~ con dinero en efectivo** to pay cash, 3
página principal/inicial *(f.)* home page, 1
Páginas amarillas/blancas *(f. pl.)* Yellow/White Pages, 5
paila *(f.)* large pan, 9
paisaje *(m.)* landscape, 10
pájaro *(m.)* bird, 9
palabra *(f.)* word; **~ clave** keyword, 2; **~ relacionada** related word, 12
palanca *(f.)* lever, 9
paleta *(f.)* palette, 10
pálido/a pale, 6
palito de madera *(m.)* wooden stick, 9
palmera *(f.)* palm tree, 5
palo *(m.)* club, 6
paloma *(f.)* pigeon, dove, 9
palomitas de maíz *(f. pl.)* popcorn, 11
pan *(m.)* bread, 3
panadería *(f.)* bread bakery, 3
panameño/a Panamanian, P
pantalla *(f.)* screen, 11
pantalones *(m. pl.)* pants, 2; **~ cortos** shorts, 2
paño *(m.)* cloth, 7
papa *(f.)* potato *(Lat. Am.)*, 3
papagayo *(m.)* parrot, 6
papel *(m.)* paper, 1; role, 11; **~ sanitario/higiénico** *(m.)* toilet paper, 9
papelería *(f.)* stationery store, 7
papelito *(m.)* little piece of paper, 4
paquete *(m.)* package tour, 4
par *(m.)* pair, 7
para for, to, 4; by, 6; **~ que** in order to, so (that), 9
parabrisas *(m.)* windshield, 7
parada de autobús *(f.)* bus stop, 2
paraguas *(m.)* umbrella, 2
paraguayo/a Paraguayan, P
paraíso *(m.)* paradise, 7
parar to stop, 7; **~ de** to stop (doing), 4
Pare Stop, 7
parece it seems; **~ mentira** it seems unreal, 7; **~ que** it seems that, 3
parecer (zc) to seem, appear to be, 4
pared *(f.)* wall, 1
pariente *(m., f.)* family member, relative, 5
parlante *(m.)* speaker, 6
parra *(f.)* grapevine, 9
participación *(f.)* participation, 10
participar to participate, 10
partido *(m.)* game, 6
partir to leave; **a ~ de** starting from, 12
parto *(m.)* birth, delivery, 9
pasaje *(m.)* ticket, 4
pasajero/a *(m., f.)* passenger, 4
pasaporte *(m.)* passport, 4, 5
pasar (una película) to show (a movie), 11
Pascua *(f.)* Easter, 10
Pase por... Pass by . . . , 7
Paseo del Río Riverwalk (in San Antonio), 11
pasillo *(m.)* hallway, 2; hall, 9

paso *(m.)* step, 6; **no hay ~** do not enter, 7; **~ peatonal** pedestrian crossing, 7
pastel *(m.)* cake, 3
pastilla *(f.)* pill, 8
patata *(f.)* potato (*Spain*), 3
patear to kick, 6
patinaje (sobre hielo) *(m.)* (ice) skating, 6
patinar to skate, 6
patines *(m. pl.)* skates, 6
pato *(m.)* duck, 9
patria *(f.)* country, 11
patrimonio de la humanidad *(m.)* human heritage, 9
pavo *(m.)* turkey, 9
peaje *(m.)* toll, 3
pecho *(m.)* chest, 5
pechuga *(f.)* breast (of an animal), 8
pedido *(m.)* order, 3
pedir (i, i) to ask for, 3; to request, 7; **~ favores especiales** to ask for special favors, 10; **~ prestado** to borrow, 8
pegajoso/a catchy, sticky, 6
pegar to hit, smack, 4
peinarse to comb one's hair, 3
película *(f.)* movie, 11; **~ cómica** comedy, 11
peligro *(m.)* danger, 3, 12; **estar en ~** to be in danger, 2
pelirrojo/a red-head, 1
pelo *(m.)* hair, 3, 5
pelota *(f.)* ball, 6
peluquero/a *(m., f.)* hair stylist, 5
penca sávila *(f.)* aloe vera, 8
pendiente *(m.)* pendant, 8
pensamiento *(m.)* thought, 5
pensar (ie) to think, plan, intend, 3, 8
pensión *(f.)* boarding house, 1; **con media ~** with breakfast and lunch, 3
peor worse, 7; **es ~** it's worse, 8; **lo ~ de todo** the worst part of all, 12
pepino *(m.)* cucumber, 3
pequeño/a small, 1, 7
pera *(f.)* pear, 3
perder (ie) to lose, 3, 6, 7; **~ de vista** to drop from sight, 5
perdido/a lost, 12
perdón *(m.)* pardon, P
perdone la molestia I beg your pardon, 7
perezoso/a lazy, 1
perfecto/a perfect, 1
perfume *(m.)* perfume, 7
perfumería *(f.)* perfume store, 7
perico *(m.)* parrot, 9
periódico *(m.)* newspaper, 2
periodista *(m., f.)* journalist, 5, 11
perito/a *(m., f.)* expert, 9
perla *(f.)* pearl, 8
permanecer (zc) to remain, 10
permiso *(m.)* permission; **con ~** excuse me, P
pero but, 10
perro/a *(m., f.)* dog, 5
perseguir (i, i) to follow, pursue, 3
persistente persistent, 1
personaje principal/secundario *(m.)* main/secondary character, 11
peruano/a Peruvian, P
pesa *(f.)* weight, 4
pesado/a heavy, 6
pertenecer (zc) to belong to, 12
pesadilla *(f.)* nightmare, 11
pescadería *(f.)* fish market, 3
pescado *(m.)* fish, 3
pescar to fish, 4, 5
pesimista pessimistic, 1
peso *(m.)* weight, 3
peste *(f.)* plague, 11
picar to chop, 9
pico *(m.)* peak, 7
pie *(m.)* foot, 5; **a ~** on foot, 3
piedad *(f.)* mercy, 6
piedra *(f.)* stone, 7, 8
pierna *(f.)* leg, 5
pieza *(f.)* piece, 8, 10
pila *(f.)* battery, 7; pile, 9
píldora *(f.)* pill, 8
piloto *(m., f.)* pilot, 5
pimienta *(f.)* (black) pepper, 3
pimiento verde/rojo *(m.)* red/green pepper, 3
piña *(f.)* pineapple, 3
pincel *(m.)* brush, 10
pingüino *(m.)* penguin, 9
pintado/a painted, 10
pintar to paint, 1, 10
pintor/a *(m., f.)* painter, 5, 9, 10
pintoresco/a picturesque, 2
pintura *(f.)* painting, 10; **~ al óleo** oil paint, 10; **~ corporal** body painting, 8
pirámide de la alimentación *(f.)* food pyramid, 8
piscina *(f.)* swimming pool, 2, 3
piso *(m.)* floor, 2
pista *(f.)* rink (ice skating/hockey), track, 6
pitar to beep the horn, 7
pito *(m.)* horn, 7
pizarra *(f.)* blackboard, chalkboard, 1
placa *(f.)* license plate, 7; plaque, 10
placer *(m.)* pleasure, 5
plancha *(f.)* iron, 9
planchar (la ropa) to iron (clothes), 9
planeta *(m.)* planet, 9
planicie *(f.)* plains, 7
planta *(f.)* plant, 1
plata *(f.)* silver, 8
platanera *(f.)* banana tree, 9
plátano *(m.)* banana, 3, 8
platillo *(m.)* saucer, 3
plato *(m.)* dish, 3; **~ principal** main dish, 3
playa *(f.)* beach, 2
plaza *(f.)* city square/plaza, 2; place/seat, 4
pleito *(m.)* fight, 6
plomero/a *(m., f.)* plumber, 5
pluma *(f.)* pen, 1; feather, 10
población *(f.)* population, 11, 12
poblado/a populated, 12
poblar (ue) to populate, 12
pobreza *(f.)* poverty, 11
poco a poco little by little, 4
poder (ue) to be able to, 3
poderoso/a powerful, 8, 10
policía *(f.)* police force, 11; *(m., f.)* police officer, 11
polifacético/a multifaceted, 6
pollo *(m.)* chicken, 3
poner to put, place, 2; **~ la mesa** to set the table, 2; **~ una carta en el correo** to mail a letter, 2
ponerse to put on (clothing), 3, 6; to become, 6; **~ a +** *inf.* to start doing something, 6; **~ las pilas** to charge up one's batteries, to get a wake-up call, 11
por for, 4; around, by, 6; **~ correo** by mail, 8; **~ ejemplo** for example, 6; **~ encima de** above, 9; **~ favor** please, P; **~ fin** finally, 3, 5; **~ la (mañana, tarde, noche)** in the (morning, afternoon, night), 1; **~ qué diablos** why in the world, 10; **~ si acaso** just in case, 4, 11; **~ su propia cuenta** on her/his own, 10; **~ supuesto** of course, 3, 5; **~ último** finally, 5
porción *(f.)* portion, 8
portátil portable, 6
portugués *(m.)* Portuguese language, 1
portugués/esa Portuguese, P
posible possible, 1
postal *(m.)* post card, 2
posteriormente later, 6
postre *(m.)* dessert, 3
practicar to practice, 1; **~ deportes** to play sports, 1
precio *(m.)* price, 7; **los precios están por las nubes** the prices are high (in the sky), 3
preciso/a necessary, 7; **es ~** it's necessary, 7
predecible predictable, 6
predecir to predict, 9
preferible preferable, 7; **es ~** it's preferable, 7
preferir (ie, i) to prefer, 3
preguntar to ask a question, 4
premiar to award, 12
premios *(m. pl.)* honors, 6
prenda *(f.)* garment, 7
prendedor *(m.)* brooch, 8
prender to turn on, 6
prensa *(f.)* press, news, 2, 11
preocupado/a worried, 2
preocupante worrisome, 11
preocupar to worry, 4, 8

preocuparse to worry, 3; **no se preocupe** don't worry, 4
preparar to prepare, 4
presentación *(f.)* introduction, P
presentador/a *(m., f.)* presenter, 11
presentar to introduce, 12; **~ una película** to show a movie, 11
presión sanguínea *(f.)* blood pressure, 8
presionar to press, 6; to click with the (computer) mouse, 6
préstamo *(m.)* loan, 8; borrowing, 12
prestar to lend, 8
presupuesto *(m.)* budget, 8
prevenir to prevent, 10
primar to predominate, 9
primavera *(f.)* spring, 2
primer/o/a first, 4
primero *(m.)* first (day), 1; **~ que todo** first of all, 5
primo/a *(m., f.)* cousin, 5
prisa *(f.)* haste, hurry; **tener ~** to be in a hurry, 2
prisión *(f.)* prison, 11
probador de hombres/mujeres *(m.)* men's/women's dressing room, 7
probar (ue) to try, taste, 3; to prove, 11
probarse (ue) to try on, 3, 6; **voy a probármelo/la** I'm going to try it on, 7
problema *(m.)* problem, 1
procesador de comidas *(m.)* food processor, 9
producido/a por produced by, 11
producir (zc) to produce, 2
profesional professional, 1
profesor/a *(m., f.)* teacher, 1
profesorado *(m.)* faculty, 1
programa *(m.)* program, 1, 6; **~ de prevención contra el SIDA** AIDS prevention program, 11; **~ educativo** educational program, 11; **~ semanal** weekly program, 11; **~ social** social program, 11
programación matinal *(f.)* morning programming, 11
programador/a de computadoras *(m., f.)* computer programmer, 5
promedio *(m.)* average, 8
promocionarse to promote itself, 9
pronóstico del tiempo *(m.)* weather forecast, 2
propina *(f.)* tip, 3, 4
proporcionar to supply, 8
propósito *(m.)* resolution, 10; **a ~** by the way, 7
protagonista *(m., f.)* main character, 11
protector solar *(m.)* sunscreen lotion, 5
proteger to protect, 10
protegerse to protect onself, 5
próximo/a next, 4, 11
prueba *(f.)* test, exam, 8; proof, 9
psicología *(f.)* psychology, 1
psicólogo/a *(m., f.)* psychologist, 5
psicopedagogía *(f.)* psychology of teaching, 6
psicosis *(f.)* psychosis, 1
publicado/a published, 9
público/a public, 10
pueblo *(m.)* town, 12
puente *(m.)* bridge, 11
puerta *(f.)* door, 7; **~ de salida** departure gate, 5
puerto *(m.)* port, 7
puertorriqueño/a Puerto Rican, P
pues well, 12
puerco *(m.)* pig, 9
puesto *(m.)* position, 6; put, placed, 9
pulgada *(f.)* inch, 3
pulpo *(m.)* octopus, 3
pulsar to click on something, 6
pulsera *(f.)* bracelet, 8
punto *(m.)* dot, 5; degree, 8; **a ~ de** about to, 9; **en ~** exactly on the hour, 1
pupitre *(m.)* writing desk, 1

que than, 7; that, which, who, 10
¿Qué? ¡Qué! What, 1; **~ alivio!** What a relief!, 4; **~ fecha es hoy?** What is today's date?, 1; **~ gusto!** What a pleasure!, 4; **~ hambre!** I am very hungry!, 3; **~ hora es?** What time is it?, 1; **~ lástima!** What a pity!, Too bad!, 1; **~ nervios!** How frightening, 11; **~ quiere decir ... ?** What does . . . mean?, P; **~ susto!** What a scare!, 4; **~ tengan un buen viaje!** Have a nice trip!, 4; **~ tiempo hace?** What's the weather like?, 2
quebrar (ie) to break, 7
quechua *(m.)* Quechua language, 8
quedar to remain, 6; to be left over, 7
quedarle to fit someone, 7; **no ~ remedio a alguien** to have no choice, 12
quedarse to stay, 3; to remain behind, 6
quehaceres *(m. pl.)* chores, 9
quejarse to complain, 5
quemar to burn, 9
quemarse to burn, get a sunburn, 5
querer (ie) to want, 3
querido/a dear, 3
queso *(m.)* cheese, 3
quien(es) who, whom, 10
¿quién(es)? who?, 1
quilate *(m.)* karat, 8
química *(f.)* chemistry, 1
químico/a *(m., f.)* chemist, 5
quince fifteen, 1
quinceañero/a *(m., f.)* fifteen-year-old
quinientos five hundred, 3
quinto/a fifth, 4
quirófano *(m.)* operating room, 9
quisiera I would like, 3
quitarse (la ropa) to take off (one's clothes), 3
quizás maybe, perhaps, 8, 9

radio *(m.)* radio, 1, 7
radiografía *(f.)* x-ray, 8
raíz *(f.)* root, 6
rápidamente rapidly, 3
rápido/a fast, 1
raqueta *(f.)* racket, 6
raro/a strange, 2
rastro *(m.)* trace, 10
rata *(f.)* rat, 9
ratón *(m.)* mouse, 6, 9
rayas *(f. pl.)* stripes; **de ~** striped, 7
raza *(f.)* race, 12
razón *(f.)* reason; **tener ~** to be right, 2
reaccionar to react, 4
realista realistic, 1
realizador/a *(m., f.)* creator, 11
realizar to make, 3; to do, 12
rebaja *(f.)* discount, 8
rebanada *(f.)* slice, 8
rebotar to bounce, 12
recepción *(f.)* reception, 3
recepcionista *(m., f.)* receptionist, 3
receta *(f.)* prescription, 8
rechazado/a rejected, 11
rechazar to reject, 11
recibir to receive, 1, 6
recibo *(m.)* receipt, 7
recoger to pick up, 4
recomendar (ie) recommend, 3
recordar (ue) to remember, 3; **~ un hecho histórico** to remember a historic event, 10
recorrer to travel all around a place, 4; to tour, 11; **~ mucho camino** to come a long way, 12
recorrido *(m.)* route, 3
recreo *(m.)* recreation, 4
recuerdo *(m.)* memory, 5
recurrir a to turn to, 10
recursos hidroeléctricos naturales *(m. pl.)* natural hydroelectric resources, 9
red *(f.)* the net, Internet, 1; network, 6
reemplazar to replace, 9
refresco *(m.)* soft drink, 8
refrigerador/a *(m., f.)* refrigerator, 9
regalar to give a gift, 4
regañar to scold, 10
regatear to bargain, 8
regla *(f.)* ruler, 1; rule, 3
regular OK, P
relajación *(f.)* relaxation, 8
relajado/a relaxed, 8
religioso/a religious, 10
reloj *(m.)* watch, clock, 1, 8
remedio *(m.)* remedy, 8

renacentista *(adj.)* Renaissance, 4
rendimiento *(m.)* performance, 6
rendirse (i, i) to give in, 7
renunciar to quit (a job), 6
réplica *(f.)* replica, 10
repollo *(m.)* cabbage, 8
reportero/a *(m., f.)* reporter, 11
represa *(f.)* dam, 8
representación política *(f.)* political representation, 11
reseña *(f.)* critique, 11
resfriado *(m.)* cold; **estar ~** to have a cold, 8
residencia *(f.)* dormitory, 1
respetar to respect, 6
respirar to breathe, 8
responsabilidad *(f.)* responsibility, 6; **~ ecológica** *(f.)* ecological responsibility, 9
respuesta *(f.)* answer, 12
restaurante *(m.)* restaurant, 2
resuelto/a resolved, 9
retirar to withdraw money, 8
retrato *(m.)* portrait, 10
reunido/a reunited, 9
reusar to reuse, 9
revés *(m.)* back, reverse; **al ~** backwards, 12
revisar to check/examine, 8
revista *(f.)* magazine, 5
revoltillo *(m.)* scrambled eggs, 8
revolver (ue) to turn, 9
reyes *(m. pl.)* king and queen, 4
rezar to pray, 10
rico/a rich, 1; delicious, 3
ridículo/a ridiculous, 8; **es ~** it's ridiculous, 8
rienda suelta *(f.)* free rein, 11
río *(m.)* river, 7
rincón *(m.)* corner, 11
riqueza *(f.)* richness, 6; wealth, 9
ritmo *(m.)* rhythm, 6
rito *(m.)* ritual, 10
robo *(m.)* robbery, 4, 11
rodeado/a surrounded, 3
rodilla *(f.)* knee, 5
rogar (ue) to beg, 4; to plead, 7
rojo/a red, 1
romper to break, 7; **~ con** to break up with, 7
romper(se) (el brazo) to break (one's arm), 8
ropa *(f.)* clothing, 3; **~ de hombre/mujer** menswear/womenswear, 7; **~ interior** underwear, 7
ropero *(m.)* closet, 2
rosa *(f.)* pink, 1; rose, 9
rosado/a pink, 1
roto/a broken, torn, 9; **esta ~** it's ripped, 7
rubio/a light-complexioned, blonde, 1
rueda *(f.)* tire, 7; wheel, 10
ruido *(m.)* noise, 5
ruidazo *(m.)* loud noise, 5
ruinas *(f. pl.)* ruins, 12
ruso/a Russian, P

S

sábado *(m.)* Saturday, 1
saber to know, 2; to find out, 5; **no sé** I don't know, P
sabroso/a delicious, 9
sacar to take (away), 4; **~ dinero** to withdraw money, 8; **~ fotos** to take photos, 10; **~ la basura** to take out the garbage, 9; **~ la lengua** to stick out one's tongue, 8
saco *(m.)* blazer, suit jacket (for men), 7
sacrificio *(m.)* sacrifice, 10
sacudir to shake, 4 **; ~ los muebles** to dust the furniture, 9
sagrado/a sacred, 12
sal *(f.)* salt, 3
sala *(f.)* living room, 2; **~ de clase** classroom, 1; **~ de emergencia** emergency room, 8; **~ de espera** waiting room, 5
salado/a salty, 3
salario *(m.)* salary, 6
salida *(f.)* departure, 4
salir to leave, go, 2; **~ con destino a** to leave/depart with destination to, 2; **~ de** to leave from a place, 2; **~ limpio** to be cleared of blame, 12; **~ para** to leave for a place, 2
salitre *(m.)* salt residue, 8
salón de conferencias *(m.)* conference room, 3
salsa *(f.)* salsa music, 6
salto *(m.)* waterfall, 7
salud *(f.)* health; **tener buena/mala ~** to be in good/bad health, 8
salvadoreño/a Salvadoran, P
salvar to save, 9
sancocho *(m.)* chicken and meat soup, 7
sandalia *(f.)* sandal, 5, 7
sangrar to bleed, 8
sangre *(f.)* blood, 8
sanitario *(m.)* toilet, 9
sano/a healthy, 8
santuario *(m.)* altar, 12
sartén *(f.)* frying pan, 9
saxofón *(m.)* saxophone, 6
sazón *(f.)* flavoring, seasoning; **buena ~** tasty cooking, 9
secador de pelo *(m.)* hair dryer, 9
secadora *(f.)* clothes dryer, 9
secar la ropa to dry the clothes, 9
secarse to dry off, 3
secretario/a *(m., f.)* secretary, 5
secuencia *(f.)* sequence, 11
secuestrador/a *(m., f.)* kidnapper, 6
secuestro *(m.)* kidnapping, 6
sed *(f.)* thirst; **tener ~** to be thirsty, 2
sedentario/a sedentary, 8
seguir (i, i) to follow, 3; **~ derecho/recto** to go straight, 7
según according to, 4
segundo/a second, 4; **segunda clase** *(f.)* second class, 4
seguro/a sure, 2; **no estar ~** to be unsure, 8
seis six, 1
seiscientos six hundred, 3
sello *(m.)* (record) label, 6; hallmark, 10; stamp
selva *(f.)* jungle, 7; **~ tropical** rainforest, 7
semáforo *(m.)* stoplight, 7
semana *(f.)* week; **~ pasada** *(f.)* last week, 4; **el fin de ~ pasado** *(m.)* last weekend, 4; **Semana Santa** Holy Week, 10
sencillo/a simple, 3
sentar (ie) to seat someone; to place, 3
sentarse (ie) to sit down, 3, 6
sentir (ie, i) to feel, sense, perceive, 6; to be sorry, lament, regret, 8
sentirse (ie, i) to feel (*i.e.*, well, bad), 3, 6
señor *(m.)* gentleman, Mr., P, 1; lord, 12
señora *(f.)* lady, Mrs., P, 1
señorita *(f.)* young lady, Miss, Ms., P, 1
separado/a separated, 5; **estar ~** to be separated, 5
separador *(m.)* bookmark, 10
septiembre *(m.)* September, 1
séptimo/a seventh, 4
sequía *(f.)* drought, 9
ser to be, 1; **~ adulto** to be an adult, 5; **~ alérgico/a a...** to be allergic to . . . , 8; **~ chismoso/a** to gossip, 10; **~ mayor** to be older, 5; **~ menor** to be younger, 5; **~ soltero/a** to be single, 5
serio/a serious, 1
seropositivo/a HIV positive, 11
serpiente *(f.)* snake, 9
servicio *(m.)* service, 3; **servicios de salud** *(m. pl.)* health services, 11
servilleta *(f.)* napkin, 3
servir (i, i) to serve, 3; **¿En qué le puedo ~?** How can/may I help you ?, 3, 4, 7
sesenta sixty, 1
setecientos seven hundred, 3
setenta seventy, 1
sexto/a sixth, 4
si if; **~ me lo propongo** if I put my mind to it, 12; **~ no fuera por ti** if it weren't for you, 9
sí yes, 1
SIDA *(m.)* AIDS, 8, 11
siempre always, 3
sierra *(f.)* mountain range, 7
siete seven, 1
siglo *(m.)* century, 11
significar to mean, 6
silla *(f.)* chair, 1

sillón *(m.)* arm chair, 1
silvestre wild, 8
símbolo *(m.)* symbol, 10
simpático/a nice, friendly, 1
sin without, 4; **~ duda** without a doubt, 5; **~ embargo** nevertheless, 5; nonetheless, 12; **~ que** without, 9
sino but, rather, on the contrary, 10
sinónimo *(m.)* synonym, 12
síntoma *(m.)* symptom, 8
sintonizador *(m.)* tuner, 6
sistema *(m.)* system, 1
sitio *(m.)* site, 9; **~ favorito** bookmark, 10; **~ web** Web site, 1
sobre about, 3; over, on top of, 4
sobrepoblar (ue) to overpopulate, 9
sobrino/a *(m., f.)* nephew/niece, 5
sociedad *(f.)* society, 1
sociología *(f.)* sociology, 1
sofá *(m.)* sofa, 9
sol *(m.)* sun, 5; **hace ~** it's sunny, 2
solamente only, 4
solicitar (un trabajo/puesto) to apply (for a job), 6
solicitud *(f.)* application, 6
soltero/a *(m., f.)* single person, 4; **ser ~** to be single, 5
solución *(f.)* solution, 11
sombrero *(m.)* hat, 2, 7
sombrilla *(f.)* umbrella, 5
sometido/a bound, 11
sonar (ue) to ring, 6; to play, 6; to sound, 6
sonido *(m.)* sound, 11; **~ digital** *(m.)* digital sound, 6
sonrisa *(f.)* smile, 9
soñar to dream, 3
soñar con to dream about, 3
sopa *(f.)* soup, 3
soroche *(m.)* altitude sickness, 8
sorprender to surprise, 8
sótano *(m.)* basement, 3
subir to climb, go up, 1; **~ al tren** to board the train, 4; **~ por** to go up (a street), 7; **al ~** upon boarding, 5
subrayado/a underlined, 10
suceder to happen, 5; to occur, 11
sucio/a dirty/shady, 4; **esta ~** it's dirty, 7
sudadera *(f.)* sweat suit, 7
sudor *(m.)* sweat, 7
suegro/a *(m., f.)* father-/mother-in-law, 5
sueldo *(m.)* salary, 6; **~ mínimo** minimum wage, 11
suelo *(m.)* ground, 6
sueño *(m.)* dream, 1, 3; **tener ~** to be sleepy, 2
suerte *(f.)* luck; **mala ~** bad luck, 3
suéter *(m.)* sweater, 2; **~ de lana** wool sweater, 7
sugerir (ie, i) to suggest, 7
sujeto *(m.)* subject (of a sentence), 1
suicidio *(m.)* suicide, 11
sumamente very, 12
superastro *(m.)* superstar, 3
superficie *(f.)* surface, 6
supervisor/a *(m., f.)* supervisor, 5
suplicar to beg, 9
suponer to guess, 12
sur *(m.)* south, 4
surcar to go through, 3
sureste *(m.)* southeast, 4
suroeste *(m.)* southwest, 4
sustantivo *(m.)* noun, 5
sustentar to support, 10
susto *(m.)* scare; **¡Qué ~!** What a scare!, 4

T

tableta *(f.)* tablet, 8
tal vez maybe, perhaps, 8
talco *(m.)* powder, 7
talla *(f.)* size, 7
tamaño *(m.)* size, 3
también also, too, 3
tambor *(m.)* drum, 6
tampoco neither, either, 3
tan as; **~ ...como** as . . . as, 7; **~ pronto como** as soon as, 9
tanda *(f.)* set, 8
tanque de gasolina *(m.)* gas tank, 7
tanto so much, 9; **~ como** as much as, 7
tanto/a/os/as... como as much/many . . . as, 7
tapado/a covered, 5
tapar to cover, 9
tapas *(f. pl.)* appetizers (*Spain*), 3
tapete *(m.)* rug, small carpet, tapestry, 8
tapiz *(m.)* tapestry, 8
taquilla *(f.)* ticket window, 4
tardar en llegar/salir to take (too much) time to arrive/leave, 4
tarde *(f.)* afternoon, 1; **por/en la ~** in the afternoon, 1
tarjeta *(f.)* card; **~ de crédito** credit card, 2, 3; **~ de sonido** sound card, 6
tasa de cambio *(f.)* rate of exchange, 8
tatuaje *(m.)* tattoo, 8
taza *(f.)* cup, 3
té *(m.)* tea, 3
teatro *(m.)* theatre, 1
teclado *(m.)* keyboard, 6
tecnología *(f.)* technology, 9
tejedor/a *(m., f.)* weaver, 12
tejido *(m.)* weaving, 8; synthetic tissue, 11
teléfono *(m.)* telephone, 1
telenovela *(f.)* soap opera, 11
televidente *(m., f.)* TV viewer, 11, 12
televisar to televise, 11
televisión *(f.)* television, 1; **(cadena) de ~** cable TV, 11
televisor *(m.)* television set, 9
tema *(m.)* theme, 1
temer to fear, be afraid of, 8
temible fearsome, 7
temperatura *(f.)* temperature, 2
tempestad *(f.)* storm, 1
templado/a temperate, 2
temporada *(f.)* season, 3
tenedor *(m.)* fork, 3
tener to have, 2; **~ alergia a...** to be allergic to . . ., 8; **~ apetito** to have an appetite, 8; **~ buen/mal clima** to have a good/bad climate, 2; **~ buena/mala salud** to be in good/bad health, 8; **~ calor** to be hot, 2; **~ catarro** to have a cold, 8; **~ celos** to be jealous, 5; **~ cuidado** to be careful, 7; **~ dolor** to have pain, 8; **~ escalofríos** to shiver, have a chill, 8; **~ éxito** to be successful, 11; **~ frío** to be cold, 2; **~ ganas de** (+ *inf.*) to feel like (doing something), 2; **~ gripe** to have the flu, 8; **~ hambre** to be hungry, 2; **~ miedo (de)** to be afraid (of), 2; **~ náuseas** to be nauseous, 8; **~ prisa** to be in a hurry, 2; **~ que** to have to, 2; **~ razón** to be right, 2; **~ resfrío** to have a cold, 8; **~ sed** to be thirsty, 2; **~ sueño** to be sleepy, 2; **~ ... años** to be. . .years old, 2
tenis *(m.)* tennis, 6
tensión nerviosa *(f.)* nervous tension, 8
terapia *(f.)* therapy, 11
tercer/o/a third, 4
terminar to complete, finish, 1
ternera *(f.)* veal, 3
terraza *(f.)* terrace, 2
terremoto *(m.)* earthquake, 3, 12
terrestre (of) earth, earthly, 6
terrible terrible, 1; **es ~** it's terrible, 8
territorio *(m.)* territory, 12
tesoro *(m.)* treasure, 5
testigo *(m., f.)* witness, 10
textura *(f.)* texture, 10
tiempo *(m.)* time; **~ completo** full-time, 6; **~ parcial** part time, 6; **estar a ~** to be on time, 4, 5; **hace buen/mal ~** the weather is good/bad, 2; **¿Qué ~ hace?** What's the weather like?, 2
tienda *(f.)* store, 2
tierra *(f.)* Earth, 8; land, 12
tigre *(m.)* tiger, 9
tintorería *(f.)* dry cleaners, 7
tío/a *(m., f.)* uncle/aunt, 5
tiquete *(m.)* ticket, 4
tirar to throw, 4, 11
titulares *(m. pl.)* headlines, 1
tiza *(f.)* chalk, 1
toalla *(f.)* towel, 5
tobillo *(m.)* ankle, 8
tocar to play (an instrument); to touch, 1, 6
tocarle a uno to be one's turn, 11
todavía still, 3
todo/a everything, 3; **~ tipo (de)** all kinds (of), 6
todos/as everybody, all, 3; **todos los días**

every day, 3
tolerante tolerant, 1
tomar to take; **~ conciencia** to be(come) aware, 9; **~ el sol** to sunbathe, 5; **~ en cuenta** to take into account, 7; **~ fotos** to take photos/pictures, 10
tomate *(m.)* tomato, 3
tonto/a stupid, 1
toque *(m.)* touch, 7
torcerse (ue) to twist, 8
torre *(f.)* tower, 4
tortuga *(f.)* turtle, 5
toser to cough, 8
tostadita *(f.)* chip, 9
tostadora *(f.)* toaster, 9
tostones *(m. pl.)* fried plantains, 5
trabajador/a hard-working, 1; **~** *(m., f.)* worker, 5; **~ social** social worker, 11
trabajar to work, 1
trabajo *(m.)* labor, 4; work, position, 6; **~ social** social work, 1
tradicional conventional, 1
traición *(f.)* betrayal, 10
traicionar to betray, 9
traído/a brought, 9
traducir (zc) to translate, 2
traer to bring, 2; **~ buena suerte** to bring good luck, 10
tráfico de drogas *(m.)* drug trafficking, 11
traidor/a *(m., f.)* traitor, 10
traje *(m.)* suit, 7; **~ de baño** bathing suit, 2
tranquilízate calm down, 10
transgénico/a transgenic, 11
transmitir to transmit a TV/radio program, 11
transparente transparent, 1
transplantado/a transplanted, 9
tras after, 10
tratar(se) de to deal with, be about, 1, 11
trece thirteen, 1
treinta thirty, 1
tren *(m.)* train, 3; **~ interurbano** commuter train, 4
trenza *(f.)* braid, 7
tres three, 1
trescientos three hundred, 3
triste sad, 2
tristeza *(f.)* sadness, 5
triturar to grind, 9
triunfar to succeed, 11
trombón *(m.)* trombone, 6
trompeta *(f.)* trumpet, 6
truco *(m.)* trick, 12
tulipán *(m.)* tulip, 9
turno *(m.)* turn, 9
turquesa *(f.)* turquoise, 8

U

ubicación *(f.)* location, 6
último/a last, final; **por último** finally, 5
un rato a little while, 9
unas veces sometimes, 5
único/a only, 3; **lo único** the only thing, 9
unidad *(f.)* unit, 6
unido/a united, 5
uniforme *(m.)* uniform, 6
unir to combine, 6; to unite, 12
universidad *(f.)* university, 1
uno/a one, 1; **el uno al otro** each other, 6
urgente urgent, 7; **es ~** it's urgent, 7
urna sellada *(f.)* sealed box, 11
uruguayo/a Uruguayan, P
usar to use, 1
usuario/a user, 6
utensilio *(m.)* utensil, tool, 9
uva *(f.)* grape, 3
¡Uy! Jss!, 6

V

vacaciones *(f. pl.)* vacation, 4; **estar de ~** to be on vacation, 4; **ir(se) de ~** to go on vacation, 4
vacío/a empty, 7
vagón *(m.)* train car, 4
valentía *(f.)* bravery, 9
valer to be worth, 11; **~ la pena** to be worthwhile, 5; **no vale la pena** it's not worth it, 4
valioso/a valuable, 12
valle *(m.)* valley, 7
valorar to value, 4
vámonos let's go, 4
vapor *(m.)* mist, 3; **al ~** steamed, 8
vaquero/a cowboy/cowgirl, 7
varios/as several, 3
vasco/a Basque, 4
vasija *(f.)* bowl/pot, 10
vaso *(m.)* glass, 3
veces *(f. pl.)* times (occasions); **a ~** sometimes, at times, 3; **otras ~** other times, 5
vecindario *(m.)* neighborhood, 5
vecino/a *(m., f.)* neighbor, 5
vegetales *(m. pl.)* vegetables, 8; **~ de hoja** leafy greens, 8
veinte twenty, 1
veinticinco twenty-five, 1
veinticuatro twenty-four, 1
veintidós twenty-two, 1
veintinueve twenty-nine, 1
veintiocho twenty-eight, 1
veintiséis twenty-six, 1
veintisiete twenty-seven, 1
veintitrés twenty-three, 1
veintiuno twenty-one, 1
vela *(f.)* candle, 3, 8
veleta *(f.)* weathervane, 4
vencer to conquer, defeat, 12
vendedor/a *(m., f.)* salesperson, 5, 8; **~ ambulante** street vendor, 8
vender to sell, 1, 4
venezolano/a Venezuelan, P
venir to come, 2
venta *(f.)* sale, 7
ventaja *(f.)* advantage, 6
ventana *(f.)* window, 1
ventanita *(f.)* little window, 7
ventoso/a windy, 8
ver to see, 2
verano *(m.)* summer, 2
verdad *(f.)* truth, 8; **es ~** it's true, 8; **no es ~** it's not true, 8
verdadero/a true, 4
verde green, 1
vestido *(m.)* dress, 7
vestir (i, i) to dress, 6
vestirse (i, i) to get dressed, 3, 6
veterinario/a *(m., f.)* veterinarian, 5
vez *(f.)* time (occasion); **a la ~** at the same time, 3; **de ~ en cuando** from time to time, 11; **de una ~** once and for all, 5
vía *(f.)* track, 3
viajar to travel, 1, 4
viaje *(m.)* trip, 3; **¡Buen/Feliz ~!** Have a nice trip!, 4; **¡Que tengan un buen ~!** Have a nice trip!, 4
víbora *(f.)* snake, 9
video digital *(m.)* digital video/movies, 6
videoteca video store, 11
viejo/a old (for a person or thing), 1, 7
viento *(m.)* wind; **hace (mucho/un poco de) ~** it's (very/a little) windy, 2
viernes *(m.)* Friday, 1
vigía *(m.)* watchman, lookout, 7
vigilancia del vecindario *(f.)* neighborhood watch, 11
vigilar to watch, 4, 8
villano/a *(m., f.)* villain, 11
vino tinto/blanco *(m.)* red/white wine, 3
violento/a violent, 11
violeta *(f.)* violet, 9
violín *(m.)* violin, 6
visitar to visit, 1
víspera *(f.)* the day before, 10
vista *(f.)* view, 4
vistazo *(m.)* glimpse, 12
visto/a seen, 9
vivir to live, 1
volante *(m.)* steering wheel, 7
volcán *(m.)* volcano, 7
volibol *(m.)* volleyball, 1
volumen *(m.)* volume, 3
voluntad *(f.)* will, 10
volver (ue) to come back, return, 3
vomitar to vomit, 8

vuelo *(m.)* flight, 4
vuelto/a returned, 9

Y

y and, 1
ya now, already, yet, 5, 10; **~ hecho/a** ready made, 8; **¡~ lo verán!** you'll see!, 8
yerno *(m.)* son-in-law, 5
yeso *(m.)* cast, 8
yogur *(m.)* yogurt, 8
yuca *(f.)* yucca, 5
yucateco/a from the Yucatan, 12

Z

zamarros *(m. pl.)* heavy pants, 7
zanahoria *(f.)* carrot, 3
zapatería *(f.)* shoe store, 7
zapatos *(m. pl.)* shoes, 7; **~ de tacón alto/bajo** high-heeled/low-heeled shoes, 7; **~ de tenis** sneakers, 7
zapoteca Zapotec, 2
zócalo *(m.)* city square/plaza, 2
zona central *(f.)* central zone, 12
zorro *(m.)* fox, 9
zumo *(m.)* juice (*Spain*), 3

English-Spanish Vocabulary

A

a un/a
about sobre, 3, 4; **~ to** a punto de, 4, 9
above encima de, arriba de, 4; por encima de, 9
abstract abstracto/a, 10
academic subject materia *(f.)*, 1
accelerate acelerar, 7
acceptable aceptable; **not ~** deficiente, 3
accessories accesorios *(m. pl.)*, 7
accomplish alcanzar, 11
accomplishment logro *(m.)*, 8
according to según, 4; conforme a, 6
account cuenta, *(f.)*, 8; **checking ~** cuenta corriente, 8; **savings ~** cuenta de ahorros, 8
accountant contador/a *(m., f.)*, 5
achieve lograr, 7, 11
achievement logro *(m.)*, 10, 11
acquire adquirir (ie), 6
across from enfrente de, 4
act actuar, 10; hecho *(m.)*, 12; **delinquent ~** acto delictivo *(m.)*, 11
acting actuación *(f.)*, 11
action *(adj.)* de acción, 11
active activo/a, 8
activity actividad *(f.)*, 1
actor actor *(m.)*, actriz *(f.)*, 11
add añadir, agregar, 9
addiction adicción *(f.)*, 11
address dirección *(f.)*, 3, 7
adequately adecuadamente, 9
adjective adjetivo *(m.)*, 5
adolescence adolescencia *(f.)*, 5
adolescent adolescente *(m., f.)*, 11
adore adorar, 10
adult adulto/a *(m., f.)*, 5; **to be an ~** ser adulto, 5
adulthood edad adulta *(f.)*, 5
advantage ventaja *(f.)*, 6
advice consejo *(m.)*, 11
advise aconsejar, 7
afraid asustado/a; **to be ~ (of)** tener miedo (de), 2
affair asunto *(m.)*, 4
after después, 3, 4; después (de) que, 9; tras, 10
afterwards después, 4
against contra, 3; **to be ~** estar en contra de, 10
age edad *(f.)*, 4
ago hace + *time* + que + *preterite*, 6
agree ponerse de acuerdo; **I agree** estoy de acuerdo con, 4
agreed de acuerdo, 11
AIDS SIDA *(m.)*, 8, 11; **~ prevention program** programa de prevención contra el SIDA *(m.)*, 11
air bag bolsa de aire *(f.)*, 7
air conditioning aire acondicionado *(m.)*, 7
airport aeropuerto *(m.)*, 2
alone a solas, 2
all todo/a; **~ kinds (of)** todo tipo (de), 6; **~ Saints Day** Fiesta de Todos los Santos *(f.)*, 10
allergic alérgico/a; **to be ~ to . . .** ser alérgico/a a ..., tener alergia a ..., 8
alleviate (pain or symptoms) aliviar, 8
alligator caimán *(m.)*, 9
aloe vera penca sávila *(f.)*, 8
alpha wave onda alfa *(f.)*, 8
already ya, 10
also también, 3
altar santuario *(m.)*, 12
although aunque, 5
altitude sickness soroche *(m.)*, 8
always siempre, 3
amaranth amaranto *(m.)*, 8
among entre, 3, 4
amuse (someone) divertir (ie) (a alguien), 6
anatomy anatomía *(f.)*, 1
ancestor antepasado *(m.)*, 12
and y, e, 1; más, 1
angry enojado/a, 2; **to be ~** estar enojado/a, 8; **to get ~** enojarse
anguish angustia *(f.)*, 11
animal animal *(m.)*; **stuffed ~** muñeco de felpa *(m.)*, 9
animation animación *(f.)*, 11
ankle tobillo *(m.)*, 8
announce anunciar, 11
announcer anunciador/a *(m., f.)*, locutor/a *(m., f.)*, 11
annoy molestar, 4
anonymity anonimato *(m.)*, 11
answer contestar, 4, 6; respuesta *(f.)*, 12
answering machine contestador automático *(m.)*, 10
anthropology antropología *(f.)*, 1
antibiotic antibiótico *(m.)*, 8
antidote antídoto *(m.)*, 8
antique store/dealer anticuario *(m.)*, 11
anxiety angustia *(f.)*, 10
anxious ansioso/a, 11
anything algo *(m.)*, 3
anyway de todos modos, 4
apartment apartamento *(m.)*, 2
appear aparecer (zc), 5, 11; **~ to be** parecer (zc), 4
appetizer entremés *(m.)*, 3; tapa *(f.)* *(Spain)*, 3
apple manzana *(f.)*, 3
applicant aspirante *(m., f.)*, 6
application solicitud *(f.)*, 6
apply (for a job) solicitar (un trabajo/puesto), 6
appointment cita *(f.)*, 8
approach acercar(se), 11
April abril, 1; **~ Fool's Day** Día de los Inocentes *(m.)*, 10
archaeology arqueología *(f.)*, 1
architect arquitecto/a *(m., f.)*, 5
architecture arquitectura *(f.)*, 10
archive (document collection) archivo *(m.)*, 4
area entorno *(m.)*, 3
Argentinean argentino/a, P
arm brazo *(m.)*, 5
armchair sillón *(m.)*, 1
army ejército *(m.)*, 9
around por, 6
arranged arreglado/a, 5
arrest arrestar, 11, 12
arrival llegada *(f.)*, 4
arrive llegar, 1; **~ late** llegar tarde, 4; **~ on time** llegar a tiempo, 4
arrogant arrogante, 1
art arte *(m.)*, 1; **contemporary ~** arte contemporáneo, 10; **modern ~** arte moderno, 10
artisan artesano/a *(m., f.)*, 10
artist artista *(m., f.)*, 1, 5, 10
as tan, 7; **~ . . . as** tan... como, tanto/a/os/as... como, 7; **~ long as** mientras que, 9; **~ much as** tanto como, 7; **~ soon as** en cuanto, luego que, tan pronto como, 9; **~ soon as possible** cuanto antes, 11
ash ceniza *(f.)*, 10
ask (a question) preguntar, 4; **~ (for)** pedir (i, i), 3; **~ for special favors** pedir favores especiales, 10
aspirin aspirina *(f.)*, 8
assassinate asesinar, 11
assassination asesinato *(m.)*, 11
assure asegurar, 8
asterisk asterisco *(m.)*, 11
astonished asombrado/a, 9; **to be ~** asombrarse, 11
astronomer astrónomo/a *(m., f.)*, 12
at en, 4; **~ a distance** a lo lejos, 7; **~ last** por fin, 5; **~ the same time** a la vez, 3;

at *(continued)*
~ this moment en este momento, 3; **~ this very moment** ahora mismo, 3; **~ your service** a sus órdenes, 3
athlete atleta *(m., f.)*, 5; deportista *(m., f.)*, 6
ATM machine cajero automático *(m.)*, 8
atom átomo *(m.)*, 1
atmosphere ambiente *(m.)*, 6
attend (a class) asistir a, 1
attract atraer, 10; **~ attention** llamar la atención, 8
attractive llamativo/a, 7
August agosto, 1
aunt tía *(f.)*, 1, 5
authentic auténtico/a, 10
autumn otoño *(m.)*, 2
average medio/a, 2; media *(f.)*, 6; promedio *(m.)*, 8; **~ temperature** temperatura media *(f.)*, 2
available disponible, 6
avoid evitar, 7, 8
award entregar, premiar, 12
aware consciente; **to become ~** tomar conciencia, 9

B

baby boy/girl bebé *(m., f.)*, 5; niño/a *(m., f.)*, 5
bacillus bacilo *(m.)*, 8
back espalda *(f.)*, 5; **~ door** puerta de atrás *(f.)*, 8
backpack mochila *(f.)*, 1
backwards al revés, 12
bad malo/a, 1; mal *(adv.)*, 7; **~ luck** mala suerte *(f.)*, 3; **it's ~** es malo, 8
bag bolsa *(f.)*, 7, 8
bake hornear, 9
baked al horno, 8; **~ clay** barro cocido *(m.)*, 9
balcony balcón *(m.)*, 2
ball balón *(m.)*, 6; pelota *(f.)*, 6
ballad balada *(f.)*, 6
balm bálsamo *(m.)*, 8
banana plátano *(m.)*, 3; banano *(m.)*, 8; **~ tree** platanera *(f.)*, 9
band conjunto *(m.)*, 6
bank banco *(m.)*, 2
barbecue churrasco *(m.)*, 8
bargain regatear, 8
bark ladrar, 5
Baroque barroco/a, 2
baseball béisbol *(m.)*, 6
based basado/a, 9
basement sótano *(m.)*, 3
basin cuenca *(f.)*, 8
basketball básquetbol *(m.)*, baloncesto *(m.)*, 6
Basque vasco/a, 4
bat *(sports)* bate *(m.)*, 6; murciélago *(m.)*, 12
bathing suit traje de baño *(m.)*, 2
bathroom cuarto de baño *(m.)*, 2
bathtub bañera *(f.)*, 2
battery batería, pila *(f.)*, 7
bay bahía *(f.)*, 6
be ser, 1; estar, 2; **~ able to** poder (ue), 3; **~ about** tratar de, 11; **~ afraid (of)** tener miedo (de), 2; **~ against** estar en contra, 10; **~ allergic to . . .** ser alérgico/a a..., tener alergia a, 8; **~ an adult** ser adulto, 5; **~ angry** estar enojado/a, 8; **~ appetizing** apetecer (zc), 7; **~ astonished** asombrarse, 11; **~ aware** tomar conciencia, 9; **~ born** nacer (zc), 5; **~ careful** tener cuidado, 7; **~ cleared of blame** salir limpio, 12; **~ cold** tener frío, 2; **~ divorced** estar divorciado/a, 5; **~ dizzy** estar mareado/a, 8; **~ familiar with** conocer (zc), 2; **~ happy** alegrarse 5, 8; estar contento/a de, 8; **~ hot** tener calor, 2; **~ hungry** tener hambre, 2; **~ in a hurry** tener prisa, 2; **~ in charge of** estar a cargo de, 7, 11; **~ in danger** estar en peligro, 2; **~ in good/bad health** tener buena/mala salud, 8; **~ in love** estar enamorado/a, 5; **~ in style** estar de moda, 7; **~ in the way** estorbar, 9; **~ jealous** tener celos, 5; **~ late** estar atrasado/a, 4; **~ left over** quedar, 7; **~ left (to do)** faltar, 4; **~ married** estar casado/a, 5; **~ mistaken** equivocarse, 6; **~ nauseous** tener náuseas, estar mareado/a, 8; **~ of concern** importar, 4; **~ of interest** interesar, 4; **~ older** ser mayor, 5; **~ on time** estar a tiempo, 5; **~ one's turn to** tocarle a uno/a, 11; **~ pregnant** estar embarazada, 8; **~ quiet** callarse, 11; **~ ready** estar listo/a, 3; **~ right** tener razón, 2; **~ separated** estar separado/a, 5; **~ single** ser soltero/a, 5; **~ sleepy** tener sueño, 2; **~ sorry** sentir (ie, i), lamentar, 8; **~ successful** tener éxito, 11; **~ thirsty** tener sed, 2; **~ unsure** no estar seguro/a, 8; **~ worth** valer, 11; **~ worthwhile** valer la pena, 5; **~ wrong** estar equivocado/a, 6; **~. . . years old** tener ... años, 2; **~ younger** ser menor, 5
beach playa *(f.)*, 2
beachball balón *(m.)*, 5
bean frijol *(m.)*, grano *(m.)*, 8
bear oso *(m.)*, 9
beat batir, 9
beautiful bello/a, 10; **very ~** bellísimo/a, 5
beauty belleza *(f.)*, 5
because porque; **~ of** debido a, 3
become ponerse, 6; **~ +** *profession* hacerse + *profession*, 5; **~ aware of** darse cuenta de, 6; **~ happy** alegrarse, 6
bed cama *(f.)*, 1, 3
bedroom dormitorio *(m.)*, alcoba *(f.)*, 2
beef carne de vaca (res) *(f.)*, 3
beep (the horn) pitar, 7
beer cerveza *(f.)*, 3
before antes de, 4; antes (de) que, 9
beg rogar (ue), 4, 7; suplicar, 9
begin comenzar (ie), empezar (ie), 3
behavior comportamiento *(m.)*, 9
behind detrás de, 4
believe creer, 1
bellhop botones *(m.)*, 3
belong to pertenecer (zc), 12
below debajo de, 4
belt correa *(f.)*, 10; **leather ~** cinturón de cuero *(m.)*, 7
beside al lado de, 4
besides además de, 3
bet apuesta *(f.)*, 5
betray engañar, 6; traicionar, 9
betrayal traición *(f.)*, 10
better mejor, 3, 7
between entre, 4
big grande, 1; amplio/a, 2
bike bicicleta *(f.)*, 3
biking ciclismo *(m.)*, 6
bill cuenta *(f.)*, 3; billete *(m.)*, 8
biology biología *(f.)*, 1
bird pájaro *(m.)*, 9; ave (el) *(f.)*, 7
birth parto *(m.)*; nacimiento *(m.)*, 10
birthday cumpleaños *(m.)*, 1
bite morder (ue), 5
bitter amargo/a, 3
black negro/a, 1; **~ and white** en blanco y negro, 10; **~ pepper** pimienta *(f.)*, 3
blackboard pizarra *(f.)*, 1
blazer saco *(m.)*, 7
bleed sangrar, 8
blender licuadora *(f.)*, 9
block cuadra *(f.)*, manzana *(f.)*, 7
blood sangre *(f.)*, 8; **~ pressure** presión sanguínea arterial *(f.)*, 8
bloom floración *(f.)*, 9; florecer (zc), 10
blond rubio/a, 1
blouse blusa *(f.)*, 7; **silk ~** blusa de seda, 7
blow golpe *(m.)*, 10
blue azul, 1
board (the train) subir (al tren), 4
boarding house pensión *(f.)*, 1
boat barco *(m.)*, 3
boil hervir (ie, i), 9
Bolivian boliviano/a, P
bone hueso *(m.)*, 8
book libro *(m.)*, 1
bookbag mochila *(f.)*, 1
bookmark separador *(m.)*, indicador *(m.)*, sitio favorito *(m.)*, 10
bookshelf estante *(m.)*, 1
bookstore librería *(f.)*, 2, 7
boots botas *(f. pl.)*, 2
border borde *(m.)*, 3; límite *(m.)*, 7
boring aburrido/a, 1
borrow pedir (i, i) prestado, 8

borrowing préstamo *(m.)*, 11
boss jefe/a *(m., f.)*, 4
both ambos/as *(m., f.)*, 6
bother molestar, 4, 8
bounce rebotar, 12
bound sometido/a, 11
bowl vasija *(f.)*, 10
box caja *(f.)*; **sealed ~** urna sellada *(f.)*, 11
boxing boxeo *(m.)*, 6
boy chico *(m.)*, 1; muchacho, *(m.)*, niño *(m.)*, 5
boyfriend novio *(m.)*, 1
bracelet pulsera *(f.)*, 8
braid trenza *(f.)*, 7
brain cerebro *(m.)*, 8
brake freno *(m.)*, 7
bravery valentía *(f.)*, 9
Brazilian brasileño/a, P
bread pan *(m.)*, 3; **~ bakery** panadería *(f.)*, 3
break descomponerse, 5; quebrar (ie), romper, 7; **~ (one's arm)** romper(se) (el brazo) 8; **~ up with** romper con, 7
breakfast desayuno *(m.)*, 3; **to have ~** desayunar, 3; **with ~** con desayuno, 3; **with ~ and lunch** con media pensión, 3
breast (of a bird) pechuga *(f.)*, 8
breathe respirar, 8
brick ladrillo *(m.)*, 2
bridge puente *(m.)*, 11
briefcase maletín *(m.)*, 1
bring traer, 2; **~ good luck** traer buena suerte 10
broadcasting station emisora *(f.)*, 11
broccoli bróculi *(m.)*, 8
brochure folleto *(m.)*, 4
broiled asado/a, 9
broiler asador *(m.)*, 9
broken roto/a, 9
bronze bronce *(m.)*, 10
brooch prendedor *(m.)*, 8
broom escoba *(f.)*, 9
brother hermano *(m.)*, 1, 5; **~ in-law** cuñado *(m.)*, 5
brought traído/a, 9
brown café, marrón, 1
browser navegador *(m.)*, 1
brush cepillarse, 3; pincel *(m.)*, 10
bucket cubeta *(f.)*, 7
buckle up (seat belt) abrocharse (el cinturón), 7
buddy compadre *(m.)*, 11
budget presupuesto *(m.)*, 8
build construir, 10; **~ sand castles** hacer castillos de arena, 5
builder constructor/a *(m., f.)*, 12
building edificio *(m.)*, 2
bureau aparador *(m.)*, 9
burn quemar, 9
bus autobús *(m.)*, 3; **~ stop** parada de autobús *(f.)*, 2
bush arbusto *(m.)*, 8
business negocio *(m.)*, 4, 6
businessman/woman hombre/mujer de negocios *(m., f.)*, 6
busy ocupado/a, 7
but pero, 10; sino, 10
butter mantequilla *(f.)*, 8
butterfly mariposa *(f.)*, 9
button botón *(m.)*, 6
buy comprar 1
by por, para, 6; **~ hand** a mano, 10; **~ mail** por correo, 8; **~ means of** a través de, 6; **~ the way** a propósito, 7

C

cabbage repollo *(m.)*, 8
cabinet gabinete *(m.)*, estantería *(f.)*, 9
cable cable *(m.)*, 11; **~ TV** televisión (cadena) de cable *(f.)*, 11
cadaver cadáver *(m.)*, 1
cake bizcocho, pastel *(m.)*, 3
calabash calabaza *(f.)*, 12
calculator calculadora *(f.)*, 1
calendar calendario *(m.)*, 1
call llamar, 1
calm calmado/a, 2; **~ down** cálmate, 3; tranquilízate, 10
calorie caloría *(f.)*, 8
camera cámara *(f.)*, 10
campaign campaña *(f.)*, 9
Canadian canadiense *(m., f.)*, P
canary canario *(m.)*, 5; **the ~ Islands** Las Canarias *(f. pl.)*, 11
candle vela *(f.)*, 3, 8
canyon cañón *(m.)*, 7
cap gorra *(f.)*, 2, 6
capable capaz, 12
capsule cápsula *(f.)*, 8
car coche *(m.)*, 3; auto(móvil) *(m.)*, carro *(m.)*, 7
careful cuidadoso/a; **to be ~** tener cuidado, 7
carnation clavel *(m.)*, 9
carnival Carnaval *(m.)*, 10
carpet tapete *(m.)*, 8
carpenter carpintero/a *(m., f.)*, 5
carrot zanahoria *(f.)*, 3
carry llevar, 1
cash moneda en efectivo *(f.)*, 8
cashier caja *(f.)*, 8; cajero/a *(m., f.)*, 8
cast yeso *(m.)*, 8
cat gato/a *(m., f.)*, 5
Catalan catalán/ana, 4
catastrophe catástrofe *(f.)*, 10
catchy pegajoso/a, 6
cattle ganado *(m.)*, 8
cave caverna *(f.)*, 10
cayman caimán *(m.)*, 9
cedar cedro *(m.)*, 9
celebrate celebrar, festejar, 10
celery apio *(m.)*, 3
central zone zona central *(f.)*, 12
century siglo *(m.)*, 8, 11
ceramics cerámica *(f.)*, 10
ceremony ceremonia *(f.)*, 10
certain cierto/a, 8; **it's not ~** no es cierto, 8
certainty certeza *(f.)*, 8
chain cadena *(f.)*, 8, 11
chair silla *(f.)*, 1
chalk tiza *(f.)*, 1
chalkboard pizarra *(f.)*, 1
challenge desafiar, 11
change cambio *(m.)*, 8
channel cadena *(f.)*, el canal *(m.)*, 11
chapel capilla *(f.)*, 2
charge cobrar, 7, 8; **~ up one's batteries** ponerse las pilas, 11
check cuenta *(f.)*, 3; revisar, 8; **certified ~** cheque certificado (*m.*), 8; **~ in luggage** facturar el equipaje, 5
checking account cuenta corriente *(f.)*, 8
cheese queso *(m.)*, 3
chef cocinero/a *(m., f.)*, 5
chemist químico/a *(m., f.)*, 5
chemistry química *(f.)*, 1
chest pecho *(m.)*, 5; **~ of drawers** cómoda *(f.)*, 9
chicken pollo *(m.)*, 3; **~ and meat soup** sancocho *(m.)*, 7
chickpeas garbanzos *(m. pl.)*, 9
child niño/a *(m., f.)*, 1, 5; chico/a *(m., f.)*, 5
childhood niñez *(f.)*, 5
children niños *(m. pl.)*, 1
Chilean chileno/a, P
Chinese chino/a, P; (*lang.*) chino *(m.)*, 1
chip tostadita *(f.)*, 9
chocolate chocolate, cacao *(m.)*, 12
chop picar, 9
chores quehaceres *(m. pl.)*, 9
chorus coro *(m.)*, 10
Christmas Navidad *(f.)*, 10; **~ Eve** Nochebuena *(f.)*, 10
chronicle crónica *(f.)*, 11
church iglesia *(f.)*, 2
city ciudad *(f.)*, 2; **~ square** plaza *(f.)*, 2, zócalo *(m.)*, *(Mex.)* 2
clarinet clarinete *(m.)*, 6
class clase *(f.)*, 1; **coach ~** clase turística *(f.)*, 5
classic art arte clásico *(m.)*, 10
classmate compañero/a de clase *(m., f.)*, 1
classroom sala de clase *(f.)*, 1
clay barro (*m.*), 9, 10; arcilla *(f.)*, 10; **baked/glazed ~** barro cocido/vidriado (*m.*), 9
clean (the room) ordenar (el cuarto), 9
clear (up) aclarar, 11; **it's ~** está despejado, 2; **that's ~** eso sí que está claro, 3

clerk dependiente *(m., f.)*, 7
clever ingenioso/a, 10
click with the mouse (computer) presionar, pulsar, hacer clic, 6
climate clima *(m.)*, 1
climb subir, 1
clock reloj *(m.)*, 1, 8
close cerrar (ie), 3, 6; **~ to** cerca de, junto a, 4
closed cerrado/a, 3
closet ropero *(m.)*, armario *(m.)*, 2
cloth paño *(m.)*, 7
clothes dryer secadora *(f.)*, 9
clothing ropa *(f.)*, 3
cloud nube *(f.)*, 8
cloudy nublado; **it's ~** está nublado, 2
club palo *(m.)*, 6
clue pista *(f.)*; **I haven't got a ~** ni idea, 4
coach class clase turística *(f.)*, 5
coast costa *(f.)*, 7; litoral *(m.)*, 8
coat abrigo *(m.)*, 2, 7
codex códice *(m.)*, 2, 12
coffee café *(m.)*, 3; **~ maker** cafetera *(f.)*, 9; **~ table** mesita *(f.)*, 9
coincidence casualidad *(f.)*, 11
cold catarro *(m.)*, 8; **it's ~** hace frío, 2; **to have a ~** tener catarro/resfrío, 8; estar resfriado/a, 8; **to be ~** tener frío, 2
collector coleccionista *(m., f.)*, 10, 11
Colombian colombiano/a, P
color en color(es), 10; **primary ~** color primario *(m.)*, 10; **secondary ~** color secundario *(m.)*, 10
column columna *(f.)*, 11
comb one's hair peinarse, 3
combine unir, 6
come venir, 2; **~ a long way** recorrer mucho camino, 12; **~ back** volver (ue), 3; **~ near/close** avecinar, arrimarse, 11
comedy película cómica, 11
comfort consolar (ue), 6; comodidad *(f.)*, 6
comission comisión *(f.)*, 8
commemorate conmemorar 10
commemoration conmemoración *(f.)*, 10
commentator comentador/a *(m., f.)*, 11
common común, 12
commuter train tren interurbano *(m.)*, 4
compact disc disco compacto *(m.)*, 6
company compañía *(f.)*, empresa *(f.)*, 6
complain quejarse, 5
complete terminar, 1
compose componer, 10
composition composición *(f.)*, 10
compromised comprometido/a, 12
computer computadora *(f.)*, 1; **~ file** archivo *(m.)*, 6; **~ programmer** programador/a de computadoras *(m., f.)*, 5
concentrate concentrarse, 5
concert concierto *(m.)*, 10
concierge conserje *(m., f.)*, 3
conceived engendrado/a, 10
conclude concluir, 7
condor cóndor *(m.)*, 9
conference congreso *(m.)*, 3; **~ room** salón de conferencias *(m.)*, 3
confirmation confirmación *(f.)*, 3; **Here is my ~** Aquí tiene mi confirmación, 3
confront enfrentar, 11
conjugate conjugar, 3
connect enlazar, 3
connection lazo *(m.)*, 12
conquer vencer, 12
conquest conquista *(f.)*, 12
consequences consecuencias *(f. pl.)*, 9
conserve conservar, 9
construct construir, 10
Construction En obras, 7
consume consumir, 8
consumption consumo *(m.)*, 9, 11
contaminate contaminar, 9
contemporary art arte contemporáneo *(m.)*, 10
content contento/a, 2; contenido *(m.)*, 11
contest concurso *(m.)*, 5
contour orografía *(f.)*, 3
contrast contraste *(m.)*, 10
convenient conveniente, 1
conventional tradicional, 1
convert convertir (ie, i), 11
cook cocinar, 9; cocinero/a *(m., f.)*, 5
cooked cocido/a, 8
cookie galleta *(f.)*, 3
cooking cocina *(f.)*, 2; **tasty ~** buena sazón *(f.)*, 9
cool enfriar, 9; **it's ~** hace fresco, 2
copper cobre *(m.)*, 8
copy copiar, 6
cordless inalámbrico/a, 6
corn maíz *(m.)*, 9; **~ on the cob** mazorca *(f.)*, elote *(m.) (Mex.)*, 9
corner esquina *(f.)*, 7; rincón *(m.)*, 11
corrected corregido/a, 12
cosmetics cosméticos *(m. pl.)*, 7
cost costar (ue), 3; **How much does it ~?** ¿Cuánto cuesta/vale?, 8; **How much does . . . ~?** ¿Cuánto cuesta...?, 8
Costa Rican costarricense *(m., f.)*, P
costume disfraz *(m.)*, 10; **~ jewelry** joyas de fantasía *(f. pl.)*, 8
cotton shirt camisa de algodón *(f.)*, 7
cough toser, 8
counsel aconsejar, 7
counselor consejero/a *(m., f.)*, 5
count contar (ue), 3; **~ on** contar con, 7
counter mostrador *(m.)*, 5, 9
country patria *(f.)*, 11
countryside campo *(m.)*, 7
court cancha *(f.)*, 6
courtship noviazgo *(m.)*, 3
cousin primo/a *(m., f.)*, 5
cover cubrir, 7; tapar, 9
covered tapado/a, 5; cubierto/a, 7, 9
cowboy/girl vaquero/a, 7; **~ boots** botas de vaquero *(f. pl.)*, 7
crab cangrejo *(m.)*, 3
crafts artesanía *(f.)*, 10
crash choque *(m.)*, 7
create crear, 10
creator realizador/a *(m., f.)*, 11
credit card tarjeta de crédito *(f.)*, 2, 3
crime crimen *(m.)*, 11
criticism crítica *(f.)*, 11
criticize criticar, 11
critique reseña *(f.)*, 11
cross cruzar, 7; cruz *(f.)*, 10
crossed cruzado/a, 5
crown corona *(f.)*, 12
Cuban cubano/a, P; **~ American** cubanoamericano/a, P
cucumber pepino *(m.)*, 3
cuisine cocina *(f.)*, 3
cultivate cultivar, 12
cultural group grupo cultural *(m.)*, 12
cup taza *(f.)*, 3
cure curar, 8; cura *(f.)*, 11
current actual, 12
currently actualmente, 10
curtains cortinas *(f. pl.)*, 9
custom costumbre *(f.)*, 3
customer cliente *(m., f.)*, 7
customs aduana *(f.)*, 5; **~ agent** aduanero/a *(m., f.)*, 5
cut cortar, 9
cyberspace surfer cibernauta, internauta *(m., f.)*, 3

daily diariamente, 8
daisy margarita *(f.)*, 9
dam represa *(f.)*, 8
damage dañar, 7
dance bailar, 1, 6
dancer bailarín/ina *(m., f.)*, 6
danger peligro *(m.)*, 3, 12; **to be in ~** estar en peligro, 2
Dangerous curve Curva peligrosa, 7
dare atreverse, 9
dark oscuro/a, 10; **~ complexioned** moreno/a, 1
darkness oscuridad *(f.)*, 12
Darn! ¡Diablos! 8
data datos *(m. pl.)*, 11
date fecha *(f.)*, 1
daughter hija *(f.)*, 5; **~ in-law** nuera *(f.)*, 5
dawn amanecer *(m.)*, 8
day día *(m.)*, 1; **the ~ before** víspera *(f.)*, 10; **the ~ before yesterday** anteayer, 4
dazzle deslumbrar, 7
dead muerto/a, 9; **to be ~** estar muerto/a

deal with tratar de, 11
dean decano/a *(m., f.)*, 7
dear querido/a, 3
death muerte *(f.)*, 3, 11
debt deuda *(f.)*, 12
deceit engaño *(m.)*, 10
deceive engañar, 8
deceived engañado/a, 9
December diciembre, 1
deception engaño *(m.)*, 12
decide decidir, 1
decoration adorno *(m.)*, 10
dedicate dedicarse, 5
deed hecho *(m.)*, 7, 12
deep hondo, 9
defeat vencer, 12
degree (centigrade/Celsius) grado (centígrado/Celsio) *(m.)*, 2; punto *(m.)*, 8; **in some ~** hacia cierto punto
delay demora *(f.)*, 4
delicious rico/a, 3; sabroso/a, 3, 9
delight encantar, 4; delicia *(f.)*, 11
delinquency delincuencia *(f.)*, 11
delivery parto *(m.)*, 9
dentist dentista *(m., f.)*, 5
deny negar (ie), 8
depart (with destination to) salir (con destino a), 4
department store almacén *(m.)*, 7
departure salida *(f.)*, 4; **~ gate** puerta de salida *(f.)*, 5
depend (on) depender (de), 2
dependent dependiente, 1
deposit (money) depositar (dinero), 8
depressed deprimido/a, 2
depression depresión *(f.)*, 11
deputy diputado/a, 12
descendant descendiente *(m., f.)*, 12
describe describir, 1
described descrito/a, 10
deserve merecer (zc), 9, 11
design diseño *(m.)*, 6; diseñar, 10
designed diseñado/a, 2
desired deseado/a, 6
desk escritorio *(m.)*, 1
despair desesperarse, 11
desperation desesperación *(f.)*, 5
dessert postre *(m.)*, 3
detail detalle *(m.)*, 10
deterioration deterioro *(m.)*, 9
detonate (a bomb) detonar, 6
detour desviarse, 9
devastating devastador/a, 7
developed desarrollado/a, 12
development desarrollo *(m.)*, 12
device dispositivo *(m.)*, 6
devote oneself dedicarse, 5
diagram plano *(m.)*, 9
diamond diamante *(m.)*, 8
die morir (ue), 3
died muerto, 9
diet dieta *(f.)*, 8
difficult difícil, 1
digital digital, 6; **~ audio** audio digital *(m.)*, 6; **~ image** imagen digital *(f.)*, 9; **~ music** archivos MIDI *(m. pl.)*, 6; **~ sound** sonido digital *(m.)*, 6; **~ video/movies** video digital *(m.)*, 6
dimension dimensión *(f.)*, 10
dining room comedor *(m.)*, 2
dinner cena *(f.)*, comida *(f.)*, 3; **to have ~** cenar, 3
directory directorio *(m.)*, 6
dirty sucio/a, 4
disappear desaparecer (zc), 7
disappeared desaparecido/a, 12
disappointed desilusionado/a, 2
discarded desechado/a, 9
discotheque discoteca *(f.)*, 2
discount descuento *(m.)*, 3; ganga *(f.)*, oferta *(f.)*, 7; rebaja *(f.)*, 8
discourage descorazonar, 12
discover descubrir, 1
discovered descubierto/a, 9
dish plato *(m.)*, 3
dishwasher lavaplatos *(m.)*, 9
dislike (a person) caer mal, 4
disorganized desorganizado/a, 1
dispel alejar, 10
display case mostrador *(m.)*, escaparete *(m.)*, 7
distinguish distinguir, 12
disturbing inquietante, 10
divorced divorciado/a; **to be ~** estar divorciado/a, 5
dizziness mareo *(m.)*, 8
dizzy mareado/a; **to be ~** estar mareado/a, 8
do hacer, 2; realizar, 12
doctor doctor/a *(m., f.)*, 1, 5; médico/a *(m., f.)*, 5
document documento *(m.)*, 6
documentary documental *(m.)*, 11
dog perro/a *(m., f.)*, 5
dolphin delfín *(m.)*, 9
Dominican dominicano/a, P, 5
done hecho, 9
donkey burro *(m.)*, 9
door puerta *(f.)*, 7
dormitory residencia *(f.)*, 1
dot punto *(m.)*, 5
double duplicarse, 6
doubt dudar, 8
doubtful dudoso/a; **it's ~** es dudoso, 8
dove paloma *(f.)*, 9
dragon tree dragón *(m.)*, 9
dramatic dramático/a, 11
draw dibujar, 10
drawer dibujante *(m., f.)*, 10
drawing dibujo *(m.)*, 10
dream sueño *(m.)*, 1, 3
dress vestir (i, i), 6; vestido *(m.)*, 7
drink beber, 1; bebida *(f.)*, 3
drive conducir 2, 7; manejar, 7
driver conductor/a *(m., f.)*, 7
driver's license licencia de manejar *(f.)*, 7
drizzle llovizna *(f.)*; **it's drizzling** llovizna, 2
drought sequía *(f.)*, 9
drug droga; **~ addiction** drogadicción *(f.)*, 11; **~ trafficking** tráfico de drogas *(m.)*, 11
drum tambor *(m.)*, 6; **~ set** batería *(f.)*, 6
drunk borracho/a, 2; bebido/a, 7
dry secar, 9; **~ cleaners** tintorería *(f.)*, 7; **~ off** secarse, 3
duck pato/a *(m., f.)*, 9
during durante, 4
dust (the furniture) sacudir (los muebles), 9
dwelling domicilio *(m.)*, 4

E

E-mail correo electrónico *(m.)*, 6
each cada, 4; **~ other** el uno al otro, 6
eagle (el) águila *(f.)*, 9
ear oreja *(f.)*, 5
earring arete *(m.)*, 8; pendiente *(m.)*, 8
earth tierra *(f.)*, 8, 12
earthly terrestre, 6
earthquake terremoto *(m.)*, 3, 12
ease (pain or symptoms) aliviar, 8
easily fácilmente, 3; hábilmente, 6
east este *(m.)*, 4
Easter Pascua *(f.)*, 10; **~ bunny** conejito de Pascua *(m.)*, 10
eastern oriental, 7
eat comer, 1
echinacea girasol rojo *(m.)*, 8
economical económico/a, 4
economics economía *(f.)*, 1
Ecuadorian ecuatoriano/a, P
editor editor/a *(m., f.)*, 5
edge orilla *(f.)*, 7
educational program programa educativo *(m.)*, 11
effort esfuerzo *(m.)*, 10
egg huevo *(m.)*, 3; **scrambled eggs** revoltillo *(m.)*, 8
egotistic egoísta, 1
eighth octavo/a, 4
either tampoco, 3; **~ ... or** (o)... o, 3
election elección *(f.)*, 1
electric eléctrico/a, 8; **~ appliance** electrodoméstico *(m.)*, 9
electrician electricista *(m., f.)*, 5
elegant elegante, 1
elephant elefante/a *(m., f.)*, 9
elevator ascensor *(m.)*, 3
eliminate evitar, 9
embroidery bordado *(m.)*, 7
emerald esmeralda *(f.)*, 8
emergency room sala de emergencia *(f.)*, 8

emit emitir, 8
emotional emocional, 1
empire imperio *(m.)*, 12
employee empleado/a *(m., f.)*, 5
employment empleo *(m.)*, 11
empty vacío/a, 7
enchant encantar, 4
encounter encuentro *(m.)*, 12
endorse endosar, 8
energy energía *(f.)*, 9
engineer ingeniero/a *(m., f.)*, 5
engineering ingeniería *(f.)*, 1
English inglés/esa, P; *(lang.)*, inglés *(m.)*, 1
enjoy disfrutar, 3; gozar 4, 6; **~ oneself** divertirse (ie, i), 3
enjoyable divertido/a, 1
enter entrar; **Do not ~** No hay paso, 7
entertaining entretenido/a, 10
entertainment entretenimiento *(m.)*, 8, 11
enthusiastic entusiasmado/a, 2
entree entrada *(f.)*, 3
environment medio ambiente *(m.)*, 9
equal equivaler, 3
equipment maquinaria *(f.)*, 6
eraser borrador *(m.)*, 1
essay ensayo *(m.)*, 5
essential esencial; **it's ~** es esencial, 7
estuary estuario *(m.)*, 8
ethnic étnico/a, 12
evaluation evaluación *(f.)*, 6
event evento *(m.)*, 10; acontecimiento *(m.)*, 11
every day todos los días, 3
everything todo, 3
evident evidente, 1; **it's ~** es evidente, 8
evil maldad *(f.)*, 9; males *(m. pl.)*, 10
exactly on the hour en punto, 1
exam prueba *(f.)*, 8
examine revisar, 8
excellent excelente, 1
exceptional fuera de serie, 12
exchange cambiar, 8; cambio *(m.)*, 8; **I want to ~ it for another** Quiero cambiarlo/la por otro/a, 7; **Where can I ~ money?** ¿Dónde puedo cambiar el dinero?, 3
excuse me con permiso, P
execute ejecutar, 12
exercise hacer ejercicio 1; ejercicio *(m.)*, 8
exhaust agotar, 9
exhibition exhibición *(f.)*, 10
existence existencia *(f.)*, 9
expense gasto *(m.)*, 8
expensive caro/a, 2
expert perito/a *(m., f.)*, 9
explain explicar, 4
expansion ampliación *(f.)*, 3
exploit explotar, 9
exploration exploración *(f.)*, 12
expose exponer, 10
exposed expuesto/a, 9
expressway autopista *(f.)*, 3
eye ojo *(m.)*, 5

F

face cara *(f.)*, 3, 5
factory fábrica *(f.)*, 6
faculty profesorado *(m.)*, 1
fail fallar, 9; fracasar, 11
failure falla *(f.)*, 10
fair feria *(f.)*; **World's ~** exposición mundial *(f.)*, 10
faith fe *(f.)*, 9
faithful fiel, 7
fake fingir, 9
fall caerse, 6; caer, 7; caída *(f.)*, 10; **~ asleep** dormirse (ue), 3, 6; **~ in love with** enamorarse (de), 5, 6; **~ in the trap** caer en la trampa, 11
Falling Rock Derrumbe, 7
false falso/a, 4
family *(adj.)* familiar; familia *(f.)*, 5; **~ member** pariente *(m., f.)*, 5
fan aficionado/a *(m., f.)*, 6
far from lejos de, 4
farewell despedida *(f.)*, 6
farm finca *(f.)*, 9
fascinate fascinar, 4
fascinating fascinante, 1
fast rápido, 1
fat gordo/a, 1; grasa *(f.)*, 8
father padre *(m.)*, 1, 5; **~ in-law** suegro/a *(m.)*, 5
faucet llave *(f.)*, grifo *(m.)*, 9
fault culpa (f.); **it's not your ~** no es culpa tuya, 3
fear temer, 8
fearful temible, 7
feature film largometraje *(m.)*, 11
February febrero, 1
feel sentirse (ie, i), 3; **~ like (doing something)** tener ganas de *(+inf.)*, 2
feet pies *(m. pl.)*, 3
fertility fertilidad *(f.)*, 10
field cancha *(f.)*, 8
fifth quinto/a, 4
fight pleito *(m.)*, 6
figure figura *(f.)*, 10; **small figures** figuritas *(f. pl.)*, 10
file archivo *(m.)*, 6
finally por fin, 3; finalmente, por último, 5
financial aid ayuda financiera *(f.)*, 8
find encontrar (ue) 2, 3; hallar, 10; hallazgo *(m.)*, 12; **~ out** averiguar, 4, 11, 12; saber (in the preterite), 5
finger dedo *(m.)*, 5
finish acabar, terminar, 1, 6
fire despedir (i), 6; **~ fighter** bombero/a *(m., f.)*, 5
fireworks fuegos artificiales *(m. pl.)*, 10
first primer/o/a, 3, 4; **~ day of the month** el primero *(m.)*, 1; **~ of all** primero que todo, 5
fish pescado *(m.)*, 3; pescar, 4; ir de pesca, 5; **~ market** pescadería *(f.)*, 3
fits queda; **it ~ you well/poorly** te/le queda bien/mal, 7
fix arreglar, 5
flag bandera *(f.)*, 10
flamingo flamenco *(m.)*, 9
flat tire llanta pinchada *(f.)*, 7
flattened achatado/a, 7
flight vuelo *(m.)*, 4; **~ attendant** aeromozo/a *(m., f.)*, 5
floor piso *(m.)*, 2
florist florería *(f.)*, 7
flourish gracia *(f.)*, 5
flower vase florero *(m.)*, 1
flu gripe *(f.)*, 8
flute flauta *(f.)*, 6
fly mosca *(f.)*, 3
focus foco *(m.)*, 11
fold bolero *(m.)*, 9
folder carpeta *(f.)*, 1
folk art artesanías *(f. pl.)*, 8
folklore folclor *(m.)*, 10
folkloric folclórico/a,10
follow seguir (i, i), perseguir (i, i), 3
food comida *(f.)*, 3; **~ group** grupo de alimentos *(m.)*, 8; **~ processor** procesador de comidas *(m.)*, 9; **~ pyramid** pirámide de la alimentación *(f.)*, 8
foot pie *(m.)*, 5; **on ~** a pie, 3
football fútbol americano *(m.)*, 6
for por, para, a, 4; **~ example** por ejemplo, 6
foreign extranjero/a, 3
forest bosque *(m.)*, 7, 9
forge forjar, 8
forget olvidar, 7; **~ it** olvídelo, 4
forgive disculpar, 9
fork tenedor *(m.)*, 3
form forma *(f.)*, 10
formula fórmula *(f.)*, 1
formulate a query formular una consulta/una búsqueda, 8
fortify fortalecer (zc), 12
found fundar, 12
fourth cuarto/a, 4
fox zorro *(m.)*, 9
fracture fractura *(f.)*, 8
fractured fracturado/a, 8
frame marco *(m.)*, 10
free gratuito/a, 3; libre, 4; **~ associated state** estado libre asociado *(m.)*, 5; **~ rein** rienda suelta *(f.)*, 11; **~ time** ocio *(m.)*, 11
freezer congelador *(m.)*, 9
freezing helado/a, 7
French francés/esa, P; *(lang.)* francés *(m.)*, 1
Friday viernes *(m.)*, 1

fried frito/a, 9; **~ plantains** tostones *(m. pl.)*, 5
friend amigo/a *(m., f.)*, 1, 5
friendly amable, simpático/a, 1
frightened asustado/a, 4
frightening espantoso/a, 4
from de, desde, 4; **~ here** desde aquí 3; **~ time to time** de vez en cuando, 11
frozen helado/a, 7
fruit fruta *(f.)*, 3; **~ stand** frutería *(f.)*, 3
fry freír (i), 9
frying pan sartén *(f.)*, 9
fuel combustible *(m.)*, 9
fulfill cumplir, 8, 9
full-time tiempo completo, 6
fun divertido/a; **to have ~** divertirse (ie), 6
funny cómico/a, 1, 11

G

Gallician gallego/a, 4
game partido *(m.)*, 6
garbage basura *(f.)*, 9
garden jardín *(m.)*, 2
gardener jardinero/a *(m., f.)*, 5, 9
garment prenda *(f.)*, 7
gas/gasoline gasolina *(f.)*, 7; **~ pedal** acelerador *(m.)*, 7; **~ tank** tanque de gasolina *(m.)*, 7
generally generalmente, 5
generation generación *(f.)*, 11
generous generoso/a, 1
gentleman señor *(m.)*, 1
German alemán/ana, P; *(lang.)* alemán *(m.)*, 1
get conseguir (i), 3; **~ a sunburn** quemarse, 5; **~ a tan** broncearse, 5; **~ along** llevarse bien, 5; **~ angry** enojarse, 6; **~ better** aliviarse, mejorarse, 8; **~ down (from)** bajar (de), 4; **~ dressed** vestirse (i) 3, 6; **~ married** casarse (con)., 5; **~ rid of** deshacerse de, 4; **~ sick** enfermarse, 6, 8; **~ up** levantarse, 3, 6; **~ upset** alterarse, 10; **~ washed** lavarse, 3; **~ worked up** inquietarse, 10;
giraffe jirafa *(f.)*, 9
girl chica, muchacha *(f.)*, 5
girlfriend novia *(f.)*, 1
give dar, 4; **~ a gift** regalar, 4; **~ in** rendirse (i, i), 7
glove guante *(m.)*, 2, 6, 7; **~ box** guantera *(f.)*, 7
glass vaso *(m.)*, 3
glazed clay barro vidriado *(m.)*, 9
glimpse vistazo *(m.)*, 12
go ir, 2; andar, 5; **~ away** irse, 3; **~ bicycling** montar en bicicleta, 5; **~ camping** acampar, 9; **~ down (a street)** bajar por, 7; **~ horseback riding** montar a caballo, 5; **~ off** apagar(se), 9; **~ out** salir a, 2; **~ sailing** navegar en velero, 5; **~ shopping** ir de compras, 5, 7; **~ skindiving/snorkeling** bucear, 5; **~ straight** seguir (i) derecho/recto, 7; **~ through** surcar, 3; **~ to bed** acostarse (ue), 6; **~ up, climb** subir, 1, 7; **~ water skiing** hacer esquí acuático, 5
goal gol *(m.)*, 4; meta *(f.)*, 6
goat cabrito *(m.)*, 3; cabra *(f.)*, 9
godmother madrina *(f.)*, 9
godson/goddaughter ahijado/a *(m., f.)*, 9
going to ir a (+ *inf.*), 2
gold oro *(m.)*, 8
golden dorado/a, 10
good bueno/a, 1, 7; **~ spirit** buen espíritu *(m.)*, 10; **~ grief!** ¡Dios mío santo!, 10; **~ looking** guapo/a, 1; **it's ~** es bueno, 8
gossip ser chismoso/a, 10; dimes y diretes *(m. pl.)*, 11
grace gracia *(f.)*, 5
grade calificación *(f.)*, 6
grandfather/grandmother abuelo/a *(m., f.)*, 1, 5
grandson/granddaughter nieto/a *(m., f.)*, 5
grapes uvas *(f. pl.)*, 3
grapevine parra *(f.)*, 9
gray gris, 1
great grandfather/great grandmother bisabuelo/a *(m., f.)*, 5
greedy envidioso/a, 1
green verde, 1; **~ pepper** pimiento verde *(m.)*, 3; **leafy greens** vegetales de hoja *(m. pl.)*, 8
grill barbacoa *(f.)*, 9
grind moler (ue) 9; triturar, 9
ground suelo *(m.)*, 6
group grupo *(m.)*; **cultural ~** grupo cultural, 12
grow crecer (zc) (una persona), 5; cultivar (una planta), 7
guava guayaba *(f.)*, 5
Guatemalan guatemalteco/a, P
guess adivinar, 5; suponer, 12
guide guía *(m., f.)*, 4; **~ book** guía *(f.)*, 4
guilty culpable, 7
guitar guitarra *(f.)*, 6
gymnastics gimnasia *(f.)*, 6

H

habits hábitos *(m. pl.)*; **eating ~** hábitos alimenticios, 8
hair pelo *(m.)*, 3, 5; **~ dryer** secador de pelo *(m.)*, 9; **~stylist** peluquero/a *(m., f.)*, 5
half (hour) media, 1; mitad *(f.)*, 11
hallmark sello *(m.)*, 10
Halloween Día de las Brujas *(m.)*, 10
hall(way) pasillo *(m.)*, 2, 9
hand mano *(f.)*, 3, 5; **by ~** a mano, 10; **on the other ~** en cambio, 3
handcuffs esposas *(f. pl.)*, 11, 12
handy a la vista, 9
handsome guapo/a, 1
hang (up) colgar (ue) 6, 9, 10, 11
happen suceder, 5
happiness alegría *(f.)*, 5; felicidad *(f.)*, 9
happy alegre, 2; **to get ~** alegrarse, 5, 8; estar contento/a de, 8
hard duro/a, 10; **~ drive** disco duro *(m.)*, 6; **~ hit** golpe fuerte *(m.)*, 5; **~ roll** bollo *(m.)*, 3; **~ working** trabajador/a, 1
harm (someone) hacerle daño (a alguien), 6
harmonious armonioso/a, 9
hassle lío *(m.)*, 7
hat sombrero *(m.)*, 2
have tener, 2; **~ a picnic** hacer un picnic, 5; **~ a chill** tener escalofríos, 8; **~ a cold** tener catarro/resfrío 8; estar resfriado/a, 8; **~ a good time** divertirse (ie), 6; **~ a good trip!** ¡Que tenga(n) un buen viaje!, 4; **~ a large audience** estar muy concurrido/a, 12; **~ a nice trip** ¡Buen viaje!, ¡Feliz viaje!, 4; **~ an appetite** tener apetito, 8; **~ an opinion** opinar, 8; **~ breakfast** desayunarse, 3; **~ dinner** cenar, 3; **~ fun** divertirse (ie), 6; **~ just done** acabar de, 1; **~ lunch** almorzar (ue), 3; **~ no choice** no quedarle remedio a alguien, 12; **~ no clue** ni idea, 4; **~ pain** tener dolor, 8; **~ the flu** tener gripe, 8; **~ to** tener que, 2
head cabeza *(f.)*, 5
headboard espaldar *(m.)*, 9
headlights luces *(f. pl.)*, 7
headlines titulares *(m. pl.)*, 1
headphones audífonos *(m. pl.)*, 6
headrest apoyacabeza *(m.)*, 7
healer curandero/a *(m., f.)*, 8
health salud *(f.)*, 11
healthy sano/a, 8
heard oído/a, 9
heart corazón *(m.)*, 8
hearth hogar *(m.)*, 8
heat calefacción *(f.)*, 2; calentar (ie), 9
heaven cielo *(m.)*, 8
heavy pesado/a, 6; gordo/a, 10
height estatura *(f.)*, 3; altura *(f.)*, 8
helmet casco *(m.)*, 6
help ayudar 1; ayuda *(f.)*, 6; **How can/may I ~ you?** ¿En qué le(s) puedo servir/ayudar?, 3, 4, 7
hen gallina *(f.)*, 9

here aquí, 3
heritage herencia *(f.)*, 5, 7
Hey! ¡Oye!, 4
hidden guardado/a, 5
hide esconder, 4
hieroglyphics jeroglíficos *(m. pl.)*,12
high elevado/a, 11; **~ heeled shoes** zapatos de tacón alto *(m. pl.)*, 7; **~ plateau** altiplano *(m.)*, 7; **~ speed** de alta velocidad, 4
highest máximo/a, 9
highway carretera *(f.)*, **divided ~** carretera/autovía de doble calzada, 3
hill colina *(f.)*, 7
hint indirecta *(f.)*, 10
hip cadera, 6
historic histórico/a, 10
history historia *(f.)*, 1
hit pegar, 4; golpear, 11
HIV positive seropositivo/a, 11
home hogar *(m.)*, 10; **~ page** página principal, página inicial *(f.)*, 1
hommage homenaje *(m.)*, 10
Honduran hondureño/a, P
honest honesto/a, 1
honor honrar, 10
honors premios *(m. pl.)*, 6
hope esperar, 8; esperanza *(f.)*, 11; **I/Let's ~** Ojalá, 8
horn pito *(m.)*, 7
horror de horror *(adj.)*, 11
horse caballo *(m.)*, 9
host anfitrión/ona *(m., f.)*, 10
hot caliente, 9; **~ springs** aguas termales *(f. pl.)*, 5; **to be ~** tener calor, 2; **it's ~** hace calor, 2
house casa *(f.)*, 2
household manager administrador/a de hogar *(m., f.)*, 5
housewife (el) ama de casa *(f.)*, 5
How? ¿Cómo?, 1; **~ can/may I help you?** ¿En qué le(s) puedo servir/ayudar? 3, 4, 7; **~ do I get to . . . ?** ¿Cómo llego a...?, 7; **~ do you want to pay?** ¿Cómo quiere Ud. pagar?, 3; **~ does it fit me?** ¿Cómo me queda?, 7; **~ many?** ¿Cuántos/as?, 1; **~ much?** ¿Cuánto/a?, 1; **~ much does it cost?** ¿Cuánto vale?, ¿Cuánto cuesta?, 8; **~ much does . . . cost?** ¿Cuánto cuesta...?, 3; **~ much is it?** ¿Cuánto cuesta?, ¿Cuánto es?, 4
How frightening! ¡Qué nervios!, 11
hug abrazo *(m.)*, 5
human heritage patrimonio de la humanidad *(m.)*, 9
humble humilde, 8
hunger (el) hambre *(f.)*, 3
hungry hambriento/a; **to be ~** tener hambre, 2; **I am very ~** ¡Qué hambre!, ¡Tengo mucha hambre!, 3
hurt herir (ie, i), 6; doler (ue), 8
husband esposo *(m.)*, marido *(m.)*, 5
hymn himno *(m.)*, 10

I

ice hielo *(m.)*; **~ cream** helado *(m.)*, 3; **~ skating** patinaje sobre hielo *(m.)*, 6
idea idea, *(f.)*; **not even the least ~** ni la menor idea, 9
idealistic idealista, 1
identity identidad *(f.)*, 12
idiomatic expression expresión idiomática *(f.)*, 5
if si; **~ I put my mind to it** si me lo propongo, 12; **~ it weren't for you** si no fuera por ti, 9
ill mal, 7
illegal ilegal, 4
illness enfermedad *(f.)*, 8; **psychological ~** enfermedad (p)sicológica, 11
illustration ilustración *(f.)*, 10
illustrator dibujante *(m., f.)*, 10
immigration emigración *(f.)*, 5
immortal imperecedero/a, 11
impatiently impacientemente, 3
imperfect imperfecto/a, 1
important importante, 1; **it's ~** es importante, 7
imposing imponente, 12
impossible imposible, 8; **it's ~** es imposible, 8
impressive impresionante, 6
imprison encarcelar, 11
improvement mejora *(f.)*, 3
in en, 4; **~ accordance with** conforme a, 9; **~ addition to** además de, 12; **~ case** en caso (de) que, 9; **~ charge of** encargado/a de, 11; **~ fact** de hecho, 9; **~ front of** delante de, 4; **~ groups** en grupos, P; **~ honor of** en honor de, 10; **~ length** de largo, 5; **~ love** enamorado/a, 2; **~ no way** de ninguna manera, 8; **~ order that** a fin (de) que, 9; **~ order to** para, 4; para que, 9; **~ pairs** en parejas, P; **~ relationship to** en cuanto a, 9; **~ search of** en busca de, 11; **~ the center** en el centro, 3; **~ the (morning, afternoon, night)** por la (mañana, tarde, noche), 1; **~ the world** bajo los cielos, 5; **~ use** en uso, 2; **~ width** de ancho, 5
Incan incaico/a, 7
inch pulgada *(f.)*, 3
inconvenience incomodidad *(f.)*, 10
inconvenient inconveniente, 1
increase aumentar, 11
index indexar, 9
indigenous indígena, 5
inexpensive barato/a, 2
infection infección *(f.)*, 8
influence influir, 7
inhabited habitado/a, 12
injection inyección *(f.)*, 8
injure dañar, 7
inner ear oído *(m.)*, 8
inside of dentro de, 4
instrument equipo *(m.)*, 9
insufficient insuficiente, 1
intelligent inteligente, listo/a, 1
intend to pensar (ie) + *inf.*, 3
intensify avivar, 8
interest interesar, 4
interesting interesante, 1
international internacional, 1
Internet red *(f.)*, 1, Internet *(m.)*, 1; **~ domain** dominio Internet *(m.)*, 4; **~ guide** guía Internet *(f.)*, 2, 5; **~ surfer** internauta *(m., f.)*, 3
Intersection Intersección, 7
interview entrevista *(f.)*, 6
introduce presentar, 12
introduction presentación *(f.)*, P
introvert introvertido/a, 1
invention invención *(f.)*, 12
investigative de investigación, 11
investment inversión *(f.)*, 3
involve involucrar, 6
involved involucrado/a, 9
iron plancha *(f.)*, 9; **~ the clothes** planchar la ropa, 9
island isla *(f.)*, 4, 7
Italian italiano/a, P; *(lang.)* italiano *(m.)*, 1
itinerary itinerario *(m.)*, 4

jacket chaqueta *(f.)*, 2
jail cárcel, prisión *(f.)*, 11
January enero, 1
Japanese japonés/esa, P; *(lang.)* japonés *(m.)*, 1
jealous celoso/a; **to be ~** tener celos, 5
jewelry joyas *(f. pl.)*, 8; **~ store** joyería *(f.)*, 7; **costume ~** joyas de fantasía *(f. pl.)*, 8
Jewish judío/a, 4
joke broma *(f.)*, 2
journalist periodista *(m., f.)*, 5, 11
joy alegría *(f.)*, 12
Jss! ¡Uy!, 6
juice jugo *(m.)*, zumo *(m.)* *(Spain)*, 3
July julio, 1
June junio, 1
jungle selva *(f.)*, 7
just in case por si acaso, 4, 11

karat quilate *(m.)*, 8
keep away alejar(se), 10
kernel grano *(m.)*, 9

key llave *(f.)*, 1, 3
keyboard teclado *(m.)*, 6
keyword palabra clave *(f.)*, 2
kick patear, 6
kidnapper secuestrador/a *(m., f.)*, 6
kidnapping secuestro *(m.)*, 6
kill matar, 11
kiln horno *(m.)*, 10
king and queen reyes *(m. pl.)*, 4
kiss besar, 4; bes(it)o, 8
kitchen cocina *(f.)*, 2
knee rodilla *(f.)*, 5
knife cuchillo *(m.)*, 1, 3; navaja *(f.)*, 12
know saber, 2; conocer (zc), 2; **I don't know** no sé, P
knowledge conocimiento *(m.)*, 6
Korean coreano/a, P

L

label (record) sello *(m.)*, 6
labor trabajo *(m.)*, 4; **~ Day** Día del trabajo *(m.)*, 10
laboratory laboratorio *(m.)*, 1
lack faltar, 4
ladder escalera *(f.)*, 10
lady señora *(f.)*, 1; **young ~** señorita *(f.)*, 1
lake lago *(m.)*, 7
lament lamentar, sentir (ie, i), 8
lamp lámpara *(f.)*, 1
land aterrizar, 5; tierra *(f.)*, 12
language idioma *(m.)*, 1
landscape paisaje *(m.)*, 10
large grande, 1
last pasado/a, 4; **~ month** el mes pasado, 4; **~ night** anoche, 4; **~ week** la semana pasada, 4; **~ weekend** el fin de semana pasado, 4; **~ year** el año pasado, 4
late tarde; **to be ~** estar atrasado/a, 4; **to become ~** hacérsele tarde a uno, 7
later luego 3; posteriormente, 6
laugh reír (i), 8
launch lanzar, 11
lawyer abogado/a *(m., f.)*, 5
lay off despedir (i,i), 6
layover escala *(f.)*, 5
lazy perezoso/a , flojo/a, 1
leader jefe/a *(m., f.)*, 5; líder *(m., f.)*, 6
leafy greens vegetales de hojas *(m. pl.)*, 8
learn aprender, 1; enterarse de, 9
leave salir, 2; irse, 3, 6; **~ behind** dejar, 3; **~ for a place** salir para, 2; **~ from a place** salir de, 2; **~ with** salir con, 2; **~ with destination to** ir/salir con destino a, 4
left izquierda *(f.)*; **to the ~** a la izquierda
leg pierna *(f.)*, 5
lend prestar, 8
length longitud *(f.)*, 3
lengthen alargar, 10
lens lente *(m.)*, 5
Lent Cuaresma *(f.)*, 10
less menos, 1
lesson lección *(f.)*, 1
let (someone) know avisar, 4
let's go vámonos, 4
lettuce lechuga *(f.)*, 3
level altura *(f.)*, 3; nivel *(m.)*, 8, 11
lever palanca *(f.)*, 9
liar mentiroso/a, 1
liberty libertad *(f.)*, 1
library biblioteca *(f.)*, 2
license plate placa *(f.)*, 7
lie mentir (i, i), 12
lie down acostarse (ue) 3
lift levantar, 6
light luz *(f.)*, 1; ligero/a, claro/a, 10; **~ complexioned** rubio/a, 1; **the ~ went out** se fue/se cortó la luz, 10
lightbulb bombillo *(m.)*, 9
like gustar, 4; **~ (a person)** caer bien, 4; **~ that** así, 9; **~ very much** encantar, 4; **I would ~ . . .** Me gustaría..., Quisiera, 3; **I would like to order...** Quisiera pedir..., 3; **you ~** te gusta(n), 1
limit limitar, 2; delimitar, 7
linguistic lingüístico/a, 2
linguistics lingüística *(f.)*, 12
link enlace *(m.)*, 3
lion león *(m.)*, 9
listen escuchar, 1
Listen! ¡Oye!, 4
literature literatura *(f.)*, 1
little pequeño/a; **a ~** un poco, 7; **~ by little** poco a poco, 4; **~ piece of paper** papelito *(m.)*, 4; **~ window** ventanita *(f.)*, 7
live vivir, 1
living room sala *(f.)*, 2
lizard lagarto *(m.)*, lagartija *(f.)*, 9
loan préstamo *(m.)*, 8
lobster langosta *(f.)*, 3
location ubicación *(f.)*, 6
London Londres, 4
long largo/a, 1; **~ sleeved** de manga larga, 7
look (at) mirar, 1; **~ (for)** buscar, 1
loose flojo/a, 7
lord señor *(m.)*, 12
lose perder (ie), 3, 6; **~ sight of** perder de vista, 5
lost perdido/a, 12
love *(adj.)* de amor, 11; **to be in ~** estar enamorado/a, 5
lover amante *(m., f.)*, 10
loving cariñoso/a, 6
low bajo/a; **~ heeled shoes** zapatos de tacón bajo *(m. pl.)*, 7
lowest mínimo/a, 2, 9
loyal fiel, 7, 9
lunch almuerzo *(m.)*, comida *(f.)*, 3
lush frondoso/a, 3
luxury lujo *(m.)*, 7

M

made hecho/a, 9; **~ of gold** de oro, 10
magazine revista *(f.)*, 5
magic mágico/a, 6; magia *(f.)*, 8
magnificent magnífico/a, 10
maid criada *(f.)*, 5
mail correo *(m.)*; **by ~** por correo, 8; **~ a letter** poner una carta en el correo, 2; **~ carrier** cartero/a *(m., f.)*, 5
mailbox buzón *(m.)*, 3
main principal, 8; **~ character** protagonista *(m., f.)*, 11; **~ dish** plato principal *(m.)*, 3
maintain mantener, 8; **~ oneself** conservarse, 8
majestic majestuoso/a, 7
major especialización *(f.)*, 1
make hacer, 2; realizar, 3; **~ a collect call** hacer una llamada por cobrar, 3; **~ a long distance phone call** hacer una llamada de larga distancia, 3; **~ a plan** idear, 12; **~ an appointment** hacer una cita, 8; **~ fun of** burlarse, 7; **~ someone angry** enojar, 6; **~ someone happy** alegrar, 6; **~ someone sick** enfermar, 6; **~ the bed** hacer la cama, 9; **~ up (comprise)** comprender, contener, 12
Mallorcan mallorquino/a, 4
mammal mamífero *(m.)*, 9
man hombre *(m.)*, 1
manager gerente *(m., f.)*, 5
management manejo *(m.)*, 6
manufacture fabricar, 11
map mapa *(m.)*, 1
marble mármol *(m.)*, 10
March marzo, 1
marigold caléndula *(f.)*, 9
market mercado *(m.)*, 2; **fish ~** pescadería *(f.)*, 3
married casado/a; **to be ~** estar casado/a, 5
mask máscara *(f.)*, 10
Mass misa *(f.)*, 5
massage (therapeutic) masaje terapéutico *(m.)*, 4
Master's degree student estudiante de maestría *(m., f.)*, 1
mathematics matemáticas *(f. pl.)*, 1
matter importar, 4; asunto *(m.)*, 11
May mayo, 1
maybe quizás, tal vez, 8
meal comida *(f.)*, 3
mean significar, 6
means medio *(m.)*, 11; **by ~ of** a través de, 6

measure medir (i), 6, 7
measurement medida *(f.)*, 7
meat carne *(f.)*, 3; **~ market** carnicería *(f.)*, 3
meatball albóndiga *(f.)*, 3
mechanic mecánico/a *(m., f.)*, 5
medical science ciencias médicas *(f. pl.)*, 1
medium mediano/a, 7
megawatt megavatio *(m.)*, 3
memory recuerdo *(m.)*, 5
men's dressing room probador de hombres *(m.)*, 7
menswear ropa de hombre *(f.)*, 7
menu carta *(f.)*, menú *(m.)*, 3
merchandise mercancía *(f.)*, 3
mercy piedad *(f.)*, 6
message mensaje *(m.)*, 6
messenger mensajero/a *(m., f.)*, 8
Mexican mexicano/a, P; **~ American** mexicanoamericano/a, P
microwave oven micro(ondas) *(m.)*, 9
Middle Ages medioevo *(m.)*, 11
MIDI archives (digital music) archivos MIDI *(m. pl.)*, 6
midnight medianoche *(f.)*, 1
milk leche *(f.)*, 3; **skim ~** leche descremada, 8
millennium milenio *(m.)*, 11
million millón *(m.)*, 3
miniature miniatura *(f.)*, 10
minimum wage sueldo mínimo *(m.)*, 11
miniskirt minifalda *(f.)*, 7
minivan camioneta *(f.)*, 7
minority minoría *(f.)*, 12
minus menos, 1
mirror espejo *(m.)*, 9, 12
Miss señorita *(f.)*, P, 1
mist vapor *(m.)*, 3
mistaken equivocado/a; **to be ~** equivocarse, estar equivocado/a, 6
mistreat maltratar, 6
mix mezcla *(f.)*, 5; mezclar, 9
mixer batidora *(f.)*, 9
model modelo *(m., f.)*, 10
modern moderno/a, 1; **~ art** arte moderno *(m.)*, 10
Monday lunes *(m.)*, 1
money dinero *(m.)*, 3; **~ exchange** cambio de moneda *(m.)*, 3; **~ order** giro postal *(m.)*, 8
monkey mono *(m.)*, 9
monument monumento *(m.)*, 2
Moors moros *(m. pl.)*, 3
more más, 7
morning programming programación matinal *(f.)*, 11
mosaic mosaico *(m.)*, 10
mosque mezquita *(f.)*, 4
mother madre *(f.)*, 1, 5; **~ in-law** suegra *(f.)*, 5
motorcycle moto, motocicleta *(f.)*, 3
mountain montaña *(f.)*, 7; **~ range** cordillera *(f.)*, sierra *(f.)*, 7
mouse ratón *(m.)*, 6, 9
mouth boca *(f.)*, 5
move mover (ue), 6
movie película *(f.)*, 11; **~ programming** cartelera de cine *(f.)*, 11; **~ star** estrella de cine *(f.)*, 11; **~ theater** cine *(m.)*, 2
Mr. señor *(m.)*, P, 1
Mrs. señora *(f.)*, P, 1
Ms. señorita *(f.)*, P, 1
multifaceted polifacético/a, 6
murder asesinato *(m.)*, 11; asesinar, 11
murderer asesino/a *(m., f.)*, 11
muscle músculo *(m.)*, 8
museum museo *(m.)*, 2, 10
music música *(f.)*, 6; **~ store** tienda de discos *(m.)*, 7
musician músico/a *(m., f.)*, 5
Muslim musulmán/ana, 4
My goodness! ¡Dios mío!, 3, 8
mystery *(adj.)* de misterio, 11

name calificar, 6
napkin servilleta *(f.)*, 3
narration narración *(f.)*, 11
national nacional, 10
native autóctono/a, 7
Native American amerindio/a, 7
natural natural, 1; **~ hydroelectric resources** recursos hidroeléctricos naturales *(m. pl.)*, 9; **~ sciences** ciencias naturales *(f. pl.)*, 1
nature naturaleza *(f.)*, 3, 9
nauseous mareado/a; **to be ~** tener náuseas, estar mareado/a, 8
near cerca de, 4
necessary necesario/a, 7; **it's ~** es necesario, es preciso, 7
necklace collar *(m.)*, 8
necktie corbata *(f.)*, 7
need necesitar, 1; faltar, 4
neighbor vecino/a *(m., f.)*, 5
neighborhood vecindario *(m.)*, 5; **~ watch** vigilancia del vecindario *(f.)*, 11
neither tampoco, 3; **~ . . . nor** ni...ni, 3
nephew sobrino *(m.)*, 5
nervous nervioso/a, 2; **~ tension** tensión nerviosa *(f.)*, 8
Net red *(f.)*, 1
network red *(f.)*, 6
neutrals neutros *(m. pl.)*, 10
never nunca, jamás, 3
nevertheless sin embargo, 5
new nuevo/a, 1; **~ Year's Day** Día de Año Nuevo *(m.)*, 10; **~ Year's Eve** Nochevieja *(f.)*, 10
news prensa *(f.)*, 2; noticias *(f. pl.)*, 11; **~ program** noticiero *(m.)*, 11
newspaper periódico *(m.)*, 2
next próximo/a, 4, 11; **~ door** de al lado, 5
Nicaraguan nicaragüense *(m., f.)*, P
nice simpático/a, amable, 1
niece sobrina *(f.)*, 5
night noche *(f.)*, 1; **~ stand** mesita de noche *(f.)*, 9; **the ~ before last** anteanoche, 4
nightly nocturno/a, 4
nightmare pesadilla *(f.)*, 11
ninth noveno/a, 4
no no, 1; **~ one** ningún, ninguno/a, 3; **~ parking** No estacionar, No aparcar, 7; **~ smoking** No fumar, 3, 4
nobody nadie, 1, 3
noise ruido *(m.)*, 5; **loud ~** ruidazo *(m.)*, 5
nomination nominación *(f.)*, 11
none ningún, ninguno/a, 3
nonetheless sin embargo, 12
noon mediodía *(m.)*, 1
north norte *(m.)*, 4
northeast noreste *(m.)*, 4
northwest noroeste *(m.)*, 4
nose nariz *(f.)*, 5
note nota *(f.)*, 2
notebook cuaderno *(m.)*, 1
nothing nada, 3
notice darse cuenta de, 6
noun sustantivo *(m.)*, 5
novel novela *(f.)*, 5
November noviembre, 1
now ahora, 3; ya, 5
nowadays hoy en día, 7
number número *(m.)*, 1
nurse enfermero/a *(m., f.)*, 5
nutritious nutritivo/a, 8

obtain conseguir (i), 3; obtener, lograr, 11
occupation oficio *(m.)*, 12
occur ocurrir, 7; suceder, 11
ocean mar *(m.)*, 3, 7; océano *(m.)*, 7
October octubre, 1
octopus pulpo *(m.)*, 3
of de, 1, 4; **~ course** cómo no, P; por supuesto 3, 5; claro que sí, 7
offender infractor/a *(m., f.)*, 7
offer ofrecer (zc), 4
office oficina *(f.)*, 2
often a menudo, 5, 10
oil aceite *(m.)*, 7; **olive ~** aceite de oliva *(m.)*, 3; **~ paint** pintura al óleo *(f.)*, 10
OK regular, P; **~ OK** está bien, está bien, 3; **He's ~** No me cae nada mal, 4
old (for a person or thing) viejo/a, 1; **to be . . . years ~** tener...años, 2
older grande, 1, 7; mayor, 7; **to be ~** ser mayor, 5

Olympic Games Juegos Olímpicos *(m. pl.)*, 10
on en, 4; encima de, 4; **~ board** a bordo, 4; **~ foot** a pie, 3; **~ her/his own** por su propia cuenta, 10; **~ the contrary** sino, 10; **~ the left** a la izquierda, 4; **~ the other hand** en cambio, 3; **~ the right** a la derecha, 4; **~ top of** sobre, encima de, arriba de, 4; **~ vacation** estar de vacaciones, 4
once and for all de una vez, 5
onion cebolla *(f.)*, 3
only único/a, 3; solamente, 4; **the ~ thing** lo único, 9
onyx ónice, 2
open abrir 1, 6; abierto/a, 9; **~ air** al aire libre, 8
operating room quirófano *(m.)*, 9
opportunistic oportunista, 1
optimistic optimista, 1
orange anaranjado/a, 1; naranja *(f.)*, 3
order pedido *(m.)*, 3; mandar, 7
organized organizado/a, 1
other times otras veces, 5
Ouch!, Ow! ¡Ay!, 6
ought to deber, 1
ounce onza *(f.)*, 3
out of fuera de, 9; **~ (their) reach** fuera de su alcance, 9
outgoing extrovertido/a, 1
outside al aire libre, 4; **~ of** fuera de, 4; afuera de, 6
outstanding fuera de serie, 7
oven horno *(m.)*, 9
over sobre, encima de, 4; **~ there** allá, 3
overpopulate sobrepoblar (ue), 9
owe deber, 1
owner dueño/a *(m., f.)*, 2, 11
oxygen oxígeno *(m.)*, 1
oyster ostra *(f.)*, 3

P

pack empacar, 1
package tour paquete *(m.)*, 4
pain dolor *(m.)*, 5
paint pintar, 1, 10
painted pintado/a, 10
painter pintor/a *(m., f.)*, 5, 9
painting pintura *(f.)*, cuadro *(m.)*, 10
pair par *(m.)*, 7
pale pálido/a, 6
palette paleta *(f.)*, 10
palm tree palmera *(f.)*, 5
pan paila *(f.)*, 9; **frying ~** sartén *(f.)*, 9
Panamanian panameño/a, P
pants pantalones *(m. pl.)*, 2
paper papel *(m.)*, 1; **little piece of ~** papelito *(m.)*, 4
parade desfile *(m.)*, 10
paradise paraíso *(m.)*, 7
Paraguayan paraguayo/a, P
pardon perdón, P; disculpa *(f.)*, 10
parents padres *(m.)*, 5
park estacionar, 7
parking aparcamiento *(m.)*, 3
parrot papagayo *(m.)*, 6; perico *(m.)*, 9
part parte; **~-time** tiempo parcial, 6; **the best ~** lo mejor, 12; **the most horrible ~** lo más horrible, 12; **the worst ~ of all** lo peor de todo, 12
participate participar, 10
participation participación *(f.)*, 10
party fiesta *(f.)*, 10
Pass by . . . Pase por…, 7
passenger pasajero/a *(m., f.)*, 4
passport pasaporte *(m.)*, 4, 5
password contraseña *(f.)*, código personal *(m.)*, 6
pasta pasta *(f.)*, 8
patient *(adj.)* paciente, 6; paciente *(m., f.)*, 8
pay pagar, 1; **~ attention** hacer caso, 12; **I want to ~ cash** Quiero pagar con dinero en efectivo, 3; **How do you want to ~?** ¿Cómo quiere Ud. pagar?, 3
peak pico *(m.)*, 7
peanut butter crema de cacahuate *(f.)*, 8
pear pera *(f.)*, 3
pearl perla *(f.)*, 8
Pedestrian crossing Paso peatonal, 7
pen bolígrafo *(m.)*, pluma *(f.)*, 1
pencil lápiz *(m.)*, 1
pendant pendiente *(f.)*, 8
penguin pingüino *(m.)*, 9
people gente *(f.)*, 1
pepper *(spice)* pimienta *(f.)*, 3; *(vegetable)* pimiento *(m.)*, 3
perfect perfecto/a, 1
perform desempeñar, 12
performance rendimiento *(m.)*, 6; interpretación *(f.)*, 11
perfume perfume *(m.)*, 7; **~ store** perfumería *(f.)*, 7
perhaps tal vez, 8; quizás, 8, 9
persistent persistente, 1
person persona *(f.)*; **young ~** joven *(m., f.)*, 4; chico/a *(m., f.)*, 5
personal personal, 1; **~ items** aseo personal *(m.)*, 7
Peruvian peruano/a, P
pessimistic pesimista, 1
pharmacist farmacéutico/a *(m., f.)*, 5
pharmacy farmacia *(f.)*, 7
phenomenon fenómeno *(m.)*, 10
philosophy filosofía *(f.)*, 1
photo foto *(f.)*, 1
photograph fotografía *(f.)*, 10
photographer fotógrafo/a *(m., f.)*, 5, 10
physical físico/a, 8; **~ exam** examen físico *(m.)*, 8
physics física *(f.)*, 1
physiology fisiología *(f.)*, 1
pick up recoger, 4
picturesque pintoresco/a, 2
piece ficha *(f.)*, 5; pieza *(f.)*, 8, 10
pig cerdo *(m.)*, cochino *(m.)*, puerco *(m.)*, 9
pigeon paloma *(f.)*, 9
pile pila *(f.)*, 9
pill píldora/pastilla *(f.)*, 8
pillow almohada *(f.)*, 9
pilot piloto *(m., f.)*, 5
pineapple piña *(f.)*, 3
pink rosa, rosado/a, 1
pitcher jarra *(f.)*, 3
pity lástima *(f.)*, 11
placate (the gods) aplacar a (los dioses), 10
place lugar *(m.)*, 2; plaza *(f.)*, 4; poner, 2; sentar (ie), 6; colocar, 9
placed puesto/a, 9
plague peste *(f.)*, 11
plaid de cuadros, 7
plains llanos *(m. pl.)*, llanura *(f.)*, planicie *(f.)*, 7
plan plan *(m.)*, 2; pensar (ie) + *inf.*, 3
plane avión *(m.)*, 3
planet planeta *(m.)*, 9
plant planta *(f.)*, 1
plaque placa *(f.)*, 10
play *(games)* jugar (ue), 1, 3; *(instrument)* tocar, 6; **~ a part** desempeñar, 6; **~ a role** desempeñar un papel, 8; hacer el papel de, 11; **~ sports** practicar deportes, 1; **~ volleyball** jugar al volibol, 1
player jugador/a *(m., f.)*, 6
plaza plaza *(f.)*, zócalo *(m.)*, *(Mex.)* 2
plead rogar (ue), 7
pleasant agradable, 1
please por favor, P
pleasure placer *(m.)*, 5; **the ~ is mine** el gusto es mío, P
plot argumento *(m.)*, 11
plumber plomero/a *(m., f.)*, 5
police policía *(f.)*; **~ force** policía *(f.)*; **~ officer** policía *(m., f.)*, 5, 11; **~ station** comisaría *(f.)*, 12
political político/a; **~ representation** representación política *(f.)*, 11; **~ science** ciencias políticas *(f. pl.)*, 1
polka dotted de lunares/puntos, 7
popcorn palomitas de maíz *(f. pl.)*, 11
populate poblar (ue), 12
populated poblado/a, 12
population población *(f.)*, 11, 12
pork chop chuleta de puerco *(f.)*, 3
port puerto *(m.)*, 7
portable portátil, 6
porter maletero/a *(m., f.)*, 4
portion porción *(f.)*, 8
portrait retrato *(m.)*, 10
Portuguese portugués/esa, P; *(lang.)*, portugués *(m.)*, 1
position puesto *(m.)*, 6
possible posible, 1

postcard postal *(f.)*, 3
post office correo *(m.)*, 2
poster cartel *(m.)*, 1
pot olla *(f.)*, 9; vasija *(f.)*, 10
potato patata *(Spain)*, papa *(Lat. Am.) (f.)*, 3; **~ soup with avocado and cheese** locro de queso *(m.)*, 7
pound libra *(f.)*, 3
poverty pobreza *(f.)*, 11
powder talco *(m.)*, 7
powerful poderoso/a, 8, 10
practice practicar, 1
praise halago *(m.)*, 10, 12
pray rezar, 10
predict predecir, 9
predictable predecible, 6
predominate primar, 9
prefer preferir (ie, i), 3
preferable preferible; **it's ~** es preferible, 7
pregnancy embarazo *(m.)*, 11
pregnant embarazada, 8; **to be ~** estar embarazada, 8
premiere estreno *(m.)*, 11
prepare preparar, 4
prescription receta *(f.)*, 8
presentation entrega *(f.)*, 12
presenter presentador/a *(m., f.)*, 11
press prensa *(f.)*, 2, 11; presionar, 6
pretend aparentar, 7
pretty bello/a, 5
prevent prevenir, 10
price precio *(m.)*, 7; **The prices are high.** Los precios están por las nubes., 3
primary colors colores primarios *(m. pl.)*, 10
print imprimir, 1, 6
printer impresora *(f.)*, 1, 6
prison cárcel, prisión *(f.)*, 11
problem problema *(m.)*, 1
produce producir (zc), 2
produced by producido/a por, 11
professional profesional, 1
profitable lucrativo/a, 4
program programa *(m.)*, 6; **AIDS prevention ~** programa de prevensión contra el SIDA, 11; **educational ~** programa educativo, 11; **news ~** noticiero *(m.)*, 11; **weekly ~** programa semanal, 11
promote itself promocionarse, 9
proof prueba *(f.)*, 9
protect proteger, 10; **~ oneself** protegerse, 5
prove comprobar (ue), 9; probar (ue), 11
provide brindar, 8
provided that con tal (de) que, 9
psychological illness enfermedad (p)sicológica *(f.)*, 11
psychologist psicólogo/a *(m., f.)*, 5
psychology psicología *(f.)*, 1; **~ of teaching** psicopedagogía *(f.)*, 6
psychosis psicosis *(f.)*, 1
public público/a, 10
published publicado/a, 9
Puerto Rican puertorriqueño/a, P
pupil alumno/a *(m., f.)*, 1
purple morado/a, 1
purse bolsa *(f.)*, 1, 7
pursue perseguir (i, i), 3
push empujar, 7
put poner, 2; puesto/a, 9; **~ (in)** meter, 12; **~ on clothes** ponerse la ropa, vestirse, 3; **~ on makeup** maquillarse, 3; **~ to bed** acostar (ue), 6

qualifications calificaciones *(f. pl.)*, 6
quantity cantidad *(f.)*, 1, 8
quarter (hour) cuarto *(m.)*, 1
quartet cuarteto *(m.)*, 6
query consulta *(f.)*, 8
quiet callado/a; **to be ~** callarse, 11
quit (a job) renunciar, 6

rabbit conejo *(m.)*, 5
race raza *(f.)*, 12
racket raqueta *(f.)*, 6
radio radio *(m.)*, 1, 7
rain llover (ue), 3; lluvia *(f.)*, 5; **it's raining** llueve, 2
raincoat impermeable *(m.)*, 2
rainforest bosque pluvial *(m.)*, 6; selva tropical *(f.)*, 7
raised criado/a, 6
rapidly rápidamente, 3
rat rata *(f.)*, 9
rate of exchange tasa de cambio *(f.)*, 8
rather sino, 10
raw crudo/a, 8
reach alcanzar, 11
react reaccionar, 4
read leer, 1; leído/a, 9
ready listo/a, 2; **~ made** ya listo/a, 8; **to be ~** estar listo/a, 3
real estate bienes raíces *(m. pl.)*, 9
realistic realista, 1
realize darse cuenta de, 7
really de veras, 4, 7, 12
rearview mirror espejo retrovisor *(m.)*, 7
receipt recibo *(m.)*, 7
receive recibir, 1, 6
reception recepción *(f.)*, 3
receptionist recepcionista *(m., f.)*, 3
recommend recomendar (ie), 3
records discos *(m. pl.)*, 7
recreation recreo *(m.)*, 4
red rojo/a, 1; colorado/a 7; **~-headed** pelirrojo/a, 1; **~ pepper** pimiento rojo *(m.)*, 3; **~ wine** vino tinto *(m.)*, 3
reef arrecife *(m.)*, 5
refine the search delimitar la búsqueda, 7
refrigerator refrigerador/a *(m., f.)*, 9
refuse no querer (ie), 6
regarding en cuanto a, 3
registered matriculado/a, 3
regret lamentar, sentir (ie,i), 8
reject rechazar, 11
rejected rechazado/a, 11
related words palabras relacionadas *(f. pl.)*, 12
relative pariente *(m., f.)*, 5
relax cálmate, 3
relaxation relajación *(f.)*, 8
relaxed relajado/a, 8
relieved aliviado/a, 2
religious religioso/a, 10
remain quedar, 6, 7; permanecer (zc), 10; **~ behind** quedarse, 6
remaining demás, 9
remedy remedio *(m.)*, 8
remember recordar (ue), 3; **~ a historic event** recordar un hecho histórico, 10
Renaissance *(adj.)* renacentista, 4
rent alquilar, 1; alquiler *(m.)*, 2; **~ videos** alquilar videos, 1
replace reemplazar, 9
replica réplica *(f.)*, 10
reporter reportero/a *(m., f.)*, 11
research investigar, 1; investigación *(f.)*, 9; **archaeological ~** investigaciones arqueológicas *(f. pl.)*, 1, 12
reservation reservación *(f.)*; **Do you have a ~?** ¿Tienen Uds. (una) reservación?, 3
resolution propósito *(m.)*, 10
resolved resuelto/a, 9
resort balneario *(m.)*, 8
respect respetar, 6
responsibility responsabilidad *(f.)*, 6; **ecological ~** responsabilidad ecológica, 9
restaurant restaurante *(m.)*, 2
résumé hoja de vida *(f.)*, 6
retired jubilado/a, 9
return volver (ue), 3; (an object) devolver (ue), 7, 9; **I want you to ~ my money** Quiero que me devuelvan el dinero, 7
returned vuelto/a, 9
reunited reunido/a, 9
reuse reusar, 9
rhythm ritmo *(m.)*, 6
ridiculous ridículo/a; **it's ~** es ridículo, 8
rice arroz *(m.)*, 8
rich rico/a, 3
richness riqueza *(f.)*, 6
ride andar, 1
right correcto/a; **~ away** en seguida (enseguida) 3, 4, 7, 9, 10; **~ in front of** enfrente de, 4; **~ now** ahora mismo, 3; **to be ~** tener razón, 2; **to the ~** a la derecha, 4
ring sonar (ue), 6; anillo *(m.)*, 8
rink (ice skating/hockey) pista *(f.)*, 6

ripped roto/a; **it's ~** está roto/a, 7
ritual rito *(m.)*, 10
river río *(m.)*, 7
Riverwalk (in San Antonio) Paseo del Río, 11
River Mansion (café on the Riverwalk) Mansión del Río, 11
road carretera *(f.)*, 3
roast pig lechón asado *(m.)*, 5
robbery robo *(m.)*, 4, 11
role papel *(m.)*, 11
rolling hills ondulaciones *(f. pl.)*, 8
room cuarto *(m.)*, 2; habitación *(f.)*, 3
roommate compañero/a de cuarto *(m., f.)*, 1
rooster gallo *(m.)*, 9
root raíz *(f.)*, 6
rose rosa *(f.)*, 1, 9
rough accidentado/a, 3
round trip de ida y vuelta, 4
route recorrido *(m.)*, 3
rows (of beads) hileras (de cuentas) *(f. pl.)*, 7
rubber caucho *(m.)*, 6; hule *(m.)*, 12
rug alfombra *(f.)*, 1; tapete *(m.)*, 8
ruins ruinas *(f. pl.)*, 12
rule regla *(f.)*, 3
ruler regla *(m.)*, 1
run correr, 1; **~ the risk** correr el riesgo, 10
Russian ruso/a, P

S

sacred sagrado/a, 12
sacrifice sacrificio *(m.)*, 10
sad triste, 2
sadness tristeza *(f.)*, 5
safe caja fuerte *(f.)*, 8; **~ from** a salvo de, 9
saffron azafrán *(m.)*, 3
said dicho/a, 9
salad ensalada *(f.)*, 3
salary salario *(m.)*, sueldo *(m.)*, 6
sale oferta *(f.)*, ganga *(f.)*, venta *(f.)*, 7
salesperson vendedor/a *(m., f.)*, 5, 8
salsa music salsa *(f.)*, 6
salt sal *(f.)*, 3; **~ residue** salitre *(m.)*, 8
salty salado/a, 3
Salvadoran salvadoreño/a, P
sample muestra *(f.)*, 11
sandal sandalia *(f.)*, 5, 7
Saturday sábado *(m.)*, 1
saucer platillo *(m.)*, 3
save archivar, guardar, 6; ahorrar, 8; salvar, conservar, 9
savings account cuenta de ahorros *(f.)*, 8
saxophone saxofón *(m.)*, 6
say decir (i), 3; **~ good bye** despedirse (i), 5
scale balanza *(f.)*, 9
scarce escaso/a, 9
scarf bufanda *(f.)*, 2, 7
scene escena *(f.)*, 11
schedule horario *(m.)*, 4; **work ~** horario de trabajo, 6
School (in a university) facultad *(f.)*, 1
science fiction *(adj.)* de ciencia ficción, 11
scold regañar, 10
scrambled eggs revoltillo *(m.)*, 8
screen pantalla *(f.)*, 11
script guión *(m.)*, 11
sculptor escultor/a *(m., f.)*, 5, 10
sculpture escultura *(f.)*, 10
sea mar *(m.)*, océano *(m.)*, 7
sealed box urna sellada *(f.)*, 11
season temporada *(f.)*, estación *(f.)*, 3
search búsqueda *(f.)*, 1; buscar, 1; **~ engine** motor de búsqueda, *(m.)*, buscador Internet *(m.)*, 2
seat plaza *(f.)*, 4; asiento *(m.)*, 4, 7; sentar (ie), 6
seatbelt cinturón de seguridad *(m.)*, 7
second segundo/a, 4; **~ class** segunda clase *(f.)*, 4
secondary secundario/a; **~ character** personaje secundario *(m.)*, 11; **~ colors** colores secundarios *(m. pl.)*, 10
secretary secretario/a *(m., f.)*, 5
sedentary sedentario/a, 8
see ver, 2; **you'll ~!** ¡ya lo verán!, 8
seem parecer (zc), 4; **it seems that** parece que, 3; **it seems unreal** parece mentira, 7
seen visto/a, 9
self-portrait autorretrato *(m.)*, 10
sell vender, 1, 4
send enviar, 4, 6, 8; mandar, 1, 6
September septiembre, 1
sequence secuencia *(f.)*, 11
serious serio/a, 1; gordo/a (problema), 10
servant criado/a *(m., f.)*, 5
serve servir (i, i), 3
service servicio *(m.)*, 3
set tanda *(m.)*, 8; **~ the table** poner la mesa, 2
seventh séptimo/a, 4
several varios/as, 3
shack cabaña *(f.)*, 7
shady (dirty) sucio/a, 4
shake sacudir, 4
shame lástima *(f.)*; **it's a ~** es una lástima, 8
share compartir, 5
sharp (clever) astuto/a, 9
shattered deshecho/a, 10
shave afeitarse, 3
shawl fachalina *(f.)*, 7
sheep oveja *(f.)*, 8, 9
sheet of paper hoja de papel *(f.)*, 9
shell concha *(f.)*, 5
shine brillar, 12
ship barco *(m.)*, 4
shirt camisa *(f.)*; **cotton ~** camisa de algodón, 7
shiver tener escalofríos, 8
shoe zapato *(m.)*, 7; **~ store** zapatería *(f.)*, 7
shop window escaparate *(m.)*, 7
shopper cliente *(m., f.)*, 3
shopping district centro comercial *(m.)*, 2
shore orilla *(f.)*, 4
short *(height)* bajo/a, 1; *(length)* corto/a, 1; **~ -sleeved** de manga corta, 7; **~ notice** corto plazo *(m.)*, 11
shorts pantalones cortos *(m. pl.)*, 2
should deber, 2
show mostrar (ue), 3, 10; **~ a movie** presentar/pasar una película, 11
shower ducha *(f.)*, 2
shrimp gamba *(f.)* *(Spain)*, camarón *(m.)* *(Lat. Am.)*, 3
shut off apagar, 7
sick enfermo/a, 2
side cara *(f.)*, 9; **~ to side with** junto a, 4
sign firmar, 8; **~ up** apuntar(se), 11
signature firma *(f.)*, 8
silk blouse blusa de seda *(f.)*, 7
silver plata *(f.)*, 8
simple sencillo/a, 3
since desde, 4
sing cantar, 1, 6
singer cantante *(m., f.)*, 6
single solo/a; **~ file** en fila, 12; **to be ~** ser soltero/a, 5
sink lavabo *(m.)*, lavamanos *(m.)*, fregadero *(m.)*, 9
sister hermana *(f.)*, 1, 5; **~ in-law** cuñada *(f.)*, 5
sit down sentarse (ie), 3, 6
site sitio *(m.)*, 9
sixth sexto/a, 4
size tamaño *(m.)*, 3; talla *(f.)*, 7
skate patinar, 6
skates patines *(m. pl.)*, 6
skating patinaje *(m.)*, 6
sketch bosquejo *(m.)*, 10
ski esquí *(m.)*, 6
skiing esquí *(m.)*, 6
skillful hábil, 10, 12
skim milk leche descremada *(f.)*, 8
skirt falda *(f.)*, 7
sky cielo *(m.)*, 8; firmamento *(m.)*, 12
sleep dormir (ue), 3, 6
sleepy cansado/a; **to be ~** tener sueño, 2
slender esbelto/a, 11
slice rebanada *(f.)*, 8
slow lento/a, 1
slowly despacio, 7
smack pegar, 4
small pequeño/a, 1, 7; **~ figures** figuritas *(f. pl.)*, 10
smother with sweetness empalagar, 12
snake víbora *(f.)*, culebra *(f.)*, serpiente *(f.)*, 9
sneakers zapatos de tenis *(m. pl.)*, 7

sneeze estornudar, 8
snow nevar (ie), 3; **~ -capped mountain** nevado/a, 7; **it's snowing** nieva, 2
so así; **~ much** tanto, 9; **~ that** para que, 9
soap jabón *(m.)*, 7; **~ opera** telenovela *(f.)*, 11
soccer fútbol *(m.)*, 6; **~ player** futbolista *(m., f.)*, 1
social social, 1; **~ program** programa social *(m.)*, 11; **~ work** trabajo social *(m.)*, 1; **~ worker** trabajador/a social *(m., f.)*, 11
society sociedad *(f.)*, 1
sociology sociología *(f.)*, 1
socks calcetines *(m.)*, 7
sofa sofá *(m.)*, 9
soil ensuciar, 9
solution solución *(f.)*, 11
some algún, alguno/a, 3
somebody alguien, 3
someone alguien, 3
something algo, 3
sometimes a veces, 3; unas veces, 5
son hijo/a *(m.)*, 5; **~ in-law** yerno *(m.)*, 5
sorry lamentable; **I'm ~** lo siento, 3, 4; **to be ~** sentir (ie), lamentar, 8
soul (el) alma *(f.)*, 7
sound sonido *(m.)*, 11; sonar (ue), 6; **~ card** tarjeta de sonido *(f.)*, 6; **~ effects** efectos de sonido *(m. pl.)*, 6
soup sopa *(f.)*, 3; **chicken and meat ~** sancocho *(m.)*, 7; **the ~ is cold** la sopa está fría, 3; **potato ~ with avocado and cheese** locro de queso *(m.)*, 7
sour ácido/a, 3
south sur *(m.)*, 4
southeast sureste *(m.)*, 4
southwest suroeste *(m.)*, 4
spa balneario *(m.)*, 8
Spanish español/a, P; *(lang.)* español *(m.)*, 1; **~-speaking** de habla hispana, de habla española, 11
speak hablar, 1
speaker parlante *(m.)*, 6
special effects (F/X) efectos especiales *(m. pl.)*, 11
specialty especialidad *(f.)*, 3
species especie *(f.)*, 9
spectacle espectáculo *(m.)*, 10
spectator espectador/a *(m., f.)*, 6
sphere esfera *(f.)*, 7
spirit (el) ánima *(f.)*, 10
spit escupir, 12
spoon cuchara *(f.)*, 3
sports enthusiast deportista *(m., f.)*, 6
spot mancha, 11
spring primavera *(f.)*, 2
square cuadrado/a, 4; cuadro *(m.)*, 10
squid calamar *(m.)*, 3
squirrel ardilla *(f.)*, 9
stable estable, 1
stadium estadio *(m.)*, 2
stain mancha *(f.)*, 7
stand out destacarse, 11
star estrella *(f.)*, 6; astro *(m.)*, 11
start empezar (ie), 3; arrancar, 7; **~ doing (something)** ponerse a + *inf.*
starting from a partir de, 12
starving hambriento/a; **I'm ~** estoy muerto/a de hambre, 3
statesman/woman estadista *(m., f.)*, 12
stationery store papelería *(f.)*, 7
statue estatua *(f.)*, 10
stay quedarse, 3; estadía *(f.)*, 5; **~ (in a hotel)** alojarse, hospedarse, 3; **~ behind** quedarse atrás, 6; **~ in shape** mantenerse en forma, 8
steamed al vapor, 8
steering wheel volante *(m.)*, 7
stellar estelar, 6
step paso *(m.)*, 6
stepbrother/sister hermanastro/a; **stepfather/mother** padrastro/madrastra; **stepson/daughter** hijastro/a, 1
stew guiso *(m.)*, 5
stick out (one's tongue) sacar (la lengua), 8
still todavía, 3; **~ life** naturaleza muerta *(f.)*, 10
stock prices precios de acciones *(m. pl.)*, 6
stockbreeding ganadero/a, 7
stockings medias *(f. pl.)*, 7
stomach estómago *(m.)*, 5
stone piedra *(f.)*, 7, 8
stop parar, 7; *(sign)* Alto, Pare, 7; **~ (doing)** parar de + *inf.*, 4; dejar de + *inf.*, 9
stoplight semáforo *(m.)*, 7
store tienda *(f.)*, 2; **~ clerk** dependiente *(m., f.)*, 3
story cuento *(m.)*, 5
stove estufa *(f.)*, 9
strange raro/a, 2; extraño/a, 6; **it's ~** es extraño, 8
stream arroyo *(m.)*, 7
street calle *(f.)*; **~ block** manzana *(f.)*, cuadra *(f.)*, 7; **~ vendor** vendedor/a ambulante *(m., f.)*, 8
strength fuerza *(f.)*, 10
stress estrés *(m.)*, 8
strip faja *(f.)*, 8
striped de rayas, 7
stroke campanada *(f.)*, 10
stucco estuco *(m.)*, 2
student estudiante *(m., f.)*, alumno/a *(m., f.)*, 1; **~ crossing** Escolares en la vía, 7
study estudiar, 1
stuffed animal muñeco de felpa *(m.)*, 9
stupid estúpido/a, tonto/a, 1
subject sujeto *(m.)*; **academic ~** materia *(f.)*, 1
subway metro *(m.)*, 3
succeed triunfar, 11
success éxito *(m.)*, 6
successful exitoso/a, 6; **to be ~** tener éxito, 11
suddenly de repente, 5
sugar azúcar *(m.)*, 3
suggest sugerir (ie, i), 7
suicide suicidio *(m.)*, 11
suit traje *(m.)*, 7; **~ jacket** saco *(m.)*, 7
suitcase maleta *(f.)*, 3
summit cumbre *(f.)*, 7
summer verano *(m.)*, 2; estival, 9
sun sol *(m.)*, 5; **it's sunny** hace sol, 2
sunbathe tomar el sol, 5
Sunday domingo *(m.)*, 1
sunflower girasol *(m.)*, 9
sunglasses gafas oscuras *(f. pl.)*, 1; gafas de sol *(f. pl.)*, 2; gafas negras *(f. pl.)*, 2
sunscreen lotion protector solar *(m.)*, 5
superstar superastro *(m.)*, 3
supervisor supervisor/a *(m., f.)*, 5
supply proporcionar, 7
support apoyar, 9; sustentar, 10
sure seguro/a, 2
surf hacer surfing, 5; **~ the Internet/web** navegar por Internet, 1
surface superficie *(f.)*, 6
surprise sorprender, 8
surround envolver (ue), 11
surrounded rodeado/a, 3
survey encuesta *(f.)*, 7
swear jurar, 6
sweat sudor *(m.)*, 7; **~ suit** sudadera *(f.)*, 7
sweater suéter *(m.)*, 2
sweep (the floor) barrer (el piso), 9
sweet dulce, 3
sweets dulces *(m. pl.)*, 8
swim nadar, 5
swimming natación *(f.)*, 6 ; **~ pool** piscina *(f.)*, 2, 3
swing mecerse (zc), 9
symbol símbolo *(m.)*, 10
symptom síntoma *(m.)*, 8
synonym sinónimo *(m.)*, 12
synthetic tissue tejido sintético *(m.)*, 11
syrup jarabe *(m.)*, 8
system sistema *(m.)*, 1

T

T-shirt camiseta *(f.)*, 6
table mesa *(f.)*, 9; **coffee ~** mesita *(f.)*, 9
tablespoonful cucharada *(f.)*, 9
tablet tableta *(f.)*, 8
take coger, 12; **~ (too much) time to arrive/leave** tardar (demasiado) en llegar/salir, 4; **~ a bath** bañarse, 3; **~ a shower** ducharse, 3; **~ a walk** dar un paseo, 1; **~ aback** desconcertar (ie), 10; **~ away** sacar, 4; **~ care** cuidar, 4; **~ care of** atender (ie), 8; **~ care of oneself** cuidarse, 8; **~ into account** tomar en cuenta, 7; **~ off** despegar, 5;

~ off one's clothes quitarse la ropa, 3; **~ out the garbage** sacar la basura, 9; **~ photos/pictures** sacar/tomar fotos, 10; **I'm going to ~ . . .** Voy a llevarme..., 7
talk hablar, 1
tall alto/a, 1
tape grabar, 6; **~ recorder** grabadora *(f.)*, 6, 10
tapestry tapiz *(m.)*, tapete *(m.)*, 8
taste probar (ue), 3, 6
tasty cooking buena sazón *(f.)*, 9
tattoo tatuaje *(m.)*, 8
tax impuesto *(m.)*, 4; **~ benefits** beneficios tributarios *(m. pl.)*, 6
tea té *(m.)*, 3
teaspoon cucharita *(f.)*, 3
teacher profesor/a *(m., f.)*, 1
team equipo *(m.)*, 6
tear lágrima *(f.)*, 5
teaspoonful cucharadita *(f.)*, 9
technology tecnología *(f.)*, 9
teeth diente *(m.)*, 3
telephone teléfono *(m.)*, 1
televise televisar, 11
television televisión *(f.)*, 1; **~ set** televisor *(m.)*, 9; **~ viewer** televidente *(m., f.)*, 12
tell decir (i), 3; contar (ue), 4; **Can you ~ me how to get to. . . ?** ¿Me puede decir dónde está...?, 7
temperate templado/a, 2
temperature temperatura *(f.)*, 2
tenant inquilino/a *(m., f.)*, 2
tenderize ablandar, 8
tennis tenis *(m.)*, 6 ; **~ court** cancha de tenis *(f.)*, 2
tenth décimo/a, 4
terrace terraza *(f.)*, 2
terrible terrible, 1; **it's ~** es terrible, 8
territory territorio *(m.)*, 12
test prueba *(f.)*, 8
texture textura *(f.)*, 10
than que, 7
thank agradecer (zc), 4, 11
thanks gracias *(f. pl.)*, P
that ese/esa, 3; aquel/aquella, 3; **~ which** lo que, 10
that one ése/a, aquél/aquélla, 3
the el/la/los/las, 1
theater teatro *(m.)*, 1
theme tema *(m.)*, 1
then entonces, 3; luego, 3, 5
therapy terapia *(f.)*, 11
there allí, 3; **~ has been** ha habido, 6; **~ is/are** hay, 1; **~ was/were** había, hubo, 5
these estos/as, 3
these ones éstos/as, 3
thief ladrón/ona *(m., f.)*, 4
thin delgado/a, 1
think pensar (ie) 3, 8; creer, opinar, 8
third tercer/o/a, 4
thirsty sediento/a; **to be ~** tener sed, 2
this este/a, 3
this one éste/a, 3
those esos/as, 3; aquellos/as, 3
those ones ésos/as, aquéllos/aquéllas, 3
thought pensamiento *(m.)*, 5
thousand mil *(m.)*, 3
thriller *(adj.)* de suspenso, 11
through a través de, 7, 8
throughout a lo largo y ancho, 9
throw tirar, 4, 11
Thursday jueves *(m.)*, 1
ticket billete *(m.)*, boleto *(m.)*, tiquete *(m.)*, pasaje *(m.)*, 4; entrada *(f.)*, 11; **~ window** taquilla *(f.)*, 4
tied atado/a, 7
tiger tigre *(m.)*, 9
tight estrecho/a, 7
tile azulejo *(m.)*, 2
time tiempo *(m.)*; **to have a good ~** divertirse (ie), 5; **to be on ~** estar a tiempo, 5
timid introvertido/a, 1
tip propina *(f.)*, 3, 4
tire llanta *(f.)*, rueda *(f.)*, 7; **flat ~** llanta pinchada, 7
tired cansado/a, 2
to a, para, 4; **~ the left** a la izquierda, **~ the side of** al lado de, 4; **~ whom** a quién(es), 10
toaster tostadora *(f.)*, 9
today actualmente, hoy en día, 5
toddler niño/a *(m., f.)*, 5
toe dedo *(m.)*, 5
toilet inodoro *(m.)*, sanitario *(m.)*, 9; **~ paper** papel sanitario/higiénico *(m.)*, 9
tolerant tolerante, 1
toll peaje *(m.)*, 3
told dicho/a, 9
tomato tomate *(m.)*, 3
tongue lengua *(f.)*, 8
too también, 3; **~ bad!** ¡Qué lástima!, 1; **~ much** demasiado, 9
tool utensilio *(m.)*, 9
tooth diente *(m.)*, 5
toothed dentado/a, 9
top cima *(f.)*, 4; cumbre *(f.)*, 7
torch antorcha *(f.)*, 12
touch toque *(m.)*, 7
tough duro/a, 3
tour excursión *(f.)*, 4; recorrer, 11; **~ guide** guía *(m., f.)*, 4
toward hacia, 4
towel toalla *(f.)*, 5
tower torre *(f.)*, 4
town pueblo *(m.)*, 12
trace rastro *(m.)*, 10
track vía *(f.)*, 3; (*sports*) pista *(f.)*, 6
train tren *(m.)*, ferrocarril *(m.)*, 3; (*adj.*) ferroviario/a, 3; **~ car** vagón *(m.)*, 4; **~ platform** andén *(m.)*, 4; **~ station** estación de tren *(f.)*, 2
training entrenamiento *(m.)*, 6
traitor traidor/a *(m., f.)*, 10
transgenic transgénico/a, 11
translate traducir (zc), 2
transmit (a TV or radio program) transmitir, 11
transparent transparente, 1
transplanted transplantado/a, 9
trap atrapar, 11
travel viajar, 1, 4; **~ agent** agente de viajes *(m., f.)*, 5; **~ all around a place** recorrer, 4
travelers' checks cheques de viajero *(m. pl.)*, 3, 8
treasure tesoro *(m.)*, 5
tree árbol *(m.)*, 6; **dragon ~** dragón *(m.)*, 9; **palm ~** palmera *(f.)*, 5
trick broma *(f.)*, 10; truco *(m.)*, 12
trip viaje *(m.)*, 3; **Have a good ~!** ¡Que tenga(n) un buen viaje!, 4; **Have a nice ~!** ¡Buen viaje!, ¡Feliz viaje!, 4
tripe mondongo *(m.)*, 5
trombone trombón *(m.)*, 6
trouble lío *(m.)*, 3
true verdadero/a, 4; **it's (not) ~** (no) es verdad, (no) es cierto, 8
trumpet trompeta *(f.)*, 6
trunk baúl *(m.)*, 7
trust confiar, 10
try probar (ue), 6; **~ on** probarse (ue), 3, 6, 7; **Can I ~ on the ...?** ¿Puedo probarme el ...?, 7; **I'm going to ~ it on** Voy a probármelo/la, 7
Tuesday martes *(m.)*, 1
tulip tulipán *(m.)*, 9
tuner sintonizador *(m.)*, 6
turkey pavo *(m.)*, 9
turn dar la vuelta, doblar, 7; revolver (ue), 9; turno *(m.)*, 9; **Do not ~** No doblar, 7; **~ off** apagar, 6, 9; **~ on** prender, encender (ie), 6; **~ to** recurrir a, 10; **~ to the right/left** doblar a la derecha/izquierda, 7; **it's your ~** te toca a ti, 3
turquoise turquesa *(f.)*, 8
turtle tortuga *(f.)*, 5
TV viewer televidente *(m., f.)*, 11
twin gemelo/a, *(m., f.)*, 1, 11; mellizo/a *(m., f.)*, 11
twist torcerse (ue), 8
type escribir a máquina, escribir en la computadora, 2
typewriter máquina de escribir *(f.)*, 9

U

UFO OVNI *(m.)*, 6
ugly feo/a, 1
uh-huh ajá, 5
umbrella paraguas *(m.)*, 2, 5

unbearable insoportable, 3
uncertainty incertidumbre *(f.)*, 6, 11
uncle tío *(m.)*, 5
uncomfortable incómodo/a, 9
under bajo, 4; **~ the influence** en estado de ebriedad, 10
undergraduate estudiante de pregrado *(m., f.)*, 1
underlined subrayado/a, 10
underneath debajo de, 4
understand comprender, 1; entender (ie), 3
understanding comprensivo/a, 10
underwear ropa interior *(f.)*, 7
unemployment desempleo *(m.)*, 6
unequal desigual, 9
unexplainable inexplicable, 12
unfair injusto/a, 6
unforgettable inolvidable, 2
unforgiveable imperdonable, 3
unfortunately desgraciadamente, 4
unfounded infundado/a, 9
unfriendly antipático/a, 1
uniform uniforme *(m.)*, 6
unit unidad *(f.)*, 6
unite unir, 12
united unido/a, 5
university universidad *(f.)*, 1
unknown desconocido/a, 5, 7
unless a menos que, 9
unpleasant desagradable, 1
unsure inseguro/a; **to be ~** no estar seguro/a, 8
unsympathetic incomprensivo/a, 10
untie desatar, 7
until hasta, 4; hasta que, 9; **~ we meet again** hasta la vista, P
untouchable irreprochable, 12
up arriba de, 4
upcoming entrante, 11
upon sobre, por; **~ arriving** al llegar, 5; **~ boarding** al subir, 5
upset alterado/a, 2, 10
urgent urgente; **it's ~** es urgente, 7
Uruguayan uruguayo/a, P
U.S. *(adj.)* estadounidense *(m., f.)*, P, 5
use usar, 1; **~ up** gastar, 12
user usuario/a *(m., f.)*, 6
utensil utensilio *(m.)*, 9
utilize aprovechar, 6

V

vacation vacaciones *(f. pl.)*, 4; **to go on ~** estar/
irse de vacaciones, 4
vacuum (the carpet) aspirar (la alfombra), 9; **~ cleaner** aspiradora *(f.)*, 9
Valentine's Day El día de San Valentín *(m.)*, 10
valley valle *(m.)*, 7
valuable valioso/a, 12
value valorar, 4
vase florero *(m.)*, 1; vasija *(f.)*, 10
veal ternera *(f.)*, 3
vegetable legumbre *(f.)*, 3; vegetal *(m.)*, 8
Venezuelan venezolano/a, P
very muy, 1; sumamente, 12; **~ beautiful** bellísimo/a, 5
veterinarian veterinario/a *(m., f.)*, 5
video video *(m.)*; **~ player/recorder** videograbadora *(f.)*, 6; **~ store** videoteca *(f.)*, 11
view vista *(f.)*, 4
villain villano/a *(m., f.)*, 11
violent violento/a, 11
violet violeta *(f.)*, 9
violin violín *(m.)*, 6
visible a la vista, 9
visit visitar, 1
volcano volcán *(m.)*, 7
volleyball volibol *(m.)*, 1
volume volumen *(m.)*, 3
vomit vomitar, 8

wagon carreta *(f.)*, 10
waist cintura *(f.)*, 6
wait esperar, 2; aguardar, 11; **~ in line** hacer cola, 5
waiting room sala de espera *(f.)*, 5
waitperson camarero/a *(m., f.)*, 3
wake up despertarse (ie), 3, 6; **wake (someone) up** despertar (ie), 6
walk caminar, andar, 1; caminata *(f.)*, 9
wall pared *(f.)*, 1
wallet cartera *(f.)*, 1
want querer (ie), 3
war guerra *(f.)*, 10
warm abrigado/a, 7
warn advertir (ie), 12
wash lavar, 1; **~ the clothes** lavar la ropa, 9; **~ the dishes** lavar los platos, 9
washing machine lavadora *(f.)*, 9
waste desperdicios *(m. pl.)*, 9; **~ basket** basurero *(m.)*, 1
watch reloj *(m.)*, 1, 8; vigilar, 4, 8; **~ (television)** mirar (la televisión), 1
watchman vigía *(m.)*, 7
watercolor acuarela *(f.)*, 10
waterfall cascada *(f.)*, 5; catarata *(f.)*, salto *(m.)*, 7
wave ola *(f.)*, 6
way camino *(m.)*, 2; **by the ~** a propósito, 7; **to be in the ~** estorbar, 9
wealth riqueza *(f.)*, 9
weapons armas *(f. pl.)*, 11
wear llevar, 1, 7
weather tiempo *(m.)*, 2; **~ conditions** condiciones del tiempo *(f. pl.)*, 2; **~ forecast** pronóstico del tiempo *(m.)*, 2; **the ~ is bad/good** hace mal/buen tiempo, 2
weathervane veleta *(f.)*, 4
weaver tejedor/a *(m., f.)*, 12
weaving tejido *(m.)*, 8
Web site sitio Web *(m.)*, 1
wedding boda *(f.)*, 3
Wednesday miércoles *(m.)*, 1
weekly program programa semanal *(m.)*, 11
weight peso *(m.)*, 3; *(sports)* pesa *(f.)*, 4
welcome bienvenido/a; **you're ~** de nada, P
well bien, 7; pues, 12; **~ being** bienestar *(m.)*, 8
west oeste *(m.)*, 4
western occidental, 7; de vaqueros, 11
wet empapado/a, 7
whale ballena *(f.)*, 9
what lo que, qué, cuál(es), 10
What?/What! ¿Qué?/¡Qué!, ¿Cómo?/¡Cómo!, 1; **~ a pleasure!** ¡Qué gusto!, 4; **~ a relief!** ¡Qué alivio!, 4; **~ a scare!** ¡Qué susto!, 4; **~ do I wear?** ¿Qué llevo?, 2; **~ does. . . mean?** ¿Qué quiere decir ...?, P; **~ is the (today's) date?** ¿Cuál es la fecha (de hoy)?, 1; **~ is the weather like?** ¿Qué tiempo hace?, 2; **~ season (month) is it?** ¿En qué estación (mes) estamos?, 1; **~ time is it?** ¿Qué hora es?, 1; **~ would you recommend?** ¿Qué recomendaría Ud.?, 3
wheel rueda *(f.)*, 10; **steering ~** volante *(m.)*, 7
when cuando, 9
when? ¿cuándo?, 1
where? ¿dónde?, 1; **~ from?** ¿de dónde?, 1
which lo que, 4; qué, cuál(es), 10
which? ¿cuál?, 1
while mientras, 4; **a little ~** un rato, 9; **a little ~ ago** hace poco, 11
whip batir, 9
white blanco/a, 1; **~ Pages** Páginas blancas *(f. pl.)*, 5; **~ wine** vino blanco *(m.)*, 3
who el/la cual, quien(es), 10
who? ¿quién(es)?, 1
whom *preposition* + quien(es)
whose? ¿de quién(es)?, 2
why? ¿por qué?, 1; **~ in the world** por qué diablos, 10
wife esposa *(f.)*, 5
wild silvestre, 8; **~ card** comodín *(m.)*, 11
will voluntad *(f.)*, 10
win ganar, 6; **~ someone's love** enamorar, 6
winner ganador/a *(m., f.)*, 12
window ventana *(f.)*, 1; **~ display** escaparate *(m.)*, 7; **little ~** ventanita *(f.)*, 7; **ticket ~** taquilla *(f.)*, 4

windshield parabrisas *(m.)*, 7; ~ **wipers** limpiaparabrisas *(m. pl.)*, 7
windy ventoso/a, 8; **it's (very)** ~ hace (mucho) viento, 2
wine vino *(m.)*, 3; ~ **glass** copa *(f.)*, 3; **red** ~ vino tinto *(m.)*, 3; **white** ~ vino blanco *(m.)*, 3
winter invierno *(m.)*, 2
wish for desear, 1
with con, 1, 4; ~ **a lot of hype** con bombos y platillos, 9; ~ **me** conmigo, 4; ~ **you** contigo, 4
withdraw (money) sacar/retirar (dinero), 8
without sin, 4; sin que, 9; ~ **a doubt** sin duda, 5
witness testigo *(m., f.)*, 10
wolf lobo *(m.)*, 9
woman mujer *(f.)*, 1
wonder maravilla *(f.)*, 2; **it's no** ~ no es para menos, 9
women's dressing room probador de mujeres *(m.)*, 7
womenswear ropa de mujer *(f.)*, 7
wood madera *(f.)*, 10
wooden stick palito de madera *(m.)*, 9
wool sweater suéter de lana *(m.)*, 7
word combination combinación de palabras *(f.)*, 12
work trabajar, 1; trabajo *(m.)*, puesto *(m.)*, 6; ~ **of art** obra de arte *(f.)*, 10; ~ **schedule** horario de trabajo *(m.)*, 6
worker trabajador/a *(m., f.)*, 5
World's fair exposición mundial *(f.)*, 10
worried preocupado/a, 2
worrisome preocupante, 11
worry preocuparse, 3; preocupar, 4, 8; angustia *(f.)*, inquietud *(f.)*, 11; **don't** ~ no se preocupe, 4
worse peor, 7
worth valor *(m.)*; **it's not** ~ **it** no vale la pena, 4; **to be** ~ valer, 11; **to be worthwhile** valer la pena, 5
wrap envolver (ue), 8
wrath furia *(f.)*, 6
wreck chocar, 7
write escribir, 1; ~ **by hand** escribir a mano, 2; ~ **letters** escribir cartas, 1; ~ **on the computer** escribir en la computadora, 2
writer escritor/a *(m., f.)*, 2
writing escritura *(f.)*, 12; ~ **desk** pupitre *(m.)*, 1
written escrito/a, 9
wrong equivocado/a; **to be** ~ equivocarse, 6

x-ray radiografía *(f.)*, 8

yellow amarillo/a, 1; ~ **Pages** Páginas amarillas *(f. pl.)*, 5
yesterday ayer, 4
yes sí, 1
yet ya, 5
Yield Ceder el paso, 7
yogurt yogur *(m.)*, 8
young joven, 1, 7; ~ **lady** señorita *(f.)*, 1; ~ **person** joven *(m., f.)*, 4; chico/a *(m., f.)*, 5; ~ **virgin** doncella *(f.)*, 10
younger menor, 7; **to be** ~ ser menor, 5
youth juventud *(f.)*, 11
Yucatan Yucatán; **from** ~ yucateco/a, 12
yucca yuca *(f.)*, 5

Z

Zapotec zapoteca, 2
zip code código postal *(m.)*, 6

Index

This index includes grammar topics and functions, as well as readings, cultural notes, vocabulary topics, and reading, writing, and Internet strategies. Readings are listed alphabetically under **Lecturas**; cultural notes are listed alphabetically under **Enlaces culturales.** Strategies are listed alphabetically under their corresponding headings (reading, writing, or Internet strategies).

Permissions and Credits

The authors and editors thank the following authors, publishers, and others for granting permission to use excerpts from copyrighted material.

Text

Chapter 3: Pages 113-114: From ESPAÑA AYER Y HOY: ITINERARIO DE CULTURA Y CIVILIZACIÓN, by Víctor Bellón Alonso and Eugenio Roncero Doña (Madrid: Editorial Edinumen, 1997), pp. 30-31; page 134: "Placido Domingo Restaurant," from *Cristina, la revista*, Año 7, November 1997, p. 18. Copyright © 1997 by Editorial Televisa.
Chapter 6: Page 228: *People en español*, Invierno de 1997, p. 97; page 228: "Patty Cabrera – bella y de las nuestras," from *Cristina, la revista*, Año 7, February 1997, p. 74. Copyright © 1997 by Editorial Televisa; page 248: From E^3,Vol. 2, No. 2, March/April 1997, p. 8; p. 248: From E^3,Vol. 2, No. 2, March/April 1997, p.12.
Chapter 8: Page 318: "Buena idea para el estrés" from *Vanidades*, Año 37, March 25, 1997, p. 36. Copyright © 1997 by Editorial Televisa.
Chapter 9: Page 358: "Fobia a la cocina" from *Cristina, la revista* Año 7, May 1997, p. 16. Copyright © 1997 by Editorial Televisa; page 371: "Así cualquiera cocina" from *Vanidades continental*, Año 36, No. 18, p. 67. Copyright © by Editorial Televisa; page 372: "Shakira" from *Vanidades continental*, Año 37, No. 12, p. 127. Copyright © by Editorial Televisa; page 377: Grupo Interconect © 1998; pages 388-389: "Árboles con historia—el último dragón," from *El país semanal*, no. 1077, May 18, 1997, p. 118.
Chapter 10: Pages 412-413: Adriana Herrera, "El Rostro Mestizo de la Navidad en América" from *Revista Credencial*, December 1994, pp. 39-40. Used by permission of *Revista Credencial*.
Chapter 11: Page 434: Adapted from http://www.infosel.com.mx/elnorte/especial/jovenes/intro1.htm; page 436: "Un viejo amigo" by Alejandro Higuita Rivera from *El colombiano*, July 27, 1997. Adapted by permission of the author; pages 437-438: Derechos Reservados © 1995-1998 Informacíon Selectiva, S.A. de C.V.; pages 448-449: From *El colombiano*, July 7, 1997. Adapted by permission of the author; page 450: From *Gente*, Año 30, No. 1659, May 8, 1997, p. 138; page 453: Adapted from *Gente*, Año 30, No. 1659, May 8, 1997, p. 96; page 453: "Se ve en TV" from *Cristina, la revista*, Año 7, May 1997. Copyright © 1997 by Editorial Televisa; page 465: "Ídoles Mexicanos," from *Vanidades continental*, Año 34, No. 21, p. 104. Copyright © by Editorial Televisa.

Photos

p. 9: John Mitchell/DDB Stock Photo; p. 12: Beryl Goldberg; p. 35: Frerck/Odyssey/Chicago; p. 46: Frerck/Odyssey/Chicago; p. 47: t, Beryl Goldberg; b, Frerck/Odyssey/Chicago; p. 53: t, Suzanne Murphy-Larronde/DDB Stock Photo; p. 57: Frerck/Odyssey/Chicago; p. 70: Suzanne Murphy-Larronde/DDB Stock Photo; p. 71: Frerck/Odyssey/Chicago; p. 74: Robert Frerck/Tony Stone Images; p. 87: t, Cliff Hollenbeck/Tony Stone Images; m, Beryl Goldberg; b, Frerck/Odyssey/Chicago; p. 93: t, Beryl Goldberg; p. 117: Frerck/Odyssey/Chicago; p. 120: Frerck/Odyssey/Chicago; p. 133: Joe McNally/Sygma; p. 141: t, Frerck/Odyssey/Chicago; p. 142: both, Beryl Goldberg; p. 144: Beryl Goldberg; p. 160: Frerck/Odyssey/Chicago; p. 167: t, Beryl Goldberg; b, Frerck/Odyssey/Chicago; p. 178: tr, Frerck/Odyssey/Chicago; l, Frerck/Odyssey/Chicago; br, Beryl Goldberg; p. 183: t, Frerck/Odyssey/Chicago; p. 186: t, Ulrike Welsch; b, Suzanne Murphy-Larronde/DDB Stock Photo; p. 189: tr, Ulrike Welsch; bl, Gary Williams/Gamma-Liaison; br, Frerck/Odyssey/Chicago; p. 203: K. McGlynn/The Image Works; p. 207: Frerck/Odyssey/Chicago; p. 227: Beryl Goldberg; p. 229: Frerck/Odyssey/Chicago; p. 231: Raymond A. Menendez/Animals Animals; p. 246: M. Algaze/The Image Works; p. 250: Frerck/Odyssey/Chicago; p. 266: Ulrike Welsch; p. 271: D. Donne Bryant/DDB Stock Photo; p. 273: Suzanne Murphy-Larronde/DDB Stock Photo; p. 277: Ulrike Welsch; p. 291: both, Frerck/Odyssey/Chicago; p. 292: t, Robert Fried; m, Frerck/Odyssey/Chicago; b, Robert Crandall/Stock Boston; p. 298: Craig Duncan/DDB Stock Photo; p. 299: David Welling/Earth Scenes; p. 308: Dreyfuss/Monkmeyer Press; p. 315: Craig Duncan/DDB Stock Photo; p. 321: Robert Fried; p. 335: t, Frerck/Odyssey/Chicago; b, Beryl Goldberg; p. 336: t, Frerck/Odyssey/Chicago; b, Robert Fried; p. 337: Robert Fried; p. 341: Robert Fried; p. 346: t, Chad Ehlers/Tony Stone Images; b, Frerck/Odyssey/Chicago; p. 347: t, Michael Moody/DDB Stock Photo; b, Peter Timmermans/Tony Stone Images; p. 353: t, John Mitchell/DDB Stock Photo; p. 356: Frerck/Odyssey/Chicago; p. 359: t, Amy Reichman/Envision; all others, Frerck/Odyssey/Chicago; p. 376: D. Donne Bryant; p. 378: Gary Braasch/Tony Stone Images; p. 395: t, Gay Bumgarner/Tony Stone Images; p. 397: t, Denise Marcotte/Stock Boston; b, Alejandro Balaguer/Sygma; p. 398: Jeremy Homer/Gamma-Liaison; p. 399: Tim Graham/Sygma; p. 401: L. Mangino/The Image Works; p. 412: Frerck/Odyssey/Chicago; p. 416: t, Christie's Images, NY; b, Schalksijk/Art Resource, NY; p. 417: m, D. Donne Bryant/DDB Stock Photo; b, Castellazzo/Latin Stock/DDB Stock Photo; p. 418: t & mr, Suzanne Murphy-Larronde/DDB Stock Photo; ml & b, Frerck/Odyssey/Chicago; p. 419: Ulrike Welsch; p. 427: both, Christie's Images, NY; p. 428: "La Granja" by César López, Colombia; photo by Ana B. Chiquito; p. 433: Chuck Pefley/Stock Boston; p. 438: Sipa Press; p. 450: t, Gramercy Pictures/The Kobal Collection; b, The Kobal Collection; p. 452: The Kobal Collection; p. 455: r, Susan Greenwood/Gamma-Liaison; l, John Spellman/Retna, Ltd; p. 471: John Curtis/DDB Stock Photo; p. 475: Museo d'América, Madrid/Scala/Art Resource, NY; p. 476: Robert Fried/DDB Stock Photo; p. 494: t, The Kobal Collection; m, Evan Agostini/Gamma-Liaison; b, Photofest.

All other photos by Video Publishing Group, Inc.

Realia

Page 88 (left): Courtesy of La Abuelita, Oaxaca, Mexico; p. 88 (right): Courtesy of El Patio, Oaxaca, Mexico; p. 236 (top): Courtesy of Discotronics, Jorge Alberto Restrepo Moreno, Medellín, Colombia; p. 236 (bottom): Courtesy of *Semana*, Santa Fé de Bogotá, Colombia; p. 248: Courtesy of E^3, Miami, FL; p. 251: Courtesy of *El Tiempo*, Casa editorial, Santa Fé de Bogotá; p. 372: Courtesy of *Vanidades continental*, Virginia Gardens, FL; p. 389: Courtesy of *El país semanal*, Madrid, Spain; p. 465: Courtesy of *Vanidades continental*, Virginia Gardens, FL.

Illustrations

Leslie Evans: pages 272, 274, 297 (top), 298, 354, 357, 374, 375, 377, 474
Uli Gersiek: pages 111, 255
Patty Isaacs/Parrot Graphics: pages 4, 45, 85, 148, 165, 198, 388, 472, 491
Randy Jones: pages 294, 295, 296, 436, 448
Susan Ferris Jones: pages 316, 317, 399, 400
Tim Jones: pages 281, 286, 297 (bottom), 304, 319, 333, 343, 362, 365, 367, 381, 410, 422, 425, 426, 444, 458, 461, 462
Daniel Powers: pages 414, 477, 485, 489, 492
Anna Veltfort: pages 6, 7, 10, 11, 15, 16, 21, 22, 23, 29, 30, 31, 33, 34, 38, 43, 44, 54, 56, 60, 63, 64, 68, 69, 72, 73, 74, 75, 76, 80, 82, 84, 95, 96, 100, 103, 105, 108, 109, 115, 118, 119, 123, 125, 126, 127, 131, 145, 147, 151, 156, 158, 159, 162, 170, 174, 180, 184, 188, 192, 195, 196, 201, 204, 210, 213, 214, 215, 216, 220, 230, 234, 237, 257, 258, 265, 284, 289, 324, 327, 356, 384, 406, 408, 441, 445

Mar Caribe
Barranquilla
Cartagena
Maracaibo
Caracas
TRINIDAD
Puerto España
VENEZUELA
R. Orinoco
Georgetown
Paramaribo
Cayena
GUYANA
SURINAM
GUAYANA FRAN.
Medellín
COLOMBIA
Bogotá
Cali
CORDILLERA DE LOS ANDES
Otavalo
Quito
ECUADOR
Guayaquil
Iquitos
Ecuador
R. Negro
Manaus
R. Amazonas
Belem
R. Madeira
BRASIL
Recife
PERÚ
Machu Picchu
Lima
Cuzco
Lago Titicaca
La Paz
Arequipa
BOLIVIA
Sucre
Salvador
Brasília
R. Paraguay
R. Paraná
Arica
Iquique
PARAGUAY
Belo Horizonte
São Paulo
Santos
Rio de Janeiro
Trópico de Capricornio
Antofagasta
Salta
Asunción
Tucumán
OCÉANO PACÍFICO
CHILE
CORDILLERA DE LOS ANDES
R. Uruguay
Pôrto Alegre
OCÉANO ATLÁNTICO
Córdoba
Rosario
URUGUAY
Valparaíso
Santiago
Mendoza
Buenos Aires
Montevideo
La Plata
Río de la Plata
Concepción
ARGENTINA
Bahía Blanca
Puerto Montt
Islas Galápagos
ECUADOR
San Salvador
Santa Cruz
San Cristobal
Isabela
Quito
Guayaquil
América del Sur
0 500 1000 1500 Kilómetros
0 500 1000 Millas
Estrecho de Magallanes
Islas Malvinas
Punta Arenas
Tierra del Fuego
Cabo de Hornos